EGYPT
GREECE
AND ROME

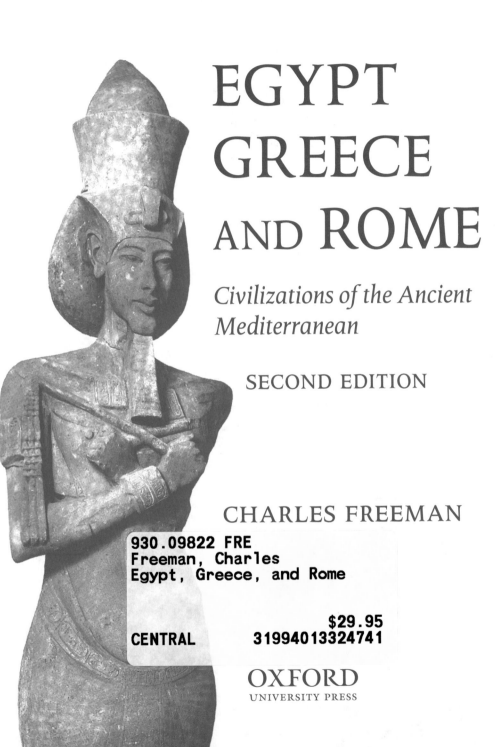

EGYPT
GREECE
AND ROME

Civilizations of the Ancient Mediterranean

SECOND EDITION

CHARLES FREEMAN

OXFORD
UNIVERSITY PRESS

OXFORD
UNIVERSITY PRESS

Great Clarendon Street, Oxford OX2 6DP

Oxford University Press is a department of the University of Oxford.
It furthers the University's objective of excellence in research, scholarship,
and education by publishing worldwide in

Oxford New York

Auckland Cape Town Dar es Salaam Hong Kong Kuala Lumpur
Madrid Melbourne Mexico City Nairobi New Delhi Taipei Toronto
Shanghai

With offices in

Argentina Austin Brazil Chile Czech Republic France Greece
Guatemala Hungary Italy Japan South Korea Poland Portugal
Singapore Switzerland Thailand Turkey Ukraine Vietnam

Oxford is a registered trade mark of Oxford University Press
in the UK and in certain other countries

Published in the United States
by Oxford University Press Inc., New York

First edition published in hardback 1996
First paperback edition 1999

British Library Cataloguing in Publication Data
Data available

Library of Congress Cataloging in Publication Data
Data applied for
ISBN-13: 978-0-19-926364-6
ISBN-10: 0-19-926364-7

10 9 8 7 6 5 4 3

Typeset in Minion
by Hope Services (Abingdon) Ltd.
Printed in Great Britain
on acid-free paper by
Ashford Colour Press Limited, Gosport, Hampshire

To my mother, in memory of an August day in 1957 when a climb we made together up to the Roman fort on Wardlaw Hill, Dumfries, Scotland, first sparked off my fascination with the ancient world, and in memory, too, of my father John Freeman (1913–86) who loved the Mediterranean and its peoples.

FOREWORD TO THE SECOND EDITION

by Oswyn Murray

It is only eight years since I welcomed the appearance of the first edition of Charles Freeman's *Egypt, Greece and Rome*; and it is a great pleasure to see how in that short time the book has established itself as the best and most reliable one-volume history of the ancient near east and the Mediterranean world. In this new edition Charles has made some substantial changes of emphasis in response to the requests of readers, and he has also systematically updated the reading lists to include all the latest work. One of his new chapters is especially important, that on the civilizations of the ancient Near East (chapter two): as today we anxiously await firm news of the survival of the Mesopotamian museums and archaeological sites, we need always to remember that the story of western civilization began in Iraq.

As I said in the preface to the previous edition, Charles Freeman has tried to give a narrative account of the main events within each period, but also to highlight the developments in cultural and social history, and to show something of the evidence on which his judgements are based. He has indicated where the evidence is uncertain, or where his interpretation may be controversial; but he has not avoided the responsibility of making decisions about the evidence in order to present a clear account. The aim of all of us who struggle to write in that most difficult of historical genres, the introduction to the study of a period, must always be to combine the current state of information with excitement and encouragement to study the subject further. History aims at producing narratives and explanations, but it is the methods by which these aims are achieved which constitute the most interesting aspect of being a historian; and making historians is at least as important as writing history. For history is a creative activity that must be renewed in each generation: there will never be a fixed and final narrative, partly because our evidence is incomplete and growing all the time, and partly because our explanations of events and the ways they interconnect reflect our own interpretation of our present world, and so are always changing. As the philosopher and historian R.G. Collingwood insisted, it is not the facts that are interesting in history, but the questions and their answers—and these can never be fixed.

The aim of Freeman's book has not changed. What distinguishes it from most of its rivals is the way that before writing a narrative that belongs to himself alone, Charles Freeman has consulted the experts in each area of the ancient world; although he makes his own mind up and judiciously steers between the various hypotheses with which those at the forefront of scholarship tend to play for the sake of argument, he is always in touch with the latest thinking in each area. In a world where specialism too often obscures the broader view, much as Fernand Braudel did a generation ago, Charles Freeman reminds all of us of the importance of the wide perspective. Both for the general reader and for the student who intends to embark on serious specialist study, he offers a firm starting point.

Oxford
November 2003

PREFACE TO THE SECOND EDITION

I am delighted that *Egypt, Greece and Rome* has found a niche for itself as an introductory text at undergraduate level as well as for the general reader. For this second edition I have taken into account the many comments made by reviewers and others but primarily have relied on the comments of those actually using the book at university level in Britain and the United States.

The most insistent demand was for more on the Ancient Near East and so I have doubled the text here. I have also added a new chapter on the ancient Mediterranean for those not familiar with the area and interludes on the 'Amarna Letters', 'Classical Art', and on 'Rhetoric'. While there was general approval of the level and scope of the text, I have reworked it in some areas to make it more coherent and to add 'new' material which I think deserves to be included. The reading lists have now been transferred to the end of each chapter.

There was some disagreement amongst reviewers as to whether quotations should be footnoted and to whether the text should spend more time on controversies. The first suggestion was rejected by a majority of teachers, the second virtually unanimously. This is a subject where the mass of new material remains overwhelming and it was clear that students appreciated a running text in which they could ground themselves before progressing to more controversial areas. This 'grounding text' is what this book aims to provide for student and general reader alike. I hope above all that it engages those who read it enough to act as a springboard for further studies or travels to see the sites mentioned.

As much of the text remains unchanged I would like to repeat my thanks to those who advised me on the first edition, Averil Cameron, John Drinkwater, Amelie Kuhrt, Oswyn Murray, John Ray, John Rich, Nigel Spivey, and Ruth Whitehouse. For the second edition John Drinkwater has advised on a rewriting of three of the central Roman chapters and Ben Garstad and Nigel Nicholson have read the revised section on the Ancient Near East. I am most grateful to them for their comments and support. I would also like to thank Oswyn Murray for contributing yet another Foreword.

During the shelf-life of the first edition my family have become increasingly used to the ancient Mediterranean, from the bustle of modern Rome to the more remote of Greek islands. I hope it provides a springboard to their own further interests.

Once again I am delighted to dedicate this book to my mother who, in her eighty-ninth year, still had the energy and interest to visit the site of the Anglo-Saxon ship burial at Sutton Hoo with me this summer.

Charles Freeman

July, 2003

ACKNOWLEDGEMENTS

This has been a large book to prepare and I am grateful to Ruth Anderson at Oxford University Press for her mastery of the art of setting deadlines and coaxing me successfully towards them. In production Matthew Cotton has been efficient and unflappable while all the subsidiary work of copy-editing (Edwin Pritchard), proofreading (Colin Baldwin) and indexing (Richard Owens) has been of high standard. It has all helped make the writing of this second edition much less daunting than it might have been.

CONTENTS

LIST OF PLATES

LIST OF MAPS

LIST OF FIGURES

BIBLIOGRAPHICAL NOTE

This is a particularly exciting time for the study of ancient history and the mass of new material is overwhelming. Since the first edition of this book the use of the Internet has grown enormously although sites come and go rapidly. Readers are recommended to use a good search engine to get up-to-date material. (Many reputable sites listed in a book published in 2001 were already defunct when accessed in 2003.) It need hardly be said that in certain areas, the Egyptian pyramids, Atlantis, etc., there is a great deal of misleading material on the Internet and sites on these subjects need to be approached with caution.

I have provided a reading list at the end of each chapter which I have tried to make as up to date as possible. In addition to the works cited readers will find it useful to have access to the *Oxford Classical Dictionary* (3rd revised edition, edited by Simon Hornblower and Antony Spawforth, Oxford, 2003) and to the *Cambridge Ancient History* which is now virtually complete in its second edition. More accessible in price is the *Routledge History of the Ancient World*. Individual volumes will be cited in the texts but the *History* is up to date and particularly useful for its analysis of texts. There is no reason why subsequent volumes should not maintain this high standard. As an introductory atlas see John Hayward's *The Cassell Atlas of World History* (London, 1997) or Colin McEvedy's *The New Penguin Atlas of Ancient History* (2nd edition, London, 2002). These are dwarfed by the superb *Barrington Atlas of the Greek and Roman World*, edited by Richard Talbert (Princeton, 2000).

General books on the main civilizations covered in this book will be cited at the end of the first chapter on each civilization: Egypt, Chapter 3; Greece, Chapter 8; Rome, Chapter 20. Books mentioned by title in the text will be given their citation there.

It is now relatively easy to find translations of key texts on the Internet but a good library will have a full set of the Loeb Library which provide translations on Greek and Latin texts alongside the originals. Some of the translations are dated but the standard is high. There is now a wide-ranging selection of texts at reasonable prices in the Penguin Classic series.

1 | Approaching the Classical World

In 1901 my great uncle, Kenneth Freeman, then aged 18, sat the papers for a prestigious prize offered by his school, Winchester College, Goddard's Scholarship. It was an awesome challenge with no less than thirteen papers for him to complete. Their subject matter offers an insight into the education offered at a traditional English public school of the day. There was a paper on English history, specifically on the reign of Queen Elizabeth I, but every other paper had some connection with Latin or Greek. There were individual papers on the Latin poets Catullus and Virgil and, from the Greek world, Homer, Sophocles, and the historian Thucydides. All these contained passages to be translated and then questions on the way the writer used his language. ('Consider the advantages and disadvantages of Catullus' fondness for diminutives, and quote examples', runs one.) A general paper asked further questions on the uses of Greek and Latin and this went so far as to include a question on law-making in Athens and Rome, one of the very few requiring knowledge outside the texts. Translation papers required Latin and Greek passages to be translated into English and English passages, including one from Shakespeare's *Henry V*, to be translated into Greek verse, or Latin elegiacs. The scholarship concluded with a Divinity paper which began with passages from Paul's First Letter to the Corinthians to be translated from the original Greek.

This was not the whole curriculum—other examinations dealt with maths, physics, and German and French literature—but it reflected the dominance of classical languages in a traditional education of the period. Young Freeman won the scholarship (and collected and bound his examination papers for posterity, which is why I have them) and then went on to study classics at Cambridge, where he won many further awards, including the Senior Chancellor's Medal. Tragically he died aged only 24, leaving the drafts of his first book, on Greek education, which was published as *The Schools of Hellas* in 1907 (republished in the United States as recently as 1969).

The study of the classics (the word 'classic' itself, derived from the Latin *classicus*, 'of the highest class'—of the five into which the Roman citizenry were divided when meeting in the assembly known as the *comitia centuriata*) had became the core of education for the upper and middle classes of both Europe and the United States. Quite apart from the importance of the Roman empire in western history there were good educational reasons for this. Latin had been the language of the western church since the fourth century, and remained essential for the Catholic clergy so long as the liturgy and all major church pronouncements remained in Latin as they did until the 1960s. With the coming of the Renaissance Latin became the language of international scholarship, particularly in the sciences where almost every major work in the sixteenth or seventeenth century was published in Latin. However, the study of Latin became the mark not just of the scholar but of society's elites. Initiation in its mysteries had become enshrined as a rite of passage to be undergone by all those who wish to be accepted as well educated. (This was, of course, mostly men but one notes the achievement in the classics of some women like Queen Elizabeth I of England who was able to complete an English translation of Boethius' *Consolation of Philosophy* in seventeen days.) In her excellent *Latin or the Empire of a Sign* (London, 2001) Françoise Waquet explores the rise and fall of an education centring on Latin from the Renaissance to today. For many it was sheer drudgery and few progressed further than a hesitant understanding of a few basic texts. For those who persisted on the other hand it became an initiation into a pre-Christian world of great heroes who could be drawn on for further inspiration. During the Renaissance almost every aspect of life was seen afresh through the eyes of the ancient authors. The founders of the American Constitution and the leading figures of the French Revolution were steeped in the achievements of the Roman republic. Although Greek texts were available in Europe in the fifteenth century, it was not until the nineteenth century, under the leadership of the Germans, that the study of ancient Greek became part of the curriculum although its very difficulty served as another way in which the educated minority were segregated from the mass of the population. The ancient Greeks were for many the ideal civilization to which all those of the ruling classes should aspire.

As the examination papers show, the focus of studies was on the translation and analysis of texts. The sheer amount of academic energy which this could demand is well described by the scholar Sir Kenneth Dover in his stimulating introductory book *The Greeks* (London, 1980, and Austin, Texas, 1989). He tells of a commentary he made on Books VI and VII of Thucydides' *The Peloponnesian War*. It involved him 'in some six thousand hours of work altogether, much of it on the minutiae of chronology, grammar, and textual criticism', and, on one occasion, he looked up 'all six hundred examples of a certain common preposition of Thucydides in order to elucidate the precise sense of one passage'. This might sound excessive (and it shows just how painstaking work in this area can be) but in creating a fuller understanding of the mentality of cultures alien to our own it has undoubted value.

Yet, traditionally the texts chosen for such detailed study were limited to history and literature. It is worth noting the complete absence among the 'set' authors at Winchester of Greek philosophers such as Plato and Aristotle, although Aristotle's *Nicomachaean Ethics* and Plato's *The Republic* formed an important part of university level education. (They were assumed to instil the values of enlightened leadership for those whom nature had called to rule over others.) Ancient Greek science and mathematics were almost totally ignored, even though they represent some of the classical world's finest intellectual achievements. Students may have known something of Catullus' fondness for diminutives; they would have known nothing of Hipparchus' astonishing plotting of the precession of the equinoxes, Archimedes' contributions to pure and applied mathematics, the ingenuity of Ptolemy's astronomical findings or his contributions to the founding of geography.

The preoccupation with the texts had other consequences. It tended to give them a sacred quality and an authority, as historical sources for instance, which was simply not justified. As Moses Finley complained in his *Ancient History, Evidence and Models* (London, 1986): 'Sources written in Latin and Greek occupy a privileged status and are immune from the canons of judgement and criticism that are applied to all other documentation.' (Moses Finley, an American Marxist, arrived in Cambridge in 1953 as a refugee of the McCarthy era. Adept at asking the big questions about the ancient world which no one else seemed, in his eyes at least, prepared to confront he invigorated the study of the ancient world and his influence remains strong.) So Julius Caesar's *History of the Gallic War* gives what is apparently an objective report of his campaigns (note the way the author speaks of himself in the third person), a report all the more easy to accept as there is no major alternative source for the war. Yet its political motives, the need to present Caesar as man of action and resolution who simply carries out his duty as a Roman commander without emotion and achieves enormous success, shape its content and approach. As will be seen (Chapters 22 and 23) this is a man who needs, in the 50s BC, to sell himself to a suspicious ruling class at home and this is what the account is designed to do. It is now a commonplace of textual criticism to see how a work has been constructed and for what motives, and few would now accept an ancient historical text as necessarily an accurate account of what happened.

Another assumption has been that the Greeks and Romans themselves gave supreme importance to the written word. The extent to which they actually did so is the subject of intense debate—there were areas in which words were given a privileged status (a law code, for instance, might have had authority through its public written expression—see Deborah Steiner's *The Tyrant's Writ* (Princeton, 1993)) and others in which they were denigrated. Certainly, it was in the cut and thrust of oral debate that the Greek mind flourished. As Plato himself remarked, one cannot engage in debate with the written word, 'if you ask them [words] anything about what they say . . . they go on telling you the same thing over and over again forever', and he makes the point by presenting his works as dialogues in which the participants argue opposing views through together. In short, most of what the Greeks and Romans knew came to them directly via the human voice with all its capacity to inspire or deceive. One of the most important achievements of this, as Geoffrey Lloyd, an authority on the development of Greek science and mathematics, has pointed out, was to stimulate the development of rational thought. Being able to use words to persuade is a means of achieving status whether in politics or intellectual life, and goes hand in hand with an ever more sophisticated understanding of what makes a good argument. The achievements of Greek science and mathematics are the result. (See Geoffrey Lloyd, *Magic, Reason and Experience* (Cambridge, 1979), especially chapter 4.) In recent scholarship there has been a new interest in rhetoric, the art of public speaking whether displayed in the Athenian assembly, intellectual discourse, the raucous political and legal confrontations of the Roman republic, or the Christian sermon, which was often preached by a bishop steeped in the traditions of pagan education in rhetoric.

Despite all this the texts of the canon of authors remain essential to the study of the classical world. The histories of Herodotus, Thucydides, Polybius, Tacitus, and, in late antiquity, of Ammianus Marcellinus and Procopius, as well as many others, all provide detailed narratives which are unlikely to be surpassed by any other form of evidence. The works of philosophers and poets, at both a private and a public level, survive in some quantity, making it possible to reconstruct something of the mentality of the small cultured elite who produced them. Even if few scholars would now show the dedication of Sir Kenneth Dover these works need continual probing and revaluation if their full meaning is to be squeezed out.

However, just as it is important not to reject the texts it is also essential to place what survives into context. The amount of ancient writing which has been lost is staggering, and it may be the best of what was written. Geoffrey Lloyd suspects that much of the finest work in Greek science and mathematics was discarded because it was simply too difficult for later generations to grasp. The physician Galen and the astronomer Ptolemy, both working in the second century AD, gained such authority that much work from before their day was considered inferior and not preserved. The picture we have of the achievements of the ancient world is inevitably distorted, and it is tempting to think how it might have been affected if a different pattern of texts had survived—the later books of Tacitus' *Annals* instead of the earlier ones, or the earlier books of Ammianus Marcellinus instead of the later ones. Again, how would twentieth-century culture have been different if Sophocles' *Oedipus*, one of only seven of his 130 plays to have survived, had not been there to inspire Freud's 'Oedipus Complex'? (The theme of a man who kills his father and marries his mother is so atypical of family life in Greek mythology (*pace* Freud's insistence that the wish to do so represents the norm) that one wonders where traditional Freudian analysts would have been without the play. Sophocles' concern may rather have been to explore the consequences of a man committing a particularly shocking crime without being aware of it.)

So the voices of the vast majority of the Greek and Roman populations and their subjects have vanished unheard. In his study of Roman slavery, *Slavery and Society at Rome* (Cambridge, 1994), Keith Bradley records only one freed slave, the philosopher Epictetus, who actually describes the indignities of slavery from the point of view of one who had endured them. Women's voices have also been lost. There are the few surviving poems of Sappho but then virtually nothing until the Christian era and the diary of the martyred Perpetua (AD 203). Any assessment of the position of these disenfranchised groups has to be decoded from the texts that survive. (See A. Cameron and A. Kuhrt (eds.), *Images of Women in Antiquity* (revised edition, London, 1993), Elaine Fantham and others (eds.), *Women in the Classical World* (Oxford, 1994).)

To some extent archaeology is coming to the rescue. The canon of established texts has been challenged by new finds. One can cite the gradual publication of the vast papyri cache (100,000 fragments) from Oxyrhynchus in Egypt which dates from the Hellenistic and Roman periods. Its discovery has helped revise the rigid picture of ancient literature which had prevailed since the Renaissance. There are over a thousand fragments from Homer, an indication of his immense popularity as a 'classic' throughout the Greek and Roman era, which show how variant readings were gradually reduced in favour of a finalized text by the end of the second century BC. Homer is not the only author who had achieved such a high status; Euripides was second to him and, interestingly, the twenty most popular authors in the cache were all writing before 200 BC. In other words we are dealing with a literate culture at home with a favourite set of earlier 'classic' texts. The second-century AD Plutarch may have derided the people of Oxyrhynchus as 'barbarians', but they were reading his sophisticated works within a generation. Books provided solace for many living in remote Egyptian villages. 'If you have already copied the books, send them, so that we have something to pass the time, because we have no one to talk to', reads one letter. Quite apart from what the Oxyrhynchus cache tells us of 'colonial' culture, an immense amount of background knowledge has been added. A tragedy by Aeschylus, *The Suppliants*, had long been considered one of his first and used to make statements about the early nature of tragedy until a text from Oxyrhynchus showed that it was actually relatively late! (The finds from Egypt also show the slow adoption of the *codex*, sheets of papyrus bound in book form, at the expense of the papyrus roll. The *codex* appears in the first century AD but only 1.5 per cent of texts are presented in this form. By AD 300, the percentage is 50 and by AD 500, 90. The roll gradually becomes obsolete as the book takes its place.)

As will be seen the climate of Egypt is ideal for the preservation of papyrus and much else besides but it is not the only source of new texts. There is a whole library of philosophy found in charred and brittle form in Herculaneum, a casualty of the volcanic eruption of AD 79 which also buried Pompeii. Then there is the remarkable selection of human voices surviving from wooden writing tablets found preserved in waterlogged pits at the Roman fort of Vindolanda near what was to become Hadrian's Wall in northern Britain. These letters not only bring the reader face to face with life as it was lived in a frontier garrison at the end of the first century AD but provide details of economic life, the organization of the army, the Latin language at its most vernacular, and the extent of literacy.

The most abundant source of new texts comes from inscriptions on stone, pottery, metal, or, in rare cases such as Vindolanda, wood. Possibly half a million inscriptions from the Greek and Roman world have now been published. Epigraphy, which is concerned not only with the recovery, translation, and editing of ancient inscriptions but with the placing of them, like other texts, in the political and social context in which they were written, is now a subject in its own right. Not only is the range of epigraphic texts much wider than those of the traditional canon of literature, but often they are discovered in their original settings, on the walls of public buildings, for instance. Some have provided a key to a whole civilization. The decree inscribed in three scripts and two languages on the Rosetta Stone, now in the British Museum, led to the decipherment of Egyptian hieroglyphics. Many have a direct historical value (the 'Decree of Themistocles' discovered in 1959 at Troezen or the Athenian Tribute Lists, for example, discussed in Chapters 12 and 15 respectively). Others give a flavour of city life, the dates of buildings, and the names and status of those who built them. Some of the more personal (although the 'personal' nature of any public inscription needs to be assessed with care) reflect marital harmony and commitment as in the famous *Laudatio Turiae*, a Roman funeral eulogy from the first century BC for one Turia by her husband who praises her constancy during the upheavals of the civil wars. (Childless, she even offers to divorce him so that he can beget heirs, a proposal he angrily rejects.)

A group of inscriptions which give a full picture of provincial life in a city of the Greek-speaking Roman empire comes from Aphrodisias in modern southern Turkey. It is a city which is hardly mentioned in other sources, but from the many inscriptions that have been found *in situ* there it has been possible to reconstruct the history of the city over centuries, the structure of some of its leading families, and the degree to which pagan culture survived into the Christian era. Among the finds has been the fullest extant text of any *senatus consultum* (a formal resolution of the Roman senate). Then there is a record (? third century AD) of ninety Jewish benefactors to the city whose status in the city seems to have been linked to Gentile members of the city council who are listed as 'god-fearers'. It is a good example of how such a community, vulnerable to attack for its exclusiveness, negotiated its survival and status in the provinces. In Anatolia, inscriptions left by Christian communities are showing just how diverse in belief these communities were and how immune to declarations of orthodoxy promulgated by distant 'ecumenical' councils. The languages of inscriptions also provide essential evidence of the relationship between Latin and Greek and local languages, and the survival of these through the centuries. In Palmyra, the great trading city on the far east of the empire, one can spot how Greek and Roman terminology was adopted within local Semitic languages. In north Africa, Punic speakers struggle with their Latin, incorporating grammatical structures from their own languages into their efforts. In short, the value of epigraphic material is immense, and it is often the only context in which voices outside those of the upper classes survive.

It is clear from this that the demise of traditional classical education does not mean that textual analysis should be discarded. It remains as essential a part of classical scholarship as it has ever been and it requires new skills, such as the decipherment of Roman cursive script for the Vindolanda tablets, for instance. It is, quite simply, important to tease out the full meaning, within the context of the culture which produced it, of any text which survives. So there will always be a need for those specialist linguists who revel in the dissection of ancient texts. However, new questions arise on how texts are to be interpreted, not just in the sense of analysing the meaning of the language but in the wider philosophical sense of what is meant by meaning. At the simplest level the student of any text needs to know when it was written, for whom and with what intent. As the case of the Gallic Wars suggests very few texts are what they seem at first reading and so there needs to be a process of uncovering different layers of meaning.

The recovery, and, as important, the preservation and decipherment, of the Vindolanda tablets rely on the skills of the archaeologist. Archaeology is primarily concerned with the recovery of material culture and buildings and their interpretation as evidence of past human behaviour. Traditionally the archaeologist has dealt largely in stone, pottery, and metalwork, as these are the materials most likely to survive in a temperate or tropical climate. In recent years a much wider range of materials, in particular those relating to plant and animal life, have proved recoverable, and so much more can be said, about agriculture and diet, for instance. The archaeologist remains preoccupied with the vulnerability of the materials he deals with (archaeological excavation necessarily involves the destruction of the context in which artefacts are found), as the looting in Iraq in 2003 reminds us. Virtually every bronze statue from the ancient world has been melted down, many for the value of their metals, others because, as 'pagan idols', they offended Christian sensibilities. It was only in the Renaissance that the urge to preserve an item because of its antiquity or aesthetic quality becomes a powerful force in Europe again with the result that ancient art begins to be idealized. Yet human destruction sometimes works in the archaeologist's favour. The burning down of the palaces of the Ancient Near East hardened the clay tablets that were piled in their archives so that they have survived to be read! Even so the archaeologist is still normally left with only a small and unrepresentative sample of what originally existed.

There are many areas where the archaeologist can make a significant contribution. In a typical excavation layers of occupation are uncovered, the older ones below the more recent. If these layers can be dated—from coins, for instance—so can other material, such as pottery, found in the same layer. Similar pottery uncovered in other contexts can then be used for dating a layer of occupation. This has been particularly important in the study of pre-dynastic Egypt. There are certain features of life which are seldom well documented—houses, patterns of trade and exchange, and developments in technology—and here the work of archaeologists has proved indispensable. Excavations and surveys along the borders of the Roman empire have revealed the successive programmes of fortification there as the empire came under the pressure of invasion. It has even proved possible to say something about political developments. Excavations in the Roman Forum have shown an increase in the space reserved for the public assemblies as the tribunes became more influential in the mid-second century BC, and a corresponding diminution in this space at the expense of that given to the senate house under the dictator Sulla. Archaeology can be used to confirm or challenge literary evidence. Coin hoards in Germany correspond almost exactly with details of the composition of such hoards given in Tacitus' *Germania*. (The study of ancient coins is another major area of scholarship in its own right.) On the other hand, the impression given in Greek texts that cities were walled and graced with public buildings from early times has been shown to be false. It was often more than a hundred years after its foundation that a city acquired its first set of walls, and the spaces set aside for public buildings were then often still unfilled.

A particularly important development has been underwater archaeology. It is an expensive and sometime hazardous business, and added to the costs of excavation are those of the preservation of artefacts when on dry land, but the expansion has been spectacular. In a study of 1957 there were only some fifty Mediterranean wrecks to work from, now the number is up to 1,500. Chronologically there is a dramatic increase in wrecks after 200 BC with a peak from 100 BC to AD 100 and a major tailing off after AD 400. Simplistically this can be seen as a record of the fluctuations of trading activity but as always when working with what has survived one must be cautious. One reason so many Roman cargo ships have been found is because they transported wine and oil in heavy amphorae which anchored the boat in the seabed when they sank. An amphora filled with wine weighs some 50 kilos and a large ship such as one excavated at Madrague de Giens near Cannes between 1972 and 1976 carried between 6,000 and 8,000 of them (a tonnage of 300–400). When wooden barrels replaced amphorae at the end of the classical era the ships would not rest so heavily on the seabed and many must have broken up. Despite this caveat shipwrecks have proved invaluable for the plotting of trade routes and trade (and occasionally a spectacular treasure such as bronze statues). A particular publicity success has been the excavation of the harbour of Cleopatra's Alexandria by Franco-Egyptian teams of divers. While traditionally scholars have stressed that Alexandria was a Greek city, culturally apart from the Egyptians (there are decrees banning all Egyptians from the city 'with the exception of pig-dealers and river boatmen and men who bring down reeds for heating the baths'), the finds show that large quantities of Egyptian statues had been transported into the city from the towns of the Delta. Displaying native Egyptian art was, it appears, a symbol of status. (It is worth noting that material from Cleopatra's era received much more publicity than that of the Roman period, another indication of how perceptions of the ancient world are shaped, in this case by the modern media.)

Advances in scientific techniques have made the evaluation of evidence more precise. Trace elements in metals allow their origin to be pinpointed. Lead isotope analysis from lead, copper, and silver ores enables a particular find to be traced back to where it was originally mined. The distinctive 'oxhide' shape copper ingots of the Late Bronze Age found in many sites in the Aegean were made of metal mined in Cyprus. The earliest Athenian coins were made of silver from Thrace, not, as might be expected, from the Laurium mines near the city. The analysis of residues found in Roman amphorae has enabled their contents to be identified, while comparison of the stamps on the amphorae themselves has been used to map trade routes. (The amphorae of one potter, Sestius, were distributed from Cosa in Italy throughout central and southern France.) Dendrochronology, the analysis of tree rings, is an effective way of exploring climate from one year to the next and it has been even shown that the year 218 BC was a mild one, which helps explain why Hannibal was able to progress through the Alps into Italy that year!

The sophistication of, but also the difficulties presented by, such methods can be shown in the attempts to provide a date for the eruption on the Aegean island of Thera, which buried the thriving Minoan port of Acrotiri, luckily preserving it as fully as Pompeii. It is not merely a historical question—the eruption has been linked to legends of a vanished Atlantis which has inspired so many fantasies about 'lost civilizations'. A date of around 1500 BC could be supported by datings from the pottery sequence and pumice apparently from the eruption found in a datable Egyptian archaeological layer of this date at Tell el-Dab'a in the Nile delta. (For the excavations at Tell el-Dab'a see Chapter 3.) However, carbon dating on samples from the site tended to go earlier—1615 BC is a mean date from samples but this can only be tentative and variations either side are possible. Then a dendrochronology based on tree rings from Californian bristlecone pines (the effect of the eruption would have been felt even this far afield as the dust in the atmosphere affects solar radiation) was used to fix a date specifically to 1628 or 1627 BC and there is some evidence to support the same dates from tree rings in Anatolia. Another approach, studying the acidity of ice cores, which reflect eruptions, in Greenland found a peak around 1645. This was flexible enough to be correlated with the 1628 date. If this date is correct what happens to Egyptian chronology? It is now suggested that the pumice found at Tell el-Dab'a was actually raw material being worked by craftsmen and so could date from before 1500!

Traditionally the focus in classical archaeology has been on the large city sites or, in the Greek world, sanctuaries. In fact much of nineteenth-century European 'archaeology' was preoccupied with the rediscovery of the major sites (the German financier Heinrich Schliemann's assault on the site of Troy, launched in 1871, was one of the best publicized, while the German excavation of Olympia 1875–81 with its 500 workers set the model for the 'big dig') and the transport of their treasures to national museums in London, Paris, or Berlin. The Germans were able to transport 350 tonnes of material from Pergamum, then sited in the decaying Ottoman empire, to Berlin as late as 1880. Although much of value has been found—how could one write the history of Rome or Athens without extensive excavation on the sites?—the concentration of popular monuments or periods of history left important areas unresearched. There has been a shift of emphasis from the city to the countryside (where, after all, the majority of the population continued to live). The field survey (based on the collection of surface finds) has proved a relatively economical and efficient way of plotting the nature of settlement across a wide area. An important field survey was that carried out by the British School at Rome in southern Etruria. (It was prompted by the widespread destruction of the ancient landscape by modern farming methods and new building.) One result of this and other surveys of Republican Italy was to challenge the view put forward in the literary sources that peasant plots had disappeared in Italy in the second century BC. Field surveys in Greece have shown how small and unpredictable the surpluses of produce were, and how precarious, as a result, was the survival of city life. Evidence of the planting of olives has proved a good indicator of political stability as the tree takes several years to mature and therefore is only planted when its maturity can be hoped for. On urban sites the geophysical survey is particularly useful in plotting the traces of buildings. A good example is the major survey of the Roman city of Wroxeter, the fourth largest city of the province of Britannia. The city is lucky not to be below modern occupation and it has proved possible to plot its outline, including industrial and market areas, and even to accumulate evidence, through discordant magnetic feedback, of destruction by fires, without any disturbance of the soil.

Field surveys, insofar as they are concerned with collecting and interpreting material, are carried out within the parameters of conventional archaeology. In the past thirty years, however, archaeologists have become much more ambitious in their objectives. The traditional approach was to accumulate evidence, describe it, and then use it to piece together a picture of the past. This inevitably produced a rather static picture of a society and one in which people often seemed less important than the objects they had left behind. The so-called 'New Archaeology' (a term originating in the United States in the 1960s) adopted a more proactive approach. The 'New Archaeologists' moved into the areas traditionally covered by anthropology. They were concerned to understand how individuals within a society related to each other and to the outside world and, in particular, how cultural change took place. They went to live among hunter-gatherer societies to observe patterns of living which might help explain the evidence left by similar societies of the past. They set up hypotheses and then examined a number of sites specifically to find evidence to support or disprove these hypotheses. They then attempted to put forward 'laws' of human behaviour. ('In such and such circumstances human societies turn from hunter-gathering to farming,' for instance.)

The 'New Archaeologists' focused overwhelmingly on the environment, which they believed to be the main instigator of social change. (For example, new patterns of social cooperation might emerge if different food sources had to be exploited.) Their approach earned the name 'processual', from the emphasis given to isolating and studying the different 'processes' which conditioned social change. More recently, some archaeologists, particularly in Britain, have found the 'processual' approach too functional. They claim that the emphasis on the environment underestimates the capacity of societies to make their own values and to sustain them, in particular through the manipulation of the cultural symbols which are important to them. This new approach has been termed 'post-processual'. One risks losing sight of the traditional concerns of archaeology under the weight of these conceptualizations (and often they were promulgated in jargon which was incomprehensible to all but the most determined readers), but perhaps a synthesis has emerged which shows a deepened understanding of how societies create their own ideological framework within which cultural change takes place. So one might see how a new Roman emperor ensures his legitimacy by using symbols from great emperors of the past, one reason why Constantine, for instance, incorporated reliefs from monuments in honour of the earlier emperors Trajan, Hadrian, and Marcus Aurelius into his own triumphal arch in Rome.

The study of the history of the ancient world is one in which traditional discipline boundaries are breaking down. To take one example the distinction between archaeology and art history is increasingly blurred. The Greek and Roman world poured an astonishing amount of its surplus into expensive monuments and elaborate public images. Since the Renaissance there has been a tendency to study ancient art as a set of individual masterpieces to be attributed if possible to named artists. In the second half of the eighteenth century the German art historian Johann Winckelmann developed a sequence of artistic periods with peaks of achievement (the fifth century BC in Greece) followed by decline and decadence (the Hellenistic and then Roman periods). (For a fuller discussion of Winckelmann's importance see below, p. 243.) More recently the British scholar Sir John Beazley (1885–1970) spent a lifetime attributing surviving Attic Greek painted pots to specific painters—or 'hands' when no names were on the pots. The influence of Renaissance scholarship on his approach was clear. There will always be a place for the definition of individual excellence (how could one not applaud the achievement of an artist like the sixth-century black-figure painter Ezekias?) but there was a risk of divorcing art from its original context. The reaction against Winckelmann began in the late nineteenth century with a re-evaluation of both the Archaic and Hellenistic periods and an appreciation that the art of any period is a creation of specific historical and cultural forces in that period, and above all reflects the needs of audiences. It should not be judged by its date alone. The trend is towards placing art back into its original setting and examining how it reflected society and the needs of the viewer in the period it was made. Art is a cultural symbol which requires the diversion of resources into its creation. What does that say about the society which created it?

A fine example of how cultural symbols might be used in the Greek world is provided by Andrew Stewart in his *Art, Desire and the Body in Ancient Greece* (Cambridge, 1997) which reflects on the way in which the body was presented in sculpture and painting to the onlooker in order to reflect specific political and social ideals. There are ways of showing political heroes, 'the ideal' citizen or philosopher, and the warrior hero. Even nudity had its own cultural contexts, being the 'costume' in which a hero, whether a victorious athlete or a challenger of tyranny could be portrayed. A more focused use of art as propaganda is explored by Paul Zanker in his *The Power of Images in the Age of Augustus* (Ann Arbor, 1988). Zanker shows how certain images of traditional Roman life—the grand public building, for instance—were used by the emperor Augustus to sell himself as the restorer, not the destroyer, of the Roman republic. Every statue of himself was composed so that even the scenes on the breastplates had a cultural significance which tied him to the past, while in the *Ara Pacis*, the Altar of Peace, Augustus is shown as a simple family man, offering sacrifices to the gods as his republican ancestors might have done. Political change could be achieved through the manipulation of cultural symbols, many of which held enormous emotive power. The term 'cognitive archaeology' has been coined to describe the attempt to create the mentality of the past from its surviving cultural objects.

This recovery of 'mentality' is one of the most difficult, if most fascinating, challenges for the ancient historian. What were the parameters within which thinking took place? It is a particularly difficult area in that it is virtually impossible to discard our own prejudices and cultural preconceptions enough to enter fully into the world of another. What did it mean for an Athenian to sit and listen to a tragedy and how far would he, or she, use the experience for emotional release or to more fully understand the ethical challenges that faced the city? To what extent did a citizen feel he was genuinely part of his city community—or was his public behaviour adopted for show, a series of learned experiences so that he would appear a perfect citizen to his fellows? Why did the classical world have to wait so long before a writer felt able to explore his innermost thoughts as Augustine did in his *Confessions* in the AD 390s? How far, in general, could personal feelings be shown and if one felt emotionally disturbed how should this be dealt with? In his fine study *Emotion and Peace of Mind: From Stoic Agitation to Christian Temptation* (Oxford, 2000), Richard Sorabji shows how the Stoic philosophers were all too aware of the threat of stress in public life and how they evolved means of dealing with it. The study goes further to show how the impact of the outside world was transformed by Christians into specific temptations. Yet in what ways did Christians think differently from their pagan contemporaries? Is the *Confessions* of Augustine evidence that they did so?

There have been attempts to understand the mentalities of the ancient world through its surviving mythologies. As every child knows, these are rich and varied. There remains, however, immense controversy over what myth can tell us about the society which produced it. There is some hesitation in using the myths of any culture to provide universal meaning—the search for understanding of a myth must start with the specific context in which it grew. (In other words Freud's universalization of the Oedipus myth, which in any case is not even typical of Greek myth, must be treated with suspicion.) The French anthropologist Claude Lévi-Strauss, and his fellow 'structuralists', proposed that the world picture of any studied society can be mapped ('structured') in terms of defined objects and categories whose meanings and significance are expressed and defined through myth. A 'Paris school' led by J.-P. Vernant and P. Vidal Naquet has made elaborate interpretations of Greek myths, teasing any possible nuance of meaning from the surviving versions. A 'British school' has tended to be more pragmatic and less willing to assume that a story must have a purpose and every detail of a story a significance. Yet myths do say something about the culture which produces them, and myths shared across scattered communities sustain cultural cohesion. In some cases myths are used to rationalize behaviour. The myth of Prometheus' trick on Zeus provides a reason for preserving the meat from sacrifices for the sacrificers to eat rather than dedicating it to the gods. Other myths, particularly those relating to the foundation of a city, may contain historical information. Others again portray the dilemmas of everyday life (whether loyalty to a family should come before loyalty to a city, for instance), presenting them in a 'distanced' form which might be easier for an audience to assimilate and assess. It is impossible to say, however, how far myths had the power to condition the way individuals behaved in their everyday lives.

So far this chapter has presented a traditional view of the history of the ancient Mediterranean as dominated by the civilizations of Greece and Rome. As Martin

Bernal has argued out in the first volume of his *Black Athena* (subtitled 'The Fabrication of Ancient Greece 1785–1985' (London, 1987)) the nineteenth century saw a narrowing of perspectives in that the civilization of ancient Greece, in particular, came to be seen as ethnically pure and distinct from those around it and this had its effect on scholarship. Up to 1975 classical archaeology seemed overwhelmingly preoccupied with its own concerns and it has been noted how many of the famous classicists avoided the trend towards 'world archaeology' which was sweeping the world of their colleagues in these years. The domination of John Beazley led to the survival of classical scholarship as an intense study, often in the dusty storerooms of museums, of artefacts deemed to be aesthetically valuable. (This is not so much a criticism of Beazley as of a system which allowed one such approach to predominate.) By the late 1970s the methods of the new archaeologists, described above, began to permeate classical archaeology and one result was to break down the ethnic barriers between Greece and Rome and their surrounding cultures whose artificiality became ever more obvious. The scholar is now much more aware of how precarious a Greek ethnic identity was, how much it was one forged by the Greeks themselves, above all in the psychological 'high' achieved by victory over the Persians in the early fifth century BC. Even then 'Greekness' remained a somewhat fluid and artificial concept which embraced an enormous variety of communities, many of whom were persistently hostile to each other. There were common attributes, in language, religion, and customs, but the homogeneity of these attributes seems to have been overstressed (partly as a result of the predominance of surviving written material from just one city, Athens).

Martin Bernal's later work, in the second volume of *Black Athena* (London, 1991) in particular, which went so far as to argue, in stark contrast to the traditional view, that Greek culture grew from roots provided by Egypt and the Ancient Near East, has not received much scholarly support (responses of scholars to Bernal are to be found in M. Lefkowitz and G. Rogers (eds.), *Black Athena Revisited* (Chapel Hill, 1996)) but it is now accepted that the study of Greece and Rome has to take place within the context of a wider Mediterranean world. This is indirectly the result of the shift of emphasis away from the exclusive study of the texts, which, written as they were by a small cultured elite, tend to give an impression of Greece and Rome as distinct and homogeneous cultures. The influence of historians such as Fernand Braudel, whose celebrated *The Mediterranean and the Mediterranean World in the Age of Philip II* (2nd edition, London, 1972) treated the Mediterranean as a whole, stressing the complex interrelationships between its peoples and cultures against a little-changing geographical background, has also been important. His approach, and that of the French *Annales* school of history in general, has equal relevance for earlier periods. More recently Nicholas Purcell and Peregrine Horden have attempted a similar comprehensive overview in their *The Corrupting Sea: A Study of*

Mediterranean History (Oxford, 2000). The greater emphasis given to the findings of archaeology have allowed these relationships across the Mediterranean world, through trade, migration, and other cultural contacts, to be plotted more fully. The old diffusionist approach, the view that 'superior civilizations' somehow passed on their cultures to other more stagnant societies (an approach which had its ideological home in European imperialism), has been replaced by approaches which stress how local cultures have the power to absorb and adapt foreign cultures to their own use. (A good example is the relationship between the Etruscans and the Greeks: see Chapter 20.) Intrinsic to this study has been a growing awareness, in the works of François Hartog, for instance, in not only how one culture, the Greeks, perceived another, the Egyptians or the 'wild Scythians', but how they used those cultures as 'an opposite' against which to define their own. (For an excellent introduction see François Hartog, *Memories of Odysseus: Frontier Tales from Ancient Greece* (Edinburgh, 2001).)

One result of this shift of emphasis has been to recognize the contribution of the Ancient Near East and Egypt to the making of classical culture. The Near East provided the Mediterranean world with the alphabet, probably some of the elements of Greek philosophy, possibly, through Phoenician examples, the concept of the *polis*, and the world's three great monotheistic religions, all of which became prominent across the Mediterranean. As John Boardman has put it (speaking of Greek art in particular), 'I find it easier to view Greece before the fifth century as the westernmost extension of the eastern world than as the easternmost of the western world.' Although Egypt was largely isolated from the Mediterranean world before the seventh century, it too came to exercise a powerful influence, both material, in its grain exports, and cultural. Egypt was still seen as a fount of ancient wisdoms and its deities such as the goddess Isis became highly popular in the Roman period. Egypt provides monumental buildings as well as exquisite craftsmanship in jewellery and patterns of Greek stone working and the 'lost wax' method of making bronze statues derive from Egypt. No study of Greece and Rome can now afford to neglect these civilizations, and the next chapters as well as parts of later chapters are devoted to them.

While the barriers between civilizations and subject disciplines have been broken down so have boundaries set by date. There have been traditional markers, 323 BC for the boundary between classical and Hellenistic, AD 300 for that between the ancient and medieval world. (The first, pre-Second World War, edition of the *Cambridge Ancient History* ended, for instance, in AD 324.) The beginnings of the Greek world were set in the eighth century. George Grote, writer of one of the great nineteenth-century histories of Greece, talked of the period before this as 'a past that was never present—a region essentially mythical, neither approachable by the critic nor measurable by the chronographer'. If there is one symbolic moment which shattered this conception it was the announcement in 1952 by Michael Ventris that the language of the Mycenaean

Linear B tablets, which date from the thirteenth or possibly fourteenth century BC, was Greek, giving it the longest continuous history of any language spoken today. While, as will be seen, the eighth century did mark a fundamental turning point, it was no longer a starting point but a continuation, if in new forms, of an earlier culture.

The AD 300 boundary had dissolved more gradually with the rise of interest in late antiquity. It is now appreciated how far the patterns of classical civilization continued into the fourth, fifth, and even sixth centuries. Constantine's commitment to Christianity used to be seen in terms of a new beginning (a view conditioned by the panegyrical source for his life by the Christian bishop Eusebius) but it is now appreciated how he saw his commitment to the Christian gods in terms of the religious practices of his predecessors. (The Edict of Milan (see p. 563), which gave toleration for Christians, was a new start for them but as toleration for all was promised it could also be seen as a culmination of earlier Roman policies towards religion.) In giving patronage to Christians in the shape of large buildings, Constantine was acting as a pagan emperor would have done to his favoured religion—it was the Christians who had to react to this unexpected, and to the more ascetic, shocking, display of opulence. (See Dominic Janes's excellent study, *God and Gold in Late Antiquity* (Cambridge, 1998).) Even the Christian commitment to the poor is being reinterpreted, by scholars such as Peter Brown, as continuation and development (if extension) of traditional giving patterns. Yet by the sixth century there *is* something different, two patterns of Christianity, the theocratic Christianity of Byzantium, the more diffuse Christianity of the western bishops, which have refocused spiritual energies. With the foundations of recognizable European states and the shattering impact of Islamic invasions there is a new phase of history in the making. Even these developments have not deterred some scholars from stressing the continuing underlying patterns of Mediterranean life.

Western society, its culture, its religious beliefs, its consciousness, has been shaped for good or bad by Greece and Rome and the earlier cultures on which they drew. Fifty per cent of everyday English words have a Greek or Latin origin and they are expressed in a sequence of symbols (the alphabet) which, from its origins in the Near East, reached its final form in the Latin world. The debt of the Romance languages to Latin is even greater. The conflicts between France and her neighbours to the north over centuries may be seen as the legacy of the Roman frontier, although, equally, it can be argued that the idea of a European community, one which has finally brought France and Germany together, also has its roots in the Roman concept of universal citizenship. Then there is the legacy of Roman law, Greek political theory (and, to a lesser extent, practice), an architectural heritage, and a literature which, whatever its own merits, has bequeathed theatre and even the concepts of psychoanalysis to western culture. The classical ideal of sculpture has appeared and reappeared throughout western history and still provides an ideal of the human body, both male and female. Every four years the world is reminded, in the Olympic Games, of how central success in sport was to the ancient Greeks. In the philosophical tradition the works of Plato and Aristotle have fuelled what Richard Tarnas in his *The Passion of the Human Mind* (New York, 1991, London, 1996) has called 'the intellectual basis, at once unstable and highly creative, for what was to become an extremely dynamic evolution lasting over two and a half millennia'. It is inconceivable that Christianity would have taken the institutional or doctrinal form it did if its institutions had not matured within the late Roman empire and its doctrine within the Greek philosophical world (unless one takes a Christian Platonist view that 'correct' doctrine exists independently of social or historical context but even that view is Greek in origin). To say the Greeks and Romans are of no importance is essentially to say that one can live without any knowledge of one's past (and even the methods used to explore that past are largely Greek in conception).

Likewise, in a world where violence continues to leave its scars, it is hard to believe that Homer's depiction of the pity of war (as Hector leaves his family for battle or Priam comes to retrieve Hector's dead body from Achilles) does not find some universal echo, while Thucydides' account of the civil war in Corcyra holds no surprises for those who have seen spirals of terror and counter-terror in the twentieth century. The theme of Thucydides' 'Melian dialogue', in which he suggests those with power distort words to their advantage, has been developed by George Orwell in *Animal Farm* and *1984*. The corruptions of power analysed by Tacitus in the second century AD have all too many contemporary equivalents. Greek tragedy presents ethical dilemmas—the conflict between the individual and community, for instance—which remain central ones in political life today. In his *From Melos to My Lai, War and Survival* (London, 2000) Lawrence Tritle contrasts the Greek experience of war with that of US veterans in Vietnam. The Greeks were, after all, peoples as intelligent and ingenious as us, facing many of the same challenges, and often formulating sophisticated responses to them.

In conclusion it has to be stressed that the ancient Mediterranean was a place of great cultural complexity, and its re-creation in the hands of historians has become all the more of a challenge. It is easy to be overwhelmed by the sheer range of materials and texts and the continual widening of horizons and reinterpreting of the evidence. However, this in itself makes the study of the ancient Mediterranean an exciting place to be in so much as it ranges over so many concerns and draws in so many different kinds of scholars, the scientific archaeologist, the lover of art and literature, the traditional historian and the student of ideas. All benefit from the interaction of one approach with another in an attempt, never fully realized, of understanding the ancient world. There can be few better ways of broadening the mind.

FURTHER READING

In addition to books cited in the text. *Classics: A Very Short Introduction* by Mary Beard and John Henderson (Oxford, 1995) successfully shows that 'Classics' now means far more than the analysis of texts. T. P. Wiseman (ed.), *Classics in Progress: Essays on Ancient Greece and Rome* (Oxford, 2002), is a recent survey of the area. R. Bolgar, *The Classical Inheritance and its Beneficiaries* (Cambridge, 1954), is a scholarly introduction to the subject and concludes with a defence of the classics.

The revival of ancient Greek in the nineteenth century is covered in three excellent books: Richard Jenkyns, *The Victorians and Ancient Greece* (Oxford, 1980); Frank Turner, *The Greek Heritage in Victorian Britain* (New Haven, 1981); and Suzanne Marchand, *Down from Olympus: Archaeology and Philhellenism in Germany, 1750–1970* (Princeton, 1996). See also Simon Goldhill, *Who Needs Greek? Contests in the Cultural History of Hellenism* (Cambridge, 2002).

For the decoding of texts see A. Cameron (ed.), *History as Text: The Writing of Ancient History* (London, 1989); M. Crawford (ed.), *Sources for Ancient History* (Cambridge, 1983); and Malcolm Heath, *Interpreting Classical Texts* (London, 2002), a lively introduction. *Epigraphic Evidence: Ancient History from Inscriptions*, edited by John Bodel (London, 2001) is an excellent overview. On coins there is Christopher Howgego, *Ancient History from Coins* (London, 1995). The Routledge series, *Approaching the Ancient World*, of which these last two books are part, has a number of other valuable titles.

For the debate over Greek literacy see W. Harris, *Ancient Literacy* (Cambridge, Mass., 1989) who argues that the degree of literacy has been overestimated, and the essays in Harvey Yunis (ed.), *Written Texts and the Rise of Literate Culture in Ancient Greece* (Cambridge, 2003), which suggests that writing meant different things in different contexts. See also Rosalind Thomas, *Literacy and Orality in Ancient Greece* (Cambridge, 1992).

For the contribution of the Oxyrhynchus papyri to a revaluation of classical literature, see Peter Parsons, 'New Texts and Old Theories', in T. P. Wiseman (ed.), *Classics in Progress*, cited above.

To get started on archaeology try *Archaeology: A Very Short Introduction*, by Paul Bahn (Oxford, 2000). A wide-ranging and stimulating introduction is provided by Colin Renfrew and Paul Bahn, *Archaeology: Theories, Methods and Practice* (3rd edition, London, 2000). On the way ideology conditions the concerns of archaeologists see B. Trigger, *A History of Archaeological Thought* (Cambridge, 1989). On changing perspectives in Greek archaeology see Part I of James Whitley, *The Archaeology of Ancient Greece* (Cambridge, 2001).

On myth, see G. S. Kirk, *The Nature of Greek Myths* (Harmondsworth, 1974). More recent overviews of this highly complex area include Geoffrey Buxton, *Imaginary Greece* (Cambridge, 1994); Ken Dowden, *The Uses of Greek Mythology* (London, 1992); and, forthcoming, Mary Lefkowitz, *Greek Gods, Human Lives, What We Can Learn from Myths* (New Haven, 2003).

For an overview of the legacies of the classical world: R. Jenkyns (ed.), *The Legacy of Rome* (Oxford, 1992); M. Finley (ed.), *The Legacy of Greece* (Oxford, 1984).

2 | The Civilizations of the Ancient Near East, 5000–1200 BC

The word 'culture' is central to any discussion of human society, yet it is one of those words which is used in so many different contexts that it needs to be handled with some caution. In a very broad sense it concerns a set of shared values and traditions which is passed on in some coherent form from one generation to another. These might include a body of knowledge and beliefs, including moral behaviour, styles of art, patterns of relationships, ways of conducting government, all the specific aspects of a society by which it may be distinguished from another. Cultures are seldom frozen, it is simply not possible for a culture to remain unaffected by changing political and economic conditions, but often cultural symbols are used again and again by rulers or ruling classes in order to reassert authority or establish their legitimacy. These symbols become important rallying cries when a culture is under threat. It is normal, however, for cultures to be in a tension between forces for change and forces for continuity. Understanding how and why cultural change takes place, and how it is managed, is an important part of any history. In some areas, an open sea like the Mediterranean or one with many trade networks, there is continuous cultural interchange. Incoming cultures can be welcomed and adapted by their recipients or emphatically rejected by them. Cultures can collapse completely or be transformed into something virtually unrecognizable from what went before. A massive if slow transformation of the Mediterranean world took place with the coming of Christianity, for instance, as life was shaped to new purposes. (The issues raised here are, in the context of the 'Romanization' of Gaul, well discussed by Greg Woolf in his *Becoming Roman* (Cambridge, 1998).)

Just as it is difficult to give a clear definition of what is encompassed in a culture, so it is difficult to say what gives a particular culture the status of a civilization. The word 'civilization' itself is often used as a term of cultural and political superiority, an attitude which was shaped by the Egyptians, Greeks, and Romans as they compared themselves to other 'barbarian' peoples around them. Yet as every culture tends to think itself superior to its neighbours, it is important to move beyond such value judgements to give a broader definition of 'civilization' which can provide the setting for the cultures discussed in this book. Inherent in the notion of civilization is political and cultural stability and this normally means a state, a defined territory over which a king, a religious ruler, or some other form of government, claims control. From earliest times civilization and city life have appeared to be inseparable, although what makes a city varies from generation to generation. One may, at its foundation, be a religious centre, the focus for the worship of a god, another the setting in which a ruler displays himself, through monumental buildings perhaps; another may gain its energy from trading, be primarily a centre where people meet to buy and sell, where goods are unloaded from water, for instance, or where trade routes cross. Often functions overlap—a capital may become a port or a ruler draw his authority from the ancient religious meaning of a site. In a trading city there are opportunities for craftsmen to transfer raw materials into textiles, metal implements, or works of art for the elite so manufacturing quarters grow up, often close to the market place, and there are finished goods to be sold back to visiting traders.

In order to survive the inhabitants of cities spawn creative solutions. They have to, in order to deal with the basic administration of day-to-day survival, when so many have to be fed and given fresh water, and their waste safely removed. The way of life, the rules of trading have to be regulated, order imposed through a defined authority, the ruler, his officials, or even the people themselves. Records have to be kept and so means of transferring information into a permanent, comprehensible form, writing, develops. The city reinforces its own status through its buildings. Its walls may be as much a mark of its power as a means of defence. (This was certainly true of ancient Mesopotamia where the normal and often exaggerated boast of conquerors was that they had destroyed an enemy city's walls even if archaeological evidence shows that they had not!) As many examples from Egypt and the Near East show, walls provide an excellent setting for reliefs which can proclaim the power of a ruler or his gods. Yet a city is more than its rulers. The interaction of the people themselves encourages the exchange of ideas and their diffusion. So begins the complex interchange of cultures which will be such an important theme of this book.

No city can exist if it does not draw on surpluses of food and in most cases this comes from the surrounding land. Civilization and the control of food surpluses go hand in hand, but the process of accumulation can occur in different ways. A state may have control over valued sources, tin, silver, iron ores, which it can trade for food. It may win resources through war and then use them to fuel further expansion. It may simply develop a highly efficient bureaucracy centred on the king which channels surpluses up to his court in 'taxation' (as in ancient Egypt). A question which has to be asked of all the civilizations in this book is how surplus was accumulated and used to sustain the civilization discussed.

For the Mediterranean world the beginnings of civilization are normally placed in the Ancient Near East. The Ancient Near East is here defined as covering the area which now stretches from Turkey eastwards across to the Caspian Sea and southwards from there to take in modern Iran and Iraq. In the south-west it includes the modern Syria, Israel, Jordan, and the Lebanon. In the period covered here and in Chapter 6 there were major centres of civilization in Mesopotamia, Palestine, Phoenicia, to the north of Palestine (the modern Lebanon), Syria, and Anatolia, on the central plain of modern Turkey. Egypt was in continuous interaction with the area but as its civilization had many unique features it will be dealt with separately.

The legacy of this area both to the other civilizations of the ancient world and to the modern world is immense. It includes the earliest examples of settled agriculture, the first cities and temples, and with them systems of administration that fostered the earliest forms of writing. The alphabet originated in the Levant in about 1500 BC. The world's first kingdoms and empires, the beginnings of metalwork, and building in brick are found in Mesopotamia. Three major world religions, the only monotheistic ones, Judaism, Christianity, and Islam, have originated in the area. As the civilizations of the Ancient Near East were not isolated from each other nor from the outside world, all these developments spread to the Mediterranean world and beyond. The extensive records kept by Babylonian mathematicians and astronomers entered the Greek world in the third century BC and the data allowed the plotting of the movements of the stars over time.

The landscape of the Near East is a varied and often formidable one. In southern Iraq there were marshes (although much of the Iraqi marshland has been drained in recent years), in Jordan and Syria desert, in Iran mountains topped with snow. In southern Mesopotamia there is a flat plain rich in silt brought down by the Tigris and Euphrates (the name Mesopotamia itself comes from the Greek for 'between two rivers'). To the north and east of the plain lie mountain ranges, whose melting snows provide these two rivers with their annual floods. There are high plateaux—Anatolia, 500 metres above sea level, and Iran with its inhospitable central deserts, and more mountain ranges, north and south of Anatolia and along the Lebanese coast. These different environments have hosted both sophisticated city states and nomadic peoples whose relationships with each other have added to the complexity of the area's history. The more resilient Near East economies combined cereal production, and thus a settled population, with pastoralism, the husbanding of goats, sheep, and cattle. Typically successful city states of the Ancient Near East grasped a territory around them and consolidated their position through the control of trade, often over routes which remained unchanged for centuries. It was a precarious existence, there were few easily defensible borders, and many states collapsed after only a century or two. However, it was probably just this changing pattern of cultures which made the area such a rich source of innovation.

The rediscovery of the Ancient Near East began in the nineteenth century. The pioneers were a mixture of European diplomats, gentleman scholars, soldiers, and colonial administrators. Their motives were varied but among the most important were the determination to prove the truth of the Bible through finding backing for

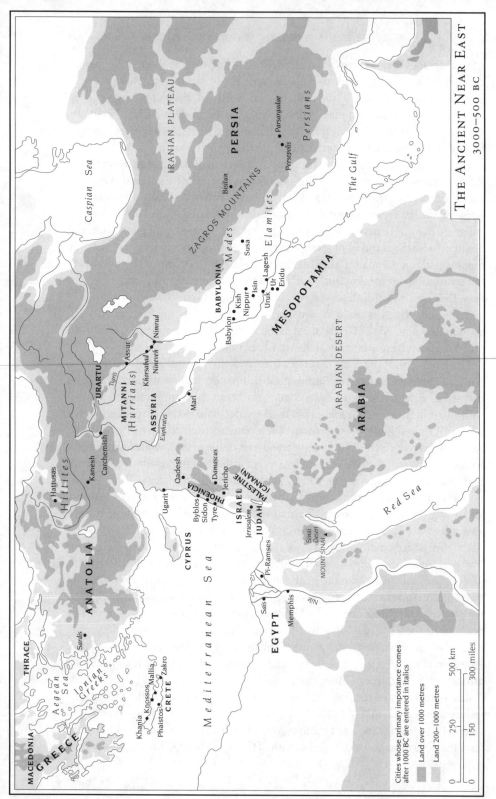

THE ANCIENT NEAR EAST
3000–500 BC

MACEDONIA
THRACE
GREECE
Aegean Sea
Ionian Greeks
Sardis
Khania
Knossos
Mallia
Zakro
Phaistos
CRETE
Mediterranean Sea
CYPRUS
ANATOLIA
Hittites
Hattusas
Kanesh
Carchemish
Ugarit
Byblos
Sidon
Tyre
PHOENICIA
Qadesh
Damascus
Jericho
Jerusalem
ISRAEL
JUDAH
PALESTINE (CANAAN)
Pi-Ramses
Sais
Memphis
Nile
EGYPT
Red Sea
Sinai Desert
MOUNT SINAI
ARABIA
ARABIAN DESERT
Mari
Euphrates
Tigris
ASSYRIA
MITANNI (Hurrians)
URARTU
Assur
Khorsabad
Nineveh
Nimrud
Babylon
Kish
Nippur
Isin
Uruk
Lagesh
Ur
Eridu
BABYLONIA
MESOPOTAMIA
Susa
Elamites
Medes
PERSIA
Persians
Bisitun
ZAGROS MOUNTAINS
IRANIAN PLATEAU
Parsargadae
Persepolis
Caspian Sea
The Gulf

Cities whose primary importance comes
after 1000 BC are entered in italics

Land over 1000 metres
Land 200–1000 metres

0   250   500 km
0   150   300 miles

MAP 1

its historical accounts and to accumulate collections of treasures for their own national museums. The great palaces of Assyria, Khorsabad, Nimrud, and Nineveh were stripped of their magnificent reliefs, which are now to be found in British and French museums. One of the great discoveries was the vast library of the Assyrian king Ashurbanipal at Nineveh with its collection of Mesopotamian literature. The cuneiform script in which the tablets were written was deciphered eventually by an Englishman, Henry Rawlinson (1810–95), from a trilingual inscription carved by the Persian king Darius on a rock at Behistun. The literature and complex history of the region could now start to be unravelled and, in fact, it is only recently that the large quantities of cuneiform tablets accumulated in western museums have been tackled. A defining moment came in 1872 when George Smith, working on Assyrian tablets in the British Museum, found a text describing a great flood and instantly placed the Bible in a wider cultural context. In the late nineteenth century the British archaeologist Flinders Petrie pioneered the use of stratigraphy in Palestine. By isolating the different layers of occupation at a site he was able to correlate his finds with datable material from Egypt and work out a chronology of events which is still usable today. The twentieth century saw in the Ancient Near East, as elsewhere, a much more meticulous and scientific approach to excavation, and very steadily its histories and cultures are being revealed and related to each other and the wider world. However, so many sites have been concealed under the shifting soil of Mesopotamia, or obliterated by later building on the same site, that there remain enormous gaps in knowledge.

A major blow, the full extent of which is still unknown, to the history of the Ancient Near East, has been dealt as a result of the looting in Baghdad and elsewhere on ancient sites in Iraq which followed in the aftermath of the British-American invasion of Iraq in 2003. It is clear that irreplaceable artefacts have either been destroyed or stolen for private resale.

Mesopotamia and the First Cities

The earliest of the city states appeared at the southern end of the Mesopotamian plain and their civilization is known as Sumer. The Akkadian (Akkadian was a Semitic language used in the area from about 2600 BC) word for this part of Mesopotamia was *Sumerum* and it is this which was adopted in modern times to name the civilization. Sumerian civilization was based on a group of cities which emerged about 3000 BC and its most important distinguishing feature is its language, Sumerian. This language is difficult to place because it seems unrelated to any other of the region and how it originated is a mystery. It has proved impossible to find any material base for a Sumerian people who were distinct from those around them but the word Sumerian is still used as a general name for the culture of the region between 3000 and 2300 BC.

The antecedents of Sumerian civilization can be tracked in Mesopotamia very much earlier than 3000 BC. At first sight the plain did not appear to be a likely home for a civilization. There were few natural resources, no timber, stone, or metals. Rainfall was limited, and what water there was rushed across the plain in the annual flood of melted snow. As the plain fell only 20 metres in 500 kilometres the beds of the rivers shifted constantly. It was this which made the organization of irrigation, particularly the building of canals to channel and preserve the water, essential. Once this was done and the silt carried down by the rivers planted, the rewards were rich: four to five times what rain-fed earth would produce. It was these conditions that allowed an elite to emerge, probably as an organizing class, and to sustain itself through the control of surplus crops which could be used in exchange for the raw materials which it lacked.

It is difficult to isolate the factors which led to the next development, the emergence of urban settlements. The earliest, that of Eridu, which grew up in the fifth millennium BC, centred on an impressive temple complex built of mudbrick (these mounds of accumulated remains are known as 'tells'), within a small depression which allowed water to accumulate. Its position, close to the Euphrates but at the intersection of marsh, desert, and alluvial soil gave the site access to farmland and fishing with some scope for pastoralism but it was its constant supply of water which appears to have given it a sacred quality. In the 1940s, excavators working their way through layer after layer of occupation eventually found a small 'chapel' built of sun-dried brick on a base of undisturbed sand. It was dated, incredibly, to 4900 BC. The height of the tell was explained as it became clear that for a thousand years temple followed temple, each built on the preserved remains of its predecessor. (This thousand-year period to the beginning of the fourth millennium is known as the Ubaid period, from a site of this period excavated in the 1920s, Tell Ubaid, near Ur.) The larger and later temples showed that they had been centres of ritual worship and that worshippers had brought simple offerings such as fish (again perhaps reinforcing the sacredness of water and all it gave life to). Pottery dishes suggested that communal meals had been part of the rituals. So the shrine had achieved a status which persisted from generation to generation. Well might later Babylonian texts talk of the creation of Eridu by the god Marduk as the first city, 'the holy city, the dwelling of their [the other gods] delight'.

Close by the temple complex was found a cemetery and the excavation of graves dating from about 3800 BC suggests that it was reserved for an elite. Their grave goods were well made and some, such as obsidian beads, had come long distances. Older burials had been marked and preserved. The assumption is that this elite was somehow associated with the maintenance of the temples and gained privileges as a result. Eridu, which was the southernmost of the Mesopotamian settlements, may have been, in fact, primarily a centre for pilgrimage. Its mythological links to creation and its association with permanent supplies of water, so yearned for in the desert, preserved its status so that modern Iraqi governments still see it as the founding city of their civilization.

Eridu could hardly be called a city in the full sense of the word but its neighbour Uruk, to the north-west, has a better claim. The most significant period in Uruk's history is between 3800 and 3200 BC for which there is a mass of evidence of monumental building, in stone and a primitive concrete for some periods, in mudbrick for others. The building sequence has been difficult to clarify because large buildings seem to have been demolished and then new ones built on their levelled remains (there is no evidence that this was as the result of destruction through warfare) but the impression is of public ceremonial areas which allowed for easy access by crowds. What is remarkable is that architectural styles change when rebuilding takes place—there is no attempt to perpetuate the same style of building—although there are enduring design features such as attractively coloured clay cones which were set into walls and pillars. This was an innovative people and hand in hand with this goes evidence of more sophisticated bureaucracy. Officials had their own seals, their individually chosen designs inscribed on cylinders which could then be rolled across damp clay to identify goods of which they were owners or for which they were responsible. A primitive form of writing, again inscribed on damp clay, was used to record goods, administrative decisions, and the use of labour. Some signs were simply representations of the commodity itself, an ear of corn, water, or numbers of containers (these are known as logograms). The evidence that this was an ordered society is reflected in the Warka (Warka is the modern Arabic name for the site) vase in which a procession of naked men carry containers of goods in some form of ritual procession probably associated with Inanna, the goddess of love and war. (The vase was reported missing in the immediate aftermath of the invasion of Iraq in 2003 but thankfully it was returned to the Baghdad museum.)

The development of Uruk, a site which eventually covered some 550 hectares, about half the size of Rome at its height in AD 100, goes hand in hand with the diffusion of artefacts which are recognizably in the style of those from Uruk far beyond southern Mesopotamia, into southern Anatolia and northern Syria. This has given rise to intense debate among scholars about the nature of Uruk society. Was it, as some have argued, essentially an imperialist state which set up colonial outposts (the sites with Uruk materials) in the north which acted as centres for the control of trade or was it a more egalitarian society, with relatively little in the way of a hierarchy, which simply organized its trading activities more efficiently than its rivals? The easy access to the ceremonial buildings and the generous open spaces in the centre of the city do suggest an open society, certainly when these are compared to the closed-off temple sanctuaries of Egypt. The constantly changing styles of architecture is a contrast to those societies, many of which will be discussed later in this book, which reproduced traditional styles as a means of asserting their authority and links to the past. So Uruk might have been home to a genuinely egalitarian society which was dedicated to promoting and sustaining an economy based on exchange, possibly using its public spaces for rituals celebrating the fact. (One unusual discovery within the buildings were sealed containers with ritual objects associated with trade inside them.) One even finds that of the two leading administrative officials, one (*en*) was a man and one (*nin*) a woman. Perhaps Uruk's greatest achievement was to find ways of sustaining its economic vigour over centuries. However, in about 3100 BC its trading links disappear, perhaps, it is suggested, because the water supplies around Uruk began to dry up or the land was so intensively cultivated that the rural economy necessary to support the city collapsed. Even so, the precedent for city life had been set and Uruk's demise went hand in hand with the rise of many smaller city states each exploiting its own access to water and surrounding land.

The use of writing had now become a feature of many of these Mesopotamian city states. As suggested above, the earliest script was based on logograms, a symbol which is used to express a whole word. Two thousand logograms have been recorded from these early centuries of writing and insofar as many represented what it was wished to record (an ear of corn for corn, for instance), they were relatively easy to read and could be comprehensible across different language groups, an important consideration so far as a trading state such as Uruk was concerned. About 3000 BC, however, writing is found expressed in Sumerian. As already noted the origins of the Sumerians are obscure and their language has no links with any other known language but it clearly had some kind of status so that for centuries texts written in Sumerian were considered superior to those in other languages. (One might note the similarity with the status given to Latin in Europe described in Chapter 1.) Hand in hand with the adoption of Sumerian came an important development, the use of Sumerian words of one syllable (which was common in the language) in longer words where the sound of that syllable was needed. To take an example: the Sumerian word for 'head' was *sag*. Whenever a word including a syllable with the sound *sag* was to be written, the sign for *sag* could be used to express that syllable with the remaining syllables of the word expressed by other signs. By 2300 BC the number of signs required had been reduced to 600 and the range of words which could be expressed had widened. There were still complications. Scribes had to make clear whether the *sag* sign was the whole word 'head' or part of a longer word. Texts dealing with economic matters predominated, as they always had done, but now works of theology, literature, history, and law appear. The writing was no longer incised (on damp clay tablets) with a pointed stylus but one with a wedge shape at its end. (The Romans called the shape *cuneus* and this gives the script its name of cuneiform.) Gradually the signs diverged from their pictorial roots and became more abstract but it is remarkable that the changes spread uniformly between cities suggesting the continuing importance of trade links between them. In fact, texts found in a large cache at Shuruppak, north-west of Uruk, show that six neighbouring cities of the period worked well together, even raising men from each to work on communal projects and allowing each others' citizens free access to their territories.

Analysis of the texts from Shuruppak suggest a conservative society. A father exhorts his son not to drink or consort with prostitutes or even to speak in public to a woman he is not married to. He should respect those of higher social status, protect his family, and work the land carefully. In other texts there is an emphasis on lists, fish, birds, plants, officials, even mathematical terms. This is an indication that naming an object is seen as a way of keeping control of it, putting it in a manageable order and thus creating psychological security. The lists were compiled with the objects listed according to status (higher officials before lower ones, the sheep as the highest of animals reflecting the importance of wool in the community).

Other innovations of the late fourth millennium include the wheel, probably developed first as a more efficient way of making pottery and then transferred to transport. A tablet incised about 3000 BC provides the earliest known example, a roofed box-like sledge mounted on four solid wheels. A major development was the discovery, again about 3000 BC, that if copper, which had been known in Mesopotamia since about 3500, was mixed with tin, a much harder metal, bronze, would result. Although copper and stone tools continued to be used, bronze was far more successful in creating sharp edges which could cut anything from crops and wood to human bodies and it had the extra advantage that its melting point was very much lower than that of copper. The period from 3000 to 1000 BC, when the use of iron becomes widespread, is normally referred to as the Bronze Age. It spread right across Europe and even when iron replaced bronze for weapons and tools bronze remained important for statues and ceremonial goods.

The use of bronze requires access to copper and tin sources and these now became important. The people of Sumer probably imported their tin from mines in central Asia. It was one stand of a busy network of trade routes, some running north and south along the rivers, others eastwards through the city of Susa on the edge of the Iranian plateau to Afghanistan, the home of lapis lazuli. Timber and aromatics came from the mountains of Turkey and Syria, granite and dolerite from Egypt, cedarwood from the mountains of Lebanon. The sophistication of Sumer's society can be seen in the finds made in the so-called Royal Cemetery of the city of Ur by the British archaeologist Leonard Woolley in the 1920s and 1930s (and the best of which are now in the British Museum). The richest of the graves, which date from around 2500 BC, contain what appear to be cult figures of men and women (there is no firm evidence that they are actually kings or queens), buried with other bodies around them. There is a mass of finely crafted goods, harps and lyres fashioned in inlaid wood, gaming boards, drinking cups, and jewellery in gold and silver. The so-called Standard of Ur, one of the finest artefacts, is a two-sided sounding box with scenes of war on one side and peace on the other, beautifully inlaid with shell and lapis lazuli. The relationship between the elite corpses and those around them has been the subject of fierce debate. Woolley constructed an elaborate explanation based on royal attendants being drugged and then laid alongside their masters in a single ceremonial burial. More recently it has been thought that the cult figures had such prestige that others wished their bodies to be buried as close to them as possible at the time of death (or even had their bodies preserved to be later placed in such a prestigious context).

The plains of Mesopotamia were not peaceful. Ceremonial weapons of gold were found among the finery of the Royal Graves of Ur, suggesting a high status for those successful in war. On the so-called Vulture stele from the city of Lagesh (like the Royal Graves dated possibly to about 2500 BC), a king is portrayed first in a wheeled battle-wagon leading ranks of helmeted infantry and then a second time with the infantry striding over a defeated enemy. The city leaders were not necessarily all war chieftains—some of the terms used to describe them refer to them as religious or administrative rulers—but there is no doubt that this was an age of increasing inter-city rivalry and conflict. The emergence of war leaders is associated with northern Mesopotamia where the Euphrates and the Tigris come closest to each other. The river beds are stable and land routes well established. Hence control of the area becomes highly attractive and anyone in charge will need to be able to defend himself against rivals. It is the city of Kish which has one of the first recorded kings, one Mesilim, who ruled in about 2400 BC.

In line with these developments palaces now become more prominent in the cities. At Kish, the entrance of the palace was fronted by fortified towers and surrounded by a perimeter wall. There is evidence of growing inequality in society. There is an increasing disparity between the houses of the rich and the poor, and a system of rations appears in which the amount given out depends on the status of the recipient. Slavery makes its first appearance in the historical record, with female slaves recorded as working as spinners and weavers in the temple workshops.

As seen in Chapter 1, one of the trends of epigraphy has been a shift from a literal translation of documents or inscriptions towards more nuanced interpretations of them as public relations exercises. Texts from Sumer in the late third millennium, often inscribed on slabs or statues and displayed in temples for all to see, evoke an image of society in which the ruler is upheld as the chosen one of the gods, who maintains peace and security for all and sustains prosperity, not least as an overseer of irrigation. Cities flourish under his rule and the population grows under his 'shepherding'. (This image of the Good Shepherd reappears throughout the ancient world and is eventually incorporated into Christianity.) This may well have been idealization but the first law codes suggest that there may have been some reality in the picture of the benign ruler. The earliest surviving code, that of Urukagina, ruler of Lagesh about 2350 BC, seems aimed at restricting the power of the bureaucrats and wealthy landowners. The poor are protected against their excesses and there is evidence from Sumer in general that a system of law, with courts and respected local citizens sitting as judges, operated.

The *Epic of Gilgamesh* (see further below) contributes the idea that the king is a superior being created as such by the god Ea and the Mother Goddess.

> Ea opened his mouth to speak, saying a word to the Lady of the Gods:
> 'You are Belet-ili, the mistress of the great gods,
> You have created man the human,
> Fashion now the king, the counsellor-man!
> Gird the whole of his figure sweet,
> Make perfect his countenance and well formed his body!'
> The Lady of the Gods fashioned the king, the counsellor man!
> They gave to the king the task of doing battle for the great gods,
> Anu gave him his crown, Enlil gave him his throne,
> Nergal gave him his weapons, Ninurta gave him his corona of splendour;
> The Lady of the Gods gave him his features of majesty,
> Nuska commissioned counsellors, stood them before him.
>
> (Translation: Andrew George)

The rise of an ordered kingship was a development with immense implications for later history. Throughout the following centuries, with the Hellenistic kingships (Chapter 19), the pagan Roman emperors and then the Byzantine emperors, this emphasis on the ruler as the chosen of the Gods, whether pagan or, in the case of the Byzantine emperor, Christian, reasserts itself. In each case success in war is intrinsic to the rulers' survival, as it clearly is here.

The Akkadians

Continuing conflict between the cities was debilitating and made the southern plains vulnerable to outsiders. In about 2330 BC southern Mesopotamia was conquered by history's first recorded emperor, Sargon of Akkade. Sargon's origins were among the Semitic-speaking peoples of the north. (One legend records that his mother, a priestess, placed him in a wicker basket and left him to float downstream where he was rescued. There are obvious parallels here with the story of Moses, an indication of how these legends spread and reappear within the Near East. Another tells of his having come to power as the result of an upheaval in the palace at Kish where he was serving as a royal cupbearer.) The site of his capital, Akkade, has now been identified at the junction of the Tigris and Diyala rivers, in a suburb of modern Baghdad. It seems to have acted as a focus for trade routes and attracted a cosmopolitan population. The text of the so-called Curse of Akkad talks of 'foreigners cruising about like unusual birds in the sky' and monkeys, elephants, buffalo, ibexes, and sheep 'jostling each other in the public square'. At the height of the city's prosperity it abounds in gold, silver, copper, and tin and 'blocks' of that most precious commodity of all, lapis lazuli. From this bustling metropolis Sargon created an empire which stretched as far north as Anatolia and east as the Iranian plateau. (The site has never been fully excavated so it is hard to say whether the prosperity of the well-placed city funded the conquests or were the consequence of them.) Uruk was among the cities subdued by his armies, its walls broken down and its ruler, Lugalzagesi taken off north in triumph. The walls of Ur too were destroyed. Sargon and his successors idealized kingship by presenting themselves in reliefs as dominant over their enemies who are shown as tiny in comparison to their semi-divine conquerors. Akkadian, a Semitic language, eventually became the dominant language of the empire and most surviving cuneiform documents are written in it. Sumerian remained as the language of the priesthood and religious texts.

Sargon's empire was a personal conquest but it was preserved by his successors for another seventy years. It eventually fell apart during the rule of his great-grandson, Shar-kali-sharri, when invaders, the Gutians, swept down the Zagros mountains to destroy the rich city of the plain. The Curse of Akkad mentioned above tells how the god Enlil withdrew his protection from the city and the Gutians destroyed the trade routes and scattered the flocks. 'For the first time since cities were built and founded, the vast fields did not produce grain, the inundation ponds produced no fish, the irrigated orchard yielded neither syrup nor wine.'

The beneficiaries of this collapse of power in the north were the southern cities of Mesopotamia now able to regain their independence. After some decades of turmoil, the Sumerians achieved one final burst of glory. In the so-called Third Dynasty of Ur (c.2150–2004 BC) a highly efficient bureaucratic state emerged in southern Mesopotamia under one Ur-Nummu and his son Shulgi. The dynasty is remembered for its ziggurats, massive stepped platforms ascended by ramps. It is possible that they were symbolic homes of the gods, whose preservation high above any conceivable flood, ensured the psychological well-being of all. Even though the upper layers of the ziggurats have now disappeared they were well built with an outer layer of baked brick steeped in bitumen to give it strength and rushmatting placed between layers to spread the weight of the brick and absorb moisture. The ziggurats speak of the dominance of the gods who, as has been seen, are linked to the survival of the rulers and used by them as such. The so-called royal hymns from Ur stress the respect shown by rulers for the gods and their role in leading the main ceremonies of the city, some of which were doubtless held on the summit of the ziggurats. Like most religious texts they were written in Sumerian and may even have been used as a ritualistic means of preserving distance between ruler and ruled. One of the most attractive features of the hymns is the value placed on musical accomplishment.

This Third Dynasty is also remarkable for its literature, which included the earliest recorded epic, that of Gilgamesh, a warrior king of Uruk. (Although the epic dates from this time, the version that survives is several hundred years later and it is not certain what transformations of the text took place during these years.) The

Epic of Gilgamesh relates the relationship, first of antagonism and then of comradeship, of Gilgamesh and a wild creature, Enkidu. Their adventures together end when Enkidu slays a monster and is killed in retaliation by the gods. Gilgamesh, now beset by thoughts of death, goes on a quest to find immortality. Among the stories recorded is that of a great flood and excavations at Ur itself do contain a layer of undisturbed clay some 2.5 metres thick which Leonard Woolley believed was linked to the great flood of the Bible. It has to be said that the very nature of the low level plains of southern Mesopotamia was such that flooding was common and many cities were either lost or abandoned as the river courses shifted closer or further away from them. One flood recorded at Shuruppak was survived by 'a wise man' who took to an ark when the god Enlil unleashed his wrath on the city.

Gilgamesh was a favourite of the Sumerians and was translated into other languages of the Near East, including Hittite and Hurrian. Some scholars have suggested that it may have been an influence on Homer's epics. Parallels have been drawn between its opening sentence and that of the *Odyssey*, and with the way similar themes of mortality are dealt with in the *Iliad*. In *Gilgamesh* the goddess Ishtar goes to complain to her father and mother, gods in heaven, when rebuked by Gilgamesh. In the *Iliad*, Aphrodite, the goddess of love, whose ancestry seems linked to Ishtar, also complains to her divine parents when injured. When Penelope prays to Athene in the *Odyssey* that her son Telemachus might return safely, she ascends to an upper storey to make the sacrifice. Such a ritual is unknown in Greek life, but finds an echo in *Gilgamesh*, where there is a sacrifice to the sun god by Gilgamesh's mother from a rooftop. Just as the *Epic of Gilgamesh* is found fragmented across the cultures of the eastern Mediterranean, so too do flood stories spread throughout the Near East.

The 'Royal' burials at Ur suggest a society in which some women are given high status in their own right. Another famous text from this period tells the story of the priestess Enheduanna who had been appointed to an elite position in the religious life of Ur by Sargon. (She enjoys the honorary title 'daughter of Sargon'.) After a later revolt by Ur against Akkad, Enheduanna, not surprisingly, loses her position and is expelled from the city, whose local god Nanner is restored to prominence. Enheduanna retaliates by linking herself to the goddess, Inanna, from the nearby city of Uruk who is somehow linked to the Akkadian goddess Ishtar. She manages to return to Ur and persuade the populace that the sky god An, who has supremacy among the gods, has given judgement in favour of Inanna, who now supplants Nanner in the city. Some later texts even describe Inanna as enjoying love-making with the king of Ur. The story suggests that women of exceptional ability such as Enheduanna were able to exert influence, especially through the manipulation of the gods in their favour. Yet women as a whole had no special status. Alongside the story of Enheduanna is a text describing the textile workers of Ur, who are listed as the humblest workers of all, and then, as in many parts of the world now, made up of women and children.

By 2000 BC the power of the Third Dynasty was faltering. It is not certain why. The fertility of the land was being undermined by an influx of salt brought down in the annual floods but the rulers seem to have been able to maintain its yield. It may have been that the bureaucracy of the state became too complex: it is known that sesame oil was classified in four grades, while a single sheep's existence is found recorded on three separate tablets. Inter-city rivalry began again. Ur was sacked by invading Elamites in 2004 and *The Lamentation over the Destruction of Ur* records the razing of the residential areas and how weeds now grew where crops once had. The devastation was contrasted with an ideal state in which the rivers watered the lands and farmers went about their business in joy with all protected by the care of the gods. Other conflicts followed as another powerful city, Isin, struggled to hold Nippur, the most prestigious religious centre of Sumer, against outside attack.

The Old Babylonian Period (2000–1600 BC)

The most important conqueror of the period was Hammurapi, a king of the city of Babylon. As the deeper layers of the site of Babylon became waterlogged there is virtually nothing remaining from this period and Hammurapi's rise to power is obscure. He seems to have begun his career in alliance with other kings but in the 1760s he broke free and defeated the major cities of the southern plain, Isin, Nippur, Ur, and Uruk, thus making himself overlord of the region. He now expanded east to the Tigris, gaining control of the trade routes through to the Iranian plateau, and then in 1760 captured the major trading city of Mari, further north on the Euphrates, whose walls he demolished. Following the sack of Mari, Hammurapi moved westwards, until he came up against the border of the major state of Yamhad.

Hammurapi is best remembered for his 'law code'. It has been found beautifully inscribed in a stone stele at Susa, apparently looted and taken there by Elamite kings in the thirteenth century where it was found by French excavators. (It was believed originally to have been in the temple of the sun god Shamesh in Sippur, an important trading city on the Euphrates north-west of Babylon, and its removal shows the symbolic power of such steles.) It is written in literary Akkadian. As with many such texts, its purpose is now seen as royal propaganda. Late in his reign (it may have been inscribed just two years before Hammurapi died), the king wishes to proclaim himself as a benign ruler who has secured justice for his peoples. The laws which follow are not complete and it has been suggested that they represent actual cases where the king believes he has acted wisely. In particular he has to untangle a mass of tricky problems associated with marriage and inheritance. So we read that if a husband has children by a slave girl at the same time as he has them by his wife he can recognize them as his and they will eventually share his goods with his 'legitimate' children. Other texts show how elaborate the marriage rituals had become with a gradual harmonizing of the homes of bride and groom through a complex pattern of gifts of food. The groom lived in the bride's house for four months before returning to his home with her.

Other than his law code the most important legacy of Hammurapi's reign are the massive archives from the defeated city of Mari, which archaeologists have found, and have now begun to publish. (The palace in which they were discovered was particularly extensive and opulent and suggests that palaces had become major status symbols.) The texts provide a vivid picture of the precariousness of these small trading states. They have to be open to the outside world to exploit the possibilities for trade, yet this same dependence on open trade routes makes them acutely vulnerable. The Mari archives are full of accounts of raids on the city's territories by outlaws and nomadic tribes and the kings had to develop sophisticated survival skills. Borders were difficult to hold and there was continual interaction between the palace and the herding peoples of its outlying regions who could be given land or manufactured goods in return for their loyalty and availability for military service. Relationships between neighbouring states were maintained through a series of shifting alliances in which dynastic marriages or the exchange of goods (tin was a favourite for Mari) were used to maintain security. At the same time the economy had to be fostered. The palace itself encouraged trade, oversaw the irrigation of crops, and managed the production of textiles (in which even the queen took part). Alongside royal activity other landowners and traders helped to sustain the prosperity of the state. The archives are important also for their documentation of religious life with details of local prophets (on the model of Israel) and the skilled art of liver divination, even the rituals of the river ordeal by which guilt or innocence was 'proved' when no witnesses to an alleged crime were available. The accused, or a substitute chosen by him, could prove innocence by swimming for a defined length in the river. There is no doubt that once the publication of the archive is completed it will prove one of the richest sources of information on life in Mesopotamia. Yet it has another message. There are numerous other states mentioned in the texts for some of which there is no other documentary or archaeological evidence. For instance, the state of Yamhad is given great prominence, yet the site, under the modern city of Aleppo, has never been excavated. It is a reminder that in many aspects the study of the history of the Ancient Near East remains in its infancy.

Despite the break-up of Hammurapi's empire Babylon survived as an important city and was to have revivals of power and prosperity for many centuries to come. It appears from surviving records of private contracts, loans, and property sales that Babylonian society allowed more freedom of enterprise than that of Sumer. Trade was conducted by individuals rather than the state and landowners were free to exploit their land. A major source of information for this period is the archives from Sippur. Here a group of women, known as the *naditu*, drawn from some of the city's wealthier families, lived in a segregated area of the city, the *gagum*, as a sort of religious order. They were described as betrothed to the god Shamash but their sexually ambiguous position allowed them to openly engage in commerce. They traded in land and cattle and even, through intermediaries, commodities such as tin. Whatever their relationship with the god, it did not require asceticism. Juniper oil, myrtle oil, and other perfumes were sought in exchange for silver.

These centuries were a time of prosperity and also a period of rich cultural and intellectual development in Mesopotamia. In literature the story of Atrahasis, 'outstanding in wisdom', outlines the doings of the gods in a way which finds parallels in Homer's *Iliad*. In both works the gods are described as drawing lots to parcel out the heaven, earth, and the sea between them. The Babylonian epic of creation, the *Enuma Elish* (scholars differ as to whether it was composed in the fifteenth or twelfth century), talks of the oceans as being the first creations before heaven and earth—an idea that was possibly taken up by the Greek philosopher Thales of Miletus as the basis for his own cosmogony (see p. 189).

The Babylonians excelled in astronomy and mathematics, although their achievement is difficult to assess. They developed a calendar, based on the moon with regular additions of months to keep it in line with the solar year. Their calculations became so exact that eventually the Babylonian astronomer Kidinnu (*c.*380 BC) calculated the length of a lunar month to within one second of its true length. The Babylonian calendar later passed to the Jews (at the time of the Babylonian captivity: see below). On tablets from the period 1800–1600 BC there is evidence of multiplication, division, the calculation of squares and cubes, and even some logarithms. The Babylonians were able to calculate the value of the square root of 2 to within 0.000007 and it now seems certain that they knew of Pythagoras' theorem a thousand years before the followers of Pythagoras discovered it (although there is no evidence that they would have been able to prove it deductively as the Greeks were able to do). Mathematics was tied in with the practical needs of engineering and surveying, and instructions survive for calculating the areas and volumes of different figures. The most striking innovation was positional notation, two numbers following each other (as in 12, the 1 standing for the base of ten, the 2 for the extra units). The Babylonians used 60 as their base. Seventy, for instance, is one base unit of 60 plus 10 extra units. The use of 60, a number useful because it can be divided by so many others, still survives to measure time—seconds in a minute, minutes in an hour—and angles. It arrived in the west through Hindu-Arabic intermediaries. Another innovation of the Babylonians, the musical scale, seems to have appeared about 1800 BC and passed via the Phoenicians to the Greeks in the first millennium BC.

The Invention of the Alphabet

Far to the west of Babylon lay the land of Canaan, the ancient name given to Palestine. Here another important contribution to the western world was being made, the invention of the alphabet. Cuneiform and, to a much lesser extent, hieroglyphs were used in Syria and Palestine as early as the third millennium BC, but they were equally unwieldy and took many years of training to master. By the beginning of the second millennium new independent city states appeared in the region and they began to experiment with their own simpler ways of writing. One script originated in the important coastal town of Byblos. Only about a dozen examples survive, but these are enough to show that it was syllabic and consisted of about a hundred signs. Some of these were borrowed directly from Egyptian hieroglyphs (for which see pp. 58–9 below). It was, in fact, with hiero-glyphs that the solution to an alphabet lay. The Egyptians had already evolved some signs which were exclusively consonantal (for instance, when they wanted to create a 'd' sign, they drew the hieroglyphic sign for a hand, *ad* in Egyptian). The step the Egyptians failed to take was to extract all the consonantal signs and create an alphabet from them. This was done by a Canaanite about 1500 BC. What this scholar did was to take an Egyptian hieroglyph and use it to express a consonant in his own Semitic language. The Semitic word for 'water' is *maym*. The scholar took only its first consonant *m* and found the Egyptian hieroglyph for 'water', which happens to be a wavy line. He then assigned this sign to the sound *m*. Similarly with 'house', in Semitic *bet*. To get a sign for *b*, the scholar took the Egyptian hieroglyph for 'house', a quadrilateral, and assigned it the sound *b*. Once the concept was grasped that consonantal sounds could be written down and that any word could be written using a selection from just over twenty consonants, any culture could evolve its own signs to represent each consonantal sound. In the Syrian town of Ugarit on the Mediterranean coast, for instance, writing had been traditionally expressed in Babylonian cuneiform. Once the concept of the alphabet was grasped in Ugarit, it was written with cuneiform signs. By the thirteenth century BC the writers of Ugarit were using only twenty-two consonants. At some point (scholars have put forward dates as early as 1300 BC and as late as 1000 BC), the Phoenician cities developed their own alphabet, and probably transmitted it to the Greeks in the ninth or eighth cen-tury BC. Perhaps because they wished to use the alphabet primarily for the recording of poetry, the Greeks introduced vowels. (See further below p. 132.)

The Assyrians and the Hittites

The northern boundary of Babylonia was normally Gebel Hamrin, the Red Mountain. Beyond this mountain ridge another state, Assyria, emerged at the beginning of the second millennium BC. Ashur was set on a limestone cliff which was given natural protection by the Tigris flowing round it. There was fertile land nearby and easy access to a trade route through the Zagros mountains into Iran. The early prosperity of Ashur rested on its success as a trading centre whose tentacles reached into Anatolia for silver, into Babylonia for textiles, and perhaps as far east as Afghanistan for its tin. The early Assyrian kings appear to have made Ashur a centre which the merchants of the cities of southern Mesopotamia could visit to buy supplies of precious metals. They paid in fine textiles which were then taken north to Anatolia by donkey caravan to exchange for more metals. What is interesting is that although the Assyrian kings of this period were important ceremonial figures (described in formal texts as viceregents of the god Ashur) day-to-day administration of Ashur was in the hands of a committee apparently of the heads of the merchant families. Anything to do with prosperity of the city, from taxation to relations with neighbouring states, was under their control. The Assyrian merchants had their own quarters in the cities of northern Syria and Anatolia and their rights here were negotiated by the Ashur committee with the local Anatolian princes. The records, in cuneiform, of one of these communities, found at Kanesh in central Anatolia and dated to between 1900 and 1830 BC, illustrate the sophistication of the traders and include calculations of their prices, profits, and turnover, and even arrangements for credit. A common practice was for the merchant to be based in Anatolia while his wife stayed in Ashur supervising the collection and production of cloth. It was accepted that while abroad the merchant could acquire a local wife so long as both his wives were supported and back in Ashur many of the wives seemed to have retained the profit from their own activities.

In the early eighteenth century BC this network of Anatolian trade was disrupted by power struggles between rival Anatolian princes. An important moment seems to have been the overthrow of Kanesh by another principality, Kussara. The dynasty of Kussara then appear, about 1830, to have taken over the ruined city of Hattusas and transferred their archives here. This was the genesis of what became the empire of the Hittites, or the 'people of the Land of Hatti' as they called themselves. The word Hittite is that used in the Bible, but only of a period when the Hittites had been reduced to tribespeople after the collapse of their civilization in 1200. The fact that the predecessors of the biblical Hittites had in fact controlled a great empire in the second half of the second millennium was only recognized in the late nineteenth century. Much about the Hittites remains obscure and the history of the empire is continually being rethought. A recent classification of the empire defines two phases, the first from 1650 to 1400 BC, the Old Kingdom, the second from 1400 to 1200 BC, the New Kingdom, when the Hittites became a major player in the Ancient Near East.

The Hittite capital remained Hattusas (the modern Boghazkoy), in north central Anatolia. It was a rocky and easily defended site with one of the few good sources of water in what is an arid region. The Hittites faced a long struggle for survival against the surrounding peoples of the Near East, in particular the Hurrians, who in the fifteenth century united in the state of Mitanni in northern Syria. The records of the Old Kingdom show intense rivalries between branches of the royal family, interspersed with and often linked to, periods of military triumph or disaster. What is remarkable is that a coherent state survived at all but it was the tenacity of the Hittite rulers which was one the most remarkable features of their state.

Some form of more successful expansion begins in the reign of Tudhaliya I at the end of the fifteenth century. He is found in control of the rich copper deposits of Isuwa which had normally been subject to Mitanni, and the Hittites appear as players on the wider diplomatic scene. They were still not secure, however. Even Hattusas appears to have been sacked by a mountain people, the Gasga, at one point. It was only under the rule of Suppiluliuma I (c.1380–1345) that the Hittites overcame Mitanni and installed a puppet ruler there, using the state as a buffer between themselves and Assyria, which by now had revived and become the most powerful nation of northern Iraq. They also subdued large tracts of Anatolia and it is possible that one of the peoples they came into contact with, the Ahhijawa, were, in fact, the Mycenaean Greeks. As the Hittites expanded southwards into Syria towards the Euphrates they met the Egyptians. The two states clashed at the major battle of Qadesh (1275 BC: see p. 74). The outcome was the consolidation of a border between Egypt and the Hittites in southern Syria.

The Hittite kings were powerful and autocratic figures whose status ultimately rested on their success in war. Even debilitating campaigns along the borders were led by the king in person. Once territory had been won, the empire was sustained by a series of treaties between the king, whose semi-divine status was emphasized by a great ceremonial complex constructed in Hattusas (which had been recaptured and strongly fortified by Suppiluliuma I), and his defeated rivals. The territory of each was strictly defined and the supremacy of the 'Great King' was underlined by recounting how fortunate the subject king was to enjoy his mercy. Each had to come in person to Hattusas once a year with his tribute, supply troops when needed, and report any disturbances in his region. The Great King cemented his own relationships with his people through frequent travel in central Anatolia where he would preside at major festivals to emphasise his own close relationship with the gods. While alive he was their representative, on death he became a god himself.

The Hittites dealt lightly with neighbouring cultures. In the royal archives of their capital Hattusas there are texts in eight different languages. This was a truly multilingual empire (although an Indo-European language known as Nesite, usually referred to as Hittite, was the language of imperial administration) and it was also multicultural in that it seems to have borrowed freely from the other cultures around it and it may have in its turn transmitted its borrowings to the eastern Mediterranean. The Hittites adopted cuneiform writing for their language, and their system of law may have been influenced by law codes from Babylon and elsewhere. Some of their religious beliefs—the worship of a powerful sun goddess, for instance—also show Mesopotamian influence. The *Epic of Gilgamesh* has been found at Hattusas in Akkadian, Hurrian, and Hittite versions. The Hurrians were a particularly strong influence. The most important Hittite epic, that of Kumarbi, is borrowed directly from the Hurrians. (Kumarbi was a Hurrian god.) The epic is remarkable for describing sets of gods following on from each other in generations: Anu (heaven) is overthrown by his son Kumarbi, the father of the gods, who becomes a king and is overthrown in his turn by Teshub, a weather god. A similar story of conflict between gods is found in the *Theogony* of the eighth-century Greek writer Hesiod (see p. 139). In both cases a father god is castrated by his son, and it is assumed that the Kumarbi epic is yet another of the Near Eastern myths which filtered into Greece.

While the core of the Hittites' prosperity seems to have rested on agriculture and the exploitation of metal resources in Anatolia itself, it was, like every state of the period, linked into wider trading networks. Just how extensive these were at the time of Hittite power can be seen from one of the most exciting underwater finds of the past, a shipwreck from this period from Uluburun, near Kas in southern Turkey, which dates from the fourteenth century BC. The wreck is of a cargo ship which may have started its journey in the Levant and engaged in a circular voyage which took it northwards up the coast of the Levant, across to Cyprus along the southern Anatolian coast, where it met its end, possibly on to Mycenaean Greece before taking advantage of the prevailing winds to head south to Crete, across to Egypt and then back to the Levant. It is the extraordinary variety of goods it carried which is most impressive. The cargo included ivory, glass (first invented about 1600 BC but still a precious commodity), cylinder seals, and pottery which came from throughout the Near East. Alongside these were copper ingots from Cyprus, ebony from south of Egypt, and bronze tools of Egyptian, Levantine, and even Mycenaean Greek design. This is trade conducted at a sophisticated level with commercial acumen and presumably mature systems of credit.

Yet a hundred years later this complex network of trade and traders was disrupted. The end of the thirteenth century BC saw a cataclysmic collapse of the societies of the eastern Mediterranean. The fortified cities of Mycenaean Greece are destroyed as are settlements on Cyprus. About 1200 Hattusas itself was burned. Although Hittite principalities remained in Syria, the capital was abandoned and parts of the Anatolian plain deserted. So Hittite civilization collapses. The Egyptians seemed to have been forewarned of the unrest and successfully fought off a collection of invaders, Libyans, 'northerners coming from all lands', and the mysterious 'Sea Peoples' who attacked the Delta. Even so in the dislocation which follows Egypt withdraws to the Nile valley. The economic networks of the eastern Mediterranean and Near East are broken up so comprehensively that a so-called 'Dark Age' sets in and continues for some centuries.

The original explanation based on the Egyptian texts which describe the invasions suggests that the Sea Peoples were some kind of invading force. More careful analysis of the evidence suggests that these wandering bands may have been the result of the breakdown rather than its cause and that some of them were not so much marauding hordes as mercenaries fighting for the Libyans and others. Scholars are now exploring the possibility that the complex trading relationships between the peoples of the region had become too extended and precarious, that taxation had alienated rural peoples on whom the civilizations ultimately depended and a form of system breakdown had taken place. Whatever, the cause, it shook out the cultures of the regions. The world which emerges is very different, but before it is described, another major civilization of the region, that of Egypt, needs to be explored.

FURTHER READING

The background to the emergence of early agriculture and the first cities in this area is well covered by Brian Fagan, *Peoples of the Earth* (9th edition, New York, 1998). A very good general survey of the area is M. Roaf, *The Cultural Atlas of Mesopotamia and the Ancient Near East* (New York, 1990), but the authoritative work is now A. Kuhrt, *The Ancient Near East, c.3000–330 BC* (London, 1995), which can be backed by J. Sasson and others (eds.), *Civilizations of the Ancient Near East* (London, 1995), four volumes of essays. An excellent introduction is provided by Gwendolyn Leick, *Mesopotamia: The Invention of the City* (London, 2001). In *Ancient Mesopotamia: The Eden that Never Was* (Cambridge, 1999), Susan Pollock turns an anthropologist's eye to the region. The emergence of social control is dealt with in Michael Mann's *The Sources of Social Power*, vol. i (Cambridge, 1986). It includes studies of Assyria and Persia. See also N. Postgate, *Early Mesopotamia, Society and Economy at the Dawn of History* (London, 1992); Marc Van De Mieroop, *A History of the Ancient Near East* (London, 2004); and P. Bienkowski and A. Millard, *Dictionary of the Ancient Near East* (London, 2000).

A recent overview of the art of the area is to be found in Dominique Collon, *Ancient Near Eastern Art* (London, 1995). On alphabetic writing see chapter 20a in the *Cambridge Ancient History*, vol. iii, Part 2 (Cambridge, 1991) by B. Isserlin, 'Earliest Alphabetic Writing'. A useful overview is also provided in *World Archaeology*, 17/3 (1986), 'Early Writing Systems'. Translations of Akkadian texts can be found in Benjamin Foster, *Before the Muses* (two volumes, 2nd edition Bethesda, Md., 1998), and of Sumerian in Thorkild Jacobson, *The Harps That Once: Sumerian Poetry in Translation* (New Haven, 1987). A recent translation of the *Epic of Gilgamesh* is that by Andrew George (London, 1999). M. L. West, *The East Face of Helicon: Western Asiatic Elements in Greek Poetry and Myth* (Oxford, 1997) deals with the literary links between the Near East and the Greeks.

On the Hittites, see Trevor Bryce, *The Kingdom of the Hittites* (Oxford, 1998) and *Life and Society in the Hittite World* (Oxford, 2002), and J. MacQueen, *The Hittites and their Contemporaries in Asia Minor* (London, 1986).

For the Kas shipwreck see G. F. Bass, 'Oldest Known Shipwreck Reveals Splendors of the Bronze Age', in the *National Geographic*, 172, no. 6 (Dec. 1987). On the Sea Peoples see N. K. Sandars, *The Sea Peoples: Warriors of the Ancient Mediterranean* (London, 1978) although this is now dated.

3 | Egypt, the Gift of the Nile, 3200–1500 BC

When, in AD 80, the Roman emperor Titus was portrayed on a temple wall in Egypt, one of the provinces of his empire, he was shown standing with a mace raised menacingly in his right hand. An earlier ruler of Egypt, King Narmer, had been portrayed in the same pose 3,200 years earlier. The worship of the goddess Isis can be traced back to 2400 BC, 2,000 years before the rise of Rome. The cult still had enough vitality for worship of the goddess to spread throughout the Roman empire (there was a temple to Isis as far west as London), with her temple at Philae on the upper Nile closed by the emperor Justinian as late as AD 536, sixty years after the Roman empire had 'fallen' in the west. Egyptian religion, in short, entered its most expansionist phase when it was already far older than Christianity is now. These are striking reminders of the longevity and continuity of early Egyptian history. This does not mean that Egyptian society was always stable—the Egyptians were particularly adept at masking change by overlaying it with the appearance of continuity—but there were consistent forces which shaped Egyptian life.

The most influential of these was the result of the unique set of circumstances arising from the ecology of the Nile valley. The valley had virtually no rainfall of its own. The water for its irrigation came down the Nile in annual floods, most of which originated in summer rains in the Ethiopian mountains. With the floods came silt, and the combination of fertile soil and ready water could produce yields of crops three or four times those from normal rain-fed soil. As important as the wealth of water and soil was the regularity with which the floods came. The Nile started to rise in May, and from July to October was high enough to flow out over the flood plain of the valley. This was *akhet*, the time of inundation. Four months later, by the beginning of November, the waters had begun to fall. The land could be marked out and ploughed and sowed. This was *peret*, the time 'when the land reappeared'. The final four months of the year, *shemu*, from March to June, brought the harvest.

In a normal year the fields along the Nile produced a large surplus of grain. Effectively gathered up it could be used to sustain rulers, palaces, craftsmanship, and great building projects and these are the achievements of the early kingdoms of Egypt, maintained, despite periods of breakdown, over twenty centuries. By the first millennium BC, however, the country had become weaker and fell prey to a series of conquerors—Assyrians, Persians, Greeks, and Romans. All were eager to exploit its riches, and as a result Egypt became drawn into the world of the Near East and the Mediterranean. For the Greeks Egypt was the fount of wisdom, and some believed that Egypt was the origin of their own civilization. The Egyptians probably provided them with models for their own monumental temples and early sculptures. (The evidence is discussed in Chapter 11.) Under the the Greek dynasty of the Ptolemies Alexandria became one of the great cities of the Mediterranean and an important centre of Greek learning. After the defeat of the last of the Ptolemies, Cleopatra, the early Roman emperors used Egypt's grain to sustain their rule and to contribute to feeding their oversized capital, Rome. When Constantinople was founded in AD 330 the grain supply of Egypt was diverted there, thus allowing the city to become established and to flourish as the capital of the eastern empire while in the late empire Egypt was an important centre of Christianity and home to the first monasteries. The 'ancient wisdom' of Egypt has haunted Europe for centuries and the spectacular rediscovery of Egypt's remains in the nineteenth century has made it one of the most popular civilizations of the ancient world.

Beginnings

One of the most persistent Egyptian creation myths relates how at the beginning of all things was the sun, Ra. Ra scattered his semen and out of it sprang Shu, the god of dryness, and Tefnut, the goddess of humidity. Shu and Tefnut produced a new generation of gods, the sky goddess Nut and the earth god Geb. They in their turn gave birth to four children, Isis and Osiris, Seth and Nepthys. Isis and Osiris, husband and wife, became the first rulers of Egypt. However, Seth overthrew his brother, cutting him into pieces. Isis devotedly put him together again, adding a new penis (the original having been eaten by fish) with such success that she was able to conceive a son, Horus. She kept Horus hidden in the marshes until he was strong enough to overthrow Seth. Osiris meanwhile had become god of the underworld, where he acted as a symbol of rebirth. Seth continued in Egyptian mythology as a potential threat to order, while Horus remained as the protector of the earthly kings who were his successors.

This creation myth brought together several elements of early Egyptian history and beliefs. The 'family' was a composite one, made up of early gods from different cult centres along the Nile, while the conflict between Horus and Seth may well have echoed memories of a real struggle between two early states. It is a reminder that Egypt was not a natural unity. The country had two distinct ecologies. The valley was thin, often only a few kilometres wide in some areas, and stretching for 1,000 kilometres from the Nile Delta to the first cataract at Aswan. In the north, on the Delta, the river spread out over marshland and

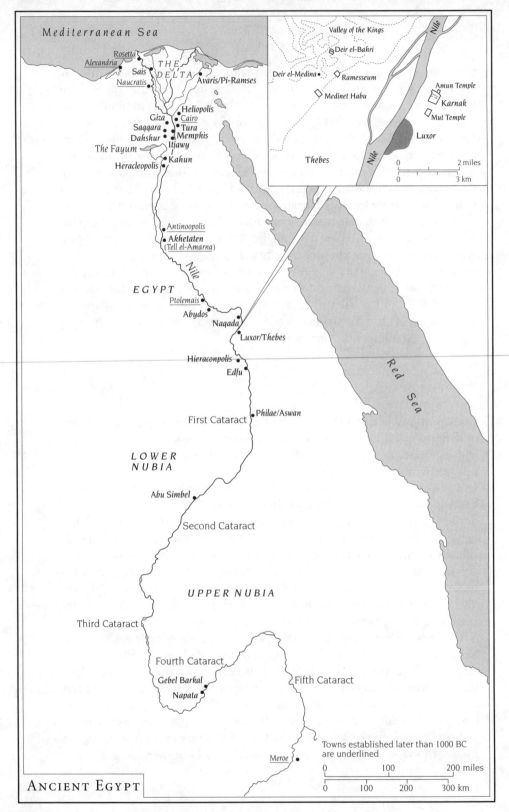

Mediterranean Sea

Rosetta
Alexandria
Sais
Naucratis
THE DELTA
Avaris/Pi-Ramses

Heliopolis
Giza
Cairo
Saqqara
Tura
Dahshur
Memphis
Itjawy
The Fayum
Kahun
Heracleopolis

Antinoopolis
Akhetaten
(Tell el-Amarna)

EGYPT

Ptolemais
Abydos
Naqada
Luxor/Thebes

Hieraconpolis
Edfu

First Cataract
Philae/Aswan

LOWER NUBIA

Abu Simbel

Second Cataract

UPPER NUBIA

Third Cataract

Fourth Cataract

Gebel Barkal
Napata

Fifth Cataract

Meroe

Nile

Red Sea

Valley of the Kings
Deir el-Bahri
Deir el-Medina
Ramesseum
Medinet Habu

Amun Temple
Karnak
Mut Temple

Luxor

Thebes

Nile

0   2 miles
0   3 km

Towns established later than 1000 BC
are underlined

0   100   200 miles
0   100   200   300 km

ANCIENT EGYPT

MAP 2

swamps which were rich in bird and animal life. From earliest times each area developed its own culture, with separate traditions of pottery-making and burial customs. There is no evidence that the Delta region actually ever formed an independent state, but the insistence that Egypt was made up of two distinct kingdoms, one in the north on the Delta, the other south along the valley, lasted in Egyptian tradition long after the first unification in about 3000 BC. They are represented as the lands of reeds, the valley, and the lands of papyrus, the Delta, with different crowns and protecting gods.

Egypt was comparatively isolated from the outside world. Deserts surrounded the valley. In the south the country was bounded by the cataracts, whose granite rocks in the Nile made travel further upstream difficult. Beyond the cataracts was Nubia. The climate here was harsher than in Egypt and agriculture never developed to such a high level. The more successful of the Egyptian kingdoms controlled Nubia and exploited its raw materials—gold, copper, semi-precious stones, and what for the Egyptian were exotic animals, including giraffes, leopards, and ostriches. In the north there is some evidence for direct contact with the Mediterranean, although much of it is now probably buried in the silt of the Delta. The most vulnerable part of Egypt was the north-east, from where potential invasion routes led across the desert from Palestine but the scattered kingships of the region were relatively easy to control. Overall the country remained remarkably secure until the end of the second millennium.

The Unification of Egypt

Archaeological evidence shows that the foundations of Egyptian civilization were laid long before the first recorded unification of the country in 3000 BC. Emmer wheat, barley, and flax, the staples of Egyptian farmers, were being cultivated well before 4000 BC. By that date burials in Upper Egypt were already being made with the body on its side facing west, the home of the setting sun, with provisions, food offerings, and hunting equipment being left for the afterlife. During the second half of the fourth millennium, the four to five hundred years before the first recorded unification of Egypt, the scattered agricultural communities of the valley grew larger. At the important site of Naqada north of Hieraconpolis there was a walled town as early as 3600 BC. The growth of settlements such as Naqada and Hieraconpolis may reflect their position on the trading routes to the gold mines of the eastern desert. Their rise coincides with more sophisticated craftsmanship. Graves are becoming richer, with goods now made in gold, copper, and a variety of stones.

It may have been this need for finer raw materials which acted as the catalyst to open Egypt to a wider world. The Nile valley provided clay for pottery and mudbricks but little wood. Flint was the only immediately accessible stone.

Anything else, the fine white limestone from the rocks which lined the valley, the hard stones, granite and diorite, gold, copper, or semi-precious stones, had to be quarried or mined from the surrounding desert or traded from further afield. This required an ordered society able to organize expeditions across the inhospitable desert. By the end of the fourth millennium contact had been made as far as Mesopotamia. Cylinder seals have been found in Egypt which echo those of Sumer, and designs from them or from actual buildings may have inspired the form of the façades of Egyptian mudbrick tombs. Many scholars argue that the concept of writing, first found in Egypt on a set of inscribed labels in a royal tomb in Abydos dating from about 3100 BC, may have been borrowed from Mesopotamia. Both Sumerian cuneiform (see above, p. 26) and Egyptian hieroglyphs (see below) used the same convention of combining signs to represent the sound of a word with others to represent its meaning. It was the idea, not the script, which was borrowed in that from the beginning the Egyptians developed their own hieroglyphic script. Hieroglyphs ('sacred carved letters') appear to derive from pictures found on much earlier Egyptian pottery. At first writing appears to have been confined to court use, used to record economic activities recorded by the state, the name of the king (in a format known as the *serekh*) and in formal commemorative art such as the Narmer Palette (below).

As the early Egyptian settlements grew, so did tensions between them. They were probably exacerbated by a period of increasing aridity after 3300 BC which intensified settlement in the Nile valley and possibly by competition between rulers over luxury resources, copper, gold, and hard stone. It is reflected in the art of the period. A painted tomb at Hieraconpolis shows a man struggling with two lions, while other palettes (the so-called Hunters' and Battlefield palettes) show contrasting scenes of conflict and harmony among animals. (The palettes were flat stones used originally as grinding surfaces which later acquired some kind of ritual significance.) The story of Horus and Seth seems to represent an actual struggle between Hieraconpolis, a cult centre for Horus, and Naqada, whose cult god was Seth. There was probably no one moment of unification but in later tradition it was from this disorder that a king named Narmer finally achieved some kind of dominance over Egypt just before 3000 BC. On the so-called Narmer palette the king is apparently shown as a southerner conquering the north, the Delta, though his enemies may well have included neighbouring peoples such as the Libyans. At some point, perhaps soon after unification, Narmer's successors established their capital at Memphis, strategically placed at the junction between the Delta and the valley.

The Narmer palette is a remarkable survival. It was found carefully preserved at Hieraconpolis, and it portrays Narmer, on one side of the palette wearing the crown of Upper Egypt and on the other that of Lower Egypt. The king is shown subduing his enemies, some of whom lie decapitated before him, their heads between their feet. Quite apart from its historical importance, the palette shows that many conventions of Egyptian art are already in place. Status is represented by the comparative size of the figures. Narmer is the largest figure throughout. In one scene an official is shown as smaller than Narmer but still much larger than the accompanying standard-bearers. The artist is not concerned so much with providing a proper representation as with passing on detail, even if this means distorting normal perspectives. The face of the king, for instance, is shown in profile but his eye is shown in full and the shoulders are viewed from the front. Both hands and feet are shown in full.

Horus continued throughout Egyptian history as the special protector of the kings. He was always portrayed as a falcon. On a magnificent statue of Khafra (often known by the Greek version of his name, Chephren), one of the pyramid-building kings of the Old Kingdom, now in the Cairo Museum, he is shown perching on the king's back, his wings around the king's shoulders. Each king took a 'Horus name' in addition to his birth-name and other titles. It was often a reflection of how he saw his political ambitions—'He who breathes life into the heart of the Two Lands' or 'Bringer of Harmony', for instance.

From this moment Egyptian history is divided into dynasties of kings. In the past, historians have adopted a list of thirty-one dynasties compiled by an Egyptian priest, Manetho, on the orders of King Ptolemy II about 280 BC. They stretch from Narmer to the overthrow of Persian rule by Alexander in 332 BC. However, Manetho's list leaves much unresolved. It makes Narmer's unification appear much more sudden than archaeological evidence suggests. It is not always clear when one dynasty ends and another begins or why a change has taken place. Manetho's aim was to produce an ordered sequence, and at times of breakdown, when dynasties may have ruled alongside each other, Manetho puts them one after another, providing a source of much confusion to historians. Some of Manetho's dynasties, such as the Seventh, have remained obscure. So as a background for dating, historians have used other methods, radiocarbon, stratigraphy (which has produced sequences of pottery styles which have been dated for instance), astronomical records and, of course, other written sources. This still leaves discrepancies, periods, and reigns of individual pharaohs where the chronology is still debatable. There are so-called 'high', 'middle', and 'low' chronologies. In order to avoid confusion the chronology used here is that of the *Oxford History of Ancient Egypt* as described in Chapter 1 of the *History* by Ian Shaw, 'Chronologies and Cultural Change in Egypt'.

The First Dynasties

The appearance of writing, the unification of the country, and the establishment of a capital at Memphis, mark the beginning of what is known as the Early Dynastic period, the First to Third Dynasties (*c.*3000–2613 BC). This is the world's first stable monarchy and it stands in marked contrast to the battling city states of Mesopotamia. In these 400 years a model of kingship was developed which was to last over centuries. By 2500 the myth had developed that the king was the direct heir of the sun god Ra. Ra, it was said, impregnated the ruling queen (appearing to her usually in the guise of her husband). Thoth, the herald of the gods, then appeared to her to tell her that she was to give birth to the son of Ra. The royal couple thus acted as surrogate parents for their successor, and 'son' succeeded 'father' without a break. The king's wife was traditionally referred to as 'the one who unites the two Lords'. The earlier tradition of Horus as protector was absorbed into the myth by making Horus a member of Ra's family, and the god continued as the special protector of the king against the forces of disorder personified by Seth. In essence the king had a dual nature, the divine emanating through his human form.

On the succession of a new king there was a coronation ceremony, the *kha*, also the word used for the appearance of the sun at dawn, when the king was given his divine name which was afterwards written together with his existing personal name in a cartouche which also contained the symbols of Upper Egypt (a sedge plant) and Lower Egypt (a bee). After thirty years of a reign there was the jubilee ceremonial of *sed*, when the king received the renewed allegiance of the provinces of Egypt wearing first the White Crown of Upper Egypt and then the Red Crown of Lower Egypt. Each province brought their local gods for him to honour. Part of the ceremony involved the king running a circuit as if to confirm his fitness to rule.

Ceremonial was important but not enough. Although the ideology of the divine king was imposed in Egyptian life from the earliest times, his survival rested on being able to keep order (any loss of control was traditionally rationalized as a sign that the gods had withdrawn their support), and this involved bureaucratic expertise. From early times taxes were collected in kind by the court and then stored in granaries before being rationed out to support building projects and the feeding of labourers. The sophistication of the system can be shown by the annual records of the height of the Nile floods from which the expected crop yield for the year seems to have been calculated. It was these developments that must have encouraged the development of a writing system. The king may also have controlled foreign trade, as it was the court which was the main consumer of raw materials and centre of craftsmanship.

The administrative complex around the royal court at Memphis was known as *Per Ao*, The Great House, a name used eventually, from about 1400 BC, for the king himself, pharaoh. Heading the administration was the vizier, whose roles included overseeing the maintenance of law and order and all building operations. Then there were a host of other officials, with titles, such as 'elder of the gates', 'chief of the secrets of the decrees', and 'controller of the Two Thrones', whose functions have been lost. It can be assumed that there were strong links with the provinces, as without these order could not have been maintained or resources channelled upwards to the court. However, nothing is yet known about how local administration functioned in this early period.

Resources were not needed solely to sustain the king and his officials in life. From the earliest dynasties it was believed that at the death of a king his divinely created spirit, the *ka*, would leave his body and then ascend to heaven, where it would accompany his father, the sun god, Ra, on the boat on which Ra travelled through each night before reappearing in the east. However, certain formalities had to take place if the king was to reach his destination safely. The body of the king had to be preserved, its name recorded on the tomb, and the *ka* had to be provided with all it needed for the afterlife. It could not survive without nourishment.

These basic requirements were the same for all Egyptians, but only the kings could normally travel to the other world. Others, at this period, had to be content with an existence within the tomb or possibly in a shadowy underworld underneath it. However, those officials who had enjoyed his special favour might be able to rise with the king, and the custom grew of placing their tombs next to those of the kings in the hope that they would go to heaven with him as his attendants in the afterlife. It was a shrewd way of encouraging loyalty from leading nobles and officials.

Originally the bodies of the kings had been buried in mudbrick chambers. These gradually became more elaborate, the body being buried deeper and deeper in the ground, probably to protect the fine goods that were now buried with it. The deeper the body was buried, however, the more likely it was to decay (a body left in sand near the surface normally dried out from the warmth of the sun), and so there developed the process of embalming to fulfil the requirement that the body should be preserved. The viscera from Queen Hetepheres of the Fourth Dynasty, mother of Khufu (Greek Cheops), the great pyramid-builder, have survived from *c.*2580 BC but no full mummy now survives earlier than one from the Fifth Dynasty (*c.*2400 BC). By the New Kingdom the art of embalming was to have developed into a complex ritual providing the world with one of its most enduring images of Egyptian civilization.

The early kings were buried in the sacred city of Abydos, far up in Upper Egypt, a recognition of their origin as southerners. Typically the tombs had a central burial chamber, walled with timber and surrounded by store-rooms for goods and subsidiary graves for officials. Near each tomb was a walled funerary enclosure where, it is believed, rituals relating to the cult worship of each king were carried out. Despite plundering over the centuries, enough material survives to show that the tombs were filled with pots (containing food and drink for the afterlife), well-crafted stone vessels, sometimes finished in gold, and objects in copper and ivory. Another burial ground developed at Saqqara near Memphis. It used to be believed that the graves of the early kings were actually here, with those at Abydos being merely cenotaphs. Now it seems that the tombs at Saqqara, finely constructed though they might be, are in fact those of leading officials. The need to provide fine goods for the king's and his courtiers' survival in their afterlife appears to have been the catalyst for a major explosion in the arts during the Early Dynastic period.

Once the shafts of the tomb had been dug out and the surrounding chamber completed, the whole was finished off with a rectangular building over the tomb at ground level. These constructions have been nicknamed 'mastabas', after the benches which are found outside modern Egyptian houses. The mastabas of early tombs, royal and otherwise, were often constructed in the form of a model palace. It was the convention to build in a false door through which it was believed the *ka* would be able to cross. Within the door a stone gravestone known as the stele was placed. On the stele were inscribed the names and titles of the deceased, often with a representation of him seated at a table enjoying his offerings. Sometimes a list of the offerings was included, the idea being that the mere act of reading the list by the deceased could cause them to materialize and sustain the *ka* even if there was nothing real to eat.

The Building of the Pyramids

Around 2650 BC an architectural revolution took place, a rare occurrence in Egyptian history. It involved the tomb of the Third Dynasty king Djoser at Saqqara, a site which had now become used by the kings as their burial place. One of Djoser's advisers, Imhotep, had been entrusted with the supervision of the building of the royal tomb, a task which was always begun well before death. Above ground the tomb started as an ordinary mastaba (in other words was a continuation of earlier models), but this was extended and built upon so that eventually a stepped 'pyramid' of six layers emerged. On the southern side were two courtyards, and it has been assumed that these were copies of courtyards from the king's own palace at Memphis. The largest has been seen as a royal appearance court, a carefully designed forum for showing off the king, perhaps first at his coronation and then at other great festivities. (This process reached its culmination in Egypt at the great ceremony thrown by Antony and Cleopatra in Alexandria in 34 BC where Cleopatra appeared robed as the goddess Isis: see below, p. 442.) The smaller court seems to have been a copy of that used for the *sed* festival, with mock chapels for the provincial gods and two thrones, one to represent each kingdom of Egypt. It is as if the king is provided not only with goods, set out in elaborate chambers under the pyramid, but with the setting which would allow him to continue as ruler in the afterlife.

Nothing like Djoser's funerary complex had been seen elsewhere. It was faced in the fine limestone from the quarries at Tura, and this makes it the earliest known large stone monument built anywhere in the world. (The earlier great temples of Mesopotamia were built in mudbrick.) The builders remained under the influence of earlier wooden models. The stone columns in the entrance colonnade are fluted, the first known examples of a design which persists into classical architecture. The flutes represent either bound reeds or carved tree trunks, copying wooden originals. The complex introduces another innovation in the *serdab*, a room attached to the main building in which offerings were placed. It had a slit in the inside wall opening on to an inner room where a statue of Djoser was placed in such a way as to be able to see the offerings. For the first time, too, the reliefs show the king not as a conqueror, as is the earlier convention, but as undertaking the rituals of kingship. One shows him running, perhaps as part of the *sed* ceremony.

There is continued speculation among scholars as to why this revolutionary design was adopted. One simple view is that Imhotep wanted to make the building more imposing. In its finished state the stepped pyramid was 60 metres high. Another view is that the king was associated with a star cult and the steps were the means by which he was to ascend to heaven. Inscriptions from later pyramids, the so-called Pyramid Texts, support this suggestion. One reads, 'A staircase to heaven is laid for him (the king) so that he may mount up to heaven thereby.' Whatever the reason, the Step Pyramid continued to inspire reverence for centuries. It was a popular place of pilgrimage and was being restored 2,000 years after it was built. Imhotep himself was later deified as the son of Ptah, the god of craftsmen.

Djoser's dynasty, the Third, brings to an end the Early Dynastic period. With the Fourth Dynasty (*c*.2613) begins the Old Kingdom proper, which was to last to about 2130 BC. The Old Kingdom is dominated by the building of the Pyramids, one of the great administrative feats of history. For the Great Pyramid of Khufu (Cheops) alone, 2,500,000 limestone blocks with an average weight of 2.5 tonnes, were hauled up into position. One of the mathematicians accompanying Napoleon on his expedition to Egypt in 1798 calculated that the stones of the three pyramids of Giza could enclose France within a wall 3 metres high. It goes without saying that the Old Kingdom was a period of prosperity and stability, with power focused overwhelmingly on the king.

The transition from step pyramid to pyramid for the royal tomb can be seen at Meidum, some 50 kilometres south of Memphis, where there are the remains of what was built as a seven-stepped pyramid on the model of Djoser's. It was then enlarged to eight steps and finally the whole was encased in Tura limestone to form a true pyramid. For the first time a causeway was provided leading to a valley temple. (The king's body would have been brought up the causeway for final burial after rituals in the valley temple.) The pyramid is attributed to King Sneferu, first of the Fourth Dynasty, but it may not be his as he built two pyramids of his own at Dahshur nearby as well as another at Meidum. (In terms of volume Sneferu was the greatest pyramid builder of them all.) These were the first pyramids planned as such from the start. However, there was still much to be learnt. The desert surface on which the first of Sneferu's pyramids was based was unsuitable, and, in order to prevent the collapse of the structure, its weight was reduced by decreasing the angle of the incline of the upper blocks, earning it the name 'the bent pyramid'.

The transition from a stepped to a true pyramid was a difficult one for the builders to make. They could no longer rely on each step providing a base for the next layer. It is unclear why the transition took place, but it may have been the result of changing religious beliefs. It has been argued, for instance, that Sneferu adhered to a sun cult. One major change in the complex surrounding the true pyramids was that the mortuary chapel was now moved to the eastern side (from the traditional northern side) so that it received the first rays of the sun. The whole shape of the pyramid can be seen as the rays of the sun coming downwards. (There is an echo of this at Heliopolis, centre of a cult of the sun god, where a stone construction roughly in the shape of a pyramid, the so-called *benben*, was used as a symbol of the sun.)

It was Sneferu's son Khufu (Cheops) who emulated his father's building and started the first of the three great pyramids at Giza. The very fact that he chose a completely new spot suggests he was determined to make his own impact, and the tradition that he was a tyrannical megalomaniac lasted for centuries. (The Greek historian Herodotus passed on the story that he even sent his daughter into a brothel to raise more money for his projects. She hit on the idea of charging each of her customers a stone and was so successful in her trade, the story went, that she was able to use the total to build a small pyramid of her own.)

The Giza plateau held three major pyramids, the Great Pyramid of Khufu, a slightly smaller one to his son, Khafra (Chephren in Greek), and the third, about half the size of the larger two, to Menkaura (Mycerinus in Greek), whose reign was short. The burial chambers of each pyramid have been located but they were robbed in antiquity. (Khufu's burial chamber was unusual in being in the middle of the pyramid rather than below ground.) The building of the pyramids needed great technical skills but relatively little technology. The site was important. The rock had to be firm enough to sustain the massive weight of the building yet close enough to water for the stone to be brought in during the time of inundation. (Fifty-tonne blocks of granite, used to line the burial chambers and the lower courses of some pyramids, would have had to be brought from Aswan, hundreds of kilometres distant. Limestone, the main casing stone, was much more readily accessible.) The Great Pyramid of Khufu was built on ground which was carefully levelled round the planned edges of the pyramid with a mound of higher rock left in the middle. Each side measured almost exactly 230 metres and the whole was aligned perfectly to the north. This appears to have been done by taking the mid-point between the rising and setting position of a northern star.

The most probable building method was by the use of ramps (pulleys were not known until Roman times). A suggested gradient along which even a massive stone (and some pyramid stones weighed as much as 200 tonnes) could be shifted was about one in twelve. A ramp with this gradient could be built perpendicular to the pyramid base and as each level rose it would be heightened and lengthened to maintain the gradient. The stones themselves seem to have been loaded on to sledges which were then attached to ropes and pulled over timbers by gangs of men. Recent experiments at Giza with stone blocks suggest a workforce of some 25,000 would have been able to complete the Great Pyramid in twenty years.

The pyramids were only part of the funerary complex. At its fullest extent, best seen in the remains around Khafra's pyramid, it included a mortuary temple along the eastern side of the pyramid, where the body of the king was received for the final ceremonies before burial and where later offerings could be left. Leading up to the temple was a covered causeway nearly 600 metres long, its walls carved with reliefs. It led from the valley temple, where the king's remains were first received and probably given ritual purification before entering the final journey to its burial place.

Around Khufu's pyramid were a large number of traditional mastaba tombs arranged in ranks to the east and west. The eastern cemetery was the most favoured. It seems to have been reserved for the royal family, while officials had to take their place in order on the west. There is no more vivid example of a king, of vastly superior status to his subjects, arranging for his comforts in the afterlife. One other important find associated with Khufu is his ceremonial boat, found dismantled into over 1,200 pieces in a pit alongside the pyramid. It took some fourteen years to reassemble into a vessel 44 metres long complete with its oars and deckhouse. It may have been the actual boat used to convey the king's body to its burial place, or, alternatively, one for him to use in his afterlife when he would have to accompany Ra in his journey through the night.

Another famous monument of the Giza plateau is the Great Sphinx, the largest stone statue from the ancient world. (The word 'sphinx' is Greek, as many terms describing ancient Egypt are, probably derived from the Egyptian *shesep-ankh*: 'living image'.) It was fashioned from an outcrop of rock left unquarried during the building of the Great Pyramid, possibly because of the poor quality of the stone. It probably represents King Khafra as a man-headed lion. The lion was associated with the sun god and was believed to have guarded the gates of the underworlds of both the eastern and western horizons. The monument thus suggests some kind of guardianship of the pyramids themselves, linked to Khafra in his role as son of Ra.

As the Egyptologist Barry Kemp has pointed out, it is easy to be so overwhelmed by the sheer size of the pyramids themselves that one forgets the extraordinarily complex problems involved in managing the men and materials needed to build them. A steady supply of stone had to be quarried, shaped, moved, and put into position. The pyramid shape made its own demands. A small error in positioning in the lower layers would cause horrendous problems in the higher ones. Shaping the outside casing called for particular expertise. The whole operation, stretching, as it would have to, over many years, needed organizers of vision. It also required total confidence in the labour force. What incentives were needed to keep so many men toiling for so long can only be guessed at. Contrary to popular opinion, they were not slaves but ordinary peasants, presumably drafted in when their fields were under water from the annual inundation.

Even though the background to the building of the pyramids is well known particularly through the study of their evolution from Saqqara, this area has been rich hunting ground for fantasists. They have been encouraged by a lack of any Egyptian references to the function of the pyramids. In the nineteenth century these fantasists earned themselves the nickname Pyramidiots for their extravagant stories in which the measurements of the pyramids were interpreted to prove everything from the origins of British weights and measures to an outline of history to come. The positioning of the pyramids has been related to star patterns, they have been given a history dating back to 12000 BC, or even been said to have been built in two stages many thousands of years apart. Most of these fantasies centre on the Giza pyramids and ignore the many other smaller pyramids which fail to fit the proposed theory. It is just one way in which ancient Egypt continues to exercise its power over the present.

The simplest explanation for the Giza pyramids is that the pharaohs had become obsessed with the maintenance of their status for all time, an expression in fact of their divinity, and the monumentality of their burial places was the best way of achieving this. Yet the diversion of resources into such great buildings could not be sustained. By the Fifth Dynasty there is some slackening of this intense concentration on the king. Pyramids continue to be built, but these are much smaller and more human in scale. Some Fifth Dynasty kings now transferred their energies to building temples to Ra, taking as their model an original temple at an important cult centre to this god at Heliopolis at the entrance to the Delta. There is some evidence that the temple priests were becoming more involved in government (or possibly that leading nobles themselves were becoming priests in the service of Ra).

The Sixth Dynasty and the Collapse of the Old Kingdom

The most important development of all in the Fifth Dynasty was the growth of the power of provincial nobles. Whether as a deliberate royal policy or as the result of a weakening centre, many administrative posts became hereditary and their holders began to live on estates in the provinces they administered. This led to a gradual but inexorable decline in the authority of the kings. Now that they lived in the provinces, the nobles also built their own tombs there. Many were of great opulence and on a scale which would have been completely unacceptable in earlier times. The achievements of each official were proclaimed in an auto-biography carved on the wall of the tomb, a justification of his right to enjoy offerings from others for eternity. As the owners could no longer rely on their links with the kings for an afterlife, a new philosophy began to emerge which focused on the relationship of the deceased with the god Osiris. Osiris had orig-inally been associated with agriculture and the reviving power of the annual flood and he now became linked to continuing life of the deceased who, it was said on their tombs, were 'honoured' by Osiris as reward for their good behav-iour on earth. The word for honour, *imakhu*, came to mean the sense of respect and protection that a man would feel for those inferior to him and thus an important ethical concept in Egyptian society.

A number of factors may have been important in bringing a collapse in cen-tral authority in the next dynasty, the Sixth, about 2180 BC. Rainfall had been diminishing in northern Africa, and it may have been that the Nile floods were lower. Certainly there are reports of famine from this time. The long reign of Pepy II of the Sixth Dynasty, traditionally put at over ninety years but probably between fifty and seventy years, seems to have led to a gradual fossilization of political affairs with provincial nobles further consolidating their positions. Control over Nubia weakened, with expeditions there in search of gold meet-ing strong opposition from the local population. Signs of decline can also be seen with the tombs of Pepy's courtiers. They surround his pyramid at Saqqara as in earlier times, but now they are in mudbrick rather than in stone. At the same time there are reports of raids from nomadic tribes on the borders of the kingdom.

The First Intermediate Period

With the end of the Sixth Dynasty comes what has traditionally been called the First Intermediate Period (*c*.2160–2055 BC). Central government was less assertive and although a dynasty based on Heracleopolis in Middle Egypt claimed to be the successors of the Old Kingdom dynasties and retained power up to the end of the Intermediate Period (some eighteen or nineteen of its kings are known) a rival dynasty established itself in the south of the kingdom at what was then a remote provincial capital, Thebes. Its kings extended their power fur-ther south into Nubia. In retrospect this was to prove the most important polit-ical development of the period but there was nothing inevitable about the eventual success of what was to be the Eleventh 'Theban' Dynasty (discussed below). At the time the most obvious development was the continuing rise of the provincial administrators as important powers in their own right. By this time the system of administration was well established and the local officials highly experienced in running it. These officials would have wanted to keep order not only to maintain their own position but to give them the opportunity to provide tombs and offerings for their own afterlives.

An excellent example of the confidence of these provincial rulers comes from the tomb of Ankhtifi (found at el-Mo'alla, south of Thebes). Typically for the period Ankhtifi's position was one which combined 'overlord' status of two nomarchs—the administrative divisions of Egypt, another word which is Greek in origin (*nomos*, law)—as well as a religious role as 'overseer of priests'.

His 'autobiography' from the tomb is bombastic:

I was the beginning and the end [i.e. the climax] of mankind, since nobody like me existed before, nor will he exist; nobody like myself was ever born nor will he be born. I surpassed the feats of the ancestors, and coming generations will not be able to equal me in any of my feats within this million of years.

I gave bread to the hungry and clothing to the naked; I anointed those who had no cosmetic oil, I gave sandals to the barefooted; I gave a wife to him who had no wife. I took care of the towns of Hefat and Hor-mer in every [situation of crisis when] the sky was clouded and the earth [was parched(?) and when everybody died] of hunger.

[When there was trouble in the neighbouring nome of Thebes] I sailed downstream with my strong and trustworthy troops and moored on the west bank of the Theban nome . . . and my trustworthy troops searched for battle throughout the Theban nome, but nobody dared to come out through fear of them.   (Quoted by Stephan Seidlmayer in *The Oxford History of Ancient Egypt*)

Until recently the picture presented of the First Intermediate Period has been pessimistic. This is because it has been associated with a series of texts which detail social breakdown and despair. One talks of a world turned upside-down, with a resulting famine, and rich and poor in upheaval. 'Gold and lapis lazuli, silver and turquoise, carnelian and bronze are hung about the necks of slave girls while noble ladies walk in despair through the land . . . Little children say [to their fathers] he should never have caused me to live.' (Translation: Rosalie David.) The trouble with this approach is that archaeological evidence does not support it. A more careful examination of surviving texts shows that many actually originate after the period and may have exaggerated the disorder to justify the reassertion of power by the rulers of the Middle Kingdom. Recent revaluations of the period stress that the weakening of central control was successfully countered by the rise of efficient local officials who, as has been seen in the case of Ankhtifi, had no inhibitions about proclaiming their achievements. Insofar as cultural vitality and craftsmanship spread outside the court to the provinces, it can even be viewed as a period of positive achievement, not least in that it showed that Egyptian society could respond creatively to change.

The Emergence of the Middle Kingdom

In about 2055 BC one of the Theban princes, Mentuhotep II of the Eleventh Dynasty, launched a campaign north and defeated the kings of Heracleopolis. Their power disintegrated and it seems likely that most of the nomes acquiesced in Mentuhotep's rule as there is no archaeological evidence of prolonged warfare. The reunification marks the beginning of the Middle Kingdom. Mentuhotep's progress in reuniting Egypt can be seen in three successive Horus names he took for himself. 'He who breathes life into the heart of the Two Lands' was the first expression of his desire to unify the country. Then, as if to stress his southern origins, 'Divine is the White Crown [of southern Egypt]', and finally, in the thirty-ninth year of his reign when he felt totally secure, 'He who unifies the Two Lands'. His success was reinforced by the declaration of himself as a god and in reliefs he is shown wearing symbols of different deities.

Mentuhotep's concerns went further than unification. He secured the borders of Egypt against raiding nomads and then extended Egyptian influence down into Nubia with all the riches it offered. He and his successors of the Twelfth Dynasty aimed at a total domination of the area and its peoples. Their power was expressed in a series of elaborately constructed forts on the Nile between the First and Second Cataracts. When Mentuhotep died he was buried in one of the finest monuments of the Middle Kingdom, a great funerary complex set against a natural amphitheatre of rock on the west bank at Thebes. It is a combination of old styles and new (not least in its recognition of the 'peoples' cult of Osiris). As if establishing its links with an older Egypt, the complex has a valley temple, a causeway, 950 metres long, flanked by statues of the king in the form of Osiris, and a mortuary temple. Terraces and walkways give it further spaciousness and it was surrounded by groves of sycamore and tamerisk trees. What it lacks is a pyramid (although some experts believe that one may have been built on the roof of the mortuary temple). The body was buried under the cliff face itself, while alongside the main complex are the tombs of six 'queens', wives or concubines of Mentuhotep. Close by archaeologists have found a tomb with the remains of sixty men who had been killed in battle. It is possible that these were heroes of the final battle for control of Egypt given the status of lying beside their leader. The complex is a further sign of the ability of the great rulers of Egypt to express their links to the past without compromising their individuality but it is also a sign of the growing skills of the stone masons as well as engineers and architects. Sophistication of design rather than monumentality for its own sake is a major feature of the Middle Kingdom building projects.

For the time being no more royal burials took place at Thebes. The Eleventh Dynasty was replaced by the Twelfth about 1985 BC when one Amenemhat seized power. Amenemhat I, who was probably originally a vizier, and his successors were among the most successful kings in Egyptian history. Seeking to strengthen his position strategically (there was increasing fear of raids from Asia which a headquarters so far south as Thebes was not well placed to deal with), Amenemhat founded a new capital at Itj-tawy just south of Memphis in Middle Egypt (its full name reads 'It is Amenemhat who has conquered the Two Lands'). The new foundation also reflects Amenemhat's determination to establish his own identity and a comparison might be made with another strategically placed capital of later times, Constantinople. Amenemhat may have also set a new tradition of installing his son as co-regent so that power could pass more smoothly on a king's death but some scholars now doubt whether this is a correct interpretation of the texts.

The Middle Kingdom: The Years of Stability

For the next 200 years (c.1985–1795 BC) Egypt enjoyed a period of equilibrium. These were the great years of the Middle Kingdom. The reassertion of royal authority is shown by the extension of monumental building by pharaohs such as Senusret (ruled c.1956–1911 BC) in all the major cult centres of the land. This extension of power to the regions is one of the most important political developments of the period—the pharaoh is, in fact, challenging the power of local temple elites by overshadowing their buildings with his. There was much closer control of the local nomarchs by state officials and nomarchs were given specific responsibilities, defending a border or leading an expedition overseas, which emphasized their position as servants of the pharaoh. At the beginning of the period nomarchs' tombs (and their coffins, in particular) are among the finest in existence. The walls are covered with scenes of hunting, fishing, and the harvesting of abundant crops which they hope to enjoy in their afterlife while the tombs themselves are fronted by pillared façades and placed higher on the hillsides than those of more lowly officials. As time progresses the ranking of tombs becomes less obvious and the number of smaller ones increases. Here architecture reflects the shifting realities of power.

The kings imposed their influence well beyond the traditional boundaries of Egypt. They controlled Nubia more effectively than ever before and opened up new areas of cultivation in the Fayum, a large oasis area to the west of the river, through an impressive system of dikes and canals. They made the first significant contacts with Asia and the east through expeditions by boat and overland across the Sinai desert. The most important trading centre was Byblos, on the coast of Lebanon, from where cedarwood and resin (used in embalming) were shipped to Egypt. The contacts were so close that the local rulers at Byblos adopted Egyptian titles and used hieroglyphs. However, many texts show a distinct hostility towards Asians in general—Senusret describes himself as 'the throat-slitter of Asia' and the story of Joseph's brothers selling him as a slave to an Egyptian master (Genesis 37: 28–36) rings true. There were also some trading contacts with Crete. It would be wrong, however, to overstate Egyptian influence in this period. There is virtually no evidence in the archaeological record of influences from further overseas, while among the records preserved in the great archive at Mari on the Upper Euphrates (destroyed about 1760 BC, see p. 33 above) there is not even a mention of Egypt.

The administrative elite of the Middle Kingdom reached an impressive standard of efficiency. Officials were expected to be versatile, at one moment leading an army, the next organizing an expedition to bring back stone from a desert quarry, and then supervising justice in a courtroom. There was meticulous supervision by the state over every aspect of life. The carpenters in the royal boatyard recorded the movements of even planks and goatskins. The forts on the Nubian border, hundreds of kilometres from the capital, were garrisoned and fed. When workmen had to be assembled to build a pyramid for King Senusret II between the Nile and the Fayum at Kahun, an artificial town was built which could house 9,000 of them, complete with their stores.

The rulers of the Middle Kingdom evolved an ideology which underpinned their rule. It centred on the concept of *ma'at*, harmony achieved through justice and right living. (*Ma'at* was personified as a goddess.) The kings claimed that their duty was to act with restraint so as to preserve the balanced relationship between ruler and gods on which *ma'at* depended. One text put it as follows: the king is on earth 'for ever and ever, judging humanity and propitiating the gods, and setting order [*ma'at*] in place of disorder. He gives offerings to the gods and mortuary offerings to the spirits of the blessed dead.' This involved generosity and forgiveness. A famous story is that of Sinuhe, a minor official in the retinue of Senusret I. Sinuhe has fled Egypt, fearful of the king's anger after some minor incident, and taken refuge in Syria. Years later he is nostalgic for home. He returns to Egypt to throw himself on the mercy of the king and is pardoned and allowed to live with the royal family again and even enjoy a tomb near the king. Such was the image the kings were pleased to portray. Even their statues have moved away from the purely monumental to allow hints of their individuality to emerge through the conventional poses.

For the individual administrator the key to personal contentment lay in moderation, and texts survive in which fathers preach to their sons:

Do not bring down the men of the magistrates' court or incite the just men to rebel. Do not pay too much attention to him clad in shining garments, and have regard for him who is shabbily dressed. Do not accept the reward of the powerful man or persecute the weak for him. (Translation: T. James)

Some of this so-called 'Wisdom Literature' may date from before the Middle Kingdom, but it reflects the ethical spirit of this age.

The same ideas are reflected in the 'Tale of the Eloquent Peasant', one of the most popular texts of the Middle Kingdom. A peasant is on his way with his loaded donkeys from the Delta to the Nile Valley. He is waylaid by a covetous landowner who tricks him into leading his donkeys over his barley. When one of the donkeys eats a mouthful of barley, the landowner triumphantly confiscates it. The rest of the story is taken up with the peasant's search for justice, which he achieves after long-winded displays of eloquence in front of the local magistrate. In a nice touch, the peasant is fed a daily ration while his case is being heard. At the same time his wife is also secretly sent provisions. Despite the enormous persistence required from the wronged peasant, the lesson is that the state will uphold justice and even support the oppressed during their ordeals.

Writing was fundamental to the status of the administrator. 'Be a scribe. Your limbs will be sleek, your hands will grow soft. You will go forth in white clothes honoured with courtiers saluting you,' was the advice given in a Middle Kingdom text, *The Satire of Trades*, which ridiculed all other occupations. The process of learning was a long one—twelve years according to a later Egyptian text. Most prestige attached to the ability to write hieroglyphs. There were many hundreds of signs to learn and, like the calligraphy of Japan and China, the writing of hieroglyphs became an art form in itself.

Hieroglyphs were a formal script used mainly for carving sacred texts on stone. At their simplest level individual hieroglyphs were pictures of what the scribe wanted to express, a figure of a man for a man, a pyramid for a pyramid (pictograms). The sound of the pictogram could be used also as a syllable in a longer word. The mace was *h(e)dj*, and so the pictogram for a mace was used whenever the sound 'hedj' appeared as a syllable in a word. Some hieroglyphs were used to represent single consonants but the Egyptians had no vowels. In fact, the symbol for mace was used to express not only the sound 'hedj', but the sound and words represented in 'hadj', 'hidj', 'hodj', and 'hudj'. Extra hieroglyphs often had to be added to make it clear what actual word was being expressed. A mace with a necklace after it, for instance, represented 'silver'. Pictograms could also represent abstract concepts. A papyrus roll stood for writing. The hieroglyph for 'to travel south', against the current of the Nile, was a boat with a sail, while that for 'to travel north', with the current, was a boat with an oar and its sail down.

For the day-to-day administrative and legal texts which formed the bulk of Egyptian written material, scribes used the hieratic script. Hieratic was a form of shorthand in which the most common hieroglyphic symbols were abbreviated. As time went on it became more and more condensed, in effect a different script from hieroglyphs altogether. Many of the texts were inscribed on papyrus, made from the stem of a marsh plant which was cut into strips which were then pasted together to form a smooth surface. Each sheet measured about 48 × 43 centimetres and could be joined with others in rolls of up to 40 metres. Writing was with a reed, using black carbon with important words highlighted in red ochre.

Texts from the Middle Kingdom suggest a love of learning for its own sake. One father, Khety, from a humble background himself, talks to his son. 'I shall make you love writing more than your mother—I shall present its beauties to you. Now, it is greater than any trade—there is not its like in the land.' (Translation: R. Parkinson.) The Middle Kingdom was seen as the classical age of literature, and its most celebrated stories, such as the two outlined above, were copied and recopied by later generations. Literary texts were, however, only a small part of the total output of administrative documents, medical treatises, funerary inscriptions, and accounts of religious ritual which have also survived.

Another major cultural achievement of the Middle Kingdom was its jewellery. Jewellery had many functions. It served as a sign of status and wealth as well as of royal approval. The king would make presentations to favoured courtiers in a tradition which has lasted to present times. The Order of the Royal Collar, given for bravery in battle, is found as early as the Old Kingdom. Jewellery was also assumed to have magical properties, helping to ward off evil spirits and disease. Certain stones, turquoise and lapis lazuli, for instance, had particular importance. The master craftsmen of the Middle Kingdom have left marvellous examples of crowns and pectorals from the tombs of royal women. Their speciality was *cloisonné* work, the inlay of precious stones within a gold frame.

From earliest times the framework of order and a shared sense of community was maintained by religion. The Egyptians were sensitive to the complexity of spiritual forces and the need to propitiate those gods who could protect them against disorder, destruction, or everyday misfortune. The coherence of religious belief was maintained by absorbing gods into a family and conflict could be rationalized through myths of inter-god conflict such as that between Osiris, Horus, and Seth. The threat of political disunity could be neutralized by merging gods, Ra from Heliopolis in the north with Amun from Thebes further south, for instance. Spiritual forces were represented in human or animal form. Ra is hawk-headed (a hawk soars upwards to the sun) with a sun-disk on his head. Thoth, the god of wisdom, with an ibis head and a scribe's tools in his hand. Seth was always presented as a mischievous creature with a long snout and a forked tail. Overall Egyptian religion provided a particularly sophisticated approach to the mysteries of life and was instrumental in underpinning its overall stability.

At the level of popular religious belief the Middle Kingdom is the period of Osiris. His story, his death and suffering, and rebirth as a saviour who welcomes those who have lived by his rules to another world, is grounded in the ancient ritual of annual renewal found in many other cultures. By the Middle Kingdom the main shrine to Osiris was at Abydos, where tradition had it that his body was reassembled after its mutilation by Seth. In tomb paintings the body of the deceased is often portrayed visiting Abydos before its final burial. It became the custom for visitors to Abydos to build a small chapel or cenotaph to act as a permanent memorial for the giver.

Osiris judges each soul as it comes to him after death. In the texts which explain what is required of a good man, there is the same emphasis on behaviour centred on moderation and harmony with the natural world. The deceased promises not only that he has not killed, fornicated, or offended the gods, but that he has not taken milk from children, dammed up flowing water, or taken herds from their pastures. It is an attractive code of life, with affinities to a later philosophy, Confucianism, and it represents what has been described as a 'democratization of the afterlife' (John Wilson) in that the afterlives of pharaohs and subjects are no longer so distinct.

In every society there is a yawning gap between its ideals and the actual achievements. Whatever their protestations, there is no doubt that the rulers of the Middle Kingdom were formidable men unwilling to brook any opposition to their rule. The only words which have come to us are those of the elite, perhaps 1 per cent of the population, those who would have most benefited from a period of strong government. It is known that the middle and lower classes were enlisted to undertake fixed tasks, service in the army or labour, with those attempting to evade service being sent to remote parts of the empire or to work in the stone quarries. Little is known of the mass of peasantry and even less of those peoples such as the Nubians who were colonized during this period, although it is clear that punitive expeditions into Nubia were brutal. However, there is no doubt that the Middle Kingdom does represent one of the pinnacles of Egyptian civilization. After the megalomania of the Fourth Dynasty, there is something refreshing about the more human scale of life in these centuries. In the words of Gae Callender, it was 'an age of tremendous invention, great vision and colossal projects, yet there was also careful and elegant attention to detail in the creation of the smallest items of everyday use and decoration'. It is this combination which attracts.

The 'Hyksos' and the Second Intermediate Period

The decline of the Middle Kingdom, like that of its predecessor, appears to have been gradual. The Twelfth Dynasty came to an end about 1773 BC, and then there was a succession of kings with short reigns. As they have different lineages, it is possible that power circulated among leading families. Slowly they began losing their grip on the borders of Egypt. In the eastern Delta there was an influx of migrants from Palestine, which was enjoying a period of particular prosperity. By the late eighteenth or early seventeenth century a ruling elite which combined Egyptian and Asian cultural traits took charge of the city of Avaris on the eastern Delta, the site of which, long lost, has now finally been identified as the modern Tell el-Dab'a.

The Egyptians to the south called the new ruling dynasty the 'Hyksos', literally 'chiefs of foreign lands', thus stereotyping them as invaders, but archaeology is suggesting that this is too simplistic a portrayal and needs further exploration.

The settlement at Tell el-Dab'a has been expertly excavated by the Austrian archaeologist Manfred Bietak. Originally it was a frontier city marking the border between Egypt and Asia. In the Middle Kingdom it seems to have had both a defensive and a trading role and in the latter it attracted an influx of outsiders from Lebanon and Syria, Palestine, and even Cyprus who, it seems, intermarried with local Egyptians. There is a cosmopolitan air to the range of artefacts found in the city which include Minoan pottery and jewellery and cylinder seals from Syria. The chronology of the site is hotly contested (in that it is difficult to link the variety of artefacts found to outside chronologies) but about 1710 there appears to have been an epidemic in the city—bodies have been found buried unceremoniously in large pits. It is in the period of recovery that a new wealthy elite appears to have gained control, just as the Thirteenth Dynasty kings at Itj-tawy were in decline. Their last effective ruler was Sobekhotep about 1725 BC. In Tell el-Dab'a (Avaris) one Nehesy, who was probably Egyptian but may have been Nubian, appears to have seized power and adopted many traditional royal epithets such as 'lord of the two lands'. He linked himself to the 'local' god Seth, normally a god of disorder but now appropriated for the new regime. The 'Hyksos' kingdom of Nehesy and his successors mixes features of both Egyptian and Syro-Palestinian cultures and gained immense prosperity from trade. The texts speak of imports of 'chariots and horses, ships, timber, gold, lapis lazuli, silver, turquoise, bronze, axes without number, oil, incense, fat and honey'. Tell el-Dab'a expanded fast—eventually to three times the size of any contemporary site in Palestine. Then came expansion to the south. Itj-tawy and Memphis were overrun in the early seventeenth century (the native Egyptians presenting it as a ruthless attack although there is no archaeological evidence to back this) and a border with Upper Egypt defined at Cusae on the Nile some 200 kilometres south of Memphis. While Avaris remained the home town of the dynasty, control of northern Egypt was enforced from Memphis, which was much better placed strategically than Avaris to control the Nile. The Avaris kings appear to have established links across the desert into Nubia, where the weakening of Egyptian power had led to the emergence of the independent kingdom of Kush.

In recent years scholars have been able to sort out the confusions surrounding Manetho's list of dynasties for this period. Manetho's Fourteenth and Fifteenth Dynasties are believed to represent the Avaris kings while the Sixteenth and Seventeenth represent a rival set of kings who maintained power in Thebes. These were hemmed in by the Avaris rulers to the north and the kingdom of Kush in the south. The Theban kings were isolated and vulnerable at a time when order seems to have deteriorated with the fragmentation of the kingdom and there is a heavy stress in their inscriptions on military prowess. At first they seem to have coexisted with the Hyksos rulers. There is some evidence of trading contacts, and the 'Hyksos' king Apepi may even have married into the Theban royal family. However, at some point about 1550 BC, the Theban kings marched north. They first broke the links between the 'Hyksos' and Nubia, then Ahmose I entered the Delta itself, capturing first Memphis and isolating Avaris from Palestine so that he could capture it. The archaeological evidence shows that the 'Hyksos' were armed only with copper weapons while the Thebans had the much harder bronze. Perhaps the 'Hyksos' had become too confident in their prosperity but there seems to have been no slaughter when they surrendered. There is instead a resumption of Egyptian artefacts on the site suggesting that the Asian population had simply left. The excavators also found that the rebuilt palace of Avaris was decorated with Minoan frescos. Although these are in fragments and will take many years to reconstruct, they have led to the revival of an ancient tradition that Ahmose married a Cretan princess. Finally Ahmose struck eastwards into Palestine itself and then, the borders with Asia secure, he returned south to restore Egyptian control over Nubia. The scene was now set for the New Kingdom, a period of stability which lasted for 500 years and involved a massive expansion of Egyptian power into Asia.

FURTHER READING

For general overviews see Ian Shaw (ed.), *The Oxford History of Ancient Egypt* (Oxford, 2000), which has a full reading list; N. Grimal, *A History of Ancient Egypt* (Oxford, 1992); S. Quirke and J. Spencer (eds.); *The British Museum Book of Ancient Egypt* (London, 1992); *The British Museum Dictionary of Ancient Egypt* (London, 1995); and J. Baines and J. Malek, *Atlas of Ancient Egypt* (Oxford, 1984), the last for good maps and illustrations. Rosalie David's *Discovering Ancient Egypt* (London, 1993) includes details of the excavation of Egypt as well as a gazetteer of the main sites and a historical outline. Challenging, but also stimulating, is B. Kemp's *Ancient Egypt: Anatomy of a Civilization* (London, 1989). For reference there is the three-volume *Oxford Encyclopaedia of Ancient Egypt*, edited by D. Redford (Oxford, 2001).

For Egyptian art see W. Stevenson Smith, *The Art and Architecture of Ancient Egypt* (revised edition, New Haven, 1981); Gay Robins, *The Art of Ancient Egypt* (London, 1997); and J. Malek, *Egypt: 4000 Years of Art* (London, 2003). Richard Wilkinson, *Reading Egyptian Art* (London, 1992), provides an aid to understanding Egyptian iconography.

On early Egypt see A. J. Spencer, *Early Egypt: The Rise of Civilization in the Nile Valley* (London, 1993), and Toby Wilkinson, *Early Dynastic Egypt* (London, 2001). The authoritative work on the pyramids is I. Edwards, *The Pyramids of Egypt* (revised edition, London, 1993) but see also M. Lehner, *The Complete Pyramids* (London, 1997), and for a comprehensive study of the Sphinx, P. Jordan, *Riddles of the Sphinx* (Stroud, 1998).

For hieroglyphs there is Mark Collier and Bill Manley, *How to Read Hieroglyphs* (London, 1998), and the thoughtful study by Erik Iversen, *The Myth of Egypt and its Hieroglyphs in European Tradition* (Princeton, 1961).

For a study of the impact of Egypt through history see Charles Freeman, *The Legacy of Ancient Egypt* (New York, 1997).

4 | Egypt as an Imperial Power, 1500–1000 BC

The Emergence of the New Kingdom

With the triumph of Ahmose I of the Eighteenth Dynasty over the 'Hyksos', unity and stability returned to Egypt. There was a very different atmosphere to the New Kingdom (c.1550–1069 BC). The memory of the Hyksos dynasty was exploited through the rulers of the New Kingdom becoming warrior kings, building an empire in Asia which at its height reached as far as the Euphrates. The forces of Seth, the ruling god of Avaris, normally seen as undermining the power of the kings, were now considered to have been subdued by them and redirected at Egypt's enemies. It was Thutmose I (1504–1492 BC) who reached the Euphrates and defeated the state of Mitanni in Syria. With control established over the cities of Palestine, local princes, with Egyptian troops to oversee them, were used to maintain the new empire intact.

As in previous dynasties, the kings of the New Kingdom also established firm control over Nubia. It is Thutmose I who is credited with the defeat of the Kingdom of Kush. 'The Nubian bowmen fall by the sword and are thrown aside on their lands; their stench floods their valleys . . . the pieces cut from them are too much for the birds carrying off the prey to another place,' the king records on a rock face near the victory. Egyptian rule was imposed further south than ever before, down to the Fourth Cataract and probably beyond. A frontier post was established at Napata, under the shadow of a table mountain, Gebel Barkal, which acted as a landmark for traders coming across the desert. For the first time the Egyptians could now directly control the trade routes with their rich harvest of exotic goods coming from central Africa. The Nubian gold mines were also worked so intensively that by the end of the New Kingdom they had become exhausted.

Martin Bernal in his *Black Athena* suggested that the Egyptian empire also extended into the Mediterranean, with Egypt exercising what he called 'suzerainty' over the Aegean between 1475 and 1375 BC (with contact also at earlier periods). So far little evidence has been found to support the argument. It is true that a growing number of Egyptian artefacts have been found in the Mediterranean, but hardly enough to support the claim of 'suzerainty'. A survey made in 1987 found a total of only twenty-one artefacts carrying Egyptian royal cartouches, most of which were discovered in Crete, the nearest part of the Aegean to Egypt. It seems that many of these may have been traded through the Levantine ports. Egypt had no city on the Mediterranean coast until Alexandria was founded by Alexander the Great in 332 BC, and no seagoing navy is recorded before the seventh century. It is hard, therefore, to see how Egypt could have maintained any form of control over the Aegean, and Bernal's thesis has received little scholarly support.

It took some time for the New Kingdom to build up its strength. Despite his military successes, Ahmose of the Eighteenth Dynasty did not reopen the limestone quarries at Tura until late in his reign. His own buildings were all in mudbrick. His successor, Amenhotep I (1525–1504 BC), portrayed himself as an aggressive warrior king (his Horus name was 'Bull who conquers the lands'), but the evidence is of twenty years of peace and stability. All the usual signs of Egyptian prosperity now returned. New temples were built in Thebes and Nubia, and raw materials started to flow in to support a resurgence of artistic activity. Thebes was particularly honoured as the city from which the dynasty had sprung and the god Amun was appropriated as its protective god.

Shortly afterwards the dynasty produced a rarity in Egyptian history, a ruling queen. There had been signs of the growing power of the queens early in the Eighteenth Dynasty. Both Ahmose's mother and wife seem to have been formidable women who had cults dedicated to them at Thebes. Hatshepsut, the niece of Amenhotep I and daughter of his successor Thutmose I, went further. Hatshepsut had married her half-brother, King Thutmose II. She had no sons, but Thutmose II had one by a concubine who, although still only a boy, succeeded as Thutmose III on the death of his father in 1479 BC. Hatshepsut was accepted as co-regent. Many early reliefs show her dutifully accompanying the young king as he fulfils the royal rituals but she was only biding her time. She soon took absolute power for herself, claiming that she was ruler by right as the heir of Thutmose I.

Every successful Egyptian ruler had to establish himself within a well-established ideology of kingship. For a woman this presented an almost insurmountable problem and Hatshepsut had to define her image carefully. In some representations—sculptures, for instance—Hatshepsut was happy to present herself as female, and she took a female Horus name, 'The She-Horus of fine gold'. In more conventional settings, however, such as temple reliefs, she is shown as male, even being shown with a pharaonic beard! She also made great play of her divine ancestry, spelling out the details of her conception by Amun in the temple she built at Deir el-Bahri. Here she referred to herself as the son of Amun, the most forceful way in which she could proclaim her legitimacy. In one inscription she even rewrites history to suggest that it is she who finally brought the rule of the Hyksos to an end and is now in a position to restore Egypt to its original purity. It is a fascinating example of the ways in which Egyptian rulers, particularly those who were outsiders, were able to define themselves within conventional ideologies of power without masking the reality of the situation. Comparisons have been made with a similar adept manipulation of her courtiers by Queen Elizabeth I of England.

Hatshepsut ruled for over twenty years. It was a successful and stable reign and a peaceful one too, perhaps because the one section of Egyptian society Hatshepsut could not trust entirely was the army and so she never used it. For the first time in the New Kingdom a ruler had effective control over Middle Egypt, and a mass of new temples were built there. Hatshepsut was blessed with an outstanding chief official, Senenmut, a man of humble family who worked his way up to a position of far-reaching power. (Inevitably there were suggestions that he was the queen's lover. Graffiti of the time have even been found showing a female pharaoh with a lover. The intimacy of his relationship with the royal family is confirmed by a charming statue, now in the British Museum, of him nursing the queen's only child, her daughter by Thutmose II.)

Senenmut's talents and interests were wide-ranging, as was typical for leading officials of the court. His tomb was decorated with astronomical symbols and contained the classics of Middle Kingdom religious literature. One of his greatest achievements, in his role of chief architect, was the mortuary temple he built for his queen at Deir el-Bahri, running along the northern side of the imposing tomb of Mentuhotep, founder of the Middle Kingdom. A succession of terraces supported by colonnades led up into the natural amphitheatre of the hillside with side chapels commemorating Thutmose I, Amun, and the goddess Hathor, the most popular of the Egyptian goddesses. Finally, a passage cut in the rock face contained an inner sanctuary. The complex echoes that of Mentuhotep but again it is unique and reinforces the theme of continual reinvention in pharaonic iconography. Hatshepsut was not buried in the complex herself. She prepared two tombs for herself in the valleys behind, an indication, perhaps, of her fears that her body would not be left undisturbed.

One of the most celebrated reliefs on Hatshepsut's complex commemorates an expedition to the land of Punt, possibly staged as a publicity stunt to make up for her lack of military activity. (It certainly aroused enormous excitement at the time.) There are references to this mysterious land as early as the Old Kingdom. Punt was probably along the African shores of the southern Red Sea, although no one site has ever been identified. Hatshepsut's reliefs suggest a journey through the Red Sea, and at Punt itself there are pictures of tree houses and tropical fauna (as well as the queen of Punt, depicted with a swollen and curved body). The fruits of these expeditions included aromatic plants, used for incense, ebony, electrum, and shorthorned cattle, and it seemed that the traders lingered there for about three months at a time, perhaps waiting for favourable winds with which to return home. The exotic goods were used to glorify Amun, her 'father', whose temples at Karnak received yet more embellishment.

Hatshepsut disappears from the record about 1458 BC. There is some suggestion that Senenmut turned against her and engineered the return of Thutmose
III to power. Some years into his reign the hieroglyphs representing Hatshepsut's
name were systematically erased from every monument, even from the tips of
obelisks. This was a devastating fate for any Egyptian, as the survival of their
inscribed name was one way in which an afterlife could be ensured. The comprehensive removal of Hatshepsut's name may be a sign of the spite of Thutmose
for his powerful stepmother, but probably the main objective was to restore an
ordered and comprehensible past focused once again on male kingship.

In the reign of Thutmose III as sole ruler (1458–1425 BC) the New Kingdom
was threatened with the loss of control in Asia. The kingdom of Mitanni, earlier defeated by Thutmose I, was now challenging Egypt for the control of the
Levant. It attempted to undermine Egyptian rule by stirring up rivalries
between the cities of Palestine. Thutmose led no less than seventeen campaigns
in Asia, proudly recording their results on the walls of the temple of Amun at
Karnak. One of his most famous battles was at Megiddo, where the king,
against all professional advice, took his armies through a difficult mountain
pass to emerge behind his enemies and defeat them. The booty was magnificent and meticulously listed at Karnak, 894 chariots, 200 suits of armour, 2,000
horses, and 25,000 other animals. With control over Palestine re-established,
Thutmose took on Mitanni itself, even launching a successful crossing of the
Euphrates. He also imposed his rule forcefully on Nubia. The land was now
being exploited directly by Egyptian institutions, with the result that much of
the indigenous culture was eradicated.

In royal mythology Thutmose was portrayed as one of the great kings of
Egypt. He was far more than a successful conqueror. He had an acute sense of his
place in history as the successor of a long line of Theban kings. A list of his ancestors was set up in the temple at Karnak and was treated with special reverence.
He was also a man of culture and curiosity. He was an enthusiastic reader of
ancient texts, and is believed to have composed literary works of his own. In contrast to his predecessors he was clearly impressed by Syrian culture and his three
wives may have been Syrian themselves. Marbled glass from Syria becomes a
popular luxury item. Thutmose even brought back examples of the flowers and
plants of Syria, depicting them in a botanical scene on the temple wall at Karnak.
There is, in short, a much more relaxed and positive approach to the outside
world.

There is an interesting contrast between the imperial propaganda of the
pharaohs and the reality of their actions. A pharaoh had to incorporate an aura
of invincibility into his image. Thutmose's successor, Amenhotep II (1427–1400
BC), gloried in the role of war hero. His ebullient Horus name, 'Powerful bull
with great strength', is echoed in legends which tell how he hunted lions on foot
and killed Syrian princes with his own hands. However, much of this was for

home consumption. In the twenty-seven years of Amenhotep's reign, there were actually only two Syrian campaigns and gradually the pharaohs began to realize the importance of diplomatic solutions. Under Amenhotep's successor Thutmose IV (1400–1390 BC), peace was made with Mitanni. The Mitannians were worried about the rise of the Hittite empire to the north, and they were quite content to hold northern Syria against the growing threat while allowing Egyptian rule to continue in Palestine. It is in Thutmose's reign that one sees a shrinking in the number of military officials and the consolidation of civil administration. Peace was secured when Amenhotep III (1390–1352 BC) married the daughter of the Mitannian king. The reality of international relations in this period can be seen in the Amarna letters (see the Interlude below).

The Administration of the New Kingdom

The reign of Amenhotep III marked the zenith of the New Kingdom. The structure of its administration is fairly well known. The king presided over three departments of government. The first was his own family. This could be large: Rameses II (1279–1213 BC), for instance, was said to have fathered 160 children. While the royal family had immense status, not many of its members seem to have been given political power. The king was presumably careful not to encourage those with royal blood to build up positions of influence. There were exceptions, however. The heir might be given command of the army, and there was a traditional role for the queen, or eldest daughter of the king, as Chief Priestess of Amun. (As it was believed that the eldest son of the queen had been conceived in her by Amun, who, by this time, had replaced Ra in this role, this was no more than her due and made her position unassailable.) Through her the king had access to much of the wealth of the temples.

The second department of government oversaw the empire in Nubia and Asia. Apart from Nubia, where the ecology was very similar to what they were used to, the Egyptians were not successful colonizers. Their world was so dependent on the ordered environment of the Nile valley that they found it very difficult to adapt to life outside. When Egyptian armies reached the Euphrates they were completely bewildered by it, never having encountered water flowing southwards. In words reminiscent of the political newspeak of George Orwell's 1984, they described the river as 'water that goes downstream in going upstream'.

Ultimately the Egyptians depended on military force to sustain their rule, and for the first time in Egyptian history the kings raised a large army, of perhaps between 15,000 and 20,000 men. It was divided into battalions of infantry and charioteers, each battalion fighting under the name of a god. A large proportion of the troops consisted of levies raised within the empire itself. However, the army was expensive and difficult to maintain and soldiering was never popular. In practice most kings contented themselves with punitive raids into Asia or Nubia early in their reigns, as much for propaganda purposes as for suppression of rebels, and then returned to a more settled life in their courts. The normal pattern of administration was indirect, with Egyptian governors, supported by envoys and garrisons, ruling through vassal princes. The governors were responsible for maintaining order and collecting taxes, tribute, and raw materials. Thutmose III, the most successful conqueror of Asia, initiated a policy of bringing back Palestinian princes to Egypt as hostages for the good behaviour of their home cities.

The empire was an important source of raw materials. This had always been the case with Nubia, but Asia also provided booty from the wars and openings for trade. The grain harvests of the plain of Megiddo were appropriated by Thutmose III, tin came from Syria, copper from Cyprus, and silver, valued in Egypt more highly than gold, from Cilicia in southern Anatolia. If the temple inscriptions are to be believed, prisoners were brought back to Egypt in their thousands, and foreigners are to be found as artisans, winemakers, servants, and mercenaries. With them came Asiatic gods and goddesses, among them Astarte, the goddess of horse-riders, who were adopted within the Egyptian pantheon.

The third department of government was concerned with internal administration. This was subdivided into four offices, one each for the administration of the royal estates, the army, the overseeing of religious affairs, and internal civil administration. Each was headed by a small group of advisers, perhaps twenty to thirty at any one time, who were often intimates of the king. The country was divided into two administrative areas, one, Upper Egypt, based on Thebes and the other on Memphis. The success of civil administration was dependent on the personality of the ruler. It was he and only he who could infuse the necessary energy into maintaining the links with the provincial governments stretched out along hundreds of kilometres of valley. Smaller centres had mayors, who were responsible for collecting taxes, probably a tenth of total produce, and carrying out orders from above, although it is not clear how far mayors exercised power over the countryside outside their towns. Criminal cases and the countless property disputes which arose over land which disappeared under water for four months of the year were dealt with by councils of soldiers, priests, and bureaucrats.

Kings and Temples

Once his kingdom was secure Amenhotep III was free to concentrate his energies on a vast new building programme. The most magnificent of his creations were the temples to Amun and the 'mother goddess' Mut at Thebes. Thebes was sacred as the base from which the kings of the Eleventh and Twelfth Dynasty and later the Eighteenth Dynasty had unified Egypt. It was the most popular place for burial for the kings, as the great funerary complexes to Mentuhotep and Hatshepsut at Deir el-Bahri show. King Thutmose I, father of Hatshepsut, was the first king to choose for his own tomb a desolate valley behind Deir el-Bahri. Later to become celebrated as the Valley of the Kings, it was to be home to sixty-two tombs, nearly all of them of royalty.

The god native to Thebes was Amun. He was an unseen god of the air (the word Amun means 'the hidden one'), though in his 'animal' form he was portrayed as a human being. As has been mentioned, in the Middle Kingdom Amun had been syncretized with the traditional sun god Ra to form a composite god Amun-Ra. Temples to the god had been built in the Middle and Old Kingdom at Luxor and Karnak, 'suburbs' of Thebes, but they had been on a relatively small scale. Now Amun was credited with the victories of the New Kingdom, and the exploits of the warrior kings were proclaimed in reliefs on the massive temples for which Amenhotep III, among others, was responsible.

The temples of Luxor and Karnak were built as residences of the gods with all the exclusivity that that implied. They were approached by long avenues, lined in the case of Amun by ram-headed sphinxes. (The ram was the sacred animal of Amun.) Their entrances were guarded by pylons, massive stone gateways, and through them was a series of courts and colonnades which led to the sanctuary of the god. As this holy of holies was approached through anterooms, ceilings became lower and the floors higher to represent the original mound from which creation was believed to have emerged. The light was also restricted so that when the sanctuary was reached the cult statue of the god stood almost in darkness.

In theory the king was the only person of sufficient divinity to be able to undertake the rituals involved in feeding and sustaining the *ka* of the god. In his absence select priests were allowed in to act as his representatives. To purify themselves for entry, they and the vessels they used were ritually washed in the sacred pool which was an important feature of each temple. Then they would make a dignified approach to the sanctuary, breaking the door seals which protected the god each night. Each day the statue was anointed and clothed in fresh linen and the prescribed prayers recited before it.

The only chance the public had to participate in the temple rituals of Thebes was at the great festivity of Opet which took place each year at that joyful time when the Nile floods reappeared in the valley. The statue of Amun at Karnak, clothed in gold and jewels, was taken from its sanctuary, mounted on a sacred barque, and carried to the side of the Nile. It was then sailed down to visit the temple of Amun at Luxor. Along the bank of the Nile the spectators, overcome by religious fervour, danced and sang, waved standards, or prostrated themselves before the passing god.

The temples were not simply religious institutions in the modern sense of the word. They were an integral part of the administration of the state. The High Priest of Amun at Thebes might be a priest who had been promoted, but he could also have been picked from the senior courtiers or army generals. Among his responsibilities were the granaries, the artisans working on the royal tombs, and public works in general. The temples enjoyed vast wealth, much of it from endowments made by the king, probably in the expectation that a proportion of the resulting produce would be paid back to the state. An estimate of the land belonging to the temple of Amun at Karnak alone in the late New Kingdom is 2,400 square kilometres, almost a quarter of the total cultivated land of Egypt. A labour force of over 80,000 is recorded. The temples of Amun at Thebes had a total income of nearly 2 million sacks of grain a year.

The Cult of Aten

By the end of the reign of Amenhotep III (*c.*1350 BC), the temples were so rich that they had become political and economic rivals of the king. The first signs of strain can already be seen in Amenhotep's reign. He seems to have distanced himself gradually from the influence of Thebes. He brought up his own son, also Amenhotep, in Memphis and is found patronizing other cults in northern Egypt—that of the sacred bulls at Saqqara and the sun god at Heliopolis, for instance. For the first time in Amenhotep's reign a new cult appears, the worship of the sun in its physical form, Aten. It was Amenhotep's successor, Amenhotep IV, better known as Akhenaten, 'Pious Servant of Aten' (1352–1336 BC), who was to attempt a religious and social revolution, installing Aten as a single god in place of the traditional gods of Egypt.

The worship of a sun god was well established in Egyptian religion. Each sunrise was seen as a symbolic re-enactment of the first creation and sun worship was also common among the cultures of the Middle East over which Egypt ruled. If Akhenaten had done no more than emphasize Aten among the other gods of Egypt he would probably have caused no stir. However, he chose to launch an attack on all other gods, in particular Amun, and to install himself as a direct mediator between his people and Aten. Iconographically the shift is shown by depicting Aten as a disc with rays ending in hands that touch the king and his family. The family is emphasised by the elevation of Akhenaten's wife Nefertiti so that the royal couple appear as the twin children of Aten. Akhenaten's motives for this religious revolution are not clear. He may have been under the influence of his father, with whom he had possibly been co-regent before he had died (not all scholars agree on this), or his mother, the formidable Queen Tiy, who lived on into the new reign. He may simply have been trying to assert his own independence from the power of the temples or genuinely have developed his own religious beliefs. Whatever his motives he had set himself a massive task. Religious belief was so deeply embedded in the Egyptian world picture that Akhenaten was, in effect, challenging the intellectual structure of the state.

The impact was profound. Many temples were closed down and their goods were confiscated. The economic structure of the state was upset as lands were transferred directly to the king. The masses lost their festivals so that the rhythm of the year was disrupted. As the reign went on the persecution of Amun became more intense. His name and even any reference to 'gods' in the plural was erased from the temples. Such a dramatic revolution could never have been effected if Akhenaten had not kept the support of the army.

The first temple to Aten was built by Akhenaten at Thebes. Judging from the quality of its reliefs it was constructed in haste. It proved too close to the stronghold of Amun. Five years after his accession Akhenaten moved his capital downriver to a virgin site in Middle Egypt. It was named Akhetaten but is better known under its modern name Tell el-Amarna. The move presumably reflected the king's desire to break free completely from the weight of Egyptian tradition but there were other reasons. Among the cliffs of the east bank at Tell el-Amarna there was a natural opening into a valley and through this could be caught the first glimpse of the rising sun. The city's main temple was aligned with the valley, and unlike the traditional closed sanctuaries of Amun was left open to the skies. Aten was always used to emphasize the positive aspects of life, day rather than night, rebirth rather than death, light rather than darkness. Most of the reliefs and paintings of Akhenaten show him directly under the sun, whose rays, each capped with a small hand, reach down to him.

A hymn to Aten survives, inscribed on a tomb in Amarna. The first verse reads:

> Earth brightens when you dawn in lightland,
> When you shine as Aten of daytime;
> As you dispel the dark,
> As you cast your rays,
> The Two Lands are in festivity.
> Awake they stand on their feet,
> You have roused them;
> Bodies cleansed, clothed,
> The arms adore your appearance.
> The entire land sets out to work,
> All beasts browse on their herbs;
> Trees, herbs are sprouting,
> Birds fly from their nests.
> Their wings greeting your *ka*.
> All flocks frisk on their feet,
> All that fly up and alight,
> They lived when you dawn for them,
> Ships fare north, fare south as well,
> Roads lie open when you rise;
> The fish in the river dart before you,
> Your rays are in the midst of the sea.

> (Quoted in Amelie Kuhrt,
> *The Ancient Near East* (London, 1995), vol. i)

The new religion did not catch on. For the mass of people there was no incentive to turn away from traditional religious practices which were so deeply integrated into everyday life. Egyptian religion was astonishingly flexible at a popular level. There was a plethora of gods which could take on different identities and attributes to meet different human and spiritual needs. They were grouped together or merged as composite gods in a rich mythology which covered creation and the afterlife. To replace them by a single physical entity, available only in one form, was a cultural shock far greater than the Egyptians could absorb. Even the workmen building at Tell el-Amarna stayed loyal to their traditional gods.

The failure of Aten does not make the reign of Akhenaten any less interesting. He was a strong king who focused the kingdom on himself as the only mediator with his god. By confiscating the goods of the temples he strengthened his political position and he appears to have been well in control of the administration. He was one of those rare Egyptians who introduced important cultural changes. He was represented with his wife Nefertiti and his family in much more informal and realistic poses than was conventional. It was as if the royal family now replaced the mythological families of the gods. Some portraits even show him with a unique physiognomy including a bloated stomach, an extraordinary departure from the accepted portraiture of a king. He also moved away from the classical language conventionally used in texts to introduce his own artificial language, half classical, half in the popular idiom, to further emphasize his own identity. In short, there was a loosening of Egyptian traditions to allow a much more freely expressive style of art.

Tell el-Amarna was situated well away from the floodline of the Nile. It was carefully planned out within a large area defined by fourteen boundary stelas. The city was largely destroyed after Akhenaten's death but enough remains to plot out the royal palaces, the adjoining harems, the Great Temple to Aten, and the administrative offices. There is a set of gardens, and suburbs containing the homes of the administrators. A workmen's village, complete with walls that enclosed its inhabitants at night, is reminiscent of that further south at Deir el-Medina. (See Chapter 5.)

The plan of Tell el-Amarna has much to tell about the nature of royal administration. The king and his family had their private residence set well apart from the rest of the city in the north. In the ceremonial centre of the city, connected to the residential palace by a processional route, was another grander and more public palace which seems to have been designed for the king's public appearances and his reception of foreign envoys. Its core was an enormous courtyard with colossal statues of the king surrounding it. Amarna may have been the home of a particularly forceful and independent king, but its layout shows how carefully the power of a ruler could be stage managed for effect and linked closely to control of its officials.

When Akhenaten died in about 1336 BC the country was left in some confusion. His successor (who may have been Nefertiti 'disguised' with a male name, Smenkhara) lived only a few months and it was a boy, Tutankhaten, the son of Akhenaten by another wife, who succeeded. His name suggests that the worship of Aten was still officially practised, but within a year the king's name had been changed to Tutankhamun and the city at Tell el-Amarna had been abandoned. There was a major reaction to the cult of Aten. Nobles, for instance, now built their tombs as small temples as if to reassert public control of religion and filled them with wall paintings and statues of the traditional gods. (Osiris quickly reasserted his position as the most important funerary god.) With Akhenaten now being presented as having betrayed his people and the cosmic order, it is possible that no pharaoh was ever given the same degree of respect as his predecessors. The god Amun becomes a universal transcendent god manifested through the other gods of Egypt but approachable by those who believe in him. 'Far away he is as one who sees, near he is as one who hears,' as one text put it and Amun is seen as able to intervene directly in believers' lives.

Tutankhamun never emerged as ruler in his own right. By the age of 19 he was dead, possibly from a cerebral haemorrhage. It was by sheer chance, probably because the site of the tomb was forgotten and blocked by the debris from later tunnelling, that his tomb in the Valley of the Kings survived intact until rediscovered in 1922 by the British archaeologist, Howard Carter. The completeness of the finds, the rich array of grave goods, and the poignant story of the king who had died so young led to a wave of 'Tutmania' which swept across the world in the 1920s.

The Nineteenth Dynasty: The Last of the Great Egyptian Dynasties

On the death of Tutankhamun the Eighteenth Dynasty was virtually exhausted. The land was still in disruption, and it is hardly surprising that it was a general, Horemheb, who eventually succeeded. Horemheb saw himself as the restorer of traditional order. He even extended his reign backwards so as to delete that of Akhenaten and his successors and is officially recorded as a member of the Eighteenth Dynasty. Horemheb built heavily at Karnak, tearing down Akhenaten's temple to Aten and using its blocks for his own needs. With no male heir, he passed on the kingdom to a fellow general who, as King Rameses I, was to be the founder of the Nineteenth Dynasty, the last to see Egypt as a great power.

Rameses' family was from the eastern Delta and the centre of power now shifted back towards the north. The priests of Thebes may have regained their temples, but during the remaining years of the New Kingdom they were never to be allowed to rebuild their political influence. The family had no royal blood, and when Rameses' son Sety I succeeded him about 1294 BC he shrewdly tried to conceal this by having himself portrayed on a stone relief (from the Temple of Abydos and now in the British Museum) alongside sixty-nine predecessors in a line stretching back to Narmer, the supposed founder of a united Egypt. Significantly, Hatshepsut and Akhenaten and his immediate successors were omitted. The past had to be ordered within the traditional ideology of kingship. To reinforce his position, and complete the restoration of the old gods, Sety built temples in all the major religious centres of Egypt. Avaris was revived as a northern capital and its temple to Seth restored.

The Egyptian empire was now under the threat of a new enemy, the Hittite empire, which at its height in the late fourteenth century extended across the central Anatolian plateau, over much of what had been the kingdom of Mitanni and south into the Levant. (See Chapter 2 for further details of the Hittites.) Conflict along the northern boundaries of the Egyptian empire seemed certain, and already in the reign of Sety I new campaigns had to be launched into Asia to reimpose Egyptian control there. The most famous battle against the Hittites was that waged in about 1275 BC by Sety I's son, Rameses II (c.1279–1213 BC), at Qadesh, the town in Syria which had been unofficially recognized as the border of the Egyptian empire. Rameses presented it on the temple walls of Egypt as a crushing victory, but with accounts surviving also from Hittite sources it is possible to see that the Egyptian army was lucky to escape intact from the mass of Hittite chariotry. In fact, the campaign was a stalemate, and Rameses was sensible enough to realize the dangers of campaigning against such a strong empire so far from home. About 1263 BC he made a Treaty of Alliance with the Hittites and brought his military career to an end.

Rameses is remembered because of the vast building programme he carried out during his long reign. Nearly half the temples which still stand in Egypt date from his reign. One of his most famous legacies is the great temple of Abu Simbel, rescued and rebuilt by UNESCO in the 1960s when Lake Nasser threatened to engulf it after the building of the Aswan dam. Four colossal statues of Rameses, each 21 metres high, sit alongside each other in the rock face. Between them the temple entrance opens into a great hall and far inside there are four further statues of the gods. Twice a year the rays of the rising sun would strike inwards to illuminate the gods. The temple, at the southern extremity of Egyptian rule, was clearly designed to show off the reality of the king's power over his Nubian subjects.

The Disintegration of the New Kingdom

To glorify his home area in the Delta, Rameses constructed an impressive new capital at Pi-Rameses, close to the earlier Avaris. Here he had his palace and there were major temples to Amun, Seth, and Ra. As the king neared the thirtieth year of his reign he built a massive set of Jubilee Halls for the ceremony of *sed*, the celebration of thirty years of power. Naturally Rameses could not neglect planning for his death, and he followed the tradition of building a great royal tomb, perhaps the most opulent of them all, in the Valley of the Kings. As a more visible memorial he constructed a vast mortuary temple, the Rameseum, on the west bank of the Nile at Thebes. Its granaries alone were so huge that 3,400 families could have been fed for a year from their contents.

The excavators at Pi-Rameses have established that the city was well protected by waterways and that there were at least three barracks to house soldiers. Despite the public grandeur and outward confidence of the reign there were already signs that the state was becoming more defensive. After the death of Rameses external pressures on Egypt grew. The Sahara continued to become drier, encouraging the raids of land-hungry nomads on the wealth of the valley. Raids from the west by Libyans are mentioned for the first time in Egyptian history in the Nineteenth Dynasty. About 1200 BC the Mediterranean itself became troubled in the great upheaval which led to the attack of the so-called Sea Peoples on the Delta (see p. 38 above).

In the next Dynasty, the Twentieth, only one able king, Rameses III (*c.*1184–1153 BC), stands out. He carried out a series of brilliant victories against the intruders and managed to build some fine monuments, including a massive temple at Medinet Habu near Thebes, but his state was crumbling. The temples appear to have been accumulating land at the expense of the state, eventually controlling a third of all cultivable land in Egypt, with a consequent fall in tax revenues. This may reflect the shift, begun after the Amarna period, of trust away from earthly rulers to the supreme god Amun. Even Rameses II, when he was in trouble at the battle of Qadesh, forgot his own 'divine' status so completely as to call on Amun for help. By the end of Rameses' reign there were growing signs of internal unrest with the atmosphere of insecurity heightened by raids from Libya. An assassination attempt was hatched within the royal harem, while, in a rare bureaucratic breakdown, grain rations failed to arrive for the craftsmen working on the royal tombs. In retaliation the workmen organized the first recorded strike in history.

The last nine kings of the Twentieth Dynasty all took the name Rameses, as if they hoped it would prove a lucky token against further decay, but they could do little to stop the decline. Part of the problem was that many were already elderly when they came to the throne. Their reigns proved too short and their energies too diminished for them to enforce their power. The average Twentieth Dynasty reign lasted under twelve years, compared to an average of nearly twenty years in the Eighteenth Dynasty. The resources available to the kings were also contracting. The gold mines of Nubia were exhausted by the end of the New Kingdom. Rich areas such as the Fayum, a cultivated part of Egypt since the Middle Kingdom, gradually became indefensible against the Libyans. As central government faltered under ageing kings with diminishing resources, the empire disintegrated. The Asian empire was lost by the time of Rameses VI (1143–1136). The population of Nubia fell as gold mining ceased there and its provincial administration withdrew at the end of the Twentieth Dynasty. By 1060 Egypt had withdrawn into its original valley boundaries.

A vivid picture of the collapse of society within Egypt comes from records of tomb robberies. Such robberies had always taken place, but now their scale seems to have increased dramatically. It was the impoverished inhabitants of western Thebes who seem to have been most prominent in siphoning off grain supplies from the temples and robbing tombs of their furniture. Even royal tombs were not immune, a sure sign that respect for authority was crumbling. Among the goods recovered by officials were not only gold and silver but linen, vases of oil, wood, copper, and bronze. Corruption spread. Even the officials themselves became involved, and Nubian troops brought up to help deal with the problem themselves joined in despoiling tombs and monuments. In a desperate, but successful, attempt to preserve the bodies of the kings, their mummies, among them them that of the great Rameses II, were collected from their original tombs and gathered in a new hiding place in the hills behind Deir el-Bahri, where they lay undiscovered until the nineteenth century.

A lament from an earlier banquet song catches the mood of the last years of the New Kingdom:

Those gods who existed aforetime, who rest in their pyramids, and the noble blessed dead likewise. The builders of the chapels, their places are no more, like those who never were. None returns from there to tell us of their condition, to tell their state, to reassure us, until we attain the place where they have gone.   (Translation: R. Parkinson)

This was a devastating moment for a society which prided itself so much on its good order and respect for the past. Despite moments of national revival, the Egyptian state was never again to enjoy such power and sustained prosperity as it had in the New Kingdom.

FURTHER READING

See the general histories cited in Chapter 3. On individual kings/queens see the following: Joyce Tyldesley, *Hatshepsut: The Female Pharaoh* (London, 1996); C. Aldred, *Akhenaten, King of Egypt* (London, 1988); N. Reeves, *The Complete Tutankhamun* (London, 1990); K. Kitchen, *Pharaoh Triumphant: The Life and Times of Ramesses II, King of Egypt* (Warminster, 1982); and Joyce Tyldesley, *Ramesses, Egypt's Greatest Pharaoh* (London, 2000).

The Amarna Letters

To the king, my lord, my sun, say: message from Shuwardata, your servant, the ground for your feet. At the feet of the king my lord and my sun, seven and seven times I throw myself. The king my lord has permitted us to make war against Qiltu, and I have made war: it is saved for me, my city has been restored to me. Why ever did Abdi-Heba write to the men of Qiltu: 'Take silver and be my followers!'? Let the king my lord know that Abdi-Heba took my city from my hands. Further, Lab'aya is dead who took our cities, but here is Abdi-Heba who is a second Lab'aya, and takes our cities. May the king think of his servant regarding this fact. I will do nothing, until the king responds with a word to his servant!

(Translation: Ian Hutchesson)

In the New Kingdom, the Egyptians held a loose but determined hold over the land of Canaan. Shuwardata was one of the vassal kings in the region, apparently ruling a small state in the south of the region. He was one of many in Canaan whose cities had been harassed by rival kings, first Lab'aya of Shechem, and then after Lab'aya's death by Abdi-Heba, ruler of Jerusalem. Yet rather than defend himself, he waits on the pharaoh before making a move.

This is the world of the Amarna letters, some 350 documents discovered in the abandoned palace of Akhenaten at El-Amarna in 1887 (and thus datable to c.360–335). The letters are written in Akkadian cuneiform, the *lingua franca* of the region, and this in itself is a sign that no one power is strong enough to insist on the use of its own language. (None of the letters, even from the vassals, are in Egyptian, for instance.) The letters record the complex and fluid relationships between the pharaohs Amenhotep III and Akhenaten and the states of the Ancient Near East, including both 'great powers' and vassal states of the pharaoh in Canaan. (See the map on p. 22.) So the state of Mitanni, in northern Syria between the Tigris and Euphrates, once an enemy of Egypt, is now, in the surviving letters from its king Tushratta, an ally and the royal families have intermarried. Less stable is the relationship with the Hittites during the reign of Suppiluliuma (see p. 37 above) especially after Suppiluliuma invades Mitanni and reduces it to a vassal state. It is an instability which is eventually to lead to war between Egypt and the Hittites in the following century (see p. 74 above). The Hittites faced another challenge in the resurgent power of Assyria under King Ashur-uballit (1356–1330) who was determined to exploit the power vacuum left by the collapse of Mitanni. This resurgence led to protests from another power the Kassite kingdom of Babylonia which was quelled by a marriage alliance in which Ashur-uballit's daughter married the son of the Kassite king.

As between the 'great powers' the letters show a readiness to use force but also an understanding of the fears among rival powers that such force would provoke. Rulers know when they ought to compromise. The sensitive way in which diplomacy is exercised by a rising power is well shown in the two letters in the archive to the pharaoh from Ashur-uballit. In the first he has just asserted his authority and is testing his relationship with Egypt carefully. Will he be accepted by Akhenaten as an equal?

Say to the king of Egypt: This speaks Ashur-uballit, king of Assyria. May everything be well with you, your house, your land, your chariots and your troops. I am sending a messenger to you to visit you and to visit your country. Until now my predecessors did not write; but today I am writing. I am sending you a beautiful chariot, two horses, and a date stone of authentic lapis lazuli, as your greeting gift. Do not delay the messenger whom I have sent to you for a visit. May he pay his visit and then come back to me. (Translation: A. K. Grayson)

This cautious approach makes no mention of the Assyrian king's own status and does not go so far as to ask for a gift in return as was the custom between equal kings. Yet by the time of the second letter, Ashur-uballit is sure of his position. He refers to himself by the title of 'great king' and addresses the pharaoh as his 'brother'. What is more he feels confident enough to complain that the pharaoh did not even send him enough gold in a gift to cover the cost of sending his own messengers!

The vassal states of Canaan are in a different position. The area was fragmented between mountain ranges and gorges and no king was likely to become strong enough to become a great power. Yet this was clearly Egypt's sphere of influence and no outside power would be allowed to threaten her hegemony (hence the eventual confrontation with the Hittites at Qadesh). Egyptian rule was comparatively light, there were local Egyptian administrators, expeditionary forces, and scattered garrisons. It was common for Canaanites to be brought up in the Egyptian court and then transferred as rulers of an important city in the hope that they would remain loyal. Abdi-Heba, for instance, had been educated in Egypt and placed on the throne of Jerusalem by the pharaoh. Akhenaten seems to have chosen carefully how to exercise his power. A certain amount of rivalry between kings was tolerated but there were limits to the expansion of any one vassal king. So Lab'aya had been eventually captured by the Egyptians, ostensibly to be taken back to Egypt, but killed on the way there by his captors. As Shuwardata's letter shows vassals knew it was better to ask the pharaoh first before seeking revenge!

The *realpolitik* of diplomacy was underpinned by exchanges, of sons and daughters in marriage, of gifts between kings and by trade. This helped to cement what could otherwise have degenerated into interstate anarchy. What is remarkable is how successful the Amarna system was in avoiding war. While it was usual for rulers of the great powers to proclaim their strength aggressively, each state seems to have accepted that this was often no more than rhetoric and any tensions could be eased by working through diplomatic conventions. There was an understanding that it was in all the states' interests to keep trade on the move. While the Amarna system was never formalized into a set of stable alliances, it worked remarkably well on an ad hoc basis and has been seen by some historians as representing the birth of international diplomacy.

FURTHER READING

W. L. Moran (ed. and trans.), *The Amarna Letters* (Baltimore, 1992); Raymond Cohen and Raymond Westbrook (eds.), *Amarna Diplomacy: The Beginnings of International Relations* (Baltimore, 2000).

5 | Daily Life in New Kingdom Egypt

The New Kingdom has left more information about daily life in Egypt than any other period of Egyptian history. The tombs of the nobles and kings were now normally cut deep into the rocky hillsides (probably as a response to tomb robbers), and the halls, courts, and chapels which formed the entry to the burial chambers were richly decorated with reliefs and paintings. They presented the way of life the dead man hoped for in the future, a re-creation of life at home, on his estates or hunting in the marshes. Although they are idealized and have an ordered serenity which must have been very different from the bustle and misfortunes of real life, they are a rich source for details of everyday activities.

The New Kingdom is also rich in written sources. As only a tiny elite could write effectively, these again are the views of an unrepresentative minority. (The finds at Deir el-Medina, described below, suggest, however, that many craftsmen could manage simple jottings.) Many texts are purely concerned with administration, but even these often give a vivid picture of everyday life. The accounts of the state's campaign against tomb robbers towards the end of the New Kingdom make absorbing reading. Others are more immediately personal. There are, for instance, moving love lyrics from the last years of the New Kingdom which echo across the centuries with astonishing freshness. 'I yearn for your love by day and night,' pleads one girl. 'I lie awake for long hours until dawn. Your form revives my heart. My desire is entirely for you. Your voice it is which gives my body vigour.' (Translation: K. Kitchen.) A young man remembers how he has braved a lurking crocodile to cross the river in flood to reach his beloved, while a girl lures her lover to the water's edge with the promise that she will let him see her undress and bathe.

Archaeology has been able to make an exceptional contribution to the understanding of the Egyptian past because of the richness of its tombs and temples and the dryness of the climate which has helped preservation. Lucky finds such as the almost untouched tomb of the boy king Tutankhamun have enjoyed worldwide publicity. Once again, however, the discoveries of archaeology have focused on the elite. The poor lived in mudbrick villages along the Nile and most of these have been lost under the silt of later floods. It is only recently that the focus of Egyptian archaeology has turned to the settlements in which the Egyptian peasants and craftsmen lived their everyday lives.

The Villagers of Deir el-Medina

One of the more successful excavations of a less opulent community has been that carried out by the French Institute of Oriental Archaeology at the so-called workmen's village at Deir el-Medina. The village was believed by its inhabitants to have been founded close to the Valley of the Kings west of Thebes by Amenhotep I of the New Kingdom about 1500 BC. (There is some evidence, in fact, that it was founded slightly later by Thutmose I.) For 500 years it contained a skilled workforce, numbering at its height about 120 craftsmen with their families and supporting staff, perhaps a total population of some 1,200. The excavation of the site has been enriched by the discovery of papyrus records and thousands of potsherds on which the villagers have made rough jottings about daily life. Although the village was an artificial settlement and not at all typical of those lived in by the mass of the farming peasantry, it provides the richest and most coherent record of how ordinary Egyptians lived and thought.

Deir el-Medina was a closed community. Its sole purpose was the tunnelling and decoration of the royal tombs in the barren Valley of the Kings. Its workers, possessed as they were of the secrets of the tombs, were cut off from the rest of Egyptian society, isolated in the walled village at night when they were not away working in the valley. The village relied on being provisioned from the outside with grain from the stores of the local temples and water brought up on the backs of donkeys by its own water-carriers. Marriages took place within the community and skills were passed on within families from one generation to the next. Families were not large, in one 'census' only one household is recorded as having as many as five members and there are several men living on their own. Older children seemed to have moved out of their parents' house, left the village, or set up their own homes.

Deir el-Medina was a microcosm of Egyptian artisan society. Among its workmen were painters, plasterers, woodcarvers, sculptors, masons, and scribes as well as unskilled labourers. The village had its own police force and a 'domestic staff' of launderers, slave women to mill flour, doorkeepers, and messengers. Its houses, which opened on to the main street of the village, were built on a common pattern. There were three or four main rooms one behind the other, a front parlour, a main living-room, often with columns and a skylight, a sleeping area, and an open kitchen at the back. A cellar would hold the family treasures (the master of the house often placed his bed over its entrance) while the roof was also used as space for living or sleeping. The walls had niches for the household gods. Bes, the dwarf god, the protector of families and women in childbirth, was usually the most prominent, but Taweret, the goddess of pregnancy, childbirth, and breastfeeding, represented as a pregnant hippopotamus, and Hathor, guardian of womenfolk and domestic bliss, were also common. (Hathor, the daughter of Ra, combined several attributes in her personality—the tenderness of a mother caring for her children and the fury of a lioness protecting them, as well as, in a sensuous human form, female sexuality.) Furnishings were well built but simple—low stools, wooden bed-frames, pottery, with mats and baskets of woven rush.

The workmen were given one day free in every ten. Later in the New Kingdom this seems to have been increased to two. These 'weekends' could be used for the workmen's own craft and building work. Many had their own sets of tools. They decorated their houses and often left their names on the doorposts. They also worked on their own family tombs, and a cemetery grew up on a hillside to the west of the village. It was carefully planned. The tombs of the ordinary workmen were grouped around that of their Chief Workman and aligned with the royal tomb they had been building in the valley beyond. The burial chambers were quarried into the hillside or under the ground. Chapels of mudbrick, painted white and often surmounted by a small pyramid, stood outside each entrance.

The jottings on the potsherds cover every aspect of daily life, letters, records of work done, accounts of disputes, snatches of hymns or literature, and magic spells against illness. They give a lively picture of life in the village, wives walking out on husbands, celebrations on the feast days of the gods or favoured kings, workmen being stung by scorpions, heavy drinking on birthdays, the mourning of a lost friend. Inevitably there were tensions and disputes and these were resolved by a village council. When matters appeared deadlocked there was a ritual in which a heavy statue of the founder, the deified pharaoh Amenhotep, was carried in procession through the village by the village elders. This ritual seems to have concentrated minds and a verdict was eventually produced which was written down by a scribe and signed by the elders. Punishments could, however, be harsh, a hundred blows with a stick, branding, or hard labour. Some cases were sent out of the village to be judged by a higher authority. Whatever the internal tensions they were dissolved in a shared hostility to the outside world if the rations on which the village was dependent failed to come through.

One of the most interesting finds at Deir el-Medina was the 'library' of a village scribe, one Kenher-khepshef. Just after it was discovered in 1928 many of the papyri were stolen but some forty works have survived or been recovered. Papyrus itself was cheap—a roll cost about the same as a pair of sandals—so it was clearly possible for texts to circulate widely among those who could read. Kenher-khepshef's choice of texts is broad. There is one which celebrates earlier authors suggesting an interest in literature for its own sake, while sacred texts are mingled with secular ones. A manual to the morning, midday, and evening rituals to be performed at the shrine dedicated to Amenhotep (Kenher-khepshef may have been a priest of the cult) shows that these have been modelled on the more elaborate rituals of the great temples. The fact that the sacred texts are not stored separately from others indicates a relaxed attitude to religion and other texts from Deir el-Medina suggest that there was quite a range of attitudes among the villagers, from those who were deeply pious to those who were sceptical about the mythology of the gods and were even ready to question the utterings of oracles.

Economy and Enterprise

Despite the records of the squabbles of the villagers at Deir el-Medina, life in ancient Egypt is often presented as if it was a serene paradise. In fact, Egyptian civilization depended on what must have been a highly efficient, perhaps even ruthless, transfer of the surplus crops produced by the peasantry to an administrative elite who may, with their families, have numbered less than 5 per cent of the population. Whatever the ideals proclaimed by the administrators, there was no attempt to provide services for the community as a whole. (An exception may have been some form of dole of grain in years of famine. Large quantities of grain were certainly stored and several provincial governors boasted of their kindness to the poor.) When the peasants were not working the fields, many must have been conscripted as labour on the great building projects of the kings. Tombs, temples, and palaces were exclusive places from which they were barred.

The texts do occasionally show some recognition of the misfortunes which could befall the peasantry. *The Satire of Trades*, for instance, whose main objective was to ridicule all occupations other than that of a scribe, warns the student of the miseries of rural life:

Remember the state of the peasant farmer faced with registry of the harvest-tax, when the snake has taken one half of the crop and the hippo has devoured the other half. The mice overrun the field, the locust descends and the cattle eat up. The sparrows bring poverty upon the farmer. What is left on the threshing floor falls to the thieves . . . The tax-official has landed on the river bank to register the harvest tax, with his janitors carrying staves and the Nubians palm rods. They say 'Give up the grain' . . . although there is none. They beat him up . . . he is thrown head first down a well . . . So the grain disappears.   (Translation: K. Kitchen)

The situation must have been even worse at times of disorder when officials were left unsupervised. However, the more successful farmers and artisans did seem able to accumulate some income. The letters of one farmer from the Eleventh Dynasty, Hekanakht (*c.*1950, although some scholars date it later) to his family (they were written when he was away on business) detail some of his dealings and this gives some idea of how a surplus could be used. He did not own his land but had some accumulated 'capital' of grain, copper, oil, and flax which he could use for barter or to pay his rent in advance. He had a second income from his position as *ka*-servant, responsible for keeping an eye on the tomb of one Ipi, the vizier of Mentuhotep II. By the time of the letters, he is getting on in years and he has delegated work on the land to his sons, especially one by the name of Merisu, whom he berates in the letters for his slackness. 'Put your back into the ploughing, do your utmost, look after my seed corn, look after all my property. See, I consider you responsible for it! . . . Hoe all my land, sieve with the sieve, hack with your noses into the work.' (Translation: John Ray.) He is a querulous old man. He complains that Merisu had sent him dried-out old barley instead of the season's new crop and does not treat the youngest son, Sneferu, his father's favourite, with enough care. Sneferu is to be sent home to his father as soon as the ploughing is complete. He is equally annoyed by his sons' failure to respect his new young wife, Iutenheb, whom in some way they have abused. In short, life for Hekanakht's family may have had its tensions but with steady work they clearly had enough to live on.

The workmen at Deir el-Medina too seem to have accumulated some surplus from their rations, perhaps from selling their skills in their free time or manufacturing simple objects such as beds. One money-maker was the hire of donkeys to the local water-carriers. There are also some New Kingdom paintings of traders sitting by the dockside selling goods which seem to have come off moored boats. Traders such as these (they were known as *shuty*) were often in the employ of the state or a temple, but their job seems to have given them access to spare goods which they could then sell on the side. Records of grave robberies in the late New Kingdom suggest it was the *shuty* who were the most likely middlemen for the goods stolen. An actual record of the range of goods involved in what appears to be a bill of lading of a Nile riverboat from about 1137 BC includes jars of sesame oil and wine, olives, gourds, salt, gutted fish (no less than 5,000 of them) and the heads of gutted waterfowl, 110 bundles of sedge, and fifty papyrus rolls. It confirms the picture given by the Kas shipwreck in which trade involves many small quantities of different commodities.

The system of exchange for surplus goods was based on a unit of weight, the *deben* of about 90 grams. A *deben* could be calculated in gold, silver, or copper, with the value the greater the more precious the metal. A *deben* in silver, for instance, was worth about a hundred times one in copper. A transaction by a certain scribe Penanouqit has survived. He wanted to sell an ox which was valued, in copper, at 130 *deben*. In return he accumulated a linen tunic valued at 60 *deben*, two others worth 10 *deben* each, 30 *deben* worth of beads for a necklace, and the remaining 20 *deben* in grain. The Egyptians never developed any exchange system involving coins.

Egyptian Medicine

Life in ancient Egypt was, typically, short, certainly shorter than most parts of the world today. A large number of embalmed bodies have now been examined, alongside the skeletons of those not rich enough to afford the process. There was a peak in death rates at about the age of 3 when children transferred from breast milk with its protective powers to solid food. The average life expectancy for those who survived childhood is calculated at 29 with few individuals surviving beyond 60. Life expectancy was longer for the elite, but one survey of twenty-six royal mummies (whose findings have not been universally accepted) suggested that only three of them lived beyond 50. Many Egyptians were afflicted with parasites, acquired probably from polluted water sources, while lungs suffered from sand and coal dust (probably inhaled from the smoke of fires). Tuberculosis was also widespread. Teeth were worn down, probably by the silicone from the stones used for the threshing or grinding, and gum abscesses were common. The analysis of bones also suggests painful and debilitating handicaps. Many individuals who survived to 40 had spinal osteophytosis, excrescences on the spine caused by excessive strain. Such lesions are missing from the richer burials, although many of these show signs of arteriosclerosis, originating from a diet rich in fat. Cancer was rare, probably because few Egyptians reached the ages at which it becomes common.

Homer wrote in the *Odyssey* that medicine in Egypt was more developed than anywhere in the world, and Herodotus, writing some three centuries later, agreed with him. The Egyptian physicians certainly had some expertise, fostered by the practice of specialization and the meticulous examination of disorders. In one papyrus different kinds of snake bites are described in tiny detail each with a prognosis. 'As for the cobra serpent, with the hue of sand, if it bites a man he suffers on the side that was not pierced and does not suffer on the side with the bite; it is an illness I can treat'—apparently with emetics and bleedings. The Ebers papyrus has some 700 prescriptions for internal diseases set out according to the organ affected. The Edwin Smith surgical papyrus shows a profound empirical knowledge of different kinds of injuries with recommendations for treatment. It contains the earliest known description of a brain. If a skull is smashed open in an accident, you find an organ 'like the corrugations which appear on molten copper in the crucible, and something therein throbs and flutters under your fingers like the weak place in the crown of the head of a child when it has not become whole'. Other texts concentrate on dislocated joints. Egyptian physicians seem to have been able to mend broken bones and treat open wounds, while there are skeletons whose trepanned skulls have healed over, suggesting that the recipients of surgery sometimes survived.

However, effective treatment was hindered because there was no proper understanding of how the human body worked, despite the close examination the practice of embalming allowed. The heart was considered the centre of the body, and from it flowed all bodily fluids, not only blood but saliva, urine, and semen. It was believed that all internal illnesses were caused by obstructions of their flow, often due to the malevolence of a god. Successful freeing of these obstructions relied on complicated techniques and potions, most of which would have had no effect whatsoever on any illness. Nile mud, dirt from a patient's fingernails, and mouse droppings were used alongside a variety of herbs and extracts from animals. Recovery from most illnesses would only have been through natural healing or chance fitting of a particular remedy to the right disease (the application of mouldy bread, an anticipation of penicillin, for instance).

In short, Egyptian medicine operated in a context in which empirical approaches (sometimes, as with the effects of snake bites, accurate, sometimes as with the internal workings of the body, hopelessly misguided) mixed with what could be called magic. No treatment could be effective without reciting an incantation over the patient. One should not decry this. It is known today that the very act of consulting a doctor can help towards healing while what might appear to be an irrational precept, that a medicinal plant must be gathered before daybreak as some texts required, for instance, is shown to be 'rational' in that alkaloids such as morphine vary in strength in particular parts of a plant during the daily cycle. However, there was little incentive to reach a deeper understanding of the body. Texts often achieved a sacred quality in themselves and were passed on from generation to generation without questioning. The Edwin Smith papyrus dates from the Second Intermediate (Hyksos) Period but has material which is a thousand years older. The older a treatment the more respect it was given. The Greek historian Diodorus, who visited Egypt in the first century BC, wrote that the doctor who followed a text exactly would not be blamed if the patient died, but if he disregarded it and the patient suffered he could even be sentenced to death.

Astronomy and Mathematics

It was the needs of administration and building, both essential if the status quo was to be maintained, which encouraged the development of skills in astronomy and mathematics. The stars were used both to align buildings and to calculate time. A calendar was developed based on the rise of the 'Dog Star', Sirius. Sirius remains below the horizon in Egypt for some seventy days, reappearing at sunrise around 19 July. By chance this coincided with the beginning of the Nile floods and so for the Egyptians marked the beginning of a new year. This 'solar' calendar had a full cycle of 365 days and 6 hours, in other words, every four years an extra day would have to be added to the year to keep it synchronised with the sun. However, the Egyptians used another calendar based on the night sky. They observed how the stars seen on the horizon as the night passed into day moved in relation to the horizon in a regular pattern. They divided the stars in thirty-six groups, each of which rose above the horizon for ten days before being supplanted by another group. This led to a year of 360 days and five extra days, birthdays of the gods, were added to make up 365, but this, of course, did not include the extra six hours. It has been calculated that both calendars, solar and lunar, set off together about 2773 BC. However, as the years passed it must have become clear that the lunar calendar was falling behind the solar calendar at the rate of one day every four years. By this time the system was so embedded that the two calendars were never reconciled and it took 1,460 years (i.e. four times 365) for them to coincide again.

The Egyptians' problem has proved the Egyptologists' asset. A Roman historian happened to record that in AD 139 there was a coincidence between the rising of Sirius and the start of a civil year. By going back in jumps of 1,460 years other coincidences have been calculated for 1322, 2782, and 4242 BC. On a few occasions written sources have recorded the discrepancy between the rising of Sirius and the civil year. One document from the reign of King Sesostris III, for instance, mentions that Sirius will rise on the sixteenth day of the eighth month of the seventh year of the king's reign (dated here on the lunar calendar), and from this the year, 1866 BC, can be calculated. Other reigns can be dated from this, and a partial chronology of Egyptian history reconstructed.

In order to measure time during the day the Egyptians used sun clocks. One surviving example had a pillar standing at right angles to a base. The shadow of the sun then fell on the base and the time of day was read from lines drawn on the base. The day and night were each divided into twelve hours but these varied in length according to the season. It was the Greeks who adopted this twenty-four-hour 'clock' and then improved it by making the twenty-four hours equal in length, the system still used today.

As mathematicians the Egyptians were pragmatic. Arithmetic and geometry, which were not distinguished, were used to add up wages, to calculate the volumes of granaries and the areas of fields (particularly important when the floods went down and the land had to be marked out again), to collect taxes and to calculate the number of bricks needed for a planned building. The basic procedures appear to have been in place as early as 3500 BC and remained essentially undeveloped until the arrival of the Greeks more than 3,000 years later. The two major mathematical texts, the Moscow and Rhind papyri (the latter now in the British Museum) are essentially lists of problems and their solutions which a scribe would have consulted when he needed to. A typical problem was how to share out a fixed number of loaves of bread or jugs of beer between people of different status, some of whom had the right to more than others. The Egyptians were hampered by their inability in general to use fractions with a numerator higher than one, so that if they wanted to record $\frac{7}{8}$, for instance, they had to build it up as $\frac{1}{2}$ plus $\frac{1}{4}$ plus $\frac{1}{8}$, while $\frac{5}{7}$ becomes $\frac{1}{2}$ plus $\frac{1}{4}$ plus $\frac{1}{4}$ plus $\frac{1}{28}$. Quick calculations were only possible through the use of prepared tables.

There was more success with geometry. The Egyptians knew that triangles in the ratio of 3 : 4 : 5 had a right-angle opposite the hypotenuse and there is a story that they used ropes with these proportions marked by notes when they wanted to create a right angle. They could calculate the areas of triangles, and in the measurement of circles calculated *pi* to the decimal equivalent of 3.16, remarkably close to the actual figure of 3.1416. They could also work out the angles of pyramids. Measurements were in the 'royal cubit', about the same length as a man's forearm, a picture of which was used for the hieroglyph for cubit. An area of 100 royal cubits, known as a *setjat*, was used as a measure of land.

In general, however, Egyptian mathematics always focused on the solution of specific administrative and architectural problems. Although this included the solution of equations with one unknown quantity, the Egyptians never developed any conception of mathematics as a science. In his history of mathematics, Morris Kline sums up their limitations. 'There was almost no symbolism, hardly any conscious thought about abstraction, no formulation of general methodology, and no concept of proof or even plausible argument that might convince one of the correctness of a procedure or formula.' This sober assessment has to be borne in mind when reading about some of the more extravagant claims for Egyptian science. The 'wisdom' of the Egyptians, expressed in much of their literature, did not lie in this area.

Home and Family

There were many incentives for accumulating wealth. The first was the immediate needs of a family. The family was the living unit of Egyptian society. Wall paintings and sculptures show contented couples with their arms around each other, and there was an ideal of care of young for old. 'Repay your mother for all her care to you,' writes one scribe. 'Give her as much bread as she needs and carry her as she has carried you . . . For three years she suckled you, nor did she shrink from your dirt.' The evidence from Deir el-Medina suggests, however, that things did not always run smoothly in family life. Infidelity and jealousy were as common in ancient Egypt as elsewhere.

Marriage took place for women at the onset of puberty, between 12 and 14, while men seem to have been older, perhaps 20, with those in the administrative elite having already begun to earn a living by then. It seems that both families had to provide goods before a marriage contract could be made, another incentive for gathering wealth. Within the royal family it was possible for a brother to marry a sister. (The legend of Isis and Osiris legitimized, or was developed to legitimize, the practice.) For commoners brother–sister marriages were almost unheard of, although marriages between cousins and uncles and nieces were quite common.

Women normally followed what would now be seen as a highly traditional pattern of life, running the household and being expected to produce a male heir to carry on the family and to take responsibility for the family tomb. It was wives who, either personally or through servants, ground corn, baked bread, spun flax, and wove cloth from it. The job was not without its status and there was some acceptance of women's rights. Men were specifically warned to leave the running of the house to their wives, and women did have the right to own and manage property and could bring a case in court if they were dispossessed of it. A woman who was divorced by her husband became entitled to his continued support. As the love lyrics quoted above suggest, there may have been some emotional equality between the sexes.

In wall paintings women are usually portrayed as much lighter-skinned than their husbands. This may partly be convention but also presumably reflects the longer hours they spent within the home. (Light skin, a sign that a woman did not have to work in the sun, suggested high status.) Women are shown helping their husbands in the fields, and an inscription from the late New Kingdom suggests they could travel around freely outside the home. However, there are very few examples of women earning a living independently. There were some openings in the temples as junior priestesses or leaders of choruses but a more likely role was as an entertainer at feasts or as a member of the royal harem. (The kings had elaborate harems and one portrayal of Rameses III shows him relaxing in one.) The reaction to Queen Hatshepsut has already been described. It has rightly been said that Egypt can be compared with Mediterranean society where, even if women do not appear to be dominant in public life, behind the scenes they exercise considerable influence.

It was not expensive to keep children. They could run around naked in the warm air and live on papyrus roots. However, the mortality rate was high, especially at the moment of weaning. When boys reached the age of 14 they passed into adult life after a religious ceremony which included circumcision. On one occasion, in the First Intermediate Period, 120 boys are recorded as being circumcised at the same time, an indication that this was an important rite of passage recognized by the whole community. Girls stayed at home, and seem to have had no equivalent ceremony other than that of marriage.

By the age of 14 boys would already have received some training in their father's occupation, either through learning on the job or through formal instruction in a temple school. (Some records suggest formal education may have begun as early as 5.) For future administrators the course was a demanding one and total commitment was expected. 'I am told you neglect your studies and think only of pleasure. You wander through the streets, stinking of beer and have been found performing acrobatics on a wall,' was the poor report given by a scribe to one of his students. It may have taken twelve years to master all the skills required to be a scribe. (The skills demanded went far beyond learning to write. A scribe would be expected to master all the details of administration, what rations a soldier should be given, how many bricks were needed to build a ramp, and how many men to pull and erect a stone statue, for instance.)

Another important use of wealth was the construction of a home. The houses of Deir el-Medina have already been described. At Akhenaten's capital at Tell el-Amarna the homes of the administrators were much larger. They were built within a surrounding rectangular enclosure which left space for an open court-yard and a side chapel. The main rooms were decorated with painted plasters. In one house there was a ceiling of brilliant blue, columns of reddish brown, and walls predominantly in white but with a frieze of blue lotus leaves on a green background. Among the comforts enjoyed by the owners were bathrooms, in which the bather stood on a limestone slab and had water poured over him, and shaped stone lavatory seats. There was ample storage space for grain next to a kitchen court at the back of the house. Some wall paintings show houses with ponds and gardens well stocked with a variety of trees. The family could grow its own vegetables. Onions and leeks were particular favourites while the most pop-ular fruits were grapes, figs, and dates. One study of seeds from a Middle Kingdom site discovered poppies, lupins, mignonette, jasmine, heliotrope, and irises among the flowers and peas, beans, radishes, and cucumbers among the vegetables. Among the contributions of the Hyksos era to Egyptian diet were apples and olives.

Such elite homes and their accompanying lifestyle required a mass of domes-tic help. When a wealthy man went out on business he might be accompanied by two servants. One carried a mat and a fly-whisk, the other a pair of his sandals. His destination reached, the master would have his feet washed, his fresh sandals put on, and then he would settle down on his mat with the flies being flicked from him. Within the home, cooking, cleaning, and waiting at table would be done by servants or by slaves captured in military campaigns.

Social life for the elite was sophisticated. Their homes were furnished ele-gantly, the furniture carved with animal heads or inlaid with ivory, ebony, or glass. Every care was taken with personal appearance. A box belonging to one Tutu, who lived at the time of the Eighteenth Dynasty, the height of the New Kingdom, was filled with her cosmetics, eye paint, a mixing palette, an ivory comb, and pink leather sandals. Banquets were an important feature of this lifestyle and they were conducted according to elaborate rituals. The host stood at his gate and was greeted formally by his guests as they arrived. He responded in kind and then led them indoors where both sexes settled down for the meal. Music was an essential part of any feast. Dancing girls would perform to the sound of harps, lutes, oboes, or flutes.

The Rituals of Death

Among the songs that have survived from these banquets are laments on the shortness of men's lives and the inevitability of death. The subject was an appropriate one. The serenity and sophistication of life for the richer classes cannot conceal the fact that death was often sudden. Texts survive from the beginning of the first millennium in which the gods are petitioned to protect a child against the dangers of everyday life, which are spelt out in detail. There is the threat of disease, of course, but also walls that fall on one, scorpion and snake bites, drowning or being eaten by crocodiles. Among those who can bring harm are Syrians, Nubians, and western nomads and there was a fear of being spoken to in foreign languages, presumably because evil words could be passed on without the Egyptian listener recognizing them. Then there are more mysterious powers to guard against—gods who can seize people in the countryside and kill them in the town and a general fear that *heka*, a creative power which can be used for good or ill, will be turned against the child. These texts need to be set within the growing sense of personal piety found in the New Kingdom after the disruption brought by Akhenaten. It is ultimately the gods, not a strong pharaoh, who will protect and so they must be petitioned to do so. There is a rise in the use of oracles in an attempt to find out the will of the gods.

The awareness of the inevitability of death can be seen in the custom of planning one's own tomb from about the age of 20. In the New Kingdom, as has already been mentioned, these tombs consisted of a court in front of the rock face (in the hills west of Thebes, for instance), a series of chambers, halls, and chapels cut into the rock where offerings could be left, and then a descending tunnel to the underground chambers where the body was to rest. As in earlier periods, the tomb contained a stele, a gravestone, with the name and exploits of the deceased on it.

The deceased hoped that he would be accepted by Osiris as worthy of life in the Field of Reeds, a lush fertile land somewhere beyond the western horizon. The life he would lead there would be a more carefree version of what he had already endured, and his hopes were portrayed in paintings on his tomb's walls. The farming year is regular, peasants plough fields, gather the crops of a rich harvest, and thresh the corn. Craftsmen prepare fine goods for his use. Banquets with dancing girls and musicians lighten the evenings.

In more sombre mood were paintings of the meeting of the dead man with Osiris, who presided over the trial which decided his future in the afterlife. The ritual was formalized in the *Book of Going Forth by Day* (usually known as *The Book of the Dead* and first found in the Middle Kingdom), a copy of which was left in the tomb. There were forty-two judges before whom the dead man had to plead his case. High standards were expected and covered every area of moral behaviour. He had to prove he had not killed or stolen, committed adultery, or had sex with a boy. He must never have insulted the king, trespassed, damaged a grain measure, or harmed his neighbours' land. At the end of the trial the heart of the dead man, the seat of the emotions and the intellect, was weighed against a feather. If it was too heavily weighed by sin and the scale tilted downwards the heart was devoured by a monstrous animal. If not, the way was open to the Field of Reeds.

There was no possibility of an afterlife without a preserved body. The skills of the embalmers reached their peak in the New Kingdom. Soon after death the brain and internal organs of the body were removed, although the heart, as the core of the body, was left in place. All were packed with dry natron, a mineral obtained from deposits west of the Delta, which absorbed the fluids. The body was left to dry out for forty days and then was repacked with linen or sawdust so that its shape was retained. The other organs, including the natron now impregnated with body fluids, were packed separately, the organs in so-called Canopic jars, which were placed under the protection of four sons of Horus. The body was then bound in cloth. This was an important ritual in itself, taking as many as fifteen days. The head had a funerary mask, in the case of a king in gold, placed over it. The hope was that this would allow the body to be recognized by the *ka*, the spirit, on the occasions it returned to the tomb.

The completed mummy (the word comes from the Arabic word for bitumen, *mummiya*, a substance not in fact used for embalming until much later) would then be placed in a coffin. In the case of a royal burial there would be three coffins, the first of gold, the other two of gilded and inlaid wood. The whole would be secured in a stone sarcophagus. The coffins of New Kingdom commoners tended to be only of wood. All coffins were decorated with ritual texts. Common too were a pair of eyes, on one side of the box, supposedly to allow the occupant to see the sun rising in the east. The whole process from death to completion of the mummy was prescribed to take place within seventy days. If the death was sudden this was the only time the workmen had to finish off the tomb. In some there are clear signs of the building having been finished in haste to meet the deadline. The sarcophagus was sealed at the base of the burial shaft.

The tomb would also be stocked with the possessions a man might need in the next life. The wealthy elite took no chances and provided themselves with tables, beds, chairs, even chariots and boats. In the tomb of Tutankhamun, the only royal tomb to have been found largely intact, there was a throne of gilded wood, clothes, writing palettes, gaming boards, fans, and jewellery in addition to his sarcophagus and full set of three coffins with the gold mask which covered his head. There was an obsessive fear that the deceased might demean his status by having to engage in physical labour, and so *shabtis* were included as a model labour force. By the last years of the New Kingdom it had become usual to provide 365, one for each day of the year together with thirty-six supervising *shabtis*. They were made in pottery, glass, or metal and could even be provided with their own equipment—hoes, baskets for grain, or water-pots on yokes.

There is no more lasting reminder of the underlying prosperity of ancient Egypt than its capacity to divert so much of its wealth into closed tombs. The art of balancing the needs of the living with those perceived ones of the dead is a fine testimony to the stability and sophistication of the state. Life in ancient Egypt had as many tensions and fears as in any other society but the Egyptians had evolved ways of coping with insecurity and accepting the realities of life. One must live within one's limits. As *The Instruction of Ptah-hotep*, an early text revived in the late New Kingdom, puts it: 'Have no confidence that you are a learned man. Take counsel with the ignorant as with the wise, for the limits of excellence cannot be reached and no artist fully possesses his skill.' This is perhaps where Egyptian wisdom was to be found.

FURTHER READING

Everyday life in ancient Egypt is now fully dealt with by E. Strouhal, *Life in Ancient Egypt* (Cambridge, 1992), and L. Maskell, *Private Life in New Kingdom Egypt* (Princeton, 2002), and medicine in J. Nunn, *Ancient Egyptian Medicine* (London, 1995). For Egyptian mathematics, see the overview in Morris Kline, *Mathematical Thought from Ancient to Modern Times*, vol. i (Oxford, 1972). Specifically on Deir el-Medina see the texts and commentary in A. G. MacDowell, *Village Life in Ancient Egypt: Laundry Lists and Love Songs* (Oxford, 1998). Translated literature is to be found in R. Parkinson, *Voices from Ancient Egypt: An Anthology of Middle Kingdom Writings* (London, 1991), and R. Faulkner, *The Ancient Book of the Dead* (edition revised by Carol Andrews, London, 1985). A wider selection of translations can be found in M. Lichtheim, *Ancient Egyptian Literature*, 3 vols. (Berkeley, 1973–80).

Anything by T. James is also worth reading. See, for instance, his *Pharaoh's People: Scenes from Life in Imperial Egypt* (London, 1984). A well-respected social history is B. Trigger, B. Kemp, D. O'Connor, and A. Lloyd, *Ancient Egypt: A Social History* (Cambridge, 1983).

On religion see Rosalie David, *Ancient Egyptian Religious Beliefs and Practices* (London, 1982); B. Shafer (ed.), *Religion in Ancient Egypt* (Ithaca, NY, 1991); and S. Quirke, *Ancient Egyptian Religion* (London, 1992). For women, G. Robins, *Women in Ancient Egypt* (London, 1993), and J. Tyldesley, *Daughters of Isis* (London, 1994). A lively selection of biographies is provided by John Ray, *Reflections of Osiris: Lives from Ancient Egypt* (London, 2001).

6 | The Ancient Near East, 1200–500 BC

The Neo-Assyrian Empire

In the long term it was the Assyrians who were the beneficiaries of the collapse of the Hittites and the weakening of Egypt at the end of the New Kingdom. Despite the break-up of their Anatolian trade networks, the Assyrians had survived as a kingdom and their royal family was still able to trace its lineage back to the sixteenth century. This gave it a sense of legitimacy which underlay periods of dynamic revival in the later centuries of the second millennium BC—the so-called Middle Assyrian period (c.1400–c.1050). The myth of an extensive Assyrian state survived throughout Assyrian history so that in their campaigns kings usually did not see themselves so much as conquerors as simply reasserting their right to their own territory. Even in periods when the kingdom had retreated to its heartland, the open country around Assur, the continual need to defend the area against nomadic raiders led to the maintenance of a military tradition.

By the ninth century kings such as Adad-Nirari II, Ashurnasirpal II, and Shalmaneser III were able to launch wars of aggression. The Assyrian state god, Assur, now proclaimed the right of the state under its king, his representative on earth, to expand its borders without limit. So there are campaigns to the west to Syria, the Levant, and southern Anatolia, and into the foothills of the Zagros mountains in the east. In the flush of his own victories (he had reached the Mediterranean which he called 'the Great Sea') Ashurnasirpal initiated an artistic revolution. In the great new palace he constructed for himself at Kalhu north of Assur (the modern Nimrud), he covered the walls with a mass of finely carved reliefs. Comparison of designs suggests that the idea came from the wealthy state of Carchemish which had offered him tribute. Subsequent Assyrian palaces at Khorsabad (the modern Dur-Sharrukin), and Nineveh follow the tradition. At Nineveh, Austen Layard, the nineteenth-century excavator of the palace, found 2 miles of reliefs in the seventy-one halls of the palace. (After a somewhat unseemly struggle for control of the site with rival French excavators many of them were hurriedly shipped off to London where they remain among the treasures of the British Museum. The French appropriated the reliefs from the palace at Khorsabad and most are now in the Louvre.) Many scenes show cities being stormed (the Assyrians were masters of siege warfare, their expertise not equalled until Hellenistic times) and then plundered without mercy but the kings also show off their prowess as builders and hunters of lions. While the reliefs are undoubtedly propaganda, they also provide an unrivalled picture of everyday life in town and country.

By now iron had superseded bronze as the metal of war (see further p. 129), but the real strength of the Assyrians lay in their cavalry, made up of faster and heavier horses bred and pastured on the rich grazing lands of the plain. By the end of the century, the whole of northern Mesopotamia was under Assyrian control and Babylon, whose independence had at first been respected, had been devastated. The fortunes of the neo-Assyrian empire ('neo' to distinguish it from the earlier Assyrian state) fluctuated. Its heartland and outlying areas was always difficult to hold and its borders were seldom all peaceful at the same time. Within the royal family there were continual struggles for power. Yet at its height, under kings such as Tiglath-pilaser III (745–727 BC) and his successors Sargon II and Sennacherib in the late eighth and early seventh centuries, the empire reached as far as Cyprus and southern Anatolia, Palestine and Syria, Mesopotamia and the routes leading to the Iranian plateau. For a brief period it even controlled Egypt. Between 705 and 630 this empire remained relatively stable.

The motives for the revival of Assyrian power are difficult to gauge. There were, of course, the ancient traditions of control of extensive territory to maintain but these have to be set within the context of a mass of neighbouring states who represented an apparent or real threat to the Assyrians. Like the Prussians many centuries later the military ethos of the empire may have rested on the need to defend a vulnerable central plain from enemies real or imagined. Tiglath-pilaser III reformed the Assyrian army so that it was maintained as a standing professional force of foot soldiers backed by mounted forces, chariots, and cavalry. This gave it an immense advantage over its rivals who were raised year by year. Much of its reputation rested on fear of its brutality. The exploits of the conquerors are recorded in the Royal Annals, as the following example shows:

I felled 3,000 of their fighting men with the sword. I carried off prisoners, possessions, oxen and cattle from them. I burnt many captives from them. I captured many troops alive, I cut off some of their hands and arms; I cut off of others their noses, ears and extremities. I gouged out the eyes of many troops. I made one pile of the living and one of heads. I hung their heads on trees around the city. I burnt their adolescent boys and girls. I razed, destroyed, burnt and consumed the city.   (Quoted in J. Oates, *Babylon*)

The plundering of cities and the crushing of peoples was followed by the deportation of the survivors. (The sad lines of deportees, their possessions on carts and the women carrying children, are recorded on the palace reliefs.) Their declarations of war were presented within a standard formula which suggested that they, the kings, had done everything to avoid battle but the intransigence of their opponents had roused the anger of the god Ashur. It was the sacred duty of the king to intervene to preserve the harmony of all. After the horror of suppression, a myth was promulgated that the gods of the conquered peoples had abandoned them because of their behaviour, that these gods had even called on the Assyrians to wreak their vengeance. So during a siege of Jerusalem (in 701), the Judaean court was told by the Assyrian commander that it was quite clear that they had offended Yahweh and that he had abandoned them to their fate. However, the Assyrians would return the gods (literally, it seems, in that cult statues would be removed from a city after its defeat and then returned) and natural harmony would be restored. Moreover the treaties between the Assyrian kings and subject rulers were upheld by oaths in which both the Assyrian and the local gods were evoked. If the treaty was broken it was treated as an act of madness—no one sane would risk the anger of the gods. Again it would be the duty of the king to restore their favour by destroying the rebels.

However, the empire would not have survived as long as it did if suppression had been its only strategy. The kings portrayed themselves as fathers of their people who cared for the well-being of all and it is known that they would listen to appeals. Plunder was brought back to the Assyrian heartland and distributed freely. A letter to the king Ashurbanipal (668–627), the last of the great Assyrian rulers, describes the prosperity which was the result. 'The old men dance, the young men sing, the women and girls are happy; women are married, adorned with earrings, boys and girls are brought forth, the births thrive . . . Those who were sick for many years have got well, the hungry have been sated, the parched have been anointed with oil, the needy have been covered with garments.' In addition to the sharing out of booty, the Assyrians seem to have had a deliberate policy of agricultural expansion, the bringing into cultivation of new areas, and a state-sponsored distribution of iron ploughs to the peasantry. This was enforced, however, by the deliberate policy of settling deportees in depopulated parts of the empire. In their new homes the deportees were often described as Assyrians as if their original nationality had been erased. The empire also seems to have been given coherence by the shared values of its ruling elite in the same way as is found in the Roman empire a few centuries later. Favoured courtiers are found holding land throughout the empire, a guarantee of shared involvement in its security.

In the final century of the empire a new capital was created at Nineveh (the modern Mosul), hitherto a fairly minor religious centre. The king responsible was Sennacherib (705–681), who was determined that the city would not only be impressive (it was to hold 'a palace without rival', an ambitious enterprise in a region known for its magnificent royal buildings) but would also enjoy the latest technology. Its hydraulic engineering works were so sophisticated that some of its tunnels and dams are still in use today. They watered orchards and parks and then extended out to the arable land around. (It may be that the famous hanging gardens of Babylon were in fact at Nineveh.) Meanwhile a mass of deported workmen laboured on the palace and the squares and avenues of the city. While Sennacherib could be as brutal as his predecessors—he diverted his considerable technical skills to work out a means of flooding Babylon after he had sacked it—he was clearly something more than this. The reliefs at Nineveh show his informed interest in the vast territories he controlled.

His successor but one, Ashurbanipal, went further in proclaiming himself as a scholar. 'I can solve the most complicated divisions and multiplications,' he boasted. 'I have read intricate tablets inscribed with obscure Sumerian and Akkadian, difficult to unravel, and examined sealed and obscure inscriptions on stone from before the flood.' He is remembered as the founder of one of the first libraries in a form recognizable today, a systematically arranged set of books available for consultation. The tablets in Ashurbanipal's library recorded their provenance, often as 'Palace of Ashurbanipal, King of the World, King of Assyria'. There may have been some 1,500 titles in all, omens and religious texts, scholarly works, even including dictionaries for translating Sumerian into Akkadian and works of literature such as the ubiquitous *Epic of Gilgamesh*. Many seem to have been accumulated as trophies of war from defeated cities, a precedent to be followed by the Romans after they defeated Greek states and took off their libraries as plunder. The collection seems to have been personal to the king but texts warning against theft suggest it was also open to other readers. The perennial problems of librarians are recorded in other tablets from the period in which readers are warned against breaking tablets, placing them in water, or rubbing out the text, and the most persistent problem of all, not returning them!

In a few short years at the end of the seventh century the Assyrian empire succumbed to the combined forces of the Medes and Babylonians and as an empire disappeared suddenly and completely from the historical record. Ashur was sacked in 614, Nineveh fell in 612. Why the Assyrian collapse was so sudden is not clear. There had been power struggles between rival kings in the 620s and these may have caused some weakening of the state with Babylon recovering its independence in this decade and then, under its king Nabopolassar, going on the offensive, but this is hardly enough to explain the defeat of an empire which had developed such sophisticated survival skills. What seems to have tipped the balance against Assyria is the intervention of the Medes. It is possible that Assyria's weakening grip on eastern trade routes threatened to undermine the prosperity of the Medes, who took retaliatory action, and the combination of two enemies proved too much. The records suggest the shock waves of the collapse were felt throughout the Near East. Herodotus records the fall of Nineveh in his history of the Persian wars (as part of the rise of the Medes) and it became part of the founding myth of the Persian empire itself. The arrogance of Assyria was mocked by the sage Phocylides of Miletus in an epigram. 'A city which is small but on a lofty promontory and well-ordered is stronger than foolish Nineveh.'

The Neo-Babylonian Empire

The Babylonian king Nabopolassar (626–605) recorded his triumph in an inscription. 'I slaughtered the land of Assyria, I turned the hostile land into heaps and ruins. The Assyrian, who since distant days had ruled over all the peoples, and with his heavy yoke had brought injury to the people of the Land, his feet from Akkad I turned back, his yoke I threw off.' Babylon enjoyed its finest period as an independent state between 625 and 539 BC. Its greatest king, Nebuchadrezzar II, who ruled from 604 to 562 and who was responsible for a final defeat of the Assyrians at Carchemish, won a great empire. Egypt was contained, Judah was subdued, and the major Phoenician trading city of Tyre captured after a siege of, according to legend, thirteen years. Not much is known about the administration of this new empire but there is no doubt about the importance of Babylon as a centre of royal splendour. Massive walls and gates surrounded the city with a processional way leading from the main temple, past the palace of the king and outside the city to the ceremonial building where the New Year was celebrated. Gold, silver, and lapis lazuli were used to decorate the walls. Display for its own sake replaces the more subtle propaganda of the reliefs of Assyrian palaces. Nebuchadrezzar also built to last. The bricks and other building materials are so well made that they are still reusable. Buildings were designed to be placed on vast foundations so that they would be safe from the floods of the Euphrates which flowed through the middle of the city—the river was crossed by a graceful bridge. Dominating the city was a great ziggurat to the god Marduk, whose cult centre this was, of which the foundations survive. It may be the original of the Tower of Babel mentioned in the Book of Genesis and needed some 17 million bricks for its completion. Like earlier ziggurats its purpose seems to have been to provide a link between earth and heaven, to tie the city to the world beyond. Babylonian mathematics and science flourished with ever more accurate recordings of historical and astronomical events.

The Land of Israel

Among the peoples conquered by both the Assyrians and the Babylonians were Israelites (also known in the earliest period of their history as Hebrews). The origins of the Israelites are obscure. Outside their own writings there is virtually no mention of them as a people before the ninth century BC (there is a single reference to them from Egypt of about 1200 BC) and many of the events recorded as history in the Hebrew scriptures have no separate archaeological or documentary evidence to confirm them. This has made any discussion of their history intensely difficult. From the nineteenth century there have been western scholars preoccupied with fitting the stories of the Old Testament to historical evidence, some of them implying that the existence of the Christian God could be substantiated if such links were found, while the establishment of Israel as a state in 1948 brought new pressures to confirm the link of the Jewish people with their territory back to figures such as David. Much depends on the status given the Hebrew scriptures/Old Testament as a historical source. The scholar Amélie Kuhrt gives a balanced assessment. 'Like many accounts of the past, it was not intended to provide a critical historical study; rather it contained stories detailing the interaction of a people, Israel, with their god, Yahweh, who had chosen them to work out his divine plan. It is a complex, ideologically driven compilation, within which stories were refashioned to drive home particular lessons of the past.' In other words, the historian should read the Hebrew scriptures as texts in which historical events have been shaped to provide a coherent understanding of how the Israelite people came to be, above all in relationship to their god, Yahweh. In this the scriptures remain the only account of a Near Eastern people that describes how they themselves visualized the emergence of their people. Increasingly scholars are insisting that the history of Israel can only be fully understood if the first Israelites are placed among their neighbours of the region and seen as facing many of the same challenges.

After the creation and the birth of humankind came the age of the Patriarchs when Abraham emerges as the father of Israel leading his people through the lands of the Near East. It is his grandson Jacob who is first associated (by Yahweh) with the name Israel and with the begetting of twelve sons who become the ancestors of the twelve tribes. Jacob's son Joseph is sold into slavery in Egypt but then rises to a high position with the pharaoh and settles his family there. After oppression by the pharaohs the Israelites fulfilled their promised destiny by being led out of Egypt by Moses across the Sinai desert (the celebrated 'Exodus') and eventually after forty years of wandering to the edge of 'the promised land', Canaan. It was in this time that Yahweh gave Moses the Ten Commandments, part of the covenant through which he linked himself to his chosen people. It is Joshua who completes the journey into Canaan.

The Israelites may have been able to establish themselves in Canaan because of the depopulation caused by the disruptions of the thirteenth and twelfth centuries (although the archaeological evidence for the early settlement is hard to interpret) but they found little security. This is the era of the Judges, one in which the Israelites enjoyed no central administration or religious or cultural coherence. The 'judges' were in fact mainly war leaders who struggled to keep an Israeli identity alive at a time of turmoil. Among their early opponents were the Philistines, who may have been other casualties of these upheavals, perhaps even, some have suggested, sea peoples themselves who had come to settle along the south-western coast of Canaan. (It is from the Philistines that the name Palestine is derived.) Eventually the twelve tribes gave allegiance to a single king, first Saul, then David, and, much later, Solomon. David is the Israelite king *par excellence*, unifier of the twelve tribes, defeater of the Philistines, and conqueror of Jerusalem, which became the capital of the kingdom. As yet little mention of David has been found in any document or inscription of the period outside the Hebrew scriptures. The reputation given to Solomon in the Book of Kings as a builder has, however, received some support from archaeologists who have found extensive rebuilding of several cities of the region in the tenth century BC.

After Solomon's death his kingdom was split into two. In the north ten tribes preserved the name Israel, in the south the kingdom of Judah emerged, with Jerusalem a short distance within its territory. The citizens of Judah were known in Hebrew as *yehudi*, and from this, by way of the Greek *ioudaios* and the Latin *judaeus*, comes the English 'Jew'. The two kingdoms coexisted for two centuries, although they were often at war with each other. In 722 BC the Assyrians annexed the northern kingdom and extinguished its national identity. Judah survived, but as a subject kingdom of the Assyrian empire.

The Israelites rejoiced in a rich and varied body of sacred literature, much of it drawn from the common literary and religious heritage of the Near East. There is a creation story, narrated in the Book of Genesis, which has parallels with a similar account in the Babylonian epic *Enuma Elish*. In both myths God (Yahweh) fashions the world from a primordial abyss and his work of creation lasts six days after which he rests on the seventh. The story of the flood is, as has already been said, Sumerian in origin. The Garden of Eden seems rooted in a Near Eastern tradition, probably Mesopotamian, of an idyllic garden from which rivers flow. The theme of the righteous sufferer found in the Book of Job, perhaps the most profound and penetrating book of the Hebrew scriptures, is paralleled by similar stories in Babylonian literature. The range of the scriptures is wide, from the historical accounts of the formation of Israel and Judah to the gentle eroticism of the Song of Solomon, from the intensity of the Book of Job to the exultations and thanksgivings of many of the Psalms. As a varied collection of texts they evolved over a period of some 600 (some scholars would say 800) years and were eventually brought together as a single body of writings, the Hebrew scriptures, about the second century BC.

The most outstanding feature of these writings and what gives them a coherent theme is that they focus on one god, Yahweh, the protector of the people of Israel. As we have seen, it was Yahweh who led the Israelites from Egypt and into Canaan, the promised land, having given them, through Moses, the Ten Commandments. Early accounts of Yahweh see him as the supreme god among many. In Psalm 82, for instance, Yahweh asserts his dominance over a council of other gods. Gradually Yahweh becomes associated with the national identity of the Israelites, and other gods are seen as those of Israel's enemies, to be despised as such. (This is one of the themes of the eighth-century Book of Hosea.) A century later in the Book of Deuteronomy Yahweh is identified not only with the people of Israel but with a place, Jerusalem. Woven into Deuteronomy is a concern for social justice. All men are brothers and there should be special concern for the poor. The development of an ethical tradition is an essential element of the Hebrew scriptures and is underpinned with a concern for ritual purity expounded in meticulous detail in the Book of Leviticus.

Central to the worship of Yahweh was the concept of covenant. A covenant, an agreement which bound two people together, was widespread in the Near East. In this context it was an agreement made between Yahweh and his people, Israel. In its earliest recorded form it presents Yahweh as the protector of Israel who will remain faithful to his people for ever. Later, from Moses onwards, the covenant is seen as dependent on the good behaviour of the people of Israel. If they desert Yahweh he can punish them in retaliation. The books of the prophets, Isaiah and Jeremiah, for instance, are dominated by warnings of the catastrophe about to fall on Israel because of its wrongdoings. The prophets themselves are burdened figures (Jeremiah talks at one point of being seduced and overpowered by Yahweh when asked to spread the bad news that the Israelites will be overrun by the Babylonians), and they try hopelessly to avoid the task Yahweh imposes on them.

Jeremiah's prophesies came true. Judah had retained a precarious independence among the surrounding city states but Nebuchadrezzar proved too strong. Jerusalem appears to have been conquered twice by him, in 597 and 587, and according to the Book of Kings 10,000 inhabitants were carried off to Babylon. Although recent research suggests that the depopulation might not have been so great as the Hebrew sources suggest, from the psychological point of view this exile was a crucial moment in Jewish history and underlined the new image of Yahweh as one who could abandon his people to their suffering. It may have been seen as a time of desolation, but the exile was in many ways a creative one, and it was in this period that the early Hebrew scriptures were first consolidated as a single collection. The first dispersion of the Jews was to establish an experience of exile which was to recur throughout Jewish history. Even when Jerusalem was restored to the Jews by the Persians many did not go back. The Temple was rebuilt about 516 BC, but Jerusalem remained a relative backwater for centuries.

The Jews had created the world's first sustained monotheistic religion. (The Egyptian king Akhenaten's dominant sun god had died with him.) As the writings of the Old Testament show, it was a concept which left many unsolved philosophical problems about the nature of the one God. For some he was the source of both good and evil. ('I am Yahweh unrivalled, I form the light and create the dark. I make good fortune and create calamity,' writes the prophet Isaiah.) He was a protector god but also a god of retribution, able to destroy not only Israel's enemies but also Israel itself when it offended him. The lesson of the Babylonian exile was that only through the admission of guilt and the acceptance of just punishment could the relationship be restored in a new covenant. There is some hope that this new covenant might be brought by an earthly ruler: in the prophesies of both Isaiah and Jeremiah a messiah is talked of, one who will bring everlasting justice and peace.

The monotheism of Israel needs to be contrasted with the different religious traditions of the other peoples of the Ancient Near East. The more common pattern was to have a mass of different deities living alongside each other (polytheism). At times one emerges as supreme over others. This is known as henotheism and perhaps best describes the position of Amun in New Kingdom Egypt, or Ahura-Mazda in the Persian empire (below). The relationship between the supreme god and others varies. He may be linked to them through family ties, as with Zeus in Greece, he may absorb their identities (syncretism), or he may rule over them as distinct but subordinate deities. His supremacy may be maintained by presenting them as manifestations of his own power. Many of the successful civilizations described in this book were pragmatic in their religious policies, keeping their own gods as supreme, but tolerating the existence of others.

The Phoenicians

These centuries also saw a transformation along the Levantine coast. There were cities here such as Byblos which had a history stretching back thousands of years. In the second millennium Ugarit, Tyre, and Sidon were all important trading centres. Before 1200 BC the economies of these cities were linked to those of the inland city states, through which they served as intermediaries with the outside world. During the disruptions associated with the sea peoples, however, the original inhabitants of Canaan (from whom the Israelites distinguished themselves) lost much of their coastline and inland territories so that by the tenth century they controlled only 200 kilometres of coast (from an original 500) and the narrow strip of land which ran between the coast and the mountains which quickly rose to some 3,000 metres. This proved, in fact, their salvation as they were well protected from invaders from the east, yet had good access to timber on the mountain slopes. The cities were well sited in bays and inlets while two cities, Tyre and Arvad, were on islands and virtually impregnable.

Gradually trade revived and there is a record of an Egyptian official, Wenamum, visiting Byblos in about 1100 in search of timber. With Egypt's status in decline he is treated with some condescension but his account suggests that the king of Byblos has a fleet of twenty cargo ships with access to another fifty coastal vessels in nearby Sidon. So there is already some trading activity although Wenamun's account also mentions pirates along the coast. The city which is to take the lead in expanding trade is, however, Tyre. It may well be that the city had a more flexible approach to commerce than Byblos with individual merchant families, rather than the king, taking the initiative. By the ninth century, it is clear that it is individual merchants from Tyre who have, through their agents, set up outposts in

Babylonia. Tyre's reputation spread widely. Writing some 300 years later, after Tyre had fallen to the Babylonians, the prophet Ezekiel laments 'that city standing at the edge of the sea, doing business with the nations in innumerable islands . . . your frontiers stretched out far to sea, those who built you made you perfect in beauty . . . Then you were rich and glorious surrounded by the seas.' (This evocation of a prosperous city was so powerful that the Venetians later adopted it for themselves!) Ezekiel details (chapter 27) all the many peoples from as far east as beyond the Euphrates to as far south as the Arab peninsula that dealt with the city.

The Canaanites would probably have always been traders. Although the coastline was fertile it could never have supported their population. However, it has been argued that the boost to the revived trade was given by the Assyrians, who demanded tribute of the cities particularly in metals which they could only raise by trading overseas. It is certainly true that by the ninth century the Canaanites were penetrating deep into the Mediterranean, and it was here that they came into contact with another trading people, the Greeks, who shared with them a trading post at al-Mina on the Orontes river through which contacts could be made with Mesopotamia. The Greeks whose own trading activities were still undeveloped found it difficult to distinguish the traders they worked with and they gave them the collective term Phoenician, which is probably derived from the reddish purple dye extracted from molluscs for which they were famous throughout the Mediterranean. The mingling of Greeks and the Phoenicians, who had absorbed much of the cultural heritage of the Ancient Near East, was to be of profound importance in the history of the western world (although the Greeks may have had other contacts; from the eighth century their shields and helmets suggest the direct influence of Assyria).

Egypt in the First Millennium

The most distant of the conquests of Assyria was Egypt. After the death of Rameses XI, 1069 BC, Egypt underwent a period (the so-called Third Intermediate Period, c.1070–664) of increasing fragmentation as provincial families and, above all, the priests of Thebes strengthened their local bases against the power of the central ruler. At times in the ninth and eighth centuries BC there were as many as eleven rulers competing for power. By the mid-eighth century southern Egypt was controlled by a foreign dynasty originating from Nubia. This Nubian dynasty, the Kushites, originated far in the south, although they used Napata, the furthest point of Egyptian control in the New Kingdom, as their Nubian capital. The Kushites were therefore well aware of the cultural and political heritage of Egypt, and their rulers sensed how they could exploit it for their own ends. In 727 BC their most ambitious king, Piankhi, marched against the rulers of the north, claiming that he was leading a campaign on behalf of Amun against rebels to the god. When he reached the Delta he shrewdly declared his allegiance to the sun god Ra, always stronger in the north than Amun, by ritually purifying himself at the temple at Heliopolis. He was then acclaimed ruler of all Egypt (founding the Twenty-Fifth Dynasty). Piankhi proved adept at manipulating the traditions of the past. He even built a pyramid tomb for himself and his family at Napata (although in a form different from those at Memphis). This search for roots in the Egyptian past as far back as the Old and Middle Kingdom continued under Piankhi's successors. They built at all the ancient religious sites of Egypt, including Memphis and Thebes, used traditional royal titles, and decorated their temples with themes from the Old Kingdom. They even expanded into Asia again.

It was just at this time of relative unity that Assyria struck. A conquest of Egypt had long been among its ambitions, and Egyptian incursions into Palestine provoked the empire further. In the early seventh century the Assyrian king Esarhaddon was able to invade Egypt across the Sinai desert. Memphis was sacked in 671, and the Egyptian ruler, Taharqo, was forced to retreat south. In 664/663 the Assyrians attacked again, and this time reached as far as Thebes. The religious capital of Egypt, sacred and inviolate for so many long centuries, was sacked. This was a humiliating blow to the Kushites and they withdrew south (where they maintained a kingdom around the city of Meroe for several hundred more years).

The Assyrians were too far from their homeland to be able to maintain permanent control of Egypt and they were forced to rule through collaborators. They chose one Psamtek (in Greek Psammetichus), ruler of a small Delta kingdom based on the town of Sais, as their instrument of control. Psamtek was as adept in his manipulation of the Egyptian past as the Nubian kings had been. He sent his daughter Nitocris to Thebes and installed her as the 'wife' of Amun-Ra, thus ensuring his own control over the south. Artistic styles were modelled on those of the Old and Middle Kingdoms and Memphis was confirmed as the country's capital.

Through a mixture of diplomacy and force Psamtek eventually established his rule over the whole of Egypt, founding a new Dynasty, the Twenty-Sixth (also known as the Saite Dynasty). Luckily for him, the power of Assyria was waning and Psamtek remained unchallenged by his nominal overlords. He was to rule for over fifty years, and he and his immediate successors saw a period of unity, wealth, and cultural renaissance. Nobles were buried in magnificent tombs and once again temples were built on a colossal scale. For the first time Egypt built a navy (probably as an aid to defending its interests in Palestine—it was equipped with Greek-style war galleys) and was able to compete on equal terms with other trading nations of the Mediterranean and Black Sea. The dynasty was also highly receptive to foreigners. About 620 BC Greek traders were allowed by Psamtek I to set up a trading centre at Naucratis on a branch of the Nile near Sais. Greek mercenaries soon formed part of the Egyptian army (together with Phoenicians, Syrians, and Jews, many of whom were refugees from the Assyrian conquests). A thousand kilometres up the Nile some of their signatures have been found inscribed on the leg of a colossal statue of Rameses II. As was noted earlier Greeks began visiting the country as tourists and were so overawed by what they saw that some came to believe that their own civilization was descended from Egypt's.

The Rise of the Persian (Achaemenid) Empire

In the mid-sixth century an empire finally arose which managed to conquer and consolidate its hold over the entire Ancient Near East, including, for much of the period, Egypt. It is known as the Achaemenid empire, the name being derived from the legendary founder of its ruling family, a king known as Achaemenes (although this name is often applied only from the rule of Darius I (522–486)). The empire was remarkable for establishing a stable system of government which held together a wide range of subject peoples and cultures for 200 years. Even if its federal system of government was vulnerable when broken at the centre, as happened when Alexander the Great defeated and hunted down its last 'king of kings', Darius III, in the 330s, the empire deserves to be recognized as a major achievement. The fact that the Seleucids, the Macedonian dynasty which succeeded Alexander in the area, ruled through its original structure of government, used local languages rather than Greek in its administration, and borrowed many customs of its royal family is evidence of that.

One reason why the empire has been dismissed so easily in the west is that the main accounts of it come from Greek historians, above all Herodotus, who saw it in a hostile light after the empire's two attacks on the Greek world in 490 and 480 BC (detailed in Chapter 12 below). The failure of the empire could be blamed by the victorious Greeks on the autocratic ways of its rulers and the lethargy of its peoples as well as on the inherent cultural superiority of the Greeks. Herodotus is particularly harsh on Cambyses, the conqueror of Egypt, branding him as a ruthless despot, although native Egyptian sources suggest he was respectful to the Egyptian gods. For much of the empire Herodotus' negative assessment cannot be countered by any significant historical sources although there are monumental inscriptions erected by its rulers on rock faces, notably the account of his coming to power by Darius I (522–486) at Behistun which is largely concerned with justifying his right to kingship. Much of the work on the empire relies on the patient building up of a picture from local sources. The *lingua franca* of this widespread empire was Aramaic and texts written in a variety of other local languages have survived. However, while some of them have been useful in showing how local administration worked, labour was organized, and land held in particular areas, there are still vast tracts of the empire, particularly in the east, of which almost nothing is known. As has happened elsewhere the archaeologists began work at the great capitals of the empire, Pasargadae, Persepolis (remarkable for the remains of its palace burnt and looted by

Alexander), and Susa. Smaller towns have been neglected by archaeologists and many have been buried under modern cities such as Damascus. Even in the western parts of the empire, the picture is fragmentary.

The Persian empire was founded by one of the great conquerors of history, Cyrus II (ruled 559–530 BC). Cyrus was descended from a line of kings which had emerged at Persis (modern Fars) on the Iranian plateau in the late seventh century out of the earlier Elamite state. (The Elamites whose state was based on the southwestern part of modern Iran had been a major player in near eastern politics, especially during the second millennium BC.) However, he represented a distinct Persian people who had possibly arrived as pastoralists from central Asia as the Elamite state was in decline. To his north were another people, the Medes, who controlled the fertile valleys which led down into the Iranian plateau and who had recently shown their military prowess in the wars against the Assyrians. In 550 the Medes attacked Cyrus possibly as a reaction to his growing power. Their defeat led to the incorporation of the Medes and their wealthy capital, Ecbatana, within the Persian state. The land of the Medes offered rich grazing and fine horses as well as more manpower and other neighbouring states began to resent the growing power as it expanded further both to the west and east. King Croesus of Lydia, a state which had been consolidated in the seventh century in western Anatolia, attacked the Persians in the mid-540s but he too was defeated and his capital, Sardis, brought into what was now an empire. The prosperous Greek city states of the coastline of Anatolia were bullied into accepting Persian control.

Cyrus' conquest of the Greek coast was probably followed by campaigns as far east as central Asia and Afghanistan. Finally, he turned back to Babylonia in the fertile plains of Mesopotamia. Following the glorious reign of Nebuchadrezzar, the state had lost some of its vigour. Its last king Nabonidus (succeeded in 555) was not of royal lineage but had been a state official. He seems to have been accepted by the nobles but threats to his kingdom meant that he spent many years of his reign campaigning abroad, particularly in Arabia. One result was that he was accused of neglecting the god Marduk, whose rituals required an annual ceremony at each New Year in Babylon itself. Confronted by Cyrus, the Babylonian state fell after one major battle (Opis in 539 BC), and Cyrus found himself master as far west and south as the borders of Egypt. It was now that he showed his political abilities. Despite carrying out a massacre of his opponents at Opis he managed to legitimize his rule by claiming that he was restoring traditional order to Babylon after Nabonidus had threatened its prosperity through his lack of religious orthodoxy. So it was that 'all the inhabitants of Babylon, as well as the entire country of Sumer and Akkad, princes and governors, bowed to Cyrus and kissed his feet, jubilant that he had received the kingship, and with shining faces happily greeted him as a master through whose help they had come to life from death and had all been spared death and disaster, and they worshipped his name'. He was accepted by the Babylonian elite while the defeat of the city allowed him to liberate the Israelites from their bondage and be acclaimed by them as a deliverer. Traditional accounts link him to the rebuilding of the temple at Jerusalem. Among his new subjects were the Phoenicians, whose sailors were to provide the manpower for an imperial navy.

The Achaemenid empire now stretched over 4,000 kilometres from east to west and 1,500 from north to south, 6 million square kilometres with an estimated population of some 35 million. Its territories were so varied and, in many cases, so uncontrollable that it was impossible to impose authoritarian rule but, as the treatment of Babylon showed, this was not Cyrus' way. So long as the ultimate authority of himself as 'King of Kings' and the Persian god Ahura-Mazda were recognized, local cultures and religions were free to thrive. In Persian art foreigners are shown as dignified people, some of whom were allowed to bear arms in the presence of their emperor. Taxes were kept relatively low—it has been noted that Cyrus' capital at Pasargadae was nothing like so lavish as those of the Babylonian or Assyrian kings. Foreign craftsmen at the city were free to display their own styles. Palaces show the influence of Assyrian art, the Greeks brought their own traditions of stone working while Cyrus' own tomb echoes models from Anatolia. (A later Greek account of the tomb tells how Cyrus' body was encased in a gold sarcophagus with a tapestry from Babylon as coverlet.)

The maintenance of such a vast empire depended heavily on the energy and charisma of Cyrus. On his death his successor, his son Cambyses, was successful in extending the empire yet further through the conquest of Egypt and Cyprus. The Persian armies invaded Egypt in 525 BC, defeating king Psamtek III and besieging his capital at Memphis. The city fell and the last of the native Egyptian kings was, according to some sources, carried off in triumph to the Persian capital at Susa (other sources say he was executed in Memphis). As mentioned above, Egyptian sources suggest that, like his father, he was shrewd enough to integrate himself into local custom. At Sais he restored the temple of Neith, the mother of Re, to the native priesthood and then carried out the traditional rituals of homage. He seems to have used the local elites to sustain his rule. A new phase in Egyptian history had begun, one in which foreign rulers, Persians, Greeks, and Romans, would exploit the centuries-old traditions of loyalty to a central ruler to serve their own ends.

By 525 BC, therefore, the Persian empire extended over the whole of western Asia. However, Cambyses faced considerable internal unrest while he was still in Egypt and shortly before his death in 522 there was a coup by one of his generals, Darius. This could have been the moment when the empire collapsed but Darius himself proved a military and organizational genius and, by 520, he had subdued the revolts and stabilized the empire. Without any justification, it seems, Darius claimed descent from Achaemenes, and successfully exploited his background to gain the allegiance of the heartlands of the empire. Perhaps more than his predecessors, he consolidated the Persian nobility behind him and used them as a ruling elite. It is his achievements which were proclaimed on the great inscription carved on a rock face 80 metres high at Behistun in north-western Iran in three languages, Elamite, Akkadian (the script used by Babylonians and Assyrians), and Old Persian. (As already noted, one of the major feats of nineteenth-century archaeology was the copying and deciphering of Akkadian from this inscription by the Englishman Henry Rawlinson.) Campaigns followed in the east, where control was consolidated over the vast stretches of plains and mountains which form Afghanistan, Pakistan, and the eastern parts of modern Iran. About 514 Darius crossed the Hellespont into Thrace and fought some inconclusive campaigns against the native Scythian peoples.

Darius legitimized his rule through the one god, Ahura-Mazda, who was prepared to preside benignly over the lesser gods of the peoples Darius controlled. King and god reinforced each other's legitimacy. 'A great god is Ahura-Mazda, who created the earth, who created yonder sky, who created man, who created happiness for man, who made Darius king, one king over many, one lord of many,' runs part of the inscription on Darius' tomb and reliefs on this and later royal tombs show king and god each raising a hand to each other in greeting. A myth of succession is created that through the deceit of rival pretenders the empire had fallen into disorder and the god and Darius had restored both righteousness and good order. In a royal inscription, of which two copies have been found suggesting it proclaimed the official ideology of the empire, Darius prides himself on his calm temper which enables him to dispense justice for all his people with fairness and equanimity.

The empire was divided into twenty satrapies, or administrative regions, each under an imperial appointee, normally a Persian. (Rather as the French were to make it possible for an educated African subject of their empire to become 'French' through education, so it seems to have been possible for an outsider to be given honorary status as a 'Persian'.) In line with the generally tolerant attitude to local peoples, ancient capitals, Memphis, Sardis, Ecbatana, Babylon, were preserved as centres of local government and many of the resources gathered in taxation or tribute were stored locally. (Massive amounts of silver were found by Alexander's men in the citadel in Babylon, for instance.) Each capital kept its own records of administrative decisions and there are even cases of local officials writing in to check the details of royal decrees from the local archives. It was a system flexible enough for the kings to keep contact with the more remote tribal peoples whose loyalty was essential if free passage through the empire was to be preserved (normally through buying their allegiance with gifts).

Communications were good with a network of roads criss-crossing the empire. The celebrated Royal Road, the backbone of the empire's communications, ran from Susa to Sardis, the former capital of Lydia, in the west with any dangerous stretch or crossing continuously guarded. Along it messages could be carried more than 300 kilometres a day. Official travellers were given a pass allowing them to draw rations for the next day from each station on the road, and the record that this had been done was then sent up to the capital. This effective and well-policed communications system allowed wealth to be channelled upwards, to the great palaces of Pasargadae and Persepolis in the homeland of the dynasty and to Susa, the ancient capital of the Elamites, which Darius made the administrative capital of the empire. As before the dynasty drew freely on the resources and skills of its subject peoples. Darius' palace from Susa was built of cedars from the Lebanon with other timbers brought from Afghanistan. Lapis lazuli came, as it had always done, from the east, gold from Sardis and Bactria. Egypt provided its most common precious metal silver, as well as ivory which also came in from Nubia and India. Once again it was the Greeks who were the expert stone cutters, the Medes and the Egyptians the finest craftsmen in gold and wood, while the Babylonians were responsible for baking bricks for the palace.

Despite the overall efficiency and good order of the empire it could hardly be maintained in absolute peace for decade after decade. In 499 BC the western part of the empire was shaken by a major revolt by the Greek cities of the Ionian coast. Darius was forced into confrontation with a people who were to prove the match of his empire. For the next 150 years, the empire and its Greek neighbours were to have a complicated relationship which was finally to end in the overthrow of the empire by Alexander. Before the story of this relationship goes further, an introduction must be made to the Greeks and their sea, the Mediterranean.

FURTHER READING

See reading list after Chapter 2 for the main surveys. Here again Amélie Kuhrt is essential. On the Assyrians, H. Saggs, *The Might that was Assyria* (London, 1984), and also the essays in vol. iii, Part 2, of the *Cambridge Ancient History*; J. Oates, *Babylon* (London, 1979) and H. Saggs, *The Greatness that was Babylon* (London, 1963). For a general introduction to the history of the Jewish people and their sacred writings see John Rogerson and Philip Davies, *The Old Testament World* (Cambridge, 1989), and Michael Coogan (ed.), *The Oxford History of the Biblical World* (Oxford, 1998). There is also John Rogerson, *Atlas of the Bible* (Oxford, 1989), and N. de Lange, *Atlas of the Jewish World* (Oxford, 1984). For the archaeological background see J. Tubb and R. Chapman (eds.), *Archaeology and the Bible* (London, 1990), and John Laughlin, *Archaeology and the Bible* (London, 1998). B. Metzer and M. Coogan (eds.), *The Oxford Companion to the Bible* (Oxford, 1993), provides authoritative background material. Karen Armstrong's *A History of God* (London, 1993) charts the rise of the concept that there is one male God. On the Phoenicians, S. Moscati, *The World of the Phoenicians* (London, 1999), and as editor, *Phoenicians* (London, 2001). See also Maria Aubet, *The Phoenicians and the West* (Cambridge, 1994), and G. Markoe (ed.), *Phoenicians* (London, 2002). For the later history of Egypt, N. Grimal, *A History of Ancient Egypt* (Oxford, 1992) and chapters 12 and 13 of *The Oxford History of Ancient Egypt* (Oxford, 2000). Persia is covered in the *Cambridge Ancient History*, vol. iv, chapters 1–3 and at an introductory level in Josef Wiesehofer, *Ancient Persia from 550 BC to 650 AD* (translated by Azizeh Azodi, London, 2001), but the definitive study is now Pierre Briant, *From Cyrus to Alexander: A History of the Persian Empire* (translated by Peter Daniels, Winona Lake, 2002). On how Persia was 'barbarized' by the Greeks see E. Hall, *Inventing the Barbarian* (Oxford, 1989).

7 | The Setting for Mediterranean Civilization

The first draft of this chapter was begun in a room overlooking the head of the Adriatic near the remains of the major provincial city of Aquileia. It was February and a bitterly cold wind, the notorious bora, was slicing its way down through the mountain passes towards the sea. Capricious and sometimes reaching over 100 knots an hour the bora can bring havoc on land and sea. It was this same wind which sprang up nearby in September AD 394 and threw the army of a pagan usurper Eugenius into such disarray that it was considered to have been sent by God against him. (September is early for the bora at its worst—it normally starts in November and reaches its height in January and its unexpected arrival this early doubtless made it easier to claim it as a miracle.)

Despite the winter cold, this part of the Mediterranean was fertile and well watered and there was easy access to clay, stone, and even gold. Aquileia, which had been settled in 181 BC as a Roman colony to defend the area against invading Celts, had good access to the sea and served as the end point for trading routes from the north. Roads led from it westwards across the Po valley, southwards, towards central Italy and over the Alps to Austria. As a result it had grown enormously prosperous from trade and its own industries of which glass making and gem cutting were the most prominent. (There is a record of a ship leaving Cyrenaica (Libya) bound for Aquileia with no less than 3,000 measures of oil and 8,000 bushels of wheat on board.) In the fourth century its wealth sustained a massive basilica complex whose mosaics, recovered from under silt only in the last century, are among the glories of early Christian art. However, all this depended on the security provided by the *pax romana* and as the empire disintegrated in the fifth century it was sacked by the Huns in AD 452, some of its scattered citizens possibly being among the founders of Venice.

A few months before I had been in a very different part of the Mediterranean, the island of Symi close by Rhodes and the coast of modern Turkey. It was very hot and the island was so limited in resources of water that in the summer season it had to be brought in by tanker. Crossing the island on foot one came across the stone walls and terraces which showed how centuries of peasant knowledge and cunning had been used to divert the meagre resources of rainfall to where it was needed. It was an acute reminder that much of the Mediterranean has always lived on the edge of drought. (There is a record of a seven-year drought in Thera in the seventh century BC, for instance.) On outlying, and now virtually deserted, beaches smooth expanses of rocks just under the water may well have been those on which boats were beached two or three thousand years ago. Looking out over the small bays one was reminded of Homer's description of Odysseus arriving at the land of the Cyclops (although with water meadows and rich crops of grain their land was no Symi):

There's a snug deep water harbour there, what's more, no need for mooring gear, no anchor stones to heave, no cables to make fast. Just beach your keels, ride out the days until your shipmates' spirit stirs for open seas and a fair wind blows.   (Translations of Homer: Robert Fagles)

There had been a further consequence of Symi's isolation, it was scattered with monasteries, most now deserted.

On the Turkish mainland across from Symi there had been another major city, Cnidus, occupying a magnificent position at the head of a peninsula. Its land had been fertile enough to make it a centre of wine-growing and its wines were traded as far as Athens, where they were a favourite among connoisseurs in the Hellenistic period. Cnidus also had a famous medical school and one of its doctors, Ctesias, had served in the Persian court in the fifth century BC and written the first known work by a westerner on India. (Like most Greek cities of Asia Minor Cnidus had been part of the Persian empire in the sixth and again in the fourth century.) In the fourth century another citizen, Eudoxus, proved an outstanding mathematician and astronomer, responsible for ensuring the primacy of geometry in Greek mathematics and working out a mathematical system which apparently explained the movement of the planets. As was typical of the times he travelled widely, studying in Athens and Egypt and finally returning to Athens to teach alongside the philosopher Plato. Then there was Sostratus, the architect of the famous lighthouse at the entrance to the harbour at Alexandria. In the city itself the great tourist attraction was Praxiteles' statue of Aphrodite, of the fourth century BC, the first example of the goddess being shown life size in the nude (see further p. 245).

The Mediterranean, and its neighbour the Black Sea, are inseparable from the lives of most of the civilizations of this book. One of the most famous cries of ancient history, *Thalatta, thalatta*, 'the sea, the sea', recorded by the historian Xenophon as the defeated mercenaries he had led into Persia (401 BC) reached the shores of the Black Sea, is a reminder of how reassuring its presence must have been for those who had travelled too far inland. What is remarkable about the sea is that with its many harbours, bays, and islands it is safe enough for everyday travel but large and volatile enough in its behaviour always to contain the unknown and unexpected. This is well represented in Greek myth. The legend of Jason and the Argonauts, reworked in the third century BC by Apollonius Rhodios, draws on ancient tales of the prince who braves his way into magical lands (here the Black Sea which, in Homer's time, was believed to be limitless) in search of a prize, the Golden Fleece, and inevitably gets entangled with a woman, in this case Medea, who is the archetype of the scheming barbarian temptress. (In Euripides' play *Medea*, she kills her own children to spite Jason when he deserts her for a Greek wife.) In the *Odyssey*, Odysseus is engaged in a voyage of return from Troy to his home Ithaca, where his loyal wife Penelope is waiting unsure whether he is alive or dead. (One of the greatest fears of Homer's heroes was to die unknown and unburied at sea.) Homer stretches out the experience to an improbable ten years, so one could say that Odysseus is forced to become an explorer in spite of himself. Between Troy and Ithaca, he is imprisoned by the seductive nymph, Calypso, helped or hindered (shipwrecked even) by gods and goddesses, and subject to clashing rocks, monsters or whirlpools. Yet when he is washed ashore on the fertile island of the Phaeacians, he encounters a civilized people benignly ruled by their king Alcinous. He is welcomed and given every courtesy and the Phaeacians offer to escort him onwards. They have even managed to control the sea. They boast:

Our ships know in a flash their mates' intentions, know all ports of call and all the rich green fields. With wings of the wind they cross the sea's huge gulfs, shrouded in mist and cloud— no fear in the world of foundering, fatal shipwreck.

Yet in contrast there are the Cyclops. Their land is every bit as fertile as that of the Phaeacians but they lack all the attributes of civilization and good order:

Lawless brutes, who trust to the everlasting gods. They never plant with their own hands or plow the soil. Unsown, unplowed, the earth teems with all they need ... they have no meeting place for council, no laws either. No, up on the mountain peaks they live in arching caverns—each a law unto himself ruling his wives and children, not a care in the world for any neighbour.

One can read into this something which flows through the Greek mentality, the possibility of good order and harmony (a harmony which can extend to the home and life on the land) but always the underlying fear of disorder, from a Medea or the Cyclops, a vengeful god or the vagaries of the weather.

For the Greeks another important psychological element of life in the Mediterranean was the constant awareness of the great civilizations of the east. The Phoenicians acted as middlemen through which the rich cultural heritage of these states was passed on, partly through word of mouth, myth, and the alphabet, partly through goods such as textiles and metals. The palace of Phaeacia had walls 'crowned with a circling frieze glazed as blue as lapis', the precious stone which came from Afghanistan, although no Greek palace could ever rival those of the kings of the more powerful trading states. However, these came and went as their precarious hold on the trading routes on which their prosperity depended waxed or waned and it was Egypt, with its more sustained civilization, that came to predominate in the minds of the Greeks. The Greeks were visiting and settling in Egypt by the seventh century. Here was a link to the very distant past and by the time of the Greek historian Herodotus, mid-fifth century BC, Egypt is being credited as the fount of ancient wisdoms, which had been carefully preserved, so Herodotus reports, in writing in temple archives by their priests. The Egyptians, he goes on, were the first to define the relationships between man and the gods and the Greeks had absorbed their own religion from them. They had invented writing and mathematics (according to Aristotle) and were the most learned of doctors. Yet Egypt was something other—the dependence of the Egyptians on the pharaohs made them 'barbarian' rather than Greek to a fifth-century 'intellectual' like Herodotus and he has tremendous problems in finding a way of categorizing the complexities of Egyptian society. He ends up making them opposites to the Greeks. In a famous passage from Book II of his *History* he writes:

The Egyptians in their manners and customs seem to have reversed the ordinary practices of mankind. For instance, women attend market and are employed in trade, while men stay at home and do the weaving . . . Men in Egypt carry loads on their heads, women on their shoulders; women pass water standing up, men sitting down . . . Sons are under no compulsion to support their parents if they do not wish to do so, but daughters must . . . Elsewhere priests grow their hair long; in Egypt they shave their heads . . . When writing or calculating, instead of going like the Greeks, from left to right, the Egyptians go from right to left . . . (Translation: Aubrey de Selincourt)

The Egyptians, and other peoples such as the Persians, who were a brooding presence after the invasions of 490 and 480 BC by the empire, found themselves being used by the Greeks as a means of defining the attributes of their own culture. The wild Scythians of the Black Sea, were used in the same way but in their case, like the Cyclops, as a contrast to stable government. In short, the Greeks and other Mediterranean cultures were in a continuous process of evaluating themselves through the definition of others.

So the Mediterranean and its surrounding lands provided a psychological setting but it was also of course a geographical entity. In his work on the Mediterranean at the time of Philip II Fernand Braudel looked at the different rhythms of the sea and its seasons. He explored it not just as a sea but as a whole which encompassed all the surrounding ecologies, plains, valleys, mountains, deserts, each of which was related to each other. The Mediterranean is a relatively sheltered environment and what gives it its focus is the possibility it offers of unrestricted communication, from the mouth of the Black Sea to the Straits of Gibraltar (and of course beyond these limits into the Black Sea and the Atlantic). 'We have long seen that vast stretch of sea from the Ocean to the furthest shore of Pontus held as if it were a single safe and closed harbour,' as the Roman statesman Cicero was to put it. Many parts of it, especially among the islands of the

Aegean, offer safe sailing. So 14,000 years ago the obsidian deposits on the island of Melos were being exploited by seafarers from the Peloponnese and by the second millennium BC there is widespread trading activity as confidence among the peoples of the sea grows. This confidence was destroyed by the upheavals associated with the Sea Peoples (see p. 38 above) but by the eighth century it is back. The more adventuresome of the sea's peoples are now probing its shores for minerals and fertile niches where there is surplus of grain to be had or even the possibility of settlement.

Mobility and Mediterranean life went hand in hand. This was partly because it was relatively easy to travel but also because specific parts of the Mediterranean met specific needs and had to be reached by traders to be exploited. If grain is the basis for nutrition (and up to two-thirds of a diet might be provided by it) then access to the more fertile areas, those in particular which had enough rainfall to support the more nutritious wheat—Egypt, Sicily and southern Italy, the Black Sea and, later, north Africa—would always be important. The Ancient Near East, and its far-flung trade routes, provided luxury goods and textiles, the northern Aegean timber, Cyprus copper, Etruria (central Italy) iron, copper, and silver, and Tartessus, the hinterland inland from Cadiz in southern Spain, silver (the commodity required to meet the demands of the Assyrians for tribute). As political contexts changed, so new possibilities of trade and settlement arose. The Black Sea, which had once been seen as beyond civilization, was by the fifth century settled with prosperous Greek cities, trading with each other, the native peoples, and through the Bosporus the wider Greek world. When, under the Ptolemies, Egypt became open to settlement, colonists from no less than 200 Greek cities are recorded among its new inhabitants. So there is a continual interaction between different economic niches and sometimes a distinct civilization emerges from the contact, as with the Etruscans in central Italy.

It was essential that there should be some overall security if markets were to be freely exploited. In many periods piracy, often organized and extensive, disrupted trade routes. The *pax romana* established by Augustus across the Mediterranean after the turmoil of the civil wars of the first century BC led to a major increase of activity. The writer Suetonius tells of the passengers and crew who, meeting the dying Augustus off the coast of Campania, 'wished him the greatest of good fortune because, they said, they owed their lives to him and their liberty to sail the seas: in a word, their entire freedom and prosperity'. The archaeological evidence for trade backs up this picture. By Roman times there is extensive trade, in grain, wine, oil, and in heavyweight cargoes such as marble and granite. It was underpinned by the shipping of the *annona*, the food supply of grain for the enormous populations of Rome and, later, Constantinople. Some historians such as Moses Finley played down the extent of trade but recent research is showing that even peasant farmers were ready to trade their surplus if they had any.

This positive picture has to be immediately qualified by a reminder that the Mediterranean is always capricious—watching the build-up of a Mediterranean summer storm is as dramatic an experience as any. For half the year the Mediterranean was unsailable. Between the September and March equinoxes the Atlantic spreads depressions across the Mediterranean, unsettling the climate and causing troublesome winds such as the bora. The transition from summer to winter is well described by the accounts of Paul's voyage from Caesarea, the provincial capital of Judaea, to Rome in Acts, chapter 27. Paul, accused by the Jews of infringing the Law, had used his status as a Roman citizen to gain the right to appeal to the emperor in Rome and so he set off from Caesarea accompanied by a centurion. The first stop was the ancient trading port of Sidon on the Levantine coast. Then with wind blowing down against them they had to cross under the lee of Cyprus, then across open sea to the southern coast of Asia Minor. Again the winds were against them and when they reached Cnidus they were unable to put into harbour but had to continue across open sea to the southern coast of Crete. By now the voyage had taken so long they were past the autumn equinox. They should have sheltered for the winter in Crete but the centurion accompanying Paul refused to stop. As they headed out into the open sea there followed a hazardous journey with the storms so powerful that all the cargo and ship's gear had to be jettisoned as the ship was left free to run before the gale. Eventually, and it seems by sheer luck, they made landfall at Malta where their ship was forced aground. The Maltese welcomed the shipwrecked travellers with genuine hospitality but it was a further three months before they could continue their journey to Sicily and up the western coast of Italy to Rome.

In settled times trading routes were defined by wind and currents. As ships in the ancient Mediterranean were square sailed they did best in a following wind and in the eastern Mediterranean these prevailed from north to south. So while it took three days to sail from Athens to Rhodes and a further four days on to Egypt, the journey back would take twice as long. (This was one of the problems faced by Paul.) Detailed studies of voyages between Venice and the Holy Land in the sixteenth century show that it took an average of forty-three days to reach the Holy Land, ninety-three to return. Working one's way up from Athens to the grain supplies of the Black Sea through the swift southward current of the Bosporus at its mouth would take so long that only a single passage a year was possible. In Apollonius Rhodius' reworking of the legend of Jason and the Argonauts Jason and his men have to resort to rowing up through the Bosporus to reach the Black Sea along 'the narrow strait of the winding passage, hemmed in on both sides by rugged cliffs, while an eddying current from below was washing against the ship as she moved on'. There were other difficult passages. The crossing between the Ionian sea and Sicily was always challenging as even in midsummer it could be disrupted by unfavourable winds. The meeting place between the Adriatic and the Ionian Sea was particularly tricky. In the western

Mediterranean the Straits of Gibraltar became impassable when the winds were from the west and ships often had to wait for up to two months for them to change. With lighter cargoes it was often quicker to bypass the Straits by taking them by land.

The winds are more troublesome than the currents, which in a land-locked sea such as the Mediterranean are relatively light outside narrow passes such as the Straits of Gibraltar and the Bosporus. The water which runs in from the Straits of Gibraltar (there is a continual current entering the Mediterranean here as it is the only way in which water lost by evaporation can be replenished) tends to flow along the northern coast of Africa and then turn upwards along the coast of Palestine and round Asia Minor. It then turns westwards and the current from the Black Sea meets with it and the two combine to make a current which runs back along the northern shores of the Mediterranean, past Dalmatia, Italy, and on to Spain. This anticlockwise movement is, of course a major oversimplification as there are eddies and small counter-currents around the islands.

The heavier the cargo—if one wants to see how heavy observe the monumental granite columns, 40 feet high, on the façade of the Pantheon in Rome which were transported all the way from Aswan in Egypt (and it seems that even larger ones were planned for)—the more important it was to use currents rather than fight against them and it was the merchant ships, particularly those laden with metal or marble, which needed to exploit their support. So that if one traces, from archaeological finds on land and shipwrecks, the routes of metal-bearing ships of the Late Bronze Age, they run from Cyprus to Asia Minor then across the Ionian Sea to Sicily and finally along the Spanish coast. Ships setting out westwards from north Africa towards the Straits of Gibraltar would find it easier to cross northwards to the Spanish coast and then hug it on their journey west. Those heading east towards Sicily kept along the north African coast, then headed northwards to the coast of Sardinia from where they could approach Sicily from the west. While one would imagine, from looking at a map, that the port of Carthage on the north African coast would be a port of call for Phoenician ships heading west, it was the opposite. They would only approach it when coming back from the west and this may be one reason why it was able to establish its independence from the home cities of Phoenicia (see pp. 383–4). Some of the most important ports, such as the island of Ibiza off the Spanish coast and the port of Motya on the coast of Sicily, prospered because they were where routes crossed.

The sea defines the land. Strabo (writing in the first century BC and the most important source of ancient geography) suggests that 'most of all it is the sea that delineates precisely the layout of the land, creating gulfs, and sea basins, traversable narrows, and, in the same way, isthmuses, peninsulas and capes, in this the rivers and mountains also play their part.' The rugged coastline means that although the Mediterranean is about 3,800 kilometres from east to west, there are some 22,000 kilometres of shoreline. About a thousand harbours have been plotted along the coast, an average of some 30 to 40 kilometres apart. One can find early (medieval) maps which bristle with their names. If relationships between cultures are peaceful and pirates have been subdued a boat can journey from one port to another within a day. The word port can mean anything from a major centre such as Alexandria to a beach of the kind described by Herodotus where Carthaginian traders would lay out their cargo and then see whether the natives would offer enough gold for it but essentially there was ample opportunity to stop off to rest, take in fresh water, and trade. Then there were the rivers which allowed trade networks to penetrate inland so that one finds major cities growing up at the point either where a river becomes fordable or where navigation ends. Even in Roman times, it was water transport which defined routes of communication.

Three major peninsulas run down into the Mediterranean, the Iberian (modern Spain and Portugal), the Italian, and the Greek, which is extended outwards into the Aegean through a pattern of islands. So this is also a fragmented sea. All three peninsulas are dominated by mountains. Mountains make up three-quarters of the land surface of Greece and there are relatively few areas of fertile lowland—the plain of Thessaly is the largest. In the Peloponnese in the 1930s only a sixth of the land was being cultivated. Italy can be seen as a long ridge (the Appenines) broken in the north by the Po valley, the most fertile area of the peninsula. In Spain there is a strong contrast between the fertile plains of the coasts and the mountainous interior. Mountains have proved important in that they limit the area for cultivation, fragment communities, and provide a further incentive to travel by sea. They also define agriculture in another way. When rain does fall, and in the Mediterranean this is normally in the winter rather than summer months, it tends to cascade downwards destroying top soil. In response the farmer has to terrace soil so that it is not lost. It is not only that rainfall varies by season, there are quite dramatic variations year by year. To take one modern example, in the 1960s the annual rainfall in Kavala, the ancient Neapolis on the northern Aegean, varied between 252 and 897 millimetres, and research suggests the climate was little different in classical times. This means that a 'good' year might produce far more than is needed while a 'bad' year far less. It was coping with this variability which was important and as it could not be planned for every year had to be focused on overproduction. Successful farming always needed ingenuity and this is being increasingly recognized as a result of field surveys. The famous Mediterranean trio of crops, vines, olives, and grain, were grown together in an attempt to maximize return. The best combinations for each ecological niche, whether plain, valley, or grazing land, evolved through trial and error. Being hardier and more dependable, barley was a more popular, if less nutritious, crop to grow than wheat which was the preferred grain of the elite. If a landowner was lucky and accumulated more land, it made more sense to choose a plot with a different ecological make-up so that the chances of some crop coming up somewhere were increased. So one finds wealthier farmers moving from one plot to another often quite long distances. A single large estate was an extravagance (or alternatively a status symbol).

The ingenuity needed to survive in such a climate extended to the selling of surplus if there was any. There was no advantage in having a good year and then wasting the extra produce. In that sense every crop was potentially a cash crop, although the ease with which it could be sold depended on the wider political and economic setting. One study of the southern Argolid (in the Peloponnese) from the eighth century BC shows how the local population had concentrated on providing grain with which to feed themselves. As population grew the only way they could expand production was through more intense fertilization and the cultivation of hitherto marginal land. In the fourth century, however, there were major disruptions in the Greek world—in Athens, for instance, much of the olive crop seems to have been destroyed. The Argolid was relatively well protected and the farmers responded by increasing their own olive production at the expense of grain. As new settlements on the coast show they had become orientated towards the outside world. By the third century there is evidence of increased piracy as the struggle between the successors to Alexander's empire disrupted the eastern Mediterranean. With the loss of security, the olive trade of the Argolid goes into decline and its farmers return to grain farming. (See T. van Andel and C. Runnels, *Beyond the Acropolis: A Rural Greek Past* (Stanford, 1987).)

In Roman times the pull of demand for grain, wine, wool, and leather was more sustained and much larger, particularly because of the needs of the army. The legions not only ensured the security within which settled agriculture could be maintained over decades, they provided the demand for its products and, more than this, the labour, through captured slaves, to meet it. The Mediterranean economy became something very different from that known by the Greeks where no one city was able to exercise stable control over the sea or land. So it is not surprising that many parts of Italy developed medium or larger estates, the so-called villa economy, in which the landowner was able to flaunt his growing wealth through display. By the fourth century this had also become the economic pattern in many of the provinces and with the stability of the empire these are able to draw on a wide range of products from fish paste to works of art from what was genuinely a Mediterranean-wide economy.

Braudel's famous work was focused on the sixteenth century. Recently Peregrine Horden and Nicholas Purcell in their *The Corrupting Sea: A Study of Mediterranean History* (the first of a promised two volumes, Oxford, 2000) have concentrated on the ancient and medieval period. It is a complex but important book which emphasizes the necessity of seeing the Mediterranean as a series of microregions each exploiting its own ecological niche. The authors stress the range of these, not only arable and grazing land, but woodland and wetland. Wetlands have been largely neglected in studies of Mediterranean agriculture but as Horden and Purcell show they provide a welcome variety of plant and animal life, more permanent and dependable sources of water than rainfall, and the water can be directed through channels as a means of communication. It is this diversity of microeconomies—which demand a wide range of skills if they are to be exploited to the full—which underpins Horden and Purcell's stress on the ingenuity and adaptability of the Mediterranean peasant. It was not only his skills within the microeconomy which were important. Each region was connected to the wider whole and an ever-changing set of relationships were in play.

The Roman empire was to extend far beyond the bounds of the Mediterranean. It was not only to include the lands occupied by the civilizations described in the last chapter but it was to expand into the more temperate climate of western Europe. The notion of the Mediterranean as the civilized world and those living beyond it as barbarians persisted. Even as late as the early third century AD when the empire had centuries of contact with northern Europe the historian Cassius Dio is able to able to write of Pannonia, a region he himself had visited:

The Pannonians dwell near Dalmatia along the bank of the Danube from Noricum to Moesia, and live of all men the most wretchedly. Both their soil and climate are poor; they cultivate no olives and produce no wine except to a very slight extent and of a very poor quality, since the climate is mostly extremely harsh. . . . For having nothing to make a civilized life worthwhile, they are extremely fierce and bloodthirsty.

The Roman and Greek view of the 'Celts' was similar (one factor to be borne in mind when discussing them, p. 355 below). In his *Facing the Ocean: The Atlantic and its Peoples* (Oxford, 2001) Barry Cunliffe turns this picture of barbarism on its head by stressing the importance of the long Atlantic sea channel which runs from the coast of west Africa up through the British Isles to Greenland with many rivers running into it. 'It is like a broad corridor with many doors opening into it along which people, carrying with them beliefs, knowledge, and commodities, have constantly scurried over ten thousand years.' These are not people without a history, nor without sophisticated survival skills honed in the harsh Atlantic environment. Inevitably links with the Mediterranean, by sea through the Straits of Gibraltar and overland, developed which ultimately were to lead to the incorporation of the 'Celts' into the Roman empire. It was now that the Germans were burdened with taking on the role of barbarians. Just how misguided the Romans were in denigrating those peoples living beyond the Mediterranean was shown in the third and fourth centuries when it was a series of tough Balkan generals and their men who saved the empire.

The story of the Mediterranean economy is one in which there was a continual interplay between forces of stability and those of instability. At no point did its peoples ever achieve any technological or economic breakthrough which transformed production of either food or goods and throughout the period covered by this book the parameters within which life had to be lived remained constant. It could be argued that it was the natural ingenuity of its peoples in attempting to improve the stability of the environment at the expense of forces pushing the other way which is the motivating power that lies behind many of the cultures described in the rest of this book.

FURTHER READING

Fernand Braudel, *The Mediterranean and the Mediterranean World in the Age of Philip II* (2nd edition, London, 1972), and Horden and Purcell, cited above, are fundamental. Neal Ascherson, *Black Sea: The Birthplace of Civilization and Barbarism* (London, 1995), is excellent. François Hartog, *Memories of Odysseus* (Edinburgh, 2001), deals with the 'psychology' of the Mediterranean. Moses Finley's thesis of the limited nature of the Roman economy is to be found in his *The Ancient Economy* (Berkeley, 1985). See further P. Garnsey and others (eds.), *Trade in the Ancient Economy* (Berkeley, 1985); H. Parkins and C. Smith (eds.), *Trade, Traders and the Ancient City* (London, 1998); and D. J. Mattingly and J. Salmon (eds.), *Economies Beyond Agriculture in the Classical World* (London, 2001). A useful survey of the economy of the Roman empire is to be found in P. Garnsey and R. Saller, *The Roman Empire, Economy, Society and Culture* (London, 1997). See also Peter Garnsey, *Food and Society in Classical Antiquity* (Cambridge, 1999).

8 | The Early Greeks, 2000–700 BC

The Minoans

The island of Crete occupies a central position in the eastern Mediterranean. It is accessible from Egypt, the Near East, mainland Greece, and from the west. The island is fertile and well wooded and towards the end of the third millennium was able to sustain several urban settlements. In some of these, about 2000 BC, large 'palace' complexes appeared. The 'palaces', which have large central courtyards and a series of public rooms, acted as centres for the storage of surplus grain, wine, oil, and other produce. Whoever controlled the 'palaces' recorded the goods stored on clay tablets, first in a hieroglyphic script and later in the island's own syllabic writing, known to scholars as Linear A.

The monumental architecture of the palaces and their system of bureaucratic administration are reminiscent of Egypt and the Near East. Yet, even though there may have been some influence from the east, this was no culture imposed from the outside. It depended for its survival on the well-organized exploitation of the local countryside, something which could only have evolved over a long period of time. It is known as Minoan, after a king, Minos, reputedly the son of Zeus, who, according to later legends, was given Crete to rule. These legends must reflect memories of the Cretan past which passed down the centuries to later Greeks.

Minoan civilization was rediscovered when an English archaeologist, Arthur Evans, intrigued by carved seal-stones from the area, began digging at the site of Knossos in 1900. It was here that he discovered the grandest Minoan palace of all and evidence of a sophisticated civilization whose craftsmanship was as fine as any in the eastern Mediterranean. Excavators from France and Italy working on other sites, among them Mallia and Phaistos, soon showed that it was a civilization which extended across the island. 'The recent discoveries in Crete have added a new horizon to European civilization,' exulted Evans, 'a new standpoint has been at the same time obtained for surveying not only the Ancient Classical World of Greece and Rome, but the modern world in which we live.'

Who lived in the palaces is unknown. Evans claimed that they were seats of royalty, assuming that the Minoans had kings, as later legends suggested. However, it is only later that there is any record of Minoan leaders (in the Linear B tablets, see below) and it has been argued that early Minoan society was not heavily centralized and even that the 'palaces' were, in fact, religious centres. The earliest burials suggest society was organized around clans or extended families, and excavations in towns surrounding the palaces have shown that there were large independent households in control of their own stores. Even so, there must have been an administrative elite, and the efficiency with which the palace economies were organized does suggest a controlling leader. Surplus produce was carefully recorded and stored, apparently to exchange for goods from overseas, in particular metals and stone. On seals are found designs of ships with sails (not galleys as in other earlier civilizations) and this suggests extensive sea trade.

Some evidence for this trade in the Aegean has recently been uncovered on the island of Thera (modern Santorini). At Acrotiri there was a flourishing commercial town with between 8,000 and 12,000 inhabitants. In the seventeenth century BC it seems to have undergone a catastrophe as earthquakes and a subsequent volcanic eruption destroyed the town and then covered it in ash. (See p. 9 above for the dating problems involved.) Acrotiri appears to have been independent of Crete with pottery in local rather than Minoan styles. However, the walls of the houses, some of which still stand to two or three storeys high with internal floors intact, are covered in frescos and there is certainly Minoan influence here, with lively scenes of animals and flowers. The most famous of the frescos, the 'Ship Fresco', shows the first ever recorded town scenes. Settlements run alongside a shoreline with boats, dolphins, and humans in the sea beyond and crowds assembled on the shore. It is assumed that the houses are those of merchants and the 'Ship Fresco' a record of their overseas contacts. Yet the number of imports from Crete remains small and there is no evidence of Minoan control.

Someone in Crete was also patronizing skilled craftsmen. One style of pottery of this early period (the so-called Old Palace Period, 2000–1600 BC), Kamares ware, is among the best ever found in Greece. It is eggshell-thin and covered with flowing abstract designs in white, red, and orange. Seals of jasper or rock crystal are engraved with portrayals of animals, birds, and insects. At Mallia a hoard of exquisite gold objects was discovered by looters in a cemetery. Most eventually reappeared in the British Museum, although a beautiful pendant of two bees facing each other over a honey cake was found later by excavators on the site.

About 1600 BC these early palaces were destroyed. It is assumed that an earthquake was the cause, although the causes and dates of these and later destructions of Cretan palaces are still hotly disputed. The palaces were quickly rebuilt on an even more magnificent scale than before, a clear sign of the underlying prosperity and stability of Minoan society. Again the palaces centre on a courtyard, but the public rooms on a first-floor level are magnificent, reached by grand stairways. The best of these at Knossos, which it has been possible to reconstruct, leads up to a set of 'royal apartments'. The palaces are now well constructed with timber posts inserted to give them flexibility against earthquakes.

On the walls of the palaces, particularly at Knossos, are fine frescos. Some show processions, others women, bare-breasted with flowing hair, others scenes of natural life with an abundance of flowers and animals. The most famous are the scenes of bull leaping—men and women leaping over the horns of charging bulls. (This is certainly some kind of cult activity, and later Greeks recorded the legend of the Minotaur, half bull and half man, supposedly the offspring of a liaison between Minos' wife Pasiphae and a bull, which was kept in a labyrinth below the royal palace.)

This New Palace Period (1600–1425 BC) was prosperous and well ordered. There are extensive towns with, at one site, Gournia, houses facing winding cobbled streets. Again, some houses are more substantial, suggesting they are the homes of palace officials, while in the countryside villas appear. Many are working farms, but others may have been the countryside retreats of the elite. The palaces sustained fine craftsmanship, beautifully worked stone vessels, delicate carved seal-stones, and work in gold. The celebrated Harvester Vase, carved in hard stone, shows a group of robust farmers marching out to sow their land, their movement and comradeship beautifully captured by the carver. The famous gold cups found at Vaphio in the Peloponnese, but almost certainly from Crete, show bulls being taken into captivity, in one case by brute force, in another through the lure of a female.

An atmosphere of ritual and worship pervades Minoan society but it is difficult to make much sense of it. There is a wide range of religious sites, rooms in the palaces set aside for cult worship, sacred caves, and shrines on mountain peaks. Worship, in the form of sacrifices and votive offerings, seems to have been directed at a variety of goddesses. The double axe (which originates in Mesopotamia) is a particularly potent symbol, and at Knossos snakes and bulls have some form of ritual significance. The so-called Poppy goddess (with three incised poppy seeds on her head) found at a small rural shrine suggests that opium was used to induce religious ecstasy. A darker side of Minoan ritual has emerged in recent years. In a house in Knossos a mass of children's bones have been found and it appears that the children had been sacrificed. Shortly before, at the mountain shrine of Anemospelia, a 'temple' was uncovered in which was found the body of a youth, bound, on an altar, with a bronze dagger beside him. The temple was preserved because an earthquake had brought it crashing down. Was he being sacrificed in a vain attempt to ward off the catastrophe?

The Minoans were by now trading throughout the Cyclades (the islands of the southern Aegean) and Near East. The stone they used came from Egypt, the Peloponnese, and the Aegean island of Melos. Copper, made into large ingots, came from the Laurium mines in Attica (later to be more famous as the source of Athens' silver). In Egypt there are tomb paintings of Cretans bringing cloth as tribute, while Minoan pottery is found not only in Egypt but also along the Syro-Palestine coast. In some cases the Minoan presence is more substantial.

A dramatic recent discovery of frescos of bulls and bull leapers at Tell el-Dab'a (ancient Avaris) on the Nile Delta may be evidence of a community of Minoan merchants there about 1550 BC or even, some have suggested, a marriage between a Cretan 'princess' and a pharaoh (see above, p. 62). There are three walled city sites in the Aegean—Phylakopi on Melos, Agia Eirene on Kea, and Kolonna on Aegina—where the architecture is reminiscent of that of Cretan towns, Linear A is used, and there are frescos similar to those of Crete. It is probably stretching the evidence too far to talk of a Minoan empire, as local cultures continued to flourish, but certainly the Minoan presence and influence in the southern Aegean appears to have been substantial.

Minoan society has had its enthusiastic admirers. The colourful frescos, the apparent joy and sophistication of the people, the sense of a peaceful and ordered society which revelled in the beauties of nature, have been combined to create an image of an idyllic world. In her book *The Dawn of the Gods* (London, 1968) the archaeologist Jacquetta Hawkes argued that Minoan Crete was essentially a feminine society, in contrast to those more masculine cultures of the north. There was something of a shock in 1981 when the Anemospelia sacrifice was found and a darker side of Minoan life emerged. There is some evidence too that war played a far larger part in Minoan life than was once thought. The 'carefree' Minoans may turn out to be no more than a fantasy created in the twentieth century.

The Mycenaeans

In about 1425 BC there was another wave of destruction of the Cretan palaces. Only Knossos survived intact. The rest were devastated by fire and abandoned for some time. When occupation was resumed a new culture had emerged. Its chamber tombs, those at Sellopoulo near Knossos, for instance, were similar to those of the mainland, and it was using a new script, Linear B, which borrows many of the signs from Linear A but is in a different language. What had gone on is still disputed. The palaces may have been destroyed by earthquakes followed by fires or as a result of conflict between rival centres. At some point invaders entered the island, either as conquerors or appropriators of the ruined palaces. Knossos was probably used as a base by the newcomers but was to be itself destroyed at a later date, sometime between 1400 and 1200. The invaders were the Mycenaeans, the first known civilization of mainland Greece.

In 1876 a German merchant turned archaeologist, Heinrich Schliemann, digging inside the massive stone walls of the citadel of Mycenae in the Greek Peloponnese, had uncovered a circle of stone slabs within which were six shaft graves. The graves, deep rectangular pits some of which contained several burials, were filled with an array of rich grave goods, including gold cups and face masks and a mass of weapons. Schliemann, who had immersed himself in the epics of Homer with their tales of the great Trojan War, was convinced that Mycenae was the capital of those Greeks who had sailed off to Troy and that he had found no less than the grave and funeral mask of Agamemnon, their leader.

In fact the graves were much earlier than any conceivable date for the Trojan War. They and an earlier, less rich, set of shaft graves, dated from perhaps as early as 1650 and had been used and reused until about 1500 BC. At first they seemed so distinct culturally from what had gone before that it was assumed that they were the work of newcomers to Greece. However, there are earlier stone tombs which are structurally similar to the chambers of the shaft graves, while recent work on the pottery associated with the tombs has shown that it is a direct continuation of earlier styles. There is now no doubt that Mycenaean civilization developed directly from what had gone before. What is hard to explain is why this opulence developed so suddenly and unexpectedly in an area which had no port and no great agricultural resources.

At some point local chieftains at Mycenae, and other similar sites elsewhere in the Peloponnese, appear to have begun exploiting their land more effectively so that a surplus of the enduring local staples of the Greek mainland, olive oil, wine, wool, flax, and hides, could be squeezed out and then used for exchange in overseas trade. The Mycenaeans were after metals and luxury goods, copper and tin for bronze weapons, gold and silver for the finer metalwork, amber from northern Europe, lapis lazuli and dyes from the east. These were all goods needed to meet the demands of a warrior elite, demands they were prepared to satisfy by force. Weapons found in the shaft graves include short swords suitable for thrusting and cutting in close combat which show signs of having been used in battle.

In short, Mycenaean civilization was outward-looking and often aggressive. Culturally it was much less sophisticated than that of the Minoans, but from the fifteenth century onwards it spread throughout the eastern Mediterranean. It may have been now that Crete was overrun and its culture absorbed. (Eventually it becomes impossible to distinguish between Mycenaean and Minoan craftsmanship.) A Mycenaean presence has been found throughout the Cyclades and a Mycenaean settlement with its own defensive walls has been found on the Asian mainland at Miletus. Trading routes, plotted through finds of Mycenaean pottery, ran as far west as Sardinia, Italy, and Malta and as far east as the Levantine coast and Egypt. Twenty sites in Egypt, some far up the Nile, have produced Mycenaean pottery, and it has recently been suggested that figures of warriors on a papyrus from Tell el-Amarna might represent Mycenaean mercenaries.

By the fourteenth century the Mycenaeans had become fine craftsmen, particularly in bronze and ivory but also in gold and silver. They were also accomplished builders. From the fifteenth century rulers were buried in monumental 'tholos' tombs, vaults in the shape of a beehive constructed in the sides of a hill and approached by long passageways cut through the hillside. Later in their history Mycenaean settlements were protected by massive walls of unworked limestone extracted in rough blocks from local sources and levered into place. These walls were far more imposing than was needed for defence and suggest chieftains determined to impress their subjects or neighbours. In Mycenae the citadel is entered through the celebrated Lion Gate, in which two lions flanking a column perch upon a massive lintel.

The Mycenaeans must have been aware, even before they came directly into contact with Crete, of the existence of Linear A script. By about 1400 they were writing their own language in a similar syllabic script, known to scholars as Linear B. What this language was remained unclear for many years. Most scholars believed it to be pre-Greek. In 1952, in one of the more important archaeological achievements of the century, a young architect, Michael Ventris, who had had an enthusiasm for languages and cryptography since he was a boy, made a stunning proposal. He had deciphered the values of several syllables and had recreated words which appeared close to those of the earliest surviving Greek texts, those of Homer's epics. Among them were 'shepherd', 'bronzesmith', and 'goldsmith'. Not everyone was convinced, but the next year a new batch of Linear B tablets emerged from the Mycenaean palace site of Pylos in the south-west Peloponnese. One of them was a list of furniture. Beside a vessel with three supports were Linear B syllables reading, according to Ventris' theory, TI-RI-PO. Earlier in the text two similar vessels had an adjoining text reading TI-RI-PO-DE. The Homeric Greek for a single tripod and a pair of tripods corresponded exactly. By now there were very few doubters (although one set of diehards confronted by a new batch of tablets from Pylos which confirmed Ventris' decipherment claimed that they had been deliberately forged!).

Scholars were enthusiastic to find that Greek had been spoken so early, 500 years before the first Homeric text. How much earlier still remains a matter for debate. Greek is one of the family of Indo-European languages which appear to have originated from a common source in the area north of the Black Sea and travelled from there westwards into Europe. A conventional view is that Greek entered Greece with invaders from the east about 2000 BC and gradually became dominant over local languages, traces of which remained in words to describe local features such as towns, mountains, trees, and plants. In 1987 the Cambridge archaeologist Colin Renfrew put forward a bold alternative. He argued that the arrival of Indo-European languages was associated with the first use of farming terms at the time of the Neolithic Revolution, perhaps as early as 6000 BC for Greece. His theory has so far failed to gain widespread acceptance by language scholars though some archaeologists are more sympathetic. There is some archaeological evidence for new populations, possibly from Anatolia and the Near East, moving into the Balkans and Greece around this date and it is conceivable that they brought Indo-European languages with them.

As the Linear B tablets, particularly those of the large batch from Pylos, were deciphered, new evidence for the antiquity of Greek religion appeared. Zeus was already known to have roots deep in Indo-European cultures, but there were now the first mentions of other Greek gods and goddesses—Aphrodite, Athena, Ares, the god of war, Apollo, and Poseidon. At Pylos itself the tablets suggest that Poseidon was the presiding god, and it is particularly fascinating to find Homer, several centuries later, talking of the townsmen of Pylos offering sacrifices of black bulls to him. It is worth mentioning, however, that perhaps half of the gods mentioned in the Linear B tablets do not survive into later times.

The evidence of the tablets has been supplemented in the past few years by that of archaeology. For the first time remains of free-standing temples have been found in Crete, the islands, and on the mainland. There is evidence of cult figures, possibly of Levantine origin, placed inside them. In a few cases worship at a Minoan or Mycenaean site appears to have continued through into classical times and beyond. The mountain shrine of Kato Syme in Crete continued in operation into Greek times, while the great cave to Zeus on Mount Ida, again in Crete, has cult objects from the late Minoan period and also a mass of Greek and Roman finds suggesting centuries of continuous worship. On mainland Greece the shrine at Calapodi in Phocis is another where worship appears to have been uninterrupted. Worshippers did not necessarily continue to believe the same thing or follow the same rituals simply because they worshipped in the same place, but it may be possible to track some elements of later Greek religious belief and practice back into Mycenaean times.

Independent palaces and citadels, Mycenae, Tiryns, Athens, and Pylos among them, lorded it over their local territory. (Schliemann was wrong to see Mycenae as a capital of Greece, although it may have been first among equals.) The rulers of each centre controlled trade and industrial production through an impressive bureaucracy. At Pylos there are records of the issue of bronze to the local smiths and the supervision of huge flocks of sheep. The centres certainly had trading links with each other, and Homer's description of Agamemnon as leader of a band of hero chieftains each with his own followers may have its origins in the experience of joint Mycenaean raids outside Greece.

In the thirteenth century the fortifications of the Mycenaean centres became more massive. Even Pylos, where the palace has a domestic atmosphere very different from that of the typical Mycenaean stronghold, was rebuilt to make it more defensible. A defensive wall was built across the isthmus of Corinth, probably as a protection against invasion from the north. The evidence suggests that this was a time of rising tension probably affecting the Mediterranean area as a whole. The palace of Pylos, the only Mycenaean palace without strong fortifications, came under attack about 1200. (Some scholars are now suggesting an earlier date.) The Linear B tablets, preserved by the heat of the fire which burned the palace, record hurried preparations for defence with, according to one interpretation, watchers sent to the coasts, bronze gathered in from the temples, and levies of gold. There are even hints that human sacrifices were carried out to appease the gods. It was of little use. The palace was destroyed.

It has proved impossible to disentangle the sequence of events between 1200 and 1100. The destruction of cities did not take place simultaneously. Some centres such as Athens remained largely unscathed, others were destroyed, then reoccupied, then destroyed again. It has been argued that there was a Mycenaean revival in the mid-twelfth century which was then snuffed out by further onslaughts. In some cases refugees carried their culture to other sites (such as Lefkandi on the island of Euboea and, possibly, recent excavations suggest, to the Chalcidice peninsula) and preserved it intact. However, Mycenaean civilization had depended on a combination of strong and ordered leadership and administrative efficiency. By 1100 BC this had gone. With it disappeared literacy, fresco painting, stone building, and craftwork in gold and silver.

The causes of the collapse of Mycenaean civilization have been hotly debated. The traditional view that it was the result of the marauding 'Sea Peoples' now appears to be simplistic in that the 'Sea Peoples' may themselves have been casualties of the breakdown rather than its instigators. There is increasing support for the idea that the economies of the Mycenaean centres became simply too complex, unable to sustain their prosperity as their populations rose. As resources became scarce, the Mycenaeans may have turned on each other, leading to a massive 'systems collapse', a civil war which all ultimately lost. The collapse may have been hastened by actual invasions from the sea but these may have been by those whose own cities had been destroyed. There is also a legend, preserved by the later Greeks, that Mycenaean civilization had been destroyed by invaders from the north-west, the Dorians. There is little archaeological evidence to support this invasion, though recently some archaeologists (Hector Catling, in particular) have suggested that handmade burnished pottery found on several twelfth-century sites, the so-called 'Barbarian Ware', may be that of incomers from the north. In short, there is continuing controversy over whether the reduced and impoverished communities of the twelfth and eleventh centuries were newcomers or the old populations adapting to new circumstances, although scholarship tends, in the present state of archaeological evidence, towards the latter view.

The collapse of Mycenaean civilization was followed by what scholars have traditionally called a Dark Age, from 1100 BC until the emergence of a new Greek world after 800. As with many other Dark Ages, however, the Greek Dark Age has proved vulnerable to the work of archaeologists, who are gradually finding evidence that life was, perhaps, not quite so gloomy as was once assumed. Without doubt, however, the unity of the Mycenaean world had been shattered. What did remain among the dispersed populations of the old Mycenaean centres and in the depopulated countryside was life carried on according to old traditions but at a much lower level. Contacts with the outside world were broken. One of the most important developments was the emergence of weapons in iron rather than bronze. This may have been because the sources of tin were cut off or because the collapse of trading networks saw the end of those ruling elites who had controlled trade in tin. (Copper, the other ingredient in bronze, remained available to the Greeks from Cyprus.) If trade in tin had broken down, then it would have been comparatively easy for the Greeks to have found iron ore in Greece itself and smelted it to create what proved to be a tougher and more versatile metal than bronze. Iron eventually replaced bronze for weapons and everyday implements as it had already done further east (the earliest iron technology is to be found in Anatolia and then developed in the twelfth and eleventh centuries in northern Syria).

The Migrations

The collapse of Mycenaean civilization did not mean that there was no movement of peoples across Greece and the Aegean. There are legends of widespread migrations of Greeks from the mainland eastwards, and maps of the different but mutually intelligible Greek dialects spoken in a later age help to reconstruct what may have happened. In remote areas, the mountains of Arcadia and Cyprus, the dialect known to scholars as Arcado-Cypriot appears to be the survival of Mycenaean Greek. In Cyprus the dialect must have been brought there by refugees of the turmoil of the twelfth century. In the Peloponnese generally, the old centre of the Mycenaean world, the Doric dialect is supreme. The legends that the Dorians came from the north to overthrow the citadels of Mycenaean Greece were deep-rooted in later Greek mythology, and the sense that the Dorians were different lingered for centuries. As has been seen, there is, however, little archaeological evidence to explain their appearance and their origins in the Peloponnese remain obscure. The Doric dialect is later found in Crete and across the southern Aegean from there as far as Rhodes and the south-western tip of Asia Minor.

Another distinct dialect is the Ionic. It appears first north-east of the Peloponnese in Attica and the adjoining island of Euboea. The Athenians' own tradition was that the area remained largely unscathed by the chaos of the twelfth century, but, even if there is no sign of widespread destruction, there is archaeological evidence of cultural change, in burial customs and styles of pottery, and iron makes its appearance. It is assumed that Mycenaean civilization collapsed here as elsewhere. In the tenth century there appears to have been a migration of Ionic speakers to Asia Minor, where they colonized the central part of the coast, a region later known as Ionia. From the plains of Boeotia and Thessaly another dialect, Aeolic, appears to have spread to the northern coastline of Asia Minor.

The end result of these migrations was an Aegean surrounded by Greek settlements whose relationships with each other must have been maintained by the criss-crossing of the sea by traders, craftsmen, and wandering poets.

The conventional view of the Dark Ages as totally stagnant has also been challenged in recent years by finds at Lefkandi, a Greek settlement which flourished on the coast of Euboea overlooking the Greek mainland. It is an ancient site with remains going back to 2000 BC. For a brief period in the twelfth century it was deserted, but by 1100 BC it seems to have been occupied again, and then continuously until about 825 when the settlement went into decline. Lefkandi's wealth, seen in the gold of its burials, came from trade with the east, with Cyprus and the Phoenicians on the Levantine coast.

One of the most unexpected finds at Lefkandi has been the burial of a 'hero', a local leader, cremated, alongside his wife, who was bedecked in gold. All were enclosed in a large apsidal building which was later covered by a mound. (This is the view of the main excavator, Mervyn Popham, although other archaeologists suggest the burial was dug into a pre-existing building and some even that the building might be later.) The date of burial is between 1000 and 950 BC and is remarkable for providing the skeletons of a team of four horses. Such teams (they are known as *quadrigae* (singular *quadriga*)) were always a status symbol as the horses ran alongside each other but the outer two were always trace horses with no pulling power. In effect they were there to show off the opulence of their owners. The *quadriga* as status symbol persisted throughout classical history. Greek gods, heroes, or aristocrats are portrayed in chariots these normally have four horses. The Greek games, which as we shall see was essentially an aristocratic enterprise, had four horse chariot races and these were transferred, via the Etruscans, to Rome, where they became a major entertainment in the Circus. Victorious Roman generals celebrated their triumphs in Rome in *quadrigae* and emperors presented themselves in the the same way in bronze *quadrigae* on triumphal arches. Only one full-scale team survives, that now on show in St Mark's Basilica, Venice. It probably dates from the second or third century AD.

In the present state of knowledge Lefkandi remains almost unique, perhaps a rare settlement where the earlier age of Mycenaean war chieftains lingered on. It is at least another fifty years before a comparable revival in the wealth of grave goods is found at other major sites, such as Athens, Knossos, and Tiryns. The late tenth century also sees a revival of trade from the east. It is stimulated by the expansion of the Phoenicians, who, as was suggested in Chapter 6, may have needed to trade to accumulate tribute for their Assyrian overlords. From about 850 onwards there is further evidence of Greek traders from the island of Euboea, joining in. By 825 there is permanent Greek influence (whether from a Greek community living there, or from Levantine traders with Greek contacts, is disputed) at the trading port of al-Mina at the mouth of the Orontes river on the northern coast of the Levant. The east provided luxury goods, textiles, carved objects in ivory or cast ones in precious metals, as well as iron ore and other metals. The revival in trade can only be explained by a growth in prosperity in Greece and the Aegean itself as conditions stabilized and a surplus of agricultural wealth once again became available. The Greeks may have shipped slaves, captured from the north, to the east in return for their imported luxuries.

The Eighth-Century 'Renaissance'

In the eighth century there is a much more dramatic transformation. Mainland Greece suddenly goes through a period of rapid social, economic, and cultural change. At one level the change is seen in a large rise of population, recorded in Attica, for instance, by an increase in the number of graves (although, as there are many factors governing the survival of graves, the evidence must be treated with caution, particularly if used to compute actual growth rates). Land which had been uncultivated since the twelfth century was now being reoccupied. With rising prosperity came a revival in metalworking. An increase in shipbuilding reflects renewed and growing links with the outside world. Greek pottery from the ninth century is hardly ever found outside Greece. By the eighth century it is widespread in the Mediterranean. Examples have been found at over eighty sites.

In the early Dark Age there were few resources to sustain fine craftsmanship. Weaving may have been important but all traces of cloth have vanished. Pottery, however, has survived. The finest of the period comes from Athens and the surrounding plains of Attica. In the so-called Protogeometric age, 1050–900 BC, the lingering influence of Mycenaean models disappears as Athenian pots suddenly become grander. The diameter of the typical vase increases and decoration becomes ordered and less makeshift. The neck of the vase is decorated with semicircles drawn with compasses to ensure uniformity. This style spread to some but not to all parts of Greece. In the Geometric age, from around 900, and again initiated by Athens, rectilinear decoration becomes dominant (possibly borrowing from textile designs). The painter becomes obsessed with the ordering of space to such an extent that by the middle of the ninth century many pots are covered with geometrical designs, zigzags, swastikas, and borders in an endless variety of motifs. Again the style spreads to regional workshops, but many areas of the Aegean, including Euboea and the Cyclades, are largely untouched by it. What is almost completely missing, however, is any representation of figures. An exception is, typically, from Lefkandi. Here a centaur from the tenth or ninth century has been found, an astonishingly early representation of the man-horse beast which is so common in later Greek art.

It is only in the mid-eighth century that figures appear again on pottery, and then only in one context, the large funerary pots found in the Dipylon Gate cemetery at Athens. In the works of the so-called Dipylon master, who may have been working as early as 770, figures are crammed in between the decorative motifs. There may be as many as a hundred on a single pot. They appear only in scenes connected with death. There are mourners surrounding a body on a bier or warriors fighting in battles on land or sea. The pots themselves are large, over a metre and a half tall. They are funerary memorials in which aristocratic families are using the only monumental art form locally available to glorify their exploits. Although the work of the Dipylon master is still set within the conventions of the Geometric period (the figures are stylized and arranged symmetrically), a crucial step forward had been taken and the inspiration seems to have been the east where friezes of figures and animals are found in a variety of contexts, including metalwork. One of the great art forms of Greece, the dynamic narrative of real or mythical events on fine pottery, has been born. The Dipylon master remained a pioneer and his approach vanished in about 725. However, human forms reappear on pottery and, this time, remain there from about 700 onwards.

Equally important in this period was the arrival of literacy in Greece. Linear B, used for the first written Greek texts, had been written in syllables. Over eighty different ones were needed. In the eastern Mediterranean in the fifteenth century, on the other hand, alphabets had begun emerging within the Semitic cultures of the Levant (see p. 35). Somewhere in the eighth century a Greek community, possibly that at al-Mina or one in Cyprus, picked up the Phoenician alphabet and sponsored the rebirth of Greek literacy.

Some uses of literacy are obvious, especially for a society which is becoming increasingly mobile: the marking of possessions with a personal name, the recording of commercial transactions, or the listing of goods. For all these needs a consonantal alphabet is sufficient. The range of words used is limited and fluency of speech is not required. However, in a transformation of enormous significance, the Greeks used some of the Phoenician consonants for which they had no use as vowels. It is possible that they thought some of the Phoenician consonants they heard were representations of their vowels and they used these consonants accordingly. This meant that virtually any sound could be represented in writing. The examples of seventh-century writing that survive (over 150 examples have been found in Athens alone) show that very soon writing was being used in a variety of contexts, as a mark of ownership, for public inscriptions, in dedications at shrines (overall the most common use), and as 'captions' on painted pots. At some shrines writing seems to have been added to pieces of pottery offered to the gods, as if it was seen to have some sacred quality in itself. It also seems that writing, when inscribed on a gravestone, for instance, was used as a means of perpetuating the memory of an individual.

One of the very earliest inscriptions in Greek, found on a vase at the Greek trading post at Pithekoussai on the island of Ischia off the west coast of Italy, consists of three lines of verse describing the vase as belonging to Nestor and promising sexual desire to whoever drinks from it. It dates from about 720. Nestor is a Homeric hero, and it is possible that the two great epic poems ascribed to the poet Homer, the *Iliad* and the *Odyssey*, were by this time known to the inscriber. Whether they had been actually written down by this date is unknown although it has been argued by Barry Powell (*Homer and the Origins of the Greek Alphabet* (Cambridge, 1991)) that the alphabet was adopted specifically for this task. (Even if Powell is wrong the Nestor vase does suggest a link between writing and the symposium, the aristocratic drinking parties, where poetry was recited.)

Homer

It is now generally agreed that the *Iliad* and *Odyssey* evolved over many centuries, originally as songs. Wandering around the homesteads and halls of the Greek world were the singers, men of prodigious memories who had mastered the art of communication through verse. Research in the Balkans, notably in the early part of the last century by the American scholar Milman Parry, has shown how formidable the skills of such singers could be and how sophisticated their techniques. One Bosnian Muslim was found to have held in his mind twice as many lines as the *Odyssey* and *Iliad* combined. The singers did not simply rely on memory. Serial recordings of the survivors of this tradition show they have an extraordinary ability to improvise, never repeating the stories in the same way, and continually developing their themes.

The singer may draw on folk memories but his song will also be shaped by his audiences. His living depends on his ability to maintain their interest hour after hour by the firelight, possibly night after night. His instinct will be to sense their needs and improvise accordingly. In a number of different cultures the predominant need has been to hear of the founding heroes of the nation. The *Epic of Gilgamesh* from Sumeria, the *Song of Roland* and other epics set at the time of Charlemagne, the legends of Arthur and his knights belong to the same tradition as the *Iliad* and *Odyssey*. The first written version often emerges hundreds of years after the events it claims to describe, by which time its links with actual historical events have become tenuous. (Research on the *Song of Roland*, first written down about AD 1150, has shown it to be a massive distortion of the eighth-century events it claims to record.)

What Parry demonstrated was how the internal consistency and structure of each song solidified with time. The singer relied heavily on a number of formulas, such as 'swift-footed Achilles', or full lines—'When early-born rosy-fingered dawn appeared'—which fit the metre and can be used again and again, particularly when the singer needs a pause to reflect on the next development in his plot.

What controlled the composition was the need to maintain the rhythm and power of the verse, and the words chosen by the poet to fill gaps between the formulas were those which fitted the metre rather than those which necessarily made good sense. The poet was concerned above all to maintain an emotional impact through the steady, almost ceremonial, intonation of the verse, rather than to tell a coherent story.

As a result, the recitations of the epics must have been events full of emotional charge which it is difficult for a modern audience to re-create. Peter Brook, the British theatre director who has specialized in taking his productions into traditional cultures worldwide, describes a visit of his troupe to remote villages in Iran in 1970. Here the tradition of Ta'azieh still survived. The Ta'azieh are mystery plays which deal with the martyrdom of the early Islamic prophets. The play watched by Brook was led by a musician, and as he began his chant Brook records, 'His emotion was in no way his own. It was as though we heard his father's voice, and his father's father's and so back. He stood there, legs apart, powerfully, totally convinced of his function and he as the incarnation of that figure who for our theatre is always the most elusive one of all, the hero.' As the action developed and the leading character walked off to what the audience already knew would be his death, the watching villagers became drawn in. 'I saw lips trembling, hands and handkerchief stuck in mouths, faces wrought with paroxysms of grief. First the very old men and women, then the children and the young men on bicycles all sobbed freely.' What Brook goes on to call 'the inner echo' has been found when a community identifies totally with its traditions. The same thing may have happened to the listeners of Dark Age Greece.

As an epic reaches coherence, possibly after centuries of fluid development, there may be a moment when it becomes part of the cultural heritage of the community, and then there is a strong impulse to preserve it in a more stable form for future generations. At some point a final author, 'Homer', put the *Iliad* and *Odyssey* into a coherent form, adding connecting passages and improving overall consistency. Who Homer was is still unknown and probably will remain so: it is not even certain that the same person brought both epics to their final form. Tradition made him a native of the island of Chios or the nearby coastal town of Smyrna, but more recently it has been suggested that the Ionic dialect which predominates in the final version of the poems is the native one of western Ionia, possibly the island of Euboea, rather than of the settlements of the eastern Aegean. Embedded in the verse are words and formulas some scholars date back to Mycenaean times and, as has already been suggested in Chapter 2, there are possibly even links to the epics of the Near East.

Why was there a desire to record the *Iliad* and *Odyssey* in writing? The singers moved in the world of the aristocratic chieftain and his retinue, a world described in the *Odyssey* itself where Odysseus seeks hospitality in the hall of the king of the Phaeacians. It is possible that aristocrats, feeling their own traditions under threat in the fast-changing world of the eighth century, were the prime movers in guarding their heritage through writing it down. The development of vowels made the whole process much easier.

The *Iliad* and *Odyssey* have very different themes but they are episodes of a common story, an expedition by Greeks (Achaeans, Homer calls them) overseas to the city of Troy in pursuit of the beautiful Helen, wife of Menelaus, king of Sparta, who has been carried off by Paris, a son of King Priam of Troy. It takes ten years of battle, siege, and cunning before Troy falls, leaving the surviving Greek heroes free at last to make their way homewards to their long-missed wives and families.

Tradition sets the Trojan War in Mycenaean times, long before the eighth or seventh centuries when the poems were first written down. Such an expedition by a group of Mycenaean chieftains and their men to the coast of Asia Minor ties in well with the aggressive nature of Mycenaean expansion. Troy was a prosperous settlement on the coast just south of the entrance to the Black Sea, access to which it may have controlled, and it was certainly a potential target for greedy Greek warriors. There is even evidence of destructions of the city at the time of greatest Mycenaean expansion in the fifteenth century and later in the twelfth.

However, there is no evidence to link the Mycenaeans with these destructions (one of which was almost certainly due to an earthquake). It is more likely that the core of the epics preserves more general memories of the Mycenaean age when men fought far from home and raids and sieges were part of everyday life. It is also important to remember that material may have been added very much later than Mycenaean times. The Lelantine war between rival Greek cities of Euboea split the Greek world in the later part of the eighth century (see p. 156) and the experience, possibly fresh in the mind of Homer and his audiences, could well have been woven in with the earlier folk memories.

The world Homer portrays in the *Iliad* is one of violence, often presented in a horrifying form. The bulk of the poem is taken up with the continuous ebb and flow of battle between Greeks and Trojans before the walls of Troy. The epic begins with the anger of Achilles, one of the Greek hero warriors. He has been forced by the leader of the Greeks, Agamemnon, to surrender a girl won as a prize. The real question is honour. The proud Achilles feels humiliated by the way he has been ordered about by a man whose authority he regards as less than supreme. He refuses to fight, even wishing destruction on his own side. Eventually, as the Trojans, under their great war leader Hector, son of Priam, drive back the Greeks to their ships, Achilles relents so far as to lend his war armour to his companion Patroclus. Patroclus is killed and this finally impels Achilles to revenge. In war Achilles is a machine who moves forward slashing and stabbing without mercy. He kills Hector and drags him off behind his chariot. As he broods on his victory, however, he is disturbed in the night by old King Priam, coming alone to ransom his dead son. For Achilles the myth that violence and killing leads to glory is broken as he sits with the old man and at last understands the pity of war. He has already been told that he himself will soon die, and Priam's presence makes him realize the effect his death will have on his own age-ing father.

In the *Odyssey*, the war has been won and Odysseus, one of the Greek war leaders, makes for his homeland, Ithaca. The poem opens with his faithful wife Penelope in their palace at Ithaca besieged by boorish suitors who hope to make her their wife. She is still hoping against hope that Odysseus has survived Troy. Unknown to her, Odysseus is alive but has been entrapped by the goddess Calypso. Zeus finally persuades the goddess to let him go but he is shipwrecked by the sea god Poseidon, who bears him a grudge. Odysseus is washed up in the kingdom of the Phaeacians, where he is rescued by Nausicaa, the daughter of the local king, Alcinous. Offered hospitality and entertained with games and poetry, Odysseus relates a whole series of fantastic adventures he has under-gone since leaving Troy. They include the capture of himself and his men by the Cyclops, one-eyed giants, his temptation by the Sirens, and sailing between the twin horrors of the monster Scylla and the whirlpool Charybdis. Restored to good health by the welcome of the Phaeacians, Odysseus eventually leaves for Ithaca. He lands there disguised as a beggar, but is gradually recognized by those who know him from many years before, among them his faithful dog, Argus, and his old nurse. After destroying the suitors in a scene as violent as any in the *Iliad*, he is finally reunited with Penelope in a moving scene of middle-aged love.

The world of the epic is one of superhuman heroes, many of whom are directly descended from the gods. When one of them arrives at the scene of bat-tle he can transform the whole course of events by his exploits. (Appropriately the 'great' heroes of Homer, Achilles and Hector arrive for battle in four-horse chariots.) Achilles seems able to kill men in their hundreds without pausing for rest. However, even heroes die. (This is the main difference between them and the immortal gods.) Hector and Patroclus fall in the course of the *Iliad* and the imminent death of Achilles is predicted. Homer does not even offer his heroes the possibility of an afterlife, other than in the most shadowy form. What mat-ters above all in the *Iliad* is honour, preserving dignity in the face of the horror of war, a point developed three centuries later by the tragedian Sophocles. A 'good' man is one who shows strength, skill, and courage in battle. However, Homer's heroes are no stiff-upper-lipped Englishmen. Their plight intensifies their emotions. They sob openly when companions die and are torn with grief at what might happen to their wives and children after they have died.

It is part of Homer's appeal that he is able to present another world in contrast to that of war, one of peace in which everyday life is carried on in well-ordered domesticity. Even in the midst of war Troy preserves an atmosphere of civilized living. Priam's palace is 'built wide with porches and colonnades of polished stone', and deep in its cellars are great treasures. There is courtesy and kindness among the city's inhabitants. In the *Odyssey* there is more scope for the rituals of hospitality in the aristocratic halls where local lords sustain their relationships by feasting and the giving of luxury gifts—bronze cauldrons, fine fabrics, gold and silver. The guest is welcomed. He is washed by the servant girls, fitted out in fresh clothes and fed. Later his story is listened to with respect and then he is bedded down on the porch, while the lord and his family retire to their own bedrooms.

In these homes the influence of wives is strong. They have a major role in running the household, supervising weaving and the grinding of corn by servant slave girls, watching over the stores, and bringing up their children. While the heroes expect to have women around them available simply for sex, they treat their aristocratic wives with respect. Penelope, for instance, has some sort of emotional equality with her husband. They talk together before making love and share a cosy intimacy as fellow high-status members of their society (although Penelope's son Telemachus treats his mother with less respect). Arete, wife of King Alcinous of Phaeacia, is described as honoured by her husband as no other wife in the world is honoured. 'Such has always been the honour paid to Arete by Alcinous and her children and by the people here, who gaze at her as at a divinity and greet her with loyal words whenever she walks about the town, because she is full of unprompted wisdom.' (Translation: Walter Shewring.)

In a violent and unsettled age, however, there was no doubt that women were desperately dependent on the protection of their husbands. Some of the most heart-rending scenes in the *Iliad* come when Hector's wife, Andromache, realizes what her fate will be if Hector dies. She will probably be dragged off as a captive and become a slave and unwilling sexual partner to a Greek warlord. Penelope, too, is alone. Her son, Telemachus, is at the threshold of manhood but still not assured enough to be able to offer protection to his mother against her persistent suitors. She has to rely on her own guile to delay accepting any of them as a husband, and the situation is only resolved when Odysseus, aided now by Telemachus, slaughters them.

Set against scenes of both peace and war and often woven into them is the natural world. Homer never forgets the rhythms of everyday life and the backdrop of sea, sunlight, and stars. Outside Troy the Greek armies bed down for the night by their watchfires:

As stars in the night sky glittering round the moon's brilliance blaze in all their glory when the air falls to a sudden windless calm . . . all the lookout peaks stand out and the jutting cliffs and the steep ravines and down from the high heavens bursts the boundless bright air and all the stars shine clear and the shepherd's heart exults—so many fires burned between the ships and the [river] Xanthus' whirling rapids. (Translation: Robert Fagles)

In the *Odyssey*, a poem of longing *par excellence*, Odysseus is impatient to set out on the final journey to Ithaca:

Odysseus all the while kept turning his head towards the glowing sun, impatient for it to set, because he yearned to be on his way home again. He was like a man who longs for his evening meal when all day long his two dark red oxen have drawn his jointed plough over the fallow; thankful he is when sunlight goes; he can limp home to his meal at last. (Translation: Walter Shewring)

The gods play an essential part in the *Iliad* and the *Odyssey*. Homer presents them as a closely connected family with their home on Mount Olympus: Zeus and his wife Hera, their children, Ares, the god of war, and Hephaestus and, by Zeus' other liaisons, Apollo and Athena. However, they seldom work in unity. In the *Odyssey* Athena acts as a protecting goddess for Odysseus while Poseidon, Zeus' brother, is out to upset him. In the *Iliad* the gods are even more partisan. Hera and Athena are violently against the Trojans while Apollo takes their side. The gods can also act unscrupulously with each other to get their way. Hera tires Zeus with love-making so that she can put her own stratagems in hand while he is recovering in sleep.

Human beings can try and influence the gods by sacrifice, but the gods decide whether to listen or not and have the power to intervene in human affairs at will. In the *Iliad* it is Apollo who decides on the death of Patroclus, while the gods choose not to intervene to save Hector. However, they are not all-powerful. The Greeks did not assume that every unexplained natural event was the work of the Olympian gods, while in the *Iliad* even Zeus, traditionally the most powerful of the gods, is unable to save his own son Sarpedon who is fighting for Troy. With the power of the gods less than absolute, human beings are left with some space in which to exercise free will and take responsibility for their own actions. There are instances in both epics when the heroes ponder on the best course to take. They are even free to attack the gods, as Agamemnon does on one occasion, berating Zeus for his cruelty to men. Unlike some epic poets Homer does not allow his heroes to escape their fate, by turning into an animal at a moment of crisis, for instance.

For later generations Homer remained a great moral teacher. In fifth-century Athens boys would learn the epics by heart and not only absorb a heritage but understand appropriate behaviour in different contexts from the many different types of relationship portrayed. The tragedies of the Trojan War become inextricably linked to Greek mythology and drama. The emotional power of Homer persisted into the Roman period so that he is the most popular author of the Oxyrhynchus papyri cache. Part of his enduring genius lies in his portrayal of heroes as fully human beings whose dilemmas remain real to his readers nearly 3,000 years later. Through Homer the Trojan War continues to haunt the European consciousness as the archetype of all wars.

Hesiod

The consciousness that in religious matters the Greeks had moved on from more primitive traditions of abject dependence on the gods and could move on even further is found in the poems of a contemporary of Homer, the poet Hesiod (normally dated to about 700 BC). Unlike Homer, Hesiod provides some biographical details about himself. His father had migrated back from overseas to Boeotia on the Greek mainland, where Hesiod had been born. The family estates were small, and when Hesiod and his brother inherited them they soon quarrelled over their shares. Hesiod comes over as a cynical and pessimistic figure, hardened by the experience of peasant life and with deep-rooted prejudices against women.

The earliest work of Hesiod to survive is the *Theogony*. Its aim, in Hesiod's words, is to 'tell how in the first place the gods and the earth came to be, and the rivers and the boundless sea with its seething swell and the shining stars and the wide heaven above, as well as the gods born of these givers of good things' (translation: Robert Lamberton). While Homer presents the gods of Mount Olympus as if they had always been in existence, Hesiod wants to go back further to the act of creation itself. In this he is drawing not on Greek traditions but on the creation myths of the east, with which his stories show many parallels. He evokes primitive and tempestuous gods, Uranus, god of heaven, and Gaia, goddess of earth. Their relationship is a violent one and at one point their son, Cronos, cuts off his father's genitals. They fall into the sea and, as they float in their own blood and semen, the goddess of love, Aphrodite, is born from the mixture (not that viewers of Botticelli's celebrated *Birth of Venus* (the Roman version of Aphrodite) would ever guess at this method of conception). Cronos himself fathers the Olympian gods, who under the leadership of Zeus have to do battle with the Titans, children of Uranus and Gaia, before they can reign supreme. Woven into the *Theogony* are other myths such as that of Prometheus, a champion of humankind, who stole fire from heaven. Zeus' revenge on men includes, according to Hesiod, the creation of women. He plumbs dark depths of the human psyche left untouched by Homer.

Hesiod is also known as the author of a very different poem, *Works and Days*. One theme of this work is the concept of history as moving forward through phases from ages of gold, silver, and bronze to one of heroes before reaching the unhappy present, the age of iron. This is an age, Hesiod argues, with specific reference to his quarrel over land with his brother, in which ethical standards have broken down, one when the rich landowner lords it over the poor peasant, who is defenceless against his power. (It has been argued that Hesiod is drawing on eastern wisdom literature in presenting himself and his brother as personifications of good and evil. The work, as a whole, is set within a religious framework.) However, all is not without hope. There is the possibility of justice, *dike*, and Zeus, normally seen as indifferent to the suffering of man, is invoked by Hesiod as its protector. It is up to human beings to work hard (there are echoes here of Egyptian Middle Kingdom texts) so that good order can be achieved in unity with the gods. This is ultimately a much more optimistic philosophy than any offered by Homer and it reflects the dawning of a new age, that of the city state where justice can perhaps be made a reality.

Much of *Works and Days* is concerned with life on the land and consists of what can be seen as advice on the cultivation of crops, what should be sown, when harvest should take place, and how to fill the slack times of year. (The motivation for including this may be the desire of the poet to show how the good man lives an ordered life, particularly through knowing how to cultivate the land properly.) There is some evidence, though it remains disputed, that population growth was leading to a transformation of agriculture, with the large grazing herds of the aristocracy being replaced by the more intensive arable farming described by Hesiod. Livestock was the ideal form of wealth in a time of instability. Stock could at least be rounded up and put in a secure place—a field of barley, the grain most suitable for the dry soil of Greece, could not. Stock, in large numbers, are a good way of reflecting status but a highly inefficient way of producing calories for human consumption. Most of those eaten by the animals are lost and could have been better consumed by humans directly as grain. This is why a growing population might initiate more grain-growing and by doing so undermine the traditional aristocratic way of life. Again, because an olive tree takes several years to mature, the decision to grow it is in itself a recognition of stability.

The Appearance of the *Polis*

The transition may have been easier because the aristocracy had no secure control over the local peasantries. There was, in fact, a deep-rooted prejudice against providing any form of regular labour for others. In Homer the landless labourer hiring himself out to others is presented as the lowest possible form of life, only marginally better than death. As a result the mass of the Greek population was never restricted in its mobility, and as population grew this made it possible for larger settlements, towns and cities, to emerge without hindrance, often through the merging of neighbouring villages. When they needed protection the farmers would retreat to local high ground—the Acropolis in Athens, Acrocorinth in Corinth—but some Cycladic sites may have been walled as early as 900. The walls of Smyrna, the modern Izmir, for instance, appear to date from 850. By the late eighth century there is the first evidence of paved streets (such as at Phaistos, on Crete). These towns may have taken the cities of the Phoenicians on the coast of the Levant as their model.

It was through this development that the *polis*, the essential social and political unit within which Greek life was to be lived for centuries to come, was born. The *polis* was not just the physical entity of a city, its buildings and the walls around them. In Homer this is called an *asty*. The *polis* was much more. It was a community, living primarily in a city but drawing on the lands which surrounded it for its supplies. It was also a setting within which human relationships could take new forms, where abstract concepts such as justice could be translated into practice. 'Citizen state' (a term coined by W. G. Runciman) might be a better translation. When Hesiod talks of the coming of justice he sets it in a city, and he compares a city where justice rules with one where crime predominates. The emergence of politics follows naturally from life in the ideal *polis*.

The *polis* is necessarily preoccupied with its identity. It finds a protecting god, Athena for Athens and Sparta, Hera in Samos, Apollo in Eretria (on Euboea) and Corinth. An altar is built to a god or goddess, later a temple, at first on the same model as the aristocratic hall, the *megaron*, and then more grandly with its own peristyle of columns. An early, eighth-century example is the temple to Hera at Samos. Originally built as a long narrow building with a cult statue housed at the back, it was transformed with a rectangle of wooden columns set on stone bases. The temple becomes the pride of the city, and by the seventh century cities are competing with each other to provide the grandest.

The foundation myths of individual cities speak as if they had existed as sophisticated bodies of citizens, with buildings to match, from the moment of foundation. In fact the process was much more gradual. The end of the eighth century seems to be the period when there is the first evidence of cities being confident of their identity and able to defend themselves through the use of a citizen army. Few had the resources before the sixth century to build themselves grand public buildings, and it is only in this century that many aspects of civilized city life such as paved streets and fountains appear. The *polis*, in its material form, must not be assumed to have existed earlier than it did.

The emergence of the *polis* certainly intensified local loyalties, but it appeared at the same time as a growing consciousness of what it meant to be Greek. There is a dramatic increase in the use of religious centres which were remote from any city and totally unconnected with them. At Delphi, the oracle sacred to Apollo, bronze figurines, presented as offerings, have been found in their hundreds. Only one dates from the ninth century, over 150 from the eighth. Olympia was another site which was gaining a pan-Hellenic importance. The traditional date for the founding of the games is 776 BC, although there appear to have been festivals to Zeus much earlier than this. The eighth century saw a vast increase in the number of dedications. These developments suggest increasing mobility and the formation of a coherent Greek culture alongside the growth of individual loyalties to the *polis*. The combination is one of the tensions which helped bring vitality to Greek life. Meanwhile, however, population pressures at home and a growing confidence on the sea were combining to bring about a major expansion of Greek settlements throughout the Mediterranean. This outburst of colonization is the subject of the next chapter.

FURTHER READING

Greece—general books. There are standard translations of many works in the Loeb Classical Library and Penguin Classics. Excellent translations of Homer include those by Richmond Lattimore and Robert Fagles of the *Iliad* (the second available now on cassette read by Derek Jacobi) and the *Odyssey* by Walter Shewring in prose or Robert Fagles in verse. A general source book is M. Dillon and L. Garland, *Ancient Greece* (London, 1992). Introductory one-volume histories include S. Pomeroy and others, *Ancient Greece: A Political, Social and Cultural History* (New York, 1999), and Charles Freeman, *The Greek Achievement* (London, 1999). P. Cartledge, *The Cambridge Illustrated History of Ancient Greece* (Cambridge, 1998), has an excellent set of essays on the classical period. Paul Cartledge, *The Greeks: A Portrait of Self and Others* (Oxford, 2002 and earlier editions) is an essential and readable study of the Greeks in relation to 'others'. C. Dougherty and L. Kurke (eds.), *The Cultures within Ancient Greek Culture: Contact, Conflict, Collaboration* (forthcoming Cambridge, 2003) promises to break new ground. See also A. Snodgrass, *An Archaeology of Greece* (Berkeley, 1987), and James Whitley, *The Archaeology of Ancient Greece* (Cambridge, 2001). On the sites themselves, C. Mee and A. Spawforth, *Greece: An Oxford Archaeological Guide* (Oxford, 2001). C. M. Bowra's *The Greek Experience* (London, 1957) is an enduring classic. The publishers of this book, Oxford University Press, have provided a fine array of companion studies. J. Boardman, J. Griffin, and O. Murray (eds.), *The Oxford History of the Classical World* (Oxford, 1986); M. C. Howatson (ed.), *The Oxford Companion to Classical Literature* (Oxford, 1989); John Boardman (ed.), *The Oxford History of Classical Art* (Oxford, 1993); and E. Fantham and others (eds.), *Women in the Classical World* (New York, 1994). M. Grant and R. Kitzinger (eds.), *Civilization of the Ancient Mediterranean: Greece and Rome* (New York, 1988) is a major three-volume survey with essays on most aspects of the subject. An important study of the intellectual background to Greek archaeology is to be found in the essay by Ian Morris in Ian Morris (ed.), *Classical Greece: Ancient Histories and Modern Archaeologies* (Cambridge, 1994). See also John Boardman, *The Archaeology of Nostalgia: How the Greeks Recreated their Mythical Past* (London, 2003).

General surveys of Greek literature include Peter Levi, *The Pelican History of Greek Literature* (Harmondsworth, 1985), and, more recently, A. Dihle, *A History of Greek Literature* (London, 1994). For the historians see T. Luce, *The Greek Historians* (London, 1997). The authoritative survey by M. Robertson, *A History of Greek Art* (2 volumes, Cambridge, 1975) has been distilled into his *A Shorter History of Greek Art* (Cambridge, 1981). An acclaimed study is A. Stewart, *Greek Sculpture* (New Haven, 1990). See also R. Osborne, *Archaic and Classical Greek Art* (Oxford, 1998), and N. Spivey, *Greek Art* (London, 1997) and *Understanding Greek Sculpture* (London, 1996). There is also a well-illustrated survey by J. G. Pedley, *Greek Art and Archaeology* (London, 1992).

Chapter 8. A recent overview of the Aegean is O. Dickinson, *The Aegean Bronze Age* (Cambridge, 1994). See also the chapter by K. Wardle, 'The Palace Civilizations of Minoan Crete and Mycenaean Greece, 2000–1200 BC', in *The Oxford Illustrated Prehistory of Europe* (Oxford, 1994) (and, in the same volume, Mervyn Popham on 'The Collapse of Aegean

Civilization at the end of the Late Bronze Age'). Colin Renfrew's thesis on the early transfer of Indo-European languages to Europe is in his *Archaeology and Language* (London, 1987). On the Minoans there is now J. Lesley Fitton's well-received *Minoans* (London, 2002) and for the art D. Preziosi and L. A. Hitchcock, *Aegean Art and Architecture* (Oxford, 1999). John Chadwick's *The Decipherment of Linear B* (Cambridge, 1967) describes the achievement of Ventris, and there is the more recent Andrew Robinson, *The Man who Deciphered Linear B: The Story of Michael Ventris* (London, 2002). See also W. McDonald and C. Thomas, *Progress into the Past: The Rediscovery of Mycenaean Civilization* (2nd edition, Bloomington, Ind., 1990). W. Burkert surveys Mycenaean religion and its links with later Greek religion in chapter 1 of his *Greek Religion* (Oxford, 1985).

Oswyn Murray's *Early Greece* (2nd edition, London, 1993) takes the story up to 480 BC as does Robin Osborne, *Greece in the Making, 1200–479 BC* (London, 1996). Both are lively and authoritative introductions with good bibliographies. See also A. M. Snodgrass, *The Dark Age of Greece: An Archaeological Survey of the Eleventh to Eighth Centuries* (Edinburgh, 1971), and James Whitley, *The Archaeology of Ancient Greece* (Cambridge, 2001). I. Morris, *Archaeology as Cultural History* (Oxford, 1999), studies the relationship between archaeology and ancient Greece. An important recent book on the development of Greek identity is J. M. Hall, *Ethnic Identity in Greek Antiquity* (Cambridge, 1997). For the Dark Age onwards I particularly enjoyed Jeffrey Hurwit's *The Art and Culture of Ancient Greece, 1100–480 BC* (Ithaca, NY, 1985), which makes useful connections between literature and art and is alive to the many outside influences on the formation of Greek culture, and H. Fraenkel's *Early Greek Poetry and Philosophy* (Oxford, 1975), a solid, readable introduction. John Boardman's *The Greeks Overseas* (4th edition, London, 1999) is fundamental for this chapter, and, even more so, for the next.

For a good introduction to the issues surrounding Homer and his times see C. Emlyn-Jones (ed.), *Homer: Readings and Images* (London, 1992). M. Finley's *The World of Odysseus* (Harmondsworth, 1962) provides a stimulating introduction to Homer's world. See also the essay by Oliver Taplin in the *Oxford History of the Classical World*. See Oliver Taplin, *Homeric Soundings* (Oxford, 1992); J. Griffin, *Homer on Life and Death* (Oxford, 1980); Milman Parry, *The Making of Homeric Verse* (Oxford, 1971); and J. Carter and S. Morris, *The Ages of Homer* (Austin, Tex., 1995). On Hesiod there is Robert Lamberton, *Hesiod* (New Haven, 1988) and the chapter by Jasper Griffin, 'Greek Myth and Hesiod' in the *Oxford History*. For links to the east see M. L. West's, *The East Face of Helicon: West Asiatic Elements in Greek Poetry and Myth* (Oxford, 1997).

Recent ideas on the development of the *polis* are covered in L. Mitchell and P. J. Rhodes (eds.), *The Development of the Polis in Archaic Greece* (London, 1997). The relationship between the development of peasant farming and the emergence of the *polis* is discussed in V. D. Hanson, *The Other Greeks* (London, 1995).

The Greeks in a Wider World, 800–600 BC

The Orientalizing Revolution

For the Greeks, whose lives were always frugal and where a surplus had to be painfully won from the land, the east offered a glittering lure, one which still dazzled Alexander and his men when they sacked the great cities of Persia four centuries later. Contact with the east was supported by Greece's position. The country is naturally focused towards the east. The mountain ranges run from west to east and the mountains continue as the Aegean islands, stepping-stones for eastern traders. All the best Greek harbours are on the east coast. In contrast, Italy is protected from the east by the Apennines, and this was one reason why cultural contact with the east along the western coastline was delayed.

In the nineteenth century there was some reluctance to consider that the Greeks might have owed any of their heritage to the east but the German scholar Poulsen recognized the eastern influence on Greek art as far back as 1912, and the theme was developed in the 1960s by John Boardman in his *The Greeks Overseas*. Oswyn Murray first used the term 'The Orientalizing Period' in 1980 to describe not just a revolution in art but a development in Greek society as a whole, and Walter Burkert's *The Orientalising Revolution* appeared in its German original in 1984. 'Orientalizing' was the result of a complex and varied set of relationships between the Greeks and the peoples of the east which spread over centuries. Eastern motifs appear in Cretan pottery as early as the ninth century while Egypt was an important influence on Greek architecture and sculpture as late as 600 BC. Some influences came as the result of eastern craftsmen who came to the west as refugees, others from goods which were taken west by traders and copied by local craftsmen, while the Greeks themselves may have learned directly from contacts in the east. Disentangling the various influences is made harder by the response of the Greeks themselves. In Egypt the kings had created and enforced an easily recognizable palace style. In Greece, with no single dominant state, each area could develop its own response to the east, and it took time for a more uniform Greek culture to emerge from what was absorbed. The relationship between the Greeks and the Orient is made more complex because neither Greek nor Oriental culture was a stable entity. As the earlier chapters of this book have shown there were many Near Eastern cultures.

Without doubt the most important immediate influence on the Greeks were the Phoenicians, a people the Greeks viewed with a mixture of awe and suspicion, 'famous as seamen, tricksters, bringing tens of thousands of trinkets in their ships', as Homer put it. By the ninth century they were well established in their cities along the Levantine coast and had begun to reach out into the Mediterranean itself. Their first recorded colony at Kition on the south-east coast of Cyprus was founded in the late ninth century. They were more mature and confident than the Greeks at this stage and probably ventured to the west, with its tricky crossing between the Peloponnese and the coast of Italy, some generations before the Greeks. The traditional founding date of their most important overseas colony, Carthage, on the coast of north Africa, is 814 and large numbers of trading posts were established on the southern coast of Spain in the eighth century. They were also expert shipbuilders, and the *pentekonter*, the fifty-oar warship, and the trireme were Phoenician in origin.

It was traders from the island of Euboea, at first from Lefkandi (see previous chapter) and its successor, the city of Eretria, and Chalcis who seem to have made the first tentative steps at mingling with the Phoenicians and infiltrating the east. What they had to offer in return for the luxury goods and metals they craved is not clear. There is some Euboean pottery of about 925 BC found in northern Syria, but slaves were the most likely export, one which would have left no trace in the archaeological record. By 825 the Euboeans appear to have had a foothold at al-Mina on the Orontes river, a trading-post where Greek influence survives alongside that of Phoenicians, Cypriots, and possibly other traders. Al-Mina offered the shortest caravan route to Mesopotamia via the towns of northern Syria. It was possibly here that the Greeks first picked up the Phoenician alphabet, although there is no reason why the transmission should not have taken place in Greece itself and Cyprus remains another alternative. Traders may also have brought back to Greece the example of the walled city although the concept of the citizen who participates fully in city life is unknown in the east.

From the ninth century onwards the Phoenicians and the other peoples of the Near East were increasingly under pressure from the expanding power of Assyria (see p. 94). Assyrians stood on the shore of the Mediterranean for the first time in 877. Al-Mina was overrun by about 720. One of the major Phoenician cities, Sidon, was totally destroyed in 677. The Assyrian invasions of Egypt (see p. 104) followed in the seventh century. In Assyrian sources there are some records of retaliatory Greek raids, possibly by Greek pirates based in Cilicia (southern Turkey). One result of all these upheavals was the fleeing of eastern craftsmen as refugees to Greece.

The archaeological evidence of this contact with the east is widespread. As a result of the custom that victors in the Olympic Games dedicated cauldrons to the sanctuary, more eastern bronzes have been found at Olympia than any other site yet discovered in the eastern world. These great cauldrons, with their cast animal-head attachments, originate from Assyria, northern Syria, or the state of Urartu, east of the Euphrates. There are jewellery and gems, seals in Syrian and Egyptian styles (as has been suggested, earlier Egyptian goods were probably traded in the Mediterranean through Phoenician middlemen), shells from the Red Sea, and Phoenician silver bowls. The round shield of the Greek hoplite (p. 163 below) and the horsehair crest of his helmet are similar to those of the Assyrian infantry. A large proportion of the trade must have been in fabrics, but they have perished.

These fine goods were decorated with a whole world of eastern images which were soon copied. In many cases the derivation is obvious: for instance, there are 'royal' figures on cauldrons very similar to those found in the stone reliefs in the Assyrian capitals. The later Greek portrayals of Zeus and his thunderbolt and Poseidon and his trident appear to derive from models of warrior gods from the Syro-Hittite region who are depicted brandishing weapons in their right hands. There are no lions in Greece, but they appear now in Greek art. The *chimaera*, a composite of lion, she-goat, and serpent, is linked to Hittite representations, while the Triton, a merman, seems to come straight from Mesopotamia. There is a wealth of foliage, including lotus leaves and friezes of palms. By the late eighth century these influences are transforming the art on Greek pottery into a new exoticism— 'boars, wild goats, dogs, chickens, lions, sphinxes and griffins endlessly parade around countless seventh-century vases', in the graphic words of Jeffrey Hurwit.

With the goods and their craftsmen came new skills. *Polydaidaloi*, 'of many skills', is how Homer describes the Phoenician makers of a large silver bowl awarded as first prize at the funeral games of Patroclus. The Phoenician metal-workers were clever at hammering and fashioning bronze and silver. From the east and Egypt came the technique of casting with the 'lost wax' method, in which a core of wax is surrounded by clay and then melted out leaving a mould, and ivory-working. Ivory was always regarded as a mysterious substance by the Greeks (any description of elephants and their tusks must have bordered on the fabulous), and, with faience work, was prominent among imported luxury goods.

The influence from the east was not confined to its art. The skill of writing, perhaps the most important gift from the east to the Greeks, has already been discussed. The habit of reclining at a couch for a meal or a drinking party replaced the traditional custom of sitting upright in the eighth century. It probably originated in Palestine. The cult of Adonis, the young man, beloved by Aphrodite, who was killed by a boar while hunting, has its origins in the annual death of a vegetation god celebrated in the Phoenician city of Byblos (from where it seems to have travelled first to Cyprus, the island of Aphrodite, and thence to Greece). Mount Kasios, on the Levantine coast near al-Mina and just visible from Cyprus, appears as the setting for a battle between Zeus and a hundred-headed monster, Typhoeus. It is only part of a rich mythology, seen in the works of Hesiod, for instance, which has its roots in the east. Hades, the Greek underworld, has parallels with the realm of mud and darkness described in the Mesopotamian epic *Gilgamesh*. The idea of a foundation deposit of pre-cious metals and stones placed under new buildings is found in Assyria, and the Khaniale Tekke tomb in Crete of about 800 BC appears to have had a similar deposit of gold left there by migrant Syrian goldsmiths. The custom spread in the Greek world, and later temples at Delos and Ephesus had similar deposits.

With these movements came the language of trade, a series of Semitic words some of which have made a further transfer into English. Goods would be con-tained in a *sakkos* and among them might be found *krokas* (crocus), *kannabis*, and *kinnamomon* (cinnamon). The Greek unit of weight, *mina*, comes from the Akkadian *mana*. *Plinthos*, a clay brick, originates in Mesopotamia, makes its way into Greek architecture as the base of a column, and is still used in English. The Assyrian *maskanu*, a booth or tent, reappears in Greek theatre as *skena*, the back-drop of the stage, and hence scene.

In the enthusiasm to dig out the influences of the east on the Greeks, some have gone so far as to suggest that the Greeks were simply an appendage to the eastern world during this period. Certainly the Greeks may have been diffident in the face of the opulence of the eastern civilizations and the seafaring skills of the Phoenicians, but in almost every sphere they ended up transforming what they had learned for their own ends. Greek art, literature, religion, and mythol-ogy may contain eastern influences, but ultimately they are Greek. The alphabet is borrowed, then transformed with the use of vowels into something infinitely more flexible. Homer may have absorbed elements of epic style from Mesopotamia, but the *Iliad* and *Odyssey* stand as works of literature in their own right set in an unmistakably Greek world. The Dipylon master might have borrowed eastern images for his goats and deer, but they are fitted into his own geometric design. In the art of pottery-making itself the Greeks had nothing to learn from the east.

The Western Settlements

By the eighth century, the Euboeans were also looking to the west. It was not an easy route for them to take. They had either to make a land crossing over the Isthmus of Corinth before setting out along the Gulf of Corinth or brave the dangerous coast of the southern Peloponnese. On either route there was an open crossing to the Italian coast. Once again it seems that the more adventurous Phoenicians had shown the way. By the end of the ninth century Phoenicians may have been settled on Sardinia, where there were rich deposits of copper, tin, lead, and iron ore. There are also hints of a Phoenician presence in southern Italy

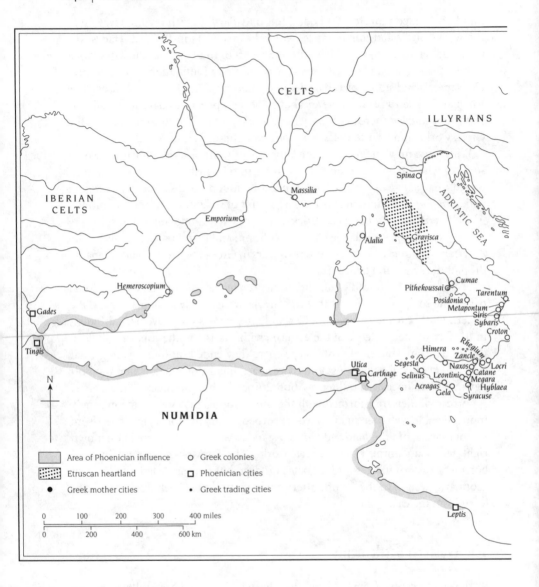

MAP 3

in the early eighth century. The Euboeans followed later, probably about the middle of the century, and also in search of metals. Sardinia appears to have been the richest source, but it may well have been that the Phoenicians were so well established there that the Euboeans made their way instead up the western Italian coast to the island of Ischia. Here at Pithekoussai they formed a settle-

THE GREEKS AND THE PHOENICIANS IN THE MEDITERRANEAN
800–600 BC

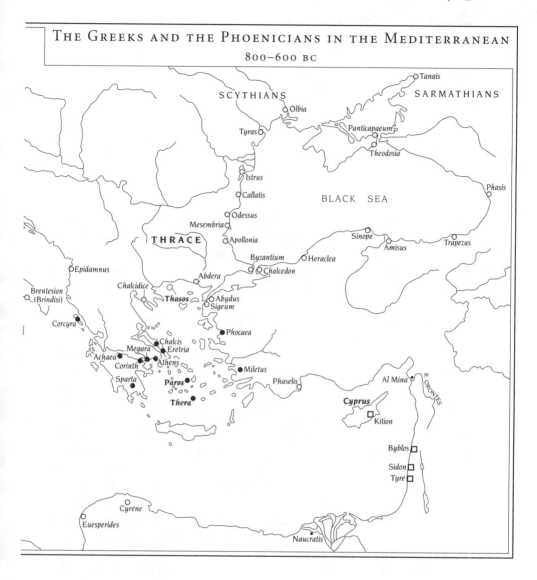

ment to trade with the peoples of the Italian mainland. It seems to have been in full operation by 750 BC.

The settlement at Pithekoussai was predominantly Greek but there is also evidence that Phoenician and perhaps other eastern traders helped make up the population. Its model was almost certainly the Phoenician trading settlements in Sardinia and Spain. Pithekoussai echoes the Phoenician Gadir (the modern Cadiz) in that it was close to important resources yet isolated enough to be secure. Its main focus was the metal ores of central Italy and beyond (tin may have come into Italy from Britain via France), and soon Greeks were face to face with the Etruscans, who had formed a loose confederation of states in the area north of Rome. The traditional view of the Greek impact on the Etruscans is stated by John Boardman, who contrasts the two cultures:

> The Greeks chose, adapted and assimilated until they produced a material culture which was wholly Greek, despite all the superficial inspiration which the east provided. The Etruscans accepted all they were offered without discrimination. They copied—or paid Greeks and perhaps immigrant easterners to copy—with little understanding of the forms and subjects which served as models.

This view has been increasingly challenged in recent years (and modified by Boardman himself in his recent *The Diffusion of Classical Art in Antiquity*), with new emphasis placed on the way that Etruscan society in fact used Greek imports for its own ends and did this so successfully that Greek potters, the so-called Perizoma Group of late sixth-century Athens, for instance, actually adapted their wares for the Etruscan market. (The Etruscans are discussed in detail in Chapter 20.)

As the Greeks became increasingly confident on the sea and as their wealth and population increased, they began to travel for other reasons, predominantly to find new homes for their surplus populations. In theory there is a distinction between the Greek *emporia*, trading-posts, and the *apoikiai*, colonies, but it is not always easy to see. Trading cities such as al-Mina and Naucratis in Egypt (see below) were definitely *emporia* because they were in areas where the Greeks had no political independence and could do little but trade. Pithekoussai is somewhere in between, a settlement under Greek control, openly trading but also earning a living from the provision of skills to foreign communities. About 725 BC, relatively soon after Pithekoussai's foundation, a breakaway settlement was founded at Cumae on the Italian coast. Important to Cumae was its own land, its safe beach, and its acropolis. It was also inhabited, it was said, predominantly by settlers whose origin was the Euboean city of Chalcis. (The split may, in fact, reflect growing tension between Chalcis and Eretria at home in Euboea.)

This was the ideal, a safe site, with a good harbour or sheltered beach and land to support its inhabitants. It was the goal of a mass of migrants from Greece who during the years 730–580 BC spread across the Mediterranean, the migration only coming to an end when the best sites had been settled. The final result was to establish a Greek presence in the Mediterranean from the Black Sea in the north-east to the coast of modern France and Spain in the west. The catalyst is assumed to be population increase in mainland Greece and to a lesser extent in the Greek cities of Asia Minor (although it has to be said that archaeology has not yet confirmed a correlation between the most energetic colonizing cities and the areas of Greece in which population growth appears to have been highest). The

impulse to trade remained as a subsidiary factor. Many colonies, even while living primarily off the land, were on trading routes, exploited their local resources,
and exchanged goods with the native peoples.

The Greek custom was for landholdings to be shared equally between sons. As
the history of nineteenth- and twentieth-century France, where there is a similar (Napoleonic) system of inheritance, has shown, the custom breeds a mass of
peasantry living in small lots which only provide a surplus in exceptional years.
The peasants inevitably are tough, hard-working, deeply conservative, and
understandably cynical about the possibilities of any improvement in their lot.
(One reason why they make such good soldiers.) With an increase in population
their future can only get worse. Settlement overseas is the best alternative, and
peasants are ideally suited to the task of taking new land in hand. (The French
colonization of Algeria in the nineteenth century comes to mind.) For those who
had mastered the art of living in Greece, the Mediterranean offered many sites
where conditions were as good as or even better than those left behind.

Later Greek sources talk of the *apoikiai*, homes from home, as if they were normally set up by a mother city. Whether the earliest settlements were part of such
an organized process is uncertain. In the eighth century the *polis* was scarcely
developed in much of Greece and migration may have taken place in a much more
haphazard way, perhaps as a result of conflict over land. Later a *polis* often did take
responsibility for organizing a colonial expedition, sometimes forcibly sending
out excess population. (One unhappy group of would-be colonists from the island
of Thera, sent out when the island was hit by a drought, were refused landing when
they returned without having founded a colony.) The cohesion of the *polis* meant
that the colonists knew each other and may already have been bound to each other
in kinship groups. A typical colonizing group would have been of 100–200 young
men. (The *pentekonter*, adopted by the Greeks from the Phoenicians, took at least
fifty men, and two or three would sail together.) Sometimes, as in the case of
Thera, each family with more than one son was ordered to provide one of them
for the colony, certainly the fairest way of dealing with land shortage and a good
indication of the well-established authority of the *polis* by the late seventh century.
(The Theran expedition is dated to 630.) Once the colonists arrived they would
maintain links with their home city, often importing its pottery exclusively and
maintaining cults and customs from home. The foundation oath of the Theran
settlement, which was eventually established at Cyrene on the north African coast,
gave any citizen of Thera who later joined the colony an automatic right to citizenship of the colony and access to unallotted land. However, insofar as the word
colony suggests political dependence on the mother city this is misleading. With
the exception of Corinth, which attempted to keep firm control over its foundations, overseas colonies quickly asserted their independence.

The rituals of colonization were well developed. The colonizing city would
provide a leader, usually of aristocratic or semi-aristocratic status. His first task,

especially if planning to head west, was to approach the oracle at Delphi where Apollo gave guidance on the sites to choose. 'Here is Taphiasos, the unploughed, on your path, and there is Chalcis: then the sacred lands of the Kouretes and then the Echinades. Great is the ocean to the left. But even so I would not expect you to miss the Lakinian cape, nor sacred Krimissa, nor the river Aisaros' is one surviving piece of advice. Armed with these instructions, the colonists would take with them 'the sacred fire' of their home city, probably in fact only ashes, with which to kindle their first sacrificial fire on arrival and confirm their spiritual links with home. (These reported oracles may in some cases be foundation myths which were developed later to rationalize the choice of site.)

According to Plutarch, writing some centuries later, the leader was entrusted by Apollo with the 'signs for recognizing places, the times for activities, the shrines of the gods across the sea, the secret burial places of heroes, hard to find for men setting forth on a distant voyage from Greece'. It seems that his role was to assess the sites with the best omens, perhaps those which had some connection with earlier expeditions (the 'burial places of heroes'). Certainly attempts were made to link a chosen site with a mythical figure from the past. Heracles, for instance, was supposed to have carried out one of his labours, the subduing of the monster Geryon, in Sicily and this was used to justify choosing sites there. Whatever the omens, however, it is hard to dispute that the final choice would have been made on purely practical grounds of survival. The best sites were those with harbours, fertile land, peaceful or conquerable natives, and a defensible hilltop for times of crisis. The leader would mark out the limits of the new city, set out the sacred areas for its temples, and divide up land. His status was so assured that after his death it was usual for a hero cult to be established in his honour. The descendants of those who had come with him would often continue as the ruling classes of the city, preserving their status against newcomers.

The first Greek colonies were in the west, and in the eighth century they were still overwhelmingly the creations of the Euboeans. Naxos, a headland site with a small fertile valley behind it, was the first landfall in Sicily for ships rounding the toe of Italy. The Chalcidians colonized it about 734. (These dates are derived from the account by the fifth-century historian Thucydides.) Leontini, set inland and thus of no trading importance, Catane and Zancle, along the north-eastern Sicilian coast, and Rhegium on the Italian coast overlooking the strategically important Straits of Messina were all Chalcidian colonies established by the end of the eighth century. It was the Corinthians, however, who settled the finest Sicilian site of all, Syracuse, in about 733 BC. It had the best harbour on the island, a permanent source of fresh water in the spring Arethusa, and access to fertile land. It was later to become the richest city of the Greek world.

With the Euboeans firmly in control of the Straits of Messina, later settlers moved on to the coast of Italy itself. The Achaeans from the north-west

Peloponnese founded Sybaris, Croton, and Metapontum on the instep of Italy and, possibly through an overland route from Sybaris, Posidonia on the west coast (in its Latin form, Paestum, known as the home of one of the finest set of surviving Greek temples). High up on the instep of Italy the Spartans founded their only colony, Tarentum. Its first settlers were illegitimate children born to Spartan wives while their husbands had been away on service. (Their illegitimacy deprived them of access to land in Sparta itself.) Tarentum retained exceptionally close ties with Sparta, enjoying its pottery and continuing its native cults.

The native population, in Sicily the Sicels and Sicanians, appear to have offered little resistance. Some of the local population must have been incorporated as labourers into the new settlements, others probably acted as middlemen for procuring resources from inland. One of the later Greek settlements, Selinus on the west coast of Italy, even set up formal arrangements for intermarriage with the native town of Segesta, with which it had good commercial ties. With such good control of local resources, the colonies became fabulously rich. There was a touch of the *nouveau riche* in the massive temples and ornate art forms of the west, while western aristocrats competed on equal terms in the chariot races at Olympia. The word 'sybaritic' remains in English to describe the luxuriance of the city of Sybaris, on the instep of Italy.

As the Greek presence in the west became more secure, relationships with the Phoenicians began to break down. The most important Phoenician colony was Carthage on the north African coast. From there the Phoenicians had colonized the west coast of Sicily, and in 580 there were clashes between Greeks and Phoenicians when a band of Greeks from Rhodes tried to settle within the Phoenician enclave. There was more trouble further west. The Phoenicians had struck out along the north African coastline and were soon settling on the Spanish coast. There was a substantial Phoenician presence there by the eighth century. When settlers from the Greek city of Phocaea, on the coast of Asia Minor, came west in the last phase of colonization they found a substantial part of the western Mediterranean already closed to them.

The Phocaeans headed up the west coast of Italy, trading with the Etruscans as they went, and then made their way along the southern coast of France. Their most important settlement was Massilia (modern Marseilles) about 600, but they also edged around the coast of northern Spain, founding a colony at Emporion (modern Ampurias). Their intrusions aroused the suspicions of both Etruscans and Phoenicians. In the 540s a fresh wave of Phocaean settlers came west after their city had been taken over by the Persians. A new colony was founded at Alalia on Corsica and this enabled the Phocaeans to bypass the Etruscans. The Etruscans, furious at losing their trade, joined with the Phoenicians in driving the Phocaeans from Alalia. There are records of further clashes, and by 500 Greeks, Etruscans, and Phoenicians were consolidating separate spheres of influence in the western Mediterranean. It was probably the blocking of traditional routes by the Phoenicians which finally encouraged the Greeks to trade up the Adriatic coast.

The settlement of Massilia enabled the Greeks to trade with the Celtic peoples of Gaul (modern France) through the river valleys. One site, Mount Lassois, overlooking the Seine, south-east of Paris, became especially important. Here tin and other goods from further north were unloaded and transferred either south to the Rhône and thence to Massilia or to northern Italy. In 1953 the excavation of the grave of a Celtic princess at Vix, the cemetery of Mount Lassois, uncovered the largest and finest Greek bronze crater (a bowl for the mixing of wine) ever found. It was 1.64 metres high and complete with its lid and a handle in the shape of a statuette of a woman. The rich decoration included reliefs of warriors and chariots and moulded gorgons. It was probably of Spartan origin. It is too grand an object to be part of normal trade and it can only be assumed that it was a diplomatic gift made to a local leader, possibly in this case a woman, to cement or establish a trading relationship.

The impact of the Greeks on the Celtic Gauls was important. According to the Roman historian Justinus (third century AD):

from the Greeks the Gauls learned a more civilized way of life and abandoned their barbarous ways. They set to tilling their fields and walling their towns. They even got used to living by law rather than force of arms, to cultivating the vine and the olive. Their progress, in manners and wealth, was so brilliant that it seemed as though Gaul had become part of Greece, rather than that Greece had colonized Gaul.

The impact must have been less widespread than described here and limited to areas of direct contact. It has also been argued, by Michael Dietler, for instance, that the Celts incorporated prestige objects from Greece and the east into their own rituals, rather than allowing their society to be changed by them. (For the Celts see further p. 355 below.)

Settlements in the Northern Aegean, Black Sea, and Libya

While successive waves of Greeks were moving west, the versatility and the exuberance of the Euboeans also led them to move northwards from their island, along the coast of Thessaly, to Macedonia and Thrace. One objective may have been timber, vital for shipping and already becoming in short supply in mainland Greece, but the land was also adapted by settlers to growing vines. Chalcis settled so many sites along the triple-pronged peninsula that juts out into the Aegean from Macedonia that it still retains the name Chalcidice. Further east, towards the entrance to the Black Sea, the native Thracians offered some resistance to Greek expansion. One of the main colonies, that established by the Cycladic island of Paros about 680 BC, was perhaps wisely placed on the offshore island of Thasos. The seventh-century poet Archilochus (see below) records the continual struggles of the settlers with Thracian marauders.

By the beginning of the seventh century Greeks were moving into the Dardanelles, the entrance to the Black Sea; Megara, a coastal city west of Athens, seems to have been the first. Her earliest settlement, Chalcedon, was on the Asian side of the straits. Native opposition may have made it easier for the Megarans to establish a position here before crossing to the much more favourable European side, where the city of Byzantium was founded about 660 BC. Byzantium's site was an outstanding one, with a headland, superb natural harbour, and good protection by the sea on the south. The city controlled the entrance to the Black Sea as well as enjoying fine fishing. A thousand years later the same site was to be chosen by the Roman emperor Constantine for his eastern capital, Constantinople, the modern Istanbul.

The Black Sea was not immediately welcoming to the Greeks. The native peoples around the shores—among them the Thracians, and the Scythians, with their reputation for human sacrifice—were hostile. The northern shores of the sea, which were the home of the best resources, had extremely cold winters. Although there is some literary evidence for settlement in the eighth century, there is little archaeological support for such an early date and it may have been the seventh century before the main colonies were established. The two cities most responsible were Megara and, predominantly, Miletus, one of the cities of Asia Minor whose hinterland was under pressure from the expansion of Lydia. Once settlements were established they could exploit not only fish and land but hides and slaves. Greek goods have been found far up the river valleys in the Russian interior and Scythian art, like Etruscan, becomes heavily influenced by that of Greece. One Scythian king, Scyles, adopted a Greek lifestyle so enthusiastically that he was killed by his own people when seen participating in Dionysiac revels.

The settling of Cyrene on the coast of north Africa by the Therans took place, after extensive searches for a good site, about 630. It was an unusual colony, one of the few to be established well inland. (Leontini in Sicily is another example.) This suggests that relations with the native population must have been good. This was not to last. There was massive opposition when the Greeks tried to introduce new settlers and dispossessed the natives in the process. However, Cyrene survived and became one of the richest areas of the Greek world. Apart from the natural resources of sheep, corn, and horses, the city had a monopoly of the silphium plant, now extinct but valued in the ancient world as a cure-all. (A particularly fine cup from Sparta (dated to c.550 BC) shows a ruler by the name of Arkesilas overseeing the weighing and packing of silphium.)

Excavations on the site of Cyrene have helped provide evidence of intermarriage between Greeks and natives. The first settlers on each site were probably men. Women from the founding *polis* may have followed them, but more likely the settlers intermarried with local women. A line of poetry by the Cyrenian poet

Callimachus talks of the belted men of war dancing with the fair-haired Libyans, and in the cemeteries there is evidence of Libyan cult practices. Herodotus mentions that the women of Cyrene followed the Egyptian practice of not eating cows' meat, suggesting they were local people. Put together this evidence suggests that intermarriage was normal. In fact, it is hard to see how colonies could have expanded otherwise.

The Lelantine War and the Emergence of Corinth

As has been seen, it was the island of Euboea, especially its two main cities, Eretria and Chalcis, which provided the main impetus for early colonization. At the end of the eighth century, however, the relationship between the two cities broke down. The conflict seems to have centred on control of the rich Lelantine plain between their territories and the war is known for this reason as the Lelantine War. Details of the war are very fragmentary, but it seems to have drawn in many cities of the Greek world. In fact, it may have acted as a cover for the many other festering border disputes which must have arisen at a time of expanding populations.

It was a war of the old aristocratic Greece. The Euboeans had become involved in trade primarily to bolster their aristocratic elites and now the heroes from these fought out their battles. In a tone reminiscent of medieval chivalry, there was even an agreement not to use plebeian missiles such as arrows and stones. The *Iliad* may draw as much on the experience of this war as on the folk memories of those of Mycenaean Greece.

The war probably ended in the exhaustion of both of the leading cities, and it appears that the influence they retained was now exercised in different spheres of the Mediterranean. Eretria may have become associated with the colonial enterprises of her allies Megara and Miletus in the Black Sea, while Chalcis was now linked to Corinth. It was, in fact, the city of Corinth which emerged as the leading city of Greece after the war. Al-Mina, the trading-post patronized by the Euboeans, was sacked at this time by the Assyrians, and the archaeological record shows that when it was rebuilt it was Corinthian, not Euboean, pottery which predominated.

Corinth was not an old foundation, despite enjoying fertile land and having the shelter of Acrocorinth, the massive fortress rock which dominates the city. In the eighth century it was still a cluster of villages, but it then expanded quickly. It has been suggested (though the evidence is weak) that Corinth gained control of the Isthmus during the Lelantine War, seizing land from Megara, one of Eretria's allies. This would have given her both timber and pasture but, more significantly, control of the main route from east to west as well as the only land route from the Peloponnese to the north. The sea voyage around the

Peloponnese with its rocky coast was dangerous, and many seafarers preferred to drag their ships and goods across the Isthmus (on a specially constructed roadway, the *diolkos*). Under the Bacchiadae, a ruling clan of perhaps 200 households, who intermarried only with each other, the city enjoyed fifty important years of stability and was able to exploit its position to the full.

In contrast to the more traditional parts of Greece where craftsmen were still despised, the Bacchiadae welcomed them and used their talents. One major industry was shipbuilding, carried out, probably by foreigners, at workshops on the coast. It seems that prospective colonists could charter their ships from Corinth, but the Corinthians also pioneered faster and more efficient warships. Their *pentekonters* were narrow and undecked, with the keel beam prolonged and fitted with bronze so that it could ram an opponent. With such ships the Corinthians could challenge any merchantman. As mentioned above, they also kept close contact with their colonies, and it is possible in the late seventh century to speak of a Corinthian empire.

The most pervasive sign of Corinth's dominance is the city's pottery. It flooded the Greek world in the seventh century and its styles are so well known that many sites can now be dated to within twenty-five or even ten years by the pottery found there. Most of it was in small domestic ware in the shape of perfume flasks (the perfume itself being another import from the east), jugs, and cups. Its decoration provides some of the best evidence for the spread of Oriental motifs. The city was far more responsive to the east than Athens was at this period, and from about 725 BC pots in the so-called Proto-Corinthian style are covered with animals, foliage, flowers, and rosettes. Human figures are less common, but one vase, the Chigi vase of about 650 BC, stands out for its magnificent representation of hoplites, armed foot-soldiers, the new mass troops of the Greek world. Another innovation, from about the same date, is black-figure drawing, figures in black with details of their anatomy incised on them set against the natural buff background of the clay. It is a process which was probably learnt from eastern metalworkers and remained exclusive to Corinth until the Athenians adopted it a hundred years later (setting their black figures against an orange background). Corinthian dominance in the pottery world lasted into the sixth century when, for reasons not fully understood, it was supplanted by that of Athens.

One Oriental import to Corinth was that of temple prostitution, a practice probably borrowed from the Phoenician city of Byblos. High up on Acrocorinth the fertility goddess Astarte, transformed into the Greek goddess of love, Aphrodite, oversaw ritual prostitution. The easy sexual mores of Corinth lasted for centuries and were encountered by the representative of another Oriental cult, the apostle Paul, during an eighteen-month stay in the city in the first century AD. The clash of two very different approaches to sexual behaviour was to inspire Paul's celebrated Letters to the Corinthians with their enormously influential teachings on Christian sexuality.

In the middle of the seventh century another part of the east became open to the Greeks. King Psammetichus (Psamtek) of Egypt, in the process of establishing the independence of his state from Assyria (p. 104), welcomed Greek mercenaries and later traders. For the Greeks the rich corn surplus of the Nile valley was the main attraction, but papyrus and linen were probably also a lure. In return the Greeks may have brought oil and wine, and silver, always rarer and more precious to the Egyptians than gold. The Greeks were given their own trading-post at Naucratis in the western Delta on a tributary of the Nile, and it appears to have been in operation by 620 BC. Soon Greeks were visiting Egypt not only as merchants but as awe-inspired tourists. The poetess Sappho's brother came as a merchant. (He was reputed to have fallen in love with an expensive courtesan in Naucratis.) Egypt was seen as the fount of traditional wisdom, and some Greeks even mistakenly believed it to have been the origin of their own culture.

Archilochus and Life on the Frontier

The world of the seventh century was a fluid one, a frontier society in which the Greeks were expanding among new peoples and influences but one in which they survived with an increased sense of confidence. It is lucky that, as a complement to the mounds of pottery and the bronze luxury goods, a few voices of the period survive to speak down the ages. The poet Archilochus, for instance, gives an extraordinarily vivid picture of life in a new colony. He was illegitimate, from the relatively barren island of Paros (its famous marble was not yet being exploited), and set out with his father and a band of settlers in the early seventh century to colonize the north Aegean island of Thasos. It was a primitive and harsh world he found there. The colony was under threat both from native Thracians and rival settlers. It was not a world of heroic values but one in which the struggle for survival was paramount. Archilochus mentions how he once threw away his shield when in flight, an unheard-of humiliation for a Homeric hero, and he talks of his distaste for the strutting commanders with their neatly shaven chins. A tough down-to-earth soldier was worth much more in the kind of everyday crisis the settlers faced.

Archilochus was direct and earthy in his passions. He conceived a love for the daughter of one of his fellow settlers but her father refused him. His invective was immediate:

> May he lose his way on the cold sea
> And swim to the heathen Salmydessos,
> May the ungodly Thracians with their hair
> Done up in a fright on the top of their heads
> Grab him, that he knows what it is to be alone
> Without friend and family. May he eat slaves' bread
> And suffer the plague and freeze naked,
> Laced about with the nasty trash of the sea.

May his teeth knock the top on the bottom
As he lies on his face, spitting brine,
At the edge of the cold sea, like a dog.
And all this it would be a privilege to watch,
Giving me great satisfaction as it would
For he took back the word he gave in honour,
Over the salt and table at a friendly meal.

(Translation: Guy Davenport)

He even spread the tale that Lycambes, the father, and his daughter committed suicide as a result of the hatred and humiliation he threw at them.

Archilochus introduces a new world of poetry, that of the lyric. At its simplest the term means no more than a song accompanied by the lyre. The lyric must have originated in the songs, now vanished, of everyday life in Dark Age Greece—wedding songs, harvest songs, work songs. It is tied in with the world of the present, in contrast to the epic, which is set in the world of the past, a world where gods and supermen act out their heroic exploits. Lyrics also bring out the personal voice of the poet. In the words of Peter Conrad, 'The lyric protagonist is not a man who does things but to whom things happen . . . if the epic is a social act, the lyric is a personal testimony, the lyric is the interior of epic, it testifies to the vulnerability of the character inside the armour.' Archilochus and his abandoned shield comes to mind.

There is probably no one reason why the seventh century is an age of lyric poetry. It may reflect a period of confusion in which the collective memories exploited by the traditional singer as he moved from hearth to hearth have been shattered. The poet without a common culture to draw on is thrown back as an individual on to his own resources. Certainly Archilochus speaks straight from his heart and has no time for conventions of behaviour and courteous living. His is the voice of one man against a hostile world.

Sappho

There were many lyric poets between the seventh and fifth centuries. The ability to compose songs may have been, in fact, an expected accomplishment of any educated person (although in the Hellenistic period nine lyric poets were picked out as supreme masters and mistresses of the art). The work of most exists only in fragments and their greatness cannot be fairly judged. From this period the most celebrated was Sappho, the poetess of the island of Lesbos.

Sappho has intrigued later generations as much because of her sexual feelings as her poetry. The nineteenth-century prejudices against eastern influence on the Greeks have already been mentioned. These prejudices went deeper. The Greeks were expected to be not only culturally pure but also sexually pure. Scholars, for instance, found it difficult to imagine that Greeks may have enjoyed a wide variety of bisexual experiences without guilt and they misread or ignored the evidence which suggested otherwise. In his study of Sappho, Richard Jenkyns quotes some of the reactions of nineteenth-century scholars to the suggestion that the poetess may have been a practising lesbian. 'It is clear that Sappho was a respectable person in Lesbos,' one puts it rather primly, while another talks assuredly of her virgin purity: 'although imbued with a fine perception of the beautiful and brilliant she preferred conscious rectitude to every other source of human enjoyment'.

Sappho was born in the late seventh century on the island of Lesbos but spent part of her early life in exile in Sicily. When back in Lesbos she seems to have become the mentor or teacher of a sacred band of women dedicated to the worship of Aphrodite. It is understandable that the feelings within the group would have become intense, but there is also a story that Sappho married and had a daughter. A legend says that she committed suicide by throwing herself off a cliff when rejected by a man she loved. A possible date for her death is about 570 BC.

Only one complete poem of Sappho's survives. It is a hymn to the goddess Aphrodite in which the poet calls on the goddess in terms of easy intimacy to help soothe her love for another woman. Once again, she tells the goddess, she has got into an emotional mess and needs help. This is typical of Sappho. She comes across as a person of intense and unguarded emotions. It is her vulnerability which is one of her main attractions ('Love, looser of limbs, shakes me again, a sweet-bitter resistless creature', as one fragment runs). In the best-known of her poems she describes her feelings when a woman she is attracted to is wooed by a young man:

> Peer of immortal gods he seems to me, that
> Man who sits beside you, who now can listen
> Private and close, so close, to your sweet-sounding
> Voice and your lovely
>
> Passionate laughter—ah, how that, as ever,
> Sets the heart pounding in my breast; one glance and
> I am undone, speech fails me, I can no longer
> Utter a word, my
>
> Tongue cleaves to my mouth, while sharp and sudden
> Flames lick through me, burning the inward flesh, and
> Sight's eclipsed in my eyes, a clamorous humming
> Rings through my eardrums;
>
> Cold sweat drenches down me, shuddering spasms
> Rack my whole flame, a greener-than-grassy pallor
> Holds me, till I seem a hair's breath only
> This side of dying.
>
> Yet all must be ventured, all endured, since . . .
>
> (Translation: Peter Green)

Sappho's feelings for the natural world are as sensual as her feelings for people. In the poem known as Fragment II, Sappho calls Aphrodite to an orchard where cool water runs through the apple trees, alongside a meadow of spring flowers and gracious breezes. As Richard Jenkyns suggests, the sounds of many of the words she uses, *keladei*, for running water, *tethumiamamenoi*, for the perfumed smoke rising from a sacrifice, *aithussomenon*, for the sparkling of light on moving leaves, combine with their meaning to create the mood of sensuous languor. It is no surprise that Sappho has exercised such power over later generations.

The eighth and seventh centuries were a period of rapid change. The old aristocratic Greek values were now under siege from a world where initiative and good luck were valued. The expansion of the Greek world offered new opportunities for those whose lives had been frustrated by poverty back home. The opportunities were keenly exploited. From being culturally open to the east Greece had now absorbed its example and was spreading its own culture throughout the Mediterranean world. With it came exciting opportunities for new trade. The feeling of success flowed back into mainland Greece and the citizens of its cities. In the next decades they were to take power into their own hands from the aristocratic elite and a whole range of new political arrangements became possible. They are the subject of the next chapter.

FURTHER READING

Fernand Braudel's masterly history of the Mediterranean has been cited (see Chapter 1 above); John Boardman, *The Greeks Overseas*, is the standard introduction (4th edition, London, 1999). Vol. iii, Part 3, of the *Cambridge Ancient History* (Cambridge, 1982) provides a detailed overview. See also G. Tsetskhladze and F. de Angelis, *The Archaeology of Greek Colonization* (Oxford, 1994), and, for the west, David Ridgway, *The First Western Greeks* (Cambridge, 1992). Barry Cunliffe's *Greeks, Romans, and Barbarians: Spheres of Interaction* (London, 1988) looks at wider aspects of the relationship. Oswyn Murray, *Early Greece* (2nd edition, London, 1993), is good on Orientalizing, as is Boardman, and I have relied heavily on Walter Burkert, *The Orientalizing Revolution: Near Eastern Influence on Greek Culture in the Early Archaic Age* (Cambridge, Mass., 1992). For this whole subject J. Boardman, *The Diffusion of Classical Art in Antiquity* (London, 1994) is now fundamental. An important recent book is S. Morris, *Daidalos and the Origins of Greek Art* (Princeton, 1992), although some feel that Morris overestimates the impact of the east. There are relevant essays in John Coleman and Clark Walz (eds.), *Greeks and Barbarians* (Bethesda, Md., 1997).

On Archilochus and Sappho see the following: Peter Green, *In the Shadow of the Parthenon* (London, 1972); R. Jenkyns, *Three Classical Poets: Sappho, Catullus and Juvenal* (London, 1982); Carol Dougherty (ed.), *Cultural Poetics in Archaic Greece* (Cambridge, 1993); Ann Burnett, *Three Archaic Poets: Archilochus, Alcaeus, Sappho* (London, 1983). There is also a chapter on lyric and elegiac poetry by Ewen Bowie in the *Oxford History of the Classical World*.

10 | Hoplites and Tyrants: The Emergence of the City State

The Hoplite Army

When an *oikistes*, the leader of a new colony, had reached foreign soil and completed the rituals of landing, his first task was to make out a defensible site for his followers. Simple stone or mudbrick houses were erected and the whole surrounded by walls. Land was parcelled out among the founding settlers, its boundaries marked by ditches. The later Greek written sources suggest that public buildings were erected at the moment of foundation but the archaeological evidence now shows the process was often delayed. Surveys of Megara Hyblaea, an eighth-century colony on the east coast of Sicily, show, for instance, that land was indeed set aside for public buildings from the start but that none was actually erected until a century later. Megara Hyblaea is different from the Phoenician settlements in that the fertility of the soil seems to have been a greater lure than trade (the harbour was a poor one).

The existence of these proto-urban settlements must have been precarious. As Fernand Braudel has pointed out, it is easy to be deceived by the charm and beauty of the Mediterranean and forget the underlying daily toil needed to make the land fertile. The fundamental fact about the Mediterranean climate is its instability. 'One can never be certain of the harvest until the last moment', as Braudel puts it (in *The Mediterranean and the Mediterranean World*) after cataloguing the threats of late frosts, droughts, and floods to soil which is already eroded. Greece now, as in ancient times, is particularly vulnerable as a result of poor soil and fluctuating rainfall. (See further Chapters 7 and 13.) Other parts of the Greek world were wealthier. Sicily and southern Italy, for instance, had soil which was rich in lava and enjoyed higher rainfall than today. In contrast to mainland Greece, the land was heavily wooded. Perhaps most importantly, however, there was room for expansion once the original foundation was secure. Relationships with the local population had to be stabilized, but it appears that in most cases this was done without difficulty. Syracuse ended up with some 4,000 square kilometres (compared with 2,500 for the whole of Attica). Acragas, on the southern Sicilian coast, planted her expansive plains with vines and became a centre for the breeding of horses. Hundreds of her citizens kept their own racing stables. From her wealth she was able to construct walls which enclosed 1,800 hectares, the largest in the Greek world, and to build a succession of massive temples. Cyrene in north Africa was another area where the combination of the shrewd use of the land and the subjection of the local population brought substantial prosperity.

The typical Greek settlement was, inevitably, obsessed with its survival. With resources so limited there was continual and debilitating conflict between neighbours. Cities fought over plains, over trade routes, over their borders. As most were relatively poor there were special problems in conducting these struggles. There was no question of a city affording a standing army, so farmers had to double as soldiers. The result was the hoplite army (the word 'hoplite' came from *hoplon*, a heavy shield with a hoop at the centre, through which the arm would go, and a grip on the rim), drawn from the richer peasants, perhaps the wealthiest third of a city's population. These could provide their own 'uniform', bronze helmet, shield, cuirass, and greaves, with a sword and stabbing spear as weapons (and possibly afford to employ labour while they were in training or fighting).

The hoplites were trained to fight in rows, one formed up behind the other, making a phalanx. The men of each row either linked their shields together and advanced with spears held over their heads or held their shields on the left and carried their spears under their right arms. Cooperation was vital because each soldier depended on the next in line for protection by his shield. Manoeuvring forward to the accompaniment of a piper with suitably bloodcurdling yells, they must have relied heavily on force of impact. (An excellent illustration of the march forward comes on the Chigi vase of *c.*650 BC now in the Villa Giulia, the Etruscan museum in Rome.) Cavalry were useless against such a force, unless they could strike from the side. The horses were too vulnerable, and riders, still without stirrups at this time would easily have been dislodged. Any traditional warrior heroes of the old school would simply have been trampled underfoot. The only effective counter-force was another group of hoplites, and this explains why hoplite armies spread throughout the Greek world from the seventh century onwards.

The normal hoplite engagement was a low level affair with a few hundred men on each side. It was primarily aimed at making a show of strength against neighbours, and the actual capture of a rival city would normally have been beyond the hoplites' capabilities. Once two sides met they would shove into each other and then prod and slash until one side gave way. (The most vulnerable parts of the anatomy were the groin, open to a successful stab under the shield, and the neck.) The successful army would then raid its opponents' crops. A large battle was rare. The Spartans fought no more than four between 479 and 404, while the historian Thucydides only records two during the entire course of the Peloponnesian War (431–404 BC). At the first battle of Mantineia (418), described by Thucydides as 'the greatest battle for some time', 20,000 men might have been involved. Only about 1,400 appear to have died (300 of these on the victorious Spartan side).

Thucydides says that the Spartan custom was to fight long and hard during a battle but not to spend much time in pursuit, the time when massacres of the defeated enemy would have been easiest. (It would have been difficult, in any case, to travel far in hoplite armour.) Hoplite warfare was perhaps more to do with the assertion of the identity and pride of a city than with killing for its own sake. Polybius, the second-century BC Greek historian whose major work was an examination of why the Romans defeated the Greeks, tells how the Greeks 'made public declarations to each other about wars and battles in advance, when they decided to risk them, and even about the places into which they were about to advance and draw up their lines'. In other words, there were well-understood rituals within which combat took place. (These were to break down towards the end of the fifth century: see Chapter 17.)

Effective hoplite armies had to be well trained. Anyone who fell over in a charge, or got his spear tangled up, would have caused chaos in the tightly knit ranks. Morale was important, and each side would have had its own methods of building up courage, just as with a modern football team before a match. According to Thucydides, the Spartans before Mantineia 'sang war songs and exchanged words of individual encouragement reminding each other of their proven courage'.

The rise of the hoplite marked an important shift in loyalties. It is arguable whether hoplite warfare was the result of a rise in community spirit or whether the growth of communities spawned hoplite warfare but certainly while the Homeric hero would have fought for his own glory or that of his family, the hoplite was expected to give his loyalty to his *polis*. The poet who catches the moods of this new world is the seventh-century Spartan Tyrtaeus. The most important virtue now is courage used in the service of the community. The death of a courageous man is remembered for all time in his home city, bringing glory both to himself and to his family. In one of the fragments which are all that survive of his work, Tyrtaeus tells how with such a man:

> Young and old alike weep for him,
> and the whole city is filled with a sad longing,
> and a tomb and children and his family survive him.
> Never has fame forgotten a brave man or his name,
> But though he is under the earth he becomes immortal,
> whosoever excelling, and standing firm, and fighting
> for his land and children, is killed by mighty Ares.

> (Translation: Oswyn Murray)

The Tyrants

Aristocratic prominence had been founded first on the ideal of the warrior chief, capable of great feats of arms, and, secondly, on control of land (without which the warrior role could not have been sustained). The more fragmented world of the seventh century, with its creation of new communities and the steady growth of trade, released new energies which undermined aristocratic power. Some cities managed to adapt peacefully to the challenge of these new forces. A government where power was in the hands of an aristocratic council or shared between aristocratic families could be broadened to include citizens of wealth or those who provided military service. In many cities, however, the tensions were not contained or defused. In Aegean Greece in particular, in the century after 650 BC, a succession of city governments were overthrown by ambitious individuals who exploited popular resentments with the aristocracy to seize power. These were the tyrants. Corinth was the first tyranny, followed by its neighbours Sicyon and Megara. The first Athenian tyrant was Peisistratus, who seized power permanently, after several abortive attempts, in 546. There were tyrannies on the Aegean islands, Samos and Naxos, for instance, and in the Ionian cities of the coast of Asia Minor.

The word 'tyrant' is another of those Greek words which originate in the east, possibly from Lydia. Originally it may have meant no more than a ruler, but as Greek democracy developed and all forms of one-man rule became abhorrent the Greeks themselves gave the word the connotations that still surround it today. In the very limited sources which survive, tyrants are often portrayed in a stereotypical way, with their individualism and lack of restraint contrasted with the cooperative behaviour expected of the 'ideal' citizen. Among their excesses were sexual ones (intercourse with a dead wife and with a mother are among those aberrations recorded). In this sense 'tyrants' become figures onto whom those excluded from power can project their aspirations or hatreds. Philip and Alexander of Macedon are branded as tyrants in fourth-century Athens and there is an echo of such a projection in the assassination of Julius Caesar. Once the stereotype is penetrated for this period, however, it becomes clear that not all tyrants were particularly oppressive. Many glorified their cities and were important patrons of the arts—although the evidence suggests that tyrants did tend to become tyrannical with time.

What were the factors which encouraged the rise of tyrants? The new overseas settlements provided a different model of society, one which showed that an aristocracy was dispensable (although there are cases in the western cities where aristocracies did emerge), and which provided opportunities for those with ambition. The growth of trade and the rise of new interest groups may have increased social tensions. Interestingly, however, from what little is known about the origins of individual tyrants, it does not appear that they were necessarily drawn from a class of new rich. Many, in fact, seem to have been men of aristocratic birth who for some reason or other had found themselves excluded from power. In the Ionian cities of Asia Minor tyrants may have been no more than leaders of conflicting aristocratic factions. In other cases there are hints that a tyrant had a successful military background before seizing power, and in this case he may have been the direct representative of the hoplites. The general pattern, however, is of determined individuals, ready to manipulate traditional or non-traditional means of support to take power unconstitutionally. The implication is that aristocratic governments refused to give way and no other alternative method of political change was available.

One of the best-recorded examples of tyranny is that of Cypselus at Corinth. As has been seen in the previous chapter, Corinth, the trading and commercial centre of the Greek world in the early seventh century, was firmly controlled by the aristocratic Bacchiadae. By the mid-seventh century, however, there were signs that their strength was faltering and that their exclusive hold on power was increasingly resented. The legends suggest that Cypselus' mother was of the Bacchiadae clan, but as she was lame she had been forced to marry outside the clan, thus depriving her son of any chance of a share in political power. This may provide a reason for his determination for revenge. Other sources suggest he may have built up popular support as a military commander. Whatever the truth, about 657 he overthrew the Bacchiadae, sent the clan into exile, and shrewdly distributed their land among his supporters.

Cypselus appears to have had a realistic approach to power. Like many tyrants, he appreciated the need to win, or at least to be seen to be winning, the support of the gods, and he made rich dedications both at Delphi and Olympia. At home he glorified himself and his dynasty through temple-building. Many of the features of Doric architecture, so widely copied throughout the mainland and the Greek west, originated in Corinth (possibly as the result of contact with Egypt: see p. 184). Cypselus and his son Periander, who succeeded him peacefully thirty years later, also successfully boosted the commercial wealth of the city. Corinthian settlements extended into the northern Aegean and the Adriatic, and were kept under closer control than the colonies of any other Greek city, sharing coinage and even having their magistrates sent out from Corinth. The influence of one trading partner, Egypt, was such that Periander called his nephew Psammetichus, after the Egyptian king.

As other tyrannies appeared in the Greek world, Cypselus and his successors built up links with them. It was almost as if the tyrants felt themselves members of an exclusive club. They would help each other seize and maintain power. Sometimes two tyrants would make a friendship which transcended what had been traditional hostility between two cities. Periander of Corinth and Thrasybulus of Miletus provide one example. This in itself suggests the vulnerability of the tyrants. They knew that in the long run their position in the *polis* was weak and their best hope lay in building up a wider network of support.

Ultimately, within the city, tyranny could not be sustained. While Cypselus is recorded as moving freely in Corinth, his successor, Periander, was forced to use a bodyguard. Herodotus recounts lurid stories of him killing his wife and attempting to castrate 300 noble youths of Corcyra (Corfu), a Bacchiadae stronghold. (The purpose was to send them in this mutilated form as a gift to Periander's ally, Alyattes, king of Lydia.) When the tyranny entered a third generation under Psammetichus it was doomed. He was assassinated some four years after coming to power (in about 582 BC). In the neighbouring city of Sicyon, which had produced one of the most flamboyant of tyrants, Cleisthenes (grandfather of the Athenian statesman of the same name), tyranny was similarly overthrown in 555. By 550, with the exception of Athens, where the Peisistratid tyranny lasted until 510, tyrannies were a thing of the past on mainland Greece. They lasted longer in Asia Minor.

For all their efforts to boost trade and glorify their cities, the tyrants never succeeded in creating an ideology of leadership which inspired loyalty from one generation to the next. Once a tyrant became a petty dictator or time dimmed the glamour of a young popular leader, there was no tradition able to sustain tyrannical rule. No tyrant had the resources needed to sustain a full-time army. The hoplites were independent men who made their livelihoods from their land and could not be forged into a passive force for upholding the power of one individual. When tyrannies collapsed, the hoplite class remained in place to take over.

This was the crucial point. As individual tyrants were overthrown, Greek city life might have degenerated into civil war between rival factions. In fact, the tyrants were usually replaced by oligarchies or even democracies. The *polis*, as has been said, was not simply a set of buildings. It was a community of citizens who shared a range of experiences, in the army, in kinship groups, in age-classes, and marriage alliances. As Pauline Schmitt-Pantel has argued in an essay dealing with this period, 'to participate in sacrifices, to belong to the group of ephebes [boys normally between 15 and 20] and then to the hoplites, to take part in choruses, funerals and assemblies are all activities peculiar to citizens. These activities', she goes on, 'form a chain: each is linked to the next.' The result was a continual round of gatherings which served to reinforce the cohesion of the citizen community (or at least its adult males), and it was precisely this cohesion that the tyrants failed to break down or organize for their own benefit. It was natural that the government of the city itself should devolve on to part or even the whole of the citizen body in the shape of oligarchical (Greek *oligos*: few; *archos*: ruling) or democratic (Greek *demos*: people; *kratia*: power) rule. It was also natural that the citizen community should define itself in contrast to the outsider. As a male body, it segregated and secluded the female. As a body of free men, it felt no inhibitions about reinforcing this status by consolidating slavery. As Moses

Finley put it, 'one aspect of Greek history is the advance, hand in hand, of liberty and slavery.' (These points will be discussed further in Chapters 13 and 15.)

Sparta

The ways in which the hoplite class adapted to changing political conditions can be seen in the history of the two most important cities of the Greek mainland in this period, Sparta and Athens. Neither were typical city states. Each had, in differing ways, access to far more resources than the smaller cities, and as a result both were able to act on a wider stage. They played a dominant role in the Persian Wars of the early fifth century and then, perhaps inevitably, they became locked into deadly conflict with each other in the Peloponnesian War of 431–404 BC, a war in which Sparta emerged victorious before collapsing a few years later from exhaustion.

The city of Sparta lay along a series of low hills overlooking the river Eurotas in the southern Peloponnese (its immediate territory is known as Laconia). The site had good natural defences, and no city wall was built around it until Roman times. The city had originated as a number of scattered villages. It never had the great public buildings enjoyed by other cities and it is now a desolate place to visit. When the villages were joined to form a city state some form of compromise must have been hammered out between two ruling families. The result was that Sparta was left with two hereditary kings. They held a whole range of traditional powers and privileges, but by the sixth century their most important role was as religious leaders and as commanders of the Spartan armies. They were also members of a largely aristocratic body of thirty councillors, the *gerousia*, elders elected by the citizen body by acclamation from those who had reached the age of 60. As in most cities, there was also a citizen assembly. Its role appears to have been consultative, listening to proposals put forward by the kings or elders and approving or disapproving them.

At some point in her history Sparta began subduing surrounding villages. Although their inhabitants, known as the *perioikoi* ('those living around' i.e. on less fertile hill-land) were totally dependent on Sparta, they retained their settlements, enjoyed some aspects of local government, and were free to engage in crafts and manufacturing. They also provided their own contingents for the Spartan army although they had no say in Spartan politics. By the eighth century the city was looking further afield, across Mount Taygetus to Messenia to the west. The motives for the expansion are unclear. The land was rich but Sparta had already enough to meet her needs in Laconia and conquest of Messenia left her with a less defensible boundary. It may have been more a matter of defining an identity through successful war. After twenty years of fighting in the late eighth century, Messenia too was subdued. Here the occupation was harsher.

The land was divided equally among Spartan citizens as if it had been no more than a new colony. The local population, the helots, were reduced to serfs cultivating their new masters' land.

It was clear from the start that the Spartan hold on Messenia was a precarious one, not only because the native population did not take to its fate easily but also because Spartan expansion aroused the suspicion of neighbours. One of these was the city of Argos to the north-east of Sparta. There are hints in the literary sources that Argos may have been the first city to use hoplites (interestingly, the earliest known hoplite helmet, of about 725 BC, has been found there). According to a much later source, the Argive army, perhaps exploiting its superiority, inflicted a traumatic military defeat on Sparta at Hysiae in 669. If so, Sparta must have been shaken to the core, especially when there is also evidence of a rebellion in Messenia which took another twenty years to subdue.

It was probably during these years that the Spartan constitution became oligarchic. The only evidence for the development is a passage by Plutarch, written many centuries later, but probably drawing on a work by Aristotle on the Spartan constitution. (The passage is very difficult to interpret: see Oswyn Murray's overview of the problems involved in his *Early Greece*, 2nd edition, pp. 165–71.) It appears that the citizen assembly had acquired some kind of sovereignty in decision-making although, the passage goes on, when this was abused the kings and the elders had the right to overrule decisions. What the passage does not say is that the assembly also had the power to elect annually five *ephoroi*, ephors, from among the citizen body. The ephors were responsible for maintaining, from day to day, the overall good order of the state, in particular scrutinizing the activities of the kings. Every month they renewed their loyalty to the kings in return for the kings' promise to respect the laws of the state. In short this was a balanced constitution in which kings, elders, ephors, and the assembly each had a role to play.

Alongside political change came social change. If the city was to survive it had to build a hoplite army of its own, and here Sparta had a distinct advantage over other Greek cities. The *perioikoi* and the helots could provide for the economic needs of the state and so this left the entire male citizen body free for war. Unlike other cities, where hoplites formed a richer minority drawn from the citizen body, in Sparta all male citizens were hoplites by virtue of their citizenship. There is evidence that the change took place under aristocratic supervision. The tightly disciplined hoplite ranks were very different from the old aristocratic warrior bands, yet in Sparta the same terminology was used to describe them both. The messes in which the soldiers ate were made up of fifteen men, the same number as in an aristocratic 'symposium'. (For the symposium, see p. 217.) It seems, therefore, that aristocratic cultural forms continued to be dominant. Certainly, once the second Messenian war was over and the city relaxed in what was a period of peace and prosperity, this is the impression that remains. There was widespread trade with the east, and bronze craters (mixing-bowls, one of the main symbols of aristocratic conviviality) from the city are found as far afield as France and southern Russia. (The Vix crater may be one of them.) Spartan athletes dominated the Olympic Games throughout the seventh century. The *gerousia* remained an integral and influential part of the political system.

It was not to last. There were pressures on Spartan society which gradually destroyed the possibility of aristocratic lifestyles. It can be sensed in the word the Spartans used of themselves, *homoioi*, 'those who are similar'. Uniformity was imposed upon them by fear, the continuous threat of revolt by those they had subjugated. The Spartan state became heavily militarized, with every aspect of the life of its male citizens defined from the moment of birth. This was hoplite society at its most extreme, the complete crushing of individual identity into the service of the state. (See Chapter 13 for a fuller discussion of Spartan society.)

It was only to be expected that such a paranoic society should gradually isolate itself from the outside world. Few Spartan victors are recorded in the Olympic Games after 570 BC. Trade contracted as the state moved towards self-sufficiency. A vivid reminder of this is the iron bars retained by the Spartans as currency long after the rest of the Greek world had moved on to silver coins. There was also an idealization of the past, and, in the sixth century, the Spartans even went so far as to associate themselves with Agamemnon, the legendary leader of the Greeks in the Trojan War. The constitution was given a hallowed status which protected it against reform. The bringing of *eunomia*, good order, was prized as its main achievement. The rituals of Sparta, those relating to the succession of the king, for instance, were also unlike anything known elsewhere in the Greek world.

Sparta provides an excellent case study in the nature of conservatism (and is a useful reminder that the Greeks were not always innovators). As a model it has continued to have sympathizers into modern times. As Richard Jenkyns has pointed out in his *The Victorians and Ancient Greece*, in Victorian times Spartan upbringing was compared to that of an English public school. In both cases, it was noted with approval, children were taken from their ancient family homes to be trained for the good of the country. Beatings and rough games were acceptable parts of the system, which finally produced reserved but steady citizens. The experience of the twentieth century has tarnished such a view. The rigid training of an elite to uphold the honour of the state against its enemies has been too prominent a feature of both communist and fascist societies to attract much support now. (Hitler, one is not surprised to learn, showed some enthusiasm for Sparta.)

The morale of the Spartan citizens (as with that of the subjects of any totalitarian state) needed to be maintained by continual mobilization. The city was not always successful. In about 560 BC at the Battle of Fetters against the city of Tegea in southern Arcadia (it was called this because the Spartans marched out with fetters with which to enslave the Tegeans when they had been overcome), it was Sparta who was defeated. She now acted in a more restrained way. When Tegea was eventually conquered she was maintained as a dependent city, but not, like previous conquests, incorporated into the Spartan state. In the 540s Sparta had her revenge on Argos and extended her influence into the eastern Peloponnese. She was now the most powerful state in the peninsula. Even Corinth was prepared to accept her dominance, partly because Argos, for centuries the most powerful city of the eastern Peloponnesian coast, had been an enemy of hers too. The cities of the northern Peloponnese were encouraged to form alliances with Sparta. Those which had tyrannical governments were helped to overthrow them and adopt an oligarchical model instead.

With her position secure in the north, Sparta's ambitions now extended across the Isthmus. She continued to champion oligarchy against tyranny. In 524, with the help of Corinth's navy, she tried, unsuccessfully, to overthrow Polycrates, tyrant of Samos. In 510 Spartan troops were to be found intervening against the tyranny of the Peisistratids of Athens. Sparta's interventions were motivated not just by her hatred of local tyrannies. She was increasingly conscious, as was all Greece, of the looming power of Persia. Embassies had come from several peoples outside Greece, the Lydians, the Scythians, and Egyptians, asking for help, but Sparta had been unable to save any of them from Persian expansionism. Persia, as a monarchy, aligned herself naturally with the tyrants of the Greek world and Sparta found herself left as the most powerful defender of Greek freedom and independence.

Sparta may have appeared powerful to the outside world but in fact her strength was limited. There were several factors which inhibited a forceful foreign policy. First, she never became a major sea power and this restricted her ability to act beyond the Greek mainland. At the same time she always remained vulnerable at home. The helots were not like the slaves of a typical Greek city who had no common heritage. Those in Messenia, at least, had a shared culture and experience of oppression. A revolt which took place while the Spartan armies were abroad could have been catastrophic, and Spartan leaders never forgot the possibility that it might happen.

There was also the question of leadership. A king who left the Peloponnese in search of military glory abroad risked upsetting the delicately balanced constitution at home. This became clear during the reign of King Cleomenes (520–490 BC). Once out of his city and with an army under his command, Cleomenes became increasingly assertive. After 510 he tried to define Spartan policy towards Athens and her ruling families with such high-handedness that even Sparta's allies balked. In 494 he crushed a reviving Argos with such brutality (6,000 Argives were reputedly burnt alive in a wood) that his city feared the revenge of the gods for this act of 'hubris' (overweening pride). Faced with the opposition of his fellow king Demaratus, Cleomenes had him deposed. When Cleomenes finally returned to Sparta he was soon dead, presumably liquidated by the oligarchy. From now on the Spartans would be reluctant to let a king out of sight.

Sparta's power was limited in another way. There was no way she could hold down the entire Peloponnese. Her policy of alliances with the northern cities showed she recognized this. However, if she was to expand across the Isthmus she had to cross their territories. At first, and typically, Cleomenes acted as if the allies would simply do what he wanted. When, however, in 506, Cleomenes' plans for another attack on Athens were resisted, notably by Corinth, the Spartans were forced to compromise. They had to accept becoming part of a federation, known to historians as the Peloponnesian League. The League was clearly under the dominance of Sparta, who had the largest and best-trained army, but its structure included a council of all member states, each with one vote. A majority could prevent any military action proposed by Sparta (as happened in 440 when the Spartan assembly voted for war with Athens but was overruled by the League). The League was an early example of inter-state cooperation. It survived (until as late as 366) because no member state could stand up to Sparta, while Sparta was increasingly dependent on the allies' manpower.

Athens in the Sixth Century

As has been seen, one of Cleomenes' expeditions, that of 510, was to overthrow the Peisistratid tyranny in Athens. Athens was to be the focus for Sparta's hostility for over a century, first as a tyranny and then as the Greek world's leading exponent of democracy. Both were inimical to the *eunomia*, good order, sustained by an oligarchical government, which was the ideal of Sparta and her allies.

Archaeologists have found signs of the occupation of the Acropolis, which dominates the city of Athens, as early as 5000 BC, and the rock had been a stronghold of the Mycenaeans. As the Mycenaean civilization collapsed in the twelfth century, Athens and its surrounding area, Attica, survived the worst of the turmoil. Occupation of the Acropolis was uninterrupted, and the inhabitants of Attica later prided themselves on their pure and undisturbed racial heritage. The area was also the springboard for the Ionian migrations (see p. 129), and links, real or imagined, with the Ionian communities of Asia Minor continued to be a factor in Athenian foreign policy well into the fifth century.

Attica was an unusually large area for one Greek city state to control. Its 2,500 square kilometres are made up of three plains, divided by mountain ranges. These are shut off from the rest of Greece by the sea and, in the north-west, by the mountains of Cithaeron and Parnes, but unity was never achieved easily. There had been struggles between Athens and Eleusis, the largest town of the western plain, at some point in the past, and it may not have been until the early seventh century that Athens emerged as the dominant city in Attica.

Even then Athens was comparatively undeveloped as a city. Although she had been one of the leading centres of Greece in the age of Geometric vase painting (see p. 131 above), by 750 she had been eclipsed as an overseas trader by emerging city states such as Corinth and Sparta. The city faced strong competition from Argos, with its fine position on the eastern seaboard of the Peloponnese, and Aegina, an island visible from the Attic coast, which had become an important trading and naval power. Aegina was able to dominate the Saronic Gulf between the island and the Attic coast and proved a serious rival to Athens as late as the fifth century.

In compensation the people of Attica looked inwards. By the sixth century there are signs of dramatic increases of population in the countryside. Attica was not particularly rich (Plato talked of 'the skeleton of a body wasted by disease; the rich soft soil has all run away leaving the land nothing but skin and bone'), but there was variety—timber (for shipbuilding as well as charcoal), grazing land, and the more fertile soil of the plains. Studies of land use in the sixth century show that the upland townships were particularly prosperous. One major centre, the largest settlement in Attica after Athens, was Acharnai, which exploited the local woodland for charcoal, the only fuel suitable for cooking and heating in the city. The wealth of Acharnai was such that she provided many of Athens' hoplites. On the lowlands the most successful crop was the olive, which by the early sixth century produced a surplus which Athens was able to spare for export. Attica also had good clay, used to make her fine pottery. Two assets still to be exploited at this date were her marble, the finest coming from the slopes of Mount Pentelicus, and, most important of all, the rich silver mines of Laurium, only mined successfully from the late sixth century (although they had been exploited in a modest way as early as Mycenaean times). The Athenian economy was thus a complex one, and it operated at several different levels, with farmers and craftsmen producing for their own needs, for those of her neighbours, and, increasingly, as it became more sophisticated, for overseas markets.

In the eighth and seventh centuries Athens remained a state controlled by the landed aristocracy. Some sixty different aristocratic clans are known by name. Between them they selected the three ruling magistrates (the archons), who after their one-year term of office joined a council which took overall responsibility for affairs of state. It was known as the Council of Areopagus, after the hill on which it met in Athens. As each clan had its own territorial base, conflict between them was probably inevitable. In about 632 one aristocrat, Cylon, tried to seize power with the help of the neighbouring city of Megara (whose tyrant, Theagenes, was his father-in-law). He failed, and his supporters were massacred at the instigation of a rival clan, the Alcmaeonids, despite a promise that they would be spared. The Alcmaeonids were expelled from Attica for this insult to the gods, and the bodies of their ancestors were dug up and thrown over the state boundaries. A curse remained attached to the clan.

This tension between clans was only one part of a wider political and social crisis in Athens. By the late seventh century the state had started to participate in the outside world. As population increased there was growing need for grain, and this may have been the reason why the Athenians began establishing colonies in the north Aegean and the Black Sea. The first was Sigeum, founded shortly before 600 BC at the entrance to the Dardanelles, but the Athenians were latecomers to the area and had to fight the Mytileneans for it. (There is continuing debate on the extent to which Athens was dependent on grain exports not only this early but in her later history. It is assumed here that the dependency at least by the fifth century was acute.) Back home there is also evidence of a diversification of the Athenian economy, with a new emphasis on trade and crafts. Although craftsmen still suffered from traditional prejudices against any activity involving physical labour, three potters from Attica became wealthy enough to dedicate sculptures with accompanying inscriptions on the Acropolis.

Rather later than many other cities of Greece, the aristocratic ruling class of Athens was thus threatened by new economic and social pressures. The authors who describe these pressures, Aristotle and Plutarch, were both writing very much later and a great deal about them remains obscure. At one level they appear to reflect conflict between the city, which was most open to outside influences, and the countryside. There were other pressures building up over land use. It has proved very difficult to define the relationships between the aristocracy and the poorer landholders, but it is certainly true that the very poor could fall into such a degree of debt as to end up as slaves who could even be sold abroad by their creditors. There was also a slightly more fortunate class of small landholders who appear to have been bound in some kind of feudal relationship with the aristocracy. It involved surrendering a part of their produce, possibly a sixth, perhaps even five-sixths, of the total annually. This may have been a traditional payment offered in return for protection. It was clearly deeply resented.

The Athenian crisis was thus a serious one involving a variety of tensions, between different aristocratic factions and between the aristocracy and a mass of poorer landowners. One clumsy attempt to deal with the tensions came in 621 when one Draco was commissioned to draw up a law code. The tradition is that this was particularly harsh (hence the term 'draconian'), and biased in the interests of the aristocracy. There is certainly some truth in this. Minor thefts could be punished by death and a debtor could become the personal possession of his creditor. However, it was a step forward that the code was published (making it harder for aristocratic judges to manipulate it in their favour). Draco was also prepared to distinguish between various forms of killings, between those done wilfully and those which were accidental—in other words, accepting the necessity to prove fault. The traditional custom had been that a killer had to bear responsibility for killings of any sort.

The Reforms of Solon

Soon after 600, however, it became clear that Draco's laws were merely palliative. Urgent action had to be taken to avoid civil war. In 594, by a process that is not recorded, the city appointed one Solon to be archon (magistrate) with full powers to reform the state and its laws. Later sources claimed that Solon was of high birth but of moderate wealth. He is supposed to have been busy in trade and to have gained his repute by encouraging the Athenians to seize the offshore island of Salamis from their neighbour, the city of Megara.

Solon has left his own accounts of his period in office. He records his view that the roots of Athens' problems lay in the greediness of the rich, and he tells of public meetings at which he was urged to become a tyrant in order to overthrow aristocratic privilege. However, he claims he had the vision and integrity to refuse and always acted constitutionally. It was not an easy path to take. It was inevitable that any programme of reform which had a reasonable chance of bringing stability was likely to raise resentments among the powerful and frustrate the hopes of the poor, and Solon later described his experience of office as that of a wolf set upon by a pack of hounds.

Solon was in fact a superb political operator. Despite a voiced commitment to the poor, once in power he shifted his ground to portray himself as a mediator between the two sides, holding, as he put it, a strong shield over them so that the honour of neither was slighted. Crucially he sensed the importance of taking an abstract principle, *dike*, justice, to guide him. He argued that *dike* was something achievable by human beings. This is the moment perhaps more than any other, when politics, the belief that human beings could consciously hammer out their own way of living together, was born.

Solon first set himself the task of destroying the privileged position of the aristocracy. All forms of debt ownership were abolished, and Solon even claims that he searched overseas for Athenians who had been sold abroad. The payment of a part of any produce also ended, and Solon rejoices over the tearing up of the stones which marked the land subject to the dues. Next followed the opening up of government to a wider class of citizens. Here again Solon's steadiness and good sense prevailed. He sensed that too radical a reform would lead to either chaos or to an aristocratic reaction (though it may also have been that his aristocratic background caused him to steady his programme). His response was to divide the citizen body into four classes on the basis of wealth. The richest class, the *pentakosionmedimnoi*, was made up of those with land which yielded 500 or more measures of grain, oil, or wine. It extended beyond the old aristocratic class. Below it the *hippeis* was made up of men with 300 measures of yield. The name suggests that they were seen as capable of raising their own horses for war. The next class, the *zeugitai*, with 200 measures or more, corresponded to those with enough wealth to equip themselves as hoplites. The final class, the *thetes*, were those with access to little or no land.

By now the city appointed nine archons annually. They were selected, probably by lot, from forty candidates from the *pentakosionmedimnoi* who had been elected by tribal groups. The breadth of the *pentakosionmedimnoi* class and the introduction of selection by lot probably ensured that the traditional aristocracy could no longer dominate. Lesser offices were open to the next two classes, but the *thetes* were excluded from office. They had to wait another hundred years, when the desperate need to use them as rowers in the expanding Athenian navy finally earned them a full place in democratic government.

The *thetes* did, in their capacity as citizens, have a role to play, as members of the Assembly. This body was the traditional one found in most aristocratic communities, with the power to express its feelings for and against any major proposal. It may have had, or been given by Solon, the power to listen to appeals for justice by aggrieved citizens either against convictions or the acts of magistrates. Now Solon set up a council of 400 citizens to oversee its business. Later the Council and the Assembly were to be the central institutions of Athenian democracy, but this was never part of Solon's plan. Full democracy was inconceivable at this time. The Council's role may have been designed as a moderating one, to make sure that powerful popular forces expressed through the Assembly did not threaten the stability of the state. The Areopagus retained its role as the guardian of the laws, the supervisor of the archons, and with general control of the state's affairs. Aristocratic influence, even though tempered by the admission of the new rich to political power, remained strong.

As important as his other reforms was Solon's new law code. It was inscribed for all to see on wooden tablets set in rotating frames which were recorded as still intact 300 years later. Here Solon's conviction that right and wrong should be defined by men rather than gods is given full play. Almost every aspect of human conduct, from murder, prostitution, and vagrancy to the correct marking of boundaries between neighbours, is dealt with. Interestingly, economic policy is also covered. The export of grain, for instance, is forbidden, no doubt in an attempt to stop greedy landowners selling such a precious commodity to Athens' neighbours. Citizenship is also offered to those with a craft skill who come to live permanently with their families in Athens.

Not least of Solon's attractions was that he left a lively if fragmentary account of his experiences in poetry. Today this would seem a rather esoteric way of writing one's memoirs, but in the early sixth century poetry was the only literary form (prose writing only began slightly later in Ionia) and it was an entirely appropriate way for a statesman to record his exploits. The 300 lines that remain confirm the portrait of a man with a broad vision and fully developed sense of humanity. His thoughts on *eunomia*, good order, are as follows.

Eunomia makes all things well ordered and fitted
and often puts chains on the unjust;
she smooths the rough, puts an end to excess, blinds insolence,
withers the flowers of unrighteousness;
straightens crooked judgements and softens deeds of arrogance,
puts an end to works of faction
and to the anger of painful strife; under her
all men's actions are fitting and wise.

(Translation: Oswyn Murray)

Again, Solon shows that an abstract principle instituted by human beings can bring harmony.

After Solon left office (probably by 590), legend says he went abroad for at least ten years, uncertain that his reforms would survive. At first it appeared he was right. Athenian politics entered a confused period of struggles between different aristocratic factions. In some years conflict was so intense that no archons could be appointed. (The word *anarchia*, hence the English 'anarchy', was used to describe the result.) The factions were based on local allegiances and are recorded as parties of 'the Plain' or 'the Coast'. It was into this debilitating struggle that a tyrant, Peisistratus, forced his way. His rise to power was a chequered one. There were fifteen years after 560 when he alternated between control of the city and exile, and it was only in 546 that he was secure, living to hand on the tyranny to his sons, Hippias and Hipparchus, in 528.

The Peisistratid Tyranny

Although many of the details are lost, Peisistratus' struggle to win power illustrates some of the factors behind the emergence of tyranny. He first appears as a military leader, winner of a successful campaign against Megara. (It was this campaign which led eventually to the confirmation of the strategically important island of Salamis as an Athenian possession.) He then set about consolidating his support in more concrete ways. He was associated by later Greek historians with a party which was either 'of the Hills' or 'beyond the Hills', and it has been suggested that this referred to the poor in general, the 'Hills' supporting less favoured landowners than the plains and coast. (On the other hand, 'the Hills' may simply have been his territorial base.) He was also something of a showman, allegedly daring to ride into the Agora on one occasion with a local girl purporting to be Athena by his side. Outside Athens he had friends among other tyrants, such as Lygdamis of Naxos, and with cities such as Thebes. One period of exile was spent in Macedonia, where he seems to have amassed enough wealth to employ mercenaries. When he arrived back after his second period of exile, he had the men and enough support from Athenians themselves to be able to crush his aristocratic rivals. Charisma from military victory, alignment with the poor, and, in the final resort, determination and lack of inhibition about using brute force, all played their part in bringing him to power.

The Peisistratid tyranny is poorly recorded, but what details survive show that Peisistratus was a shrewd, and even benign, ruler. He seems to have kept ultimate control of appointments, but the fragmentary archon lists that survive show that aristocratic families were not excluded from power. Culturally the city remained aristocratic, with the fine Athenian pottery of the period decorated in their favoured themes of myth and heroism. However, there was no attempt to tamper with Solon's reforms, and Peisistratus fostered trade and craftsmanship. The Corinthian dominance in the Mediterranean pottery trade was now eclipsed by Athens, with the finest of the Athenian pots found not in Athens but in the tombs of Etruscan Italy. (The fact that so many have survived gives a distorted picture of the size of the industry. Probably no more than a few hundred workers were employed in Athens even at the height of the trade.) Athens' own coins appear for the first time about the middle of the sixth century. At first their silver comes from Thrace, close to Peisistratus' base in exile. Soon Athens' own silver from the mines at Laurium was the main source, and this silver in effect funded the city's increasing need for imported corn. By the end of the century the coinage is graced with the head of Athena on one side and an owl, a bird sacred to the goddess, on the other. The design was to last for 300 years.

The prosperity of Athens gave the Peisistratids the chance to transform the city. It was natural that they should want to enhance the dominance of the city over the surrounding countryside, where their rivals had their territorial bases, but their ambitions went further. They set about establishing Athens as a major religious centre. It may have been before or during his first period of office that Peisistratus initiated the Greater Panathenaea (though there are other possible founders). There had long been an annual festival to Athena, but now every four years there was an especially grand display with processions, and, in imitation of the new games springing up throughout Greece in the sixth century, competitions for amphorae filled with Attic oil. Later, one of the contests was for recitations from Homer. It seems as if an attempt was made to appropriate the poet for the city so as to emphasize its cultural superiority over the rest of the Greek world.

It was also under Peisistratus that the Acropolis was transformed into a treasure house of art. Paradoxically, much of what is known about the transformation is the result of the Persians' destruction of the site in 480 BC. The Athenians brought together the shattered sculpture and buried it in pits on the Acropolis, while columns of broken temples were reused in defensive walls or in the foundations of their successors, leaving a mass of carved stone for scholars to study. Even so, the sequence of building during the sixth century has proved difficult to reconstruct. There appears to have been a temple to Athena constructed about

560, possibly by Peisistratus in his first period of rule, then another on the same site, begun in 520. In between the sacred sites stood a number of *korai*, statues of girls offered as private dedications to the goddess Athena. The largest construction of all, probably started by Peisistratus' sons, was a massive temple to Zeus, Athena's father, on a ridge south-east of the Acropolis itself. (It was only finished, by the emperor Hadrian, 600 years later.)

Archaeologists trying to piece together the great building programmes of the late sixth century have found it difficult to distinguish between the achievements of Peisistratus and those of his sons. Hippias and Hipparchus are credited with the building of a temple to the Twelve Gods (whose foundations survive in the Agora and from where all distances in Attica were measured), and a fine nine-spouted fountain (as yet unrecovered). Another fountain from the same date has been found in the south-east corner of the Agora. Fountains of clear water, replacing the stagnant and often contaminated water of wells, and drains, made of baked clay with heavy collared joints, mark the emergence of a more sophisticated city life, and similar developments have been found in other cities.

By this time, however, the tyranny seems to have lost its vigour. As had happened in Corinth, a second generation of tyrants could not sustain the popularity of the first. There was defeat abroad when Sigeum, the colony on the Hellespont, was lost to Persia. In 514 Hipparchus was assassinated, ironically while he was acting as a marshal at the Panathenaea. (It appears that his advances to a young man, Harmodius, had been rejected, and he had retaliated by refusing to allow Harmodius' sister to participate in the festival. This slight was enough to justify his death at the hands of Harmodius and his lover, one Aristogeiton. Aristotle later wrote that it was in their sexual desires that the tyrants most usually showed their lack of restraint and that this was the most common reason for their fall.) Hippias began to act more harshly, executing his opponents. In 510 the help of Spartan hoplites was called upon to finally overthrow the tyranny. Hippias left for exile, taking up residence in Sigeum, which was still under Persian control. There is no evidence of any major uprising, but the events of 514 to 510 were later regaled as a liberation of the city. A great statue, lost but re-created in the 470s, of Harmodius and Aristogeiton survives in a Roman copy, and is a fine example of the heroic in classical art, the nudity of the two men emphasizing their heroism.

The Reforms of Cleisthenes

The Peisistratids had controlled the aristocracy, but not destroyed it. In the countryside its network of support lay in the phratries. Although much about the nature of the phratries is disputed, they appear to have been associations of adjoining landowners, usually members or supporters of one aristocratic clan.

Membership of a phratry provided the only proof of citizenship, so it was a closely guarded privilege. When the tyranny was overthrown, there appears to have been an immediate aristocratic reaction, partly sustained by nobles returning from exile, in which the phratries were purged of any members considered sympathetic to the tyrants. They lost their citizenship, and the state appeared once again to be falling under aristocratic control with all the rivalries that entailed.

One of the contenders for power was Cleisthenes, a member of the Alcmaeonid clan. Cleisthenes had spent the last years of the tyranny in exile, returning to the city with the Spartans in 510. With the ancient curse still on his family, he had little support from among the traditional aristocracy, but he was clearly an ambitious man and he appealed to the people for support, probably through the Assembly. It is not quite clear how he mobilized the people to his cause, but he must have done so with astonishing effectiveness. In a coherent series of reforms, undertaken in 508/507 BC, he was to break the political power of the phratries and establish genuine equality among citizens.

What is impressive about Cleisthenes' reforms is their radical nature. He appears to have simply bypassed the phratry system, creating a completely new set of political units, the demes, some 140 of them, probably based on local descent groups. (There was also some correlation, in 507, with the place of residence, and the word *deme* is often translated as village. However, when a member of a deme moved, he did not lose his membership of that deme no matter where he later took up residence.) Demes were given responsibility for local order and thus their members were involved directly in administration. They drew up the citizen lists, enrolling young men at the age of 18. To break down regional power groups, Cleisthenes then divided Attica itself into three areas: the town itself, the coastal region, and the interior. Each area had its demes grouped into larger units known as *trittyes*. The culmination of the process was to take one *trittyes* from each region and form the three into one tribe, making ten tribes in all for the whole of Attica. These ten tribes replaced four traditional Ionian tribes. The ten tribes selected (annually, by lot) fifty members each to sit on the council of 400 founded by Solon, which was thus enlarged to 500 members. The Council (also known as the Boule) kept its role as supervisor of the business of the Assembly.

Through his new tribes Cleisthenes also produced the means by which a state army could be raised. Little is known of the sixth-century Athenian army, but, based as it was on the phratries, it must have preserved some elements of the aristocratic war-band. Now men had to train in their new tribes alongside men from other regions. The city was their only common bond and morale must have been improved. From 501, in a reform which was not Cleisthenes', each tribe had to provide a general, *strategos*, elected by the Assembly from those candidates who put themselves forward. The generals, who, unlike other state officials,

could hold their appointment from one year to the next, became the most prestigious figures in the city, gradually coming to overshadow the archons. Their
growing status emphasizes, in fact, the relative lack of power enjoyed by the
other magistrates in Athens (the contrast can be made with the enduring influence over the citizenry of Sparta by the kings and ephors). This is one reason why
the Assembly and the Council were able to consolidate their own power.

There are many gaps in the evidence that survives for Cleisthenes' reforms,
and it may be that the accounts shape them so that they appear to be a stepping-
stone for the democratic revolution of 461. It can be argued, however, that
Cleisthenes was that rare figure in political history, the reformer with a rational
plan for a fairer society which was successfully implemented and sustained. Any
less far-seeing populist reformer might well have stirred up the urban population against the country-based aristocracy. The result would almost certainly
have been a civil war. By introducing democracy in the countryside, Cleisthenes
gave citizens the opportunity to build up administrative experience locally and
also ensured that the countryside would be fully integrated into the Athenian
democracy. (Evidence from inscriptions shows that they took up the challenge
with enthusiasm.) The Assembly was the main beneficiary. The procedure for
selecting its members, the citizens of the state, was now under democratic rather
than aristocratic control. With the end of the influence of the phratries and the
old tribal system, citizens were now able, through the Assembly and Council, to
participate in city affairs as equals (although the archons were still selected from
the richest class). The word *isonomia* was coined to describe the system of equal
balance which now prevailed. Shared experiences in the armed forces must have
strengthened the sense of shared brotherhood. The next development, although
not one necessarily envisaged by Cleisthenes, was to proceed to full democracy,
with decision-making concentrated in the Assembly. (See Chapter 15 for the
process.)

FURTHER READING

For recent overviews, in addition to Murray, Whitley, and Osborne already cited see the
essays in N. Fisher and H. Van Wees (eds.), *Archaic Greece* (London, 1998).

For hoplite warfare see W. K. Pritchett, *The Greek State at War* (Berkeley, 1974), and
V. D. Hanson (ed.), *Hoplites: The Classical Greek Battle Experience* (London, 1991). The
sources on the tyrants are very poor but see A. Andrews, *The Greek Tyrants* (London, 1956),
and more recently J. McGlew, *Tyranny and Political Culture in Ancient Greece* (Ithaca, NY,
1993). G. de Ste Croix argues for the tyrants within a Marxist perspective in his monumental *The Class Struggle in the Ancient Greek World* (London, 1981). (Despite enormous problems in finding 'classes' in the economy of the ancient world, this book has a wealth of
insights into the Greek world right up to the Arab conquests.) Pauline Schmitt-Pantel's
essay is in O. Murray and S. Price (eds.), *The Greek City from Homer to Alexander* (Oxford,
1990).

On Sparta see Paul Cartledge, *The Spartans* (London, 2002) and *Spartan Reflections* (London, 2001). Jenkyns's points are in his *The Victorians and Ancient Greece* (Oxford, 1980). Solon is covered well in Murray's *Early Greece*.

The argument over Athenian grain supplies is fully reviewed by M. Whitby's essay in H. Parkins and C. Smith (eds.), *Trade, Traders and the Ancient City* (London, 1998). Jeffrey Hurwit's *The Art and Culture of Ancient Greece, 1100–480 BC* is good on Peisistratus and see also A. Andrews in the *Cambridge Ancient History*, vol. iii, Part 3, chapters 43 and 44, and vol. iv, chapter 4. On Peisistratus' embellishment of the Acropolis see chapter 6 of Jeffrey Hurwit, *The Athenian Acropolis* (Cambridge, 1999). For new thoughts on the phratries see S. Lambert, *The Phratries of Attica* (Ann Arbor, 1993). On Cleisthenes there is Josiah Ober's essay, 'The Athenian Revolution of 508/9', in C. Dougherty and L. Kurke (eds.), *Cultural Poetics in Archaic Greece* (Cambridge, 1993). See also chapter 5, by Martin Ostwald, in the *Cambridge Ancient History*, vol. iv (Cambridge, 1988). See also P. Manville, *The Origins of Citizenship in Ancient Athens* (Princeton, 1990), and Josiah Ober, *The Athenian Revolution: Essays on Ancient Greek Democracy and Political Theory* (Princeton, 1996).

11 | Cultural Change in the Archaic Age

When specialists began classifying the pottery of Greece, they labelled the material produced between 620 and 480 BC, the period between the Orientalizing and the Classical period, as Archaic (from the Greek *archaios*, old). The term has gradually been extended, first to describe the wider cultural developments of the period and then as one for the age as a whole. Conventionally, the Archaic age has been seen as a prelude to the Classical period, offering hints of what was to come, but one should be cautious in foretelling history in this way and the period is now increasingly valued in its own right as one of the more fascinating periods of Greek political and cultural history.

The age was one when, although they continued to draw on influences from the east, the Greeks increasingly determined their own patterns of development. Perhaps the dominant feel of the period is the gradual coming of order and control. 'The overriding and enduring impulse of Archaic art', writes Jeffrey Hurwit, 'was to formalise, to pattern, to remake nature in order to make it intelligible.' This can be seen in the growing naturalism of statues and the increasing control over subject matter in vase painting, with the chaotic animal parades of the Corinthian vases replaced by ordered depictions of myths. On the Ionian coast there is an intellectual revolution, with the first systematic application of rational thought to the physical world. These changes run alongside those political developments described in the last chapter. Solon and Cleisthenes, for instance, were both applying abstract principles of justice to the practical problems of human beings living in society, very much in the spirit of the cultural changes which will be described here.

The First Coinage

The sixth century was one of increasing wealth in the Greek world as trading contacts multiplied and cities, particularly those on the Ionian coast and in Italy, became more settled and prosperous. Traditionally, the appearance of coinage has been taken as a symbol of this commercial expansion. As an easily carried and stored means of establishing value and facilitating exchange, coinage has proved a fundamental part of every economy to the present day, only under challenge from other forms of transfer of wealth (cheques, and now the electronic transmission of funds) since the last century. The advantages it gave over barter are obvious when the dealings of the Egyptian scribe Penanouqit (p. 84) are recalled. In order to sell his ox he had to take a varied selection of goods in return. Every transaction which involved barter must have been cumbersome.

The historian Herodotus attributed the invention of coinage to Lydia, the wealthy state of western Anatolia which neighboured the Greek cities of the eastern Aegean, and archaeological evidence supports him. The sequence by which Lydian coins developed has been found preserved in the foundation deposit of the temple of Artemis at Ephesus (about 600 BC). The deposit includes metal lumps of a standard size. With them are similar lumps stamped on one side and others stamped on both. It appears that the Lydian kings handed their mercenaries their payment once a year in a single lump of metal (electrum, an alloy of silver and gold). Here are the forerunners of coins, thin circular pieces of metal of standard size stamped by the issuing state. When the first Greek coins appear (on the trading island of Aegina about 595 BC, in Athens about 575, and in Corinth shortly afterwards), they are already stamped on both sides, a clear indication that the Greeks adopted the practice only after it had been fully developed by the Lydians.

Originally coins had the value of the metal in which they were made. There was thus no problem in offering them for exchange because they could always be melted down without losing value. The weight and purity of each coin could be guaranteed by the stamp of the city or kingdom it came from, and an unblemished design on both signs confirmed that it had not been scraped down. Denominations remained large until the fifth century, and most coinage is found in or near the city of its origin. For these reasons it is now believed that the main use for early coins was state accounting. Coins were probably used for paying officials and mercenaries, and for expenditure on public buildings, while recipients could pay taxes, fines, or harbour dues in return. There is some evidence that cities saw their own coinage as a precious resource which should not be 'lost' overseas (though Athens, with her own large reserves of silver, was not so fussy and Athenian coins are more widely scattered than those of any other city). Certainly the persistence of city emblems on coins (those of Aegina are stamped with a turtle, those of Athens with an owl) shows that this is one more way that cities are flaunting their individual identity. It was probably not until the late fifth century that coinage became used in everyday commercial transactions.

Temples and Sculpture: The Influence of Egypt

Even if coinage may not have played a major part in commercial expansion, there is no doubt that this was an age of growing prosperity. The more successful cities flaunted their wealth through their temples, now seen as the showcases of a proud *polis.* Between 575 and 560 a vast sanctuary to the goddess Hera was laid out on the island of Samos. It was entered by a monumental gateway, and within, beside the altar (altars were always kept outside temples so that sacrifices would be accessible to a large audience and the mess and smoke kept in the open air) was a vast temple. It was 100 metres long and 50 metres wide, with a double colonnade, twenty-one columns along each side, eight at the front, and ten at the back. As was now typical of Greek temples, it had a deep porch, and this led into the cella where the cult statue of the god or goddess would stand. (The primary function of a temple was to house a cult figure. Rituals such as sacrifice which required the participation of crowds were held outside on an altar in the surrounding sanctuary (*temenos*).) The temple at Ephesus, where the Lydian coin deposits were found, was even larger, some 115 metres long. Again it had a double row of columns. At Didyma on the coast of Asia Minor there was another vast temple, dedicated to Apollo.

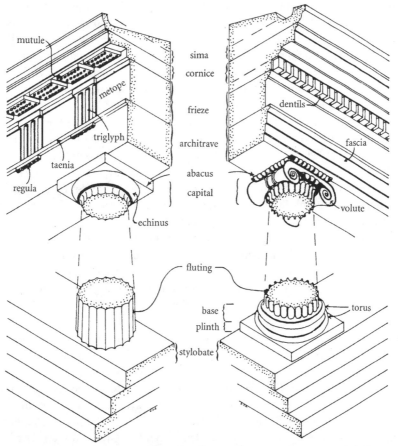

FIG. 1 The Doric and Ionic orders. This figure illustrates the essential differences between the two original classical orders.

These eastern temples carried the scrolled columns of the so-called Ionic order. The development of orders of architecture, particularly through the provision of a model which can be copied, is a typically Archaic achievement. The Ionic order appears to be a Greek invention, though the foliage and decoration that goes with the order still suggests the influence of the east. On the Greek mainland and in the west the Doric order was supreme. In this order the columns are topped by square stone slabs and the whole design is simpler. In the west the richer cities, determined to show off their new-found wealth, built their Doric temples in groups, often along ridges. There were four great sixth-century temples at Selinus in western Sicily, for instance, and two at Posidonia (Paestum) which are still in fine condition.

What were the influences on the development of these huge temples? The Greeks initiated their own tradition of building in stone. The Corinthians were carving limestone by the end of the eighth century, and there are Corinthian temples with limestone walls by the early seventh. The inspiration to be more creative and ambitious with the material possibly came from Egypt. The opening of Egypt by King Psammetichus I (Psamtek) (664–610 BC) encouraged the first major incursion of Greeks, both as traders and visitors, into his country. Inevitably they came into direct contact with its vast array of stone monuments. The pyramids of Giza, for instance, were only 120 kilometres from the Greek trading-post at Naucratis, and visitors would also have had the opportunity to see Psammetichus' own massive building programme in action. It is interesting that the majority of Greeks who settled Naucratis were Ionians, and a taste for monumental art seems to be found largely in the Ionian cities. The temple of Artemis at Ephesus with its double row of columns may be an echo of the columned halls of Egypt, while the famous row of marble lions at Delos seems an almost direct copy of the traditional sacred processional routes of the Egyptian temples.

The Ionians may not have been the only Greeks who borrowed from the Egyptians. Much of the ornament in the Doric order seems to develop directly from earlier Greek timber models (the triglyphs, for instance, are reproductions in stone of the ends of roof-beams), but a comparison can be made between the columns of the shrine of Anubis at the temple of Hatshepsut at Deir el-Bahri and the temples to Hera at Olympia (590 BC) and to Apollo at Corinth (540 BC). Some decorative mouldings on Doric temples, the cavetto, a hollowed moulding in the shape of a quarter-circle, also appear to be Egyptian in origin. The example may have spread to Greece via Corinthian traders.

Another Egyptian influence may be seen in sculpture. In the seventh century small terracotta and bronze statues, with wigged hair, a triangular face, and a flat skull, became common in Greece. They face forward in a rigid pose with both feet together. The style is called Daedalic, after a legendary Greek sculptor, Daedalus, although it originated, with so much else, from the east. By the second half of the seventh century, Greek sculptors begin making life-size Daedalic figures in marble. A famous one is the statue of Nikandre from Naxos, possibly carved as early as 650, another the 'Auxerre goddess' of 630, found in France but probably of Cretan origin. 'The origins of the Nikandre *kore*', writes Jeffrey Hurwit, 'are complex: she owes her shape to a native [Greek] tradition of large scale sculpture in wood, her style to a popular Orientalizing fashion, and her proportions to Egypt. It was probably also the Greek experience in Egypt that gave her sculptor the inspiration and confidence to transpose a large-scale wooden image into marble.'

Marble was to become the preferred material for the sculpture of the period (at least until bronze casting was perfected later in the century) and it also became popular as a building material for temples and other prominent buildings. It can be assumed that the Greeks learnt how to fashion marble after seeing Egyptians working on their native hard stones, granite and diorite. The most common sculptural form now became the *kouros*, a life-size (or even larger) nude male carved in marble, typically with the left leg in front of the right. (The female form, the *kore*, was rarer and always clothed.) It has been demonstrated that these statues were planned out on stone blocks using a similar grid to the Egyptians, but the *kouroi* are normally nude (unlike the clothed Egyptian statues) and their poses are more relaxed and natural than those of their Egyptian counterparts, even though over 150 years, 650–500 BC, their form remains much the same. The *kouroi* stood on sacred sites, often as grave-markers, but also as apparent offerings to the gods. They are most commonly found in the more aristocratic Greek cities. When an aristocratic elite is overthrown, the *kouroi* disappear. It could be said that the *kouros* is an immortalization of a hero at the height of his powers and that he represents the aristocratic male at his most confident. (Andrew Stewart explores this idea in his *Greek Sculpture* (New Haven, 1990).)

In the second half of the sixth century another skill was perfected, the art of large-scale bronze casting by the 'lost wax' method. The earliest surviving bronze sculpture, a *kouros* from the Piraeus, dates from about 525 BC (some experts date it slightly later) and marks the moment when the technical problems involved in casting and assembling bronze statues had been solved. The technique seems to have originated in Samos from models imported from Egypt and the Near East (Samos, for reasons that are not clear, was an important centre of trade) and, like many innovations in the open world of the Aegean, spread quickly. The method involved building up a model in clay and covering it with a thin layer of wax. A further coating of clay was provided which was joined to the inner core by pins which ran through the wax. The whole was then heated, solidifying the clay and causing the wax to run out. The gap between the two layers of clay could then be filled with molten bronze. It was an important revolution in that solid bronze statues often cracked when they cooled and were, in any case, too heavy to transport easily. Soon the Greeks were producing bronzes of the highest quality even though few have escaped being melted down. The Delphi charioteer, the Zeus from Artemisium, and the Riace warriors are among the few that survive from the fifth century.

Among the most engaging buildings of the Archaic age are the city treasuries given by cities, as offerings or evidence of their reverence, to the great sanctuaries of the Greek world. They were simple buildings, normally no more than a marble rectangle faced by two columns. The best known are at Delphi (see p. 239), the site of the Pythian oracle, on the slopes of Mount Parnassus. Here fragments of sculpture or walls survive from treasuries given by Sicyon (in the northern Peloponnese), Athens, and the island of Siphnos. On the sculptured friezes which run around these treasuries were portrayed the myths of the Greek world, often in narrative form. The finest, dating from about 530 BC, are from the Treasury of the Siphnians. They include a three-scene depiction of the judgment of Paris (Paris was asked to judge who was the most beautiful of the goddesses, Hera, Athena, or Aphrodite), a discussion by the gods of the fate of the defeated Trojans, and a long frieze showing a battle between gods and giants. The last was a favourite theme, symbolizing the triumph of good over evil, Greek over barbarian.

The Revival of Athenian Pottery

The emergence of a new interest in myth can also be seen in the pottery of sixth-century Athens. In the seventh century, as has been seen, Corinthian pottery, with its riot of animal life, reigned supreme in the Greek world. The Athenian Geometric style had been completely displaced by it, and in the early sixth century even the Athenian potters were adapting Corinthian styles, letting their animals run in disorder round the vases. By 570, however, the Athenians had resumed control of their pottery. On the François vase (exported to Italy and named after its finder) of this date, the painter Cleitias composed over 200 figures. There are some unrelated animals prancing around one band of the vase which echo the style absorbed from Corinth. However, most of the figures are related to each other and portray the myths surrounding the life of the hero Achilles, including the marriage of his parents, Peleus and Thetis, and the games held in honour of his dead companion, Patroclus. There seem to be two simultaneous developments. First, the painter is imposing a unity of theme. (By the 530s, painters such as Exechias are concentrating on a single event—a game of dice between the two heroes Ajax and Achilles, for instance, or the moment when the mast of the boat bearing the god Dionysus sprouts into a fruitful vine.) Secondly, there is the preoccupation with myth. On these fine pots portrayals of daily life are rare. As with the sculptures of the treasuries, this is the world of the gods and heroes. Traditionally it has been believed that the pots themselves were used for the drinking parties of the aristocracies, the symposia, and they reflect the interests of this class.

In about 525 there is another development. Instead of the figures on a vase being painted in black on an orange background, the process is reversed. Figures are now left in orange/red with the background being painted black. While the details of black figures had to be engraved in the silhouette with a sharp tool, red figures could be drawn on. By the end of the sixth century, when red-figure painting was adopted by a group of Athenian potters known as the Pioneers, the new freedom given to painters was being exploited to the full. Not only are the details of each figure more exact, the figures themselves take on a new lease of life. They jump, tumble, and race across the whole surface of the pots and some are shown foreshortened. 'The invention of the technique of showing foreshortened figures was,' writes the art historian J. J. Pollitt, 'both from a technical and conceptual point of view one of the most profound changes ever to have occurred in the history of art.' The concern of the patrons of this pottery remains, however, largely the same—representations of myth or of scenes of aristocratic life. No one would have guessed from them that the Greek world was one which depended so totally on the labour of farmers.

The phrase 'a new lease of life' is suitable for explaining what happened next. The *kouroi* gradually become more natural and relaxed in their pose. The temple sculptures become less wooden and exploit the spaces they are given—on the triangular pediments, for instance—more successfully. The sculptures of the great temple of Zeus at Olympia of about 460 BC show a real understanding of the feelings and moods of the participants. This is the dawning of a new age, when, in the famous words of the fifth-century philosopher Protagoras, 'man is the measure of all things'. It is associated with the victory of Greece over the Persians and, in Athens, with the triumph of democracy. However, it could not have happened if there had not also been a revolution in intellectual thought, a revolution which saw the birth of western philosophy. (See also Interlude Two, The Classical Age in Art p. 243.)

The Birth of Western Philosophy

In 585, according to the historian Herodotus, a battle between the Medes and the Lydians had been brought to a sudden halt when the sky darkened with an eclipse of the sun. The combatants were so overawed that they made peace with each other. An equally remarkable fact, however, was that the eclipse was said to have been predicted by one Thales, a citizen of the Ionian city of Miletus. It is impossible to say now, from the fragmentary sources, whether Thales had genuinely predicted the eclipse or simply provided an explanation for it after it had happened. He may have been simply passing on material gathered by Babylonian astronomers, and his own picture of the cosmos, described below, would hardly have provided him with a means of prediction. However, the moment is often seen as the birth of Greek philosophy, with Thales, for Aristotle at least, its founding father.

There is no one reason why Greek philosophy should have begun in the Ionian world. The cities of the Asian coast were the most prosperous of the sixth-century

Greek world. Miletus was the richest of all and, like many of the others, had had a tyrant. After he had been overthrown a civil war had broken out. One of the factions in the war was known as 'The Perpetual Sailors', and this underlines the fact that many Milesians must have travelled abroad in search of trade—to Egypt, for instance, and equally to some of the opulent and sophisticated civilizations of the east. Here they would have had the opportunity to observe different cultures and absorb the varying intellectual traditions of these surrounding peoples. This in itself may have shaken conventional assumptions and liberated fresh ways of thinking.

The scholar who has done most to illuminate the birth of 'fresh ways of thinking' within the *polis* itself is Geoffrey Lloyd. For Lloyd the *polis* acts as a cockpit for debate. In the assemblies and the law courts argument was intense, yet there seem to have been restraints on letting these degenerate into outright civil war. In order to formulate and win arguments without a breakdown of order there was every incentive to find first principles from which debate could begin. So in an argument over whether an accused man could be condemned one could be forced back into a discussion of what is meant by 'justice', how evidence is to be tested, and what is an appropriate punishment. Those who 'won' such arguments could earn status as a result and so there was an increasing premium on the facility of reasoning which could be transferred into other 'philosophical' contexts. Lloyd shows how a word such as 'witness' used in the law courts is the root of the word for 'evidence' in scientific discourse and how the term used for cross-examination of witnesses was adopted to describe the testing of an idea or hypothesis. (See, in particular, his *Magic, Reason and Experience* (Cambridge, 1979).)

The process can, perhaps, be picked up in the verse of Solon in Athens (see p. 176) in roughly the same period that Thales was beginning his speculations in Miletus. Solon talks of justice as an abstract principle which can be discussed rationally and introduced into a political system through the actions of men. What is crucial to the development of reasoning is that ideas can be debated without fear of inciting the wrath of the gods. Greek philosophy was remarkable in that it paid little attention to authority figures. As Lloyd points out in his *The Revolutions of Wisdom* (Berkeley, 1987) while in Egypt and the Near East it was unheard of to criticize earlier work, in Greece it was the norm. If earlier 'authorities' were to be challenged then coherent means of doing so had to be elaborated. This placed an emphasis on ways of finding truth and certainty (and an assessment of what 'truth' and 'certainty' actually were in specific philosophical contexts).

The early philosophers were concerned with understanding the nature of the cosmos. The names of three from Miletus survive: Thales and two followers, Anaximander and Anaximenes. All were recorded as practical men. Thales had been involved in politics and had some engineering skills. Anaximander made a map of the known world. Anaximenes was remembered for his skills of observation of everyday things, such as how an oar broke through water and scattered phosphorescence. Philosophy, in fact, may have been only a secondary interest for them. What survives of their thought is very fragmentary and subject to continuing debate. They appear to have shared a belief that the world system, the *kosmos*, was subject to a divine force which gave it an underlying and orderly background. Where they got this idea, which is a far cry from the Homeric world of gods, is unknown—possibly from eastern mythology. It proved fundamental to the speculations which followed.

Thales is known for his prediction of the eclipse, but he also seems to have been the first man to look for the origins of the *kosmos*. For Thales the basis of all things was water, on which the earth itself floated. There were Egyptian and Semitic creation stories in which the initial state was a waste of waters, but Thales may also have picked water because of its demonstrable importance to all human life. What Thales appears to have been suggesting is that everything stems from this one originating source. It is not clear, however, whether Thales thought that all existing things could be broken down back into water or whether they had changed irreversibly into their new forms. This attempt to give a single, rational account of the natural order can be seen as a key moment in the evolution of western culture with implications which still excite scientists and philosophers today.

Anaximander, a contemporary of Thales', concentrated on a problem which arose directly from Thales' speculation, the difficulty of understanding how a particular physical entity (fire is an example given) can possibly come from something which seems to be an opposite to it, water. The very fact that he spotted the problem and tried to find a reasoned solution to it is significant in itself. Anaximander's solution was to imagine an indeterminate substance from which everything developed. He called it 'the Boundless'. Anaximander saw 'the Boundless' not only as the origin of all material but with the separate function of surrounding the earth and keeping everything in balance. He seems to have believed that not only could water and fire never merge into each other but that they, like other opposites such as 'the dry' and 'the wet', were actually in conflict with each other, and only an overriding force, 'the Boundless', could keep them in check.

Anaximander's other contribution was to propose how the earth existed as a stable and unmoving object in space. Thales had argued that the earth rested on water, but this left the problem of what the water rested on. Anaximander proposed that there is no reason why anything which exists at the centre should necessarily move from that position. It cannot move in opposite directions at the same time and will thus always remain suspended in the centre. If this is Anaximander's argument (it is only recorded as such by Aristotle 200 years later), then it is the first instance in natural science of what is known as the principle of sufficient reason (the principle that nothing happens without a reason).

What Anaximander did not explain was the process by which one form of matter, 'the Boundless', became another. Was there a boundary between 'the Boundless' and the rest of the physical world or was 'the Boundless' in some form identical with the physical world? It was left to the third of the Milesian thinkers, Anaximenes, to suggest a solution. Anaximenes argued that the world consisted of one interchangeable matter, air, from which all physical objects derived. The transition of steam into water and then into ice provided an example. Harder substances, such as rock, consisted of air which had been condensed even further. For Anaximenes, air also had a spiritual quality. It was a substance which existed eternally whatever it might be temporarily transmuted into. Its special position could be seen from its importance in sustaining life, and here Anaximenes drew on a popular conception that death occurred because air had withdrawn from the human body.

If the universe did originate from one substance, the problem was how to reconcile this with the enormous diversity and sense of constant change that any observer of the physical world is confronted with. The question of diversity and disorder was posed by one of the most complex of the early philosophers, Heraclitus, who, like his forerunners, was an Ionian, from the city of Ephesus to the north of Miletus. He was active about 500 BC.

Heraclitus' work survives in about a hundred fragments, as if he wrote not in continuous prose or verse as other philosophers did but in a series of short and penetrating observations. (The more recent example of Wittgenstein comes to mind.) Many of the fragments are obscure and give the impression that Heraclitus was deliberately trying to disturb conventional views and show off his own brilliance. Certainly he was seen as an unsettling and unpopular figure by his contemporaries. He explored the contradictions he perceived in the physical world. Salt water is drinkable for fish but undrinkable and deadly for men. Two very different properties exist in the same substance. The road which leads upwards also leads downwards. If one steps into a stream on successive days is it, with its changed water, still the same stream? In many cases, Heraclitus notes, a concept is intelligible only because there is an opposite to it. The concept of war is only meaningful if there is also one of peace. They are mutually dependent on each other, as also are night and day, winter and summer. Heraclitus went on, however, to argue that there was an overall coherence, *harmonie* (the Greek word meant the coming together of two different components to make a structure greater than its parts), in this world. What appears to be diversity in nature is in fact part of a natural unity. The opposites provide tensions but all is reconciled by a divine force, God. 'God is day, night, winter, summer, war, peace, surfeit, famine.'

Heraclitus was one of those who was happy to derive his ideas from the world he could observe around him. 'All that can be learnt by seeing and hearing, this I value highest,' as he put it in one fragment. The approach taken by his contemporary and philosophical rival Parmenides could not have been more different. Parmenides was born about 515 BC in Elea, a city in southern Italy which had been founded by exiles from another Ionian city, Phocaea. He may have been consciously challenging Heraclitus when he discarded observation about the physical world in favour of taking a lonely path towards finding truths based only on reason. The physical world, Parmenides argues, in the earliest piece of sustained philosophical argument to have survived, is made up only of what can be conceived in the mind. That and that alone exists. (This is fine for something which does exist, like a piece of rock, but is less helpful for concepts which can be imagined but which do not actually exist, such as a unicorn. It is assumed that Parmenides did not intend to include them in his system.) What cannot be thought of has no existence whatsoever and nothing more can or need be said about it. Parmenides goes on from here to argue that what exists—a piece of rock, for instance—can only exist in that state. It cannot be conceived of in any pre- or post-rock state because then it would not have existed as it does now and what did not exist cannot be spoken of. Therefore, the rock and by analogy all existing things are unchangeable, caught in a perpetual present. Parmenides goes further to argue that as nothing cannot exist there cannot be empty space between objects—all things that exist are joined as one indivisible substance. The logical conclusion, therefore, is that the world is composed of one unchanging substance. This immediately contradicts what the senses have to say and opens up a chasm between the findings of reason and those of observation.

Parmenides' pupil Zeno went on to explore the paradoxes exposed by Parmenides' reasoning. One is that of the arrow in flight. To the senses the arrow appears to be moving. Yet logically, Zeno argued, it was not. The argument goes as follows. Everything is at rest when it is 'at a place equal to itself'. At each moment of time the arrow is always at 'a place equal to itself'. Therefore the arrow is always at rest. Equally a runner cannot run across a stadium until he has crossed half its length. He cannot reach half its length until he has covered a quarter and a quarter until he has covered an eighth and so on. Logically, he can never reach the end of the stadium.

Parmenides had shown that if a single incontrovertible starting point can be taken, then it is possible to proceed deductively to demonstrate some contingent truth. This was a crucial step in the development of philosophical argument. His conclusions were deeply unsettling in themselves and acted to stimulate further thought across the Greek world. Plato, for instance, acknowledged the influence of Parmenides when he argued that there are unchanging entities, the Forms, which can only be approached through reason. (See p. 282.)

One reaction to Parmenides was to enquire more closely into what it was that actually made up material objects. Empedocles of Acragas, for instance, who was at work in the mid-fifth century, aimed to reinstate the senses as a valid source for knowledge. Objects, he suggested, were not unchanging as Parmenides had argued. They come into being in their different forms according to a different mix of four elements, earth, water, air, and fire. Forces of what he called love and hate caused the perpetual disintegration and reformation of different materials but the four elements remain constant. (This theory continued to be influential in Europe as late as the seventeenth century.)

An alternative explanation to the problem of material objects was to assume that they could be divided into tiny particles which were themselves indivisible.

(The Greeks used the word *atomos* for such a particle, hence 'atom'.) The concept originated with the mid-fifth-century Leucippus, a native of Abdera, a small town in the northern Aegean founded by settlers from Ionia. Leucippus broke completely with Parmenides to assert that 'nothing' *could* exist (a good statement then as now from which to start a philosophical argument) in the sense that there could be empty space between things. If this was accepted, matter did not have to be joined together in one undifferentiated mass and objects could move as there was empty space to move through. Leucippus and his younger contemporary Democritus, also from Abdera, went on to argue that the physical world was made up of atoms which were of the same substance but differed in shape and size. These atoms move at random (exploiting the empty spaces), but atoms of like size or shape tend to be attracted to each other and form material objects (Democritus even postulated that some were conveniently provided with hooks). So the world as it exists takes shape. Every object is made of the same substance arranged differently according to the form of its constituent atoms. Where the Atomists differed from earlier cosmologists was in their belief that the formation of the world was random. There is no mention of a guiding force behind it. The only things that exist are atoms and the empty spaces between them. This was the first developed statement of materialism, the theory that nothing which can be directly grasped by the senses exists beyond the material world. It made the Atomists Marx's favourite Greek philosophers.

A very different approach was provided by Pythagoras, another Ionian in origin, a native of the island of Samos. He was forced into exile in southern Italy, probably about 525 BC. Very little is known about Pythagoras' life, although a mass of later legend attaches to it. He was clearly a charismatic figure and drew around him a band of devoted followers who continued in existence long after his death and who inspired other similar groups in the cities of southern Italy. It has proved virtually impossible to distinguish between what Pythagoras himself taught and what was added later by the Pythagoreans. 'Pythagoras' theorem' of the right-angled triangle, for instance, seems to have had no direct connection with him (and was probably known, in essence, to the Babylonians many hundreds of years earlier).

The one teaching which is most likely to have been Pythagoras' own is that of the transmigration of the soul. Pythagoras appears to have believed that the soul exists as an immortal entity separately from the body. The body is simply its temporary home, and on the death of one body it moves on to another. What kind of body it moves on to depends on its behaviour in each life, for the soul is not only immortal, it is rational and responsible for its own actions. It must never let itself be conquered by the desires of the body. If it does then it will suffer in the next. Likewise, through correct behaviour it can move on to a happier existence. The Pythagoreans were therefore ascetics, but unlike many with this leaning they never cut themselves off from the world. In fact, many Pythagoreans became deeply involved in politics, though the austerity of their beliefs often aroused opposition.

Although direct proof of any association of Pythagoras with mathematics is lacking, he is often linked with the theory that the structure of things rests on numbers. A single string spanning a sounding-box sounds a note when plucked. Halve the length of the string and pluck it again. The note is one octave higher. Metals mixed in certain proportions form new metals. The relationship between the parts of a 'perfect' human body can be calculated mathematically. Is it possible to argue from this that mathematical forms exist unseen behind all physical structures? The possibility that they do and can be grasped by a reasoning soul was to be taken up by Plato. The study of mathematics was to be the core of the education given to his aspiring philosophers.

The varied arguments of the early Greek thinkers were invigorating but deeply unsettling. Faced with the seeming absurdities of Parmenides' deductions, philosophy could be dismissed as no more than an intellectual game. It could be argued that 'truth', if the concept could be said to exist at all, was something relative, dependent on the inadequate senses of individual observers or the ways in which they constructed their reasoned arguments. In the sixth century another Ionian, Xenophanes, had already made a similar point in a famous statement about the gods:

Immortal men imagine that gods are begotten and that they have human dress and speech and shape . . . If oxen or horses or lions had hands to draw with and to make works of art as men do, the horses would draw the forms of gods like horses, oxen like oxen, and they would make their gods' bodies similar to the bodily shape they themselves each had. (Translation: E. Hussey)

If the gods, to take Xenophanes' example, are the construction of human minds, it is a short step to argue that other concepts—goodness or justice, for instance—might also be. The fundamental question is then raised as to whether there could ever be any agreement over what the gods, or justice or goodness, might be. This was to be the central issue tackled by Socrates and Plato in the late fifth and early fourth centuries (see pp. 279–86).

The achievements of these early philosophers need to be placed in context. They had not invented rational thought, which is an intrinsic element of human society, found in every culture. The study of southern African cave communities of 70,000 years ago shows that during a prolonged period of drought different kinds of stone tools were evolved to hunt the diminished supply of animals. When the drought was over the tools were discarded. The environment was being manipulated in an intelligent way even as early as this. In the *Odyssey* Odysseus fights his way through the waves after his shipwreck. He weighs up the alternative methods of getting safely to shore—going straight in and being smashed by rocks or swimming further along the shore and risking being swept off by a gust of wind. Faced with changing physical circumstances, human beings have always contemplated the alternatives for survival and made conscious decisions as to the best way forward.

The achievement of Greek philosophy was to go beyond these everyday decisions and recognize a distinct branch of reasoning which can be applied to abstract issues. The Egyptians and Babylonians had evolved a number of mathematical procedures to deal with the practical problems of building, calculating rations, and so on. These procedures had reached their final form in Babylon about 1600 BC. What was missing was any ability to use numbers in an abstract way. This was the breakthrough achieved by the Greeks. Although a systematic outline of mathematical knowledge was not produced until Euclid's in about 300 BC, it is clear that Greeks were thinking as pure mathematicians by the fifth century, able to work with axioms, definitions, proofs, and theorems. In this way, general principles could be formulated which could then be used to explore a wider range of other issues. It was the ability to work in the abstract that inspired intellectual progress, not just in mathematics but in science, metaphysics, ethics, even in politics. The reforms of Cleisthenes in Athens in the late sixth century (see p. 179) depended on a plan of bringing together a set of communities into the artificial structure of the *trittys*, a plan he must have constructed in an abstract form.

The end result, and one which was fundamental, was that there were few inhibitions on enquiry. The success of Greek philosophy lay in its critical and argumentative approach to an extraordinary range of questions. As Bernard Williams pointed out:

In philosophy the Greeks initiated almost all its major fields—metaphysics, logic, the philosophy of language, the theory of knowledge, ethics, political philosophy and the philosophy of art. [Williams here is only referring to the concerns of modern philosophers—he might have added mathematics and science, included as 'philosophy' by the Greeks.] Not only did they start these areas of enquiry but they progressively distinguished what would still be recognised as many of the most basic questions in those areas.

It is worth noting that Williams concentrates on the Greeks as question *askers*. They did not always come up with very effective answers. There were good reasons for this. First, their speculations often ran far ahead of what their senses could cope with. It is sobering to realize that no Greek astronomer had any means of exploring the heavens other than his own eyes. (There were instruments developed for measuring angles, but they still depended on the naked eye for their use.) Aristotle's theory of spontaneous generation, the idea that life could come from nowhere, which lingered on as a misconception until the seventeenth century, arose largely because he had no way of seeing small objects. (His colleague Theophrastus, in a textbook example of how no Greek philosopher was immune from criticism by his colleagues, made the point by noting tiny seeds which Aristotle had missed, thus casting doubt on the concept altogether.) Not the least of the Greeks' philosophical achievements was, however, to recognize that even though the senses were inadequate they were still crucial. The fifth-century philosopher Democritus got to the core of the problem when he constructed a dialogue between a mind and the senses. 'Wretched mind, taking your proofs from us (the senses), do you overthrow us? Our overthrow will be your fall.'

'Early Greek philosophy', writes Martin West, 'was not a single vessel which a succession of pilots commanded and tried to steer towards an agreed destination, one tacking one way, the next altering course in the light of his own perceptions. It was more like a flotilla of small craft whose navigators did not all start from the same point or at the same time, nor all aim for the same goal; some went in groups, some were influenced by the movements of others, some travelled out of sight of each other.'

In short, the Greek world of the sixth century fostered an intellectual curiosity and creativity which took many forms. The Archaic age deserves to be seen as one where a particular attitude of mind took root, perhaps, as has been suggested, because of the intensity of life in the *polis*. It involved the search for an understanding of the physical world free of the restraints imposed by those cultures which still lived in the shadow of threatening gods. It was still a fragmented world, however, one in which cities survived precariously on the limited resources available. Its vulnerability was now to be tested by attack from the east by the largest empire the world had yet seen, that of Persia. (For the Persian empire, see earlier, p. 105.)

FURTHER READING

N. Fisher and H. Van Wees (eds.), *Archaic Greece* (London, 1998). Hurwit is again good, on links with Egypt, for instance. On art see the chapter by Alan Johnston, 'Pre-Classical Greece', in the *Oxford History of Classical Art* and the survey histories cited here after Chapter 8. For coinage see the chapter by Colin Kraay in the *Cambridge Ancient History*, vol. iv and for coinage and politics, Leslie Kurke, *Coins, Bodies, Games and Gold: The Politics of Meaning in Ancient Greece* (Princeton, 1999). John Boardman has introductory books on vases, *Athenian Black Figure Vases* (London, 1974) and *Athenian Red Figure Vases* (London, 1975). See also T. Rasmussen and N. Spivey (eds.), *Looking at Greek Vases* (Cambridge, 1991); B. Sparkes, *The Red and the Black: Studies in Greek Pottery* (London, 1996) and Susan Woodford, *Images of Myths in Classical Antiquity* (Cambridge, 2003).

On early philosophy a standard introduction is E. Hussey, *The Presocratics* (London, 1972) and more recently A. A. Long (ed.), *The Cambridge Companion to Early Greek Philosophy* (New York, 1999). Translations are to be found in G. Kirk and J. Raven, *The Presocratic Philosophers* (Cambridge, 1983). See also the useful introduction by Martin West in the *Oxford History of the Classical World* and chapter 6 (by Christopher Janaway) in A. Grayling (ed.), *Philosophy: A Guide through the Subject* (Oxford, 1995). In addition to the works of Geoffrey Lloyd cited above, there is his *Early Greek Science: Thales to Aristotle* (London, 1974). A. D. Bowen (ed.), *Science and Philosophy in Ancient Greece* (New York, 1993) has a chapter, by C. Kahn, on the origins of Greek science and philosophy. See also, for Greek philosophy in general, Terence Irwin, *Classical Thought* (Oxford, 1989) and the chapter on philosophy by Bernard Williams in *The Legacy of Greece* (Oxford, 1984). For more advanced work there is W. K. C. Guthrie, *A History of Greek Philosophy* (Cambridge, 1962–81); the excellent Karsten Johansen, *A History of Ancient Philosophy: From the Beginnings to Augustine* (London, 1998) and J. Brunschwig and G. E. R. Lloyd (eds.), *Greek Thought: A Guide to Classical Knowledge* (Cambridge, Mass., 2000).

12 | The Persian Wars

Before they had been overrun by the Persians in the 540s the Ionian cities had been prosperous and confident, supporting the largest navies of the Greek world. They had dominated Greek trade with Egypt and had also traded inland to the east through Lydia. As has been seen, their contacts with the east had stimulated important cultural achievements, among them epic poetry and the birth of philosophy. Politically, however, the cities were conservative, many of them living under tyrants. Their conqueror, the Persian Cyrus, had sustained and used the tyrants to maintain control of this new part of his empire, but many Ionians had fled west as refugees, enriching the cities of the Greek mainland and Italy with their skills.

The cities had their own rivalries. One was between Miletus and the strategically important Cycladic island of Naxos. The tyrant of Miletus, one Aristagoras, had enlisted Persian support in an attack on Naxos. (He persuaded the Persians that Naxos might be used as a stepping-stone to further conquests in the Aegean, although there is no evidence that the Persians had any plans for such conquests at this date.) It failed partly because the Persian commander had warned Naxos of the attack, and in his fury at the betrayal Aristagoras turned against Persia. He exploited a growing Greek restiveness with tyrannical rule by surrendering his tyranny and proclaiming *isonomia*, equality in rights, in Miletus. The response was immediate. There was a traditional camaraderie among the Ionian cities based on their common cultural roots and the everyday contact of traders. They had suffered together from the growing demands for tax and men from the Persians and had seen their long-established trading patterns disrupted by the Persian advance. (At Naucratis, the Greek trading-post in Egypt chiefly patronized by the Ionian Greeks, for instance, the sequence of Greek pottery, and hence, it is assumed, their occupation, breaks at 525 BC.) Now they too overturned their tyrannies and met to plan action against the Persians.

First, help was sought from the mainland. Sparta was too preoccupied at the time with her rivalry with Argos, but Athens and the city of Eretria on Euboea honoured their ancient links with the Ionians. In 498 twenty ships from Athens and five from Eretria crossed the Aegean to join the massed Ionian fleets. An expedition was launched inland to Sardis and the city was set on fire before the Persians were able to drive the Ionians off. This provocative raid sparked off other revolts among the cities of the Hellespont as well as those further south on the Asian coast. Even the Greek cities of Cyprus managed to throw off the Persian yoke for a year.

To counter-attack the Persians divided their forces into three, but by 495 they had still not regained control. It was no easier, however, for the Greeks to win. It proved impossible to forge the hoplite forces of the scattered cities into a single force strong enough to defeat the Persians comprehensively (although the historian Herodotus saw the major problem as being the cowardice and laziness of the Ionians). The revolt looked like it had entered stalemate until, in 494, the Persians decided to launch an attack on Miletus, still the centre of the revolt. The Ionians massed their fleets to defend the city, but at the battle of Lade the Persians managed to fight their way through and take the city. With the core of resistance gone, other cities were then subdued one by one and the revolt was over.

After the initial brutality of revenge, Darius was shrewd enough to relax his grip on the Greek cities, and Herodotus suggests that democratic governments were allowed to emerge. However, the spirit of the Ionian world was broken and the prosperity its cities had known in the Archaic age was never recovered. The question now was whether Darius would move further into Greece. It did not seem difficult to do so. As a result of Darius' earlier expedition into Europe (see p. 108), the Persians now controlled the north Aegean coast as far south as Mount Olympus. They had the navies of Egypt and the Phoenicians to call on and faced a people who appeared preoccupied with their own internal quarrels. Darius had been given an excuse by the Athenian and Eretrian involvement in the revolt, and revenge on them, suggests Herodotus, was, in fact, his main motive. Now he sent messengers calling on the Greek cities to submit. In two cases, Sparta and Athens, the messengers were executed, an act of sacrilege which made war inevitable.

The expedition against Athens was put in the hands of Datis, a Mede, and Darius' nephew, Artaphrenes. The figures are disputed, but it seems that about 300 triremes were gathered in Cilicia and then loaded with men and horses. The former tyrant of Athens, Hippias, now 80, was included in the fleet to impose as a controllable ruler on Athens when she was defeated. In the early summer of 490 Datis began making his way along the southern Turkish coast. At first the Greeks were not alarmed. The obvious route for the invading forces was along the coast of Asia Minor and then round to Thrace, where they would arrive towards the end of the campaigning season. Suddenly, however, instead of heading north, the Persians struck directly west across the open Aegean. Naxos was attacked and this time subdued and the fleet sailed on to Euboea, where the city of Eretria was besieged until it was betrayed and taken within a week.

It was now late summer. The Persians were in a formidable position. They were in good order (they had actually managed to co-opt extra troops on their way) and had a foothold on Greek territory with a supply route that ran back to

MAP 4

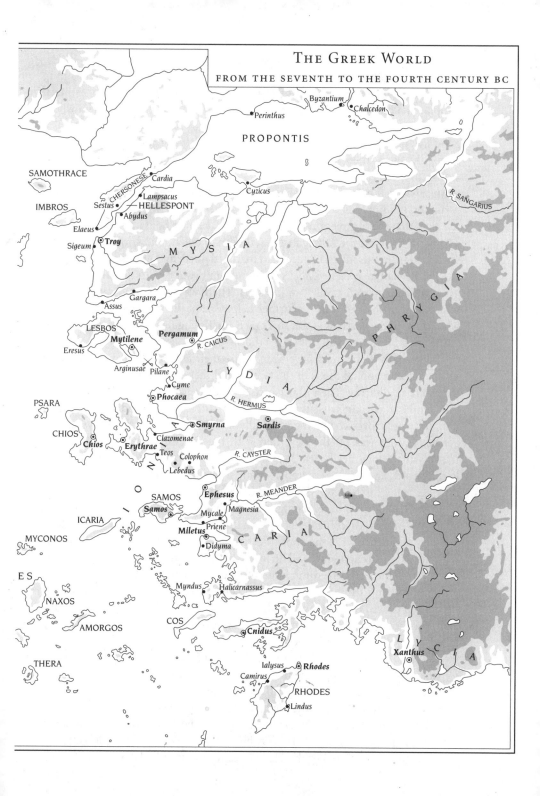

THE GREEK WORLD

FROM THE SEVENTH TO THE FOURTH CENTURY BC

Byzantium
Perinthus
Chalcedon

PROPONTIS

R. SANGARIUS

SAMOTHRACE

Cardia
CHERSONESE
Lampsacus
Sestus — HELLESPONT
Abydus

IMBROS

Elaeus
Sigeum
Troy

M Y S I A

Cyzicus

P H R Y G I A

Gargara
Assus

LESBOS
Mytilene
Pergamum
R. CAICUS

Eresus

L Y D I A

Arginusae Pilane
Cyme
Phocaea

PSARA

R. HERMUS

Smyrna
Sardis

CHIOS
Chios
Erythrae
Clazomenae
Teos
Colophon
Lebedus

I O N I A

R. CAYSTER

Ephesus
R. MEANDER

SAMOS
Samos
Mycale Magnesia

ICARIA

Priene
Miletus
Didyma

C A R I A

MYCONOS

ES

NAXOS

AMORGOS

COS

Myndus Halicarnassus

Cnidus

L Y C I A
Xanthus

THERA

Ialysus Rhodes
Camirus
RHODES
Lindus

the empire. Within a few days they had moved over to the mainland, landing unopposed on the long beach of Marathon, 40 kilometres north of Athens. Hippias had his own reasons for guiding the Persians there—it had been where he had landed with his father, Peisistratus, over fifty years before—but it was a good site in other ways. There was pasture and fresh water, and if a battle were to be fought there, there was ample room for the Persian cavalry, probably 800 strong, to manoeuvre.

Meanwhile, the Athenians learned by fire signal that the Persians had landed. A runner, Phidippides, was sent at once to Sparta. When he returned it was with the news that the completion of a religious ritual would hold up the Spartans for a week. By this time the Athenian army, of some 9,000 hoplites, joined by a thousand men from the city of Plataea, had marched north and were settled in opposite the Persian army. The Greeks were outnumbered two to one and faced an army which had both cavalry and archers. There was hot dispute over whether to attack at once or to wait for further help. One of the ten generals, Miltiades, who had seen the Persians at war in Thrace, finally engineered an agreement that battle would be joined but only if conditions were especially favourable.

The Persians' hope must have been to use their archers and cavalry to break up the massed hoplite ranks of the Greeks and then send in their infantry once they were in disarray. The only chance for the Greeks was to meet the Persian infantry head on and trust that the superior coordination and morale of the hoplites would overwhelm them. Ideally a time should be chosen when the Persian cavalry was off the field and with the Greeks as close as possible to the Persians before they began their charge. Every day they edged their defended line forward, and on 17 September 490 it seemed that the Persian cavalry had disappeared. One theory is that it had been withdrawn for watering during the night but had delayed in returning, another that it was being loaded for a direct attack on Athens. By coincidence, command for the day belonged to Miltiades and he was quick to seize the opportunity. He drew up the hoplites in a long line with the wings strengthened and he immediately ordered the attack. The Greeks ran towards the Persians in the hope of reaching their lines before the Persian archers broke up the phalanx. The two sides crashed together, but while the Persians appeared to be gaining in the centre the Greeks enveloped them in the rear and broke them up. A massacre followed with some 6,400 Persians being killed as they fled towards the beach or the surrounding marshes. Only 192 Greeks died. The surviving Persians made a final attempt to sail round the coast to Athens, but as they appeared in sight of the city, they saw that the Greeks had already marched the 40 kilometres back and were ready to oppose them. It had been a complete victory, acknowledged even by the Spartans, who arrived, as promised, a day later to cast an expert eye over the body-strewn battlefield. (The story that Phidippides ran on from Athens to take part in the battle and then ran back to Athens to tell of the victory seems, sadly, to be later invention, but it has proved a legend powerful enough to create the modern marathon, a run of 42 kilometres, the distance between Marathon and Athens. The first marathon was run at the revived Olympic Games in Athens in 1896 when it was won, appropriately enough, by a Greek, Spiros Louis.)

It has been possible to describe the Persian invasion of 490 in such detail because the events formed part of the first 'modern' work of history, the *Histories* of Herodotus. Herodotus was born in the 480s at Halicarnassus on the coast of Asia Minor, one of the Greek cities incorporated into the Persian empire. His background shows what a fluid concept 'Greekness' had become by the fifth century. Technically Herodotus was a subject of the Persian empire, while the names of his father and uncle suggest an origin among the native peoples of the coast, the Carians, who had presumably intermarried with the Greeks. Yet culturally Herodotus was Greek and could speak no other language.

Very little is known of Herodotus' life. The seizure of power by a tyrant in Halicarnassus may have driven him from the city into exile on Samos. He seems to have returned to Halicarnassus about 464, possibly as part of a liberation force. It must have been shortly afterwards that his wanderings through the Greek and Persian world began. How far his travels were inspired by his desire to write his history and how far he simply picked up information which he later realized could be woven together is not known. The *Histories* certainly give the impression of being travel notes which were later written up into a coherent form. In his later years Herodotus visited most of the mainland cities of Greece and probably gave readings at Athens. However, his final home appears to have been the Athenian colony at Thurii in southern Italy, and it was probably here that he died in about 425.

When he began to write up his *Histories*, probably in the 440s, Herodotus set himself, in his own words, the task of giving 'the great and wondrous achievements of both the Greek and non-Greek barbarians their due renown, especially the explanation of why they had fought each other'. In other words, he was not only setting out a narrative account of what had happened in the Persian wars but he was trying to understand *why* the wars had happened in the first place. He was also promising an even-handed investigation. In the circumstances, the word he coined, *historia*, enquiry or research, was an appropriate one.

This was a new departure in the study of the past. It is possible that Herodotus may have been influenced in his survey of the opposing sides by an earlier geographer, Hecataeus of Miletus (writing about 500 BC), whose work is now lost. He may also have absorbed the more rational approach to understanding the physical world pioneered by the philosophers of Miletus, a short distance up the coast. His achievement can be highlighted by looking at other contemporary traditions of recording the past. For the Jews, whose national history was being written in this same period, the past was a record of the relationship between man and Yahweh. Political events were interpreted as the result of Israel's willingness to obey or disobey the commands of Yahweh. For the Egyptian state, as has been seen (Chs. 3 and 4 *passim*), the past was in the possession of the king and he would manipulate it to protect his own position. The record of past kings was doctored so that it became an unending succession of keepers of good order at the end of which a new ruler could take his place. Truth, in the sense of an impartial and objective account of the past, was therefore dispensable in the interests of political stability.

The Greeks used myth in similar if rather more fluid ways. Myths were not simply stories handed down from the past to be used for entertainment. They could be manipulated for overtly political ends. As has already been seen, the Greeks used myths of Heraclean labours in Sicily as a justification for settling there. Similarly, foundation myths tied a people to their land and helped support their right to be there. Part of Herodotus' achievement was to question the validity of myth. As Paul Cartledge has pointed out, there are at least three occasions in his *Histories* where he describes Greek myths only to reject them as insufficient bases for finding the truth. He even derides those who believe implausible tales as simple-minded. 'Here, in other words', says Cartledge, 'is Herodotus the "scientific" historian, staking his claim to mastery of his new intellectual territory.' This has recently been emphasized by Rosalind Thomas in her *Herodotus in Context: Ethnography, Science and the Art of Persuasion* (Cambridge, 2000). If one looks at the careful way in which Herodotus assesses the possible causes for the annual Nile floods in his Book II, for instance, one finds him using reason and empirical evidence in his acceptance and rejections of specific explanations and openly deriding one solution as a myth dreamt up by poets. This does not mean that Herodotus disregards the power of religion. Throughout his *Histories* he relates how actions are shaped by the religious scruples of the participants, and he even seems prepared to accept that there are cases of divine intervention (at the Battle of Marathon, for instance—a legend survived of the hero Theseus rushing ahead of the Athenian battleline).

There is also an underlying propaganda message in the *Histories*. One of their purposes was to applaud the victory of the Greeks against the overwhelming power of the Persians and draw appropriate conclusions about the differences between free and unfree states and the consequences of unrestricted pride. The Greeks, with their simple life, cooperative political arrangements, and belief in liberty, are, in Herodotus' eyes, superior, and this explains their success.

Whatever the framework within which he worked, Herodotus made a serious effort to look at both sides, to ask questions, and to try to establish the truth. He was prepared to value the customs of other people. While he writes for a Greek world, he has the vision to understand that the Greek way of life does not necessarily appear superior to others. (He has a good story in which Indians and Greeks hear of each other's burial customs and both end up disgusted.) He also tries to avoid stereotypes. The Persians, for instance, emerge not as one-dimensional ogres but as human beings with normal, if extravagant, ambitions. Among Herodotus' greatest assets are his intellectual breadth and curiosity.

It was this curiosity that took Herodotus so far in his researches. In his preliminary study of the Persian empire he tried to understand it as a whole, a task which took him among its varied conquests from Babylonia, Egypt, the Levantine Coast, and the Black Sea. Egypt clearly fascinated him, as it did many a Greek traveller, and Book II of the *Histories* is devoted to the country. Despite their innumerable diversions into geography, folk tales, and entertaining titbits, in the last resort the *Histories* hold together as a great war story. In this sense they echo the epic tradition established by Homer and they range well beyond a narrative of events. Herodotus' successor Thucydides (see p. 297) narrowed the perspectives of history to political narrative, and it is perhaps only very recently, when total history has become the vogue, that Herodotus' achievement has been fully recognized. Like Homer, Herodotus also creates a sense of a Greek identity which transcends any city loyalty. His definition of the Greeks in terms of their common blood, language, religion, and customs still provides a useful working model for understanding that identity. The contrasts he presents between Greeks and Persians help define it further.

The most majestic piece of Herodotus' narrative comes when he describes the second Persian invasion of 480. Darius died in 486. A revolt in Egypt had prevented him from renewing his attacks on the Greeks. His son, Xerxes, succeeded comparatively easily but showed he was a much more intolerant man than his father, preferring to rule over his subject peoples in his own right, rather than sheltering, as Darius had done, behind the traditional titles of pharaoh of Egypt or king of Babylon. Although he had little experience of war, Xerxes was determined to settle the troublesome business of the Greeks, and by 484 meticulous preparations for a much larger invasion were in hand.

Xerxes' task was to bring a large army, supported by a navy, across from Asia through Thrace (the European possessions of the empire had been unaffected by the defeat at Marathon) and then down into Greece. It was a logistical nightmare, but the Persian planning was thorough. A vulnerable area was the sea around Mount Athos, which was prone to storms, so a canal, wide enough to take two triremes abreast, was dug across the peninsula. It took two years to construct. The Hellespont running between Asia and Europe was another dangerous spot, exposed as it was to high winds and rough seas. Its breadth of 2,500 metres was spanned by two pontoon bridges attached by cables to each shore. A first pair were swept away by a gale but the second held and were covered by a wooden roadway designed so that crossing animals would not see the waters below. For Herodotus, as for Aeschylus in his play *The Persians* (first performed in 472), these preparations were so grandiose as to be an affront to the gods.

This time the Greeks could not depend on a lucky turn of events on the battlefield. The great army gathered by Xerxes from the ends of his empire may have numbered 200,000, ten times the size of that at Marathon, and the navy, with 600 triremes, may have been twice as large. (Herodotus gives a figure of 1,700,000 for the army and 1,300 triremes, but these may have been conscious exaggerations to emphasize the magnitude of the task facing the Greeks.) A single city could not defeat them, and some unity had to be forged among the Greeks. It was not an easy task. The Greek cities had their own hatreds—Athens for Aegina, Sparta for Argos—which made unity difficult. Many states in the north were simply overawed by the Persians and by 481 had already submitted to Xerxes' envoys. There were aristocratic factions in many cities which saw a Persian victory as giving them the opportunity to seize power. The oracle at Delphi, whose presiding god Apollo had been given special favour by Darius, saw its best chance of survival as neutrality and its prophesies were coded accordingly. (Themistocles, the Athenian leader, had to create his own interpretation of the advice given by the oracle to Athens in order to persuade the Athenians it was favourable to them.)

It was Sparta who took the initiative in October 481 in calling the Greeks together to plan resistance. There were two urgent tasks: to coordinate resources under one central leader, and to warn off the many cities who looked like submitting to the Persians. Those who met at Sparta, over thirty states in all, agreed to end their feuds and all agreed to make Sparta supreme commander of both land and sea forces. It was decreed that any city which submitted voluntarily to the Persians would have its property confiscated, with a tenth being offered to the oracle at Delphi. Even so, in the campaign that followed many failed to join in. Argos would never fight alongside Sparta; Corcyra promised ships but they never arrived. Syracuse, probably the richest city in the Greek world, offered an enormous army but only on the condition that her ruler, Gelon, would have chief command of the Greeks. The offer was turned down. In the event, Gelon played his part by heavily defeating a Carthaginian attack on Sicily made, possibly with Persian connivance, the following year.

It was magnanimous of Athens to submit to Spartan leadership (although there is also evidence that other states would not have accepted her leadership). She had shown, at Marathon, that she had a highly competent army, and since 490 she had concentrated on building a large trireme fleet. The inspiration for this had come from Themistocles, a member of a poor but aristocratic family, the Lycomids, who since his first election as an archon in 493 had placed naval policy first. He had successfully fought for the creation of a harbour at the sheltered Piraeus to replace the open beach at Phaleron. (The Piraeus had only become an option when the island of Salamis, which overlooked its entrance, had become an Athenian possession in the sixth century.) When, in 482, a new rich strain of silver was discovered in the Laurium mines, Themistocles persuaded the Assembly to spend it on creating a new fleet rather than distributing it among the citizens as had been customary. To get his way he cleverly played on the traditional fears of the Athenians of Aegina, but it is certain that his real motive was the protection of the city against another Persian invasion. By 480 Athens was to have a fleet of 200 triremes.

By the time a second meeting of the resisting Greek cities could be held, at the Isthmus in the spring of 480, Xerxes was poised to cross into Europe. Herodotus describes his colourful army of Persians, Medes, Indians, Arabs, Ethiopians, Libyans, and Lydians, each with distinctive battledress and weapons. The core of the army was the 10,000 Persian Immortals, so-called because if one died his place was immediately filled. The navy was similarly mixed, with the largest contingent being provided by the Phoenicians and Egyptians. There was a large number of supporting triremes conscripted from the Ionian cities. Greeks were about to find themselves fighting other Greeks.

The coordination of so many nationalities, many of whom must have been lukewarm in their loyalty to Persia, was bound to be a problem. Just as serious was the task of getting the army and navy intact into Greece before the end of the campaigning season. This was normally October, a month by which winter storms had become frequent and the best of the harvest had been eaten and so was not available for invading forces to plunder. It was clear that navy and army would have to travel along the coast together. The rowers could not land to pick up fresh water without Persian control of the coastline, while the army was not secure if Greeks could land by sea and threaten it from behind.

The first choice of the Greeks was to meet the Persians as far north as Thessaly with its open plains. There was much to be said for such a forward policy, not least because it would allow the Thessalian cavalry, the best on mainland Greece, to be used on the Greek side. A small Greek force was actually sent north, but there were at least three passes to defend and the armies could easily have been outflanked. There was also doubt of the reliability of the Thessalian aristocracy. It was finally agreed that the first attempt to check the Persian army would take place at the pass of Thermopylae, which ran between the mountains and the sea east of the city of Trachis. In places the pass was only 2 metres wide and it seemed a reasonable holding place. Even here, however, was too far north for many of the Peloponnesian states, whose preference was to defend themselves at the Isthmus. By the time Xerxes finally arrived at the pass in mid-September many Greeks were being drawn to the Olympic Games, while the Spartans were once again constrained by rituals which forbade fighting. This time, however, a small Spartan force led by King Leonidas and his personal guard of 300 did set out, but, even when joined by allies, the total defending force at Thermopylae was still only 5,000.

There remained the danger that the Persian fleet might move down the coast beyond the pass and land troops in the Greeks' rear. Possibly as early as 481 the Greeks had agreed that the Persian fleet should be met off Cape Artemisium, on the northern tip of Euboea. The beach was level there and launching was easy, while, if things went wrong, a safe retreat could always be made between Euboea and the mainland. The main disadvantage was that this was open sea and the Greeks risked being surrounded by the much larger Persian fleet. Nevertheless, the naval effort was substantial. Athens sent her entire force of 200 triremes. With 200 men a trireme, this represented 40,000 men. If a fourth- or third-century inscription, 'The Decree of Themistocles', found at Troezen as recently as 1959, is to be trusted as an account of Athenian activities (it is probably a reasonably accurate copy of the original), her skilled rowers had been divided into crews in the autumn of 481, with Athenian soldiers being added to the crews so that they could have a thorough training over the winter. Another 70 triremes from the Peloponnese joined the Athenians. The whole fleet was under the control of the Spartan Eurybiades.

The Persians had lingered in the north during the summer, consolidating their supply lines and consuming the harvest as it ripened. It was early September by the time they moved towards southern Greece. Already the weather was turning. As the Persian triremes rowed their way down the coast towards Euboea they were caught in four days of storms. Many ships were sunk or wrecked on the exposed shore of Magnesia, but when the Greeks at Artemisium finally saw the survivors appear and head for the Gulf of Pagasae to refit, they could see that the fleet was still much larger than theirs.

Xerxes had now reached Thermopylae with his armies. He decided that he would launch a joint attack on land and sea on the 17th. His naval plan was to split his fleet. One part would face the Greeks directly at Artemisium while the other part, of 200 selected ships, would row round the east coast of Euboea, then move up the channel behind the Greek fleet to catch them in a pincer. It proved a disaster. A storm arose on the night of the 17th as the Persians rounded the southeastern edge of Euboea. All 200 ships were wrecked on a lee shore. The remaining Persian fleet eventually attacked on the 19th but the battle was inconclusive.

Meanwhile, Xerxes had first stormed the entrance to Thermopylae on the 17th. Throughout that day and the next hard fighting took place in the narrow entrance to the pass with each side rotating its best troops. If anything the Spartans had the better of the combat, having perfected a method of appearing to retreat and then turning to cut down their pursuers. But it was on the 18th that Xerxes learnt of a path through the mountains above the pass. He quickly exploited his knowledge. On the night of the 18th, a full moon, several thousand of the Immortals were sent on a forced march along the mountain ridge. The defending force of Phocians heard their feet rustling through fallen oak leaves, but the Phocians were pushed aside and by early the next day Leonidas knew there was no hope of saving the pass. He sent away his allies and remained with his personal guard to face the inevitable end. By the evening of the 19th the battle was over with the Spartan force wiped out. A later inscription put in the pass read:

Tell them in Lacedaemon, passer-by:
Obedient to their orders, here we lie.

As the Persian army streamed down through the pass, there was little point in the Greek fleet remaining so far north and it too fell back. Attica could not now be held—its northern frontier was simply too long. The Greek troops moved back to the Isthmus, where thousands of men were constructing a wall of defence. Athens lay completely exposed. Most of her population had already been evacuated, possibly, if one interpretation of the dating of the events of 'The Decree of Themistocles' is right, as early as the autumn of 481. The city was almost deserted as the Persians entered on 27 September. The next morning the remainder of the Persian fleet, having rowed 300 kilometres from the Gulf of Pagasae, arrived on the broad beaches of Phaleron below the city. As they rested on the beach they must have rejoiced to see the flames rising from the Acropolis, which was now being thoroughly sacked and its few defenders massacred. It would have seemed that Xerxes had triumphed.

The Greek fleet had now made its base on the island of Salamis. It was vulnerable here. One of the first commands of Xerxes when he arrived on the coast had been to order the digging of a mole across the channel. If the fleet was blocked in from the south by the mole and the Persian fleet sent round to guard the western entrance of the Bay of Eleusis, then the Greek fleet would be trapped. Time was not on the Greeks' side in any case. There were 80,000 men on the island as well as a large number of refugees from the city. They could not be fed for ever. The Spartan commander, Eurybiades, certainly felt that the best plan was to get the Greek fleet, now numbering 379 triremes, safely away to the Isthmus.

His opponent in the debate that followed was Themistocles, who knew that the abandonment of the last piece of Athenian territory would be disastrous for the city. He used the Athenian triremes as a bargaining tool, threatening to withdraw them from the Greek fleet, if the order was given to retreat. Eurybiades gave in. It was now that Themistocles showed the cunning for which he was famous. He knew that battle had to come quickly if Salamis was to be saved. His task was to make sure it came on Greek terms, in narrow waters where the Greek superiority in ramming tactics could be best exploited, if possible against tired crews. This meant forcing the Persian fleet to row its way up the Salamis Channel.

Themistocles played on the hopes and ambitions of Xerxes. He sent Xerxes a slave with the news that the Greek fleet was demoralized and full of dissension and that it was about to escape westwards by night. This was enough to raise Xerxes' hopes that he could destroy it once and for all. On the night of 28 September a squadron of Egyptian ships was sent to the western end of the bay to wait for the emerging Greeks, while at the eastern end, around midnight, Persian ships also moved across the entrance to the Channel. Themistocles now had to lure them in. As dawn broke on the 29th, a detachment of 70 Greek ships was sent northwards, as if in flight, in full view of the Persians, including Xerxes, who was watching the manoeuvres from a 'throne' on the hillside. It was enough to encourage the Persian fleet, made up mainly of Phoenicians, to move into the channel. It was in thirteen rows. By the afternoon the rowers had been more than twelve hours at sea. As they moved inexorably onwards, with no chance of retreat in the narrow waters, they saw to their horror the main Greek fleet emerging from the shelter of the shore and turning, united and fresh, towards them. At the same time a southerly wind was blowing up a swell. It caused the high-decked Phoenician ships to roll horribly, exposing their sides to the bronze rams of the Athenian triremes.

The battle is described by a messenger in Aeschylus' play, *The Persians*:

A Greek ship charged first and sheared off the whole high stern of a Phoenician ship and every captain drove his ship against another ship. To begin with the onward flowing Persian fleet held their own; but when the mass of ships was congested in the narrows, and there was no means of helping one another, and they were smashed by one another's rams sheathed in bronze, then they shivered their whole array of oars, and the Greek ships intelligently encircled them and battered them from every angle. Ships turned turtle, piles of wreckage and dead men hid the sea from sight, corpses were awash on shores and reefs, and the entire barbarian fleet rowed away in disorderly flight.   (Translation: N. G. L. Hammond)

One source claims that the Persians had lost over 200 ships as against 40 for the Greeks. Although the contribution of the Aeginetan and Corinthian triremes had been significant, the Athenian proclaimed Salamis as their victory, won by them on behalf of the people of Greece. As the lyric poet Simonides put it,

The valour of these men shall beget glory for ever undiminished,
so long as the gods allot rewards for courage,
For on foot and on their swift-moving ships they kept
all Greece from seeing the dawn of slavery.

(Translation: N. G. L. Hammond)

In fact, the war was far from over. Although Herodotus saw the Battle of Salamis as the decisive moment of the war, it was not conclusive. The Persian army was still intact and holding a substantial part of mainland Greece. The Persian navy even after Salamis, was still larger than the Greek, and it retreated for the winter to safe harbours in Samos and Symi in the eastern Aegean. Xerxes returned home for the winter, but he left his great royal pavilion behind under the care of his commander, Mardonius, suggesting he would return the next spring with fresh forces. Mardonius was left for the winter with 100,000 men, a larger force than any the Greeks could raise.

The war could now have entered a stalemate. The Peloponnesians could shelter, they hoped indefinitely, behind the fortifications of the Isthmus, leaving the Athenians as refugees on Salamis. There was little incentive for the

Peloponnesians to venture further north. When campaigning began again the next summer the Peloponnese would, however, be vulnerable to a naval attack.

It was this fear that gave the Athenians their trump card. They had been offered an alliance by the Persians on terms which included the restoration of Attica and their city ruins to them. Many Athenians were tempted (the neighbouring city of Thebes had already changed sides), but Herodotus records the Athenians turning down the Persian offer with the famous riposte which proclaimed the common identity of the Greek people in their culture, religion, language, and customs, and hence the impossibility of a betrayal of this shared heritage. The chance that Athens might accept the Persian offer could, however, be dangled before the Spartans. In the summer of 479 a high level Athenian mission to Sparta finally persuaded the Spartans that if Athens was to remain loyal she needed help. The Spartans were cautious of leaving the Peloponnese for the usual reasons, including fear of a helot uprising and suspicion that Argos, which was rumoured to be in the pay of Mardonius, might attack when the army was in the north. In the event, 5,000 Spartan hoplites, 5,000 *perioikoi*, and 35,000 helots under the command of Pausanias, the regent, moved quietly across the Isthmus. The Athenians sent 8,000 hoplites to join them.

Xerxes had never returned, but Mardonius had experience in command going back to the 490s and was probably a better general in any case. Xerxes had never allowed his cavalry, which provided him with one of his main advantages over the Greeks, to be used effectively. Mardonius withdrew north from Attica, which he had reoccupied to prevent the Athenians raising a harvest, to Boeotia, where the ground was more open and suitable for horses. The Greeks followed him, and complicated manoeuvring ensued, with each side seeking to exploit the ground most favourable to it. Mardonius stuck at first to open ground, hoping that the Greek forces, which by now were made up of hoplites from over twenty cities, would break up. The Greeks concentrated on keeping to higher ground, where they were relatively secure from cavalry charges. Finally, near the town of Plataea, the Greeks were forced to retreat from their positions to secure better sources of food and water. Mardonius carelessly interpreted the retreat as a flight and sent in his troops in pursuit. He was suddenly faced with determined resistance, above all from the Spartan contingent. By the end of the day Mardonius and the flower of his troops lay dead and the treasures of the Persian headquarters lay in Greek hands. One Persian contingent fled back to Asia so fast that it outstripped the news of the defeat that followed it. Plataea was overwhelmingly a Spartan victory. The Athenian troops played little part at all—one reason why this battle, the most decisive of all of the Persian wars, was never eulogized by their propagandists.

Ever since the demoralizing experience of Salamis, the remaining Persian fleet had been idle, staying along the eastern Aegean coast. It did not dare move back towards the Greek mainland for fear that the Ionian Greeks would rise once again in revolt as it left. With so many of the Phoenicians lost at Salamis, much of the fleet was now made up of Greek ships and they could hardly be trusted. The Greeks' own fleet now moved across the Aegean to deal with it. They found their enemies with their ships beached on the shore at Mycale and no stomach left for a fight. The ships were easily destroyed.

Victory was now complete, and the jubilant Greek fleet sailed northwards, drawing islands such as Samos, Chios, and Lesbos into the Greek alliance. It then made for the Hellespont with the aim of breaking down Xerxes' great bridge so that Persians could neither retreat into Asia nor be effectively reinforced. It had already collapsed, probably under the impact of storms. The Spartans now sailed home, but the Athenians remained to liberate the Hellespont, an area vital for them as a route through which their corn supplies came. Among the booty were the great ropes which had held the Hellespont bridge, found at Cardia. They were towed back to Athens as a trophy of war.

The impact of the Persian Wars on Greece needs to be put into perspective. Many of the essential elements of Greek culture were in place before the Persian invasions. The *polis* was well established and politics had already reached a high level of maturity. There was a fine tradition of craftsmanship shown across a wide variety of materials. The poetic tradition was a sophisticated one, and drama had been born in sixth-century Athens. In Ionia the foundations of abstract theorizing had been laid. The Persian Wars did not therefore create Greek culture. What they did do was help define this culture more sharply and boost the self-confidence of the Greeks, above all that of the Athenians.

'The fact was', writes John Herington in his book on *Aeschylus* (New Haven, 1986):

that the great Persian invasion of 480–79 BC made a unique impact on the Greek imagination. Fifth century Greek lyric poets, wall painters and sculptors, who, like the tragedians, traditionally worked through mythology alone to express their visions of life, similarly made an exception for the Persian Wars, for these were felt at once to possess the same exemplary and universal quality as the myths inherited from the far past.

The wars allowed a revival of the old aristocratic values, *arete*, glory, manliness, and valour. On the battlefield at Marathon a mound was built over the 192 heroes who had fallen, while it has been argued that the celebrated frieze of the Parthenon depicts the heroes of the battle being received by the gods. A picture of the battle adorned the Stoa Poikile, the Painted Stoa, in the Agora, and a 13-metre-high statue of Athena was erected on the Acropolis in honour of the battle. To ensure the wider Greek world appreciated what had been achieved the Athenians built a treasury at Delphi from the spoils of victory. Some years later, perhaps about 450, a bronze group of gods and heroes from Athens' past, including Theseus, the hero always associated with the coming of democracy, and Athena, with Miltiades added to them, was placed in front of the treasury. It is possible that the famous Riace warriors, two life-size bronze figures of the highest quality, later looted by the Romans and found off the coast of Italy in 1972, were from this monument. Once the second invasion had been defeated, Athens again claimed the glory. Another epigram of Simonides laments the Athenian dead at Plataea:

> If to die well is the greatest part of valour,
> fortune granted this to us above all men.
> For in our eagerness to clothe Greece in liberty,
> we lie in unaging good repute.
>
> (Translation: N. G. L. Hammond)

Poets (such as the Spartan Tyrtaeus) had talked before of the beauty of dying for one's city. Simonides (who was not an Athenian but came from the small island of Ceos) was the first to link the giving of life with the saving of liberty. Here was a rich legacy for Europe, as countless twentieth-century war memorials attest.

The maintenance of liberty became an essential element of the Greek consciousness. Herodotus, for instance, re-creates a conversation between the Athenian commander at Marathon, Miltiades, and Callimachus the war archon, who had the casting vote when the decision was made to attack. 'It is now in your hands, Callimachus, either to enslave Athens, or to make her free and to leave behind you for all future generations a memory more glorious than even Harmodius and Aristogeiton [the murderers of the tyrant Hipparchus in 514] left.' The freedom that Miltiades was referring to was the sovereign freedom of a state to conduct its affairs through its own citizens and without outside interference. The same point is made in another re-created conversation, this time between Xerxes and the exiled Spartan king Demaratus, in which Demaratus contrasts the freedom of the Spartans, a freedom restrained only by the law, with the despotism of the Persian king. Sparta hardly enjoyed what anyone could call freedom in the sense of individual liberty and human rights, but the point that Greeks lived under constitutions while the Persians lived under arbitrary rule was a fair one.

However, the contrast could easily degenerate into racism. In a denigration of the barbarian, the late fifth-century Hippocrates of Cos talked of the mental flabbiness and cowardice of the Asiatic, partly as a result of their climate and partly because they were subject to tyrannical rule: 'even if a man is born brave and of stout heart, his character is ruined by this form of government'. The same theme is used by Aristotle in his analysis of slavery. In his *Politics* he writes, 'The peoples of Asia are intelligent and skilful in temperament, but lack spirit so that they are in continuous subjection and slavery.' Hence, it follows, the Greek race, which in Aristotle's words is 'both spirited and intelligent', is justified in using Asiatics as slaves.

Another point has to be made. The Persian Wars are often seen as the moment when the Greeks acquired their true identity. For those cities who played a major part in the conflict this may have been true. However, only between thirty and forty of the 700 or so Greek cities around the Aegean are known to have resisted the Persians. The victory may have been a great one, but to see it solely in terms of Greeks versus barbarians is too simplistic, however much this may have been the image put forward in the propaganda of the victors.

Persia was not suddenly excluded from the Greek world. While it is possible to see, in hindsight, that a long period of decline set in after 480, Persia was still there to be feared or used. Persian money was sought in the endless Greek conflicts of the fifth and fourth centuries. The word 'medism' (the Greeks failed to distinguish between Persians and Medes) was used to condemn an opponent as having pro-Persian, often merely aristocratic, sympathies and was a political rallying cry for decades to come. What no one could possibly have predicted, however, was that 170 years later a military genius from the outlying regions of the Greek world, Alexander of Macedon, would actually revenge the Greeks for Xerxes' ambitions and destroy the empire that had attacked them.

FURTHER READING

The Ionian revolt is well covered by Oswyn Murray, chapter 8 of the *Cambridge Ancient History*, vol. iv and that volume also has two chapters (9 and 10) on the Persian wars by N. G. L. Hammond. See also A. Burn, *Persia and the Greeks* (2nd edition, London, 1984). J. Morrison and J. Coates look at the mechanics of naval warfare in *The Athenian Trireme* (Cambridge, 1986). On Herodotus see John Gould, *Herodotus* (London, 1989) which helped set in place a new respect for the historian. In fact, Herodotus is enjoying a renaissance. In addition to Rosalind Thomas, cited in the text, recent works include J. Evans, *Herodotus, Explorer of the Past* (Princeton, 1991), P. Derow and R. Parker (eds.), *Herodotus and his World* (Oxford, 2003), and N. Luraghi (ed.), *The Historian's Craft in the Age of Herodotus* (Oxford, 2001). E. Hall, *Inventing the Barbarian* (Oxford, 1989), looks at the impact of the wars on Greece.

13 | Everyday Life in Classical Greece

Aristocratic Survivals

One of the major developments of the Archaic period was the erosion of the political power and status of the aristocrat. With hoplite warfare becoming the military expression of city identity the aristocrat could no longer prove himself as a heroic warrior while traditional landed wealth was being challenged by the increase in trade. The aristocrat estate with its wasteful cattle economy had largely vanished by the seventh century. The poet Theognis, a Megaran aristocrat writing about 550 BC, expressed the views of a class who feel themselves under siege.

> Kyrnos, our city's still the same; its people, though, are different:
> the ones who used to have no concept of our laws or rules,
> but wrapped their ribs around with goatskin cloaks, and lived
>   like deer outside the city walls,
> it's they who are the masters now, while those who once were fine
> are cowards now. Oh, who can bear the sight.
>
> (Translation: Alan Griffiths)

High birth is the defining factor of the *agathoi*, loosely translated as 'the good ones', but with connotations of physical excellence and skill in war. The rest are *kakoi*, 'the unworthy ones'. The *agathoi* need wealth because it is the only way that their position can be sustained. For the *kakoi*, however, wealth is seen as potentially corrupting (the *kakos* has not been brought up to know how to handle it and certainly he can never use it to transform himself into an *agathos*). Intermarriage, for Theognis, is anathema. The class of *agathoi* must be kept pure. Similar attitudes were not unknown among the aristocracy of nineteenth-century Europe faced with the influx of 'new' money made in trade.

How can the *agathoi* maintain their status? One way is to mark their graves with the symbolic form of the nude hero, the *kouros* (see earlier p. 187). However a more immediate access to status was required while they were still alive. Now that the old Homeric warrior contest was no more, aristocrats became obsessed with proving themselves through other forms of contests, *agones*. The early sixth century was the period when games spread through the Greek world. The Olympic Games, held every four years, were by then officially 200 years old but probably much older still. They had originated as a festival to the god Zeus, and the great temple to the god stood in a sacred enclosure around which the stadium, the race track for chariot races, the gymnasium, and the wrestling ring were grouped. Close to it was an ancient altar at which, at the central point of the games, a hundred oxen were sacrificed to Zeus. The ashes were never cleared away but mixed into a paste, with the result that every year the altar became more monumental.

By the sixth century the games had taken their final form of nine events, among them running and chariot races, boxing, wrestling, and a pentathlon. The custom of running naked, nudity being the 'costume' of heroic identity, was already well established. The contestants would assemble at Elis, the city which managed the games, a month before they were due to start, and then two days before the first races a procession would set out for the sanctuary with officials leading the athletes, horses, and chariots. The games would last for five days and were attended by vast crowds. The events were interwoven with contests for heralds and trumpeters, speeches by well-known orators, banquets, sacrifices, and finally, on the last day, a great procession of the victors to the Temple of Zeus where they were given their wreaths of wild olive and showered with leaves and flowers. (The last games were held in AD 395, but the site had become forgotten after earthquakes changed the flow of the river Alpheaus and allowed it to be buried in silt. Much of the site of Olympia has been excavated since its discovery in 1766.)

In the sixth century the Olympic Games were joined by the Pythian Games at Delphi (in 582), in 581 by the Isthmian Games, and by the Nemean Games at Nemea in the Argolis in 573. Each year there were now one or two major festivals. However, they were, in effect, only open to those with the leisure to train for them. This preserved them for the aristocracy. The prizes were, as at Olympia, always modest—a pine crown at the Isthmian Games, a crown of wild celery at the Nemean. A victor might erect his statue at the games and hundreds of these statues still remained at Olympia when the site was visited by the Greek traveller Pausanias in the second century AD.

Among the poets of this world is Pindar (518–438 BC), a Theban aristocrat whose complex but exquisite songs were commissioned by aristocratic victors from throughout the Greek world. Pindar believed the good breeding of the aristocrat made him naturally superior, while victory in the games elevated him further, close to the gods and heroes of the past. His achievements shone with the radiance and magic of gold: 'Gold shines out like a blazing fire in the night beyond any proud wealth: and, if you wish to sing of prizes, seek no other bright star that is hotter in the day than the sun in the golden sky, nor shall we name a contest better than Olympia' (*Olympian I*; translation: Ewen Bowie). In her *The Traffic in Praise: Pindar and the Poetics of Social Economy* (Ithaca, NY, 1991) Leslie Kurke has shown how success in the games transferred itself into status in the city where victors would even be incorporated unarmed into the line of battle as if they had become talismans of their city's invincibility. In 416 BC the Athenian aristocrat Alcibiades, entered no less than seven chariot teams in the Olympics and then unscrupulously used his success to manipulate the city's democratic assembly. 'There was a time', he told his credulous audience, 'when the Greeks imagined that our city had been ruined by the war, but they came to consider it even greater than it really is because of the splendid show I made as its representative at the Olympic Games, when I entered seven chariots for the chariot race and took the first, second, and fourth places . . . It is customary for such things to bring honour, and the fact that they are done at all must give an impression of power.'

Just as victory brings its divinity so does defeat its shame. In a late ode to a wrestler, Pindar records the humiliation of those defeated:

> And now four times you came down with bodies beneath you,
> (You meant them harm)
> To whom the Pythian feast has given
> No glad home-coming like yours.
> They, when they meet their mothers,
> Have no sweet laughter around them moving delight.
> In back streets out of their enemies' way
> They cower, disaster has bitten them.

> (Translation: Maurice Bowra)

Back home after the excitement of the games, the aristocracy retreated into the private world of the symposia, drinking parties conducted within a formal and ritualized setting. The symposium had its roots in the hall-feasts of the warrior chieftains, but now they were developed into occasions of dignity and ceremony. Men reclined on couches set around the walls of the dining-room. There were always odd numbers of couches, a minimum of seven, a maximum of fifteen, often with two men to a couch. One man would preside over the proceedings, mixing the wine and overseeing the transfer of the mixture to the drinking-cups of the guests. The symposium, was, in fact, the major influence on the design of pottery and its decoration. The water was fetched in a *hydria*, the wine stored in an amphora, from which it was transferred for mixing to a *krater*, and distributed to the participants via a drinking cup, a *kylix*. Although it has proved enormously difficult to generalize about the relationship between the *symposium* and the favourite scenes on pottery, there is certainly a link to scenes from the life of Dionysus, the god of wine, and to traditional mythical scenes in general.

The symposia provided for many pleasures—food and drink, good conversation, and sex. There were girls, the *hetairai*, who often had skills in dancing and music and who could provide more in companionship than the prostitute visited for immediate sexual relief. Then there were games such as *kottabos* which involved flicking the dregs of wine at a target or favoured lover. The symposia would normally end in music and song—the *hetairai* are often shown on pots naked playing the double pipe, the instrument associated with Dionysus and abandonment—and finally the participants might take to the streets to complete an evening of drunken revelry.

In Greece music was interwoven with every aspect of life. Rosalind Thomas lists, among the many manifestations of music, 'hymns to the gods at public festivals, paeans in honour of Apollo, victory odes at the games, processional songs (*prosodia*), songs praising individuals (*encomia*), songs at funerals and marriages (*epithalamia*), maiden songs (*partheneia*), and dirges'. Typically, also, music accompanied any public performance of poetry or drama. The composing of the words was thus only part of the poet's task. Pindar stresses 'the garlands placed like a yoke on the hair exact payment of this sacred debt: to blend together properly the lyre with her intricate voice, and the shout of oboes, and the placing of words' (translation: Rosalind Thomas). The works of Pindar were choral lyrics, those of Sappho monodic lyrics, accompanied by the lyre. Music gave an emotional tone to the spoken word which is hard to re-create today. It was one which the philosopher Plato was well aware of, and when he put his case for the regulation of poetry (based on the emotions it aroused) he included dancing and choral singing as well.

Music also formed the core of a traditional education. In Athens education was originally a form of initiation into aristocratic culture. Literature and physical training were taught alongside music and all three were related to physical and moral development. Physical training allowed the development of a perfect body. 'What a disgrace it is for a man to grow old without ever seeing the beauty and strength of which his body is capable,' said Socrates. Mastery of the lyre had its place in the formation of character. 'So also the lyre teacher', records one source, 'sees to his pupils' restraint and good behaviour. Once they are able to play, he teaches them songs by suitable poets, stringing these into the lesson, and gets the rhythms and tunings into the boys' minds to make them less wild and better in tune for effective discourse and action.' (Translation: Peter Levi.) The lyre was always the symbol of restraint and respectable women are often shown on pottery seated and playing one. Once literacy had been acquired, pupils learned poetry, particularly that of Homer, by heart, as a means of absorbing moral values.

Attendance at a symposium appears to have been a part of the young boy's initiation into the values of aristocratic society. As a sign of his status he was allowed to sit, but not recline, on a couch, and was expected to pour out the wine once it had been mixed. In the same period that games became an integral part of aristocratic life, another form of competition, that of older unmarried men for the sexual attentions of young boys, appears. It is recorded without inhibition or prurience on many vase paintings.

Anthropologists have found pederasty to be a feature of many traditional societies, and it is normally related to the initiation of the boy into the warrior community. In some cases semen is passed on from the older man to the boy as if the strength of the community depends on it being preserved from one generation to the next. Usually the boy is expected to be a passive partner. In Athens, however, the essence of these pederastic relationships is not easy to discern. They certainly took place within heavily circumscribed limits. The *erastes*, the suitor, approached the *eromenos*, the loved one, according to the closely defined rituals of a courtship. The boy was expected to behave chastely, to refuse any material reward, and not to submit easily to the attentions of his lover. (This is the ideal put forward in Plato's *Symposium*.) The sexual element of the relationship appears to have been restrained, and may not have involved any actual penetration of the *eromenos*. In his essay 'Law, Social Control, and Homosexuality', which deals with the control of sexuality in Athens, David Cohen suggests that the boy, who was not yet fully a male member of the community, might be being used as a substitute for women by older men who had not yet reached the age of marriage. The courtship rituals for boys and for women were, he suggests, very similar. The boy had the right to be protected from unreasonable sexual demands and his family would be vigilant to ensure he was not being abused by his lover.

A distinction has to be made between pederasty, as described above, and homosexuality. For a Greek male to accept the submissive role in a homosexual relationship, or to be paid for this role, was considered so degrading that, in Athens at least, it resulted in the loss of citizen rights. As a surviving vase painting showing the victory of the Greeks over the Persians at the battle of Eurymedon (early 460s BC) suggests, one of the rights of a victor was to inflict sexual humiliation on those he had defeated.

For the older man pederasty appears always to have ceased with marriage, and older lovers were simply seen as ridiculous. 'What kind of life is there,' wailed the sixth-century poet Mimnermos, conscious above all of his failing sexual powers:

without golden Aphrodite, the goddess of love. May I die when I no longer take any interest in secret love affairs, in sweet exchanges and in bed. These are the flowers of youth, pleasant alike for men and women. But when painful old age overtakes a man and makes him ugly outside and foul-minded within, then wretched cares eat away at his heart and no longer does he rejoice to gaze upon the sun, being hateful to young men and despicable to women. (Translation: Robert Garland)

It was understandable that many aristocrats should hold conservative views and be reluctant to welcome the coming of democracy in a city such as Athens. Xenophon, the historian and friend of Socrates, wrote that 'the *demos* [the people] has put down the athletes at Athens and the practitioners of *mousike*'. As Josiah Ober has shown in his studies of the Athenian democratic process, *Mass and Elite in Democratic Athens* (Princeton, 1989) and *Political Dissent in Democratic Athens: Intellectual Critics of Popular Rule* (Princeton, 1998), however, aristocrats adapted to democracy in different ways. Some attempted to use enduring traditions of deference, or displays of victory in the games (as with Alcibiades above) to gain influence over the Assembly; in other words they accepted the reality of political change and tried to work with it. Others put up defences of oligarchy or, in the extreme case of Plato, highly sophisticated attacks on popular involvement in government. A tradition of reasoned objection to democracy was to be an important element in Greek political philosophy. (See further p. 285 below.)

Life on the Land

(See also Chapter 7.)

So when first the time for ploughing appears to mortal men, then set yourselves hard to it, your slaves and you yourself, ploughing in in wet and dry through the time of the plough-ing, pressing on with the task early in the morning, so your fields may be full.

Plough in the spring; earth turned over also in the summer will not let you down. (From Hesiod's *Works and Days*, translation from *The Cambridge Illustrated History of Greece*, ed. Paul Cartledge)

The dramatic events of the Persian Wars confirmed the reputation of the Greeks as effective soldiers and sailors. They tended to mask the fact that the majority of Greeks spent most of their time as farmers. In fact, as in all the pre-industrial economies discussed in this book, 90 per cent of the population of ancient Greece cultivated the land and had no other option if their city was to survive. As Robin Osborne pointed out in his *Classical Landscape with Figures*, these were the forgotten Greeks, barely mentioned in the literature and their scratchings on the surface of the soil hardly noticed by archaeologists. It is only since the 1970s that what little has survived in writing about the land has been correlated with the findings of field surveys to bring to life the farming activities of the Greek world.

The primary unit for production, the storage of goods and their consumption in the Greek world, was the *oikos*, or household. (The Greeks used the word *oikonomia* to describe the management of a household and its possessions and this is the source of the English word 'economy'.) *Oikos* was an elastic term. It might refer to the actual house itself, the household including family and slaves, or even the house with its surrounding land. The most common form of landownership in ancient Greece was the small plot, the *kleros*, a share inherited by a son from his father. The owner and his family might be the only workers on it but, as with Hesiod's farm, above, one or two slaves seem to have been usual.

In general the soil in Greece is poor, but the greatest challenge faced by all farmers in Greece is the unpredictability of rainfall. A good yield depended on frequent turning and weeding if moisture was to be retained, but instruments were primitive and the work must have been back-breaking. The ard, a rudimentary form of plough, always made of wood with perhaps an iron tip, would only cut through, not turn, the soil, and turning had to be completed as a separate task. Oxen might help with the ploughing, but most tasks, from pruning to harvesting the various crops, cereals, grapes, and olives, had to be done by hand.

The typical city state had access to plains, hillsides that might be cultivated with terracing, hillsides which could not be cultivated but might be used as pasture, and mountains which were totally barren. Each city had a different mix of lands and had to plot its survival accordingly. How land was divided is the subject of much scholarly debate. Studies of the property of a set of Athenian aristocrats in the late fifth century, for instance, showed that, typically, they had land scattered throughout Attica as well as beyond the state. Field survey evidence is now suggesting, however, that in the fifth and fourth centuries plots were being consolidated to achieve greater economy of scale and that animals were being pastured on them and their manure used for fertilizer. This suggests the emergence of a more intensive and, possibly, more market-oriented agricultural economy. However, once one looks at settlement patterns in different parts of Greece it is their variety which stands out. The ingenuity of the peasant farmer means that land is exploited in whatever way leads to survival. Survival meant not only producing a surplus of crops but actually protecting the land itself. Many surveys have shown a countryside dotted with towers. Their purpose is not always clear, they may have been watchtowers (an early warning system against attack by a neighbouring city), a strong room for valuables, or even simply a mark of ownership. It is a reminder that life on the land was never a rural idyll.

Most important in terms of calorie yield were cereals. Barley was the most popular cereal as it requires only half as much rainfall as wheat. (This made wheat bread a luxury, to be found mainly on the tables of the aristocratic symposia.) Studies of farming in Neolithic Greece suggest that a yield of 1,000 kilos of grain could be raised per hectare. There is some evidence that grains were larger by classical times, but there would still have been a significant shortfall of grain requirements in Attica each year, one reason why the trade routes to the cereal-growing areas of the north Aegean and Black Sea became so important for the city. The most widespread crop was the olive. Its deep roots and narrow leaves were well suited to a climate of hot sun and low rainfall. Its oil could be used for cooking, lighting, and even as a form of soap, and could be traded to areas such as the Crimea and Egypt where olives did not grow. It grew alongside the vine, another of the staples of the Greek economy.

As suggested in Chapter 7, the Greek farmer would plan for a small surplus, partly of course through prudence, but also to supply dowries for his daughters, contributions to collective feasts, and as a means of buying pottery, salt, fish, and metals. If the evidence that landholdings were being consolidated from the fifth century is true, this surplus might be gained from the marketing of produce. There remains, however, very little actual evidence for trading outside the

Athenian deme, for instance, and in Athens itself archaeologists have found no market buildings earlier than the late fifth century (though this does not rule out more makeshift arrangements for the transfer of goods). One could infer, from the evidence of terracing, which is labour and cost intensive, for instance, that there must have been some commercial incentive for improving production. The Argolid survey (see Chapter 7 above) provides a better example of the trading of surplus.

The Greek farming year had two periods of intensive activity. From September to November the olives and grapes were gathered, just at the same time as the ploughing and the sowing of seed took place for the next year. The harvesting of grain took place in May or June. There were two important slack times, in early spring and from July to September when the harvest was in. It was in these times that the great games of the Greek world were held, the Isthmian Games in the spring and the others in the autumn. Fighting also took place in these periods. The Persian Wars, as has been seen, were fought in the autumn; the Persian forces of 480 having entered Greece at the time when there was ample food for them to plunder. Men and their animals could also be employed in building. Accounts from the Athenian sanctuary of Demeter at Eleusis show almost all construction took place in the slack periods, particularly after the harvest. Oxen were also available then. Sixty-six are recorded as being drafted in to drag one column of marble.

Animals also formed an essential part of the agricultural economy. Sheep and goats could be pastured on higher ground or along the borders of the city state. Ownership of the land was not required, so flocks would range widely. Once these animals had passed through the rituals of sacrifice (see p. 240), they provided most of the protein needed by the population. All the raw materials for clothing were available from wool and leather. There were settlements in the hills wholly concerned with making cloth, leather goods, and cheese.

Industries, Crafts, and Trade

The largest non-agricultural concerns were the mines. Iron ore could be found locally in Greece and smelted for tools and weapons. Precious metals, gold and silver, were used by the state for large-scale enterprises such as paying mercenaries and, particularly from the late sixth century onwards, for coins to oil transactions of everyday commercial life. The silver mines in Attica are the best known as they underpinned the success of Athens as a naval and political power. The ancient remains have been carefully surveyed. Around 2,000 shafts have been located around Laurium, some over 120 metres in depth. Records from the fourth century show that 200 Athenians were then involved in taking out concessions. They could borrow the substantial amounts of money required (at 12 per cent interest in one recorded case) and then approach a slave-owner for the lease of labour. The historian Xenophon mentions one contractor with a thousand slaves available for hire, but they were often used so harshly by their hirers that their life expectancy was short. The most arduous task was crushing the silver ore, washing and separating it—the remains of the ancient washeries have been found. In an arid region the required water was stored from winter rainfall in cisterns.

Even richer than the Athenian mines were those of Chalcidice and the Rhodope massif in the northern Aegean. In addition to silver, they held the only Greek-controlled source of gold. While the total Athenian production in a year has been calculated at 65 talents, individual mines within this area are said to have produced 1,000 talents worth of precious metal each year at the height of production in the fourth century. These mines later fell under the control of Macedonia, which is one reason why this remote kingdom on the north of the Greek world became so powerful a force in the fourth century under the energetic leadership of Philip II. (See Chapter 17 below.)

Manufacturing was widespread in the Greek world. Most of it was local, drawing on raw materials such as wool, iron ore, and clay and processing them for immediate sale. Everything was done on a small scale and technology was virtually unknown. The Greeks had no tradition of applying their scientific understanding to creating more efficient ways of production. Even coins were made in an unsophisticated way with each one stamped individually. The largest workshop recorded in Athens made shields and employed 120 workers. Of two workshops owned by the father of the orator Demosthenes, one employed thirty slaves making knives, the other twenty joiners making beds. There were probably no more than 200 workers in the Athenian potters' quarter, the Ceramicus, at one time.

By the sixth century trade routes were busy, but the patterns of trade and the quantities of goods transported have proved difficult to measure. The evidence from shipwrecks, unlike that from later periods, has been too small to be of much use. All traces of slaves, grain, livestock, timber, the probable staples, have disappeared, but it is clear that commerce was based on small-scale free enterprise, with individuals taking responsibility for raising and managing their own voyages. The single largest commodity was grain shipped from those areas which had a consistent surplus, the Black Sea, Egypt, and Italy, to those which could not depend on one. Metal ores were also important, and in some cases their sources can now be pinpointed. Silver for the first Athenian coinage, for example, came from Thrace, not the Laurium mines in Athens. There was some specialization. It can be shown, for instance, that one late sixth-century group of Athenian potters, the so-called Perizoma group, produced designs specifically aimed at Etruscan tastes. They put loincloths on athletes in deference to Italian sensitivities about nudity and transformed conventional pictures of Athenian symposia into Etruscan funerary scenes.

Slavery

In many enterprises, those of building, mining, manufacturing, and work on the land, slaves carried out much of the labour. Slavery had long been widespread in the ancient world, the common fate, as Homer makes clear, of war captives and their families. However, as human beings seem to have been one of the few commodities the civilizations of the east would take from the Greeks in return for their luxury goods, a slave trade began. Thrace was the most important early source of slaves and then later the inland areas of Asia Minor. It gradually became more common for the Greeks to keep slaves for themselves, and eventually they may have made up perhaps 30 per cent of the population of many cities.

The slave had normally gone through traumatic experiences even before he or she had started work for a Greek master. The slave's family had usually been broken up and he or she had been removed from a native culture. The culture shock of entering the Greek world as an owned person must have been severe. What was added to the shock by the experience of day-to-day living as a slave is difficult to gauge. Within the home there were rituals and conventions which offered some protection to the slave. He or she was welcomed with a ceremony in the new home (and, as a symbol of the fresh beginning in life, given a new name). It was thought an act of hubris, pride, to beat a slave unjustly. These conventions and natural altruism may have combined to make life tolerable, but one cannot be too optimistic. The comedies of Aristophanes suggest casual brutality was common. Sex by men with their female slaves was tolerated and, as the evidence in one lawsuit suggested, was not considered serious enough to justify a wife's infidelity.

Slavery can take various forms. Chattel slavery, the direct ownership of the slave, was the most common, but there were other forms of servitude such as that suffered by the helots in Sparta. Some idea of their status can be seen from a remark by Thucydides that 700 helots who had been raised to campaign with the Spartan king Brasidas (see p. 299) were rewarded by being made free and allowed to live where they wanted. This implies they were normally tied to the land and were seen as the servants of the state rather than of individual owners. They differed from the mass of chattel slaves, in that they were Greeks, lived in their own communities in lands that had traditionally been their own, and were allowed to retain at least part of their produce (the rest being handed over to the state). In other ways their lives were miserable. At each new election of ephors, there was a ritual by which war was declared against helots in general, and it appears that those who looked like emerging as leaders were systematically killed. One episode in the training of adolescent Spartans for war involved placing them in the countryside and giving them free rein to kill any helots they came across.

With the possible exception of Sparta, there was no distinct slave economy in ancient Greece (as there was, for instance, on the sugar and cotton plantations of the West Indies and the American South). Those slaves with skills could work alongside freemen and even citizens. The status of eighty-six of the skilled workforce is known from the records which survive of the construction of the Erechtheum in Athens. Twenty-four were citizens, twenty-four metics (foreigners of free status), and twenty slaves. The slaves worked as masons and carpenters and their labour was paid at the same rate as free men. One disgruntled Athenian complained that it was impossible to distinguish slaves from free men in the streets.

A large number of slaves worked as domestic servants in the homes. Here a slave might achieve some identity because of his or her skills or general usefulness. Much less secure, however, were those slaves who found themselves working in larger groups in the fields, in workshops, or, worst of all, in the mines. Here there was little chance of preserving any individual identity and treatment appears to have been harsh. In the mines the slave seems to have been no more than an expendable instrument for obtaining the city's most sought-after source of wealth. Slaves also made up a large part of the population of common prostitutes.

The use of slaves was inextricably bound up with the Greeks' sense of their own identity. It was considered demeaning to be the servant of others, and by employing slaves the citizen was reinforcing his identity both as a free man and as a Greek. Slave labour also freed the citizen for political life. However, some justification had to be evolved for the practice. For the philosopher Aristotle, who explored the problem in his *Politics*, it was part of the natural order that there should be an elite who did the ruling and a slave class who carried out the labour on which civilized living depended (although he accepted that some disagreed with this view). 'One that can foresee with his mind is naturally ruler and naturally master, and one that can do these things with his body is subject and naturally a slave . . . the latter are strong for necessary service, the former erect and unserviceable for such occupations but serviceable for a life of citizenship.' However, a physical source for this slave labour had to be found, and this left Aristotle with little real option other than to define the difference in status between ruler and slave in ethnic terms. As he continued:

The nations inhabiting the cold places and those of Europe are full of spirit but somewhat deficient in intelligence and skill, so that they continue comparatively free, but lacking in political organization and capacity to rule their neighbours. The people of Asia on the other hand are intelligent and skilful in temperament, but lack spirit so that they are in continuous subjection and slavery. But the Greek race participates in both characters, just as it occupies the middle position geographically, for it is both spirited and intelligent: hence it continues to be free and to have very good political institutions and to be capable of ruling all mankind.   (Translation: H. Rackham, Loeb Classical Library edition)

According to Aristotle, therefore, slaves 'deserve' their position because they are outsiders.

Citizens and Others

As Paul Cartledge has shown in his book *The Greeks*, the world of the Greek citizen can be explored through the way it created outsiders such as barbarians, both free and slave, and, within the city, women and non-citizens in order to strengthen the identity of the citizen group. In Athens the cohesiveness of male citizen society was reinforced by a variety of associations and kinship groups. The traditional kinship group in Athens had been the phratry, which may originally have been based on allegiance to an aristocratic clan. By the sixth century, the phratry, while still aristocratic in tone, appears to have become a political grouping, controlling citizenship. Cleisthenes deprived it of its political power and undermined the individual identity of each phratry by using one of the traditional Ionian festivals, the Apatouria, to allow the phratries to meet collectively and exercise functions such as recognizing marriages, admitting infant members, and overseeing the transition of young men to adulthood as a group.

There were many other associations. Some of them were purely religious, others were connected with particular trades. Aristocrats might claim allegiance to a clan, the Alcmaeonidae, for instance, or a drinking club. The sense of comradeship that resulted is finely expressed in a speech by the Athenian Cleocritus (as recorded by the historian Xenophon). Cleocritus is leading an attack on the oligarchs in the city who wish to destroy democracy:

Fellow-citizens, why are you driving us out of the city? Why do you want to kill us? We have never done you any harm. We have shared with you in the most holy religious services, in sacrifices and in splendid festivals; we have joined in dances with you, gone to school with you and fought in the army with you, braving together with you the dangers of land and sea in defence of our common safety and freedom. (Translation: Oswyn Murray)

The Athenian citizen was thus given identity through a range of shared activities which went well beyond his involvement in the Assembly.

In contrast, life in Sparta seems uniform and regimented. It pays to be cautious in saying this because Sparta was often deliberately presented, by both admirers and detractors, as a contrast to Athens and so what was different about the city might well be unduly emphasized. The Spartans also made it difficult to establish the truth about themselves. They prided themselves on presenting an inscrutable face to the world and in hiding their true military strength. Anton Powell, in an overview of life in Sparta, suggests a comparison with Mao Tsetung's China, 'where the movement of foreigners was restricted, communication with outsiders was guarded, while much that was reported derived from the uncheckable accounts of enthusiasts'.

What cannot be denied was that Sparta was a city which idealized the state over the individual and concentrated on breaking down any activities or relationships which threatened the cohesion of the community. The process of socialization began at the age of 7 with the removal of a boy from his family. Plato remarked that all education in Sparta was carried out through violence rather than through persuasion and the emphasis was on producing hardiness through endless tests of self-reliance and endurance. At the age of 20 the boys joined messes, the *syssitia*. These were, in effect, the only associations recognized by the state and they provided a totalitarian social world. The messes ate together nightly and there was no distinction between young and old, rich or poor. It seems, though the direct evidence is slight, that homosexual relationships were the norm. Certainly there was little scope for any other form of physical affection. Men could marry, but until they were 30 all visits to their wives had to be conducted stealthily by night. (There was an interesting ritual relating to the consummation of marriage. On the marriage night the bride was dressed in a man's cloak and sandals and laid in an unlit room to await the attentions of her bridegroom. The deflowering of a woman dressed as a man may, it has been suggested, have marked a formal transition from the homosexual world of the mess to that of the heterosexual.)

The state inculcated its own values, related to its need for survival as a military machine. The greatest glory was to die in the service of the state. The families of those who had died appeared to rejoice even after a defeat. Survivors, on the other hand, were shunned. There were two from Thermopylae. When they returned to the closed society of Sparta both were humiliated and one even committed suicide. Action was valued above words. The Athenian politician Pericles puts it well when he talks of the Athenians as superior to the Spartans because they did not think that words 'damaged' actions as the Spartans did. The Spartans were famous for their brevity of speech (the word 'laconic', from Laconia, the country of Sparta, derives from this source). It is also interesting to note that they had little use for literacy. Only one classical inscription has been discovered in Sparta itself, and writing seems to have been reserved for the recording of international treaties.

Propaganda became an essential part of maintaining the public façade of the Spartan state. With so little respect given to words, it was expressed visually, particularly in the display of troops. Their hair was kept conspicuously long and they were dressed in identical red cloaks. (The historian Xenophon remarked that the Spartan army seemed to consist entirely of bronze and scarlet.) Their numbers were always kept a closely guarded secret. Other states grasped the importance of deflating this proud image. When the Spartans were finally defeated at Leuctra (371 BC), the Thebans exposed their dead separately so that all could see they were not invincible.

Citizenship in Sparta was defined through ownership of land through which membership of a mess could be sustained. In Athens no land was required, but, by the mid-fifth century, citizenship was only available to those born to parents who were both themselves citizens. Citizenship was thus a privilege and a closely guarded one. It implied duties but also economic and social advantages. In Athens only citizens could take part in government, own land, or join most of the associations. Outsiders, metics, were not, however, social rejects. In Athens they could mix freely with the intellectual elite of the city (Plato's *Republic* takes place in the house of Cephalus the Syracusan) and take part in religious processions. They had some legal privileges as well such as the right to speak on their own behalf in law courts. Unable to own land, they probably had a predominant influence in manufacturing and trade.

The shared language, culture, and values of the Greek world and the relative ease with which it could be crossed allowed those with skills every chance of exploiting them within other Greek communities. The lyric poet Pindar was born near Thebes but is reputed to have moved to Athens to study music. His travels then took him to Sicily (some of his greatest odes were in honour of the Sicilian tyrants), and he finally died in the Peloponnese in 436 at the age of 80. The philosopher Aristotle was born in northern Greece in 384. He moved south when he was 17 and spent twenty years in Athens as a pupil of Plato. Then, for twelve years, he travelled, setting up academies in two cities on the coast of Asia Minor, Assos and Miletus. He spent three years in Macedonia as tutor to the young prince of Macedon who was to become Alexander the Great, before returning to Athens for a further twelve years. He retired to the island of Euboea, where he died in 322. For neither man was lack of citizenship a barrier to a successful career outside his home community.

Women in the Greek World

> As the one who bears and cares for the children and tends house and hearth, she is at the very centre of what is secure, nurturing, life giving; but in her passionate and emotional nature and the violence of her sexual instincts which she is felt as little able to control, she is regarded as irrational, unstable, dangerous.
>
> (Charles Segal, quoted in Sarah Pomeroy, *Families in Classical and Hellenistic Greece* (Oxford, 1997))

The Greeks were deeply ambivalent about women. For the male citizen they were another 'other' against which the virtues of the citizen can be defined but they were also indispensable for a settled life and an Athenian woman who was a citizen herself and married to one was allowed to pass on the privileged status to her children.

The records suggest that sex was freely available for men in Athens. A fourth-century dramatist, Xenarchus, describes the city prostitutes 'basking in the sun, their breasts uncovered, stripped for action'. As in many such societies (Victorian England comes to mind) the purity of the wife is maintained alongside a flurry of sexual activity in the back streets. In Athens the 'pure' citizen wife, whose life is described below, contrasts with those who have to use their bodies to survive. 'Mistresses we have for pleasure, concubines for daily service to our body, but wives for the procreation of legitimate children and to be faithful guardians of the household,' as one Athenian put it.

Whatever the reality of women's lives in Greece, they themselves have left little record of it. When they speak, above all in tragic drama, they do so through men's voices. In short it is hard to know what Athenian wives really felt as they sat together in the women's quarters of the cramped and probably smelly houses which were typical of urban Athens. They may have taken some satisfaction in their status as citizens and mothers of citizens-to-be. On the other hand, they may have yearned to enjoy the freedom of the *hetairai*, the courtesans who attended the symposia and who sometimes established stable relationships with young aristocrats. However successful in the short term, however, the *hetaira*'s life depended on her looks and charm. She was vulnerable to pregnancy (and the child could never be recognized as a citizen, although the Athenian Pericles did manage to achieve citizenship for his son by his mistress, Aspasia, by special decree) and disease, and when her lover married she would be discarded. The best documented case in Athens is one Neaera. Neaera had been born a slave girl but had worked her way up so successfully that one of her lovers, an up-and-coming politician, Stephanus, tried to pass her off as his legitimate wife and her daughters by previous relationships as Athenian citizens. In the ensuing court case (brought by a rival of Stephanus, wishing to discredit him with the truth about his wife) Neaera's previous life was revealed in sordid detail and was clearly one in which she had suffered sexual abuse. One previous lover had even had sex with her openly at a symposium 'making his privilege a display to the onlookers'.

The most important moment of transition in a conventional Athenian woman's life was marriage. The experience consisted of being taken at a young age, just after puberty, into a relationship with a man, probably ten to fifteen years older, in a strange home. A fragment from one of Sophocles' plays records the experience:

Unmarried girls, in my own opinion, have the sweetest existence known to mortals in their fathers' homes, for their innocence always keeps such children safe and happy. But when we reach puberty and can understand we are thrust out and sold away from our ancestral gods and from our parents. Some go to strange men's homes, others to foreigners, some to joyless houses, some to hostile. And all this once the first night has yoked us to our husband we are forced to praise and say all is well.   (Translation: Oswyn Murray)

It is written, like almost all comments on women, by a man, but it makes the point that women, unlike men, entered a form of exile when they married.

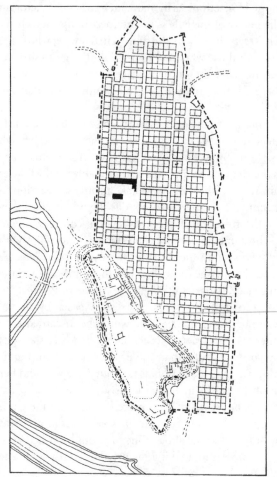

FIG. 2 The town of Olynthos, northern Greece, was razed to the ground by Philip of Macedon in 348 BC and its ruins provide the best remaining evidence of a typical Greek town and its houses. These are small (some 17 metres square) and enclosed with a courtyard, hearth (*oikos*), and men's room (*andron*). The bedrooms were on an upper storey.

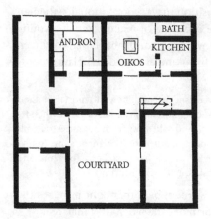

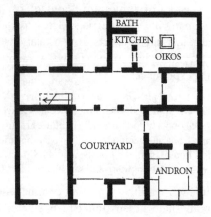

Solon had recommended that men marry between the ages of 28 and 35, when they were past the peak of their strength and should rightly consider the future of their family. Girls might be ten to fifteen years younger. This discrepancy may have been deliberate, to ensure the dominance of males who were, at their age of marriage, sophisticated and well used to public life, over women who, in the words of one source, 'had been closely supervised in order that they would see as little as possible, hear as little as possible and learn as little as possible'. There were also medical theories that childbearing was safest for a younger mother (while, in contrast, male sperm became more potent with age) and that sexual intercourse was the best answer to the emotional upheavals of female adolescence.

As in most traditional societies, love played little part in the choosing of partners. Marriage partners were usually chosen from within a relatively small circle of families known to each other. The bride's family had to provide a dowry, and it was the passing over of this, into the complete control of the bridegroom, that formalized the agreement. The preservation of property within a family was another important factor. It would normally pass only through the male line, but a woman who had no brothers was assigned a special status, that of *epikleros*, because she went with the estate (*kleros*). So that her inheritance would not be lost to the family, she could be married to the nearest of her male relations who would have her. (A paternal uncle would often come forward.) Even if she was already married, a new marriage could be formed to preserve the inheritance, so long as the first marriage was childless.

Inevitably, as with every moment of transition in Greek life, marriage involved rituals. The bride took a purifying bath before being taken in a formal procession with the bridegroom and his best friend in a cart to the bridegroom's home. The bride would be greeted by the bridegroom's mother and then go through the formalities of welcome to a new home before the couple retired for the physical consummation of the marriage. The importance of the wife as a bearer of children was underlined by the fact that her status in the new home improved once a son was born. 'When a child was born, then I began to trust her and I put her in charge of all my things, believing that the closest connections had been formed,' as one suitor in an Athenian law case put it. A marriage which was childless could be dissolved, and women did possess the right to divorce their husbands if their behaviour was particularly shameless.

The domestic arrangements of Greek families are not well documented. However, at Olynthos in northern Greece, the foundations of houses have been uncovered in a town which was destroyed by Philip of Macedon in 348. Typically, each house was closed off to the outside world, its exterior walls provided with relatively few windows. The men's room, the *andron*, was near the main door so that visitors could be entertained without having to intrude on the more secluded quarters of the women. The space of the house was itself sacrosanct— it was always a charged moment when a woman in a tragedy stepped over the threshold and a matter of great offence if an outsider entered a house and came upon its womenfolk unawares. In larger houses there would be a courtyard where the women could sew and weave on warm days, and here there would also be ample space for the storage of the family's oil, wine, and grain. Richer homes might have mosaics on the floors of the public rooms but on the whole there is little sign of luxury. In democratic Athens, in any case, it was socially and politically unacceptable to flaunt wealth. The more prosperous and comfortable bourgeois home was not common in the Greek world before the Hellenistic age.

Every Athenian woman had her protector, the *kyrios*, either a male relative before she was married or her husband. 'Her' property, outside her immediate possessions of clothes and jewellery, was in his care and she could undertake only the most modest of transactions on her own behalf. However, the Athenians do not seem to have believed that women deserved protection simply because they were the weaker sex. In fact, the opposite seems to have been true. It was claimed that women were subject to particularly strong and threatening feelings and that suppression of their instincts by men was justified through fear of the emotional havoc they could wreak. A legal example makes the point. A man who violently raped a woman was treated less severely than one who seduced a woman. The reason was that the seduction, unlike rape, threatened to create an individual able to follow her own desires. (The matter was made more complicated, however, by the fact that the seduction or rape was also an offence against the hubris, pride, of the woman's husband or family.) Women's sexual desires were assumed (by men) to be strong. Aristophanes in his play *Lysistrata* describes the consternation of the women characters when one of them suggests a sex strike. Other sources suggest that men believed that a woman allowed outside the house would soon engage in sexual adventures. Seclusion, however, was imposed not just out of sexual possessiveness. There were also fears that a woman who conceived with an unknown man would jeopardize the inheritance of the family property. She alone was the vessel through which it could be passed legitimately on to another generation.

There were occasions, mainly religious festivals, in which women could participate in their own right. The Thesmophoria, the most widespread of the Greek festivals, was celebrated entirely by women. The ritual in Athens lasted for three days, and the women withdrew to a sanctuary out of the sight of men. The sacrifices were of piglets, but there were also rituals in which phalluses were thrown into the earth and the remnants of sacrifices from earlier years brought out from the ground. This suggests elements of a fertility cult, although a period of sexual abstinence was also demanded even before the festival began. In accompanying rituals men were denounced in obscenities and there were legends of men who disturbed the rituals being castrated. 'At the core of the festival', writes Walter Burkert, in *Greek Religion* (Oxford, 1985) 'there remains the dissolution of the family, the separation of the sexes, and the constitution of a society of women;

once a year at least women demonstrate their independence, their responsibility, and importance for the fertility of the community and the land.' It could be argued that the Thesmophoria had the social function of legitimizing the oppression of women for the remainder of the year. There were other women's festivals, the Haloa in January and the Skira in July which were linked to the agricultural year (the Skira with threshing, for instance) which suggested that women were recognized as ensuring the prosperity of the land. The most abandoned was the celebration of Dionysus, described by Euripides in his play *The Bacchae*, where the women, worked up to a frenzy through dancing, tear to pieces Pentheus, king of Thebes, who has come to spy on them.

The male Greek's fantasies and fears of women could also be released in drama. Here is further evidence that the Greeks saw women as capable of intense emotion, emotions which could be manipulated by the playwright to explore the furthest boundaries of human behaviour. Greek tragedy is full of strong women, Medea, Phaedra, Antigone, Electra, who exhibit the full range of lust, defiance, and revenge which, for cultural reasons it may have been difficult to attribute to male characters. However, the playwrights were also able to show some empathy for the condition of women, as in the famous speech given by Euripides to Medea:

> Of all things that are living and can form a judgement
> we women are the most unfortunate creatures.
> Firstly, with an excess of wealth it is required
> for us to buy a husband and take for our bodies
> a master; for not to take one is even worse.
> And now the question is serious whether we take
> a good or bad one; for there is no easy escape
> for a woman, nor can she say no to her marriage.
> She arrives among new modes of behaviour and manners,
> and needs prophetic power, unless she has learned at home,
> how best to manage him who shares the bed with her.
> And if we work this out well and carefully,
> and the husband lives with us and lightly bears his yoke,
> then life is enviable. If not, I'd rather die.
> A man, when he's tired of the company in his home,
> goes out of the house and puts an end to his boredom
> and turns to a friend or companion of his own age.
> But we are forced to keep our eyes on one alone.
> What they say of us is that we have a peaceful time
> living at home, while they do the fighting in war.
> How wrong they are. I would very much rather stand
> three times in the front of battle than bear one child.

> (Translation: Simon Goldhill)

(There may be much truth in the final two lines. One calculation from the evidence of Greek skeletons suggests that the average lifespan of adult women was thirty-six years, compared to the forty-five of men (although more sophisticated analysis may raise these figures). Early death from childbearing seems the most likely explanation. There is also evidence that girl babies were more likely to be exposed to die than boys.)

The women of Sparta enjoyed (or were seen by outside observers to enjoy) a much freer life than their counterparts in Athens. Their husbands were preoccupied with their military training and often away at war and this may have left women with far greater initiative in the management of their daily lives. It is also possible that Spartan women kept their own dowries, which enabled them to own land. (Aristotle claimed that two-fifths of the whole country belonged to women.) However, there is no doubt that the state saw the main role of women as producers of male children. They were expected to undergo physical training to make then stronger for their task. (The fact that they did so naked scandalized other Greeks.) Special privileges were given to those who had three or more sons.

The death rate in ancient Greece, through childhood illness, death in battle, shipwreck, or disease, must have been high, but many Greeks survived into old age. Solon claimed that a man was at the peak of his intellect and power of speech between the ages of 42 and 56. Plato lived until he was 80, while the playwright Sophocles was still writing a year before he died aged 91. The rhetorician Gorgias, reputed to have lived to over 100, attributed his longevity to a meagre diet. (Certainly the normal Greek diet of oil, cereals, and fruit was a healthy one and modern Greeks have the highest male life expectancy in the EU.) Some even found joy in being a grandparent. One fifth-century grave-marker commemorating a dead woman called Ampharete is inscribed, 'I am holding the dear child of my daughter, which I did when we both looked on the rays of the sun, and now that we have both passed away, I hold her still upon my knees.'

And so on towards death. For those who died young there was a desire to die nobly so that burial could take place publicly with all due honours. There was a complete contrast with Egypt, where the preoccupation was with the survival of the body and possessions into another world. The Greeks cared more for their posthumous reputations, and the preservation of the body had no importance. The rituals of death were simple and moving. The body was washed and anointed in olive oil, then wrapped in two layers of cloth. A vigil was held at which songs of mourning would be sung and the body taken in procession to the cemetery. Here its final resting place was marked by a stone stele or even a statue of the dead man for those who could afford one.

In the words of an unknown poet,

> Then he will lie in the deep-rooted earth
> and share no more in the banquet, the lyre,
> or the sweet cry of flutes.

(Translation: Oswyn Murray)

FURTHER READING

A clear introduction to the Olympic games is provided by Judith Swaddling, *The Ancient Olympic Games* (London, 1980). On Pindar see D. Carne Ross, *Pindar* (New Haven, 1988).

On music see M. West, *Ancient Greek Music* (Oxford, 1992). Greek education: see H. Marrou, *A History of Education in Antiquity* (New York, 1956), and also his chapter in Moses Finlay (ed.), *The Legacy of Greece* (Oxford, 1984). Family pride impels me to include *Schools of Hellas* (3rd edition, London, 1932) by my great-uncle Kenneth Freeman, completed before he died aged only 24.

The complex issue of Greek sexuality is dealt with in K. Dover, *Greek Homosexuality* (London, 1978); J. Winkler, *The Constraints of Desire: The Anthropology of Sex and Gender in Ancient Greece* (London, 1990); D. Halperin, *The Construction of Erotic Experience in the Ancient Greek World* (Princeton, 1990); and David Cohen's *Law, Sexuality, and Society: The Enforcement of Morals in Classical Athens* (Cambridge, 1991). See also Andrew Stewart's important study *Art, Desire and the Body in Ancient Greece* (Cambridge, 1997).

The relationships of the Greeks to their land is a fast-changing subject as field surveys become more sophisticated. R. Osborne, *Classical Landscape with Figures* (London, 1987), is a good overview. See I. Morris (ed.), *Classical Greece: Ancient Histories and Modern Archaeologies* (Cambridge, 1994) for issues surrounding surveys; Alison Burford, *Land and Labor in the Greek World* (Baltimore, 1993); S. Isager and J. Skydsgaard, *Ancient Greek Agriculture* (London, 1982). A lively study is V. Hanson, *The Other Greeks, the Family Farm and the Agrarian Roots of Western Civilization* (New York, 1995). T. van Andel and C. Runnels, *Beyond the Acropolis: A Rural Greek Past* (Stanford, Calif., 1987). See chapter 14 of James Whitley, *The Archaeology of Ancient Greece* (Cambridge, 2001), 'Beyond the Polis: The Countryside of Classical Greece', for an overview of recent surveys.

On 'life' in general see R. Garland, *The Greek Way of Life* (London, 1990). See also Garland's *The Greek Way of Death* (London, 1985). For all aspects of life in Athens there is *The World of Athens* (produced by the Joint Association of Classical Teachers, Cambridge, 1984). Anton Powell, *Athens and Sparta: Constructing Greek Political and Social History from 478 BC* (London, 1988) is stimulating. A lively study on Athenian society is J. Davidson, *Courtesans and Fishcakes* (London, 1997). On slavery, Yvon Garlan's *Slavery in Ancient Greece* (Ithaca, NY, 1988) provides the best introduction. On Sparta see Paul Cartledge, *The Spartans* (London, 2002) and *Spartan Reflections* (London, 2001).

On women see as an introduction E. Fantham and others (eds.), *Women in the Classical World* (Oxford, 1994), which includes essays on women in Archaic Greece and in Classical Athens. Sarah Pomeroy's *Goddesses, Whores, Wives and Slaves* (New York, 1975) laid the foundation of serious study of the world of women. Sarah Pomeroy's *Families in Classical and Hellenistic Greece* (Oxford, 1997) and S. Blundell's *Women in Ancient Greece* (London, 1995) contain more recent assessments. S. C. Humphreys, *The Family, Women and Death* (Ann Arbor, 1993); L. Nevett, *House and Society in the Ancient Greek World* (Cambridge, 1999).

14 | Religion in the Greek World

> There is one race of men, one race of gods, both have breath of life from a single mother [Gaia, the earth, according to legend]. But sundered power holds us divided, so that the one is nothing, while for the other the brazen sky is established as their sure citadel for ever. Yet we have some likeness, in great intelligence and strength to the immortals, though we know not what the day may bring, what course after nightfall destiny has written that we must run to the end.
>
> (Pindar, *Nemean Ode 6*, translation R. Buxton)

Any people's religious beliefs are difficult to understand, those of the Greeks particularly so because they were so diversified. Almost every activity in the Greek world had its spiritual dimension. However, there had never been a divine revelation of the will of the gods. There was no central organization, no 'Church', no sacred book from which dogma could be preached, no priesthood, in the sense of a separate body of men or women who had authority to interpret what was correct belief or behaviour. (It was, however, possible for a city to define what was or was not considered sacrilegious behaviour, as the trial and death of Socrates in Athens showed (see pp. 281–2).) Instead there were religious attitudes and beliefs shared across the Greek world but supplemented by a host of local deities and cults. The Greeks feared the gods but there remained a sense that they were not that remote ('we have some likeness in intelligence and strength' as Pindar put it) and might even be supportive. 'For they say that foolish decisions are typical of this city, but the gods turn up for the best whatever mistakes you make', according to the chorus in Aristophanes' play *The Clouds*.

One possible way of understanding the religion of the Greeks is to see it as a method of coming to terms with the unpredictability of life. Every human community comes to learn that a good harvest cannot be assured, that the elements, wind, rain, and seas, are threatening to human life, that good fortune can suddenly be reversed by defeat in battle or through the sudden onset of illness. Most communities go further and have a brooding sense of powers of darkness which threaten the survival of human society. From the point of view of the anthropologist, religious belief is the attempt to make sense of this, to create a feeling of security so that life can be lived with a sense of purpose even in bad times.

Within the Greek world picture the gods of Mount Olympus take a central place. The backgrounds of the individual gods are varied. Some are found in the Mycenaean Linear B tablets or have even earlier origins. Zeus, the father of the gods, is found in pre-Greek Indo-European cultures. Many other gods and goddesses are similar to those found in the Near East. Aphrodite, the goddess of love, has her equivalents in the Sumerian Inanna and the Semitic Astarte, and probably came to Greece from the Near East via Cyprus. Apollo's origins also appear to be non-Greek. Others may have had Greek roots but had absorbed attributes from the east. Typically, each god or goddess is a composite one, taking its final form from many different sources.

According to Herodotus, it was Homer and Hesiod who 'first fixed for the Greeks the genealogy of the gods, gave the gods their titles, divided among them their honours and functions and defined their images', but the process, like most elements of the Homeric world view, must have begun much earlier. In their final form the Olympians became a family of gods, who had a common home on their mountain, were immortal (Zeus, his wife Hera, and Poseidon, god of the sea and earthquakes, might be portrayed as middle aged but no older), and who did not need human food. Zeus was, in most mythologies, assumed to be related to them all. Athena had sprung from his head. Artemis, goddess of hunting, another goddess whose origins lie in the east, becomes incorporated in the family as the daughter of Zeus by Leto, with Apollo as her twin. Aphrodite is another goddess whose original birth story (see p. 139, above) is overlain by a later myth of Zeus as her father through a goddess, Dione. Unlike in some cultures, there were no inhibitions about portraying the gods, in statues or vase paintings.

The formulation of the Olympian gods as a family worked well, as it did in Egypt. It defined their relationships with each other while allowing the possibility of disagreement and conflict among them. Between them the Olympian gods covered most human experiences, those of the changing weather and elements, harvests, love and sexuality (Aphrodite), craftsmanship (Hephaestus), war (the god Ares and the goddess Athena), intellectual pursuits (Apollo), and the home (Hestia). There was no important sphere of human experience which was not provided for. At the same time the roles of the gods were never frozen. One of the achievements, and functions, of Greek myth was to provide developing story lines so that religious needs and aspirations could always be catered for. It is interesting to contrast this approach with Christianity, where the interpretation of what Jesus Christ meant for the world can develop but the events of his life never can.

The Olympians were not unique. Hesiod had portrayed an earlier divine race, the Titans, overthrown by Zeus, and other gods from this lost epoch include Gaia, the earth mother, Uranus (Heaven), and Chaos (the Void). The daughters of Gaia were the Furies, who mercilessly avenged murders within a family. There were gods of the earth, the Chthonic gods, such as Hades, god of the underworld, darker, more morbid divinities when compared with the immortals of the mountain tops and approached by very different forms of rituals and sacrifice. A god who was not a member of the Olympian Pantheon was Dionysus, the god of wine and the patron of wild abandon in drink and sex. Halfway between the gods and men were the heroes, men whose exploits had earned them special honour and whose shrines were the object of special reverence. (Alexander the Great began his campaign in Persis at Troy with sacrifices to the supposed tombs of Achilles and Ajax.) Then there were nymphs and spirits who haunted the countryside.

The welfare of human beings was not the predominant concern of the gods. Their own quarrels and activities often took precedence. While they could act as protectors of the human race, they could equally be actively hostile. In Euripides' play *Hippolytus*, Hippolytus' chariot is smashed on the rocks by a great tidal wave sent by Poseidon, and many Homeric heroes die when the gods turn against them. The efforts of one god to protect a favoured mortal or city could be frustrated by another. (The story in the *Iliad* of Hera wearing Zeus to sleep by her ardent love-making so that she could put her plans in action behind his back is a good example.) The gods could not always control each other. In Aeschylus' *Oresteia* Athena and Apollo are hard put to it to restrain the awesome power of the Furies determined on the revenge of Orestes for the murder of his mother.

Yet while the Greeks did not believe that the gods were preoccupied with the behaviour of the human race, there was a general feeling that they would support correct behaviour and revenge bad. 'But if any man comes striding, high and mighty in all he says and does, no fear of justice, no reverence for the temples of the gods, let a rough doom strike him down . . . Can such a man, so desperate, still boast he can save his life from the flashing bolts of god?' as the chorus in Sophocles' *Oedipus Tyrannus* puts it. (Translation: E. F. Watling.) In Hesiod Zeus is seen as the upholder of *dike*, justice. There were virtues and vices which aroused the particular concern of the gods. Hubris was offensive behaviour through which one attempted to win more honour for oneself by humiliating others. *Ate* was headstrong behaviour, often induced by the gods, indulged in with no thought of its consequences. The gods were believed to punish behaviour against parents, guests and hosts, suppliants and the dead, with oath-breaking being the object of particular fury. On a more positive side, the gods supported *arete*, virtue, excellence, and *charis*, the giving of favours and the taking on of obligations.

While a fifth-century temple might be a public declaration of the relationship of a city with, say, its patron god or goddess, religious activities were not normally held within it. Temples could not contain a large congregation, and rituals, including sacrifices, almost always took place out of doors, often in the sanctuary surrounding the temple. One exception was the worship of the corn goddess Demeter and her daughter Persephone at Eleusis in northern Attica.

PLATE 1

The Scottish-born David Roberts visited Egypt in 1838 specifically to draw its monuments and his paintings are some of the most accurate that survive. This is of the portico of the temple of the goddess Isis on the island of Philae, one of the last great temples to be built (started 250 BC by the Ptolemies and a good example of how they worked within Egyptian architectural conventions). It was the last to be closed down, by the Christian emperor Justinian in AD 536. Note the use of papyrus leaves in the capitals of the decorated columns.

PLATE 2

PLATE 3

Both Egyptians and Etruscans idealized their hoped-for afterlife: in the Egyptian wall painting of the fifteenth century, an ordered life on the land; in the fifth-century Etruscan tomb painting from Tarquinia, a leisured banquet. Although the inspiration is from Greece, the Etruscans are shown dining with their wives, something unknown in Greece.

⇧ PLATE 4

Djoser's stepped pyramid of 2650 BC at Saqqara (*above*), with its ceremonial enclosure, marks a revolution in Egyptian architecture. It is the earliest surviving stone building of its size anywhere in the world and its monumental appearance provided inspiration for the pyramid builders of the Fourth Dynasty.

Magnificent though the building of the Great Pyramids at Giza (*left*) was, it was an achievement which exhausted the kingdom and disturbed the Egyptian ideal of a harmonious balance between ruler and ruled.

⇦ PLATE 5

PLATE 6

The celebrated Narmer palette of *c.*3000 BC (*left*) commemorating the victory of Narmer over northern Egypt, portrays Narmer about to club an enemy. Behind him the comparative insignificance of his foot washer is shown by his size, while Horus, the protective falcon god, is perched on papyrus stalks, the symbol of the Delta Narmer had defeated. Queen Hatshepsut (*below left*) had to accept the established conventions of royal art and portray herself as a man, here running the ceremonial circuit in a jubilee festival. Alexander the Great (*below right*) is adopted within Egyptian artistic conventions, being welcomed here at Luxor by Amun. Amun's traditional phallus has been chiselled out by Christians.

A more human side to the kings can be seen in the fine stone sculpture of Menkaure and his queen, Old Kingdom, *c.*2520 BC (*right*). It sets the tone for similar royal portrayals in the Middle Kingdom. Akhenaten (*far right*) was prepared to break through conventions, particularly by displaying a distended stomach, otherwise unknown in royal portrayals.

PLATE 7

PLATE 8

PLATE 9

PLATE 10

The question of how far the Greeks were directly influenced by the monumental stonework of Egypt is a difficult one. Certainly the Greeks were already working in stone before they had contact with Egypt as mercenaries and traders in the seventh century, but the building programme of King Psamtek (664–610 BC) may have acted as further inspiration. It is possible that the Doric order may have been influenced by columned facades such as that of the shrine of Anubis at the temple of Hatshepsut at Deir el-Bahri, *c.*1480 BC (*left*). It can be compared to a Corinthian example of *c.*540 BC (*below*).

The temples at Luxor and Karnak were linked by avenues of sphinxes, with ram heads or, as shown here in one of the later processional ways from Luxor (*facing above*), human heads. These may have proved an inspiration for Ionian Greeks, prominent among the early Greek traders, who faced the sacred enclosure of their cult centre at Delos with a similar line of lions in the seventh century (*facing below*).

⇩ PLATE 12

PLATE 13

PLATE 14

PLATE 15   PLATE 16

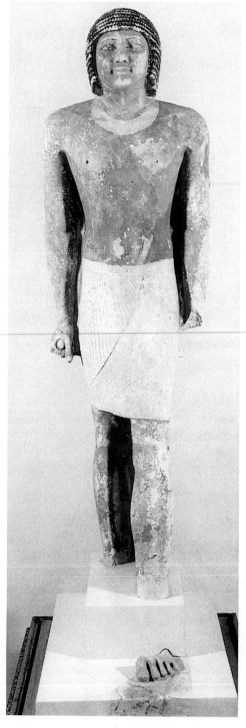

A typical Egyptian figure (*above left*) stood stiffly, his left foot forward. This is reflected in the nude *kouroi*, male 'heroes', which appear in Greece *c.*600 BC (*facing left*). The lady of Auxerre (*above right*), probably Cretan, *c.*630 BC, also shows eastern influences in her

PLATE 17 PLATE 18

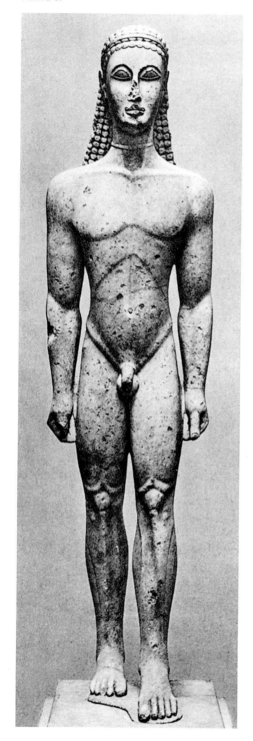

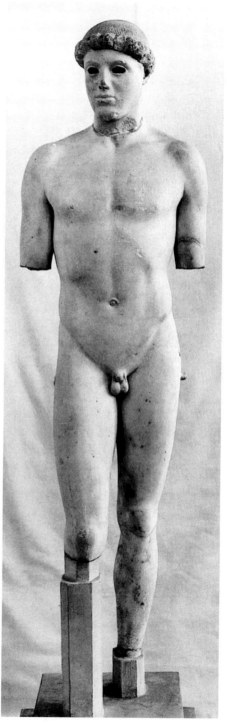

pose and hair. By the early fifth century the Greeks had broken through these conventions with the observed naturalness of the Critian boy, *c*.480 BC (*above right*). 'After this', writes John Boardman, 'all becomes possible.'

PLATE 19

PLATE 20

PLATE 21

This Sumerian chariot is from the 'Standard' from the Royal Cemetery at Ur, 2500 BC. The inlay is painted shell. This is an early example of a four-horse chariot, the model for chariots of elite figures, whether gods or men, throughout Greek, Etruscan, and Roman history. A two-horse chariot is more mobile and the extra two horses were often added as a symbol of the wealth or power of the owner. The chariot shown here would have been too cumbersome to use in battle.

This lapis lazuli cylinder seal, found in the cemetery at Ur in the tomb of Pu-abi, 'a queen', dates from 2500 BC. It shows two banqueting scenes, the upper scene being presided over by a woman, the first seated figure on the left, who is presumed to be Pu-abi herself. (The seal is Plate 21 on the right, its impression Plate 20 on the left.)

PLATE 22   PLATE 24

PLATE 23

This cuneiform tablet (Plate 22) is one of the letters found at Amarna. It is from Tushratta, king of Mitanni to the pharaoh Amenhotep III concerning the visit of a statue of the goddess Ishtar to Egypt, *c.*1350 BC. It is written in Akkadian with an ink-written note in Egyptian hieratic added to record the date of its arrival in Egypt .

This relief from Ashurbanipal's palace at Nineveh (Plate 23) shows Assyrian forces besieging a major city in Egypt in the seventh century BC. The Assyrians were the siege experts of the period. The captured Egyptians are depicted realistically with their native dress and hair styles, a reminder of how important these fine reliefs are for the historical record. Note the Nile complete with fish at the bottom of the relief.

The Rosetta stone (Plate 24 above right), discovered in 1799 at Rosetta in the Nile Delta, is the record of a royal decree of 27th March, 196 BC, through which the Ptolemies attempted to reassert control over Egypt through establishing links with the priesthood. Its significance lies in the text being written in three scripts, hieroglyphics, demotic (a popular Egyptian script) and Greek. Once the royal names Ptolemy and Cleopatra had been recognised in all three texts it became possible for the Frenchman Jean-Francois Champollion to decipher the hieroglyphs (1821) and thus make the written history of ancient Egypt available to the world.

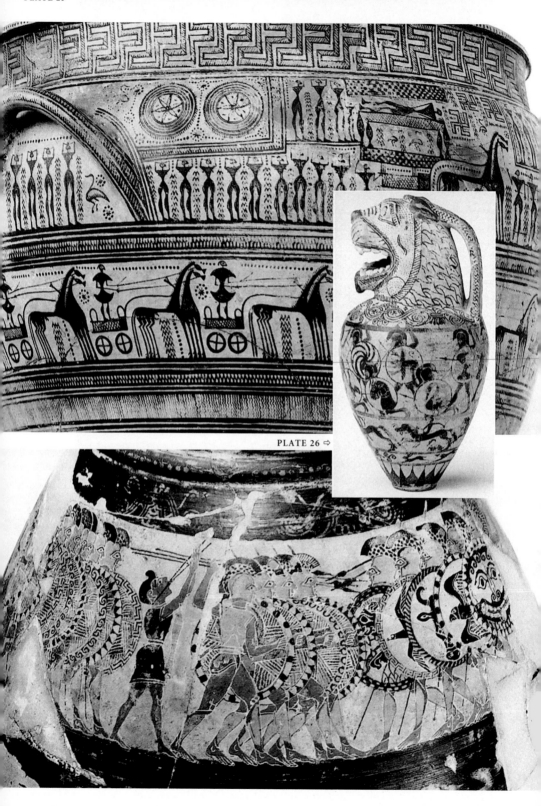

PLATE 25

PLATE 26 ⇨

PLATE 27

PLATE 28

PLATE 29

PLATE 30

The stylized geometric vase (*facing above*, Athens *c*.750 BC) is succeeded by a luxuriant and less formal style from the east in the proto-Corinthian vase (*facing inset*, 650 BC). The Chigi vase from Corinth, *c*.650 BC (*facing below*) is famous for its portrayal of marching hoplites.

By the sixth century Athenians dominate the market. The Francois vase of 570–560 BC (*above*) portrays myth as an ordered narrative. Later 'red-figure' pots use more focused themes of everyday life, an athlete purifying himself before running (*below left*, *c*.490 BC), or of myth, Europa and the Bull (*below right*, southern Italy, late fourth century).

PLATE 31

PLATE 32

The Great Sphinx at Giza of *c.*2550 BC (*above left*) shows Khafra's head on a lion's body guarding his own pyramid (the lion was traditionally seen as guardian of the entrance to the underworld). The sphinx spread from Egypt to the ancient Near East and from there, in a female form, to Greece in the seventh century BC. A Greek example (*above right*) comes from an offering of the island of Naxos to Delphi, sixth century BC. The sphinx again features in the Roman world, as in this brazier (*left*) found in a temple dedicated to Isis in Pompeii (?first century BC).

At Palestrina in Italy a great mosaic of the Nile in flood was commissioned, possibly by a Ptolemaic ruler, in the second century BC (*facing above*, detail). It shows the Hellenistic fascination with geography.

Obelisks were among the plunder brought back to Rome by Augustus from Egypt. One stood in Nero's circus, traditionally the place where St Peter was martyred. In 1586 it was transferred for this reason to its present position in front of the great basilica of St Peter on the Vatican Hill (*facing below*).

PLATE 33

PLATE 34

PLATE 35

PLATE 36

PLATE 37

PLATE 38

Sculpture proved a fine way of applauding the heroic. Harmodios and Aristogeiton, killers of the Athenian tyrant Hippias in 514 BC, stand defiant (*facing inset*), while the Prima Porta statue of Augustus (*facing*) is crowded with propaganda images. Alexander (*above*) is created as a youthful hero, akin to Achilles and Heracles, and from him Pompey (*right*) 'borrows' his style of hair.

PLATE 39

PLATE 40

PLATE 41

The limestone temple of Poseidon at Paestum, mid-fifth century (*above*), shows the weight and authority appreciated by the opulent Greek cities of Italy. The slightly later marble Parthenon at Athens (*below*) is altogether more refined. The celebrated frieze ran along the inner row of columns.

PLATE 42

Delphi, centre of the world, was visited by travellers from all over the Mediterranean in search of the guidance of Apollo through its oracle. Shown here is one of the finest of the temples dedicated to the shrine, the fourth-century *Tholos*.

PLATE 43

The sixth century was the great age of Athenian black-
figure vases. This example is by the master Exekias (third
quarter of the century). Captured by pirates, the god Dionysus
turns their crew into dolphins, while the mast of the ship miraculously
sprouts as a vine. Dionysus, the god of wine, was a favourite subject for the
pottery of the *symposia*.

Here a mystery cult centred on the rebirth of the corn crop each year (symbolized by a myth of the return of Persephone to her mother from the underworld). Initiation of new adherents took place each September through ceremonies within a Hall of Mysteries, in essence a temple, built on a site held sacred for well over a thousand years.

The gods might be approached directly by prayer. A celebrated example comes from the *Iliad*. Chryses, priest of Apollo, seeks revenge from the god for the humiliation put on him by Agamemnon. The god's titles are recited and reminders given of the sacrifices that Chryses has offered.

> Hear me,
> lord of the silver bow who set your power above Chryses
> and Killa, the sacrosanct, who are lord in strength over Tenedos,
> Simintheus, if ever it pleased your heart that I built your temple,
> if ever it pleased you that I burnt all the rich thigh pieces
> of bulls, of goats, then bring to pass this wish I pray for:
> let your arrows make the Danaans [Greeks] pay for my tears shed.
>
> (Translation: Richmond Lattimore)

Another approach to the gods was through an oracle. The intentions of the gods were, as has been suggested above, always uncertain. It was possible unwittingly to arouse their anger (as the story of Oedipus, p. 274, showed). Thus it made sense to use an oracle to test out whether a planned action was likely to bring retribution. The oracle's response might not provide a clear answer, but at least a neutral or positive answer could reassure or bring confidence. Many enterprises must have been brought to success largely through the belief that the gods favoured them, a belief gained through consultation with an oracle.

The oracle of Apollo at Delphi is the most celebrated example. The sanctuary stood high on the mountain of Parnassus overlooking the gulf of Corinth, and suppliants, who came from all over the Greek world and beyond, made their way up the mountainside from the sea. (The modern road deprives the visitor of the sense of the height and remoteness of the site. It is worth walking down the mountainside on the path from the modern village to be able to look back up at the sanctuary and catch some sense of its isolated splendour.) The cities and richer individuals who had come with their questions left dedications, often in the shape of small temples or treasuries filled with smaller votive offerings, which lined the last part of the approach to the temple of Apollo. Above the whole cluttered complex was a stadium where the Pythian Games were held every four years. (Python was a serpent which, according to myth, belonged to the original goddess of the site and was killed by Apollo when he took possession.) The sanctuary was under the control of no single city but an association of states of central Greece and the northern Peloponnese. It could reasonably claim to be unbiased in its pronouncements (although a pro-Persian bias can be detected in the 480s).

According to one hymn, Apollo explained that he wished to give unfailing advice to people from all over Greece. Delphi was believed to be the centre of the world, and it was through a hole in the ground that the messages of Apollo were transmitted to the outside world. They were interpreted and relayed to suppliants by a priestess, the Pythia, who sat on a tripod above the hole in an inner sanctum of Apollo's temple on the site.

Approaching an oracle was a serious business requiring sacrifices and signs from the god that the enquirer was welcome. The questions brought by suppliants were many and varied. According to Plutarch, 'people ask if they shall be victorious, if they shall marry, if it is to their advantage to sail, to farm, to go abroad'. Would-be colonizers sought advice on the best sites. Cities would ask for guidance on political problems, how to deal with disputes with neighbouring cities, or what would happen if they went to war. The answers given were not just gibberish. They were spoken as full sentences or in verse but often they needed interpretation. This could be given in the first instance by professionals within the sanctuary but their solutions could be disregarded. An excellent example is Themistocles' interpretation of the oracle's advice on the Persian invasion, manipulated by him to support his plan of attack. Often misinterpretation was disastrous, as the Spartans found when what they believed was an oracle promising victory against the city of Tegea, proved, in fact, to be predicting defeat.

Providing the framework for all these many activities was ritual. Rituals pervaded Greek, and, later, Roman religion. There were correct procedures for almost every activity and the failure to follow correct ritual was a matter for shame. In his history of the Peloponnesian war Thucydides describes the terrible plague which hit Athens in 429:

The funeral rites which had customarily been observed were disrupted and they buried their dead as best they could. Many had resort to the most shameless methods of burial, for lack of the necessary means and because so many deaths had already occurred in their own households. They would anticipate the builders of a pyre, put their own dead on it and set it alight, or throw the corpse they were carrying on top of an already unlighted pyre and leave it.   (Translation: Rex Warner)

For Thucydides the failure to follow the correct procedures of burial were as shocking as the deaths themselves and always evoked the fear of divine retribution.

The practice which defined the Greeks' relationships with their gods more than any other was that of sacrifice, an offering of wine, water, or a burnt offering to gods above or those in the earth below. As could be expected, sacrifices were carried out according to strict rituals. In the case of animal sacrifices the victim would be a domesticated sheep, goat, or ox. A noisy procession led it to the altar creating the impression that it met its death with joy. The ritual of slaughter was well defined: barley grain was thrown at the victim, a sacred knife was used, a few hairs were taken first from the animal's forehead before the throat was cut. Once the animal was dead it was divided and burnt. The *splanchna*, the heart, lungs, and kidneys, the sources of love and hatred, were passed round for all to taste while the lean meat provided a more substantial feast. The gods were left with what appeared to be the remnants, the thighbones, and tail. A myth explains this. Prometheus made the first sacrifice but tried to deceive Zeus by concealing the best meat in entrails and the more revolting parts of the animal and offering Zeus just the bones concealed in fat. Zeus was not taken in. He took the bones but caused Hephaestus to create a woman, Pandora, who brought to earth with her a box containing all kinds of evils and diseases from which the human race had hitherto been immune. From then on sacrificers could keep their meat but suffer a life of toil in return.

Sacrifices served many functions. One suggestion is that they evolved as a ritual through which divine forgiveness was sought for the act of killing animals which had been taken into the care of man. It was certainly assumed that the gods responded to sacrifices and might even be nourished by them. In Aristophanes' *The Birds* the birds actively try and stop the flow of offerings to the gods so as to starve them into coming to terms with the birds.

The sacrifice was also an integral and essential part of any festival. The standard format of a festival was a procession, followed by the sacrifices and then feasting. In the case of major festivals this procedure was often extended so that there were several days over which feasting became interspersed with competitions, *agones*. The Olympic Games, for instance, had originally been a festival of honour to Zeus, and for the first fifty years of its history may have ended with no more than a single foot-race. The elaborate five-day festival, which drew tens of thousands of spectators and had nine major events, evolved gradually over some 200 or more years. Again, the choral competitions which ended the Athenian festival of Dionysus, the Dionysia, later developed into the dramatic competitions which came to overshadow the rest of the activities (see below, p. 270).

The festival which was the most widespread of all in the Greek world was the Thesmophoria, originally held in honour of Demeter, the goddess of crops (see Chapter 13). It is a reminder that most festivals had their roots in the countryside and were closely connected with the rhythms of the agricultural year. However, from the eighth century the cities began, increasingly, to take control. Agricultural festivals were adopted within the city and given a fixed date (so that a festival which originally celebrated the harvest would take place on its set day whether the harvest was complete or not). The festivals of Athens were many and varied (they occupied 120 days a year). Their number reflects the fact that many originated in Attica and had been integrated into city life, presumably to reinforce the power of Athens over her surrounding territory. So emerges the city as 'a sacrificial community', one where religion permeates every aspect of its activities.

Festivals fulfilled many functions and marked many kinds of transitions. The harvest was rejoiced in, all the more because its successful gathering allowed a period of leisure. The city could create or develop a festival to celebrate its own identity, as with the Panathenaea in Athens. In Athens the festival known as Apatouria was marked by a gathering of the phratries, the admission to them of new-born infants, and the introduction of boys who had reached the age of 16. This was the festival as a celebration of a rite of passage. The festivals of Dionysus or the Thesmophoria appear concerned with the overturning of conventions through drunkenness, sexual abandon, or the reversal of the subordinate roles of women. It seems that if rebellion was sanctioned within defined limits and times it made it all the more controllable for the rest of the year.

What must have been one of the most solemn festivals of the Athenian year was the annual burial of the war dead. The bones of those whose bodies had been recovered were carried through the streets in procession, while an empty bier commemorated those lost abroad. In a speech made probably on behalf of those who died fighting on Samos in 439 BC, Pericles compared the loss of young life with 'the spring being taken from the year'. The Funeral Orations that survive from Athens suggest that this was the day when the city reflected on its achievements and consolidated its own pride in being the leading city of Greece.

As has been suggested, it is impossible to re-create the degree to which the sacred pervaded Greek life, but it seems clear that Greeks used religion in a sophisticated way to rationalize the uncertainties of life. They used their beliefs to maintain the cohesion of their communities, sustain a code of ethics, and cater for the sense of awe all human beings encounter in the face of the unknown. They never pretended that their gods were always benevolent or omnipotent in human affairs, and so bad fortune could be rationalized as a natural element of existence. What was important was the maintenance of dignity and self-respect in the face of what the gods or fate decreed.

FURTHER READING

On Greek religion W. Burkert, *Greek Religion* (Oxford, 1985) is fundamental but many aspects of Greek religion are well surveyed in P. Easterling and J. Muir (eds.), *Greek Religion and Society* (Cambridge, 1985). A more recent overview is Simon Price, *Religions of the Ancient Greeks* (Cambridge, 1999), while Robert Parker's *Athenian Religion: A History* (Oxford, 1996) is the best study of Athens, a major work of scholarship in its own right. For women and religion there is S. Blundell and M. Williamson (eds.), *The Sacred and the Feminine in Ancient Greece* (London, 1998).

On myth, see G. S. Kirk, *The Nature of Greek Myths* (Harmondsworth, 1974). More recent overviews of this highly complex area include Geoffrey Buxton, *Imaginary Greece* (Cambridge, 1994); Ken Dowden, *The Uses of Greek Mythology* (London, 1992); and, forthcoming, Mary Lefkowitz, *Greek Gods, Human Lives, What We Can Learn from Myths* (New Haven, 2003).

The Classical Age in Art

The most influential art historian of the eighteenth century was Johann Winckelmann (1717–68). Winckelmann was born in Prussia, the son of a cobbler. Coming to the study of ancient Greece as a young man through reading Homer he embarked on an academic career and by the age of 31 was the librarian of an aristocratic library in Dresden. Here he wrote his first essay on Greek art, *Reflections on the Painting and Sculpture of the Greeks* (1755). Then having converted to Catholicism, he went to Rome and finally became Librarian at the Vatican. In his most celebrated work *A History of the Art of Antiquity* (1764) he developed his theory of the relationship between art and history. He took it for granted that Greek art was supreme. 'In the masterpieces of Greek art, connoisseurs and imitators find not only nature at its most beautiful but also something beyond nature, namely certain ideal forms of its beauty.' (Note the influence here of Plato.) However, Greek art was not static, it had its own rise to greatness and its own fall. The rise began with the Archaic period and reached its height ('sublimity' in Winckelmann's terminology) in the Classical age, the fifth century BC The essence of 'sublime' art was 'noble simplicity and calm grandeur'. So the art of the Classical period (conventionally 479–323 BC) was elevated to a pedestal and until well into the twentieth century remained for many the standard by which other periods of art were judged.

Insofar as there are changes in style from the sixth to the fifth century, from Archaic to what is known as Classical, they can be seen above all in its sculpture (for pottery see p. 188). The most common expression of sculpture in the Archaic age was the *kouros*, the stiff and formal male figure erected over a grave or as an offering to the gods (see Chapter 11). As has been seen the influence of Egypt on the pose was obvious and their bodies are not carved as if they were real mortals observed in the flesh. During the sixth century there were signs of a more natural pose developing, but it was not until the early fifth century that a revolution in sculpture takes place. The transition is usually symbolized by the 'Critian boy', a marble statue found on the Athenian Acropolis and attributed to Critius, a sculptor active in Athens around 490–460 BC. It is dated by experts to just before 480 BC and represents one Callias, a victor in the boys' foot race in the Panathenaic festival. The changes from the traditional *kouros* are slight, but the boy is standing as a boy might actually stand, the right leg forward of the left which bears the weight of the body so that the right can relax slightly, not as how an artistic convention decrees a hero should pose. Yet this naturalness is achieved without the loss of an idealization of the human body. Here is, in the words of the art historian, Kenneth Clark, 'the first beautiful nude in art'. As John Boardman, the authority on Greek art, puts it: 'This is a vital novelty in the history of ancient art—life deliberately observed, understood and copied. After this all becomes possible.'

There are a few clues as to why this revolution in art, from the stylized to the observed, took place. One is that bronze was becoming the most popular medium in which statues were being created. The technical problems involved in casting and assembling bronze statues had been solved by the end of the sixth century as the earliest examples show (see above p. 187). From now on bronze predominated in Greek sculpture, but as almost every statue ended in the melting pot it is hard to guess this today. The few bronzes to survive (the Riace warriors, the Delphi charioteer, and the majestic Zeus found in a shipwreck off Cape Artemisium foremost among them) suggest the scale of what has been lost in quantity and quality. Bronze allowed far greater flexibility in modelling, and the sculptors in marble must have been able to copy in stone what was now created in metal.

The revolution also suggests a preoccupation with human form. While before the artist was concerned overwhelmingly with those few human beings who had become heroes, he now seems concerned with the physical beauty of human beings as an end in itself. It was the sculptor Polycleitus, probably a native of Argos, who allied aesthetics with mathematics when he suggested that the perfect human body was perfect precisely because it reflected ideal mathematical proportions which were capable of being discovered. One of his statues, the Doryphoros, or 'spear bearer' (originally in bronze, but now known only through Roman copies in marble), was supposed to represent this ideal. If this approach was followed to its extreme, however, all statues would have had the same, perfect, proportions but the Greeks could not close their eyes to the variety of human experience. There always remained a tension in the art of the period between the abstract ideal of the human body and a particular body copied by the artist. This may be one reason for its aesthetic appeal.

Winckelmann claimed that the 'sublimity' of Classical art was the result of the atmosphere of liberty and exuberance which followed the Persian Wars. So the moderation and self-control of the Critian boy reflects the self-confidence of a city which knows it has achieved greatness. It is an assertion which it is impossible to prove. It is all too easy to read into the expression of a work of art what one hopes to see there and one must take such arguments with caution. Nevertheless there is the sense of a change of atmosphere, the readiness to reproduce what can be observed because it is worth observing, rather than relying on conventions adopted from elsewhere. This may be no more than the experience of working in bronze but it could reflect an elevation of man, as 'the measure of all things' (the term is from the fifth-century philosopher Protagoras) in line with the many other intellectual developments of the age.

The transition to an art rooted in observation can also be seen in temple sculpture. While an individual statue might continue to be the offering of a private patron (victors at games were a particularly popular subject), the temples provided setting for publicly financed sculpture. In particular, the pediment of a temple, with its wide centre and narrow corners, offered a space that called for special compositional expertise. The first and crudest attempts to fill a pediment, in the sixth century, were simply to place a large central sculpture (for instance, on the temple of Artemis at Corcyra, 580 BC, a Gorgon's head), flanked by unrelated scenes to fill in the space. Gradually greater order was brought into pediment design, and by the end of the sixth century the temple of Aphaea on the island of Aegina has a single scene, from the Trojan War, on its western pediment.

The new mood in Classical sculpture, seen in statuary with the 'Critian boy', is found on the reliefs made for the pediments of the great temple to Zeus which dominated the sanctuary at Olympia and which was built in the first half of the fifth century. It is not only that the poses of the figures are more natural than those of their stiffer Archaic forebears, but the characters exude a sense of feeling and awareness. The sculptures are all the more moving because of the relative simplicity of the figures and the designs in which they are set. The 'seer' on the east pediment is the example most often picked out to make the point. He knows, as the other figures do not, the outcome of the story which is portrayed on the pediment in which Pelops will win a chariot race for the hand of the king's daughter by foul means and thus bring a curse on his family. Others are as impressed with the Apollo who watches from the centre of the west pediment serenely over a tumultuous conflict between Centaurs and Lapiths, here order presides over disorder. The stage is set for a further development towards the finest and most majestic temple sculptures of all, those of the Parthenon in Athens (see p. 257). Pheidias, who created the large statue of Athena for this temple, also completed an even more massive one, 13 metres high, of Zeus for Olympia, now known only from coins.

Before returning to Athens it is worth mentioning another Classical statue which had an enormous impact on later generations, Praxiteles' nude Aphrodite. The statue was created about 350 for the city of Cnidus where, according to legend, Aphrodite stopped to wash off the sea foam from her body when travelling between Cyprus and Greece. The model was Praxiteles' own mistress, Phryne. Although Aphrodite is naked she is shown with no pubic hair and no hint of her vulva. She is thus protected from violation and it is this which gives her her power over the onlooker. The statue was placed in a circular temple open to the winds and became a major tourist attraction. The original is long since lost but copies survive from the Roman world and provided an exemplar for the female nude for centuries to come. The emperor Hadrian recreated the temple and the statue in his villa at Tivoli.

FURTHER READING

See the general works on Greek art cited at the end of Chapter 8, all of which discuss this crucial transition as well as chapter 11, 'Defining the Classical: Classical Art', in James Whitley, *The Archaeology of Ancient Greece* (Cambridge, 2001); Andrew Stewart, *Art, Desire and the Body in Ancient Greece* (Cambridge, 1997); J. J. Pollitt, *Art and Experience in Classical Greece* (London, 1994); and James Porter, *Constructions of the Classical Body* (Ann Arbor, 1999).

15 | Athens: Democracy and Empire

The Delian League

After the Persian invasion of 480 BC Athens lay in ruins, the city haunted by the feeling that it had been polluted by the destruction of its temples and shrines. One source suggests the Athenians swore to leave the shattered temples as a memorial to the impiety of the invaders, and there is little evidence for any rebuilding on the Acropolis for at least a generation. Much of its Archaic sculpture was incorporated into new defensive walls. Yet, despite the devastation, the Greeks were triumphant, and Athens, with her forces intact and brimming with confidence of victory and desire for revenge, was ready to continue the war with Persia.

She was sure to find supporters from among the city states of the Aegean. For the Ionian cities, in particular, memories of their subjection by Persia after the revolt of the 490s must still have been strong and they were the most vulnerable to any renewed attack. Athens was the only state with a navy large enough to offer them effective protection and, despite centuries of separation, she remained the mother city who had recently sacrificed her own sacred buildings in their common cause. The only possible rival for their attention was Dorian Sparta. However, when in 478, Pausanias, the Spartan commander at Plataea, had led a fleet back to the Aegean to drive out the remaining Persian garrisons, he had treated the Ionian cities with such arrogance that any immediate chance of Spartan influence in the area was lost.

So common fears and ties acted to bring the states of the Aegean together under the leadership of Athens. In 477 they set up the Delian League, so termed, by modern historians, because its treasury and meeting place were on the centrally placed island of Delos, a sanctuary of Apollo and a spiritual focus for Ionians. Although the Ionian cities formed the core of the alliance, it is assumed that others such as the Aeolian island of Lesbos and the Dorian Byzantium also joined this early. The members agreed that the alliance should be a permanent one and that they would each provide resources in either ships or cash. They were to meet annually on the island to make their plans in common council. At first Athens seems to have been given no special privileges, but as she was by far the most powerful member no offensive action was possible without her support. She also appointed the treasurers of the League's finances.

The question that has fascinated historians is the real motive behind Athens' interest in the Aegean in the 470s. The historian Thucydides, whose account of the League's early activities is the only one to have survived (and whose *History of the Peloponnesian War* is one of the main documentary sources for the political events of the period), suggests that they were ones of self-interest from the start. The desire for revenge and reparations from Persia was used only as a pretext (*proskhema*) for gaining control of the League. Certainly Athens had powerful economic reasons for maintaining a presence in the Aegean. For over a hundred years the city had been importing grain from the Black Sea area and was now dependent on it. The north-western coast of the Aegean with its silver mines in Thrace and its rich timber was also attractive to a city which relied so heavily on building and maintaining ships. Perhaps from the start Athens realized that the Delian League offered her the opportunities to further her own interests. She was certainly the dominant member of the League. With a war trireme needing up to 200 fit rowers, very few of the League's members could finance and man more than two at a time. Athens had 180 triremes in 480, and 300 by 431. The Spartans had no effective navy, and in any case were preoccupied in the 470s with affairs in the Peloponnese. Thucydides suggests that Sparta was happy to leave the defence of Greece against Persia to Athens.

The commander of the League's forces was the aristocratic Athenian Cimon, son of the Miltiades who launched the Athenian attack at Marathon. His policy appears to have been to use the threat of Persia to mould and maintain the unity of the League, while at the same time keeping good relations with Sparta so that Athens could maintain her forward policy in the Aegean without any threats from the Peloponnese. His first campaign was to Eion at the mouth of the River Strymon in Thrace, where a Persian garrison still held out. Then the Athenians attacked Carystus on the tip of Euboea, a city which had gone over to the Persians in the war. Cimon's most resounding success was against a Persian (in fact, largely Phoenician) fleet at the River Eurymedon, some time between 469 and 466. The enemy fleet was completely destroyed and Persia left without any offensive forces in the Aegean. A further campaign by Cimon is recorded against Persians and Thracians in the Chersonese, possibly about 468.

Athens appears to have used these campaigns to her own advantage. There were rich timber resources to be exploited around Eion, and there is one account of an Athenian force trying to fight its way inland after the city had been captured. When the island of Scyros was cleared of pirates Athenians remained to settle around its fine harbour. More significantly, when the island of Naxos tried to leave the League in about 470 it was forced back in by a League fleet dominated by Athens—the first time, says Thucydides, that the constitution of the League was broken and a member lost its independence. A few years later Athens seized gold mines belonging to another League member, the island of Thasos. When the Thasians counter-attacked, the island was besieged and forced to surrender. Both Naxos and Thasos remained under Athenian influence. Already Athens was using the League as an instrument for her own ends.

Before her surrender (probably in 463), Thasos had appealed to Sparta for help. It was a warning to Athens that some Greek cities might look to Sparta as a protection against her control. Sparta was ready to respond, but in 464 she had suffered a devastating earthquake which was followed by a helot revolt. Cimon, determined to maintain good relations with Sparta, arrived in the Peloponnese with some 4,000 hoplites to offer help. Something went drastically wrong. It seems that the Spartans feared the Athenians might actually join the helots. They sent the Athenians home and the relationship between the two cities broke down. The breakdown was consolidated in 461 when Athens underwent a democratic and patriotic revolution which intensified her hostility to the oligarchic Sparta. Antagonism between Athens and Sparta was to dominate inter-city politics for the next ninety years.

The Survival of Aristocratic Influence

The development of democracy in Athens under Solon and Cleisthenes has already been described (Chapter 10). Solon had broken the stranglehold of the hereditary aristocracy and established a state in which, in theory at least, citizens were equal before the law. Cleisthenes' newly created tribes provided members for the Boule, the council which had the role of drawing up the business to be set before the Assembly. However, the power of this Assembly was still restricted, in ways which are not totally clear, by the Areopagus, a council made up of former archons (magistrates), who were drawn largely from the aristocracy. There were now also the ten generals, the *strategoi*, introduced in 501 and elected by the citizen body. Their status was enhanced by the Persian Wars, and generalship, which, unlike other offices, could be held from year to year, now became the goal of any ambitious politician. The generals, too, tended to be drawn from the richer classes and so, in the early part of the fifth century, Athens remained under strong aristocratic influence.

Aristocratic patronage was not confined to the privacy of dining-halls. Leading Athenian families glorified their city's name by providing fine buildings both at home and abroad. The distinguished family of the Alcmaeonidae rebuilt a temple to Apollo in Delphi in marble, while in Athens itself Cimon was an important patron of the city. Some large bones found on the island of Scyros were reputed to be those of Theseus, the legendary king of Athens, and Cimon brought them home to be housed in the Theseion in the centre of the city. The Stoa Poikile, a colonnade filled with paintings of Athens' military successes by the celebrated Polygnotus of Thasos, was the gift probably of Cimon's brother-in-law. (Its foundations were discovered as recently as 1981.) Cimon is also credited with planting plane trees around the Agora.

Yet there are now signs of new popular pressures. In the 480s ostracism was used for the first time. The procedure, probably one of Cleisthenes' innovations, allowed citizens to vote individually and secretly to send any fellow citizen into exile for ten years. (The names were scrawled on pieces of broken pottery, *ostraka*, hence the word 'ostracism'.) The surviving *ostraka* contain the names of virtually every prominent politician of the period. In the 480s those ostracized were aristocratic figures who had supposed links with Persia. This suggests that popular opinion was, not surprisingly, anti-aristocratic and patriotic. One important effect of ostracism was to provide a challenge to the traditional role of the Areopagus of protecting the state against a potential tyrant.

The 480s had seen another important development, the emergence of Athens' naval power under the leadership of Themistocles. Fighting on land had been the preserve of the better-off. Hoplites had to be wealthy enough to provide their own armour and weapons. Rowers, on the other hand, needed no equipment to protect them, and so the poorer citizen class, the *thetes*, were called on to man the oars. This class was now fully involved in the defence of the state and, as important from the political point of view, gained the experience of working together in unison. A trireme has recently been reconstructed (the Greek navy's *Olympias*) and with 170 rowers on board it has been possible to re-create the psychological impact of what the rowers went through. They were stacked in threes, one above another with the two lower rows concealed from sight. The problem of coordinating each vertical set of rowers and then each top rower with his fellows on the open deck proved formidable. The trireme could not have been rowed successfully without a well-developed sense of teamwork, and it can be assumed that the *thetes* now recognized their potential political strength. (Aristotle acknowledged this link when he wrote that the Athenian leader Pericles later 'turned the state towards naval power, with the result that the masses had the courage to take more into their own hands in all fields of government'.)

It is not surprising, therefore, that Themistocles, founder of the navy, was closely linked to the move towards greater democratic rights. Aristocratic opposition was strong. On *ostraka* dating from the 480s and 470s no name appears more frequently than Themistocles', but a chance find of 170 *ostraka* all with his name on but written in only fourteen different hands suggests that the voting was being rigged. (A more prosaic view would be that those citizens who could write prepared named sherds to pass out to those who could not.) Themistocles was finally removed from the city in 471 after a trumped-up charge of being pro-Persian had been made against him before the Areopagus.

The Democratic Revolution

Ten years later, in 461, the democratic party had its chance of revenge. The moment when the aristocratic leader, Cimon, and 4,000 hoplites were out of the city (in Sparta: see above) was an ideal moment to launch a coup. It was led by one Ephialtes, of whom almost nothing is known. (He was killed in unrest that followed his coup.) He was supported by a 30-year-old member of the Alcmaeonid family (and, incidentally, through his mother, a descendant of Cleisthenes), Pericles. Between them they stripped the Areopagus of its powers, leaving it with little more than the right to sit as a court for murder cases and sacrilege. They then distributed these powers to the Council (the Boule), the Assembly, and the law courts, with the fictional excuse that they were restoring to the people powers the Areopagus had accumulated illegally. With the Areopagus demoted, the Assembly and Boule were left as supreme lawmakers. When Cimon returned to Athens from Sparta he was ostracized, not least for his role in the humiliating debacle which had taken place there. In the words of Plutarch, a hostile commentator whose *Lives* (compiled at the end of the first century AD) are a major if unreliable source for these events, the city was now 'pitched into undiluted democracy'. Even in Athens itself opposition to democracy among embittered aristocrats and intellectuals such as Plato remained strong. As the aristocratic Alcibiades was to put it, 'As for democracy, we men of sense know what it is . . . but there can be nothing new to say about what is agreed to be absolute insanity.' (See further Josiah Ober, *Political Dissent in Democratic Athens: Intellectual Critics of Popular Rule* (Princeton, 1998).)

With Cimon in exile and Ephialtes dead, Pericles emerged as the leader of the democratic party. He was a man of natural authority, reserved in manner and incorruptible. If the speeches placed in his mouth by Thucydides are to be trusted, he had a genius for playing on the self-esteem of ordinary Athenians and persuading them that he could represent their interests. It could also be argued that one component of his success was his ability to manipulate the continuing deference of the poor to aristocrats such as himself. His position rested on his continuous re-election as *strategos*, at one point for fifteen years in succession, and he used his authority and this role so effectively that Thucydides, an admirer, went so far as to say that despite its democratic pretensions the government of Athens was in effect that of one man, Pericles.

Pericles' influence certainly pervades Athenian politics over the next thirty years, although the extent of his role in specific instances is often impossible to judge. He watched over the development of democratic institutions within the city and was certainly responsible for the law of 451 which restricted those eligible for citizenship. He was a dedicated imperialist. In his celebrated 'Funeral Oration' of 430 (see below) he spoke of overseas intervention in terms reminiscent of

American foreign policy of the 1960s, and perhaps later. 'Our adventurous spirit has forced an entry into every sea and into every land; and everywhere we have left behind us everlasting memorials of good done to our friends or suffering inflicted on our enemies' (translation from Thucydides by Rex Warner). He was instrumental in consolidating Athenian power in the Aegean as an empire from which tribute flowed to sustain not only Athens' democratic institutions but the fine buildings with which he glorified the Acropolis. He was the dominant influence in the making of foreign policy and the preservation of Sparta as Athens' main enemy.

Democracy in Practice

The structure of Athenian democracy was consolidated in the 450s. The long-established right of all male citizens (over the age of 18) to sit in the Assembly now took on new meaning as the body became the centre of power at a time when demands on the city as an Aegean power were increasing rapidly. The Assembly could make laws on all subjects, raise taxes, supervise their spending, and conduct all aspects of foreign policy. As far as is known, it met at regular intervals, four times in each of the ten months of the year. The first meeting of each month had a fixed agenda which included reports on the state of the grain supply and issues of national defence. Extra meetings could be called in emergencies.

As many as 30,000 citizens were eligible to attend the Assembly, although its meeting place, the Pnyx, a hill to the west of the city, probably only had room for about 6,000 until it was enlarged in about 400 BC (after which 8,000 might have been squeezed in). Attendance must have been biased towards those living in or near the city who had the opportunity to leave their land or jobs. (An outlying area of Attica such as the plain of Marathon was 40 kilometres away by road.) It was not until the end of the fifth century that attendance became paid.

The Assembly carried out its business by majority vote (in effect a show of hands) after listening to speeches. This, and appropriate applause and heckling, must have been the limit to most citizens' participation. Josiah Ober, in his *Mass and Elite in Democratic Athens*, has shown how members of the aristocratic elite, who provided most of the speakers, adapted their rhetoric and behaviour so as to appeal to the mass of citizens. A common ploy was for a speaker to present himself as an adviser to or protector of the people in their role as the sovereign force in the city (meanwhile taunting his opponents as enemies of the people). This language of mediation, argues Ober, was essential in allowing the mass and elite to live together in relative social stability. It underlines the fact that Athens was a society in which an enormous premium rested on speaking skills. The Assembly was an unforgiving master. Even Demosthenes, arguably the greatest of the Athenian orators, had a tough time making himself heard when a young man. Plutarch has him hurrying home with his face hidden after one early humiliation in the Assembly.

Debates could become heated and volatile, particularly when the city was under stress during the Peloponnesian War. A famous example, recounted by Thucydides, was the debate on the treatment of the people of Mytilene after the city had revolted against Athens in 427. At first the Assembly, swayed by impassioned oratory, decreed that all the Mytilenean men should be executed and the women and children enslaved. A trireme was sent off with the order. The next day the Assembly, in more sober mood, reversed the decision. (A second trireme reached the city in the nick of time.) In 406 there was a debate over the fate of the generals who after a naval victory at Arginusae had left the scene without picking up survivors (their defence being that a violent storm had made this impossible). Various proposals were put forward as a means of assessing their guilt, some of which appeared to be unconstitutional. The mass of the Assembly shouted that the decision should be left to the people, even if this meant disregarding normal procedures, and went on to order the execution of those six generals who had arrived back in Athens. Later, however, but only when it was too late, the Assembly again repented of its harshness (and rather hypocritically accused the main speakers of 'forcing' the people to act they way they did).

Between the meetings of the Assembly there had to be continuity of government, and this was provided by the Boule, the Council of Five Hundred. Each of the ten tribes put forward volunteers, and fifty of these were selected by lot to make the total of 500. Each served for a year and could only serve twice in total (and then not in consecutive years). The Boule met most days of the year in its own council house. There is some evidence that membership was biased towards richer and more influential citizens, presumably because these were more likely to volunteer.

The duty of the Boule was to oversee the running of the state, and, in particular, to prepare business for the Assembly and then ensure that its decisions were carried out. No issue could be raised in the Assembly if it had not first been discussed by the Boule. When news reached Athens in 339 that Philip of Macedon was advancing into Greece, the citizens rushed to the Assembly but had to wait there until the Boule had deliberated first. It has been argued that the Boule acted as a restraining force on the Assembly through the way it chose business and framed motions, though its continually changing membership would have militated against it achieving any sustained influence over the Assembly. In between meetings of the Boule the fifty members from each tribe took it in turn to stay on permanent call. They had a small circular meeting house, the Tholos, now excavated, which stood alongside the main council house in the Agora. Here they were put up at state expense during their month of duty.

By the mid-century Athens was a wealthy and cosmopolitan city. Its citizens formed only a minority of a population which included large numbers of slaves (perhaps some 100,000 out of a total population 250,000 for Attica) and several thousand foreigners (metics, from the Greek *metoikoi*, those who had changed homes). Although the metics could not own land or become citizens, they were welcome for their skills and formed an important part of the city's labour resources. (Forty per cent of those working on the Parthenon were metics.) In 451, in a law attributed to Pericles, eligibility for citizenship was narrowed by making it a requirement that only those born to parents who were both citizens could acquire citizenship themselves. The law was doubtless passed to preserve the fruits of citizenship for a few, although it has also been suggested that it was the response of the democrats to the aristocratic custom of seeking wives from abroad. (Ironically, as already mentioned, Pericles managed to make an exception for his son, also Pericles, by his mistress Aspasia, who was given citizenship by a special decree after Pericles' legitimate sons had died.) The complexity of the city's affairs by the mid-century can be gathered from the fact that there were no less than 600 administrative posts to be filled each year. All, with the exception of the ten generals, were chosen by lot from those citizens aged 30 or more with good credentials. In the case of the generals, where proven ability was essential, election was by simple majority in the Assembly and repeatable. The ten generals exercised collective control over military affairs but a named general might be appointed to lead a specific campaign. Other posts included the nine archons, originally the chief magistrates of the city and still responsible between them for festivals, the religious life of the city, and the administration of justice; financial officials; guardians of the prisons; and, at the bottom of the scale, those responsible for cleaning the streets. All these posts eventually became paid ones.

Once selected, officials were examined before they took office and then, standing on a stone slab, had to take an oath. (The slab was rediscovered as recently as 1970.) At the end of their year all officials had to hand in accounts to be scrutinized by a committee of the Boule, but any citizen could bring a complaint against any official at any time. Pericles' son, who turned out to be hostile to his father's achievements, complained that this right only encouraged antagonism:

> They [the Athenians] are more abusive of each other and more envious among themselves than they are towards other human beings. In both public and private gatherings, they are the most quarrelsome of men; they most often bring each other to trial; and they would rather take advantage of each other than profit by cooperative aid. (Translation: Paul Rahe)

However, public accountability at this level must have been essential in maintaining the standards of public service.

Those who were accused of offences had to appeal to their fellow citizens. There was no independent judiciary in Athens and the citizen body as a whole took responsibility for enforcing the law both as judge and jury. Although the Areopagus still judged crimes of deliberate murder and of sacrilege, most cases

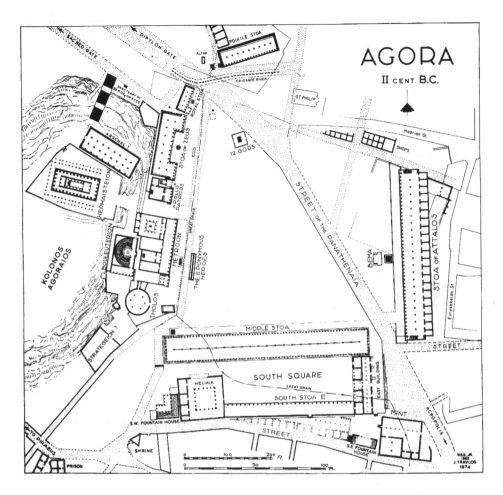

Fig. 3 The Athenian Agora. The Agora was cleared in the early sixth century and was then gradually lined with public buildings including those for officials and the council (*bouleuterion*). The larger stoas were later Hellenistic additions. The route of the Panathenaic festival, to the Acropolis, ran across the square. Note also the temple to Hephaestus on higher ground to the west.

were heard by juries of ordinary citizens. A roll of 6,000 citizens was drawn up for each year and from these a jury was selected for each case. The more serious the case the larger was the jury, with a maximum of 2,500. It was virtually a full-time job, with jurors sitting up to 200 days a year, and Pericles recognized this early in the 450s by introducing pay. The law courts were not criminal courts with clearly defined laws against which the guilt of the accused was judged. Any citizen could accuse another of an 'offence' which was usually vaguely phrased, a general charge of 'impiety' being a particular favourite, and in fact the action was often an extension of political rivalries. The aim of the prosecutor was to denigrate his opponent by bringing in a range of accusations especially that he had been disrespectful of the gods or failed in some way to be an effective citizen. 'Only recently he [one Timarchus] threw off his cloak in the Assembly and his body was in such an appalling and shameful condition thanks to his drunkenness and his vices that decent men had to look away,' was one typical taunt. Other accusations involved a man being the passive partner in a homosexual relationship, the son of a prostitute or a coward in a battle. One unfortunate defendant was said not to have shown enough sorrow on the death of his daughter (a good father would have done so, and good fathers make good citizens, the rather shaky reasoning went). One can understand why all this public throwing of dirt was so entertaining. The comic poet Aristophanes satirizes a juror who had become transfixed by his role, to the extent of sleeping in the courts and keeping a beachful of voting pebbles in his house so that he should never run short. (The speeches which survive from these cases provide excellent material on what was and what was not valued in an Athenian citizen.)

The demands of the system were heavy. It has been calculated that between 5 and 6 per cent of citizens over the age of 30 would be required each year if all the posts on the Boule, the juries, and administration were to be filled. With the ban on reselection for most posts, this meant that virtually everyone was involved in administration or government at some point in their lives. Even Socrates, who attempted to avoid political life completely, served his time on the Boule, and the playwright Euripides, who was well known for lack of sociability, went on an official embassy to Syracuse.

Literacy and Democracy

In no city of Greece have so many inscriptions survived as in Athens. There are about 1,500 dating from the middle to the end of the fifth century alone. They include treaties and decrees on political affairs, accounts, among them the famous Tribute Lists which document Athens' relationships with her empire (see below), gravestones honouring citizens who have died in war, and religious decrees.

It has been natural to assume some correlation between democracy and the public display of written material. Certainly it can be argued that a society is likely to be more egalitarian if its laws and decrees are publicly accessible, but that does not necessarily imply democratic government. The laws displayed may be those of an oppressive elite, for instance, designed to strike fear in those who see them. (See D. Steiner's *The Tyrant's Writ* (Princeton, 1993).) It can even be argued that a truly democratic society is one which values the participation of all through the spoken word, over that of the minority who can communicate through writing. The most valued political skill in democratic Athens was the ability to persuade through the art of rhetoric, not the ability to present ideas in writing. The many inscriptions found in Athens may not, therefore, have had an explicitly democratic function. One suggestion is rather that they served as reminders of the achievements of the city. The Tribute Lists were designed not so much to be read by an interested public as to display Athens as an imperial power. 'They were', suggests James Whitley, writing of inscriptions in general, 'monuments to a democratic idea, their erection and inscription a performance of public accountability—an outward, durable and visible sign of the public character of the Athenian state.'

In the fifth century Athens was a cohesive society where oral testimony was still accepted, overwhelmingly, as the best. In the fourth there are the first signs of an emphasis on documents and writing appears in new contexts. This suggests a society in which there is a breakdown of cohesion and trust. One fourth-century orator commented, 'We make written contracts with one another through distrust, so that the man who sticks to the terms may get satisfaction from the one who disregards them.' This is the dawn of a new world where the written document becomes supreme, holding for the first time a value beyond the spoken word with all its potential for manipulation and distortion by those who rely on it on a later occasion. (See further Interlude Three Rhetoric, p. 294.)

The Glorification of the City in Marble

By the 450s, the inhibition against rebuilding was also weakening and there was a determination to create a city worthy of the new democracy. An important new building from this period was the circular Tholos used as the meeting place of the Council of Fifty. It was placed next to the main meeting place of the Boule. Behind these buildings, on higher ground to the west, a temple to Hephaestus, god of fire and hence blacksmiths and craftsmen in general, rose to overlook the Agora and face the Acropolis. It remains as the best preserved of all Greek temples and reflects the growing industrial importance of the city (although Hephaestus was also honoured by Athenians as the god who cut open Zeus' head with an axe to release Athena).

The most glorious achievement of Athens in the second half of the fifth century was the transformation of the Acropolis. The great citadel had been the religious and defensive centre of the area since Mycenaean times. A major rebuilding programme for its main temples had been under way before the Persian attack. This was halted. Columns from the unfinished temples can be seen incorporated in the wall of the Acropolis itself, possibly as a memorial to the attack. Others were inserted in the walls built around the city by Themistocles in the 470s. (These were subsequently enlarged so that, as the Long Walls, they ran down to the Piraeus and made Athens impregnable.) All that was left on the rocky surface of the Acropolis were the foundations of the planned temples, and it was these that were reused to base the Parthenon, a temple to Athena, the patroness of the city in her designation as Parthenos, Maiden, and the buildings which accompanied it.

The moving spirit behind the building of the Parthenon was certainly Pericles but there was never any doubt that this was a city enterprise inspired by democratic pride. The need to honour Athena, whose massive statue in chryselephantine by Pheidias was to dominate the temple's inner sanctuary, was secondary to showing off the achievements and power of the city in the most majestic setting possible. The building was started in 447, with, in a now typical display of Athenian arrogance, money diverted from the tribute paid by members of the League. By 438 Pheidias' statue, probably already under cover within the walls and roofs of the temple, was ready for formal dedication.

It is natural to see the Parthenon as one of the world's great buildings. This may be partly the result of conditioning. In reality the Parthenon looks at first sight much like any other Greek temple. Like other temples of the period, that to Poseidon on the headland at Sunium and that to Apollo in the majestic mountain setting of Bassae, its fine position provides part of its splendour. However, the Parthenon has three features which make it of the highest quality. First, the building was made throughout from the finest marble, 22,000 tons of it, brought from Mount Pentelicus 16 kilometres from the city. Then the proportions of the building were subtly modified so as to give an illusion of lightness. The steps are curved so that the centre of each is higher than the corners. The corner columns are slightly thicker than the rest and all the columns lean slightly inwards. (They would meet, it is estimated, at a point about 1,600 metres above the temple.) Finally, the Parthenon was the most richly carved temple ever built, and the sculptures which adorn it represent the climax of the Classical revolution in art.

The development can be seen within the temple itself. The pediments of the temple have been largely lost. The eastern pediment is recorded as showing Athena herself springing fully armed from the head of Zeus and the western the goddess battling with Poseidon for the rule of Athens. The earliest surviving sculptures are the metopes, the reliefs carved between the triglyphs on the outside walls, which in this case represent the Greeks and their gods defeating foreigners. They appear varied and uncertain in quality, as if the team of sculptors was in the early stages of learning to work together. (It has been suggested that the metopes may have been designed for another, earlier, temple.)

The most complete set of sculptures is from the latest work, the frieze, which ran around the outer side of the inner wall of the temple, the only known example of a continuous composition of this kind. There is one theme, a great pro-

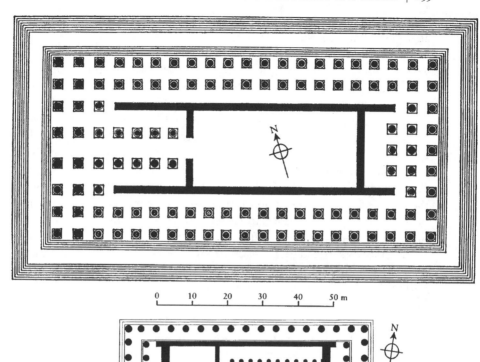

0   10   20   30   40   50 m

FIG. 4 The Parthenon and the Temple of Artemis at Ephesus. Imposing though the Parthenon (below) is, and it is the largest of the Doric temples, it was dwarfed by the vast temples of the Ionian Greeks such as the fourth century Temple of Artemis at Ephesus (above). It is possible that the Ionians were directly influenced by the massive temples of Egypt.

cession which most scholars believe can only have been the Panathenaea, the festival celebrating Athena, as patron goddess of the city. The frieze is composed as a whole. However many hands worked on it, there must have been one presiding genius, probably Pheidias, who conceived and inspired the composition. Not only is each figure beautifully executed but there is a sense of rhythm to the whole as if everyone is united by the intensity of the celebration. It is a majestic achievement even when viewed far from its natural home. (Most of the frieze is now in the British Museum, who bought it from Lord Elgin, who had removed it from the Acropolis, in 1816.)

One recent interpretation is that the frieze represents the Panathenaea of 490, after Marathon, with the 192 dead Athenian heroes, portrayed on the frieze as knights on horseback, being received by the gods in glory. Attractive and ingenious though this theory is, it involves some selective counting. The heroic-looking charioteers would have to be excluded but the marshals and grooms included if the numbers are to work. Another interpretation sees the frieze as commemorating a festival of Erectheus, a legendary king of Athens, or even, according to Professor Joan Connelly, a representation of the mythical story telling how Erectheus sacrificed his three daughters before going into battle with an invading army of Thracians. It may be more realistic to see it primarily as a celebration of the greatness of Athens and her citizen body. It is fascinating to see the chariots used in the procession are drawn by four horses, always a sign of elite or divine status. So the Athenian citizens are seeing themselves as worthy of divine or at least aristocratic status.

Once the workers had been released from the Parthenon, they were deployed to build a monumental gateway to the Acropolis, the Propylaea, and later, on the north side, the Erechtheum to house many of the oldest cults of the city. These buildings and an exquisite small temple to Athena Nike, built alongside the Propylaea in the 420s, stood among a mass of earlier buildings and shrines, but they were designed in relation to each other, with some concept of an overall harmony, the first time this is known to have happened in Greek architecture. In the cramped space of the Acropolis this was an architectural achievement in itself. The traditional setting for Greek temples was in rows or completely alone and always on flat surfaces. The Propylaea and Erechtheum both had to be designed on several levels.

According to his aristocratic critics, Pericles was 'gilding and dressing up the Acropolis like a prostitute, hanging round her neck precious stones and statues and six-million-drachma temples'. The city, however, now had a centre of outstanding beauty where religious beliefs and artistic skills met with its democratic pride in a majestic celebration of its achievements.

The Athenian Empire

This pride was also sustained by the emergence of Athens as a fully fledged empire. Without the restraining influence of Cimon, the city now became even more ruthless in its overseas affairs. Protection of the city against Sparta was a new priority. Following the breakdown of relations with Sparta the Athenians had moved quickly to make an alliance with Sparta's old enemy, Argos (460 BC). The next step was to control the Isthmus (through which any invading force of Spartans would have to pass). When the neighbouring city of Megara approached Athens for protection from Corinth, she found herself taken over and garrisoned by Athens.

Athens then dealt with her oldest rival, the island of Aegina, only a few kilometres from her coast and a trading rival for generations. Troops from the League were used to besiege her and finally to incorporate her into the League (458).

This active policy in the west took place at the same time as a major expedition by troops of the League to the east. One target was Cyprus, strategically placed close to the Asian coast and not yet a member of the League. An expedition arrived there in the late 460s, but when news came through in 459 that the Egyptians had risen against Persian rule the expedition was diverted. It was too good an opportunity to miss. Persian control over Egypt was likely to be weak and the chance of access to another source of grain irresistible. Athens' army was stationed in the Delta and occupied Memphis. About 454, however, in what appears to have been a major disaster, it was driven out by a Persian army. As many as 250 ships with most of their crews may have been lost. The details are poorly recorded, but there is no doubt that Athens was placed on the defensive and that soon afterwards the treasury of the League at Delos was moved from its exposed position in the centre of the Aegean to Athens.

In the 450s Athens also conducted a number of campaigns into central Greece. (They were known collectively as the First Peloponnesian War.) Her objectives were varied: to dominate the Isthmus and so keep the Peloponnese closed off, to bully Corinth into the Athenian rather than Spartan camp, and to exploit the fertile plains of Thessaly, the pastures of the best horses in Greece. (Control of the plains would also offer access to the timber and mineral-rich lands of northern Greece.) The campaigns brought her face to face with Sparta for the first time. In 457 Sparta had sent an army north to support her mother city, Doris, against an attack by her neighbour Phocis. As the successful Spartan army returned south, rumours reached Athens that it was in contact with anti-democratic factions in the city. The Athenians, with League support, sent an army over the Attic border to confront it. At the battle of Tanagra both sides had heavy losses but the Spartans were able to withdraw and make for home. Two months later, after the battle of Oenophyta, Athens gained control of the whole Boeotian plain with the exception of its largest city, Thebes.

The later campaigns in central Greece must have been affected by the losses in Egypt. In the event it proved impossible for Athens to sustain any long-term control over such a large territory. By the early 440s the western cities of the plain had broken free of Athenian control and an army sent to restore it was decisively defeated at Coronea (447). There were revolts in Euboea and Megara, and Megara was now lost to Athens. It was a major blow and left Athens vulnerable to direct attack by Sparta. (The Spartans did, in fact, invade Attica but soon withdrew, for reasons which have never been made clear.) Over the winter of 446/445 Athens and Sparta made a formal peace (the so-called Thirty Years Peace) by which each recognized each other's allies and promised not to interfere with their allegiances.

THE ATHENIAN EMPIRE AT ITS HEIGHT
440–430 BC

MAP 5

Although the Peace put an end to Athenian intrusions in central Greece, it did allow the city to develop an empire in the Aegean without interference from Sparta. Up to 449 Athens had been able to use the threat of Persia as a means of forcing the smaller League members into dependence on her. However, in that year it seems likely that a peace treaty was made with Persia. There is some dispute over this treaty as Thucydides makes no mention of it and the earliest reference is a fourth-century source. However, there is no further recorded hostility between Athens and Persia in the fifth century. Furthermore, there is a gap in the records of tribute paid to the League's treasury, now in Athens, for 448. This is understandable if the main *raison d'être* of the League's existence had disappeared and members refused to continue their contributions.

The Tribute Lists start again in 447, with the total collected smaller than that raised in 449. By 446 it is back to normal levels (600 talents a year). The fluctuating figures could mean that Athens insisted on renewing the collection of tribute in 447, had some difficulty in collecting from all member states in the first year, but had regained full control by 446. Certainly Athens acts from now on as if she was an imperial power rightfully exacting tribute from her subjects. As has been mentioned, the Parthenon was built out of League money. One source from the 440s talks of 'the cities which the Athenians control'. When the city of Chalcis was subdued after the revolt in Euboea of 446, she had to promise loyalty to Athens alone. No mention was made of the League. The Council of the League stopped meeting, probably during the 440s. All the evidence suggests, therefore, that Athens was now set on domination of the Aegean.

There seem to have been some 150 subject states of the empire. Virtually every island of the Aegean was a member. Athenian control stretched along the Asian coastline from Rhodes up to the Hellespont, through into the Black Sea and round southern Thrace as far as the Chalcidice peninsula. Nearer home the cities of Euboea and the island of Aegina were members. The tribute expected was not burdensome and was reduced after 445, presumably because Athens was at peace with both Persia and Sparta. The average sum was 2 talents a member, less than it took to keep an Athenian trireme in service for a year.

Athens used a variety of methods to keep control of her empire. One indirect method was to use *proxenoi*, citizens of a subject city who were expected to represent Athens' interests there. Some key cities had cleruchies (the term originates from one who is allotted land overseas while retaining citizenship at home) imposed on them. Poorer Athenians were often given preference in the allocation of places in these settlements. (Pericles' motives, claimed Plutarch, included the desire to rid the city of riff-raff.) When Lesbos revolted in the 420s, for instance, land was confiscated and then distributed to Athenian citizens, with the incentive for prospective settlers of the native population being offered as labour. The demand was such that the plots of land had to be allocated by lot. Cleruchies are recorded in at least twenty-four cities in Thrace, the Chersonese (the northern coastline of the Hellespont), and on the islands of Naxos and Andros. There is no doubt that the main motive was to strengthen Athens' control of these cities, which either had a history of revolt or were strategically important. There is also evidence of richer Athenians gaining land overseas. It may have been handed out by the state as a means of buying off aristocratic dissent. This seizure of land was imperialism at its most extreme. As J. K. Davis puts it, 'the Athenian presence in the Aegean amounts to a tremendous land-grab, carried out and protected by Athenian naval power for the benefit of Athenian citizens of all classes'.

The sources suggest other symbols of Athenian predominance. There were attempts to enforce a cultural unity centred on the worship of Athena. All members of the League were now expected to attend the Great Panathenaea bringing a cow and a shield and helmet with them and marching in the procession. (This helped reinforce the old belief that Athens was the mother city of the Ionian states.) A Coinage Decree, possibly passed in 445, required the allies to use only Athenian weights, measures, and silver coinage. This ensured the prosperity of the Athenian silver mines as well as exploiting the propaganda value of her distinctive coins. Important judicial cases were to be referred to Athens, while Athens also took an interest in supporting democracy against oligarchy. The city of Erythrae in Ionia had a 'democratic' constitution imposed on her as early as the 450s and Samos possibly went through the same experience after a revolt in 440/439.

The evidence from the 440s and 430s is of a city gradually consolidating its position wherever its trading interests required. In 443 Athens set up a colony at Thurii in the instep of Italy (on the site of the city of Sybaris, which had been destroyed by its neighbours in 510). An alliance followed with Rhegium on the Italian side of the Straits of Messina. This suggests an increasing interest in the riches of the west. Meanwhile, in the northern Aegean a new city was founded at Amphipolis, upriver from Eion, where control could be held over the river crossing. It offered access not just to timber but to the gold mines of Mount Pangaeon. Amphipolis was to acquire a mystique rather similar to that of the commercial centre of Singapore for the British empire, and its loss to Sparta in 424 was to be as deeply felt.

The Athenian empire was in many senses a conservative and even defensive one. Its main purpose can be seen as maintenance of control over trade routes. It had no internal dynamic. Despite the seizure of land in some areas, there was never the deliberate and ruthless exploitation of resources on the scale followed by later trading states such as Venice. Insofar as a transfer of resources took place, it seems to have been from the wealthier members of the subject cities to the Athenian oarsmen and Athens' own richer citizens. Athens never built up sizeable financial reserves and, since a single siege could soak up three years' worth of tribute, was particularly vulnerable to revolts. However, no revolt could be allowed to succeed or the myth of Athenian superiority would be exploded. When Samos rebelled in 440, Pericles and his nine fellow generals were sent to deal with the island. Samos was recaptured at some cost and no other city joined the rebellion. There is no doubt, however, of the resentment felt by many ordinary subjects of the empire. When some decades later, in 377, Athens tried to rebuild a naval confederacy, she could only get the Aegean cities to join by promising them that none of the impositions of empire, including the seizure of land and the payment of tribute, would be renewed.

Democracy under Strain

Sparta viewed the consolidation of the Athenian empire with some unease. In 440 many in Sparta were willing to send help to Samos, but Sparta lacked the support of Corinth, whose navy would have been essential for any expedition overseas. Events were now to push Corinth towards Sparta. Corinth had been in dispute with her former colony Corcyra (the island of Corfu), and Athens had come to Corcyra's support. Her motive may have been to prevent Corcyra's large fleet from joining Corinth's or she may have had her eye on another base in the west. In 432 another dispute broke out over the Chalcidican city of Potidaea, a colony of Corinth but also a member of the League. Athens tried to rid Potidaea of her Corinthian magistrates, but only succeeded in sparking off a revolt which forced her to retaliate with an expensive siege. It was the combination of these two intrusions by Athens which forced Corinth to seek support from Sparta. Thucydides records the Corinthian envoy taunting Sparta for her inactivity, which he contrasts with the energy of Athens.

This time Sparta responded. It seemed an excellent time to strike at Athens. Sparta had the support of Corinth at a time when the Athenian army was absent at Potidaea. Megara, which seems to have been under some form of trade ban from Athens, was eager to offer help. The way was open for Spartan forces to make a lightning raid across the Isthmus in the hope of seizing Athens. The outbreak of war was engineered by Sparta encouraging one of her allies, Thebes, to attack Plataea, an ally of Athens. (The Spartans realized that by doing this they carried the guilt for the war themselves, and when things went badly they were haunted by the belief that the gods were punishing them for their transgressions of the rules of war.)

The outbreak of a war which was to end twenty-seven years later in Athens' defeat was a turning point in the city's history. (It is covered in Chapter 17.) There was a new mood of pessimism, symbolized by a devastating plague which broke out in the city in 430. In the despair that followed, the Assembly turned against Pericles, fined him, and deposed him from his generalship (although he was soon re-elected, 'as is the way with crowds', remarked Thucydides). He died in the summer of 429 of some lingering illness probably related to the plague.

After the death of Pericles in 429, Athenian democracy had to face the stresses of plague and war. New leaders arose, the so-called 'demagogues', who were accused by their rivals of manipulating the emotions of the Assembly for their personal advantage. Sources such as Thucydides are hostile to them and the picture of them which has survived may well be a distorted one, the traditional prejudice of the aristocrat against the upstart. Certainly these leaders, of whom Cleon, Hyperbolus, and Cleophon were the most prominent, came from manufacturing rather than landed aristocratic backgrounds. Cleon owned a tannery, Hyperbolus a factory for making lamps, and Cleophon made lyres. They did not aim to become generals and concentrated their energies on building up support within the Assembly. They competed for power with the generals such as Nicias and Alcibiades whose origins were more aristocratic.

In the turmoil that followed, democracy was overthrown on two occasions. In 411, after an Athenian expedition to Sicily ended in disaster, the Assembly surrendered its power to a Council of Four Hundred. This was overthrown after four months, and an Assembly whose membership was limited to the richer 5,000 citizens was introduced. This only lasted until 410, when full democracy was restored. In 404 the Spartans, now finally victorious, imposed a Commission of Thirty on Athens, the 'Thirty Tyrants' as they became known. They could only survive with a supporting garrison of 700 men and launched a reign of terror in which some 1,500 Athenians may have died. In the winter of 404/403 the democrats, with Theban help, launched a counter-coup. The Piraeus was seized and the Thirty overthrown. These events became part of Athens' democratic mythology. The restored democracy was to last until its overthrow by Macedonia in 322.

The character of fourth-century democracy in Athens was subtly different from that of the fifth century. The city appeared sobered by the devastating experience of the Peloponnesian War, in particular by the volatility of decision-making, as shown in the Assembly, and the experience of the 'Thirty Tyrants'. A new respect was now evoked for the traditional laws (the *nomoi*) of the city. Between 410 and 399 these laws were codified and inscribed for all to see on the walls of one of the stoas. Henceforth, if any law was to be changed or a new one introduced it had to be done by a modified procedure. A legislative body, the *nomothetai*, was set up. It consisted of all members of the Boule plus 1,001 citizens drawn from the jury lists for the year. Any change in the law was first proposed by the Assembly but then had to be debated before the much smaller *nomothetai*, which decided by simple majority whether it should be accepted. The principle of democratic involvement was maintained, but modified to allow the Assembly's decisions to be reconsidered. The Assembly could still pass decrees, *psephismata*, but now these were limited in scope or only valid for a short period. Any speaker who proposed a measure which was contrary to existing laws, without going through the new procedure, could now be prosecuted and the proposed law declared invalid. The prosecution took place before jurors in the traditional way, and in effect the jurors were now deciding whether a particular decree of the Assembly was valid or not.

There is also evidence that the Areopagus, still an unelected body of former magistrates who sat on it for life, was revived as an important part of the constitution in the fourth century. By now, however, the property qualification for archons had disappeared, so the body was more broadly constituted than it had been a hundred years earlier. In 403/402 the Assembly had decreed that the Areopagus was to supervise the administration of laws by the magistrates. In the 340s the Areopagus acquired the power to try, on its own initiative, political leaders who had, in its opinion, tried to overthrow democracy or were guilty of treason or bribery. Its verdict was then passed to the jurors for confirmation. In addition there are examples, from the second half of the century, of the Areopagus actually intervening to annul the elections of officials by the Assembly.

As Mogens Hansen has argued in his *The Athenian Democracy in the Age of Demosthenes*, these changes were justified on the grounds that the traditional laws of the Athenian state from the days of Solon and Cleisthenes were simply being restored. This was nonsense, of course, but, as in 461, an appeal to some ancestral constitution' of the past, was the only way to bring about political change. 'Like many Greeks,' writes Hansen, 'the Athenians had a soft spot for the "golden age", the belief that everything was better in olden times and that consequently the road to improvement lay backwards and not forwards.' The result was that the Athenians maintained confidence in their democracy and it survived until overthrown by outsiders, the Macedonians, in 322. In many ways, with the powers of the Assembly restricted, Athenian democracy was more mature and stable in the fourth century than it was in the fifth, while the distinction made between laws (*nomoi*) and decrees (*psephismata*) was a forerunner of a similar distinction made by the Founding Fathers of the American Constitution between the clauses of the Constitution and laws proposed by Congress which could not overrule them. (Not all historians, however, agree with Hansen's view that Athenian democracy in the fourth century was significantly different from what had gone before.)

The nineteenth-century French writer Alexis de Tocqueville described Athenian democracy as 'an aristocracy of masters'. While there was always more leisure time in pre-industrial economies, particularly in the slack periods of the agricultural year, it can be argued that it would not have survived without slavery and an income from empire and, probably more important, from trade which allowed citizens to be paid as jurymen, administrators, and legislators. The Athenians believed, or allowed themselves to be convinced by Pericles, that they were superior to the citizens of other cities (although it must be remembered that there were many other democratic states in Greece whose constitutions have not survived). Here is Pericles speaking in the winter of 431/430 at the annual festival at which the Athenians commemorated their dead (the so-called Funeral Oration):

Remember that this city has the greatest name among all mankind because she has never yielded to adversity, but has spent more lives in war and has endured more severe hardships than any other city. She has held the greatest power known to men up to our time, and the memory of her power will be laid up forever for those who come after. Even if we now have to yield (since all things that grow also decay), the memory shall remain that of all the Greeks, we held sway over the greatest number of Hellenes; that we stood against our foes, both when they were united and when each was alone, in the greatest ways; and that we inhabited a city wealthier and greater than all . . . The splendour of the present is the glory of the future laid up as a memory for all time. Take possession of both, zealously choosing honour for the future and avoiding disgrace in the present.   (Translation: Paul Rahe)

Pericles is here claiming high ideals for his city. In fact, he is doing nothing less than transferring the values and achievements once prized by individual aristocrats to the citizens of Athens collectively. Already, however, he is recording the first doubts that these ideals will continue to be realized. As Bernard Knox has shrewdly pointed out, these words suggest that Athens was, like a Sophoclean hero, 'in love with the impossible'.

It is certainly true that Athenian democracy demanded a consistent involvement which is rather forbidding to modern minds. 'We do not say that a man who takes no interest in politics is a man who minds his own business; we say he has no business here at all', argues Pericles in the same Funeral Oration. The contrast with modern political thought is striking. Contemporary human rights centre on the right of the individual (every individual, not just those enjoying citizen status) to protection against the power of the state. This is a concept which the Athenians would have found difficult to grasp. They despised those who withdrew from public life. (The Greek word *idiotes*, from which the English 'idiot' is derived, meant one who put private pleasures before public duty and who was, for this reason, ignorant of everything that really mattered.) The Athenian citizen was not without protection. He could always argue his case before a jury, but ultimately a decision of a jury or the use of ostracism was final and there was no appeal to any higher principle than that of the will of the people. Socrates and the generals who survived Arginusae found this to their cost.

It is easy to point to the shortcomings and contradictions of Athenian democracy. However, it remains unique as the world's only example of a successfully functioning and sustained direct democracy. It lasted for nearly 140 years—a remarkable achievement in a period of history where instability was the norm. (The Paris Commune of 1870 did not survive long enough to offer a comparison, although during its short existence Marx and Engels compared it to the democracies of Greece.) It involved its citizens as officials, legislators, and law enforcers in a way few modern democracies would dare to do and it is remarkable for breaking the traditional connection between political power and wealth. And all this when the city was also acting as a major and innovative cultural centre. It is these achievements which are the subject of the next chapter.

FURTHER READING

The Cambridge Ancient History, vol. v (Cambridge, 1992), is fundamental for this period. A fine introduction is provided by J. K. Davies, *Democracy and Classical Greece* (2nd edition, London, 1993). There is also Simon Hornblower's penetrating *The Greek World, 479–322 BC* (revised edition, London, 1991). *The World of Athens: An Introduction to Classical Athenian Culture* (Cambridge, 1984) and Anton Powell, *Athens and Sparta: Constructing Greek Political and Social History from 478 BC* (London, 1988) have already been mentioned. Christian Meier, *Athens: A Portrait of the City in its Golden Age* (London, 1998). Mark Munn, *The School of History: Athens in the Age of Socrates* (Berkeley, 2000). On Athenian religion R. Parker, *Athenian Religion: A History* (Oxford, 1996). See generally G. de Ste

Croix's magisterial *The Origins of the Peloponnesian War* (London, 1972). On the evolution of democracy see M. Ostwald, *From Popular Sovereignty to the Sovereignty of Law: Law, Society and Politics in Fifth Century Athens* (Berkeley, 1986), and Josiah Ober, *Mass and Elite in Democratic Athens* (Princeton, 1989). For what is known about Pericles see D. Kagan, *Pericles of Athens and the Birth of Democracy* (London, 1990). For the fourth century see Mogens Hansen, *The Athenian Democracy in the Age of Demosthenes* (Oxford, 1991). The links between democracy and literacy are explored in D. Steiner's recent *The Tyrant's Writ* (Princeton, 1993), and Harvey Yunis (ed.), *Written Texts and the Rise of Literate Culture in Ancient Greece* (Cambridge, 2003). A lively study on Athenian society is James Davidson, *Courtesans and Fishcakes* (London, 1997).

Looking at the Athenian democratic achievement in a wider context, see M. Finley, *Politics in the Ancient World* (Cambridge, 1983); Eric Robinson (ed.), *Ancient Greek Democracy, Readings and Sources* (London, 2004); S. Goldhill and R. Osborne, *Performance Culture and Athenian Democracy* (Cambridge, 1999). There is much to stimulate in vol. i of Paul Rahe's *Republics Ancient and Modern: The Ancient Regime in Classical Greece* (Chapel Hill, NC, and London, 1992) and Orlando Patterson's *Freedom in the Making of Western Culture* (London, 1991). For a wider overview of Athenian democracy in relation to later democracies see David Held, *Models of Democracy* (Cambridge, 1987). J. S. McClelland, *A History of Western Political Thought* (London, 1996).

The Athenian empire is well covered in chapter 5 of Davies. See also P. J. Rhodes, *The Athenian Empire* (Oxford, 1985). Moses Finley also has an essay on the Athenian empire in his *Economy and Society in Ancient Greece* (Harmondsworth, 1981).

For the buildings of the Acropolis there are the general histories of art and architecture cited above, including Jeffrey Hurwit's *The Athenian Acropolis* (Cambridge, 1999) but see also Ian Jenkins, *The Parthenon Frieze* (London, 1994) and Jenifer Neils, *The Parthenon Frieze* (Cambridge, 2001) for a recent overview of the main theories about the meaning of the frieze. The recent restorations of the Acropolis are discussed in Richard Economakis, *Acropolis Restoration* (London, 1994) while Mary Beard, *The Parthenon* (London, 2002), looks at the building through history. John Camp, *The Athenian Agora* (London, 1992) for the archaeological development of the centre of Athens. See also chapter 13, 'The Archaeology of Democracy: Classical Athens', in James Whitley, *The Archaeology of Ancient Greece* (Cambridge, 2001).

16 | From Aeschylus to Aristotle

Athens was above all a community of shared experience and there could hardly have been a more communal activity than drama. The drama festivals were celebrations of Dionysus, god of fertility and sexual abandon. His festivities, throughout Greece, were ones in which conventions were thrown aside and women, in particular, took the chance to engage in wild dancing among the pine forests. Traditionally the cult worship of Dionysus involved participants changing identity and wearing masks. In Athens, however, for reasons to be discussed, the celebrations of the god became more formal. At the Great Dionysia, held each spring, Dionysus' statue, alongside phalluses, symbols of the sexual abandonment licensed by the god, was carried in open procession to the theatre just below the Acropolis. Then the city and its visitors congregated to hear a range of dramatic performances in which poets competed with each other for prizes. (An estimated 14,000 people, including 1,200 actors and singers, participated in the Great Dionysia, probably the largest gathering in the Greek world outside the Olympic Games.) The Dionysia had an added importance as a propaganda exercise—it was the occasion at which tribute from the empire was presented to the city and the ten generals met to offer libations. A smaller festival, the Lenaea, was held in January, a time of year when travel was too difficult for foreigners to attend. Drama brought together religion, democratic pride, and creative thought.

The supreme examples of Athenian dramatic art are the tragedies. The origins of the word is obscure. The Greek *trag-oidia* means 'goat song', and ingenious but inconclusive attempts have been made to link the plays to sacrifice of a goat or the winning of a goat as a prize. The roots of drama appear to lie in the late 500s after a border town Eleutherae had been incorporated into Athenian territory. Eleutherae had its own important festival to Dionysus 'of the black goatskin' and the rituals of this festival appear to have been transferred to Athens, where they were performed in public, as a means of confirming the integration of Eleutherae into the city state. At some point one of the chorus appears to have stood aside from the rituals to explain their relevance to the watching audience. The next step, attributed to the Athenian tragedian Aeschylus, was to introduce a second 'actor', and thus allow scenes between actors with the chorus left to introduce themes or comments on events as they unfolded. Sophocles added a third, allowing even more complex interactions between characters.

By the fifth century the rituals of the drama festivals were well established. Each festival began with twenty dithyrambs, lyric poems sung by a chorus of fifty. Each of the ten tribes of Athens entered a men's and boys' chorus. Then came the tragedies. Three poets were selected for each festival and they each produced three plays which could be linked in theme. Each trilogy was followed by a satyr play. The satyrs were the companions of Dionysus, and with large pendulous phalluses attached to their waists were represented in wild frolics. Finally, on the fourth day of the festival, five different poets offered a comedy each. The plays were financed by the *choregos*, a rich citizen who was honoured for taking this role, an element of aristocratic patronage which continued into democratic times. The final result has been described, by the classical historian J. K. Davies, as an amalgamation of upper-class lyric poetry with out-of-town bucolic Dionysiac ritual to produce entertainment of a type which hugely appealed to the newly enfranchised citizenry.

By the fifth century the first permanent theatres had developed. (The only one to survive from this period is at Thorikos in southern Attica.) The performances were held on a circular dancing floor, the *orchestra*, with a backdrop behind, the *skene* (hence the English 'scene'), which housed a dressing-room. The audience watched from the *theatron* (the name given to any space where spectators sat and the origin of the English word 'theatre'), seated in a semicircle, later provided with stone seats. Those remaining at Athens are Roman, but at Epidaurus in the Peloponnese there is a magnificent fourth-century example, its acoustics perfect for even the highest of its 14,000 seats. Actors traditionally wore masks, and many of these were stylized so that stock characters were easily recognizable. Smaller theatres were placed throughout Attica and plays could be repeated or revived in them.

The settings of tragedy, with rare exceptions such as Aeschylus' contemporary play *The Persians*, were in the myths with which Greek minds were saturated. The poet would adapt the story to suit his ends, but he could be sure that the audience would know something of the main characters and the events which unfolded. The theme usually centred on the tortured relationship between human beings and the gods. The human characters in Greek tragedy are often trapped. They have either committed some unforgivable sin or they are forced to choose between two honourable but incompatible courses of action. Either way they will offend a sacred code and are doomed. The dramatists did not take sides in the dreadful dilemmas they portrayed. Aeschylus treated the Persians, in his play of that name, with scrupulous fairness, even though his audience was sitting among the ruins of the city the Persians had sacked only eight years before. The skill lay in allowing the full horror of the story gently but inexorably to unfold.

What is lost from the surviving plays is their music. Tunes and songs were normally passed on by example and so most have vanished. Music (from *mousike*, the art of the muses), was an essential ingredient in the drama festivals. The dithythramb consisted largely of dancing and singing and the tragedies and comedies were accompanied by flutes. Sophocles, in fact, was first known for his singing and dancing, and a legend says that it was he who led the paean (the name given to a cult hymn to Apollo) after the great victory of Salamis.

Aeschylus

Only a tiny proportion of the work of the Athenian tragedians is preserved and almost all of this from three poets. The father of Greek tragic drama is Aeschylus (525–456 BC). Aeschylus was a public figure, who fought for his city at Marathon and possibly at Salamis as well. He seems to have been sympathetic to the coming of democracy. Certainly the city community takes a central place in his work. He is credited with eighty plays, but only six (there is some dispute over a seventh) survive, all from his later years. They include the only surviving play on a contemporary theme, *The Persians*, and the only complete trilogy, or cycle of three plays, which survives: the *Oresteia*.

Aeschylus was a man of deep religious sensibility with a strong belief in the underlying harmony of the world. This harmony was decreed and upheld by the gods, who would be offended by anyone who disturbed it. Crimes against harmony included destruction of the natural world, overweening pride (hubris), or breaches in the sacred conventions of warfare. However, what behaviour is actually demanded of men is not always clear. 'The paths of Zeus' mind stretch dark and tangled, impervious to sight,' as the words from one play, *The Suppliants*, put it. The possibilities of tragedy lie in men unwittingly upsetting the balance.

To make matters more complex Aeschylus allows the gods to actually tempt men into wrongdoing, as Zeus tempts Xerxes, the king of the Persians, into his invasion of Greece. Even more tragically, human beings may be placed by the gods in situations where they are forced to break one convention to uphold another. In *Seven against Thebes*, Eteocles, king of Thebes, has the sacred duty of protecting his city from attack. But one of the attackers is his brother. He can only fulfil his obligations by committing the crime of fratricide. Whichever path he chooses he is doomed.

It is one of Aeschylus' achievements as a poet to incorporate a sense of impending gloom into a tragedy from its earliest words. In *Agamemnon*, the first work of the trilogy *Oresteia*, the scene is set by a watchman who scours the night sky for the fire signalling that Troy has at last been captured by the Greeks. Something, however, makes him deeply uneasy about what should be a moment of triumph and joy. The audience learns that Agamemnon's fleet was only able to sail because a sacrifice was made, that of Agamemnon's daughter. There is more anguish waiting for Agamemnon. His wife Clytemnestra is passionately involved with a lover, Aegisthus. She kills Agamemnon on his return.

Agamemnon's crime, the murder of his daughter, is avenged, but Clytemnestra has caused another, the death of a husband, and his blood lies on her hands as she sets herself up with her lover as ruler.

This is a common theme in Aeschylus. One transgression gives rise to another. In words from the second play in the trilogy, *The Libation Bearers*, 'the blood that mother earth consumes clots hard, it won't seep through, it breeds revenge'. In *The Libation Bearers* Orestes, the son of Agamemnon and Clytemnestra, returning from exile, feels it his duty to avenge his father's death by murdering his mother and killing Aegisthus. The burden of guilt is passed on. The polluted Orestes then flees to the sacred oracle at Delphi in the hope that he can be purified. He is pursued by the Furies, urged on by the ghost of Clytemnestra.

In the final play, the *Eumenides*, 'the Furies', Aeschylus moves towards resolution. There is a trial in which Apollo appears to support Orestes' case against the Furies and argue that he was justified. (Apollo's argument was, however, irremediably sexist. It turned largely on the Greek belief that human conception depended entirely on the male sperm, while the womb was merely a receptacle in which it grew into a human being. 'The woman you call the mother of the child is not the parent, just a nurse to the seed, the new sown seed that grows and swells inside her. The man is the source of life—the one who mounts.' (Translation: Robert Fagles.) Thus, to Apollo, Clytemnestra's crime of killing a man, her husband, and with it all possibilities of future human life, was worse than Orestes' killing of a mother who had no possibilities. With a jury equally divided, it is Athena who casts the deciding vote in favour of Orestes for reasons which have been endlessly discussed by critics, but perhaps ultimately so as to uphold good order, moderation, and mercy against the unrestrained anger of the Furies. The city is also extolled by Athena as the truest security for good men. 'The stronger your fear,' says Athena, 'your reverence for the just, the stronger your country's wall and city's safety, stronger by far than all men else possess in Scythia's rugged steppes or Pelops' level plain' and the resolution of the play cannot be separated from the benefits of city government.

Aeschylus' characters are powerful figures but they are often undeveloped as individuals. It is as if they are used primarily as vehicles for the grandeur of Aeschylus' words and for stories which move relentlessly forward under their own weight to their tragic or harmonious conclusion. It is the language which is the chief glory of Aeschylus. It is both majestic and emotionally intense, well fitted to the themes of national pride and divine justice which are Aeschylus' main concerns.

Sophocles

In 468 the 57-year-old Aeschylus was defeated in the Dionysia by a man nearly thirty years his junior, Sophocles (496–406). The result almost certainly had political undertones, and suggests an aristocratic bias against Aeschylus with his democratic sympathies. Aeschylus had his revenge when he won first prize in the following year.

Sophocles may have been of a younger generation but in many ways he looks back to an earlier age than Aeschylus. With Sophocles the focus turns from the city and community to the individual, both male and female. It was Sophocles who introduced the powerful independent woman into tragedy, a revolutionary move in a city where women were kept largely in seclusion. Sophocles writes of an earlier archaic world, one of heroes where loyalties are to clans and kin rather than to a city. It is a cruel and inflexible one with the ways of the gods incomprehensible to man. Most of Sophocles' characters have flaws in their personalities which lead them inexorably to their doom, and he shows the full range of torments that human beings can undergo, symbolized perhaps in the moment when Oedipus, king of Thebes, returns to the stage just having gouged out his eyes.

In *Antigone*, the heroine, Antigone, is rooted in the kinship system in which the religious duties of the clan predominate. She finds the body of her brother Polyneices and she must bury him as sacred custom demands. But Polyneices has been a traitor to his city and the king, Creon, has forbidden his burial. Antigone, with supreme moral conviction, goes ahead, ritually scattering dust on her brother's body. She is arrested and taken off to die by being buried alive. At the last moment Creon tries to change the decision but it is too late, Antigone has committed suicide and so has Creon's own wife and his son who has been engaged to her. The tragic individual is now Creon himself, but perhaps the underlying warning of the play is that inflexibility in support of absolute values does not provide the best guide for life. A ship, suggests Sophocles, would never arrive if it tried to sail head to wind.

The acknowledged masterpiece of Sophocles is *King Oedipus*. There is a contrast here with Antigone. While Antigone is trapped by the dictates of her own conscience, Oedipus has done everything he can to escape the prophecy that he will murder his father and sleep with his mother. In what is a spare, beautifully controlled play he learns to his horror that this is just what he has done. Polluted in spite of himself, he gouges out his eyes when he comes across the body of his wife and mother Jocasta, who has committed suicide. (Nowhere else in Greek mythology is this incest/parricide theme explored, and Freud's interpretation that Oedipus unconsciously wished to kill his father is questionable, as Oedipus, an orphan from birth, did not even know that the man he killed was his father.)

In his last known play, *Oedipus at Colonus*, written when he was over 80, Sophocles comes back to Oedipus, now an old man, pathetic in his blindness, polluted by his 'crimes'. Death is near, and Oedipus makes his way to the sacred grove at Colonus, for his last days. (Colonus was where Sophocles himself was born. The spot, swallowed up in recent years by the suburbs of Athens, has only recently been replanted.) His daughters join him as others shun him and he finally meets death with nobility. That, suggests Sophocles, is the only appropriate response to the mysteries of fate.

Sophocles was writing at darker times for Athens. The city was visited by plague and in the poet's final years was succumbing to the power of Sparta. Many have seen Sophocles' emphasis on the inexorable nature of suffering as arising from these experiences. Sophocles shows little enthusiasm for the city as a political entity. He suggests that democracy presents as many problems as it solves and can do little to sustain the individual at his time of need. Among those who reject Oedipus is a representative of the *polis*.

Euripides

The third great tragic poet of fifth-century Athens is Euripides (484–406). Although Euripides was only a few years younger than Sophocles, they seem to come from different worlds. While Sophocles looks back to a pre-democratic age, Euripides is relentlessly contemporary, at home with the uncertainties and restlessness of late fifth-century Athens. His reputation is as a moody and withdrawn genius (one legend relates how he wrote his plays in a cave on Salamis) with little interest in public life. Eighteen of his plays survive from over eighty that he wrote. Although picked many times to present tragedies, he was never as successful as Sophocles, winning only five first prizes, against Sophocles' twenty.

It is in his treatment of the gods that Euripides shows that he is in tune with his times. This was a period where their relevance, even their existence, was questioned (see further below). Even if they exist, what is their nature? Why do they allow evil to occur? Why is the tyrant able to become wealthy and the pious man suffer? Despite the apparent implacability of the gods Euripides does not allow his characters to be burdened by divine power in the way Sophocles' are. In what is an important moment in European drama they actually answer back. 'You are a god full of madness or an unjust god,' is one cry in the play *Heracles*. If, as Euripides suggests, the gods might actually abandon human beings to their fate, they should not be allowed to do so unquestioned.

The result is a sharper focus on the characters themselves and their relationships with each other. They stand alone, the victims of their own emotions. In *Medea*, Medea has been abandoned by her husband, the cold and calculating Jason. She conceives of a plan to kill him and her children, partly to save them from being killed by others. Within her the conflicting forces of reason and emotion battle it out until the dreadful murders are finally committed. Here is the birth of domestic drama. The issues are on a completely different level from those public ones explored by Sophocles and Aeschylus. Medea differs from the characters of Sophocles—Antigone who is convinced she is doing right, despite the consequences of her actions, or Oedipus who suffers fate in spite of himself. Medea knows she is doing wrong but is impelled by her feelings to commit her crimes. As strong as the desire for revenge seen in *Medea* is that of obsessive love. In *Hippolytus*, Hippolytus is that rare figure in Greek life, a man who prefers celibacy. Phaedra, his stepmother, is overcome with desire for him but is angrily rejected. She kills herself, but just before she dies her distorted feelings make her declare that Hippolytus has shown incestuous love for her. Hippolytus dies after his father Theseus passes a curse on him.

Euripides' plays break through the conventions of tragedy by showing human beings alone and responsible for their own actions, however strongly they are controlled by emotional forces they cannot understand. Euripides' concerns were not confined to private emotions. With a war raging around Athens he also meditated on the nature and use of power and political violence. In *The Trojan Women*, for instance, the brutalities of war are portrayed at a time when the Athenians had captured the city state of Melos and butchered its inhabitants. In his *Helen* (412) Euripides suggests that it was not really Helen but a phantom of her that was taken to Troy and thus the war was fought for an illusion—a telling point when Athens had just suffered appalling losses in the Sicilian expedition (see below, p. 300). Euripides is continually probing below the surface with insight and imagination in an attempt to challenge the motives which drive men and women to act the way they do.

A major part of Euripides' genius, however, is his ability to switch from the most tortuous display of personal passions to pastoral beauty and lyricism. In his last play, *The Bacchae*, written in his final years when he had left Athens for Macedonia, the entire action is set in the hills and mountains. It is the choruses of *The Bacchae* which are most memorable, long and beautiful evocations of life in the woodlands and fields. The theme is the nature of the passions unleashed by religious ecstasy. A mother and her companions are caught up in the rituals of Dionysus so passionately that they prove able to turn on her son and tear him to pieces.

Euripides remained popular. In the Oxyrhynchus papyri he is by far the most widely read of the Athenian tragedians and it is interesting that in the very earliest account that survives of a man reading to himself, the text is one of Euripides' plays.

Aristophanes and Comedy

Comedy was an opposite to tragedy—the word itself, a revel or riot, suggests a moment of release. It appears much later than tragedy, in 486 for the Dionysia, 442 for the Lenaea, and the genre is openly contemptuous of its rival. Comedy in Athens was, in fact, an essential element of its democratic system in that the dramatist could ridicule virtually any aspect of life from the gods to contemporary politicians, from philosophers to other dramatists. The outrageous, even unfair, nature of many of Aristophanes' jibes, at a time when the city was under immense threat from outside, is remarkable, and helps modify the picture that Pericles' words sometimes give of a city coldly dedicated to patriotic virtue.

Very little is known of Aristophanes (c.450–385) but it is assumed he was Athenian by birth. His attitudes are elitist, and he was ready to taunt anyone who represented new values or a less than cultured lifestyle. He had the aristocrat's weakness for mocking the background of others. Euripides, for instance, was taunted for being the son of a greengrocer (even though evidence suggests his background was quite a wealthy one). Aristophanes was writing at a time when Athens was at war and he yearns for peace, presenting the past as more civilized and noble than the present. It is hard to summarize his political views because his targets were so varied, but he shows some nostalgia for the early days of democracy, a time when he considered that the 'people' were wiser than they had since become. Cleon, the dominant political figure in Athens after the death of Pericles, is portrayed in *The Knights* as a slave to an unsteady and stupid old man, Demos (The People), who is happy only when he is given handouts. Euripides is derided for betraying the traditional conventions of tragedy.

Unlike the majority of tragedies, comedies were set in contemporary Athens, though the script often quickly translates the action into an unrecognizable world. Perhaps the finest of Aristophanes' plays is *The Birds*, written at the anxious time when the Athenian expedition of Sicily (see Chapter 17, below) was under way but its fate unknown. Aristophanes creates an ideal state, an escapist kingdom of birds halfway between the world of men and that of the gods. The birds are able to cut off the flow of sacrifice to the gods and so force them to accept the primacy of the birds. In *Lysistrata*, the women of Greece launch a sex strike in order to force their men to give up war. In *The Frogs*, the theme is tragedy itself. With Euripides and Sophocles by now both dead, Dionysus has to go down to the underworld to bring back Euripides to keep the Dionysiac festivals going. In fact Aeschylus puts in a counter-claim, and in a debate between him and Euripides it is Aeschylus who wins. He is considered a better guardian of traditional morals— a reflection without any doubt of Aristophanes' own preferences.

These accounts do nothing to show the wit, outrageous double entendres, fantastic characters, and sheer hurly-burly which make up Aristophanes' work, or the lyrical quality of much of his writing. The choruses, whether made up of birds, clouds, wasps, or frogs, dress up in appropriate costumes to add to the colour and hilarity of the performances. In Aristophanes there is a marriage between the most sophisticated wit and the most unbridled vulgarity. No other comedian of the Greek world comes near to equalling it, and it is only recently that producers have felt able to revive his plays with an unexpurgated text.

The Sophists

Aristophanes' play *The Clouds* was produced for the first time in 423. It is a satire on contemporary philosophy. A dissolute old farmer, Strepsiades, has heard that philosophers can make even a bad case appear good and he is determined to have his son learn how he can do this so as to get his own back on his creditors. Part of the play takes place in a school where students engage in all kinds of meaningless intellectual exercises and where it is taught that Zeus does not exist and it is the clouds instead which produce thunder and rain.

The Clouds reflects the arrival of philosophy in Athens in the fifth century. Before this philosophers appear as isolated figures each following his own path. (See Chapter 11.) There was no coherent intellectual discipline of philosophy, and many of the early thinkers were as much poets or historians as philosophers in the modern sense of the word. By the fifth century, however, there were men who wandered from city to city teaching young men how to use their minds and voices in public service. They were known as the sophists (from *sophizesthai*, 'making a profession of being inventive and clever') and democratic Athens was quick to use their services.

At first the word 'sophist' was a neutral one, referring to anyone who had exceptional talent, but the word was later used by Plato and Aristotle in a derogatory sense. For them the sophists were those who debased true philosophy by presenting it as a series of intellectual tricks which might be taught for money. The Sicilian Gorgias, a brilliant orator who visited Athens in 427, was attacked by Plato for being able to present the arguments both for and against any motion, thus showing no reverence for objective truth. Aristophanes' attacks on the sophists were in the same vein.

Plato's attack seems rather unfair. The fifth century was a sceptical age and many believed that truth was something that could not be found. Gorgias could hardly be criticized for teaching what were in effect the skills needed for the nurturing of democracy. (See Josiah Ober's argument, referred to earlier, that it was just these rhetorical skills which ensured the stability of Athenian society.) Moreover, many of the sophists had real intellectual breadth. Hippias of Elis, who was in Athens in the late fifth century, was able to offer instruction in astronomy, mathematics, and music. Prodicus of Ceos, another visitor, analysed the meanings of words and could be said to have laid the foundations for the study of linguistics. These men were not simply purveyors of second-hand ideas.

The sophists can also be credited with pioneering the study of religion as a social and anthropological phenomenon. The Milesians had suggested that there was some divine principle at work in the universe. Heraclitus had agreed. Anaxagoras of Clazomenae, the first philosopher recorded as living in Athens and a friend of Pericles, put the matter more explicitly when he wrote, 'All living things, both great and small are controlled by mind (*Nous*) . . . and the kinds of things that were to be and that once were but now are not, and all that now is and the kinds of things that will be—all these things are controlled by Mind.' (Translation: E. Hussey.) This 'mind' was omnipresent and eternal.

The sophists were more sceptical. Protagoras, who was born at Abdera in Thrace about 490 BC and probably spent most of his life as a travelling teacher, paying several visits to Athens, summed up his doubts as follows: 'Concerning the gods I am unable to discover whether they exist or not, or what they are like in form; for there are many hindrances to knowledge, the obscurity of the subject and the brevity of human life' (translation: W. Guthrie). Protagoras' response to this uncertainty was to proclaim, in a famous outburst of optimistic humanism, 'Man is the measure of all things.' It could be taken as the slogan of democratic Athens.

Other sophists went further. Prodicus suggested that the gods originated in man's experience of nature. They had been created as personifications of natural phenomena such as the sun and the moon, rivers, water, and fire. The Athenian poet Critias, in a fragment preserved from his play *Sisyphus*, developed the theme. 'I believe', he argued, 'that a man of shrewd and subtle mind invented for men the fear of the gods, so that there might be something to frighten the wicked even if they acted, spoke or thought in secret.' (Translation: R. Muir.) In other words, the gods were purely a human creation, designed to keep men in order.

By the end of the century, however, free thinking on religious matters was less tolerable. Optimism was not possible in an age of plague and military defeat, one which saw the destruction of the Athenian expedition to Sicily in 413 and the defeat of Athens by Sparta in 404. It was natural for conservatives to see these disasters as the revenge of the gods on those who had slighted them. Already, in the 430s, a decree of the Assembly had allowed public prosecution of both those who did not admit the practice of religion and those who taught rational theories about the heavens. Protagoras was forced to flee Athens and was drowned on his way to Sicily.

Socrates

The central character in *The Clouds* was none other than Athens' most celebrated contemporary philosopher, Socrates. (Since he did not charge for his teaching he cannot strictly be called a sophist, although Aristophanes was happy to brand him as one.) Socrates was born in Athens in 470 BC and had spent almost all his life in the city, although he seems to have served as a hoplite on occasions in the Peloponnesian War. He played virtually no part in politics, claiming that to have done so would have compromised his principles. He was clearly a rather isolated, self-centred figure, capable of withdrawing from all human contact (there is one story that he once stood motionless and lost in thought for twenty-four hours) and for this reason vulnerable in a city where public participation was so highly valued.

Socrates himself wrote nothing and there are three main sources for his ideas. The first, Aristophanes' portrayal in *The Clouds*, is probably distorted by the demands of the comedy, although some have seen its references in the play to Socrates' interests in private religious cults as valid. The historian Xenophon provided some *Memorabilia* which arose from direct personal contact with Socrates and which contain a narrative with some verbatim extracts from Socrates' trial but by far the most important source, and virtually the only one for Socrates' philosophy, is Plato. Although the range of material is rich and wide-ranging, it too has its limitations. Plato was forty-five years younger than Socrates and only knew him in the closing years of a long life. Socrates is always allowed to speak directly, but it is often difficult to distinguish what are Socrates' own thoughts and what are Plato's. (Plato's works are termed 'Dialogues' because Plato records conversations in which Socrates is usually the dominating speaker. They are conventionally divided into three groups, the Early, Middle, and Late Dialogues. Socrates appears in almost every one of the Dialogues but it is assumed that Plato's views predominate in the Middle and Late Dialogues and that Plato has moved away from any historical portrayal of Socrates.)

For Plato Socrates was a hero. He is presented as someone who lives for philosophy itself, searching for the truth without any regard for material gain, in the end dying for his beliefs. These beliefs centre on the human soul and its search for 'the good'. The soul is not just a disembodied spirit, argues Socrates, it is the character of a person, an integral part of his personality. It can be corrupted by the glamour of the world and has to discover for itself that there is something called 'the good' which can be grasped through the use of reason. Once 'the good' has been found the soul will recognize and be naturally attracted to it. In effect Socrates was shifting the attentions of philosophy away from attempts to understand only the physical world towards something very different, individual self-discovery. This was a new start in the history of philosophy, and in recognition of this all earlier thinkers are conventionally described as 'pre-Socratic'.

The first step to finding 'the good' is to recognize the limitations of one's present life, and this means examining the conventions by which it is lived. ('An unexamined life is not worth living' is perhaps the most famous of Socrates' statements.) In the typical Socratic dialogue, Socrates allows the person he is talking to to express a view, about bravery or friendship, for instance. Socrates then breaks down the statement, showing how one example of friendship is inadequate as a means of understanding the essence of what friendship means. In one dialogue Socrates talks with the general Laches in an attempt to define bravery:

SOCRATES (*to* LACHES). I wanted to get your opinion not only of bravery in the hoplite line, but also in cavalry engagements and in all forms of fighting; and indeed of bravery not only in fighting but also at sea, and in the face of illness and poverty and public affairs. And there is bravery not only in face of pain and fear, but also of desire and pleasure, both fearsome to fight against whether by attack or retreat—for some men are brave in all these encounters, aren't they, Laches?

LACHES. Yes, certainly.

SOCRATES. Then all these are examples of bravery, only some men show it in pleasure, some in pain, some in desire, some in danger. And there are others who show cowardice in the same circumstances.

LACHES. Yes.

SOCRATES. Now what I want to know was just what each of these two qualities is. So try again and tell me first, what is this common characteristic of courage which they all share? Do you understand now what I mean?

Laches. I am afraid I don't.

(Translation: Desmond Lee)

Socrates assumes that there is a concept, 'bravery', which is somehow there waiting to be discovered by reason. Discovery would lead to there being real knowledge of what bravery is, at a level beyond that held in the opinions of ordinary men in the sense that the knowledge could be defended rationally. However, in the Dialogues Socrates seldom reaches this point. Socrates even suggests that it is not his job to provide this kind of knowledge. It has to be discovered by the individual for himself. (It could not, therefore, be taught.) In the *Theaetetus* he is recorded as follows: 'I cannot myself give birth to wisdom, and the criticism which has so often been made of me, that though I ask questions of others I have no contribution to make myself because I have no wisdom in me, is quite true.' On another occasion Socrates said that his wisdom lay in the fact that he was the only man who fully realized his ignorance.

It is clear from this that the experience of meeting Socrates must have been both inspiring and frustrating. Here is the portrait given in Plato's *Symposium* by a drunken Alcibiades:

When I listen to him, my heart pounds ... it's a sort of frenzy ... possessed ... and the tears stream out of me at what he says. And I can see a lot of other people that he's had just the same effect on. I've heard Pericles, I've heard plenty more good speakers, and I thought they did pretty well, but they never had an effect like this on me. My soul wasn't turned upside down by them and it didn't suffer from the feeling that I'm dirt. But that's the feeling I get from him and I know very well, at this moment, if I were prepared to lend him my ears, I couldn't hold out, he makes me admit that when there's so much I need, I don't look after myself.   (Translation: Kenneth Dover)

It was probably inevitable that Socrates would get into trouble in the deeply unsettled times of the late fifth century. In 403 the democrats had just regained the initiative in the city (after the rule of the Thirty Tyrants) and their suspicions of Socrates rested partly on his association with discredited aristocrats such as

Alcibiades. Socrates made it quite clear that he regarded popular opinion as something inferior to the reasoned findings of intellectuals. However much he professed that he himself was ignorant, the charge of intellectual elitism was bound to stick. The actual charges of 'corrupting the young' and 'neglect of the gods whom the city worships' brought by a number of his enemies in 399 may have been trumped-up ones but they reflected the uneasiness of a city where communal values continued to be strongly valued and religious sensitivities remained acute. It is certainly possible that Socrates had dabbled in private cults at a time when it was unwise to do so.

At his trial Socrates appears to have been in no mood to compromise and, in Plato's account, the *Apology*, he put his case clearly and consistently but seems only to have aroused greater anger among his listeners. He simply refused to play according to the conventions suggesting he had a mission to undermine the misguided thoughts of others and might even be supported by the city (with free meals for life!) for his efforts. (There is another tradition that Socrates said little at his trial.) The guilty verdict (apparently by 280 votes to 220) did not necessarily mean a death penalty but Socrates' refusal to suggest an alternative eventually made it inevitable. According to Plato, Socrates met his end calmly, sharing his thoughts while the hemlock steadily spread through his body (although death by hemlock was in reality painful). Plato's accounts of his last days (the *Phaedo*) have left one of the most enduring images of western cultural and political history. As the American journalist I. F. Stone suggests in his *Trial of Socrates* (London, 1988) the issues involved, community versus the individual, 'truth' and knowledge versus popular opinion, continue to 'torment' (Stone's word) the liberal conscience, although Stone himself argues that Socrates was elitist and an enemy to democracy.

Plato

The problem left by Socrates was whether the concepts he was discussing—bravery, goodness, friendship, beauty among them—could ever be defined to the satisfaction of all. This challenge was taken up by his admirer Plato (428–347 BC). Plato's background was aristocratic. It is unfair to suggest that this alone conditioned his philosophy, but he remained thoroughly unconvinced by his experience of democracy, especially as in his youth democratic rule was associated with the humiliation of his native Athens at the hands of Sparta. The trial of Socrates appears to have marked a turning point for him. Democracy for Plato was synonymous with mob rule, with decisions taken for purely emotional or mercenary motives. Furthermore, the practice of democracy implied that moral and political values were relative, subject to the atmosphere of the moment. Plato was convinced that a better foundation could be found for knowledge if absolutes, of justice and goodness, for instance, could be established, against which any specific policy could be judged. The problem lay in defining where these absolutes might exist and how they could be approached by the human mind.

A solution is explored in a famous passage in a 'Middle' Dialogue, *Meno*, where Socrates guides a slave boy, a symbol of someone with no formal learning, through a geometrical proof concerning the area of a square (a proof to show that when the length of a square's sides are doubled it quadruples in area). The slave is led inexorably onwards by Socrates through the argument towards an inevitable conclusion. The point Socrates/Plato wants to make is that the truths about the area of the square exist eternally. Each soul (Plato believed that the soul existed eternally) in fact once knew them, and the process which the slave boy has been taken through is primarily one of recollection of what has been forgotten.

Plato goes on to argue that it is not only mathematical proofs which exist to be 'recollected' in this way. Many other concepts—beauty, bravery, goodness, for instance—exist as eternal entities available to be comprehended through reason. The term Plato uses is normally translated as Form or Idea—the Form of Beauty or Bravery, for instance. Each Form can only be grasped after a long period of reflection on its nature (going through a process such as Socrates followed, meditating on every aspect of the Form chosen until its essence is defined). The Forms exist as a hierarchy, with some easier to grasp than others and with the Form of 'the good' at the apex. In his famous analogy of the prisoners in the cave (from *The Republic*), Plato has his freed prisoners first being able to see reflections of objects in water, then the objects themselves, then the stars, and finally the sun ('the good') as they progress in the use of rational thought.

The goal of the philosopher is, therefore, to understand the Forms. As the Forms are entities which exist completely independently of the human mind, they are in fact an enduring 'reality' in contrast to the transient world perceived by the senses, those few who do understand them correctly must agree on what they consist of. The Form of 'the good' will mean exactly the same to all those whose reason penetrates its meaning. Plato has moved on from Socrates' view that the goal of life is self-discovery. The Forms exist beyond the individual, and any knowledge an individual thinks he has which does not conform to a Form is by definition flawed. ('We shall approach astronomy, as we do geometry, by way of problems, *and ignore what is in the sky* [my italics], if we are to get a real grasp of astronomy,' Plato wrote in *The Republic*.)

There are many questions about the Forms which Plato leaves unresolved. This is partly because the concept is used in several different Dialogues, in a variety of contexts and to deal with different problems. Most of the Forms Plato mentions are 'good' ones, Beauty, Courage, and so on. He does not state whether there are Forms of Ugliness, Cowardice, and Evil. (In his so-called *Seventh Letter* Plato suggests that there might be Forms 'of shapes and surfaces, of the good, the beautiful, the just, of all bodies natural and artificial, of fire and water and the like, of every animal, of every quality of character, of all actions and passivities'.) Nor is it clear whether there can be Forms of physical objects, such as beds or tables. Can there be a perfect table which contains the features of all other tables in some ideal form? Some concepts are difficult to imagine as Forms, Largeness, for instance. Could a Form of Largeness be anything more than something of infinite size? Some scholars even argue that Plato came to realize that these problems were insoluble and in his later work abandoned the idea of Forms altogether.

In the best known of his Middle Dialogues, *The Republic*, Plato goes on to show how understanding of the Forms can be used to construct an ideal state. He starts from the premiss that the happiness of the individual is dependent on the happiness of the *polis*. The individual, in other words, is seen as incapable of having true happiness in his own right but only as a member of a wider community. The purpose of the community is to embody key concepts of good government such as justice and goodness. These can only be based on an understanding of the Forms. However, since only a few individuals have the intellectual ability and leisure to grasp the Forms, government must be given to them alone. Plato is turning his back on democracy, which he famously described as like a ship without a captain, and arguing for some form of rule by an elite instead.

Where did this leave the rest of the population? Plato divided them into classes, by analogy with the concept he held of the soul. For Plato, as for Socrates, the soul was something eternal existing on a different plane from the body. It had three elements: the capacity for reason, its spirit (the force which motivated it), and appetites. (The problem of whether the soul or mind can be split in this sense, a concept central to the work of Freud, continues as a major issue in philosophy.) For anyone seeking to grasp the nature of the Forms, the power of reason should gradually come to predominate over spirit and appetite. Society could similarly be divided into men of reason, the philosophers, men of spirit, to whom was given the role of soldiers, and the rest, those, prey to their appetites, who remained at the level of labourers. In the *Phaedo* Plato speaks scornfully of 'the lovers of spectacles and sounds, who delight in fine voices and colours and shapes . . . but their minds are incapable of seeing and delighting in the nature of the Beautiful itself'.

Philosophers-to-be, who could be men or women, were to be selected at an early age from those of spirit. They were first to be put through a regime of physical training and instruction in the arts to mould their character. Mathematics came next, and later a training in dialectics so that a young philosopher would be able to defend the Forms to others once he or she had grasped them. The process was a long one. Not until the age of 35 would the trainees be allowed to serve the state, and the peak of understanding of the Forms would not be reached before the age of 50.

Plato said relatively little in *The Republic* about the nature of the state which would finally emerge. It would appear to be joyless and authoritarian. Good government must not be swayed by emotion, so poetry and music are forbidden. Children are to be held in common. Sex life is to be limited, with an emphasis on eugenic breeding. The rulers must expect no gain from their position other than the satisfaction they obtain from establishing and enforcing truth. Politics, in the sense of debates between different power groups over the direction of the state, simply have no relevance (since once the Forms of Justice or Bravery, for instance, have been grasped there can be no further argument about their nature).

Plato's republic was an ideal. It seemed very far from any possible actual state, as Plato found to his cost on the only occasion he intervened in politics. He had travelled to Sicily about 388, possibly to learn more about Pythagoras from the Pythagorean communities which still existed in southern Italy. (The idea of a philosophical community fascinated Plato and inspired his own Academy in Athens.) He had met and was deeply attracted to Dion, the brother-in-law of the ruler of Syracuse, Dionysius. Dion absorbed Plato's philosophy, and some twenty years later when Dionysius' son, Dionysius II, succeeded as ruler as a young man, Dion plotted to mould him into a philosopher king on the Platonic model. Plato, now in his sixties, returned to Sicily, but Dionysius was not prepared to play along with his ideals and both Dion and Plato were forced to flee. In one of his last works, *The Laws*, Plato finally sets out a constitution. Many of its requirements are severe: strict chastity, constant supervision of children, a ban on all homosexuality. It reflects Plato's continuing pessimism about human nature, one doubtless reinforced by his experiences in Sicily.

Western philosophy, wrote the mathematician and philosopher Alfred Whitehead, 'consists of a series of footnotes to Plato'. Certainly Plato's legacy is a profound one. All those who believe that there is a reality beyond the physical world which embodies value, a view which entered Christianity via the Neoplatonists and St Augustine (see Chapter 30), fall within the Platonic tradition. Those who do not see any evidence of such a reality fall outside it. It is a crucial divide and it mirrors the divide between those who accept the possibility of moral absolutes and those who do not. The legacy of Plato in Christian theology has been especially important. As will be seen, Platonism was the most popular philosophy in the early Christian centuries and was there at hand as Christian theology developed. Once truths about the Christian faith were consolidated in the fourth century they were assumed to be, like Plato's Forms, unchallengeable. Plato's theory of the soul in which the reasoning part of the soul was under continual threat from the more sensual parts underpinned asceticism and even opulent church building was defended on the grounds that it gave an image on earth of what 'true' beauty might be in the world beyond.

The legacy of Plato so far as political thought is concerned is, inevitably, controversial, 'What is our ultimate aim? The peaceful enjoyment of liberty and equality; the reign of eternal justice, whose laws are engraved, not in marble or stone, but in the hearts of all men, even in that of the slave who forgets them [compare *Meno*] and of the tyrant who rejects them.' This statement appears to be set well in the Platonic tradition. It is, in fact, a speech of Maximilien Robespierre made at the height of the French Revolution, a speech which goes on to justify terror against all those who oppose the establishment of a Republic of Virtue. As Karl Popper has argued in his *The Open Society and its Enemies*, Plato represents a direct threat to the democratic tradition, and any ruling elite which claims that it has the right to impose its own ideals on society is his heir.

This is perhaps too harsh. Certainly Platonism can lead to dictatorship, but it can also lead to a critique of dictatorship. In a state where the majority support genocide in the name, for instance, of establishing racial purity, how are alternative values to be developed and justified other than through a rational understanding of abstract concepts such as justice and human rights? Are there not fundamental values which need to be preserved against the momentary enthusiasm of popular assemblies? (The US Constitution with its enshrined Bill of Rights accepts that there are.) In education, does a disciplined introduction to effective ways of thinking achieve more than one based on undirected creative thought? It would be arrogant, and naive, to believe that liberal democracy has solved all the problems of human existence, and to that extent Plato deserves his continuing influence in political and moral thought. It is also important to remember that he established a method of argument, the dialectic.

One of the enduring legacies of Plato was his Academy. It took its name from a nearby grove dedicated to a hero Academus (now replanted in a suburb of Athens), and Plato founded it after his return from his first visit to Sicily in the 380s. It was always a rather exclusive club, but was open to young men from throughout the Greek world, who, presumably, had to show some aptitude and commitment to philosophy before they were accepted as students. In 367 an 18-year-old from Stageira in Macedonia arrived to participate in the Academy's studies. He was the son of a doctor and had probably already picked up some medical skills of observation and possibly dissection. He also appears to have had some wealth, presumably from family land, and anecdotes suggest that despite being fragile in appearance he enjoyed dressing well. His name, one of the most celebrated in the history of science and philosophy, was Aristotle.

Aristotle

Aristotle was to stay with Plato for twenty years, although virtually nothing of this period survives in his work. It is assumed that he absorbed many of the

Platonic ideals, and he never lost the belief that rational thought was the supreme intellectual activity. However, his mind was too vigorous and wide ranging ever to be confined to mere discipleship. His instincts were different from Plato's. While Plato was always concerned with what could be discovered beyond physical reality, Aristotle was fascinated by what could actually be seen in the real world, especially what could be learnt from observation. Raphael's fresco *The School of Athens* (painted AD 1510–11) in the Vatican shows the contrast well. Plato is depicted looking heavenwards, Aristotle with his eyes towards the ground.

In 347 Aristotle left Athens, possibly after he had become dissatisfied with the teachings of the Platonic school. He spent some years teaching and researching along the Ionian coast before being summoned back by Philip of Macedon to tutor Philip's 13-year-old son, Alexander. The relationship between two of the most formidable men of the fourth century seems to have left no lasting impact on either of them. After three years Aristotle returned to his native town, Stageira, and from there, in 335, he returned to Athens. Here he founded his own school, the Lyceum. It can be seen as the world's first research institute, and the range and quality of its scientific work was only to be challenged in the ancient world by the schools of Alexandria. In 323 another outburst of anti-Macedonian feeling on the death of Alexander forced Aristotle out of Athens to Euboea, and here he died in 322, aged 62.

The range of Aristotle's work is extraordinary. While he is remembered above all for his contribution to logic and his founding of zoology as a discipline, his surviving works cover almost every aspect of knowledge. There are works on language, the arts, ethics, politics, and law. In the sciences he wrote on zoology, biology, astronomy, chemistry, and physics. He grappled with the major philosophical problems of change and causation, time, space, and continuity. In addition to his system of logic, he ranged over metaphysics and the theory of knowledge. (The word 'metaphysics' was born because the book containing Aristotle's researches on reality and the meaning of existence was placed after (Greek *meta*) the book on physics in an early edition of his works.) He clarified and defined different areas of knowledge, separating the theoretical such as mathematics and metaphysics, whose main purpose was to find truth, from the practical, ethics and politics, and the productive, those concerned with making things.

One of Aristotle's attractive qualities was that he saw himself as part of a continuing intellectual tradition. When dealing with a particular issue he first brought together all previous contributions on the subject (this is why so much of the ideas of the pre-Socratics has survived) and concentrated on the problems they left unsolved. In contrast to Plato he did not try to fit solutions into some general preconceived framework but worried away at them as he found them, never assuming there were easy answers. (In his *Aristotelian Explorations*

(Cambridge, 1996), Geoffrey Lloyd shows the ingenuity and open-mindedness Aristotle brought to such problems as finding a distinction between plants and animals when presented with sponges, jellyfish, sea anemones, and razor shells!) He also appears to be more sympathetic to public opinion. As a result there is often something provisional and speculative about his surviving works which makes them harder to read and understand than Plato's. In fact, many of his books may have been no more than notes for his lectures which he would have expanded as he talked (or notes taken by others as he spoke).

Reasoning had been an essential part of early Greek philosophy. In the hands of Parmenides and Plato it had been elevated to the supreme way of finding the truth. However, there had been no systematic thought on what makes a valid argument and, without this, progress in mathematics and science in particular would always be restricted. It was one of Aristotle's greatest achievements that he penetrated the problem and produced a system of logic which was to last unchallenged for almost 2,000 years. Its beauty and its authority lay in its simplicity.

First, Aristotle argued that the foundations of knowledge depend on propositions, statements on which all can agree. A proposition is made up of a subject, say 'cats', and a predicate which says something about the subject, say 'four feet'. The proposition then reads 'Cats have four feet'. There are other possibilities: 'No cats have five feet', 'Some cats are black', 'Some cats are not black'. Aristotle argued that almost every statement can be broken down into simple propositions such as this. (Later philosophers have found this too simplistic an approach.)

Once these propositions have been sorted out, they can be generalized by replacing the subject and predicate by letters: 'All As are B' or 'Some Cs are D', for instance. These propositions can then be used in a wide variety of situations, whichever the philosopher wants to work with. The next step, taken in Aristotle's *Prior Analytics*, is to examine how propositions can be used as the basis for deductions. One has to start with two propositions. Take 'A is a B' and 'All Bs are C'. It follows logically that A is a C. (To put in an actual example: 'Socrates is a man. All men are mortal. Thus Socrates is mortal.') This is an example of what Aristotle called a syllogism. 'A *sullogismus*', he wrote, 'is an argument in which certain things being assumed, something different from the things assumed follows from necessity by the fact that they hold.' In the *Prior Analytics* Aristotle went on to look at the instances where logical deductions cannot be made. ('A cat has four feet. A dog has four feet. Therefore a dog is a cat' does not follow logically, for instance, and the student in elementary logic has to sort out why.)

Aristotle's contributions in zoology were also to last over 2,000 years. Most of the fieldwork for his *Zoological Researches* was done while he was in Asia. It was a formidable work, bringing together observations of animals as varied as hyenas, elephants, sheep, and mice. Close examination was supplemented by dissection. When Aristotle wanted to understand the evolution of a chick embryo, he found a hen's clutch and then removed an egg each day, comparing the difference in the development of each. Sometimes Aristotle made mistakes, at other times he relied on inaccurate hearsay, but as a total enterprise the *Researches* is formidable. It remains, however, a compilation of material. Aristotle never created his own experiments to further his understanding of animals. He believed that the essence of an animal could only be grasped if it were seen in its natural habitat.

Aristotle was, in fact, primarily an empiricist. He liked collecting and interpreting facts about the physical world as it existed and could be seen around him. He asked what could actually be said about a physical object. Taking a chair, for instance, what exactly is it? Aristotle said that a proper analysis would not only consider what it was made of (wood, perhaps) and what particular shape it had to take to be classified as a chair, but who made it and what its purpose was. He distinguished between the essential attributes of a chair (without which it could not be a chair) and incidental qualities such as the colour it was painted. Here again he broke with Plato. Suppose the chair was painted white. For Plato whiteness might be a Form, existing eternally. Aristotle took a more down-to-earth view. Whiteness was a quality of a particular chair and it did not exist as something independent of that chair. It depended on the chair for its being. (Similarly the soul was an intrinsic part of the human being, as embedded in it as the impression a stamp has made on a piece of wax. This was in contrast to Plato's view that the soul was like a sailor on a ship, they worked together but one could be withdrawn from the other without the essence of either being destroyed.)

As this example suggests, Aristotle always went beyond mere observation. He does not just describe a chair, he is interested in the philosophical problems surrounding it in its existence as a chair. How, for instance, could a chair change into something else and what is the process involved? Is the capacity for change inherent in an object or does it need some outside force to initiate it? What is the cause of the chair being a chair? When looking at living animals he was fascinated by the problem of why they had the physical attributes they did. Why does a duck have webbed feet? Aristotle argued that it was because it had a role, that of being a duck, and the webbed feet were essential to fulfilling this role. The most important attribute of a human being was his ability to think rationally and so the highest state of being human was to develop this faculty to its fullest extent. Aristotle seems to be suggesting that there is an underlying purpose to nature, that of the self-fulfilment of every living being through the correct use of the attributes it possesses.

It was inevitable that Aristotle would have a great deal to say about the particular nature of man and his role on earth, and he made important studies both in ethics and politics. As has been suggested above, Aristotle saw the development of reason as the supreme goal of human existence. However, unlike Plato, Aristotle never establishes precisely how reason is to be used. In some way it was associated with the achievement of moral excellence, but in his *Ethics*

Aristotle argues that goodness cannot be achieved through reason alone. Rather a person becomes good by the disposition of goodness being trained into him as a child. Once this disposition has been gained and a person grows up oriented towards doing good, then the everyday doing of good depends on circumstances around him. Here reasoning appears to play a part in establishing the situations in which good actions are appropriate. The end result is a character which does good within a rationally integrated framework of ethical behaviour. The highest state, that all human beings should aim for, is *eudaimonia*, happiness, based on exercising one's reasoning to its fullest extent in the pursuit of moral excellence.

It is not enough for each individual to take on the search alone. 'Man', said Aristotle, in one of his more famous statements, 'is a social animal' (or 'political animal' as the phrase is often translated). Part of *eudaimonia* lies in living in harmony with those around one. Aristotle the empiricist was well aware of the political problems of the Greek city states. He compiled an account of 158 different constitutions, for instance. Insofar as he favoured one form of government it was democracy, but only in the restricted sense of government being open on equal terms to those with wealth and property. Aristotle shared the traditional contempt of the Greek for manual labour and trade, and those who indulged in them would have no part to play in government. He had no interest in the rights of women and defended slavery (see the quotation on p. 225). The goal was to establish *eudaimonia* for the city and this was to be achieved through the power of state with a particular focus on the education of the young. 'We should not think', writes Aristotle, 'that each of the citizens belongs to himself, rather that they all belong to the State', and again, in the *Politics*, 'whatever the majority [of the participating citizens] decides is final and constitutes justice.' There is no room here for human rights in the modern sense of the term.

As Aristotle's views on women and slaves show, he was in many ways a creature of his time. His views were conventional in other ways. He followed Empedocles in believing that the physical world was made up of four elements, fire, water, earth, and air, something he could never have established if he had relied on his own observations. (Aristotle did, however, modify Empedocles' views by suggesting that each element was affected by opposites of hot and cold and dry and wet contained within it.) He adopted the conventional view that the earth was the centre of the universe. As Geoffrey Lloyd has argued, he often started with a hypothesis and then shaped observations to prove it. Aristotle was not a truly original thinker in the sense of digging down to bedrock and building from there. However, the scale of his work was prodigious. He initiated the first enquiry into the natural sciences which ranged over the whole spectrum of the physical world. Even when he did not provide clear answers he was never afraid to pose the key questions about the existence and purpose of matter.

Aristotle's influence was profound not only in the western but also in the Islamic world. Between the twelfth and fifteenth centuries his scientific work dominated medieval Europe, largely through the translations of his works into Latin from Arab philosophers who had respected and preserved them and their championing within the Roman Catholic tradition by Thomas Aquinas. As with so many other great Greek thinkers, however, his work became frozen as impeachable authority which was used to uphold Catholic teaching. His power as an innovator was forgotten and it is ironic that by the seventeenth century when his science was challenged he was seen as an enemy of reason! A gradual erosion of his importance as a physicist followed. The rise of experimentation and a new emphasis on the use of mathematics in the seventeenth century challenged other aspects of his work, but his achievements in zoology remained influential until the nineteenth, as did his system of logic. Despite his shortcomings, Aristotle remains a key, perhaps the key, figure in the history of science and his reputation has revived in recent years.

By 330 BC, therefore, the Greeks had undertaken a revolution in ways of thinking. It is still easy to underestimate the revolutionary nature of what they had done. In his *The Unnatural Nature of Science*, Lewis Wolpert has convincingly argued that there is nothing obvious about looking at the world in a scientific way. All the incentives are to try and make the world work on a day-to-day basis without speculating on its wider nature. It required a particularly combative form of mind to break through the limits of conventional thinking. Whether born in the law courts, the assemblies, or elsewhere, this is what the Greeks provided.

Equally, however, it is important not to take advantage of hindsight to overestimate the effect of the philosophers on everyday life. Their influence outside the circles of their own admirers was bound to be limited. Rational thinking did not suddenly displace the irrational. As E. R. Dodds argued in a famous book, *The Greeks and the Irrational* (Berkeley, 1951) Greeks continued to behave 'irrationally' in everyday life, maintaining traditional religious practices, for instance. One reason for this was that Greek science and philosophy did not bring any noticeable improvements to life. People were not suddenly cured in their thousands by Greek physicians. No one suggested any better ways of growing crops or could improve the climate or soil. There was thus no incentive for Greeks to abandon their traditional relationships with the gods. In the fourth century there is evidence that temples (that to Asclepius at Epidaurus for instance) were actually claiming better results in healing than the 'scientific' doctors.

It is sometimes argued that the Greeks introduced rational ways of thinking which deadened the natural senses, depriving human beings of access to their emotions. This chapter has shown that in Athens at least this was not so. Plato may have insisted on the importance of reason, but in the same period the playwright Euripides was exploring the forces of unreason in his play *The Bacchae*. The achievements of the Greeks lay in making brilliant contributions to the understanding of both the rational and irrational aspects of human consciousness. (The Greeks themselves distinguished *logoi* (singular *logos*) rational accounts written in prose from *mythoi*, stories, myths and legends which were not intended to express rational truth and which were normally expressed in verse.) It is doubtful whether these breakthroughs could have taken place in a city which did not enjoy the combative and competitive atmosphere of fifth- and fourth-century Athens.

The western intellectual tradition could be said to be founded on the dual legacy of Plato and Aristotle. As Richard Tarnas puts it in his *The Passion of the Western Mind* (New York, 1991; London, 1996):

> The constant interplay of these two partly complementary and partly antithetical sets of principles [Platonism and Aristotelianism] established a profound inner tension within the Greek inheritance, which provided the Western mind with the intellectual basis, at once unstable and highly creative, for what was to become an extremely dynamic evolution lasting over two and a half millennia. The secular scepticism of the one stream and the metaphysical idealism of the other provided a crucial counterbalance to each other, each undermining the other's tendency to crystallise into dogmatism, yet the two in combination eliciting new and fertile intellectual possibilities.

Further Reading

T. Webster, *Athenian Culture and Society* (London, 1973), provides a stimulating overview of cultural life in Athens. For the origins of drama see W. Connor, 'City Dionysia and Athenian Democracy', in J. R. Sears (ed.), *Aspects of Athenian Democracy* (Copenhagen, 1990). For Greek tragedy see P. Easterling (ed.), *The Cambridge Companion to Greek Tragedy* (Cambridge, 1997), and S. Goldhill, *Reading Greek Tragedy* (Cambridge, 1986). T. G. Rosenmeyer's chapter in Moses Finlay (ed.), *The Legacy of Greece* (Oxford, 1984) is also good. For details of each play see Albin Lesky, *Greek Tragic Poetry* (New Haven, 1983). On individual playwrights: J. Herington, *Aeschylus* (New Haven, 1986); Bernard Knox, *The Heroic Temper: Studies in Sophoclean Tragedy* (Berkeley, 1966); and K. Dover, *Aristophanic Comedy* (London, 1972).

On philosophy: Terence Irwin, *Classical Thought* (Oxford, 1989) and the chapter on philosophy by Bernard Williams in *The Legacy of Greece*. For more advanced work there is W. K. C. Guthrie, *A History of Greek Philosophy* (Cambridge, 1962–81); the excellent Karsten Johansen, *A History of Ancient Philosophy: From the Beginnings to Augustine* (London, 1998); and J. Brunschwig and G. E. R. Lloyd (eds.), *Greek Thought: A Guide to Classical Knowledge* (Cambridge, Mass., 2000); Richard Buxton (ed.), *From Myth to Reason? Studies in the Development of Greek Thought* (Oxford, 1999); R. Hankinson, *Cause and Explanation in Ancient Greek Thought* (Oxford, 1998). The stimulating Oxford Very Short Introductions now includes *Ancient Philosophy* (Julia Annas), *Socrates* (Christopher Taylor), *Plato* (Julia Annas), and *Aristotle* (Jonathan Barnes). On the Sophists G. Kerferd, *The Sophistic Movement* (Cambridge, 1981); James Coliaco, *Socrates against Athens* (London, 2001). I have found R. M. Hare on Plato and Jonathan Barnes on Aristotle (included with Henry Chadwick on Augustine in *Founders of Thought* (Oxford, 1991) but also available individually in the Past Masters series (both Oxford, 1982) excellent introductions. Jonathan Lear,

Aristotle: The Desire to Understand (Cambridge, 1988) is another excellent introduction. More extended treatment is to be found in *The Cambridge Companions*, to *Plato*, ed. R. Kraut (Cambridge, 1992) and to *Aristotle*, ed. J. Barnes (Cambridge, 1995). Karl Popper's *The Open Society and its Enemies* was first published in London in 1945 and reissued in 1995 (London). L. Wolpert, *The Unnatural Nature of Science* (London, 1992). Martha Nussbaum, *The Fragility of Goodness* (Cambridge, 1986), is a fascinating (and beautifully written) analysis of ethics in the context of drama and philosophy. Bernard Williams, *Shame and Necessity* (Berkeley, 1993), is another fine study of Greek ethics.

Rhetoric

Homer's heroes not only had to fight well, they had to speak well. It was the mark of the leader that he could persuade his followers to fight for him but, as Homer's own epics show, the art of the spoken word with its capacity not only to motivate but to entertain and enthuse ran deep in Greek society. Rhetoric, the art of public speaking, was intrinsic to Greek and later Roman political and intellectual life. As the Greek city states established their own assemblies new contexts for public speaking emerged. There were not only the political debates (the setting for the deliberative speech): as has been seen the law courts offered the chance for political struggles to be played out through charging and defending key figures for assumed crimes against the state (the forensic speech recognized as a different genre from the deliberative). Here there were juries to persuade. Then there were the more formal speeches—the most famous of which is Pericles' Funeral Speech in Athens in 431/430 (as recreated by Thucydides) in which he expounds the greatness of Athens. In the city festivals there are competitive speeches, some of them involving the recitation of set texts such as Homer's epics. In his exhaustive studies of the origins of Greek science, Geoffrey Lloyd, as has been seen, sees the struggle between speakers to persuade as fostering the growth of rational argument.

It is clear that even in democratic Athens, 'aristocrats' such as Pericles could still use their status as a means of getting heard but increasingly speaking could be seen as a skill to be learned. It was the Sicilian orator Gorgias, who arrived in Athens in 427 to plead the case of his native city Leontini, who showed the Athenians how an audience could be manipulated. 'Give me a theme', he called as he entered the theatre and then would argue whatever case he was given. He understood how the spoken word had an emotional power beyond its meaning and could be exploited to this end. As he put it in a speech he made on Helen of Troy, 'The power of a speech has the same relationship to the order of the soul as the order of drugs had to the nature of bodies. For just as different drugs expel different humours from the body and some put a stop to illness, others to life, so too some speeches cause pain, some pleasure, some fear, some induce confidence in the listeners, some drug and bewitch the soul with a certain bad persuasion.' This, however, was the problem. As the debates in the Athenian assembly over the treatment of Mytilene (427) or the generals accused of letting sailors drown after a battle (406) showed, assemblies were susceptible to emotional manipulation by 'skilled' or unscrupulous speakers. In his play *The Clouds*, Aristophanes sets up a debate between 'Just Speech' and 'Unjust Speech' in which the latter triumphs through verbal trickery.

So while rhetoric became, and remained for centuries, one of the most important parts of the curriculum, the Greeks recognized that it presented moral and philosophical challenges. In his description of the Mytilene Debate in his *The Peloponnesian War*, the historian Thucydides uses a speech by one Diodotus to stress the importance of thoughtful speaking:

Haste and anger are, to my mind, the two greatest obstacles to wise counsel—haste, that usually goes with folly, anger, that is the mark of primitive and narrow minds. And anyone who maintains that words cannot be a guide to action must be either a fool or one with some personal interest at stake: he is a fool if he imagines that it is possible to deal with the uncertainties of the future by any other medium, and he is personally interested if his aim is to persuade you into some disgraceful action, and knowing that he cannot make a good speech in a bad cause, he tries to frighten his opponents and his hearers by some goodsized pieces of misrepresentation . . . the good citizen, instead of trying to terrify the opposition, ought to prove his case in fair argument; and a wise state, without giving special honours to its best counsellors, will certainly not deprive them of the honour they already enjoy; and when a man's advice is not taken, he should not even be disgraced, far less penalised. (Translation: Rex Warner)

The most influential teacher of the the early fourth century, Isocrates, stressed the importance of a speaker's moral integrity. The speaker has a duty not only to develop his own character, so that he has the respect of his audience, but an understanding of the issues which he talks about:

One who wishes to persuade others will not be negligent of his own virtue but will pay special attention to it that he may get the finest reputation among his fellow citizens. Who does not know that words seem more true when spoken by those who lead good lives than by those whose lives have been criticised and that proofs based on a person's life have greater power than those provided by speech? The stronger a person desires to persuade hearers, the more he will work to be honourable and good and to have a good reputation among the citizens.

So rhetoric is not only a practical skill, it is the expression of the educated mind at its best. This was not enough for Isocrates' contemporary Plato. In his dialogue, *Gorgias*, in which, not surprisingly, Gorgias is resurrected to play a key role, rhetoric is denounced as a mere knack, in which truth is manipulated through the emotional force of oratory. It was left to Aristotle to produce what became the most famous work on the subject, *Rhetoric*. Aristotle was an orator himself so he is able to provide practical hints but he is more interested in the specific way in which rhetoric acts to persuade. 'There are three kinds of persuasive means furnished by the *logos*, those in the character of the speaker, those in how the speaker is disposed, and those in the *logos* itself, through its demonstrating or seeming to demonstrate.' One must not only learn how to speak, but reflect on what it means to speak well. As regards style, it is the speaker's duty to be clear, fitting to the occasion and not over ornate.

Rhetoric is, inevitably, shaped by the contexts in which it is needed and Athens provided the stimulus for some of the greatest orators of all time, among them Demosthenes, whose career will be outlined later. Demosthenes, however, provides a reminder of just how difficult a practical art effective rhetoric was. His early attempts at public speaking ended in humiliation and he had to train himself through placing pebbles in his mouth to achieve his clear diction. Yet rhetoric could persuade and inspire. At the end of his long life Isocrates himself was credited, in a speech addressed to Philip of Macedon, with providing the inspiration for the spread of Greek culture as a civilizing force for Asia.

If democracies need persuasive speakers, monarchies foster the formal panegyric, the speech of welcome or praise to a ruler which often takes a highly ritualized form. These emerge in the Hellenistic period. In republican Rome, on the other hand, there was once again an electorate to be swayed or, in the law courts, a jury to be convinced. Cicero was the master of Roman rhetoric, the first man to achieve political office on his skills as an orator rather than as a soldier. His *Philippics* (44–43 BC) are the last great set of deliberative speeches before the coming of the empire eclipses political oratory. This does not mean that the skill of public speaking disappears. It was too deeply entrenched in traditional education for this and its continuing value was the theme of Quintilian's *Institutio Oratoria* (c. AD 95), a work which maintained its influence not only in the Roman empire but when classical learning was revived during the Renaissance. By the second century AD, rhetoric reappears in Greece as part of the revival by Greeks of their traditional cultural skills, but also with the specific aim of representing cities before the emperor in the hope of gaining his patronage. (For this Second Sophistic see below, p. 512.) One of the most influential teachers from a later period was Menander of Laodicea (possibly the beginning of the fourth century) who laid out the conventions for a wide variety of speeches, including the correct way to address a city or an emperor (the panegyric). Yet another context was the sermon which in the hands of a master such as Ambrose of Milan or John Chrysostom in the late fourth century became a major tool in the creation of a Christian society. Augustine, himself, it is often forgotten, was the city orator in Milan before his conversion.

FURTHER READING

The best survey is George Kennedy, *A New History of Classical Rhetoric* (Princeton, 1994). See also Robert Wardy, *The Birth of Rhetoric* (London, 1996); I. Worthington (ed.), *Persuasion: Greek Rhetoric in Action* (London, 1994); and William Dominik (ed.), *Roman Eloquence, Rhetoric in Society and Literature* (London, 1997). There is also much of interest for the late empire in Sabine MacCormack, *Art and Ceremony in Late Antiquity* (Berkeley, 1981).

17 | The Struggle for Power, 431–338 BC

The Peloponnesian War began with the declaration of war by Sparta on Athens in 431 BC. (Technically, the war is the second Peloponnesian War—the first covers the fighting in the 450s and early 440s—and even this is somewhat of a misnomer as there were two distinct periods of war between 431 and 404.) Almost immediately Athens suffered a devastating blow when plague broke out. Its spread was aggravated by the large number of country-dwellers who had crowded into the city. It is possible that a quarter of the population died, including, a year later, Pericles himself, probably from an associated disease. This is perhaps the turning point in the history of Athens, the moment when the optimism expressed so confidently by Pericles begins to fade.

Thucydides

The full horror of the plague is detailed by the historian Thucydides (*c.*460–*c.*399), and it is he who provides the only full history of the war to survive. It is a magnificent one, one of the great intellectual achievements of the fifth century. Thucydides was born in Athens but his father's name suggests the family was Thracian in origin. He served in the war, but when, as a commanding general, he failed to save the important Athenian outpost at Amphipolis from capture by Sparta he was exiled. This gave him the opportunity to visit Sparta and to collect the material for his history while the war was still being fought. He completed the story to 411, dying himself some time after 404. The bulk of his book is therefore technically a documentary account rather than a history.

Thucydides writes vividly. Many of his descriptions of the war haunt the reader. (I can still remember, as a halting Greek scholar aged 14, the impact of my first reading of his description of the Sicilian expedition.) His account is so detailed and seemingly authoritative compared to any other that exists that it has set the image of the war for every later generation. Thucydides prides himself on his accuracy, deriding those such as Herodotus who used evidence too loosely. He tries to set out the chronology of the war year by year, in what is almost a scientific way, and with the expressed ambition to provide a narrative that would last. It is only recently that there has been serious critical analysis of Thucydides' approach (whether, for instance, his description of Pericles is not too flattering and that of Cleon too harsh, and whether the expedition to Sicily was quite such a turning point as he suggests). He shows no interest in the wider cultural and social background of the antagonists nor in the underlying economic realities which conditioned their reactions. Nevertheless, no account of the war at all would be possible without his account and it will continue to dominate the source material for the period as well as providing a compulsive read.

No historian, however detached, works without an ideological framework. Thucydides is very much a man of the fifth century. Man is the 'measure of all things', and the gods play no direct part in Thucydides' understanding of how the war happened and the course it followed. He takes it upon himself to penetrate the causes of the war and find the different levels at which antagonism between states was fostered. It is this fascination with the motivations of men, their fears, and the factors which shape decision-making that makes his work so much more than mere narrative.

Thucydides has no illusions about human behaviour. No one before and few after have detailed quite so vividly the appalling cruelty with which men can act when under stress. There is little in the history of the twentieth century which would have surprised him. He is particularly adept at showing how words are manipulated by those in power (and proves himself a worthy forerunner of George Orwell in this respect). In the famous debate he reports between the people of Melos, whom Athens was trying to force into her empire, and the Athenians in Book V of his *History*, he shows how the Athenians ruthlessly exploit their superior strength. 'You know as well as we do,' say the Athenian representatives to the hapless Melians, 'that when these matters are discussed by practical people, the standard of justice depends on the equality of power to compel and that in fact the strong do what they have to do and the weak accept what they have to accept.' (Translation: R. Warner.) Reality, suggests Thucydides, is structured by those who have power, an idea with enormous implications for philosophers and social scientists.

Thucydides' detached analysis of the war does not mean that he takes no moral stance. The famous Funeral Oration of Pericles, which extols the self-confidence of the Athenian state, is presented alongside his account of the plague, as if to suggest the fragility of its supremacy. Thucydides worries away at the arguments for and against the harsh treatment of rebels, those at Mytilene in 427 (see p. 253), for instance and his recorded speech of Diodotus (quoted above p. 295) is a paean to free speech. He may have dwelt on the ruthlessness of the Athenians at Melos in 416 (the men of Melos were all executed, their women and children enslaved) so that the Athenian disaster in Sicily which followed could be presented as their just deserts.

The Peloponnesian War (For the background to the war, see pp. 264–5.)

The fundamental problem of the war was how a naval power such as Athens could defeat land-locked Sparta and how Sparta, with no effective navy, could hope to capture the well-defended Athens. The first years of the war were marked by a series of ineffective raids on each other's territories. Spartan troops ravaged Attica almost every year (but could never actually storm the city itself, which, protected by its Long Walls, maintained open access to the sea). Athens launched raids on the Peloponnesian coast and one on Megara, an ally of Sparta's. Her hope was perhaps to stimulate the helots into revolt and destabilize Sparta's alliances. She also revived her old policy of the 450s and attempted to win control of the plains of Boeotia. The policy ended in failure after a decisive defeat at the hands of Thebes and her allies at Delium in 424.

In 425, however, the Athenians had a lucky break that ended the stalemate. They managed to capture a group of some 120 Spartans who had become stranded on the island of Sphacteria on the western coast of the Peloponnese when their supporting fleet had been destroyed by the Athenians. The shock effect of the Spartan capitulation was immense, not only on Sparta but on the Greek world. Traditionally Spartans died in battle rather than capitulate and the city's reputation was seriously damaged. Sparta was ready to surrender and would probably have done so immediately if a raid by a Spartan general Brasidas in 424–422 had not succeeded in capturing a number of Athenian cities along the Chalcidice peninsula and the northern Aegean, including the vital centre of Amphipolis. After an Athenian counter-attack saw the death of Brasidas, both sides were willing to come to terms. The Peace of Nicias was signed in 421 with each side agreeing to give up its gains. Amphipolis, however, chose to stay independent of Athens.

Sparta appeared, at first, the more vulnerable of the two states. Her manpower was in decline, one reason why the loss at Sphacteria was so significant, and her control over the Peloponnese seemed to be faltering. Her ally Corinth refused to sign the treaty when land she had lost was not included in it. Athens, under the influence of a persuasive young aristocrat, Alcibiades, now began interfering directly in the Peloponnese, making treaties of mutual defence with two important cities, Argos and Elis. (Elis oversaw the Olympic Games and even banned Spartan athletes from them in 420.) Alcibiades claimed later that his strategy was to force Sparta to counter-attack and risk losing everything in one battle. The battle came in 418, at Mantineia, but it was a crushing Spartan victory. It was to be another thirty years before the Peloponnesian cities risked confrontation with Sparta again.

Athens' hopes of direct control of the Peloponnese now seemed thwarted, and her next move was to launch an expedition to the west, to Sicily and southern

Italy, as a means of strengthening her position as a Mediterranean power. Her trading interests in the west were well established and there had been an earlier expedition to Sicily in 427. This new venture was largely the brainchild of Alcibiades. Alcibiades was a complex character, egocentric and ambitious, and shrewd enough to use his status as a successful competitor in the Olympic Games (he won the chariot race in 416) and his personal magnetism to manipulate the Assembly into support for the expedition. Thucydides considered his motives were largely personal ones, the desire to make his name as a military commander and to tap the wealth of the west for himself.

The problems involved in achieving and holding even a foothold in Sicily when the opposition of such wealthy and well-protected cities as Syracuse was bound to be aroused were immense. Yet such was the confidence of Athens that there was even talk of conquering the whole island. The conflicts between the Sicilian cities were exaggerated, hopes of a native Sicel uprising talked up, and the resources of one city, Segesta, who had agreed to support the Athenians, magnified. Shortly before the fleet sailed, however, the Herms, marble pillars bearing the head of the god Hermes and an erect phallus, which were used as boundary markers and signposts and whose phallic properties were a token of good luck, were mysteriously mutilated. The hysteria that resulted and the witch-hunt that followed in the effort to find the perpetrators shows that Athens remained a deeply superstitious city despite the intellectual revolutions of the fifth century. A number of aristocrats were rounded up (and Alcibiades himself later recalled from Sicily to face trial) but the matter was never satisfactorily explained. The city was left haunted by a sense of ill omen.

The story of the expedition is Thucydides' masterpiece and deserves to be read in his own words. His account starts with a magnificent description of the fleet of 134 triremes and 5,000 hoplites setting off to the west in 415. Once the fleet had arrived in Sicily, however, Segesta turned out to have few resources and it soon became clear that conflict with Syracuse was inevitable. There were three commanders, among them Alcibiades himself, and they disagreed as to whether to launch an immediate attack, delay until they had found more allies, or return home after making a show of strength. Alcibiades was then summoned home (to defend himself against a charge of 'profaning the mysteries'), but defected to Sparta instead. His loyalties to his home community turned out to be much shallower than those to himself. By then Athens was in direct conflict with Syracuse, and another of the commanders, Lamarchus, was killed in skirmishing around the city. Nicias, who was left in charge, was the commander least committed to direct confrontation with Syracuse, whose fine position, large resources, and well-defended harbour made her a formidable enemy.

In fact, there was a time when Athens might have triumphed. Her fleet gave her the initiative at sea and she captured Syracuse's harbour. The construction of siege walls around the city was put in hand. The morale of Syracuse was, however, transformed when a Spartan commander, Gylippus, managed to infiltrate a small force into the city. Athens lost her chance. Even though reinforcements arrived from home (bringing the total commitment to half of Athens' entire navy) a land attack failed. Eventually the decision was made to evacuate the harbour, whose entrance was now blocked by the Syracusan fleet.

In one of his most gripping passages Thucydides describes the emotional impact of this decisive battle as the Athenian hoplites waited to see if they would be saved:

As the struggle went on indecisively, the Athenian soldiers revealed the fear in their hearts by the swaying of their bodies; it was a time of agony for them, for escape or destruction seemed every moment just at hand. So long as the issue of the sea-battle was in doubt, you could have heard every kind of sound in one place, the Athenian camp: lamentation, shouting, 'We're winning!', 'We're losing!', all the cries wrung from a great army in great peril. The feelings of the men on the ships were much the same, until at last, when the battle had gone on for a long time, the Syracusans and their allies routed the Athenians and fell upon them, decisive winners, yelling and cheering, and chased them to the land. And then the Athenian sailors, as many of them as had not been captured afloat, beached their ships wherever they could and poured into the camp. The soldiers were not in two minds any more, but all with one impulse, groaning, wailing, lamenting the outcome of the battle, rallied—some of them close to the ships, others to guard the rest of their defensive wall, while the greater part of them began to think now about themselves, about how they were going to survive. (Translation: Kenneth Dover)

A final attempt to urge the Athenians to give battle again with their surviving ships was met with mutiny and the only option left was to escape overland. The description Thucydides gives is one of his most gripping and heart-rending. The dead were left unburied. The wounded, desperate at being left, dragged themselves after their comrades as they moved off, overcome themselves by their own shame of betrayal. The plight of the retreating army, without food and with continual harassment by Spartans and Syracusans, was horrific. When they came to water the hoplites were so thirsty they rushed forward to drink even though enemy missiles rained down on them. They lay in a stream drinking what was turning into a mess of mud and blood before the final surrender. The survivors were herded back to Syracuse and then imprisoned in appalling conditions in the quarries which surrounded the city.

There was no doubt that this was a catastrophe. Forty thousand men may have been lost as well as half the city's fleet. Athens' democracy came under severe strain, overthrown in 411 by an oligarchical government of Four Hundred who were in favour of making peace with Sparta. The empire was also in revolt. One rebel, Mytilene, was recaptured but the island of Chios had to be abandoned after a blockade which failed. In 411 Euboea revolted and joined Sparta. However, some historians, among them Simon Hornblower, argue that Thucydides inflated the importance of the Sicilian disaster, partly to create a literary impact. The fact is that Athens was able to continue the war. The Four Hundred were overthrown when they tried to make peace on behalf of Athens and replaced by a semi-democratic government of Five Thousand. The navy remained loyal to the democracy throughout and gradually new ships were built. Despite some defections, the empire survived largely intact. The will to resist remained amazingly strong.

Once again, however, it looked as if there would be deadlock with neither city able to deliver a deathblow to the other. Sparta, on the advice of Alcibiades, had set up a fortified base at Deceleia, halfway between Athens and her frontier with Boeotia, which meant that Spartan soldiers could dominate and ravage land in Attica all the year round. They could also lure slaves away from Athens, and 20,000 are recorded as escaping from the city, a severe drain on its human resources but not enough to defeat it. Somehow new resources had to be found to bring the conflict to an end.

The only major source was Persia, and in fact from the 420s both Athens and Sparta had been hoping to secure her support. The Athenians ruined their chances by unwisely backing two satraps who were in rebellion against the monarchy and, from 411, it was Sparta who gained the money to build and equip a fleet. In return the Spartans acquiesced in the achievement of Persia's main objective since the Persian Wars, the return of the Greek cities of Asia to her control. This was the end of any pretence that Sparta was fighting for the liberation of Greece.

The closing years of the war (411–404) saw the experienced Athenian fleet locked in conflict with the newer but better-resourced Spartan one. The ambition of Sparta was now to close off Athenian supplies of grain from the Hellespont. A Spartan fleet was there in 411 and managed to capture the city of Byzantium. The Athenians were not finished, however, and won two major victories in 411 and 410 and another at Arginusae (near Lesbos) in 406. Byzantium was regained in 408. In 410 the Spartans even sued for peace, but Athens refused to negotiate.

For Athens, however, a final victory remained elusive. The Spartans now always had enough resources to rebuild their fleet. In 405 the Spartans, under their commander Lysander, captured the town of Lampsachus in the Hellespont and were able to shelter their fleet in its harbour. The Athenian fleet arrived to challenge them but had to beach on the other side of the strait at Aigospotamae where there was no harbour. This left them dangerously exposed. They sailed out day after day to challenge the Spartans, who would not come out. Lysander noticed, however, that once the Athenian ships returned across the strait they were left on the beach unmanned. He launched a sudden attack achieving complete surprise. Out of Athens' fleet of 180 ships, 170 were captured. When the news reached Athens, a howl of despair spread up from the Piraeus to the city as the implications were realized. With the Hellespont now under Spartan control, Athens was starved and forced into surrender (404). The Long Walls were pulled down, the fleet reduced almost to nothing, and a Government of Thirty imposed on the city by the victorious Spartans. Against all expectations, Athens had actually been comprehensively defeated, even though the Spartans did not destroy the city completely, afraid perhaps of creating a power vacuum in the area.

Lysander

The question now was whether Sparta would be able to exploit her victory. For ten years after the defeat of Athens the dominant figure of Spartan politics was Lysander. Traditionally Sparta's military enterprises had been led by one of her kings. Lysander was an anomaly. Of good birth but poor, he manipulated his way to power, it was said, by ingratiating himself with the kings. Once in command, as 'admiral' in the Aegean, he exploited his power ruthlessly. He installed his own supporters as rulers in Aegean cities (including the Government of Thirty in Athens), built up a friendship with Cyrus, the Persian viceroy in Asia Minor, and even intervened as far afield as Syracuse, where he backed Dionysius I (see below), and Egypt. Most remarkable of all, he encouraged a cult worship of himself as 'hero', the first time this is known to have happened in Greece. In 398 he appears to have been instrumental in securing the succession of King Agesilaus to the Spartan throne, despite the latter's lameness which many had considered a bar to his appointment.

Lysander's position was always vulnerable, however. Sparta's support in the Aegean always remained limited. She had none of the advantages Athens had enjoyed in the 470s. She had no cultural or religious links with the Aegean world and showed no interest in developing any. In the eyes of many Greeks she had compromised herself by using Persian help so shamelessly. Lysander now involved himself further in Persian politics. In 402 he backed an attempt by Cyrus, whose brother Artaxerxes (ruled 404–359) had become king, to seize the Persian throne. It was a failure and Cyrus was killed. (The Greek army had to march back to the coast, an exploit recorded by the historian Xenophon in his *Anabasis*, the March of the Ten Thousand, one of the best adventure stories in Greek literature.) The failure was a major blow for Lysander. His credibility was destroyed and Sparta lost its Persian subsidies. In 396 Agesilaus showed that he was his own man, and not just the creation of Lysander, by initiating an expedition to liberate the Greek cities of Asia from Persian rule.

The Corinthian War

The Persians now took the initiative in the Aegean. They stimulated a revolt against Sparta by Thebes and Corinth, former allies of Sparta's who had been dissatisfied by the outcome of the Peloponnesian War, from which they had gained nothing. This was the so-called Corinthian War (395–386). On land it was a series of inconclusive battles. Lysander died in one of the first in 395. (It was said that, after his death, papers were found in his house in Sparta, with details of a plot to overthrow the Spartan monarchy and replace it with a government of men of excellence.) On sea the outcome was more significant. A Persian fleet commanded by an Athenian mercenary, Conon, destroyed the Spartan navy in the Aegean, and Conon then sailed to Athens, where the source of his support was overlooked in the joy that the Spartan hold on the Aegean had been broken. Persian money was used to rebuild the Long Walls and there was even some attempt to re-create the Athenian empire.

The Corinthian War was in many ways a continuation of the Peloponnesian, and once again it was the Persians who provided the means of ending it. Artaxerxes now realized that a revived Athenian empire would be to his detriment, particularly as the Athenians would challenge his renewed control of the Greek cities of Asia. He moved back towards Sparta, and in 386, in the so-called King's Peace, the Spartans once again acquiesced in his control of the Greeks of Asia. In return Artaxerxes guaranteed the independence of every Greek city and gave Sparta subsidies to uphold it. Both Artaxerxes and Sparta were the victors, and Sparta now had the excuse and the resources to break up the alliances which were forming around her enemies Thebes and Athens. Artaxerxes had his empire restored, and threats that it would be challenged by an Athenian empire reduced.

The Fall of Sparta and Victory of Thebes

Any 'victory' was, however, short-lived, as a result of Sparta's inability to act with any kind of sensitivity. She was quick to reassert her leadership of the Peloponnese, crushing the city of Mantineia, for instance. Her greatest blunder came in 382, when her troops were sent to intervene in civil unrest in her old enemy, Thebes. The city was simply seized, to the universal condemnation of the Greek world. Even the historian Xenophon, an Athenian aristocrat, who had moved to Sparta after being exiled from Athens and developed pro-Spartan sympathies, could not defend Sparta's actions. The Spartan garrison was eventually thrown out in 379, and the Spartans did not improve their standing by launching an ill-judged attack on Athens which failed miserably.

Sparta's short-sightedness even stimulated a new Athenian 'empire', the one outcome that any far-seeing strategy should have been designed to avoid. Athens declared that her motive was 'to make the Spartans leave the Greeks to enjoy peace in freedom and autonomy' and called on allies to join her. Memories of the former Athenian empire remained strong, however, and there was some reluctance to do so. Athens had to promise not to impose settlements on member states, interfere with their internal politics, or impose tribute. (When, inevitably, contributions had to be called for from members, they were termed 'assessments' rather than 'tribute'.) Seventy states, including Thebes, eventually joined what is known as the Second Athenian League (378–377).

It was clear by now, however, that Athens was very much weaker than she had been in the fifth century and that any significant military action would put immense strain on the city's resources. It was to be Thebes, not Athens, who would humble Sparta. After regaining her independence in 379 Thebes had been rebuilding her position in Boeotia, and in 371 she insisted, in a treaty with Sparta, on signing on behalf of all the Boeotian cities. Sparta evoked the King's Peace to justify attacking Thebes. At the ensuing battle of Leuctra the Thebans smashed the Spartan army, leaving a thousand dead on the battlefield. It was a decisive battle which left the Greek world in shock. Spartan rule in the Peloponnese collapsed. (She simply had neither the prestige nor the manpower to sustain it.) From now on Sparta was no more than a second-rate power.

For ten years Thebes remained the dominant city of Greece, although this was due not so much to her own strength as to the weakness of others. Her success depended on the inspired political and military leadership of two men, Epaminondas and Pelopidas. They were supported by a core of 300 highly trained troops, the Sacred Band, who were pair-bonded in homosexual relationships. Thebes' influence spread south to the Peloponnese, where she continued to restrain any possible revival of Sparta, and as far north as Thessaly. Cities such as Corinth and Megara became what were in effect client states. When Athens became hostile (going so far as to make an alliance with Sparta to oppose Theban expansionism), the Thebans even began building a fleet. Within Boeotia itself, they finally captured the other leading city of the plain, Orchomenus, in 364, and killed all its male inhabitants, sending the surviving women and children into slavery. Theban dominance was as brutal as that of any other state.

In 362 Epaminondas was killed at Mantineia when fighting a Spartan and Athenian army in the Peloponnese. Pelopidas had died two years before. Perhaps inspired leadership was the key to Theban success, because from that moment Theban power ebbed away. A peace was made on the basis that every state should keep what it had, but Theban control of her 'empire' was gradually eroded as continual warfare wore down her resources. Xenophon, bringing his *History* to a close, remarked that 'there was even more uncertainty and confusion in Greece after the battle [of Mantineia] than there had been before'.

The Vulnerability of the City State in the Fourth Century

The fifth century had seen a comparatively stable Greek world with Athens and Sparta maintaining hegemony over large areas of the Aegean and Greek mainland. This age was now over. Sparta was now humbled, the short-lived supremacy of Thebes had faded, and Athens was unable to maintain an imperial role. Reports of the 350s show slackness and corruption in the Athenian shipyards, equipment borrowed and never returned, major shortages of sailcloth, hemp, and rope. With Sparta eclipsed, the Second Athenian League had also lost its purpose. Athens' response, as it had been a hundred years before, was to impose her control more ruthlessly. This time she was met with widespread revolt. In 357, in the so-called Social War, many of the League members broke free and others gradually drifted out of her control. In the same period Philip of Macedon was encroaching on Athenian interests in the northern Aegean.

As W. G. Runciman has argued (in an essay 'Doomed to Extinction: The *Polis* as an Evolutionary Dead-End'), there had never evolved in any Greek city a wealthy elite capable of focusing the state on the kind of ruthless economic imperialism needed to sustain hegemony over a large area. In this sense, democracy, by refusing to allow the wealthy to emerge as an uncontrolled elite, acted as a brake on ambition. At the same time, the Greek cities never broke out of their constitutional conservatism. Citizenship was a jealously guarded privilege. Rome offers a contrast. There, even slaves could be freed and incorporated into the citizen body. More significantly, perhaps, a defeated rival could be transformed into an ally with rights of citizenship and demands of military service. As Polybius, the Greek historian who tried to explain the defeat of the Greeks by Rome in the second century, understood, this gave Rome an almost unlimited supply of men. No Greek city ever adopted a similar approach, and in many cases the protected citizen body simply contracted with time. Sparta had been able to raise 8,000 citizen hoplites at the time of the Persian wars, only 1,200 a century later.

The collapse of Athenian and Spartan hegemony left a world of small scattered Greek communities. They had developed new sensitivities to outside control, as Athens' experience with the Second Athenian League showed. Furthermore, the years of continual warfare had sapped their resources, and there are universal reports in the fourth century of land hunger and debt. Many cities experienced *stasis*, civil unrest between rival factions. There was a new shifting population of poor, refugees or landless individuals, wandering the Greek world in search of sustenance.

There was one occupation which was able to take in the more able-bodied and that was service as a mercenary. The rise in the use of mercenary troops was one of the most significant developments of the fourth century. The Persians had come increasingly to rely on them, for the suppression of a major revolt in Egypt from 404 onwards, for instance. The Egyptians used mercenaries in return, and in 343 there were an estimated 35,000 in the country. The mercenary could be trained, by those who could afford to pay him, as a professional soldier able to fight all the year round. At the same time, outside influences, probably from

Thrace, led to the development of the *peltast*, who wore lighter armour and boots and who carried a longer spear. The *peltast* was more than a match for the heavy and slow-moving hoplite (*peltasts* employed by Corinth defeated a Spartan army in 390), although the hoplites continued to form the core of any city army.

The rise of the mercenary army coincided with other military developments. The Athenian orator Demosthenes describes them well:

In the old days the Spartans, like everyone else, would spend the four or five months of the summer 'season' in invading and laying waste the enemy's territory with heavy infantry and levies of citizens, and would then retire again; and they were so old-fashioned, or rather such good citizens, that they never used money to buy an advantage from anyone, but their fighting was of the fair and open kind. But now you must surely see that most disasters are due to traitors, and none are the result of a regular pitched battle. On the other hand you hear of Philip [of Macedon] marching unchecked, not because he leads a phalanx of heavy infantry, but because he is accompanied by skirmishers, cavalry, archers, mercenaries and similar troops . . . I need hardly tell you that he makes no difference between summer and winter and has no season set apart for inaction.   (Translation: J. H. Vince, Loeb Classical Library edition)

This, therefore, was the world of the new professional army, able to fight all the year round without being inhibited by the traditional conventions of warfare. (It is interesting that one of the reasons for the victory of the Thebans at Leuctra was the decision by Epaminondas to hold back his right wing, the one which traditionally launched an attack, and to attack instead with his left, which he had deliberately strengthened.) One significant development was the art of siege warfare. Traditionally, battles had been fought over land and normally cities had been left untouched. From the fourth century a more ruthless approach to warfare led to the direct targeting of cities. It was perhaps as much the desire to gain booty with which to pay the mercenaries as to crush an enemy completely that lay behind the change. All over the Greek world cities now became fortified. A new foundation, such as Messene in the Peloponnese, 369 BC, was equipped with walls from the beginning. At Gyphotokastro in northern Attica (ancient Eleutherae) there are magnificent fourth-century walls overlooking the pass from Boeotia.

Dionysius, Tyrant of Syracuse, and Jason of Thessaly

The average Greek city did not really have the resources to participate in this new warfare. By the early fourth century it was becoming clear that only determined and autocratic leaders could squeeze them out. Agesilaus had hinted at what was possible. In Syracuse in the same period a more successful leader, Dionysius, emerged, as a response to the continued pressures on the city by the Carthaginians who held the west of Sicily.

Dionysius' rule, initiated in 405, is reminiscent of that of the earlier Greek tyrants. He was primarily a soldier, and his position was underwritten by his continual mobilization of Syracuse in war against Carthage. There were no less than four wars, three of them instigated by Dionysius, in forty years. None was conclusive, and the Carthaginian hold on western Sicily remained strong. In mobilizing the Greeks, Dionysius proved ruthless. The need to have a united state, rather than personal ambition, may have been the reason for his suppression of alternative centres of power, such as Rhegium, captured in 387, and his bringing of defeated Greek populations under direct Syracusan control. He extended his authority over what remained of Greek Sicily as well as virtually every Greek city of the Italian mainland.

Italy brought Dionysius resources: tin, copper, iron, silver, and wood, as well as mercenaries. His men came not only from Sicily and the Greek cities of Italy but from mainland Greece, northern and central Italy, and Iberia. They were well armed, allowed to wear the armour and use the weapons they were most used to. The problem was finance, and here Dionysius was unscrupulous in grabbing temple silver and gold, manipulating his coinage, and confiscating the property of his enemies. He even raided the treasuries of Etruscan cities.

There was a strong personal element to Dionysius' rule. He was not simply a military commander. In his first treaty with Carthage (405) he was named personally as the ruler of Syracuse. He consolidated his position by a network of marriage alliances. (On one occasion he was said to have married two wives, one from Syracuse and one from the Italian mainland, the same day and consummated both marriages the same night.) Several of his seven children were married back into the family to make a formidable network of personal loyalties. The personal nature of his rule was underlined by the wording of his alliance. In a treaty with Athens, for instance, it was agreed that Athens would send him help if 'anyone makes war by land or sea against Dionysius or his descendants or any place where Dionysius rules'. There are also hints in the sources of the trappings of kingship—purple dress, and a golden crown. However, Dionysius' only formal title was that of 'general with full powers' and he never appeared on coins.

Dionysius never forgot that he was a Greek and that Sicily was part of a wider Greek world. He presided over symposia, wrote poems and tragedies, and sent chariots to compete in the Olympic Games. He supported Sparta in the Corinthian War, supplying her with enough ships to give her superiority over Athens. Later in his reign he was wooed by Athens and finally made a treaty with her in 368. The next year Dionysius entered his play *The Ransoming of Hector* in the Athenian Lenaea festival. The judges courteously awarded it first prize, at which news it was said that Dionysius drank himself to death.

If Dionysius had defeated Carthage, the history of the western Mediterranean might have taken a different turn. It would have left him free, for a start, to move into Italy. It was during his reign, for instance, that the Etruscans, who had dominated central Italy for centuries, began to weaken. In 390 the Etruscans and Rome had both been temporarily overrun by Celtic warbands from the north. Dionysius might have exploited the situation and stopped the recovery of Rome. In the event, Syracuse ceased to be expansionist after his death and Rome was able to consolidate its position on the mainland. Within a century the Greek cities of Italy were under her control, although Syracuse itself was not to fall until 212 BC.

The example of Dionysius showed that it was possible for a determined individual to seize power and to mobilize wealth and resources, particularly professional mercenary troops, in the service of a strong and united state. Others soon copied Dionysius. Thessaly, for instance, was taken over by one Jason, a native of the city of Pherae, in the late 370s. The area was one of rich plains and large estates. It already had a tradition of one-man rule in the shape of an elective monarch, the Tagos. Jason established himself as Tagos, organized a national army and for a short time, until he was murdered, set Thessaly up as the most powerful state in Greece. Xenophon records a speech of his in which he extols the virtues of a hand-picked mercenary army trained on hardship and richly rewarded if it shows appetite for war. He records a real fear that Jason would conquer the rest of the Greek world.

The Kingdom of Macedonia

In his speech Jason listed Macedonia, a monarchical state on his northern borders, as among his targets. Its timber would allow him to build a fleet which he would man from among the peoples he had conquered. As it turned out, it was Macedonia that was to do the conquering in the mid-fourth century. As Jason had realized, it was a fertile area with good rainfall and potentially strong if its resources were mobilized. The centre of Macedonia was the Emathian plain on the Aegean coast. It was too marshy for human settlement, but the well-watered mountain slopes around the plain had supported settlements since prehistoric times. There were other river plains, such as that of the Strymon to the east, and here again settlements were grouped on the mountain slopes. Inland, Macedonia became more mountainous, with the Pindus Mountains, for instance, forming a natural barrier with Molossis (later Epirus) to the west.

There was little natural coherence to Macedonia and many of its boundaries, particularly those to the east and north, were ill-defined. The state depended at any one time on the success of its king in holding off the states which surrounded it—Illyria to the north, Thrace to the east, Molossis to the west, and Thessaly to the south. The Athenians, in search of the same resources as Jason, were continuously probing along the coastline. As for the peoples of the region, very little is yet known about them. A condescending Athenian such as Demosthenes could talk of 'that Macedonian riffraff which could not even offer a good slave for sale in days gone by' but some may have spoken Greek dialects (the extent to which Greek was spoken in Macedonia is a subject of hot dispute) and certainly there is evidence of Greek cults in the area. It is meaningless to try and establish whether the Macedonians were, on this evidence, ethnically Greek or not. (See the good discussion in this issue in Patrick Geary, *The Myth of Nations* (Princeton, 2002).) What was important for the years to come was that Macedonia had large resources which could give it considerable power if used effectively by its rulers.

The Macedonian monarchy had shown remarkable survival skills. By the fourth century it was already some 300 years old, and its longevity seems to have depended on its success in preserving the heartland of the kingdom from invaders. The kings themselves claimed that their family was of Greek origin, although it has been argued that this claim was invented in the first half of the fifth century by an earlier monarch, Alexander I, to improve his relationships with the Greek world. The judges at the Olympic Games accepted the claim enough to make a distinction between the Macedonian royal family, who were allowed to take part in the Games, and the Macedonians as a whole, who were not. The monarchy seems to have depended on the personal qualities of each king. Treaties were made directly with him, he controlled the army absolutely, and when, as happened in the case of Philip II, he appeared at a pan-Hellenic festival, it was as an individual, not as the representative of his state.

Philip of Macedon

It was with the accession of Philip II in either 360 or 359 BC that ruler and resources became combined in a formidable expansionist force which was to transform the Greek world in less than fifty years. In the nineteenth century Philip was only known through Greek sources, above all the speeches of Demosthenes, and was often portrayed—by British liberals, for instance—as a tyrant who destroyed the liberty of Greece. The career of his son Alexander also tended to place Philip in the shadows. German historians, however, were more sympathetic to him, casting him in the role of a strong man bringing order, as Bismarck had done in Germany, to surrounding scattered and weak states. In recent years Philip has been recognized as a major historical figure who laid the foundations without which his son would probably never have succeeded in his own right.

Philip had the advantage of being the legitimate ruler within a long-established monarchy. This set him apart from the other Greek despots. He also had access, within Macedonia, to the resources to build up a mercenary army. One advantage of using mercenaries was that they could be forged into a fighting force with little reference to the conventions of the past. Here Philip proved a brilliant commander, able both to inspire and to innovate. The main weapon of his men, both infantry and cavalry, was the *sarissa*, a long pike. It enabled them to fight at long range and there was no way that hoplites could engage with it. Because the *sarissa* gave the infantry comparative invulnerability, it could dispense with the heavy and expensive armour which burdened the hoplite. Men could march fast and manoeuvre easily. Once infantry had made a gap in the hoplite ranks, cavalry was used to break through. The highly disciplined and flexible army that had emerged by 350 was to set the scene for thirty years of Macedonian conquest both by Philip and by his son Alexander. Philip also made important advances in siege warfare. It was he who was responsible for the development of the siege catapult, for instance.

The range and variety of Philip's enemies were such that military prowess could never be enough. His first task when he succeeded to the throne was to define the borders of his state. This inevitably brought him into contact with a range of different peoples and cultures, including sophisticated Greeks and rough baron kings of the north. Philip's methods were a mixture of military might and diplomacy. He realized that land to the north and west of traditional Macedonia would be difficult to hold and he never extended boundaries there further than his predecessors had done. To maintain relationships with their rulers, he embarked on a series of marriages, one each with an Illyrian, Molossian (the formidable Olympias, mother of his son, Alexander), and Thracian, and two with Thessalians. In the east, however, he was more adventurous, adding the Strymon valley to his kingdom after taking the city of Amphipolis in 357. (The city is now being excavated, and the finds suggest a Macedonian elite moved in to preside over the Greek inhabitants.) This gave him access to the rich mines of southern Thrace. Their wealth, exploited now for the first time to the full, helped him to finance his mercenaries.

It can be argued, in fact, that the continual demand for the resources with which to sustain his armies underlay the policy of expansion that followed. Amphipolis had never been regained by the Athenians after its loss in the Peloponnesian War, but in 357 and 354 Philip added two Athenian cities, Pydna and Methone on the Thermaic Gulf, to his conquests. (At Methone he lost an eye when struck by an arrow.) The Athenians reacted by declaring war in 357, but Philip was only one of their adversaries at the time and they could do nothing to save their cities. He now controlled the coastlines either side of the Chalcidice peninsula. In 348 he was to move into the peninsula itself. The great city of Olynthos, the most important in the Greek north, was sacked in 348. Athens promised it help but only a small force arrived. It was so successfully razed to the ground that it was never reinhabited, and provides the best examples of Greek house plans to have survived. Among the finds have been arrowheads evocatively bearing the name of Philip. There was now no possible source of Greek resistance to Philip in the north-eastern Aegean.

(If the finds of arrowheads at Olynthos are evocative, even more so was the discovery of the royal tombs of Macedonia at Vergina in 1976. In one tomb a middle-aged man, one eye-socket scarred but healed, lay in a chamber alongside another with a woman aged about 20. The first chamber had been hurriedly constructed, the second added later. The male body was in a gold coffin surrounded by the grave goods of a warrior. Was this the body of Philip, murdered in 336 and hurriedly buried by his son, Alexander, later joined by his last wife Cleopatra, who had been murdered in her turn by Alexander's mother Olympias?)

In these same years there had been Macedonian infiltration into her southern neighbour Thessaly. By 352 Thessaly was under Philip's control, and he had exploited alliances with Thessalian aristocrats to become, in effect, Tagos. Luck as much as opportunism played a part in Philip's next expansion south. The shrine of Delphi, oracle to the Greek world (see p. 239), was controlled by the Amphityonic League, an ancient association of central Greek peoples. In 356 a dispute broke out between the members and one of them, Phocis, seized control of the shrine itself. Thebes opposed her, as did the Thessalians. Philip was inexorably drawn into the conflict. He now chose to act diplomatically, using those opposed to Phocis to dislodge her from Delphi. In the settlement that followed he was admitted to membership of the Amphityonic League. At the next Pythian Games, it was Philip who presided.

It was Athens that felt most uneasy about the peace which followed. She had faced the humiliation of the loss of her outposts in the northern Aegean, and the logic of Macedonian expansionism to the east suggested that the Hellespont, channel for her grain supplies, would be threatened next. From 352 one of the greatest orators the city ever produced, Demosthenes, was warning of the danger of Philip and the need to resist. Yet what could Athens do? The Second Athenian League had collapsed by 355 and the city's finances were stretched. There was no way she could effectively fight in the north against such a formidable opponent as Philip. When the dispute over Delphi was on, Athens had supported Phocis, largely to spite Thebes. In 346 she had to abandon Phocis, and when Philip offered the city an alliance she hesitatingly accepted it, though fully aware of how much she had compromised her position.

Philip may genuinely have wanted to maintain peace with Athens, not least to be able to use her fleet in one of his new plans, an invasion of Asia. (J. R. Ellis, in his *Philip II and Macedonian Imperialism*, has argued that his overriding objective from the start was to invade Persia and that his main concern with the Greeks was to make sure that they did not threaten his flank while he was doing so.) In the city, however, there was increasing shame over what appeared to be capitulation to his growing power. It was exploited by Demosthenes (384–322 BC). Demosthenes had learnt his trade the hard way. His father had died when he was seven and the family resources had been frittered away by his unscrupulous guardians. He mastered rhetoric in order to retrieve what little remained and his experience shows just how difficult it was to dominate an Athenian audience. However, he succeeded. His speeches urging resistance to the barbarian invader are among the finest pieces of Greek rhetoric to have survived. Yet they are rhetoric. Demosthenes was leader of a democratic faction and was carrying out his own political struggles within the city. He used all the tricks necessary to command the attention and support of a volatile Athenian assembly, and the events described in his speeches are now discounted as truthful accounts. However distorted, the speeches remain majestic defences of liberty and democracy against the forces of tyranny. (One can, perhaps, compare his use of rhetoric with that of Winston Churchill.)

It is hard to apportion blame for the showdown between Philip and the Greeks that followed. Philip was steadily moving towards Athens' interests in the Hellespont, tightening his grip on Thrace, for instance. So Demosthenes had some excuse for continuing to make the issue of a Macedonian threat to Athens the central one of his oratory. However, Demosthenes' determination to prove that Philip was an aggressor and had betrayed the alliance was equally provocative, and Philip may have lost any faith he had that peace with Athens was possible. By 340 Philip was indeed threatening Byzantium, the key port on the Hellespont, and this was enough for Demosthenes to persuade Athens to declare war in 340. The seizure of an Athenian grain fleet by Philip soon followed. Then Philip moved into Greece itself. Athenian hoplites with Theban support faced the new-style Macedonian army at the Battle of Chaeronaea in Boeotia. The outcome was to change the nature of the Greek world.

FURTHER READING

Thucydides remains the supreme early source though he is now being approached more critically, for instance by Simon Hornblower in his *The Greek World, 479–323 BC* (London, 1991). An introduction to his work is given in Oswyn Murray, 'The Greek Historians', in the *Oxford History of the Classical World*; for a more intensive study see Mark Munn, *The School of History: Athens in the Age of Socrates* (Berkeley, 2000). A short analysis of the war is provided by Davies, *Democracy and Classical Greece*, chapter 7. The fullest survey is that of D. Kagan in four volumes (Ithaca, NY, 1969–81). Details of fighting techniques are covered in the works by Hanson and Pritchett cited for Chapter 8. On the fourth century, volume vi of the *Cambridge Ancient History* (Cambridge, 1994) is fundamental. On the question of the survival of the city state, W. Runciman, 'Doomed to Extinction: The *Polis* as an Evolutionary Dead-End' is to be found in O. Murray and S. Price (eds.), *The Greek City: From Homer to Alexander* (Oxford, 1990). On Dionysius there is B. Caven, *Dionysius I, Warlord of Sicily* (New Haven, 1990).

On the Macedonian background see E. Borza, *In the Shadow of Olympus: The Emergence of Macedon* (Princeton, 1990). N. Hammond, *The Macedonian State: Origins, Institutions and History* (Oxford, 1989), continues through to the destruction of Macedonia by the Romans. On Philip II, N. Hammond, *Philip of Macedon* (London, 1994), and the earlier J. R. Ellis, *Philip II and Macedonian Imperialism* (London, 1976).

18 | Alexander of Macedon and the Expansion of the Greek World

The Battle of Chaeronaea, 4 August 338 BC, marks one of the decisive moments of Greek history. By now, twenty years into his reign, Philip II of Macedon had strengthened his resources, perfected his army, and achieved a dominant position in northern Greece. Athens, faced with the strangulation of her grain supply, had finally declared war, and Thebes agreed to stand by her. Philip drove down into Greece, met the assembled hoplite armies on the plain of Chaeronaea, and destroyed them. The Athenians alone lost 1,000 dead and 2,000 prisoners. The cities, with the exception of Sparta, who refused to join, were now bullied by Philip into forming an alliance, the League of Corinth, of which he was the leading member. Their governments were packed with pro-Macedonian dependants and forbidden to engage in any independent activity. Philip was supreme in Greece, and, although the cities themselves may not have been aware of it, the era of the independent city state was over.

Philip's dominance had, in fact, been prefigured by an Athenian orator, Isocrates (436–338 BC). In a recitation written for the Olympic Games of 380 Isocrates had argued that the only way to bring unity to the fragmented Greek world was to launch a national crusade under one leader against Persia. In the last days of his life, he saw the triumph of Philip and congratulated him on his victory at Chaeronaea. Philip had, indeed, created a new political system, a model of monarchy whose power was based ultimately on the excellence of the monarch himself and the troops and nobles who gave personal allegiance to him. It was a model which had become totally alien to the Greek world, but now it was to prove the most successful and resilient form of government in this world for the next 200 years and even provided the model for the Roman emperors. In the first instance, the relationship between the king and his troops and war leaders depended on continual victory in war with all the benefits of booty and prestige that came with it. Philip, although in his mid-forties, was determined to maintain the momentum of success. He now embarked on the most ambitious of his plans, an invasion of Persia. The time seemed ripe. There was a power struggle for the Persian throne and both Egypt and Babylon were in rebellion. Philip harked back 150 years, disingenuously claiming the right to lead the Greeks in revenge for Xerxes' invasion and the desecration of the Greek shrines. By 336 an advance force of 10,000 Macedonians had already crossed the Hellespont and was campaigning along the Asian coast.

The Young Alexander

Whatever his triumphs in war, Philip faced frustration in one quarter, from his eldest son and presumed heir, Alexander, the child of his Molossian wife, the powerful Olympias. Through his parents, Alexander was aware of a heritage that supposedly took him back on his mother's side to Achilles and on his father's to Heracles, a heady genetic mix. As a young boy he steeped himself in Homer, and perhaps even in childhood lived in a half-fantasy world of heroic combat. For tutor legend suggests that he had the most famous intellectual figure of the time, Aristotle, though little remains to tell of the fruits of their three-year encounter (and it may have been a later invention). Alexander was self-confident, endlessly curious, and reckless. He showed every sign of being a brilliant commander. Already, when only 18, he had led the cavalry at Chaeronaea, and was not slow to claim at least part of the credit for the victory himself.

Conflict between father and adolescent son was in these circumstances inevitable. When, in 337, Philip embarked on yet another marriage, with Cleopatra, the daughter of a Macedonian noble, an appalling row broke out. Alexander doubtless feared any new sons would have a purer Macedonian heritage than himself and thus perhaps be preferred for the throne on his father's death. He was forced temporarily into exile, and even when he returned his status remained uncertain, especially when Cleopatra became pregnant.

Alexander's chance came suddenly and unexpectedly in October 336. Philip was host at the marriage of his daughter by Olympias to her uncle, the king of Epirus, one more link in the network of marriage alliances with neighbouring states in which Philip specialized. The celebrations were designed as an extravagant display of Macedonian power, and Philip seemed relaxed walking in the grand procession without a bodyguard. Suddenly a young nobleman stepped forward and stabbed him. The intrigues behind the attack are still unclear but Philip was soon dead.

There is no evidence that Alexander knew anything in advance about the attack but he had to move fast. There were speedy executions of those who had questioned his position as heir. Olympias herself returned from her native Epirus to engineer the murder of Cleopatra and her child, a baby daughter. Somehow Alexander won the acclaim of the nobility and the army, probably by claiming he would continue his father's policies with all the rewards they had brought them.

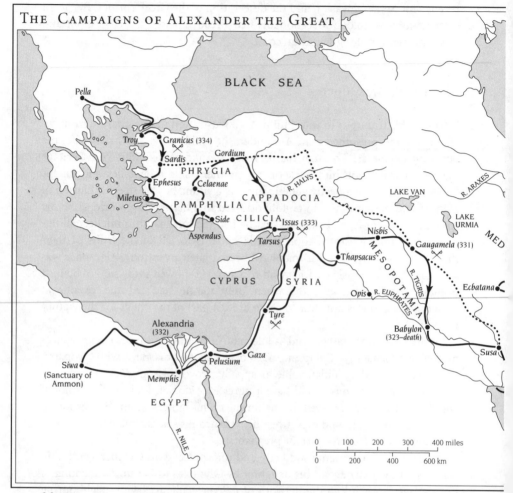

THE CAMPAIGNS OF ALEXANDER THE GREAT

MAP 6

Reasonably secure at home, he now had to deal with his neighbours. The mainland Greeks along with the Illyrians and the Thracians saw the chance to reassert their independence. Alexander marched an army southwards to overawe the leading Greek cities, Athens and Thebes, and force them to accept him as leader of the League of Corinth in his father's place. The Thracians and the Illyrians were then defeated in brilliant campaigns. While he was on the northern borders of Macedonia, Thebes chose to revolt. Alexander was always sensitive to betrayal, real or imagined. His move south was so rapid that the Thebans knew nothing of it until he was three hours' march away from the city. When the city resisted it was stormed. Six thousand Thebans died, 30,000 were enslaved,

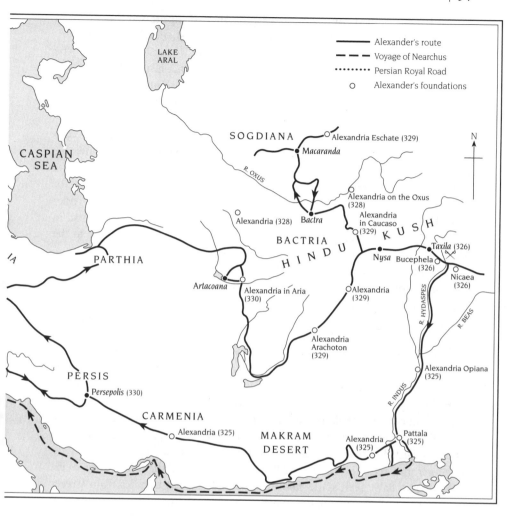

and Thebes, in effect, temporarily ceased to exist. These campaigns had taken no more than a few weeks and left the Greeks stunned. Whatever his apparent love of the world of Homer's heroes, Alexander never showed any sensitivity to the Greek culture and cities of his own time.

The Persian Adventure

It was his mastery of the Greek world that enabled Alexander to look to the east. The Macedonian forces sent into Persia by Philip were in trouble. A new king,

Darius III, had gained control of the empire. He had suppressed the revolts in Egypt and Babylon, and his commanders in the west, notably a mercenary leader, Memnon of Rhodes, had pushed the Macedonians back to the Hellespont. Alexander repeated the claim of his father that he was the avenger of the Greeks. The claim had never looked good in the mouth of the victor of Chaeronaea and did not improve by being taken up by the destroyer of Thebes.

The decision to launch a campaign into Persia seemed particularly foolhardy. It was true that the Persian empire had been in steady decline since the fifth century but it was still a relatively strong state. It had a large army and considerable resources. Its very size would ensure that any invading army could easily become isolated and vulnerable to annihilation. Nor did it make much sense for Alexander to leave Greece behind this early in his reign. There was such widespread resentment on the mainland that half of the Macedonian troops had to be left there just to keep order. Alexander had no heir, and if he were to die Macedonia and its territories were likely to collapse into anarchy.

Alexander's temperament ensured he would take the risk. The prize of Persia was simply too tempting to pass by, and it was a fine opportunity to prove himself to his father's commanders. The superb army created by his father was still intact. Its core was the Companions, an elite cavalry force of perhaps 1,800 men whose leaders traditionally enjoyed a rough comradeship with the king. They were supported by a similar number of highly trained Thessalian horsemen, and with other mercenaries there may have been a total of 5,000 cavalry. In the infantry Macedonians also formed a core, of perhaps 3,000 well-disciplined men. They were armed with their long pikes (*sarissae*) and light armour and marched in cohesive phalanxes which could be assembled in various formations according to the demands of the terrain. They were backed by light infantry. Those recorded include javelin men from the mountain regions of Thrace, archers from Crete, and Illyrians. All could be used on difficult territory. There also seem to have been some 7,000 traditionally armed hoplites from Greece itself, but after the campaign began little is heard of them. It may have been that Alexander simply could not trust them, particularly in battles where they would come face to face with the fellow Greeks that Darius was to use as mercenaries. In total, with Macedonians, Greek 'allies', and mercenaries, Alexander's was a balanced and flexible fighting force of some 37,000, not enormous in comparison to the army with which Xerxes had invaded Greece, but effective if used with imagination. It was supported by the siege machines, including the torsion catapult, which had been perfected by Philip. To accompany the enterprise there were surveyors, engineers, architects, scientists, and a historian, Callisthenes. Another 10,000 men from Philip's original invasion force awaited them across the Hellespont.

To pay for this army Alexander had to virtually empty the Macedonian treasury, and so the demand for booty with which to maintain his men was an important impulse in what followed. It was not just money which bound the troops to Alexander. The traditional loyalties enjoyed by a Macedonian monarch were reinforced by Alexander's own charismatic style of leadership which embraced the high-risk strategy of fighting at the forefront of any battle.

The accounts of the campaigns that followed come down from Roman sources. Of the five primary main sources none is earlier than the late first century BC, while the major lives of Arrian and Plutarch date from the early second century AD, three to four hundred years after the death of Alexander. (Arrian's was so popular that many of the earlier sources on which he had relied were discarded and lost to future generations.) These authors did use earlier sources, some from participants in the campaign itself, including Callisthenes, but it has proved impossible to disentangle and evaluate these accounts. As the painstaking analysis of these sources by the historian A. B. Bosworth had shown Alexander's exploits, as they have come down to us, are encrusted with later legend. This legend has persisted so that as recently as 1948 the historian William Tarn was able to argue (in his *Alexander* (Cambridge, 1948)) that 'Alexander lifted the civilized world out of one groove and set it in another'. Today historians, more attuned to imperialist propaganda, offer a more restrained assessment of Alexander's achievements.

The Conquest of the Western Persian Empire

The army marched in the spring of 334. Alexander was aware from the beginning of the Homeric nature of a campaign into Asia. Once on Asian soil he offered honours to the memory of both Ajax and Achilles, but he also remembered that through his mother he had Trojan ancestry. The Trojans were now enlisted as honorary Greeks united with the mainland Greeks against the barbarians and the small settlement on the site of Troy was showered with gifts.

Almost immediately Alexander faced his first battle. The local Persian commanders had drawn up their forces on the far side of the River Granicus. The river was a difficult obstacle with deep banks and the Persians must have hoped they would be able to pick off the Macedonians with their cavalry as they crossed. In the event the vanguard of the Macedonian cavalry managed to get across and hold off the Persian charges while Alexander and the bulk of cavalry made their crossing. Alexander led the next charge. The whole campaign was put in jeopardy when he got struck down in the mêlée, but he was rescued by Cleitus the Black, one of the commanders of the Companions, and the Persian cavalry was gradually pushed back. Then the Macedonian infantry moved in to surround the Persians. Their weapons and discipline proved so superior that the result was a massacre with perhaps nine-tenths of the enemy infantry left dead. Many were Greek mercenaries who offered to surrender. However, Alexander, determined to give a lesson to other Greeks, refused to spare them.

The victory at Granicus was so decisive that it left the coastline of Asia Minor with all the cities of Ionia in Alexander's hands. The march was now southwards, first to the administrative centre of Sardis, capital of the old kingdom of Lydia, then through some of the great cities of the coast, Ephesus, Priene, and Miletus with its fine harbour, where a Persian garrison briefly resisted until overcome and massacred. Alexander knew that these cities had to be held to prevent the Persians using them as harbours for a counter-attack in the Aegean while he was moving inland. There had to be some recognition of these cities' liberation. They were released from their Persian tribute and encouraged to set up democratic governments, but Alexander could not resist meddling in their internal affairs and 'contributions' to his campaigns soon replaced the tribute. Finally Alexander reached Halicarnassus, the home town of Herodotus, historian of the Persian wars. Here the Persian garrison under Memnon of Rhodes, recently appointed by Darius III as commander of the west, was prepared to resist. There was bitter fighting along the walls of the city and Macedonian losses were heavy. The Persians finally withdrew into two citadels which could be freely supplied by sea, and with no effective naval forces at his command, Alexander was forced to leave the city unconquered. His hopes of securing his rear were dashed. Halicarnassus held out for another eighteen months, and the Persian fleet was able to sail freely in the Aegean. It was only the death of Memnon in 333 and the call by Darius for troops to come to his aid in the east that prevented the Persians holding large areas of the Aegean and perhaps even invading Greece.

Alexander left memories of this humiliation behind him (and they were glossed over by later chroniclers such as Arrian) and moved east across the rich plains of Pamphylia to the wealthy town of Aspendus. The town was Greek in origin but it was still bullied into paying a vast sum in tribute. Troops were left to pacify the area while Alexander turned northwards, through the rocky passes and uplands of Pisidia to Celaenae, the capital of Phrygia. Finally in March 333 he arrived at Gordium on the plains of central Turkey. Here took place one of those legendary events which have become central to any account of Alexander's life. There was an ancient wagon whose yoke was tied to its pole by a complicated knot. An oracle had prophesied that anyone who untangled the knot would be lord of all Asia. The story goes that Alexander was baffled at first, and then in a fit of impatience slashed through the knot with his sword. His 'achievement' was trumpeted as evidence of divine aid for the expedition.

However, even after a full year of campaigning and one crushing victory, Alexander was still on the fringes of the empire. Its heartland and its king Darius still lay ahead. Up on the great plains of Anatolia he now began to run short of food. The crops would not ripen until August, and news was also coming through that Darius was at last gathering his forces for a counter-attack. The only hope was to move southwards again to the more fertile plains of Cilicia. This meant crossing the rocky uplands of Cappadocia and forcing a narrow pass into the coastal plain. In fact the local Persian commander was so intent on destroying the ripening crops of the Cilician plains in advance of the Macedonian arrival that the pass was left virtually undefended and Alexander was soon through. He was in the Cilician capital Tarsus before the Persians could defend it. This was the first Persian city with treasure to plunder, but the exhilaration of the troops was dampened when Alexander caught a fever while bathing in the river and hovered between life and death for days.

His troops must have been highly apprehensive. Darius had been raising levies of troops all spring and summer. The bulk of his men were Persians and Medes, but one account suggests they were joined by as many as 30,000 Greek mercenaries. The total size of the army is unknown, but it must have easily outnumbered Alexander's, and Darius, a seasoned commander, remained confident he could crush the intruder. As the army set out from Babylon towards Cilicia, it was relaxed enough to be accompanied by the royal treasure and the princesses and concubines of the court.

The two armies met in September on the eastern end of the Cilician Plain just above the Gulf of Issus. In the manoeuvres before the battle Darius tried to get between Alexander and his supply lines, and he finally drew up his armies behind the River Pinarus, which flowed into the Gulf. It was not an ideal spot as there was too little space between the mountains and the sea to allow the Persians to fully deploy their superior numbers. The Macedonian attack was launched, as always, by Alexander personally at the head of his cavalry, which he had positioned on the right of the line opposite the Persian infantry. The attack was a success and the infantry fell back, allowing Alexander to bear left towards the centre where Darius himself was to be found. Elsewhere, however, things were not going well. The Persian cavalry charged and forced back the Thessalian cavalry on the Macedonians' left flank, while the Macedonian infantry became dangerously disrupted when crossing the stream. What saved the day was the disintegration of Darius' bodyguard under the impact of the Macedonian cavalry. Darius was forced into flight and with his disappearance Persian morale collapsed. There was headlong flight, the Persian cavalry trampling back over their own infantry as they escaped. Legendary figures of 100,000 Persian dead as against 500 Macedonians are certainly an exaggeration but they suggest the magnitude of the victory. The royal baggage train and the princesses were appropriated by Alexander and he preserved them as if they had now become part of his own heritage. For the first time Alexander was able to reward his troops lavishly.

Darius' nerve was shaken by his defeat and for the first time he was prepared to negotiate. He sent to Alexander that he was prepared to treat Alexander as a friend and ally but was not ready to surrender any of his territory. Alexander refused. He would only talk when Darius came to him as a subject. This was impossible for the Persian king and he began assembling another army. Meanwhile, Alexander chose not to move further inland but to continue south along the coast of Syria and towards Egypt, one of the richest prizes of the empire. His main concern may also have been to gain control of the entire coast-line to stop it being used as a base for Persian counter-attacks on Greece.

The first Phoenician cities welcomed Alexander. However, at the city of Tyre, reached in February 332, there was a check. The old city on an island offshore housed a shrine to the city god Melqart. Alexander equated Melqart with his own 'ancestor' Heracles and demanded to be allowed to enter the shrine to worship. He was refused and in a fit of pique urged the siege of the city. It seemed an impossible task. The island was skilfully defended and could call on help from the sea. For seven months Alexander had to deploy a large force and exercise every ingenuity, including the construction of floating siege towers, before the walls were breached. The retribution was terrible. Eight thousand defenders died and a further 2,000 were crucified. The survivors were dispersed and new inhab-itants had to be sought from the interior to replace them.

The siege of Tyre suggested a lack of balance in Alexander's personality. He was beginning to see himself as something more than a human being, perhaps as a god in his own right, beyond the normal restraints of human behaviour. The sense that he was half divine was consolidated as he moved towards Egypt. By responding sensitively to Egyptian culture Alexander found himself welcomed as a liberator from the deeply resented rule of Persia. He was soon accorded the ancient honorific titles of the pharaohs, King of Upper and Lower Egypt, Son of the sun god Ra.

However, Alexander was more interested in the ancestry of Greek than Egyptian gods. In early 331 he made a difficult journey across the Libyan desert to the oracle of Ammon at Siwah. Ammon was a local god but he was commonly equated with Zeus, and in his private consultation with the priests Alexander appeared to gain the belief that Zeus had recognized him as his own son. (Plutarch's story is that the intended greeting of the priests was 'child', *paidie*, but, not being Greek-speakers, they used the wrong case, *paidios*, and Alexander thought they said *pai Dios*, 'son of Zeus'.) It echoed earlier stories which had cir-culated in Macedonia that his conception had in fact been divine. (Olympias, different sources reported, had been impregnated by either a serpent or a thun-derbolt.) At this stage conception by a god did not necessarily mean that one was a god oneself (the Homeric heroes were the offspring of gods but were mortals) but it was believed that through great exploits one could achieve divine status. The odes of Pindar spoke of victory in the games bringing an athlete close to the gods. The magnitude of Alexander's achievements already suggested he had outstripped ordinary mortals and, in the years that followed, Alexander seems to have increasingly acted as if he was half god, to the disquiet of the more conser-vative of his Macedonian commanders.

A distance between Alexander and his commanders was becoming apparent. Darius, brooding on his defeat, now offered Alexander his empire to the west of the Euphrates and an enormous ransom for his family. The commanders were eager to accept. It marked a massive extension of Macedonian territory which could now be consolidated in peace. Alexander refused. He was set on the humiliation of Darius and forced the Persian monarch to continue the war. He may have felt that his legitimacy as ruler of Persia could only be achieved by directly replacing Darius. This would explain the single-mindedness with which he was to hunt Darius down.

The Humiliation of Darius

The new army raised by Darius was almost exclusively made up of cavalry drawn from the centre and east of the empire. (What infantry there was, was of poor quality.) Arrian reported an unbelievable total of 400,000 horsemen: a more sober estimate is 37,000, still probably five times as many as Alexander could muster. Darius took his men north into Assyria, and positioned his army where the cavalry could be used most effectively on the plain of Gaugamela, in the foothills of the Zagros mountains. Here Alexander followed him to arrive in September 331. It was clearly the most frightening situation he had yet faced. After resting his men, he drew up his army as before, the infantry in the centre, the Macedonian cavalry on the right, and the Thessalians on the left.

Battle was joined on 1 October when Alexander began moving his cavalry around the flank of the Persians. They counter-attacked and Alexander had to feed in more and more troops to contain them. As the Persians responded by sending yet more troops, Alexander finally saw what he had been waiting for, a gap opening between the Persian left and its centre. Rushing his Companions forward with infantry supporting them on each side, Alexander forced his way through the gap. Within a few moments the state of the battle was transformed as the Persian army was broken into two. Once again Darius fled with Alexander after him in a hot pursuit which lasted 30 kilometres before he called it off. As the news of Darius' flight filtered through, his army, still fighting well on the right flank, disintegrated behind him. It was another crushing victory, and Alexander could now rightly claim the title Lord of Asia.

The Macedonians were now in the rich heartlands of the empire with no effective opposition to them left. The army moved southwards across the Mesopotamian plains to Babylon and here, as in Egypt, Alexander was welcomed as a liberator from Persian rule. The city was wealthy, its treasures were surrendered to him, and the army relaxed in the sybaritic surroundings of the richest and most sophisticated of the cities of the east. Then there was a march of triumph on the great cities of the empire, now undefended against Alexander's armies. Susa, the second capital of the empire, surrendered without a fight, its satrap coming out to meet Alexander with racing camels and elephants as preliminary gifts. Inside the city awaited gold and silver bullion amounting to 40,000 talents. Included was loot taken from Greece 150 years before and a hundred tons of purple cloth. This was only the beginning. The army now moved south-east, over snow-capped mountains to Persepolis, the spiritual centre of the Achaemenid empire.

The treasures of Persepolis had been accumulated over centuries and were vast. In Darius' bedchamber in his great palace alone, there were 8,000 talents of gold. Alexander now left his men free to loot, and the city was stripped of its treasures so effectively that its modern excavators have not found a single sizeable piece of gold or silver. A great column of camels and pack animals took off the treasures. Some were sent back to Susa, others stayed with the army. In total perhaps 120,000 talents of treasure was taken, a revenue that it would have taken the Athenian empire at its height 300 years to collect in tribute. Only the great palace of Xerxes was left intact, but in May 330 this too was sacked. One legend says that an Athenian courtesan, by the name of Thais, egged on the Macedonian leaders with whom she had been drinking to fire the palace in revenge for the destruction of Athens. Archaeologists working on the site this century have found the blackened remains of the roof timbers.

Alexander's preoccupation continued to be the capture of Darius. The king had taken refuge in Ecbatana, the capital of the Medes. Alexander followed him there and in a series of forced marches pursued him eastwards. As Darius fled his position weakened. He had never visited the east of his empire before, and the local satraps would give no allegiance to a man so tainted by defeat. One of them, Bessus, satrap of Bactria and a leading cavalry commander at Gaugamela, finally took him captive. As Alexander's cavalry moved in, Darius was stabbed and left to die. Alexander arrived shortly afterwards to take possession of the last of the Achaemenids. The body was sent back for burial in Persepolis. Alexander had achieved his victory.

The Campaigns of the East

As Alexander moved eastwards his own position became less strong. His men had achieved victory beyond their wildest dreams and they had little stomach for further marches into the unknown. Tension grew among the army commanders and Alexander became increasingly impatient with it. In the autumn of 330 he accused the brilliant but overbearing leader of the cavalry, Philotas, of conspiracy to murder him. The army was bullied into voting for his torture and execution. Philotas' father Parmenion, one of Philip's most seasoned commanders, who had consistently opposed what he saw as Alexander's recklessness, was also assassinated on Alexander's orders. The cavalry was gradually reorganized so that the power of individual commanders was reduced, and Alexander began to rely on local mercenaries rather than sending back to Macedonia for reinforcements.

The next two years saw campaigning of a very different nature. Alexander had reached the remotest reaches of the empire, the provinces of Bactria and Sogdiana, modern Pakistan and Afghanistan, and there were new, intense stresses on his men. The heights of the Hindu Kush were crossed in April 329 with men suffering from frostbite and breathlessness. They then had to march over 75 kilometres of desert before reaching the Oxus river, where many died from sudden overdrinking. Alexander's adversary was Bessus, who had proclaimed himself the new king of Persia. He was eventually hunted down, and taken to Bactra to have his nose and ears mutilated, the traditional punishment for a usurper of the Persian throne, before being sent back to Ecbatana for execution.

This whole area was unstable, and local magnates bitterly resented the intrusion of Alexander and his army. While Alexander was campaigning along the north-eastern borders of the empire, there was a massive insurrection in the satrapy of Bactria to the south. This region was ideal for guerrilla warfare. The insurrection spread, and for the next two years Alexander was tied up in a series of campaigns against local pockets of resistance. As ever, Alexander showed his inventiveness and flexibility. His archers and javelin men came into their own against the bands of nomadic tribesmen who circled the Macedonian armies. Even the most impregnable of citadels fell to his tactics. One noble, Ariamazes, thought himself invulnerable in his mountain fortress until Alexander sent 400 mountaineers to take it from above. However, the final conquest of the region was marked by scenes of terror as the entire male populations of captured cities were massacred and their women and children enslaved. Ten thousand infantry and 3,500 horsemen had to be left in Bactria to keep order, and a string of military garrisons was established. In a more constructive move, 30,000 young men were taken to be taught Greek and trained for Alexander's armies. Bactria was to become and remain an enclave of Greek culture for centuries to come. It was also here that Alexander selected a wife for himself, Roxane, daughter of a local noble, Oxyartes.

The combined effects of the stresses of the campaigns and Alexander's own personality were now causing serious problems within his court. When the army was resting at Macaranda (the modern Samarkand) in the autumn of 328, a row broke out at a drunken banquet, between Alexander and the cavalry commander Cleitus, who had saved Alexander's life at Granicus. It was said that Cleitus taunted Alexander. Alexander in response seized a weapon and struck Cleitus down. The row concealed more deep-rooted problems. The Macedonian kingship was one in which personal loyalty to the king persisted alongside a rough camaraderie. The king was not removed from his commanders—he ate and drank, often heavily, alongside them. The tradition of the Persian monarchy was very different. Here the king lived in unbelievable splendour and even the most senior of his courtiers were treated as subjects. The whole approach was symbolized by the act of *proskynesis*, a traditional obeisance of a subject before his king. Alexander, whose temperament was always autocratic, had now begun to insist on this for himself. The Macedonian commanders, already resentful of the way that Alexander had appropriated all credit for military success to himself, deeply resented submission to what was for them a humiliating ritual. Their open opposition was such that Alexander gave way but hostility lingered and gave rise to an assassination plan by his closest attendants. The plan was discovered, the pages involved executed, and they were followed by the historian Callisthenes who had offered the most articulate condemnation of *proskynesis*.

The tension was increased by Alexander's refusal to turn back. Still ahead of him lay India. Knowledge of the region was shadowy. Nominally it had been part of the Persian empire, but probably only the west had experienced any form of Persian control. (There were elephants from the Kabul valley in Darius' army at Gaugamela.) The Greeks had myths that both Heracles and Dionysus originated in India, and Alexander may have been spurred on to equal their exploits. In 327 he crossed the passes of the Hindu Kush and down through the Cophen valley. It was a progress marked by terror. Any city which resisted was stormed and its men massacred. The valley, the corridor between India and the west, had to be held by whatever means. Only one city, known to the Greeks as Nysa, was spared after a successful claim that it was the birthplace of Dionysus.

The wealthy kingdoms of India were now within the reach of Alexander. The Indus river was crossed amidst great celebrations and games in the spring of 326. Alexander was welcomed by the ruler of the state of Taxila, whose motives appear to have been to use the Macedonians to defeat rival princes further east. The bait worked. Hearing news that one of them, Porus, was prepared to resist him from behind the River Jhelum (Greek: Hydaspes), a tributary of the Indus, Alexander hurried eastwards before the melting of the winter snows and imminent monsoons made the river impassable.

The battle of Hydaspes proved one of Alexander's most crushing victories. The difficulty lay in crossing a river which was well guarded by Porus' troops. Alexander succeeded by crossing during a thunderstorm, and his men landed virtually unopposed. He now faced 20,000 Indian infantry, 2,000 cavalry, and a mass of elephants which could be stampeded into the Macedonian ranks. The Macedonian cavalry charged the Indian and forced it back into the infantry. The Macedonian infantry now advanced in superb discipline. They opened their ranks as the elephants charged and then jabbed at them with their *sarissae*. The crazed animals stampeded back into their own lines, trampling down anyone caught in the way. The Indian infantry was now slaughtered, only a few breaking through the Macedonians to escape. Porus was captured, still seated on an enormous elephant but wounded and almost alone on the battlefield. Alexander, impressed with his courage, confirmed him as ruler of his kingdom.

Buoyed up by yet another victory Alexander forced his men on. There were legends of rich kingdoms to the east, but the monsoons had now started. By the time the army reached the River Beas it had endured seventy days of continuous heavy rainfall and was close to mutiny. For the first time in his life, Alexander accepted defeat. He claimed that a sacrifice had shown the gods did not want him to continue further and ordered the retreat. There was a jubilation in the ranks which Alexander was never to forget or forgive.

The March Home

The route home was not to be through the conquered territories of the eastern empire but southwards on a flotilla down the Indus to the Southern Ocean, which Alexander was determined to explore. Even though the waters of the Indus were falling when the expedition set out in November 326, it still remained a hazardous journey. The tribes along the river were uniformly hostile and their cities had to be stormed. Alexander himself almost lost his life when an Indian arrow penetrated his chest when he was isolated on a city wall during one siege. He never properly recovered from the wound. Meanwhile, the frightened and exhausted army survived only by using terror. Such hatred was raised against the intruders that every Macedonian garrison left in the area was later wiped out.

The army reached the mouth of the Indus in July 325. A long march westward across the wind-scoured and dusty wilderness of the Makram desert lay ahead. Whole armies had been swallowed up in the desert in the past, and it may have been Alexander's obsession with surpassing all his forebears which drove him on. The crossing of the Makram took sixty days. Reports of the ordeal are contradictory but some suggest that losses were heavy. It was certainly a shattered and thoroughly demoralized force that finally reached the satrapy of Carmenia, north of the straits of Hormuz. From here it was a relatively short march back to Persepolis and the heartland of the Persian empire. The fleet returned separately under its commander Nearchus. This was a more notable achievement. Nearchus scavenged his way along the coast and reached the Tigris without the loss of a single ship. Alexander was so impressed he began dreaming of great future voyages—a circumnavigation of Africa and perhaps even the conquest of the western Mediterranean.

Administering the Empire

Alexander was now 31. He had survived fevers and wounds but each must have weakened his extraordinary constitution. Heavy drinking with his commanders was doing further damage. Yet the immense task of consolidating his conquests lay ahead. After his victories those Persian satraps who had pledged loyalty had been allowed to remain in place with Macedonians appointed alongside them as military commanders and collectors of taxes. However, with plunder available to meet all his needs Alexander had paid little attention to good government. In his absence corruption and oppression had increased. In a frenzied purge over the winter of 325/324, Alexander dismissed most of the Persians, replacing them with Macedonians. At the same time Macedonian commanders in Media, who were accused by local notables of sacrilege and rape, were summoned to Alexander and executed. An atmosphere of fear spread through the empire, reflecting Alexander's increasingly unbalanced behaviour.

The Macedonians may well have wondered what their position in the new empire would be. In February 324 Alexander reached Susa, and here he set himself up in the style of the Persian kings. He now wore the white-striped purple tunic of the Persian kings with the Persian diadem. The old Persian royal bodyguard was re-formed and served alongside Alexander's own Macedonian guard. Then the 30,000 Bactrian youths whom Alexander had left to be trained in Macedonian drill and tactics arrived. They were an impressive force and a potential challenge to the battleworn Macedonian forces. Yet Alexander still seemed to believe in an inherent Macedonian racial superiority which could be imposed through the mixing of Macedonian and Persian blood. He took two more Persian wives, one a daughter of Darius, for himself, and in a ceremony of glittering extravagance married off ninety of his commanders to daughters of the Persian nobility. The strategy was ill-judged and few of the marriages lasted.

In the spring of 324 Alexander left Susa for the Persian Gulf. From here he sailed up the Tigris into Mesopotamia. At one of the inland coastal towns, Opis, he announced that all Macedonians who were unfit for further service because of age or injury would be disbanded and allowed to return home. It was a sensible move. The men had been ten years away from home and there would be time to replace them with fresh troops from Macedonia before the next campaigning season began. In the circumstances it was seen as a gesture of rejection. There were shouts of anger, even taunts that Alexander should go it alone with his father Zeus. Alexander's nerve broke. Thirteen of the ringleaders were executed and replaced by Persians. At this the mutiny collapsed and, as the tension broke, there was an emotional reconciliation. Ten thousand men were discharged, but each was sent home with a handsome payment.

Alexander's behaviour became increasingly absolutist. At the Olympic Games of 324 BC a letter from him was read out which proclaimed that all Greek exiles could return to their native cities. There were many thousands whom misfortune, political upheavals, and power struggles had driven from their cities. (Twenty thousand turned up at Olympia to hear the decree being read out.) Alexander may have been trying to win popularity by sending them home, but he had made no consultation with the cities and the result was to disrupt their economies and political stability as the exiles returned. Once again he had shown how detached he had become from political reality.

The summer heat now drove Alexander and the enormous entourage which travelled with him northwards to the cooler air of the Zagros mountains. His destination was the old summer residence of the Persian kings at Ecbatana in Media. The satrap welcomed him with unparalleled extravagance and there were heavy feasting and games. A casualty of one drinking session was Hephaestion, one of the few Companions who had remained an intimate of Alexander's despite all the stresses and hardships of the campaigns. Alexander was devastated. He ordered the execution of Hephaestion's physician and, in a manner contemporaries compared to Achilles' grief for Patroclus, he fasted over the body for three days. A cult was to be set up to honour the dead hero and plans put in order for the building of a vast monument at Babylon, where the court made its way in early 323.

Alexander's grief for Hephaestion appears unbalanced, and in the last year of his life he seems increasingly to have lost touch with reality. Whether he actually believed he was a god or not, he certainly associated himself with symbols of divinity. On coins minted at Babylon he is depicted with a thunderbolt, the emblem of Zeus, in his hand. At banquets he wore the purple robes and ram's horns of Zeus Ammon, and one account talks of incense being burnt before him. There is some evidence that the Greek cities were ordered to give him divine status (a debate, the result of which is unknown, took place on the subject in Athens). What is certain is that the Hellenistic monarchs, and following them the emperors of Rome, learned from Alexander the importance of claiming and advertising divine support in a way never known before in the Greek world.

Alexander remained in Babylon to plan an invasion of Arabia. The riches of the Arabian peninsula were legendary and reconnaissance of the area suggested settlement there would be possible as well. During the early months of 323 a vast harbour, able to take 1,000 warships, was being dredged out of the Euphrates and men were being gathered from the empire. There were also rumours that once Alexander had conquered the peninsula he would turn west, and a stream of embassies, from Greece, Etruria, Libya, Carthage, and even, it was said, Spain, made their way to Babylon to offer reverence.

The end to this frenetic activity came suddenly. One evening late in May 323 Alexander was drinking with his companions. In one final bout he is said to have drunk the contents of a bowl which could take twelve pints. According to one account, which may have been trying to prove that he was poisoned, he collapsed and died almost immediately. Other sources say that he lingered on alive for several days. Whatever the reality of his illness, by June he was dead. In Athens they could not believe the news. If he was, surely the whole world would stink from his corpse, said the Athenian politician Demades. A revolt in Athens which greeted the news (a sign if any was needed of how far Alexander had alienated himself from the Greek world) was put down by Macedonian troops and it was at this moment that Athenian democracy was finally extinguished.

The New Graeco-Macedonian World

Alexander's empire was a personal conquest. It had never gained an institutional framework which could bring such diverse elements as Macedonia, Egypt, Persia, and India together into a cohesive unity. There was not even an immediate successor. When asked on his deathbed who should succeed him, Alexander apparently answered, 'To the strongest'. The legitimate heir was Alexander's half-brother, Arrhidaeus, but he was retarded. Roxane was pregnant and duly produced a son. Proclaimed as Alexander IV of Macedonia, he could never be more than a puppet figure. The inevitable result was a power struggle between Alexander's generals which was to last for twenty years. The dominant figures were first Perdiccas, the senior cavalry officer, and, after his death in 320, Antigonus the One-Eyed, a Macedonian noble who had been appointed satrap of Phrygia, who struggled to maintain overall control of the empire until he was defeated and killed in 301.

The most shrewd of the competitors for Alexander's empire was Ptolemy, who, appointed as governor of Egypt after Alexander's death, simply consolidated his position as ruler while other generals fought over the rest of the empire. He also managed to grab the most sacred relic of all, Alexander's embalmed body, which he installed at Memphis. Ptolemy could not be dislodged, and he formally declared himself king around 305. The dynasty that he established lasted until 30 BC, with the death of its final queen, Cleopatra VII, Antony's Cleopatra. Rome then took control, the conqueror, Octavian, the future Augustus, pausing to gaze on what survived of the body of Alexander, by then in Alexandria, before setting out back to Italy.

In Asia Seleucus, the commander of one of Alexander's elite regiments, emerged as victor. He declared himself king in 305, proclaiming his own divine heritage as the son of Apollo. His kingdom was an unwieldy one, with Greeks, Persians, Babylonians, and all the varied peoples and cultures of the eastern provinces under his rule. It proved impossible to keep intact. The dynasty lost land continually until it was eventually confined to a small area of northern Syria, where the last of the Seleucid kings succumbed to Rome in 64 BC.

The third kingdom and the most prestigious for the heirs of Alexander was Macedonia, the only one where kings were to rule over their native people. The land was fiercely contested until 276 BC, when Antigonus Gonatas, grandson of Antigonus the One-Eyed, achieved control. His dynasty remained in power until the Romans occupied Macedonia in the second century BC. The country never recovered after the wars of Alexander, and few of its men ever returned home. They had either died, remained as settlers, or become mercenaries.

Another of Alexander's legacies was the cities left behind him along the routes of his campaigns. At least twenty-five were founded during his lifetime. While one of them, Alexandria in Egypt, dedicated in the spring of 331, was destined to become the greatest city of the Mediterranean world, others were little more than military garrisons in the conquered territories. Most were east of the Tigris in regions where cities had been rare. Alexandria-in-Caucaso in the Hindu Kush, for instance, was made up of 3,000 Graeco-Macedonian soldiers, some volunteer settlers, others discarded soldiers, supported by 7,000 locals who worked as labourers for them. Such cities were isolated, thousands of kilometres from Greece, among a hostile population, and with all the discomforts associated with pioneer life. Many failed completely, but others maintained themselves as enclaves of Greek culture for generations.

The Legacy

> Conquering by force of arms those whom he could not bring together by reasoned persuasion, he brought men from everywhere into a unified body mixed together as if in a loving cup, their lives and characters and marriage and social customs. He commanded them all to think of the inhabited world as their fatherland, of the encamped army as their acropolis and their guard.

The hymn of praise to Alexander by the Greek writer Plutarch is still to be found quoted in biographies of the conqueror as if it represented historical truth. Yet like so many classical texts it had a different purpose. It was an exercise in rhetoric and it is clear from other writings of Plutarch that he did not believe in this adulation. Even so this image of Alexander persists and it underlies the assumption that Alexander was bringing a superior civilization from the west to a more barbarous one in the east. 'This superiority of a small, noble, and free people over all of enslaved Asia is perhaps the most glorious thing among men,' was the eighteenth-century French Enlightenment thinker Voltaire's assessment. Alexander's invasion was, from a military point of view, stunningly successful, yet, he had no aptitude for the political skills needed to stabilize the empire after his conquest. The result was debilitating wars of succession. Even when a Greek dynasty, the Seleucids, did gain control of Persia they ruled through the political structure which was already there and it is now clear that in many parts of the east Greek culture only permeated slowly during the centuries of the Roman empire. (Ironically some modern business gurus use Alexander as an exemplar despite his megalomania and lack of interest in long-term planning!) It is also important to note that Alexander's 'achievement' was not accepted uncritically in the ancient world. Cicero tells the story of Alexander accosting a captured pirate with the words, 'What is your idea of infesting the sea?' The pirate answered, 'The same as yours in infesting the earth! But because I do it in a tiny craft, I'm called a pirate: because you have a mighty navy, you are called an emperor.' Might is right. The Roman historian Livy expresses no surprise that the 'barbarian' armies of Persia were defeated so easily by Alexander. An encounter with a Roman army, he suggests, would have provided a very different result!

Alexander's immediate legacy was not, therefore, an empire. Rather it was a form of monarchy, based on absolute power, an aura of divinity, and conspicuous consumption. This was to be the model he bequeathed to the Hellenistic kings who succeeded him. For later generations he became the archetype of the world conqueror, a role model especially for those Roman generals campaigning in the east. The archetype was sustained by Alexander's projection of himself as romantic hero through the works of his favourite sculptor Lysippus. He asked to be shown beardless, a sign of youth and vigour, and his chosen pose was to look slightly upwards, his gaze distant (the so-called 'melting look'). In full-size statues, none of which has survived, Lysippus appears to have grafted the 'ideal' body of a warrior onto a head of his subject. (Alexander, like that other 'great' conqueror Napoleon, was actually quite small.) In the first century BC the Roman general Pompey added Magnus, 'the Great', to his name in emulation of Alexander and even aped his mannerisms (and in one portrait bust, his haircut!). Trajan took Roman armies to the mouth of the Euphrates and then bemoaned the fact he could not take them further and equal the exploits of his hero. At his inauguration of Constantinople, his capital in the east, the emperor Constantine portrayed himself on his coins with the 'melting look' of Alexander. The final subduer of Constantinople some 1,100 years later, the Ottoman sultan Mehmed II, was an avid reader of Arrian's panegyrical *Life of Alexander* and rejoiced that while Alexander had conquered Asia from west to east, he had completed the conquest from east to west.

FURTHER READING

Two readable biographies are Peter Green, *Alexander of Macedon* (London, 1974), and R. Lane Fox, *Alexander the Great* (London, 1973). It is easy to be overawed by Alexander's achievements and to stop there. A. B. Bosworth is responsible for a much more searching and critical look at the evidence. See his *Conquest and Empire: The Reign of Alexander the Great* (Cambridge, 1988), *Alexander and the East* (Oxford, 1996), *From Arrian to Alexander: Studies in Historical Interpretation* (Oxford, 1988) and with E. J. Baynham as joint editor, *Alexander the Great in Fact and Fiction* (Oxford, 2000). For an assessment of Plutarch's eulogy see J. R. Hamilton, *Plutarch's Alexander: A Commentary* (Bristol, 1999). See also A. Stewart, *Faces of Power: Alexander's Image and Hellenistic Politics* (Berkeley, 1993).

19 | The Hellenistic World

The Hellenistic age is the name given to the period from the reign of Alexander (336–323 BC) to the conquest of Egypt by Rome in 30 BC, a span of some 300 years. It was an age of monarchies. It was unlikely, in fact, that any other form of government would have held together the different factions, races, and cultures which now had to coexist in the expanded Graeco-Macedonian world. (The distinctions between the two cultures faded with time and a relatively homogeneous Greek culture emerged.) Inevitably, the atmosphere was very different from that of the age of the city states. Many of the old cities of mainland Greece continued to exist as important, even influential, political and cultural centres but political power now rested with the strong men who had carved kingdoms from the conquests of Alexander.

The Hellenistic Monarchies

The typical Hellenistic monarch had to be a military commander. The boundaries between each kingdom remained fluid and there were frequent disputes between rival monarchs over their extent. Armies were large, up to 80,000 men, a number which remained a maximum until modern times, and made up largely of mercenaries. The Ptolemies and the Seleucids fought no less than five wars over Syria in the third century. In addition to these internal conflicts there were constant attacks by outsiders. Macedonia had to guard her northern frontiers against the tribes of central Europe. 'Celtic' warbands (see Interlude Four below) raided down into Greece in the early third century, sacking Delphi in 279, and it was only by confronting them in 277 that Antigonus Gonatas secured the kingdom of Macedonia for himself. Another Celtic people, the Galatians, settled in central Anatolia, and it was through defeating them in 238 that Attalus I was to gain the prestige that enabled him to set himself up as king of Pergamum in the north-west of Asia Minor. One of the great sculptural pieces of the period, the Altar of Zeus at Pergamum, celebrated his achievements. On its colossal frieze, 100 metres long, gods battle it out against giants. It was quite clear that the gods were the Attalid rulers, the giants the Galatians. The celebrated statue of the Dying Gaul (the Romans knew the Celts as Gauls) was executed, originally in bronze, at Pergamum at this time. (The surviving example in the Capitoline Museum in Rome is a Roman copy in marble.)

The most harassed of the kings were the Seleucids. The history of their kingdom is one of steady loss of the territories grabbed by Seleucus I. Only two Seleucid monarchs survived to die in bed. Their control of the far east of their kingdom was lost with the breakaway of Bactria in the mid-third century. In the remote north of their kingdom a Parthian ruler, Arsaces, became prominent at the same time. His horsemen were versatile enough to fight either as cavalry or archers and they were soon raiding southwards with success. The campaigns of Antiochus III (ruled 223–187 BC) in the east did something to restore Seleucid prestige in Asia, but Antiochus' humiliating defeats at the hands of the Romans (see p. 391) lost him control of the Mediterranean coast. By the second century BC the Parthians had reached the Euphrates, and by the end of the century the Seleucids had been reduced by Roman expansionism and successful Jewish nationalism (see below) to a small area of Syria.

The Hellenistic monarchs ruled over such a variety of peoples that they had to take an active role in mobilizing support. One way this could be done was through patronage. The tradition of providing 'bread and circuses' for the masses began in this period, while at a more elevated level the kings offered hospitality to 'Friends' who might come from any part of the Greek world. Normally they would have skills, as philosophers, poets, doctors, or administrators, and gradually they became assimilated as courtiers with the court itself becoming a centre of display. The Ptolemies in Egypt were particularly successful at exploiting their surplus of resources for propaganda purposes. One festival thrown in honour of Dionysus by Ptolemy II in Alexandria in 275 was the height of extravagance. The glint of gold was everywhere, in the plates on which 120 young boys bore offerings, in great mixing-bowls for wine, and in gilded statues carried in procession. Exotic animals, including a giraffe, a rhinoceros, and elephants, mingled with an enormous phallus, the symbol of the Dionysiac orgy, which was carried through the streets decorated with gold ribbons and bows. A vast pavilion was erected for special guests at which all the fittings, even the couches, were made of gold.

The courts were extravagant places, not least in their architectural settings. The accent was on the flamboyant and monumental. At Pergamum the Attalids built their own complex of great public buildings which overlooked each other and provided a magnificent if rather overwhelming backdrop to the dynasty. The grandest capital of all was Alexandria, whose extravagance was sustained by the vast wealth of Egypt. Cosmopolitan, luxury-loving, and bustling with commercial activity, the city was also the intellectual capital of the Hellenistic world. Its celebrated library may have held nearly half a million books and contributed more than any individual institution to preserving the literary works of Classical Greece. It set out with the ambition of acquiring copies of every known text, even down to cookery books. Bookstalls were scoured, ships docking at Alexandria

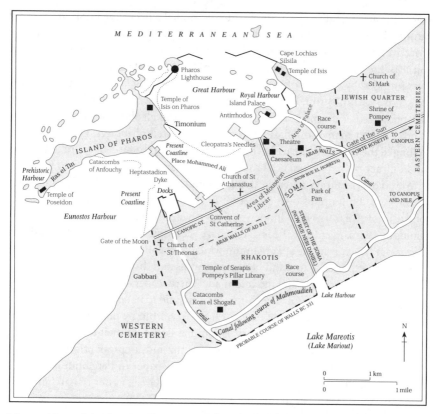

MAP 7 Alexandria, from Hellenistic capital to major bishopric. Alexandria was the capital of the Ptolemies and as such a major centre of patronage as shown in the royal palaces, which were along the sea front, and in the neighbouring Library. It was a major centre for Greek mathematics and science. It also became the major port of the eastern Mediterranean, notably through the export of Egypt's grain surpluses. Note the famous lighthouse (Pharos). The evangelist Mark was, by tradition, buried here and this made the city an important Christian city. St Athanasius (note his church) had a turbulent career as the city's bishop in the fourth century but is honoured for his championship of the Nicene creed. The Jewish community was also important and in Philo (early first century AD) produced a major philosopher.

were raided, and the official copies of Aeschylus, Sophocles, and Euripides borrowed from Athens and then never returned. Ptolemy II supported the Greek translation of the Hebrew scriptures, the so-called Septuagint, so that he could have a copy in the Library. Alexandria's is the first known library to have its works shelved alphabetically (although this only extended to the first letter of each title and one director, Callimachus, compiled a list of the books by authors grouped into the category in which they wrote, such as history, philosophy, or lyric poetry). Distinct from the Library was the Museum (the word means a place of the Muses, where the cultivation of the arts and learning takes place). It was founded by the first of the Ptolemies, Ptolemy Soter, and became the haunt of scholars from throughout the Greek world. Those who failed to gain entry lampooned it as a centre of frivolous research and alcoholism. 'In the polyglot land of Egypt many now find pasturage as endowed scribblers, endlessly quarrelling in the Muses' birdcage', as one Timon of Phlius put it, but overall Museum and Library played an essential role in keeping Greek culture alive and intact.

Alexandria's Library had a rival at Pergamum where the Attalid king Eumenes II (197–160) built up his own collection so relentlessly that there are even reports of works of Aristotle being hidden in a trench so that Eumenes could not get his hands on them. Eventually he is said to have accumulated 200,000 rolls and this is borne out by excavations at Pergamum which have found the original building. It is a strange experience to stand between its walls and distinguish the three rooms where the rolls were kept and the colonnade where readers would take out the rolls to consult them in the light. The Ptolemies were said to be so furious at this rivalry that they banned the export of papyrus from Egypt but by now the Attalids were probably already using parchment (from animal skins) for their texts. It was more durable than papyrus which rotted in the damp and its production became so linked with Pergamum that the Latin *pergemena*, 'paper of Pergamum' provides the source for the word parchment itself. If the later Greek writer Plutarch is accurate, Alexandria won out in the end. Plutarch records that Mark Antony gave the complete library of Eumenes to his lover Cleopatra in Alexandria.

Cities in the Hellenistic World

Inherent in the spread of Hellenism was the founding of cities, a tradition originally used as a strategy by the Macedonians for pacifying defeated enemies and developed by Philip as well as by Alexander. The Seleucids scattered new foundations throughout the former Persian empire, in Syria, and Palestine, on the plains of Mesopotamia, on the shores of the Persian Gulf, and as far east as modern Afghanistan. Some, Seleucia-on-the-Tigris, for example, were totally new cities. Others, such as Babylon and Susa, were older cities whose native inhabitants were now placed under Greek or Macedonian administrations. It took some time for many of these cities to become established, but by the third century adventurers, traders, and political refugees were migrating eastwards, shedding their old city allegiances to become citizens of this new world. There were new cities elsewhere: Thessalonica on the Macedonian coast was founded in 316. Greek trading ports were established along the coastline of the Red Sea.

Typically these cities were laid out on a gridiron pattern. This was not just an exercise in proportion, it was the most practical way of placing buildings which were normally rectangular in area (houses, for instance, were normally grouped around a rectangular courtyard), and the effect was not necessarily monotonous. Priene, a city resited in the fourth century, was one of the finest examples. Its streets ran up a hillside to the public buildings of the city with a fine temple gracing the summit of the acropolis. All these foundations, however distant from Greece itself, were microcosms of Greek culture. Even Alexander's military settlements had their own gymnasia and theatres. By the second century, when colonization had become more popular, a city such as that excavated at Ai Khanum on the northern frontier of Afghanistan had not only a huge theatre and gymnasium but mosaics and a library. Among the ruins were found the remnants of a piece of papyrus with a Greek philosophical text on it, while in the gymnasium a stone pillar was inscribed with moral maxims taken from the oracle at Delphi.

There was no city which could effectively defy a king armed with the latest machinery of siege warfare. (The example of Corinth, razed to the ground by the Romans in 146 BC, showed how vulnerable a city was to the determined outsider.) However, there was little sense in a Hellenistic ruler destroying the main centres of Greek culture, so in practice there had to be accommodation between king and city. Sensible kings paid lip-service to the traditions of the *polis* (it was part of the ideology of monarchical rule that a king would boast of his preservation of city independence) and city life remained vigorous. Democratic assemblies continued to meet, the city would maintain its own laws, send ambassadors to kings or other cities, and generally keep up the pretence of independence. The cities themselves realized the futility of warfare which would attract the attentions of the monarchs, and arbitration of their disputes became common instead. The third century, before the intrusion of the Romans, was the most settled the Greek world had yet seen.

The cities of the Greek mainland were not formally part of any kingdom, and some saw the advantages in joining together for common defence. The Aetolian League in central Greece gained its cohesion from a successful defence of the area against Celtic warbands. After saving Delphi in 279, the Aetolians absorbed most of the cities of the Amphictyonic Council (see p. 312). The League was a genuine federation. All its men of military age met twice a year in an assembly, there was a chief magistrate (in practice a general), and a council made up of representatives of the cities. The League became strong enough to be used by the Romans against Philip V of Macedon in the late third century (see p. 391). Another League, the Achaean, drew on traditions of cooperation in the northern Peloponnese which stretched back for centuries. Like the Aetolian League, the Achaean had a presiding general and cavalry commanders and an assembly which decided a common foreign policy. This policy fluctuated. Originally

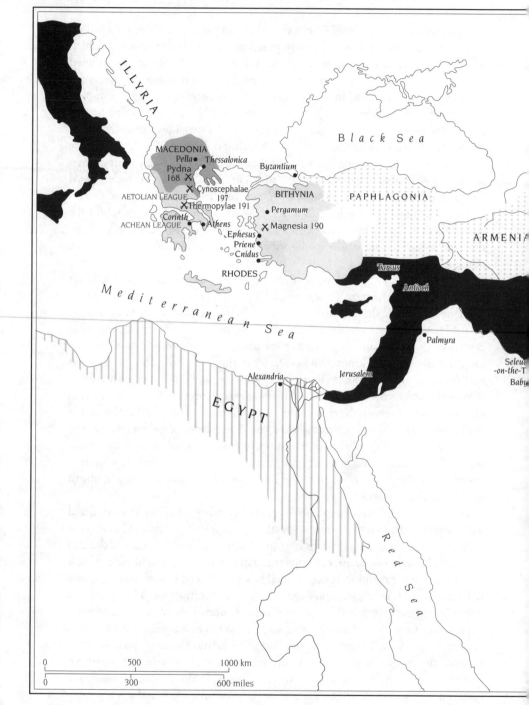

ILLYRIA

Black Sea

MACEDONIA
Pella • • Thessalonica
Pydna
168 ✗ • Byzantium
✗ Cynoscephalae
197 BITHYNIA PAPHLAGONIA
AETOLIAN LEAGUE
✗ Thermopylae 191 • Pergamum
Corinth ARMENIA
ACHEAN LEAGUE • • Athens ✗ Magnesia 190
Ephesus
Priene
Cnidus
RHODES *Tarsus*
Antioch

Mediterranean Sea

• Palmyra

• Alexandria *Jerusalem* Seleuc
-on-the-T
E G Y P T Baby

Red Sea

0   500   1000 km
0   300   600 miles

Map 8

Caspian Sea

GRAECO-BACTRIAN
KINGDOM

SELEUCID KINGDOM

Susa
(Seleucis-on-the
Eleaeua)

Persian Gulf

☐ Independent Greek States

☐ Antigonid Kingdom (Macedonia)

■ Seleucid Kingdom and Vassal States

▥ Ptolemaic Kingdom and dependencies

☐ Graeco-Bactrian Kingdom

☐ Kingdom of Pergamon

⣿ Hellenized Non-Greek Kingdoms

■ Non-Greek States

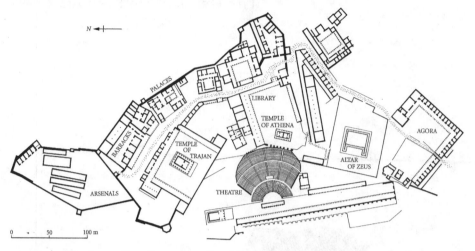

N

FIG. 5 The Acropolis at Pergamum. In addition to its temples the Acropolis shows
the typical concerns of a Hellenistic monarch, for defence (arsenals and barracks)
and for culture (a library and theatre). Unlike an earlier Greek acropolis it also holds
a royal palace.

anti-Macedonian, the League sought the protection of Macedonia when threatened by Sparta, but then switched allegiance to Rome in 200 when it became
aware of where power really lay. The switch did little good. The League was
crushed by Rome in 146 BC (see p. 393).

Athens maintained her independence for most of the period, but in the third
century the city faced an economic crisis. The details are difficult to ascertain,
but it is possible that rising grain prices and falling olive oil prices (due to new
areas of production) caused a balance-of-trade deficit (although more recently it
has been stressed that the evidence for a shift in olive production is elusive).
Furthermore, her famous pottery was now being replaced by the more fashionable silverware. The release of vast quantities of precious metals by Alexander's
campaigns drove down the price of silver, and Athens' silver mines may even
have been closed temporarily in the third century. However, the city's fame as the
traditional centre of moral philosophy (in contrast to that of Alexandria, which
became the focus for mathematicians and scientists) remained. One of
Aristotle's followers, Theophrastus, drew in 2,000 students to his lectures.
Although one third-century visitor complained of the meanness of the city's
streets, Athens benefited from the largesse of the surrounding monarchies. The
Ptolemies introduced a sanctuary of the Egyptian gods Isis and Serapis, while
Attalus II of Pergamum, a former student in the city, built a fine stoa, over 100
metres long, along the east of the Agora. (It has been reconstructed and now
houses a museum of the Agora excavations.)

One of the most interesting arenas of mutual accommodation between ruler and city was cult worship. Following the precedent set by Alexander, it soon became accepted that a monarch acquired an elevated status as the favoured of the gods. Not surprisingly, the monarchs were foremost in stressing their divine links and would associate themselves with a particular deity. The Ptolemies chose Dionysus, the Attalids of Pergamum Athena, and the Macedonian kings Heracles, the assumed ancestor of Alexander. Dead kings became the focus of elaborate dynastic cults.

Cities would respond to this by creating their own cults to the ruler. The motivations behind these cults are not easy to discover. There may have been an element of deliberate flattery, an insurance policy against the displeasure of the king, but, most important of all, the king could be targeted as the one individual who could actually get things done. This is certainly the implication of the prayer from Athens made to Demetrius Poliorcetes, son of Antigonus the One-Eyed who exercised temporary power over Athens in the late fourth century. 'O son of the most mighty god Poseidon and of Aphrodite, hail. For other gods are either far away or have not ears, or do not exist nor heed us not at all; but thee we can see in very presence, not in word and not in stone, but in truth, and so we pray to thee.' (Translation: F. Walbank.) Cult worship of kings was carried out within the framework of traditional religion, often in a temple precinct with sacrifices and libations. In Egypt the Ptolemies were integrated within the traditional framework of divine rule. The Rosetta Stone, celebrated because its three texts, hieroglyphic, demotic, and Greek, allowed hieroglyphs to be deciphered (finally by the Frenchman Jean-François Champollion in the 1820s), is a record of thanksgiving of the priests of Memphis to Ptolemy V in 196 BC. In it Ptolemy was addressed as a god who was also the son of gods.

Greeks and Others

Outside mainland Greece and Macedonia, the Greek cities were set in a sea of native peoples, Persians, Indians, Egyptians, Jews, or Celts. It is difficult to disentangle the complex relationships that evolved as a result, but in many cases social distinctions between Greek and native remained strong. In the city of Seleucia-on-the-Eulaeua (the former Persian capital of Susa), there is no record of any citizen (in the legal sense of the word) who was not Greek by birth. It takes three generations before the Seleucid rulers are found employing the first non-Greek in their administration, while it was said that Cleopatra VII, the last Ptolemaic ruler of Egypt, was the first in the dynasty to learn the local language. The formal title of her capital Alexandria was Alexandria *by* Egypt, a telling illustration of its isolation from the native culture.

Egypt provides the best-documented examples of the relationship between ruler and ruled. (Once again the survival of papyrus in the dry climate is the reason.) The Ptolemies needed revenue with which to maintain their capital city and to defend their kingdom against their Seleucid rivals and others. The Graeco-Macedonian ruling class exploited the pharaonic structure of administration to channel the surplus upward. The result was a petty and intrusive bureaucracy which aroused deep resentment among the local peoples. By the beginning of the third century Upper Egypt had broken away and accepted 'pharaohs' from Nubia in place of the Ptolemies. In a desperate attempt to keep control, the Ptolemies were forced to bring Egyptians into the administration (usually only after they had received a Greek education) and make concessions to the temples, which had always been the most independent of the Egyptian institutions. By the time of Cleopatra VII the kingdom was already disintegrating, and it was hardly surprising that the scheming queen should look to powerful Roman commanders such as Caesar and Antony to bolster up her power (see Chapter 23).

Hellenism was thus an imperialist culture. 'I am a barbarian and do not know how to behave like a Greek,' complains a camel-driver in an Egyptian papyrus. Hellenistic imperialism could perhaps be compared with French imperialism of the nineteenth and twentieth centuries, for the Greeks, like the French, chose to believe that theirs was a superior culture which could not be diluted. Those who wished to become assimilated had to do so totally, like the *evolués*, subjects of the French empire who abandoned their native religion and culture to become French citizens. It was essential to speak Greek, to attend the theatre, and show allegiance to Greek cults. The most public sign of assimilation was to strip naked for exercise in the gymnasium. Hellenistic Jews, marked by circumcision, found this particularly daunting. In practice, it appears that such a rigid approach was not sustainable and there was more cultural give-and-take than was once thought.

It was inevitable that many would absorb a veneer of Greek culture without becoming fully assimilated. Greek became the *lingua franca* of what was a highly mobile world. Greek values and customs were spread by a host of individuals and groups, traders, mercenaries, pilgrims to shrines and oracles, embassies from one city state to another, who criss-crossed the Mediterranean and the east. Native mercenaries had to pick up a smattering of Greek if they were to serve in the Hellenistic armies, and when they retired they might adopt Greek styles for their tombs and provide them with Greek inscriptions. The result of these minglings was to make Greek culture more homogeneous. The different Greek dialects which had lasted through the classical period, now became absorbed in a common language, *koine*.

The homogeneity of the Greek world was reinforced by its festivals and games. The traditional ones, at Olympia, the Isthmus, and Delphi, remained, but many new ones were founded by monarchs and cities eager to build up prestige and cash in on the trade they brought (a continuing tradition, as seen in the frenzied bidding by rival cities to host the modern Olympic Games). Their ambition was to make their games *isolympios*, equal in prestige to the Olympic Games. Some games were set up in honour of a dead king (the Ptolemeia in Alexandria, for instance, which honoured the memory of Ptolemy I), others to commemorate victories, such as the new games at Delphi established by Aetolia to celebrate the city's defeat of invading Celts in 279 BC. In a few instances non-Greeks are recorded as participating in these games and carrying off the crowns in chariot races or the athletic events. The Romans were known to compete at the Isthmian Games, and after 189 BC, when Roman influence became predominant in Greece, new festivals sprang up in honour of Rome.

One of the most important social developments of the period was the emergence of a 'new rich'. There is no evidence that the Mediterranean was any richer than it had been (in fact in many areas continuous warfare seems to have made it poorer) but what wealth there was, from landownership, trade, or a share in the influx of precious metals that were released from the cast by the conquests of Alexander, appears to have been concentrated into fewer hands. The inhibitions on public display of wealth which were so strong in, say, democratic Athens were relaxed, and the typical home of a cultured family would now boast wall paintings (landscapes were a favourite), mosaics in the reception rooms, and a host of smaller *objets d'art* in bronze or silver. The rich were also responsible for sustaining what was probably the most typical symbol of Greek culture, the gymnasium. The gymnasium was not simply a place for exercise. There were often libraries and lecture halls attached with classes held in rhetoric or philosophy. The most favoured gymnasia, especially those in the older cities such as Athens, were exclusive. They had long waiting-lists, and prospective entrants were carefully scrutinized for their suitability. Free-born citizens whose income came from land were the most favoured, and there was a distinct prejudice against trade.

The appearance of more comfortable homes reflects a trend towards a more family-centred life. Women were given a higher profile, as can be seen from the wide array of ornaments, diadems, tiaras, earrings, and necklaces which survive. Marriage contracts, of which a few have been found, show that women now gained the right to divorce their husbands if they brought home other women or had children by them. The epigraphs on grave monuments speak freely of the loss felt when a wife dies, a suggestion of mutual affection, or at least the pretence of one. This would have been unheard of in fifth-century Athens. Vase paintings now show love-making taking place in private (in contrast to the public nature of many Classical sex scenes) and in comfort in bed. What Sarah Pomeroy in her *Goddesses, Whores, Wives and Slaves* (New York, 1975) has described as 'a sophisticated etiquette of romance' was developing. Women of the upper classes also enjoyed a higher status in public life. There are examples of women holding public office, and one woman citizen of Priene donated a reservoir and aqueduct to the city. Women now seem able to deal in land and slaves, borrow money, and even enter horses in the Olympic Games. There is one early fourth-century example of a woman from Sparta being the winning owner in a chariot race at Olympia.

In the cities the richer citizens had lost many of their traditional roles as soldiers and statesmen. In recompense many became important benefactors of their cities, providing games or donating public buildings or statues, a tradition which lasted for some centuries. In Rhodes there was a long-standing tradition that, at times of famine, the richer classes would help the poor. The motives for these benefactions were varied and difficult to assess. There was undoubtedly an element of social aggrandizement involved in the public display of wealth, but the new rich may also have been defending their position against social upheavals (by the patronage of 'bread and circuses') or even profiting by hoarding grain and distributing it at times of famine. Occasionally there is even a mobilizing of the poor. In Sparta King Cleomenes III (ruled 235–219 BC), faced with a declining citizen body and ambitious for expansion in the Peloponnese, freed a large number of helots and integrated them into a citizen army.

Arts in the Hellenistic Age

Some of the spirit of this complex age can be caught in its sculpture. Most of it was in bronze and survives only in later Roman copies. If the fifth century was one of calm idealism and proportion, there now evolved a more luxuriant and ornate style which sometimes bordered on the grotesque. In architecture this was the age of the Corinthian column with its rich foliage (the earliest example found was in fact on the temple to Apollo at Bassae, built at the end of the fifth century), but there was a freedom for the patron to mix classical styles according to taste. There is a renewed interest in the personal. Figures are shown undertaking everyday tasks—a boy takes a thorn from his foot, a girl dressed in a *chiton* and mantle sits on a stool and gazes modestly at the ground. There is less inhibition in poses and often a preoccupation with movement. A superb example of a figure in motion is the bronze jockey boy found in the sea off Cape Artemisium and now in the National Museum in Athens. Figures may sprawl rather than stand in perfect balance. A favourite is Hermaphrodite, whose sexual ambivalence, male genitals, female body, was created when a nymph fell in love with Hermaphroditus, the son of Hermes and Aphrodite, and asked the gods if she could be joined to his body. Alongside the Hermaphrodites comes the appearance of the female nude in sculpture. (Female nudes were already common on vases, and could be seen in paintings after the early fourth century.) The first known is the celebrated Aphrodite by Praxiteles discussed earlier (p. 245).

A new interest in the individual, stimulated perhaps by the growth of wealthier lifestyles, is reflected in the emergence of portraiture. It originates in the coins of the period but then spreads to bronze and marble. Thousands of famous figures and local patrons, including kings, philosophers, dramatists, and athletes, were commemorated by statues in the market-places of the great cities. The monuments, which had traditionally lined the way into cities for centuries, now become more elaborate and widely spread.

The Hellenistic age was also an extraordinarily fertile and influential one for literature, although most of it has been lost. Of the enormous number of histories believed to have been written, only one, that of Polybius, survives and even then only in parts. (It is described in Chapter 21.) What does remain is mostly poetry, and vast sections of even this—tragedy, for instance—are missing. The loss is the greater as the Roman poets learnt much from the Hellenistic poets. The Roman playwrights Plautus and Terence were heavily dependent on the comic playwright Menander (342–c.292 BC), whose plots they freely adapted. Some of Menander's work does survive, including at least one full play found only recently in a cache of papyrus in Egypt. Menander is seen as the master of the so-called New Comedy, which originated in Athens in the late fourth century and became popular throughout the Graeco-Roman world. It is middle-class comedy, centring on the affairs of the well-to-do who find themselves caught up in complicated plots and coincidences. Kidnapped children reveal themselves as long-lost heirs, while well-born girls raped and made pregnant under cover of darkness at festivals emerge to find the man they wish to marry is in fact the father of their child. There is little on politics, a great deal on marriage and money. The end is always happy with even the most obstinate of problems resolved. Molière, Sheridan, the Italian Carlo Goldoni, Oscar Wilde, and George Bernard Shaw are among those who appear to be in Menander's debt.

The poets of the period seemed to enjoy a private world of intimacy based on friendship, nostalgia, and scholarship. Their poetry is self-consciously literary. The comparison has been made with the twentieth-century poets T. S. Eliot and Ezra Pound. Some of the mood has been captured in William Cory's famous, if not strictly accurate, translation of Callimachus' lament for his dead friend, Heracleitus:

> They told me, Heracleitus, they told me you were dead,
> They brought me bitter news to hear and bitter tears to shed.
> I wept as I remembered how often you and I
> Had tired the sun with talking and sent him down the sky.
> And now that thou art lying, my dear old Carian guest,
> A handful of grey ashes, long, long ago at rest,
> Still are thy pleasant voices, thy nightingales awake;
> For Death he taketh all away, but them he cannot take.

Callimachus (*c.*310–*c.*240 BC) was the most influential of the poets of the period, a particular favourite of the Romans, including Catullus and Ovid. He was a man of learning, responsible, as has been mentioned, for a massive 120-volume catalogue of the library at Alexandria and a supposed 800 volumes of other works. He set a tone for the age, one of striving after good taste and refined scholarship in an unashamedly elitist way. 'I despise neo-epic sagas: I cannot welcome trends which drag the populace this way and that. Peripatetic sex-partners turn me off; I do not drink from the mains, can't stomach anything public.' (Translation: Peter Jay.) He would have hated modern soap operas. His Hymns, of which six survive, were elaborate compositions designed to be read among discerning friends, while his epigrams, such as the most famous to Heracleitus quoted above, deal with his more personal feelings, including his love for boys. It was his range, versatility, and lively intelligence which made him the archetypal poet of the age, and he is more quoted in this period than any other poet but Homer.

Relationships between these poets was not always smooth, and Callimachus was supposed to have had a row with Apollonius Rhodius (*c.*295–215 BC), another *habitué* of the library at Alexandria who had made his home in Rhodes. While Callimachus was the supreme exponent of the short and polished epigram, Apollonius revived the epic in the form of a long account of the adventures of the Argonauts. This difference in their approach to poetry probably fuelled their quarrel. Apollonius' *Argonautica* is chiefly remembered for its portrayal of the love of Medea for Jason, 'the Greeks' most brilliant portrayal of a girl falling passionately in love', in the words of Robin Lane Fox. It may have provided the inspiration for Virgil's affair between Dido and Aeneas in the *Aeneid*, and continued to be a favourite into medieval times.

As important for European literature was the emergence of pastoral poetry. Its father is usually seen to be Theocritus (first half of the third century). Theocritus was a native of Syracuse and probably lived in southern Italy before being attracted to Alexandria by Ptolemaic patronage. He may have drawn on the traditional songs of the shepherds of southern Italy to create a world in which shepherds banter with each other, woo playful girls, or lament the death of a companion against a backdrop of the changing seasons and fertile countryside. Love-making is at first joyful and freely enjoyed on the grass or among the cypress groves, though often disillusion follows. Theocritus describes the seduction of a girl by Daphnis, a legendary Sicilian herdsman who reappears in pastoral poetry through the ages, and goes on:

> Thus did this happy pair their love dispense
> With mutual joys, and gratified their sense;
> The God of Love was there a bidden guest;
> And present at his own mysterious feast.
> His azure mantle underneath he spread,
> And scattered roses on the nuptial bed;

While folded in each other's arms they lay,
He blew the flames and furnished out the play,
And from their foreheads wiped the balmy sweat away.
First rose the maid, and with a glowing face
Her downcast eyes beheld her print upon the grass;
Thence to her herd she sped herself in haste:
The bridegroom started from his trance at last,
And piping homeward jocundly he passed.

(Translation by the English poet John Dryden, 1685)

The happiness was not to last, and Daphnis was to die of love, leading to a lament by Theocritus which was to echo down the years and provide a model for such pastoral elegies as Milton's *Lycidas*:

But O the heavy change, now thou art gone,
Now thou art gone, and never must return!
Thee, shepherd, thee the woods, and desert caves,
With wild thyme and the gadding vine o'ergrown,
And all their echoes mourn.

The attraction of the countryside as refuge is explored by another Syracusan poet, Moschus (*c.*150 BC). The translation is by the poet Shelley.

When winds that move not its calm surface sweep
The azure sea, I love the land no more;
The smiles of the serene and tranquil deep
Tempt my unquiet mind. But when the roar
Of Ocean's great abyss resounds, and foam
Gathers upon the sea, and vast waves burst,
I turn from the drear aspect to the home
Of Earth and its deep woods, where, interspersed,
When winds blow loud, pines make sweet melody.
Whose house is some lone bark, whose toil the sea,
Whose prey the wandering fish, an evil lot
Has chosen. But I my languid limbs will fling
Beneath the plane, where the brook's murmuring
Moves the calm spirit, but disturbs it not.

Science and Mathematics

In the sciences and mathematics the centre of activity was, in contrast, the very urban and cosmopolitan setting of Alexandria. The Ptolemies actively encouraged scientific research, and Hellenistic science reached levels which were not to be surpassed until the sixteenth century. It was the breadth of the achievement and the ingenuity with which difficulties were confronted which was remarkable. These were some of the greatest minds in history tackling some of its most impenetrable scientific problems. As with literature, however, what survives is fragmentary and perhaps unrepresentative of what was actually achieved.

The three great mathematicians of the day, Euclid (active about 300 BC), Archimedes (287–212 BC), and Apollonius of Perge (active about 200 BC), the last two 'original geniuses of the highest order', in the words of Geoffrey Lloyd, were all based in Alexandria. In his *Elements*, Euclid produced what has possibly been the most successful textbook in history. His method was to set out a series of axioms, propositions so basic that everyone must accept them, and then through rational argument systematically deduce theorems from them. The simplicity of his work and the method he used has made *The Elements* the foundation of all subsequent mathematics. Archimedes built further on Euclid's work. He devised sophisticated ways of measuring the area of a circle and was the first man to calculate accurately the size of *pi* and devise the formula for measuring the volume of a sphere. He virtually invented the science of hydrostatics. Overall it could be argued that Archimedes made more advances in mathematics than any other mathematician in history. (Galileo described him as 'superhuman'.) Apollonius' contribution was in geometry, where his work with conic sections taxes even the most advanced mathematician today.

The problem that these early mathematicians had to contend with was that their theoretical work advanced far beyond the technology available to them. Much of what they wrote had to remain as speculation. Hero of Alexandria (*fl. c.*60 BC) and Archimedes made water clocks and toys which worked through steam, but these were simple and had no practical value. The most fruitful area of speculation was astronomy, where there were discoveries which went far ahead of the conventional wisdom of the time. Aristarchus of Samos (*c.*275 BC), for instance, suggested that the earth went round the sun, although he failed to convince the mainstream astronomers, who continued for another 1,700 years to believe in the earth-centred universe. In the third century Eratosthenes calculated the circumference of the earth by comparing the shadow, or lack of it, thrown by the sun at two different points on the Nile at midday. Although his final result is disputed, he may have come within 300 kilometres of the correct figure. (The Greeks had no problems in accepting the world as round.)

The most influential figure in astronomy was the mathematician Apollonius (beginning of the second century BC). He started with the premiss that the earth is at rest in the centre of the universe. To the Greek astronomers this seemed the most plausible explanation as to why the position of the stars in the sky remained constant, and also accorded with Aristotle's theory that, as the evidence of gravity suggested, everything was attracted to the earth as the natural centre of the universe. From this premiss Apollonius evolved a system with which to explain the movements of the planets. He assumed that they always moved in circles but that the centre of each circle itself moved along the circumference of a second circle. Sometimes the centre of this second circle was the earth but other points were possible. The system allowed a wide range of astronomical phenomena, including the varying length of the seasons, to be explained more easily. It was Apollonius' system, as elaborated by Hipparchus of Nicaea, that was to be used in the second century AD by the greatest astronomer of all, Ptolemy (active in Alexandria AD 127–45, see below p. 514). Hipparchus (end of second century BC) achieved the remarkable feat of spotting and defining the precession of the equinoxes. As the earth is not an exact sphere its axes oscillate slightly and this means that its position as a viewing platform for the stars shifts slightly but consistently, achieving a full revolution in 26,000 years. Hipparchus spotted this and and made the first calculation of the speed of change.

Greek medicine, in contrast, claimed to give first place to observation. The earliest surviving body of texts on Greek medicine, some sixty in all, dating from between 430 and 330 BC, were traditionally attributed to Hippocrates, a physician who lived on the island of Cos in the fifth century. Even though there is no evidence that he actually wrote any of the texts, Hippocrates continues to be associated with many of the maxims outlined in them: that the patient needs to be viewed as a whole, that much healing takes place naturally, that a simple diet is conducive to good health, and that the first duty of a doctor is to his patients rather than to himself.

One of the most influential texts attributed to Hippocrates is entitled *On the Sacred Disease*. It deals with epilepsy, the disorder which was traditionally most easily associated with a direct intervention by the gods. The text points out that epilepsy occurs naturally, is rooted in the brain, has defined causes, possibly inherited, and might be cured by drugs if treated early. The text challenges those who pedal 'magic' cures for such illnesses, only the trained doctor can help. Here is the birth of modern scientific medicine.

Any serious advance in the field depended on the gathering of empirical information about the working of the human body. The Greeks were used to cutting up animals after sacrificing and to some extent they applied what they learnt of anatomy by analogy to the human body. There is a report that Herophilus of Chalcedon and Erasistratus of Ceos, both active in the 260s, went one step further in taking living criminals as the subjects of their observations and gained the first significant insights into the working of the human body. Their methods included dissection of their subjects, possibly even when they were still alive. Between them Herophilus and Erasistratus were the first to investigate the nervous system and understand the difference between sensory and motor nerves, and they came close to discovering the circulation of the blood. It was Herophilus who described and named the duodenum for the first time. Inevitably they were limited, as were all Greek scientists, by their lack of instruments. They worked only with the naked eye and had no chance of seeing bacteria or viruses. Their conception of the causes of illness was circumscribed by the theory of the four humours. Nevertheless, their work provided the foundations on which Galen, the greatest of the Greek doctors, built his pioneering studies of physiology in the second century AD (see below, p. 514).

Underlying the achievements of these 'scientists' was a lively curiosity, and it can be seen in the Hellenistic period in a passion for exploration. Alexander had inspired an interest in distant lands, and in the three centuries that followed his death Greek travellers explored the furthest reaches of the accessible world. One of the most remarkable voyages was that of Pytheas, a sea-captain from Marsilia (modern Marseilles), who sailed through the Straits of Gibraltar and then northwards to make a circumnavigation of Britain in about 320. He reached a point where the nights were only two to three hours long, a latitude of about 65 degrees. Pytheas was a genuine adventurer, a mathematician and astronomer who seems to have had no commercial interests and simply an urge to understand how the world worked. Other travellers reached the River Ganges in India and, in Africa, as far south as Somaliland, where elephants were found and brought back for the armies of the Ptolemies. One fruit of these travels was the first world map, produced by Dicaearchus of Messenia about 300. It incorporated a line of latitude. At the end of the century Eratosthenes introduced a map which showed longitude as well.

Religion and Philosophy

Although science and mathematics depended heavily on the use of reason, outside these areas it seemed as if less rational ways of thought predominated. The old loyalties to city and to the gods of Olympus were in decline in an age which was rootless and restless. The Sceptics (founder Pyrrhon of Elis (c.365–275 BC)) doubted whether anything could be said with certainty about the nature of things—the senses are too deceptive. Pyrrhon's response was to urge men to stop worrying and take refuge in tranquillity! Others extended their spiritual searches. In the place of the traditional gods, aspirations focused on Tyche, Chance or Fortune, who was worshipped as a semi-divine entity. It was an acceptance that reason could not predict the future, and it is understandable that there was a growing interest in mystery religions, several of which were imported from outside the Greek world. The goddess Isis from Egypt, and Cybele, the great mother-goddess from Anatolia, were both adopted into the Greek (and later into the Roman) world and developed their own elaborate initiation cults. Of the traditional Greek gods, worship of Demeter through her mysteries at Eleusis (see p. 238) and of Dionysus proved the most resilient. Restless though this world may have been one can also be positive about the growing range of spiritual alternatives. So long as the gods were not openly mocked and public order maintained there was freedom to explore one's spirituality in a variety of ways.

In the world of philosophy the question which haunted the philosophers was how to live 'a good life'. The question may have been given a new focus by the disappearance of so many of the traditional roles which life in the small city had provided so that energies were diverted from the vigorous debating cockpits of the *polis* towards reflection on the ultimate nature of things. One response was that of the Cynics, to withdraw from the world altogether, renouncing material possessions and turning social conventions upside-down. The founder of Cynicism, Diogenes, reputedly asked by Alexander the Great what he wanted out of life, requested no more than that Alexander get out of the way of the sun.

The two major figures of Hellenistic philosophy, Epicurus and Zeno, came from Samos and Cyprus respectively but it was to Athens that they were drawn to teach. Both tried to find a meaning for the individual in an age of angst. For Epicurus, who lived in Athens from 307 until his death in 271, the world was one in which the gods had little or no influence. He followed the materialist philosopher Democritus (see p. 194) in believing that the world was composed of atoms and that those making up each individual dissolved when that individual died and then regrouped to make up other objects. All that could be known must be based on observation and experience of this world. The only purpose of this life is to ensure survival in this world through pleasure. By this Epicurus did not mean a frenzied search for sensual enjoyment but rather peace of mind and freedom from pain. In order to achieve this it was important to escape from any fear of death and to concentrate on the pleasures of everyday living, chief amongst which Epicurus numbered friendship and rational thinking. 'The pleasant life is produced not by a string of drinking bouts and revelries, nor by the enjoyment of boys and women, nor by fish and the other items on an expensive menu, but by sober reasoning.' A retreat from the hectic, competitive life of the Greek world marked a major reversal of traditional Greek values where a man was judged by the success of his public life, and Epicureanism was never completely respectable. However, it proved popular in the last years of republican Rome and has not lost its impact today. A recent Italian edition of Epicurus sold a million copies.

The founder of the Stoics, Zeno (*c.*333–262 BC), taught from the colonnades of the Stoa Poikile along the northern side of the Agora of Athens. Like the Epicureans, the Stoics accepted that the world was made entirely of matter and knowledge of it could be gained through direct observation and reason. Unlike the Epicureans, however, for whom the world was continually changing as atoms rearranged themselves into new forms, the Stoics saw the world as a single enduring entity, a cosmos which moved forward in time under its own purpose, an evolution towards a state of ultimate goodness. Human beings were an intrinsic part of the unfolding cosmos, not separate from it. It was important to come to terms with the fact that one was part of a greater whole and also had a personal responsibility for making a contribution towards the unfolding of the future. On the one hand the Stoic learnt to accept pain and pleasure with indifference, as nothing could be done to avoid them, on the other there was a duty to live a virtuous life in accordance with one's true nature as a human being. The mature Stoic was thoughtful about his own role in society and often felt duty bound to take on public responsibilities. Stoicism was to be particularly influential in Rome, and was one of the Greek philosophical traditions which helped form early Christianity.

The Jews in the Hellenistic Period

Stoicism accepted that there was one guiding force, the *logos*, or divine reason, which shaped the destiny of the world. As has been seen in Chapter 6, a much more anthropomorphic single god had been adopted by the Jews. Under the Persians the Jews had been tolerated, and references in the Bible to the Persians are favourable. However, for the first 120 years after Alexander's death Palestine was under Ptolemaic rule and was subject to the same intrusive bureaucracy suffered by the Egyptians. One result was a new diaspora, a scattering of Jews throughout the Mediterranean world. The largest Jewish community outside Palestine was in Alexandria, but there were communities in Asia (the Seleucids were tolerant) and as far north as the Black Sea. Inevitably the scattering led to the loosening of roots with traditional Judaism. Many Jews of the diaspora became Hellenized and even forgot Hebrew. The Torah (the instruction or law of Judaism) and the Hebrew Bible were translated into Greek (the Septuagint). Even in Judaea, the mountainous region around Jerusalem, a Greek education became popular and gymnasia threatened the traditional Jewish schools. However, wherever they settled and however Hellenized they became, Jewish communities seem to have continued to live together and their faith survived. This was the world where 200 years later Paul, not only a Hellenized Jew but also a Roman citizen, was to be born, in Tarsus in Cilicia.

In Judaea itself the Ptolemies were replaced by the Seleucids in 200. While the Ptolemies had never pursued Hellenization as a policy (it had happened naturally as a result of the steady contact between administrators and administrated), the Seleucids were much more intrusive and set about imposing Greek culture. They found the richer Jews receptive, but King Antiochus IV (ruled 175–163 BC) went too far. He had been humiliated by the Romans in 168 when he tried to invade Egypt (see p. 392), and he was desperate to try to rebuild his dwindling kingdom around a unified Greek heritage. He was also short of money and soon had his eyes on the treasury of the great temple at Jerusalem. He had no understanding of the continuing depth and tenacity of the Jewish monotheistic tradition, and when he tried to ban Jewish observances and dedicate the temple at Jerusalem to Zeus (in 167), guerrilla warfare broke out under the leadership of

Judas Maccabaeus. By 141 the Seleucids were forced to accept the independence of Judaea under Judah's brother, Simon. The kingdom was extraordinarily successful, expanding to both the south and to the north as far as Galilee. The result was the confirmation and preservation of orthodox Jewish nationalism against the forces of Hellenism. This was the world into which Jesus was to be born, and from which Christianity was to spread into the other Jewish world of Paul.

Conclusion

Despite occasional revivals, such as that inspired by the Seleucid king Antiochus III, the Hellenistic kingdoms had begun to lose their vigour by the end of the third century. The decline of the Seleucids and the Ptolemies has already been charted. The Greek world might simply have disintegrated into a number of smaller states if a more united and determined power had not arisen in the west. The Greeks had heard of the city of Rome as early as the fifth century, but it was not until 280, when Pyrrhus of Epirus took a Hellenistic army over to Italy to protect the city of Tarentum against Roman expansion, that the real strength of the city was first appreciated. By 241 all the Greek cities of Sicily except Syracuse were under Roman control. Rome as yet showed no interest in Greece, but from 229 pirates originating from the rugged Illyrian coast were causing her increasing concern. They had been suppressed by 219, and by then Rome had established a protectorate over the Illyrian coast. This intrusion aroused the suspicion of Philip V of Macedon, and the stage was set for a confrontation which was to change the history not only of the ancient Mediterranean but of the world.

It used to be the custom to end courses on the Greek world with the battle of Chaeronaea in 338 or with the death of Alexander. The assumption was that after this date the 'pure' Greek world of the fifth and fourth century was polluted with foreign influences and thus, somehow, not worthy of the same respect. (This was very much the legacy of Winckelmann who saw Hellenistic art, in particular, as decadent after the sublime glories of the Classical age.) It is hoped that this chapter has shown that the Hellenistic period is not only fascinating in its own right but also of real historical significance. It can no longer be ignored in any comprehensive study of the Greek world.

FURTHER READING

An excellent introductory survey is Graham Shipley, *The Greek World after Alexander, 323–30 BC* (London, 2000). The fullest account is Peter Green's mammoth study *From Alexander to Actium* (London, 1990). It is consistently readable and provocative though many feel it underplays the achievements of the age. See also Andrew Erskine (ed.), *A Companion to the Hellenistic World* (London, 2003). On Egypt see A. Bowman, *Egypt after the Pharaohs, 322 BC–AD 642* (London, 1986), and the relevant chapters in Ian Shaw (ed.), *The Oxford History of Ancient Egypt* (Oxford, 2000). On the Seleucids, S. Sherwin-White and A. Kuhrt's *From Samarkhand to Sardis: A New Approach to the Seleucid Empire* (London, 1993) stresses the legacy of the Babylonians and the Achaemenid empire. The relationship between the Greeks and other cultures is dealt with in A. D. Momigliano, *Alien Wisdom: The Limits of Hellenization* (Cambridge, 1975).

On art see J. Pollitt, *Art in the Hellenistic Age* (Cambridge, 1986) and R. R. R. Smith, *Hellenistic Sculpture* (London, 1991). The achievements of the Greeks in science and mathematics are conveniently summarized in Geoffrey Lloyd's chapter 'Science and Mathematics' in Moses Finlay (ed.), *The Legacy of Greece* (Oxford, 1984) and covered in more detail in his *Greek Science after Aristotle* (London, 1973). More searching accounts are contained in Lloyd's other works *The Revolutions of Wisdom: Studies in the Claims and Practice of Ancient Greek Science* (Berkeley, 1987) and *Magic, Reason and Experience* (Cambridge, 1979). James Longrigg, *Greek Medicine: A Source Book* (London, 1998), and Helen King, *Greek and Roman Medicine* (London, 2001). C. J. Tuplin and T. E. Rihill have edited a recent survey *Science and Mathematics in Ancient Greek Culture* (Oxford, 2002). Morris Kline, *A History of Mathematical Thought from Ancient to Modern Times*, vol. i (Oxford, 1972). Barry Cunliffe, *The Extraordinary Voyage of Pytheas the Greek* (London, 2001).

On Hellenistic philosophy see earlier general works cited after Chapter 16. On Hellenistic ethics see Martha Nussbaum, *The Therapy of Desire, Theory and Practice in Hellenistic Ethics* (Princeton, 1994). Richard Sorabji, *Emotion and Peace of Mind: From Stoic Agitation to Christian Temptation* (Oxford, 2000) is excellent.

For the coming of Rome there is E. Gruen, *The Hellenistic World and the Coming of Rome* (Berkeley, 1984), though some feel that Gruen underestimates the scale of the impact of Rome on the Greek world, and W. Harris, *War and Imperialism in Republican Rome* (Oxford, 1979).

Celts and Parthians

The small town of Hallstatt lies at the edge of a lake in a fine mountain setting in present-day Austria. Here in the mid-nineteenth century a huge prehistoric cemetery was unearthed. The earliest graves date from about 1100 BC, but from about 700 BC there was a significant change in burial customs. The later graves were those of aristocratic warriors, each buried in a wooden chamber under a four-wheeled wagon complete with yokes and harness. Richly decorated buckles, rings, and amulets lay alongside the bodies, and pottery and amber suggested trading links with both northern and southern Europe. There was also the widespread presence of iron.

This was the first archaeological evidence for the peoples known to the Greeks as *keltoi* and to the Romans as Gauls, the Celts. Yet were these a distinct people, 'the first Europeans' as some have seen them, or were the words *keltoi* or Gaul used as a general term for the peoples living beyond the limits of Greek or Roman culture? It is astonishing to find that there is no recorded case of anyone calling themselves Celtic in the British Isles before the eighteenth century but now a Celtic identity is assumed for anyone with Welsh, Scottish, or Irish ancestry and a sense of Celtic culture, specially potent in music, is widespread. Can one dig down into the archaeological and literary evidence for any distinct and coherent Celtic people?

What is clear is that central and western Europe in the first millennium BC was occupied by a variety of tribal groups under the leadership of warrior elites, and as already mentioned one of these can be defined as a distinct culture, the Hallstatt. The so-called Hallstatt period lasted from 750–450 BC. Hallstatt peoples spread westwards through what is now central France and northern Spain, and by 500 BC some groups had even crossed into southern Britain. The culture is characterized by graves crowded with gold ornaments, brooches, jewellery, and drinking horns. Typically, Hallstatt settlements would be found along river valleys, those of the Seine, Rhine, and Danube, for instance, which provided access to the sea. Soon links were being forged with the Mediterranean, primarily the Etruscans and the Greeks. A particularly lucrative trade route was up the Rhône from the Greek colony of Massilia. The Hallstatt elites could provide gold, tin, hides and, perhaps, slaves. In return they imported Greek pottery, wine (for which they had such demand that one source records that they would exchange a slave for a single *amphora*) and, in a few cases, prestige goods such as the celebrated Vix crater, possibly a diplomatic gift (see p. 154). It was the peoples of the land around Massilia that classical writers record as calling themselves Celts.

As the importance of local Hallstatt chieftains grew, they established themselves in defended hilltop fortresses, such as Mont Lassois in Burgundy and the Heuneberg in southern Germany, which was defended by mudbrick walls with bastions, an extraordinary creation for northern Europe and one which must have been inspired by Mediterranean examples. Their artwork was becoming more sophisticated, drawing on motifs already known in the Bronze Age but also incorporating patterns and symbols from Greece and Asia.

In the middle of the fifth century the dominance of the Hallstatt elites was being undermined. It appears that less sophisticated tribal groups on the Rivers Marne and Moselle on the northern edge of the Hallstatt culture were establishing contact with the Etruscans, who, having found their routes to the west blocked by Greeks, were now trading overland to the north. One lure was the high-quality iron ore of the Hunsruck-Eifel region. The native groups now began to realize that they controlled important resources or trade routes along which tin, amber, gold, salt, or iron travelled. The impact on these tribes of their good fortune appears to have been dramatic. They accumulated fine goods for themselves and, in particular learnt the arts of metalworking. The resulting culture is known as La Tène, after a lakeside settlement of that name in Switzerland. La Tène art is distinctive but largely confined to decorative objects in metal and jewellery. Sacred symbols, such as the human head or venerated birds and animals, are woven into complex abstract patterns used to grace weapons or personal ornaments. Attempts have been made to trace influences from the Greeks, Scythians, and even the Persians on La Tène art, but it remains individual and instantly recognizable, its motifs still popular today.

Whether the La Tène elites actually wiped out the Hallstatt elites or whether their economy simply collapsed after La Tène groups closed off the supply of prestige goods is not clear, but from 450 BC La Tène was dominant and expansionist. Its graves are characterized by speedy two-wheeled chariots, apparently adopted from the Etruscans. Pressures for expansion may have come from German tribes from the north, but the evidence from cemeteries (and the ancient classical sources) suggests rapid population increase as well. Many of the migrations were simply raids of young male warriors, their status accruing from the numbers they could recruit for their war-bands and the plunder they could seize. In some cases raids were followed by settlement—across the Alps in northern Italy, for instance (where earlier Hallstatt migrants were joined by La Tène groups) from the early fifth century—or in central Anatolia where the Galatians arrived in the third century after migrations across Macedonia and Greece. The settlements were small scale, supported by intensive agriculture, and from them war-bands ranged southwards, either as raiders or mercenaries, as far as Rome and even Sicily. In Anatolia the Attalid kings of Pergamum based their prestige on the successful defeat of the Galatians.

This then is the background to many of the classical descriptions of the 'Celts'. The word, first used of one local people around Massilia, was now used generally for these European 'barbarians'. What gives the term some coherence is that there is evidence that these people shared a *lingua franca*. The evidence comes from place names, personal names, and inscriptions and suggests that there were at least three related dialects in Europe in Spain (Celtiberian), Gaul (Gaulish), and northern Italy (Lepontic). None is spoken today. They have been given the name Continental Celtic, but this is a later (eighteenth-century) imposition and is one of the ways in which a Celtic identity has been created. It would be extending the evidence to suggest that language was linked to any ethnic group, or as later commentators have called it, a 'Celtic brotherhood'.

The context in which the 'Celts' were encountered by Greeks, Romans, and Etruscans was as formidable warriors, relying heavily on surprise and ambushes and, when in direct confrontation, on martial display. The Greek historian Polybius gives an account of 'Celtic' tribes in battle at Telemon, which turned out to be a decisive Roman victory, in 225:

The Insubres and Boii wore their trousers and light cloaks but the Gaesetae had discarded their garments owing to their proud confidence in themselves and stood naked with nothing but their arms, in front of the whole array. The Romans were terrified by the fine order of the Celtic host and the dreadful din, for there were innumerable horn blowers and trumpeters and, as the whole army was shouting their war cries at the same time, there was such a tumult of sound that it seemed that not only the trumpeters and soldiers but all the country around had got a voice and caught up the cry. Very terrifying too, were the appearance and gestures of the naked warriors in front, all in the prime of life and firmly built men, and all the leading companies adorned with gold torques and armlets.

Strabo, writing in the first century BC, describes their exuberance as if they were children.

To the frankness and high-spiritedness of their temperament must be added the traits of childish boastfulness and love of decoration. They wear ornaments of gold, torques on their necks and bracelets on their arms and wrists, while people of high rank wear dyed garments besprinkled with gold. It is this vanity which makes them unbearable in victory and so completely downcast in defeat.

So far nothing has been said of the 'Celtic' British Isles. Caesar, writing in the first century BC assumed that peoples from Gaul had migrated to the south coast of Britain but the archaeological record is open to much dispute. In some cases there is linguistic evidence of migration. The Parisii of northern England seem related to the Parisi of the Seine valley in northern France. (There is also some similarity between the two tribes' grave goods.) On the whole, however, the scholarly trend has been to replace traditional diffusionist explanations of migrations with the possibility that intensive contact through trade led to many native peoples in Britain adopting La Tène culture to maintain the status of their own elites. However, most Britons spoke a dialect of Celtic known as Insular Celtic. Again it is a term used first in the eighteenth century but it does have the advantage of referring to languages which are still being spoken. It is normally divided into Q-Celtic and P-Celtic on the basis of whether the qu sound is pronounced as q- or p-. P-Celtic appears to have been spoken in most of Britain and now survives in the Welsh (and, on the Continent, the Breton) language, while Q-Celtic remains in the native Gaelic languages of Ireland, the Isle of Man and western Scotland. It is this language (and the legends and myths expressed in it) which underlies much of the existing sense of a Celtic brotherhood. It has been argued, for instance (though not without contention), that the Irish saga *Tain Bo Cuailnge* has elements which could go back to the late first millennium BC.

The Celts could never sustain themselves by war, especially after the Hellenistic monarchs and Rome became able to offer effective resistance, so agriculture remained at the core of each tribal economy. By the second century BC, however, there was a further development as some communities became concentrated in larger urban settlements, the so-called *oppida*. There is some evidence that these centres grew to protect trade routes at a time of growing external pressures, but their appearance is also suggestive of growing prosperity and stability. Coinage, adopted from Greek and Macedonian examples, appears. The *oppida* were primarily trading settlements but also, in many cases, supported local industries or were close to important natural resources. Most prominent of all was the great settlement at Manching on the upper Danube. It was set on an open plain and covered 375 hectares. It exploited local deposits of iron, but copper and bronze were also worked and high-quality pottery manufactured.

As the Romans became stronger, they were able to take the offensive against the Celts. The tribes of Gaul were defeated and their warrior elites finally broken, although some re-emerged as auxiliary troops serving in the Roman army. In the famous words of Tacitus, the Gauls were seduced by the trappings of civilization (see Chapter 26). Their many gods were merged into the Roman pantheon, and within two generations prominent Celtic families had adopted Roman names. What may have survived of a Celtic heritage in outlying areas of Europe was there to be revived by nationalists from the eighteenth century onwards.

It should be clear from the above that to make coherent links between the Hallstatt and La Tène cultures, a Celtic language with both Continental and British dialects and a mass of other peoples, some of whom may have been migratory Celts, others non-Celts who adopted elements of La Tène culture, is impossible. The term 'Celt' is generally, if loosely, used here to describe the peoples of western and central Europe as encountered by the Greeks and Romans and conquered by the latter. The Celts are also to be distinguished from the Germanic tribes beyond the Rhine and Danube although here again any clear distinction between Celt and German is difficult to make.

The Parthians

The story of the Seleucid empire, and the continuous pressures it faced, has been told in the last chapter. Its disintegration in the west at the hands of the Romans will be told in the following chapter. In the east its most formidable opponents were the Parthians. After the absorption of western Asia into the Roman empire, the Parthians were to prove one of the most persistent enemies of Rome. Their empire lasted some 400 years.

It was at the end of the third century BC that a tribal leader, Arsaces, fought his way to dominance over the many nomadic peoples of Parthia, a remote northern province of the Seleucid empire. His strength lay in his horsemen, who fought either as heavily armed cavalrymen or as archers. He proved impossible for the Seleucids to defeat, and although his kingdom remained part of the Seleucid empire, Arsaces exultantly transformed himself into an independent monarch with a fine new capital built at Hecatompylos.

It took another hard century of fighting before the Parthian empire was fully established. It had to achieve defensible frontiers in both the east and the west. Mithridates I (171–138 BC) was the first Parthian ruler to achieve full independence from the Seleucids. He penetrated as far south as Mesopotamia, but had to surrender his conquests when threatened from the east. He initiated a policy of tolerance towards the Greek culture which had now suffused Persia. (On his coins he portrayed his ancestor Arsaces as Apollo.) A successor, Mithridates II (ruled 123–88 BC, not to be confused with Mithridates VI of Pontus), won back the Parthian homeland, pushed the western boundaries of the empire as far as the Euphrates, and subdued the nomadic peoples of the east.

This was the true foundation of the Parthian empire. Mithridates was a gifted ruler who was quick to exploit the position of his empire as a middleman between his two most powerful enemies, China in the east, and, after the demise of the Seleucids, Rome in the west. The Chinese, under the Han dynasty, were happy to respond. They traded silk in return for the majestic horses provided by the Parthians, which they needed for their own defence. (The Chinese were the only people who knew the secret of the moment when to destroy the larvae of the silkworm so that the filament would form a continuous length which could be woven into thread. It was a secret only smuggled into the west in the sixth century AD.) Ambassadors were exchanged. The Parthians sent ostrich eggs and conjurors as their gift to the Chinese court, and in 106 BC the first caravan travelled west from China.

The Romans developed an insatiable desire for silk, and the Parthians were able to charge heavy dues on traffic along the overland trade route, the famous Silk Road. The first official meeting between Romans and Parthians took place on the Euphrates in 92 BC. The Romans were represented by Sulla, later the dictator of Rome. He misjudged the Parthians, assuming that their ambassadors had come to submit themselves as vassals. He treated them with such contempt that the Parthian ambassador was later beheaded for acquiescing in this humiliation. The Roman general Pompey made the same mistake referring to the Parthian monarch only as 'king' instead of the traditional 'king of kings'. At the battle of Carrhae, 53 BC, the Parthians were to have their revenge, and they followed this up with another defeat, of Mark Antony, in 34 BC (see Chapter 21). The end of the first century BC saw the zenith of the empire, and the emperor Augustus was wise enough to recognize it as an equal to Rome. Conflict with the Parthians, was, however, to continue over the centuries, until the collapse of the Parthian empire in the 200s AD.

FURTHER READING

As an introduction to the Celts see Barry Cunliffe, *The Celts: A Very Short Introduction* (Oxford, 2003); Cunliffe has also written *Facing the Ocean: The Atlantic and its Peoples* (Oxford, 2001) and *The Ancient Celts* (Oxford, 1997). A comprehensive survey is Miranda Green, *The Celtic World* (London, 1995). As background to the issues B. Cunliffe (ed.), *The Oxford Illustrated History of Prehistoric Europe* (Oxford, 1994). Also recommended is J. Haywood, *The Historical Atlas of the Celtic World* (London, 2001). On Celtic art, R. Megaw and V. Megaw, *Celtic Art from its Beginnings to the Book of Kells* (2nd edition, London, 2001). For the modern debate about Celtic identity see S. James, *The Atlantic Celts: Ancient People or Modern Invention* (London, 1999).

On the Parthians see Josef Wiesehofer, *Ancient Persia from 550 BC to 650 AD* (translated by Azizeh Azodi, London, 2001), and the chapter by R. Frye, 'Parthia and Sasanid Persia', in F. Millar, *The Roman Empire and its Neighbours* (2nd edition, London, 1981). The *Cambridge History of Iran*, vol. iii, Parts 1 and 2 (Cambridge, 1983) provides more detailed information.

20 | The Etruscans and Early Rome

> Not without reason did gods and men choose this spot for the site of our city—the salubrious hills, the river to bring us produce from the inland regions, and seaborne commerce from abroad, the sea itself, near enough for convenience yet not so near as to bring danger from foreign fleets, our situation in the very heart of Italy—all these advantages make it of all places in the world the best for a city destined to grow great.
>
> (Livy, *History of Rome*, Book V, translation: Tim Cornell)

The Roman historian Livy (59 BC–AD 17) began writing his history of Rome in 29 BC when the city's history was already glorious and its supremacy in the Mediterranean unquestioned. It was hardly surprising that he assumed that the greatness of Rome was predestined and inevitable. In fact, greatness had not come quickly. The hills of Rome had been settled for at least 700 years before the city expanded from a relatively small territory on the plain of Latium and achieved the domination of the Italian peninsula in the fourth and third centuries BC.

The Geography of Italy

The achievement, when it eventually came, was, however, a remarkable one. The most formidable obstacle to successful domination has been a mountain range, the Apennines. The Apennines stretch down the peninsula for 1,000 kilometres rising to nearly 3,000 metres in places and are often between 50 and 100 kilometres wide. There are pockets of fertile land high in the Apennines so a reasonably sized population can be supported, but the range breaks up and isolates communities. Italy, as a result, has always been a country of unexpected diversity, strong regional loyalties, and well-established local languages. Even in the twentieth century Italian remained a second language for many 'Italians'.

Around the Apennines lie the coastal plains. The richest is the Po valley in northern Italy which makes up 70 per cent of the lowland of Italy. Further north the Alps appear to close the peninsula off from Europe. In fact they are not as impassable as they look. The extraordinary find of 'The Ice Man', a body dating from 3300 BC high in the Alps in 1991 shows that individuals were crossing by foot in the earliest times, and 'Celtic' tribes, driven by overpopulation or tribal rivalry, successfully migrated across the Alps in the sixth and fifth centuries BC and settled in the Po valley. It was these resilient peoples (Gauls to the Romans) rather than the Alps who were to provide the main barrier to Roman expansion in the north.

The Romans had other people to subdue before they could achieve their 'destiny'. The most fertile land along the Apennines is that along the west coast. The soil is volcanic and the rainfall good, while between the rivers Tiber and Arno are to be found some of the richest mineral deposits in the central Mediterranean. The coast is indented and so provides a safe haven for seafarers. From the eighth century, easterners, Greeks and Phoenicians in particular, were trading inland for minerals. Their suppliers were the native peoples of Etruria, the Etruscans, who grew rich on the pickings of the trade.

The Etruscans

There have always been those who have been drawn to the Etruscans, often presenting them as a particularly mysterious people. The novelist D. H. Lawrence, for example, already tubercular and on a slow path to death, became totally immersed in the atmosphere of an Etruscan world entirely of his own making. As he wandered among deserted Etruscan tombs in the mid-1920s he fantasized:

The things they did in their easy centuries are as natural and as easy as breathing. They leave the breast breathing freely and pleasantly with a certain fullness of life. Even the tombs. And that is the true Etruscan quality: ease, naturalness and an abundance of life, no need to force the mind or soul in any direction. And death to the Etruscan was a pleasant continuance of life, with jewels and wines and flutes playing for the dance. (From *Etruscan Places*, published posthumously in 1932)

There is, in fact, no evidence to support Lawrence's belief that the Etruscans were a people without cares. Why then have they proved so attractive? One reason, perhaps, is the legend, passed on by Herodotus, of an exotic origin in the east. However, the legend has now been discredited by modern archaeology, which has established beyond doubt that Etruscan civilization originated within Italy itself. The Etruscans' language (which, unlike other languages of the peninsula, Oscan, Umbrian, and Latin, is non-Indo-European in origin) is often said to be incomprehensible and this may have added a sense of mystery. In fact, their alphabet, derived from that of the Euboean Greeks, has long been decipherable, although not every word recorded in it is yet understood and what appears to have been a solid body of literature recounting the deeds of leading families has been lost. It may be because the Etruscans are considered particularly religious and hence irrational (in contrast, said Lawrence, to the rational Romans), but every culture has 'irrational' features and, whatever Lawrence may have said, the Romans were no exception. Perhaps it is simply that so many Etruscan cities on their commanding sites are now deserted and so they are particularly atmospheric places to visit. Even the Romans caught the mood of nostalgia for the ruined cities. The poet Propertius (first century BC) wrote of the desolation of the Etruscan city of Veii, captured by the Romans in 396 BC:

> Veii, thou hadst a royal crown of old,
> And in thy forum stood a throne of gold!
> Thy walls now echo but the shepherd's horn,
> And o'er thine ashes waves the summer corn.

(Translation by George Dennis, perhaps the greatest of the nineteenth-century writers on the Etruscans.)

It is only recently that archaeology is allowing a more realistic assessment of who the Etruscans were and what they achieved. It is now clear that as early as 1200 BC the primitive agricultural economy of Etruria was becoming more sophisticated and intensive, with an increased dependence on sheep, goats, and pigs. A larger population could be supported and by 900 BC it was becoming grouped in scattered villages on the plateaux of tufa (a soft volcanic rock) which are typical of the area. Each village had its own cemetery close by. The burials of the period are easily recognizable from the biconical urns of a dark pottery incised with simple decorations in which the ashes of the dead were placed. One of the first sites of this period to be excavated, in the 1850s, was at Villanova, near the modern Bologna, and the name Villanovan was given to the period.

It used to be believed that the Villanovan culture was that of a distinct people who were taken over by the Etruscans. In fact, what later became the great cities of the Etruscan world, Veii, Tarquinia, Vulci, Cerveteri, all developed directly from these earlier Villanovan village sites. When the Greeks and Phoenicians first approached Etruria in the eighth century they found the Tyrrhenian Sea already dominated by the Etruscans, who were trading along the coast and across the sea to Sardinia. (The name Tyrrhenian comes from the Greek word for Etruscan.)

What the Etruscans had to offer the visitors from the east was metal. The Colline Metallifere, the metal-bearing hills above what became the major Etruscan cities of Populonia and Vetulonia, yielded iron, copper, and silver. The deposits were already being exploited locally but now Etruscan aristocrats began exchanging the metals for the goods of the east, pottery and finished metalwork. Local cemeteries show the results. The most extensively excavated is that at Quattro Fontanili, a cemetery of the important southern town of Veii, one of the first to make direct contact with the east. After about 760 the burials show an increased use of iron. It is beaten into the status symbols of a warrior aristocracy, helmets, swords and shields, chariots and horse-bits, and implements for

feasting. Women are buried with jewellery. The influences in this 'orientalizing' period are from the east in general, including Phoenicia and Syria, rather than simply from Greece. The easterners' settlement at Pithekoussai on Ischia (see also Chapter 9) seems to have been a cosmopolitan one.

Etruscan society appears to have been made up of clans each with its own leader. An Etruscan probably identified himself more with his clan than with a particular city or an Etruscan 'nation'. (Etruscan names, in line with those of other Italic peoples, consisted of what the Romans would later call a *nomen*, the clan, and a *praenomen*, a personal name. The Greeks, in contrast, spoke of a person and his *city*. The first Greek historian of Rome is known as Timaeus of Tauromenium, for instance.) Warfare between rival clans may have involved local chieftains fighting on horseback backed by lightly armed retainers, as with the medieval *condottiere*. Although some pieces of hoplite armour came in with Greek trade there is no significant evidence that the Etruscans adopted the phalanx and fought as equal members of a community as the Greeks did. This is warfare between individuals, and it is possible that the Roman triumph (see the end of this chapter) originated with the Etruscans as the celebration, and public assertion of his authority, by a victorious chieftain. Some sources talk of Etruscan kings, and it may be that each settlement had its own supreme ruler with 'a gold crown, an ivory throne, a sceptre surmounted by an eagle, a purple tunic threaded with gold and a cloak, also of purple, with embroidered decoration', as one later Roman account puts it.

Rivalry between local aristocrats led to the emergence of more consolidated and better-protected settlements. The tufa plateaux already offered good defence but from possibly as early as 700 BC they were fortified with tufa blocks. (Cerveteri is an example.) This initiated a tradition of building massive fortified walls which reached its peak in the fifth and fourth centuries when the Etruscan cities were threatened by both Romans and Celts. The evidence from tombs of this earlier period suggests a small aristocratic elite whose cultural life was increasingly influenced by their contacts with Greece. The Greek alphabet was adopted about 700 BC and literacy maintained by the elite as a status symbol. In the surviving tombs of Tarquinia paintings on the walls of the burial chambers show a lifestyle centring on hunting and banqueting. It is in the banqueting scenes that direct Greek influence is most evident, with couples reclining on couches in symposia and the Athenian game of *kottabos* in full swing (See Chapter 13). The couples are not, as in Athens, men with their *hetairai* but Etruscans with their wives. It is a lifestyle reminiscent of an earlier aristocratic age of Greece, the world of Odysseus and Penelope, rather than that of democratic Athens. Upper-class Etruscan women appear to have been treated with affection and tenderness and they are portrayed in carriages and as spectators at games. (Among the imports from the Greeks were chariot races which were then passed on to the Romans as their great spectator sport.) There is little indication of the homosexuality portrayed so openly on Greek vase paintings and it seems clear that the Etruscans adapted Greek ideas and fashions to their own social needs rather than slavishly imitating them.

It was the paintings of the tombs which gave Lawrence his picture of the Etruscans, but it is impossible to conclude from them that Etruscan life, even for the elite, was a parade of banquets interspersed by hunting. The pictures of banqueting, for instance, may represent the hopes of the deceased for life in the future world or may record a transitional meal between the world of the living and the world of the dead. (By the fourth century BC some banquets include demons and other symbols of the underworld in them, a development which some have linked to the increasing threat from Rome.) Similarly the Greek pottery which fills the later tombs (and provides 80 per cent of the known surviving Attic vases) may have been attractive for its associations with the world of the dead and the hopes of some afterlife for those who have carried out heroic deeds. The story of Heracles, a mortal figure who becomes immortal through his labours, is a popular theme which was probably exploited by Athenian potters working specifically for the Etruscan market. Another, the legend of the Seven Against Thebes, is more fully represented in Etruscan art than in any examples from Greece itself.

As their prosperity grew the Etruscans expanded southwards. Their influence spread over the entire plain of Campania, rich land in itself but also a meeting place with the Greeks who had crossed to the shore to set up the settlement of Cumae about 725. By the end of the eighth century the Etruscans had their own trading centres on the coast. Pontecagnano is one example. With the growing importance of trade and craftsmanship, Etruscan cities were developing on the major hilltop sites. The towns of Latium, among them Rome with its important position on the Tiber, now also came under Etruscan control and Etruscan influence spread inland. There is some evidence for urban settlement in Umbria and the peoples there used Etruscan script to record their distinctive dialect (as in the Iguvine tablets, a set of religious tracts, discovered in 1444 in the town of Gubbio, and still on display in the museum there).

One original Etruscan creation is *bucchero*, a shiny black pottery. From about 650 it was being traded along the French and Spanish coasts. In the sixth century trade in manufactured goods was given new impetus by migrants from Greece. One aristocrat, Demaratus, is recorded as fleeing from tyranny in Corinth in the middle of the century and setting up his business in Etruria. It was possibly under his influence that the Etruscans copied metal relief work in clay and so developed terracotta, used at first for the decoration of temples. It later provides some of the most attractive of Etruscan 'sculptures', married couples reclining on couches and a magnificent set of horses from Tarquinia. Particularly fascinating is a series of terracotta frieze plaques from what may be a local leader's residence at Poggio Civitate near Murlo (dated to between 650 and 575 BC). They show a horse race, a procession, possibly of a newly married couple and their attendants, a banquet, and a row of seated figures with their attendants. At Gravisca, the port of Tarquinia, a Greek sanctuary was established and offerings to Apollo, Hera, and Demeter survive. One particularly exciting find here has been an anchor with a dedication to Apollo from one Sostratus. Pots have been found in Etruria inscribed with the Greek letters SOS and it may not be wishful thinking that these are the wares of a wealthy Greek merchant of this name mentioned by Herodotus as trading in the late sixth century. Greek craftsmen now begin to settle, and Etruscan craftsmen acquired skills in working gold, silver, and ivory from them. (The cultural relationship between the Greeks and the Etruscans is fully explored by John Boardman in his *The Diffusion of Classical Art in Antiquity*.) Burial customs change to reflect a more egalitarian society. At Cerveteri from about 500 BC individual burial chambers are replaced by what is a city of the dead with tombs arranged in streets, each one with a façade in the shape of a house carved in the tufa. Family tombs are surrounded by more modest burial places for what might be servants or retainers. A similar planned cemetery has been found at the modern Orvieto (the Etruscan Volsinii).

Livy said that the Etruscans were more religious than any other people. It is difficult to give much meaning to such a statement but ritual was certainly important and the remains of sanctuaries show that the Etruscans sought divine help for their daily needs. They created a pantheon of gods drawn from many sources, some local, some Greek. (Two-thirds of the Olympian gods have an Etruscan equivalent.) Each god had his or her own place in the sky, and an understanding of the pleasure or displeasure of the gods could be gained from watching the flight of birds, flashes of lightning, or any other unusual event. The augurs, responsible for interpreting the signs, would then prescribe the correct rituals for their appeasement.

The augurs would carry out their duties standing within a sacred area set apart on high ground. (The area was known to the Romans as a *templum*, the origin of the word 'temple'.) Perhaps as early as 600 BC the Etruscans built temples immediately behind the sacred area. The model is the Greek temple but the emphasis is on a highly decorated façade and an entrance only at the front. The *podium* on which the temple rested is much higher than in Greece and the augur may have stood on its edge to make his divinations. This model was the one adopted by the Romans most notably in the great temple to Jupiter, Juno, and Minerva on the Capitoline Hill begun in the late sixth century when an Etruscan 'king' still ruled Rome. The Romans drew heavily on Etruscan beliefs, and the rules of divination, the *disciplina*, were carefully preserved by them.

Etruscan supremacy along the coast came under threat from about 550 BC as new waves of Greeks fled from Persian expansion. The Phocaean colony at Alalia in eastern Corsica was particularly threatening. In 540 BC the Etruscans, with some Phoenician support, defeated the Phocaeans at sea and forced the abandonment of the settlement, but the Phocaeans had also settled in southern France and they now blocked off Etruscan trade there. Meanwhile the Carthaginians (Phoenicians who had established the city of Carthage and made it a springboard for further colonization) had consolidated their position in Sardinia and on the western coast of Sicily and gradually forced the Etruscans off the sea. At Pyrgi, the port of Cerveteri, a famous set of gold plaques contains a bilingual dedication by a ruler of Cerveteri, Thefarie Velianas, to the Phoenician goddess Astarte, who is equated with the Etruscan Uni (the Etruscan equivalent to Hera and the forerunner of the Roman Juno). It has been suggested that Thefarie Velianas was a tyrant of Carthaginian origin who had been imposed on Cerveteri. The Etruscans were now also under pressure from the Greek tyrants in Sicily. An expedition led by Etruscans with native mercenaries against the Greek city of Cumae in about 525 BC failed and in 474 BC Hiero of Syracuse defeated an Etruscan fleet off Cumae. The Etruscan presence in Campania was eliminated in the fifth century by the Samnites, a mountain people who now began raiding into the plains.

As the Carthaginians became dominant in the Tyrrhenian Sea the coastal cities of Etruria went into decline. Inland cities including Clusium (a ruler of Clusium, Lars Porsenna, features among Rome's early enemies), Fiesole, Cortona, Volsinii (Orvieto), and Veii continued to flourish, largely because they were exploiting their land so successfully. (The remains of large irrigation schemes dating from the fifth century have been found around Veii.) These cities were grouped in a confederation of twelve city states who held an annual meeting at a shrine to the goddess Voltumna, but there does not seem to have been any political unity between them. None of them came to the help of Veii when it was attacked by Rome in the fifth and early fourth century.

What trade remained had now to be directed across the Apennines in the Po valley. A new Etruscan city near the present town of Marzabotto, at the foot of the Apennines, was laid out in about 500 BC. Its carefully planned regular streets and distinction between a public and a residential area suggest the influence of Greek town planning. Other Etruscan foundations include the modern cities of Ravenna, Rimini, and Bologna. One of the most successful trading cities was Spina on the Po delta, built, as Venice would be, on piles with bridges and canals between the buildings. Here the Etruscans met the Greeks in a city which seems as much Greek as Etruscan and which has proved the richest source of Attic vases of any Etruscan city. However, the Etruscan presence was threatened by a number of forces, including the eventual silting up of Spina and the migration of 'Celtic' war-bands across the Alps. There is some evidence of intermarriage between the newcomers and Etruscans and new trade routes were forged with the tribal groups of northern Europe (producing the La Tène culture, see p. 356) but the Etruscan cities of central Italy were now falling into steady decline and were eventually defeated and destroyed by Rome in the third century.

The decline of the Etruscans was one of the factors which made the fifth and fourth centuries an age of crisis in Italy. In the north Celtic groups were occupying the Po valley and raiding down further into the peninsula. A host of different mountain peoples began to plunder the plains. They may have been driven by population pressures but many had also acquired military skills from service as mercenaries and so had developed the confidence to attack the wealthy Greek and Etruscan cities of the lowlands. Almost every Greek city of south-west Italy was overrun in the fifth century.

The Foundation of Rome

It was in this world of turmoil and changing fortunes that Rome was to emerge as the major power in Italy in the fourth century. The earlier history of the city has proved very difficult to reconstruct. Later Roman historians drew on a variety of legends from both Greek and Roman sources to create their own version of the city's foundation. There was a Greek story, later exploited by Virgil in the *Aeneid*, of Aeneas fleeing from the fall of Troy and eventually settling in Latium, where he founded a line of kings at Alba Longa. There was a separate legend of twins, Romulus and Remus, who were abandoned by the side of the river Tiber, saved by being suckled by a wolf, and then brought up by shepherds. In the legend Romulus killed his brother after a quarrel and went on to found Rome. The two stories were linked by making Romulus and Remus the children of the daughter of one of the Alban kings and Mars, the god of war. A date for the foundation of the city of 753 BC was enshrined so effectively in national mythology that a thousand years later the emperor Philip the Arab visited Rome specifically to host an extravagant celebration of the anniversary.

There were other early histories of the city but these have been almost entirely lost. Some gave the city a Greek foundation myth, doubtless an attempt to give it status in an age when Greek culture was still pre-eminent. The first histories to survive in other than fragments date from the first century BC. The most important is that of Titus Livius (Livy). Livy was a native of Patavium (the modern Padua), and he was writing just as Rome's republican government was being transformed by Octavian, the future Augustus (Chapter 24). His aim was to glorify the dying republic, and his is a dramatic narrative account of the city's history with an emphasis on the epic. The entry of the Gauls into Rome and their butchery of the august senators who awaited them silently in their robes in their courtyards, the emotions as news of victory or defeat reaches Rome, the great battle scenes during the war with Hannibal still haunt the reader. (The hamstringing of the Roman soldiers after the battle of Cannae remained in my memory without my rereading it for over thirty years.) However, as a work of history, Livy's account is limited. His bias towards the glorification of the republic, his shaky grasp of geography, and the carelessness which which he drew on earlier sources, make the work unreliable. The historian has to draw on other fragmentary accounts, the consul lists and the histories of great families which were passed from generation to generation, as well as archaeology, to piece together the early history of the city. Even so there are periods of Rome's history (390–350 BC, for instance) about which almost nothing is known.

Rome grew up on the banks of the Tiber at a site where an island (the Tiber island) divided the river into two narrower channels and allowed bridging. The city seems to have originated, perhaps as early as the tenth century, as a scatter of villages on low-lying hills (the celebrated seven hills of Rome). The curve of the river provided a good landing place and goods could be shipped overland from Rome, both to the north and south. From early times salt was traded into the Sabine country and beyond into Umbria. Some cemeteries have survived from this period, and the site of what was to be the Forum (the city's market place but later its ceremonial centre) was used as a burial place until the early eighth century. The bodies had been burned and placed in urns.

In the eighth century, the period in which the legends place the foundation of the city, there is evidence for the arrival of Greek traders. Pottery from Euboea and Corinth has been found, and one seventh-century grave on the Esquiline Hill contained a Corinthian vase with its owner's name, Ktektos, inscribed on it. From the very earliest times Rome was open to the gods and goddesses of Greece—a vase from Athens of the sixth century BC with a representation of the smith-god Hephaestus has been found as a votive deposit at the sanctuary of the Roman equivalent, Volcanus. The archaeological evidence shows that Rome, like most successful trading cities, attracted a range of outsiders, from both Italy and the east. At the same time the city continued to share a common 'Latin' culture with some thirty communities which were scattered over the plains of Latium between the River Tiber and the Alban Hills. These communities shared a language, festivals, and the myth of a common origin (that they were all colonies of a single city, Alba Longa). They also enjoyed so-called 'Latin rights' which allowed their citizens to make a legal marriage and commercial contracts with any member of another Latin community and to acquire citizenship of another community simply by moving there.

The burial finds in Rome itself are too limited to tell much about early Roman society but 20 kilometres away an extensive study of an early cemetery of Latium, Osteria dell'Osa, has taken place at Gabbii. Here the excavator, Dr Bietti-Sestiera, has studied the graves to see what they can tell about the social relationships of a Latin community in this early period. The burial plots of two families from the ninth century have survived. In each the centre is taken up by cremated adult males accompanied by miniature weapons and models of houses. Around them other adult males, mostly young, are simply inhumed. There appears to be a clear distinction between men of rank and other male family members who remained under their father's authority. This could be an early indication of the emergence of the Roman *paterfamilias*, the powerful father figure of later Roman society, although such interpretations are all too easy to create in hindsight. Women are also grouped by rank with a particular status reserved for young unmarried females.

By the eighth century burial patterns in the cemetery have changed. Bodies are now all inhumed but placed together in groups without any distinction between bodies. If it can be accepted that each group is made up of one family it is arguable that kinship has become more important than status. This could be a sign of the emergence of the *gens*, the clan, which was to prove such an important part of Roman, as it was of Etruscan, society. Another cemetery, of the late eighth and seventh centuries, has been excavated at Castel di Decima, 18 kilometres south of Rome. The wealthier males here are buried with either spears or swords, or sometimes both, perhaps an indication that weapons denoted some form of rank but also that this was a warrior society.

In the eighth and seventh centuries some form of transformation of society was taking place in Latium, similar in many ways to what was happening in Etruria. Although it pays to be cautious with the fragmentary evidence, society may have been increasingly based on clans with some individuals emerging as aristocratic leaders. The catalyst would seem to be trade with the outside world and the increasing influence of the Etruscans.

Rome: The Age of Kings

From the eighth through to the end of the sixth century Rome was ruled by 'kings'. Almost nothing is known of the early monarchs. Kingship was not hereditary and each new king seems to have been acclaimed by the people of Rome meeting in the *comitia curiata*, an assembly of thirty groups of clans, after auspices had first been taken to ensure he had divine support. He now had *imperium*, divine authority through which he could exercise his power in political, military, and religious affairs. The symbol of *imperium* was the *fasces*, a bundle of rods bound round an axe, which was carried in front of the king. It seems to have originated with the Etruscans and it is in this same period that Etruscan influence appears to have become strong. King Tarquin I (traditional dates 616–579 BC), for instance, is recorded as having migrated to Rome from Etruria and engineered his acclamation as king. With him came the first public embellishment of the city. The Forum was paved and surrounded by ceremonial buildings, including temples and sanctuaries, and an open area cleared for assemblies of citizens. The remains of palaces suggest the city was controlled by an aristocratic elite. (However, Rome remained predominantly Latin in culture. Under the Lapis Niger, a black pavement found in the Forum (and traditionally the burial place of the shepherd who looked after Romulus and Remus) are sixth-century ceremonial inscriptions in Latin not Etruscan.)

Tarquin was murdered in 579 and his successor Servius Tullius, probably a Latin rather than an Etruscan, seized power by force. It was clearly a time of upheaval in the city and Servius Tullius might be compared with the Greek tyrants who came to power on a wave of popular resentment against an aristocratic elite. There is evidence that Servius expanded the citizen body by enfranchising the local rural population and, more important than this, creating a citizen army of all those able to afford arms. This was the first legion, with a reported strength of 4,000 men and 600 cavalry. The men were grouped into centuries (probably of ninety-six men each) and at some point, possibly in Servius' reign, it became customary to call the centuries together to meet on the Campus Martius, the Field of Mars, outside the city wall. The *comitia centuriata*, as this assembly was called later, became the most powerful of the Roman popular assemblies with the formal duty of declaring war or peace and making alliances, as well as voting on constitutional changes. (In republican times it formed the electoral body for the consuls and praetors.)

This expansion of the citizen body was crucial to Rome's later success. In Greece citizenship depended on membership of a *polis* community and it was a privilege jealously guarded against outsiders. It is certainly true that Rome was cautious about accepting citizens until they had proved themselves loyal (and to some extent Romanized) but Rome was more open about extending her citizen body than any other city of the ancient world. To the astonishment of the Greeks even the descendants of freed slaves would become citizens as a matter of course. The result was a citizen body which grew rapidly. One consequence of this, however, was that the citizen assemblies became so large that democracy on the Athenian model soon became impractical and those who did attend the assemblies were restricted to voting for or against issues placed before them.

The Foundation of the Roman Republic

In the short term Servius' hopes of creating a popularly supported monarchy were to fail. His successor Tarquin the Proud (traditional dates 534–509 BC) behaved in such a tyrannical way that he was thrown out by the outraged aristocracy in 509. The final straw, according to legend, was the rape of one Lucretia by Tarquin's son (an event which provided inspiration for many later European artists). Some kind of power struggle appears to have followed. It may have been now that Lars Porsenna, ruler of a neighbouring Etruscan city, Clusium, attacked Rome. According to one legend, immortalized by the English historian Macaulay in his *Lays of Ancient Rome*, he was foiled by one Horatius holding a bridge against him but there are some suggestions in the sources that he may have temporarily taken the city.

The final result, however, was a republican city which was now firmly under aristocratic control. The aristocracy were not necessarily anti-Etruscan. In fact Etruscan cultural influences persisted in Rome for some time. Rather, the elite proclaimed themselves the protectors of Rome against tyranny in general and this became central to the ideology through which they justified their political supremacy. From now on there would be intense suspicion of any individual who tried to use popular support to build personal power. The aristocracy's fear of tyranny was revealed in the new government they set up. Supreme power, *imperium*, in fact all the power originally enjoyed by a king, was now to devolve on two magistrates, the consuls, who would hold power for one year but who could not be immediately re-elected. Each had the right to check the other's actions. Central to *imperium* was the right to command an army and it is probably at this time that the single legion was split into two smaller legions with one available to each consul. (The centuries now became units of sixty rather than a hundred men.) *Imperium* was only effective outside the *pomerium*, the sacred central area of the city, and armed men could not be led into the city except to celebrate a triumph.

The consuls were elected by the *comitia centuriata* although their election still had to be given formal approval by the *comitia curiata*. Competition for office was intense and election depended on a shrewd manipulation of votes by the candidate which stopped short of appealing to the populace as a whole (and thus arousing the fear of tyranny among the elite). The composition of the *comitia centuriata* was arranged so that the wealthier classes of soldiers, the cavalry in particular, who voted first and by class, could overrule the poorer classes. A prospective consul thus had to build up support among the more influential citizens. He could do this through his own *auctoritas*, authority and rank achieved through military achievement and the status of his family, but a candidate also relied heavily on clients, men who would vote for him in return for protection and favours. (The word candidate is an appropriate one here as it originates with the custom of prospective consuls dressing in specially whitened togas for the election, earning themselves the name *candidati*, from the Latin *candidus*, white.)

As the needs of the city grew other magistracies were established. The quaestors were financial officials. There were originally two but, from 421, four were elected annually. Later as many as twenty would be needed. The censors took charge of the records of citizenship, probably mainly to list those eligible for military service. (The verb *censere* means to estimate.) Unlike the other magistracies new censors were appointed only every five years for a period of some eighteen months while they drew up a revised list of citizens. It was an office of great authority later reserved for former consuls. The praetor, a term originally used of the consuls, became a separate post with special responsibility for judicial affairs in 366 BC. Praetors and consuls were the only magistrates with the right to command an army.

With the magistrates normally confined to a single year of office and the *comitia centuriata* limited to voting rather than debating, discussion of policy-making increasingly became the preserve of the senate. The senate had originated as a group of advisers to the king and most senators were drawn from a group of ancient aristocratic families, the patricians, who also monopolized the priesthoods of Rome. After the fall of the monarchy the members of the senate seem to have been chosen each year by the consuls as *their* advisers, but the right to decide membership then devolved to the censors. One of them, Appius Claudius, caused outrage in the late fourth century when he tried to pack the senate with men from outside the traditional aristocratic families, and in the reaction that followed it became the custom for the senate to be made up of former magistrates who joined immediately after they had served their term of office. They then remained senators for life. The body thus contained a vast reservoir of collective experience and was to provide an impressive stability and continuity in Roman government during years of tumultuous change. The senate was presided over by a consul or praetor. It had few formal powers but it could express its feelings in a *senatus consultum*, the advice of the senate, which had no strict legal effect, but which came to be respected as if it did. The assemblies normally only passed legislation after they had heard the senate's opinion.

In the fifth century the patrician families consolidated their grip on government. Patricians took 90 per cent of the consulships between 485 and 445 BC. However, their growing power was soon challenged by the *plebs*, plebeians, the mass of citizens who by law or custom had become excluded from the magistracies and the senate. The discontent of the plebeian masses was rooted in land hunger, economic distress (in a period of almost continuous warfare), and debt, but there must have been wealthier leaders with the leisure to organize agitation against the patricians. The struggle continued for 200 years. The weapon of the *plebs* was withdrawal from the city, probably to the Aventine Hill, where they set up their own assembly, the *concilium plebis*. It elected its own officials, the tribunes, eventually ten in number, whose persons were declared sacrosanct and who acquired the right to intervene on behalf of ordinary citizens against the arbitrary use of power by a magistrate.

The battle between plebeians and patricians was marked by a steady retreat by the patricians, a retreat hastened by a decline in the number of patrician families as a male line failed. (There were 132 in 509 BC and 81 in 367.) They recognized the right of the *concilium plebis* to exist as early as 471, although it was not until 287 that its resolutions (*plebiscita*, hence the English plebiscite) were accepted as having the force of law. In the middle of the fifth century plebeian agitation resulted in the recording and publication of the Twelve Tables, the first public statement of Roman law. The magistracies were gradually opened to plebeians, the first plebeian quaestors being appointed in 409. After 342 one consul was always a plebeian. Both consuls were plebeians for the first time in 172 BC. (The patricians retained memories of their heritage and as late as AD 301 the emperor Diocletian's Edict on Prices shows that those still claiming patrician status wore distinctive shoes.)

The plebeians did not achieve a social revolution in Rome, although there were some successes such as the abolition of *nexum*, a form of debt bondage, at the end of the fourth century. What happened in effect was that the wealthier plebeians became integrated into the ruling classes, the magistracies and the senate. Access to office and hence to the senate by an outsider was possible (the term *novus homo*, 'new man', was used of the first member of a family to achieve a magistracy) but comparatively rare and so Rome saw the continued consolidation of oligarchical rule by a limited number of aristocratic families. Even the tribunes were drawn from the wealthier classes, and although the *concilium plebis* could act as a focus of popular agitation at moments of economic distress it never developed a coherent and sustained role as an opposition.

The cohesion of the state was also maintained through religious ritual. Roman religion was focused on a wide variety of gods and spirits. Many—Vesta, the goddess of the hearth, the Lares, spirits of the land who protected the household, the Penates, the gods of the store cupboard—originated in the home and reflected the needs of a community largely dependent on agriculture. Tarquin the Elder, the fifth Etruscan king, had laid the foundations of the first temple to Zeus on the Capitoline Hill. Here the magistrates offered sacrifice on taking office and the first meeting of the senate each year took place. The spoils of war were brought to the temple at the end of each triumphal procession by a victorious general. Juno, an ancient Italian goddess, associated with the needs of women, fertility, and the sanctity of marriage, also became a state goddess and was worshipped as the wife of Jupiter. Minerva, an Italian goddess of crafts, made up, with these two, the so-called Capitoline Triad. Mars, the god of war, gave his name to the month of March, originally the first in the year and the time when military campaigning could begin again after the winter. These state gods were honoured through complex rituals through which it was hoped to retain their benevolence. The rituals were overseen by priests chosen from members of the aristocratic families. Divination, particularly through the observation of the movements of birds, was also widely used to predict the future.

The Expansion of Rome

Under the kings Rome had been a successful military state and in 509 controlled about 800 square kilometres, a third of Latium. Its population has been estimated as between 20,000 and 25,000, very much bigger than that of any other Latin community, and comparable to the larger Greek cities of southern Italy. Soon after the fall of the monarchy, however, the city was challenged by the surrounding Latin tribes, who were suspicious of her continued expansion. Rome defeated them at the battle of Lake Regillus in 499 BC, but the victory was overshadowed by increasing pressures of the mountain peoples on the Latin plains. In 493 Rome agreed with the Latin communities to face the intruders together.

The most persistent enemies were two peoples, the Aequi and the Volscii, who appear to have launched a series of raids on the outlying Latin settlements. They successfully disrupted the economy of the plain, and in Rome itself there is a significant gap in public building in the middle of the fifth century. Even though the Hernici, whose land lay between the Aequi and Volscii, were added as allies of Rome, it took until the end of the century to restore order. With the situation more stable, Rome now moved on her own initiative against a very different enemy, an old rival, the once wealthy Etruscan city of Veii. The city was only 15 kilometres to the north, but its prosperity, fine hilltop position, and control of the upper Tiber through Fidenae, its outpost 9 kilometres upstream from Rome, made it a coveted prize. The legends recount ten years of siege, on the epic scale of the Trojan War, before the city fell in 396 BC.

Rome's success against Veii probably reflected its ability to mobilize its manpower in a way the Etruscan cities could never do. The war seems to have brought an enlargement of both infantry and cavalry forces. Poorer classes were now enlisted and a daily cash allowance, the stipendium, was paid while a man was away from his farm. (Only those who owned land were eligible for the army.) As the poorer citizens could not afford a full covering of armour, an oblong shield, the *scutum*, was adopted instead of the smaller circular 'hoplite' shield. In this new atmosphere a 'sack' of Rome by Celtic raiders in 390, which Livy presents as a devastating experience, was probably no more than a temporary setback caused by a band of mercenaries heading south to Dionysius' Syracuse. There is certainly little archaeological evidence for any mass destruction and only a few years later the city was able to construct a massive wall (parts of which still stand). The Celts did not seem interested in any form of permanent occupation of central Italy.

Few sources survive for this period of Roman history but it appears to have been one of consolidation. Over 500 square kilometres of land confiscated from Veii had to be integrated into the *ager Romanus* (Roman territory). There was continual low level warfare against surrounding tribes and the fortification of Ostia at the mouth of the Tiber, which archaeological evidence dates to 380–350 BC, suggests a growing interest in the sea, although no Roman navy was to exist for another hundred years.

A new period of more intensive warfare began in 343 with a short war against the Samnites, the most formidable and best organized of the inland mountain peoples. By the middle of the fourth century they had become the largest political grouping in Italy with territory covering perhaps 15,000 square kilometres. They had a well-developed system of agriculture, fortified mountain strongholds, and a history of successful expansion. (Two of the major peoples of southern Italy, the Lucanians and Bruttians, were descendants of earlier Samnite migrations.) Rome declared war on the Samnites in 343 after appeals for help by the cities of Campania. The Samnites were quickly defeated but, to the fury of the Campanians, Rome made peace with them. It was just at the moment that the Latin states were also becoming resentful of the arrogance of Roman rule. Rome suddenly found herself facing a coalition of enemies, Latins, Campanians, and once again the Volscii. Rome's reputation as a military force was confirmed when she defeated them.

It was the settlement of 338, after this war, which showed Rome's political shrewdness. Her enemies were not destroyed but instead reorganized into what has been described as a 'commonwealth' of states which stretched across the coastal plains from the Tiber to the bay of Naples. All accepted the dominance of Rome and agreed to provide armed support when called upon. Some Latin cities close to Rome now lost their independence and were incorporated into the Roman state. The ships of the coastal city of Antium, for instance, had their prows (*rostra*, literally 'beaks') cut off and displayed as trophies on the speaker's platform in Rome. (Hence the word 'rostrum' still used in English for a platform.) The members of these communities became full Roman citizens and could vote in the Roman assemblies. Other Latin communities kept their Latin rights, of intermarriage and commercial dealings, with Rome but not with each other. Their inhabitants were not made Roman citizens and remained self governing.

Among the defeated non-Latin communities, the Volscii and the Campanians, for instance, Rome developed the status of *civitas sine suffragio*, a form of Roman citizenship which involved communities in the obligations of citizenship, notably military service, but without any of the advantages, such as voting or the right to stand for office in Rome. Each of these cities was known as *a municipium*. In the passage of time the citizens of these *municipia* were given full citizenship, the last by the end of the second century BC. (For *municipia* in the empire, see further p. 510.)

In addition Rome now began to establish colonies. (The word derives from the Latin verb *colere*, to cultivate.) The citizens of each colony, who could be Romans or other Latins, gave up Roman citizenship if they had it but maintained Latin rights and formed self-governing communities. They had every incentive to defend themselves, and hence Roman hegemony, against attack, and many colonies were established in strategically vulnerable areas. Two early colonies, Cales and Fregellae, were set up in the Liris valley on the main route from Rome to the important *municipium* of Capua.

Often given less importance in the Roman sources but no less crucial were allies. By 250 Rome had made alliances with over 150 Italian communities who had either been defeated or forced through fear into surrender. Technically the allies maintained full independence, but they had to provide manpower for wars and Rome in effect decided when these wars should take place and how many men were needed. In many major battles, that of Sentinum in 295, for instance, allies provided more than half the Roman army. The soldiers of allies had, in theory, the right to share the fruits of victory on an equal basis with the legionaries.

The essence of the settlement of 338 was its flexibility. Rome could draw on a large reserve of manpower at almost no cost to herself while the defeated communities retained enough independence to dampen any desire for revolt. In any case many were controlled by aristocratic cliques who depended on Roman support for their survival. Rome herself was not burdened with vast areas of new territory. She had evolved a system of government and control which was to prove astonishingly resilient in the years to come.

Rome was soon at war again. The setting up of the new colony at Fregellae provoked the Samnites to attack. It took forty years (conventionally divided into two periods, 327–304 and 298–90, the Second and Third Samnite Wars) before they were defeated. This was guerrilla warfare in difficult mountain territory and Rome suffered a number of humiliating defeats when she ventured off the plains. A more successful long-term strategy involved consolidating a network of allies (among them, in 327, Neapolis (Naples), the first Greek city to make an alliance with Rome) around Samnite territory so that the Samnite heartland could be isolated. The first of Rome's great military roads, the Appian Way, between Rome and Capua, put in hand by the censor Appius Claudius in 312 BC, was part of the process of control. New fighting techniques had also to be developed to fight in hilly country. The hoplite formation of the Greeks was no good on rough ground so the legions were split into smaller groups, the maniples, or handfuls, of two centuries, each man armed relatively lightly with a *pilum*, a javelin which could be thrown, and a sword, *gladius*.

The last years of the Second Samnite War were marked by an expansion of Rome into the central highlands of Italy. In 304 Rome's enemies of the fifth century, the Aequi, were suppressed once and for all in a campaign of fifty days in which the inhabitants of each stronghold were massacred as it was captured. In 298 the Samnites were at war with Rome again and now they could draw on a mass of allies, Celts, Etruscans, and Umbrians, who had all been antagonized by Rome's aggression. Rome faced them at Sentinum in Umbria in 295. It was the greatest battle yet seen on Italian soil, with the Romans and their allies fielding perhaps 35,000 men. If the Romans had not diverted the Etruscans and Umbrians from the main battlefield, they might well have been defeated, but their hard-won victory broke up the alliance. After a final desperate battle at Aquilonia in 293 the Samnites were crushed and Rome was able to mop up the remaining opposition in central Italy. The defeated communities were made *municipia* or allies. In some cases their land was distributed among settlers from

Rome and their populations made slaves. (The Romans argued that those who had been defeated were at the absolute mercy of the victors and thus could be made into slaves if they were not killed.)

With Rome dominant in central Italy and the Celts hemmed in through a network of Roman alliances with the cities of Etruria, Roman attention turned south. The Greek cities were now in decline and in the 280s several began to call for help from Rome against the attacks of native populations. As Rome responded, the most prosperous Greek city of the south, Tarentum, grew alarmed at this intrusion. When a Roman war fleet (the first ever recorded) ventured into Tarentum's waters in 282 it was attacked. Rome counter-attacked and Tarentum was close to being taken. The city appealed in desperation to Pyrrhus, the king of Epirus, an ambitious ruler on the lookout for conquest and glory. Pyrrhus arrived with a large and well-equipped army of some 20,000 men. This was the first Hellenistic army the Romans had ever seen and they proved vulnerable to its power and experience. At two battles, Heraclea (280 BC) and Ausculum (279), the Romans were defeated but in each case Pyrrhus lost thousands of his own precious troops (hence the term Pyrrhic victory). Rome's allies stood firm. Even with mercenaries (and the riches of the Greek cities would have allowed him to recruit many thousands) Pyrrhus realized he could not hope to wear down the Romans. After another check at the battle of Beneventum in 275, Pyrrhus withdrew. Tarentum fell to Rome in 272 and Roman domination of the south of the peninsula was complete. There was now no area below a line between the modern cities of Pisa and Rimini (where a Roman colony, Ariminum, was established in 268) that was free of Roman control, as the city of Falerii found to its cost when it offended Rome in 241. It was crushed in a campaign lasting only six days.

Direct Roman influence over much of this territory was still limited. By 264 perhaps 20 per cent of the land surface of Italy had been made part of the *ager Romanus*, the directly controlled territory of Rome. In much of this land the local population had been enslaved or killed and it was now open to Roman settlement. Between 20,000 and 30,000 adult males may have been given plots of land to farm. Another 70,000 men and their families may have been involved in settling the nineteen new colonies recorded between 334 and 263 BC. Several of them controlled land of over 5,000 square kilometres in extent. However, these colonies and settlements lay in between cities and cultures which still retained their own languages and customs. It was to be another 200 years before Latin became the dominant language of the peninsula. Meanwhile local pride remained strong.

The Glorification of Victory

No pre-industrial society has ever mobilized such a high percentage of its male population in war over such a long period of time as Rome. It is estimated that between 9 and 16 per cent of male citizens in normal times and 25 per cent at times of crisis could be supported in her armies. (Napoleon's France may have equalled this record but only for a few years.) The supremacy of Rome in war depended not only on her manpower but on a mixture of ferocity in battle (even the dogs were cut up, recorded the historian Polybius of a Roman victory over a city in Spain) and comparative generosity in defeat. It was a formidable combination which was to underlie the strategy of Roman imperialism in the centuries to come.

In Rome itself military victory was idealized. Wars were assumed to be just and the temples built during the Samnite Wars were based on Hellenistic victory cults. There were dedications to Victoria, Jupiter Victor, Bellona (an early Roman war goddess) Victrix, and Hercules Invictus (the unconquered Hercules). The earliest Roman silver coin, probably minted in connection with the building of the Via Appia, has Mars, the god of war, on its obverse side. The religion of Rome was integrated into its political life. The priesthoods were monopolized by leading families and rituals marked the beginning and end of the war-making season. Every campaign was initiated by consultation of the gods and sacrifices. Plunder was used to dedicate and furnish new temples.

The culmination of a conqueror's success came in the triumph. A victorious general could claim the right from the senate to extend his *imperium* across the *pomerium* so that he could bring his troops in procession into the city and sacrifice at the temple of Jupiter on the Capitoline Hill. For the day, the victor even dressed as Jupiter (as Pindar's athletes became divine at the moment of victory, so did Rome's commanders) and was crowned with a laurel wreath. He was preceded by the magistrates and senate, oxen for sacrifice, war booty, and his captives. He himself rode in a chariot with his family beside him. Behind the chariot came the troops, who had the right to shout not in triumph but to denigrate their commander. (At one of his triumphs Julius Caesar was taunted with tales of his homosexuality as a young man.) As the procession reached the Capitol the prisoners would be taken off to be executed and the general continued up the hill to place his wreath on the lap of the god.

The triumph was an essential feature of Rome's militarism and can be analysed at many different levels. For a day the victor could be close to the gods. It was an occasion too for the glorification of his family who rode beside him. Yet the ritual itself was designed to make sure that the state kept ultimate control. The senate was always sensitive to any individual who used the triumph as a stepping-stone to political power (and later insisted that at least 5,000 enemy dead be counted on the battlefield before one could be granted). In a sense the triumph was a way of controlling individual ambition by allowing it one moment of exultant expression. The reality of death was also incorporated into the ritual. Not only was the victor reminded of his own mortality but the state expressed its own power over the defeated through their executions at the height of the ceremony. Not least, as Rome expanded overseas, the triumph acted as the mechanism through which the treasures of Greece and other conquered nations entered a city which in the early third century was still isolated culturally from the Mediterranean world.

FURTHER READING

General books on Rome. Once again the Loeb Classical Library and the Penguin Classics series are the best place to look for translations of the basic texts. Many of the books cited under 'The Greeks: General Books', Chapter 8 above, continue to be relevant. Perhaps the best overall history is Marcel Le Glay (and others), *A History of Rome* (2nd edition, Malden, Mass., 2001). It has a full bibliography. See also J. Wacher (ed.), *The Roman World*, two volumes (London, 1987). Source books include the two volumes by N. Lewis and M. Reinhold, *Roman Civilization: Sourcebook I. The Republic* (New York, 1951), and *Roman Civilization: Sourcebook II. The Empire* (New York, 1955). A rich range of material is also provided by Jo-Ann Shelton in *As the Romans Did: A Sourcebook in Roman Social History* (2nd edition, New York, 1998). D. Bowder (ed.), provides short biographies in *Who Was Who in the Roman World, 753 BC to AD 476* (Oxford, 1980). Two illustrated accounts of Roman civilization are T. Cornell and J. Matthews, *Atlas of the Roman World* (Oxford, 1982). Also to be recommended is L. Wilkinson, *The Roman Experience* (London, 1975).

A very useful and readable introduction written by someone who had a real feel for the landscapes of Italy is Tim Potter, *Roman Italy* (London, 1987). On Rome itself see Georgina Masson's *The Companion Guide to Rome* (London, 1965 and updated editions) and in the Oxford Archaeological Guides, Amanda Claridge, *Rome* (Oxford, 1998). For a survey of recent archaeological research in Rome, and the 1980s was a particularly fruitful decade for this, see John Patterson's article 'The City of Rome: From Republic to Empire' in the *Journal of Roman Studies*, 22 (1992).

Mary Beard, John North, and Simon Price, *Religions of Rome*, two volumes, the second a sourcebook (Cambridge, 1998) is a definitive introduction. For Roman law in everyday life, see D. Johnston, *Roman Law in Context* (Cambridge, 1999).

An overview of Roman art is D. Strong, *Roman Art* (Harmondsworth, 1976), and Mary Beard and John Henderson, *Classical Art: From Greece to Rome* (Oxford, 2001) is very stimulating. See also M. Henig (ed.), *Handbook of Roman Art* (Oxford, 1983) for articles on a wide range of arts. On sculpture, Diana Kleiner, *Roman Sculpture* (New Haven, 1992) is a thorough survey. On architecture, John Ward-Perkins, *Roman Architecture* (Milan, 1974; London, 1988) and *Roman Imperial Architecture* (Harmondsworth, 1981). *The Oxford History of Classical Art* has already been cited. J. Pollitt, *The Art of Rome, c.753 BC–AD 337* (Cambridge, 1983) looks at the written sources.

On literature *The Cambridge History of Classical Literature*, vol. ii: *Latin Literature* (Cambridge, 1982), is a solid introduction.

Chapter 20. The authority on early Italy is M. Pallottino. See his *A History of Earliest Italy* (London, 1991), which stresses the importance of not seeing the rise of Rome as inevitable. A chapter on the early peoples of Italy by E. Salmon is in vol. iv of the *Cambridge Ancient History*. The arrival of the Greeks is discussed in D. Ridgway, *The First Western Greeks*, already cited.

The Etruscans have received good attention recently. See G. Barker and T. Rasmussen, *The Etruscans* (Oxford, 1998); M. Torelli, *The Etruscans* (London, 2001); Sybille Haynes, *Etruscan Civilization: A Cultural History* (London, 2000); and N. Spivey, *Etruscan Art* (London, 1997). For a more general discussion of the relationship between the Etruscans and Greek art see J. Boardman, *The Diffusion of Classical Art in Antiquity* (London, 1994).

T. J. Cornell, *The Beginnings of Rome: Italy and Rome from the Bronze Age to the Punic Wars* (*c.1000–264 BC*) (London, 1995), is essential. On the archaeology of early Rome, see R. Ross Holloway's *The Archaeology of Early Rome and Latium* (London, 1994). For the enthusiast there are authoritative articles in the *Cambridge Ancient History*, vol. vii, Part 2: *The Rise of Rome to 220 BC* (Cambridge, 1989).

On early architecture the standard work is A. Boethius, *Etruscan and Early Roman Architecture* (Harmondsworth, 1978). C. Nicolet, *The World of the Citizen in Republican Rome* (London, 1980), looks at the emergence of citizenship and is also useful for the later republican period. How the assemblies actually worked is covered by L. R. Taylor's *Roman Voting Assemblies* (Ann Arbor, 1966); John Patterson, *Political Life in the City of Rome* (Bristol, 2000); A. Linott, *The Constitution of the Roman Republic* (Oxford, 1999). The impact of Rome on one area of Italy is the subject of T. Potter, *The Changing Landscape of South Etruria* (London, 1979), which takes the story of this area through from early times to the medieval period.

21 | Rome Becomes a Mediterranean Power

In 265 BC Rome's power extended only as far as northern Italy where the Celts provided a major barrier to further expansion. (NB. Although the term 'Celt' is used here and below, readers should be aware of the difficulties it poses—see Interlude Four, p. 355.) In the rest of the peninsula she was the dominant power in the sense that, despite the survival of local cultures and languages, there was no city or people able to challenge the combined strength of her own manpower and that of her allies. However, any expansion further afield appeared unlikely. Rome had no navy and had, in fact, already made treaties with Carthage, the major sea power of the western Mediterranean, in which she accepted Carthaginian supremacy at sea. Yet in the next 120 years Rome was to transform herself into a major Mediterranean power with interests as far west as Spain and east as far as Asia and the Aegean.

The First Punic War

The incident which set Rome on the path to becoming a Mediterranean power was a relatively insignificant one. A group of Italian mercenaries, who called themselves the Mamertines (after the Oscan name for Mars, the god of war), had seized the city of Messana (modern Messina), which overlooked the straits between Sicily and Italy. In 265 the ruler of Syracuse, Hiero, had tried to dislodge them. While some looked to Carthage for help, others appealed to Rome. The senate was reluctant to intervene as it had already condemned one group of Roman citizens who had seized a Greek city and felt it inconsistent to now uphold the Mamertines' seizure. On the other hand it was clear that a Carthaginian takeover in Messana would threaten Roman control of the straits. The debate was taken to the popular assembly (the *comitia centuriata*), and after speeches by the consuls stressing the threat to Rome and the hope of plunder it was the assembly who committed the state to action, the only example known when the citizen body, rather than the senate, set in hand a war.

Faced now with a Roman response the Carthaginians meekly withdrew their garrison from Messana and the Romans occupied the city. Although Carthage and Syracuse were long-standing enemies, the occupation was sufficiently provocative to force them into an alliance. When they besieged Messana the outbreak of war, the First Punic War (264–241 BC), was the inevitable result. (*Punicus* is the Latin for Carthaginian and refers to the joint culture of the Phoenicians and local African natives formed at Carthage.)

Carthage owed its wealth to its position. Set on a commanding site on a peninsula on the north African coast the city had started life in the ninth century as a colony of the Phoenicians. As the Phoenician coastal cities were overrun in the seventh century, in turn by Assyrians, Egyptians, and Persians, Carthage emerged as an independent city ideally suited to act as the focus for the commerce of the other former Phoenician colonies of the western Mediterranean. Her dominance over them was gradually established. She expanded into north Africa, Spain, Sardinia, Sicily, and the other islands of the western Mediterranean, successfully protecting her interests against the Greeks despite a series of debilitating wars in Sicily with Syracuse and the other Greek cities. In north Africa she may have ruled over three to four million subjects. In southern Spain she had access to some of the richest silver mines in the known world. Her wealth came from trade in metals but also from the successful exploitation of fertile land in north Africa, western Sicily, and elsewhere. Her seamen were expert and there are reports of Carthaginian voyages around Africa (unsubstantiated) and as far north as Britain and Ireland.

Carthage's main interest was the preservation of her commercial empire, and Rome, without a navy, could offer no threat to this. The only possible focus of the fighting was Sicily, and for the first three years (264–261) the campaigns were concentrated here (although the Carthaginians also made raids on the Italian coast). There were some Roman successes. Rome managed to prise Hiero of Syracuse away from Carthage and make him an ally and to take the city of Acragas, which had been held by a Carthaginian garrison. (The entire Greek population of the city—possibly 25,000 individuals—was sold into slavery.) However, the campaigns ended in stalemate. Rome's chances of subduing the coastal cities were limited so long as Carthage was in control of the sea, and it was immediately after the capture of Acragas that Rome decided to build a fleet.

No better proof could be given of the self-confidence of the city and its determination to win. There was no naval tradition, no experience of shipbuilding, no trained crews. A grounded Carthaginian ship had to be used as a model with crews being trained on land as the first hundred quinqueremes were being built, according to the historian Polybius in only sixty days. They were heavier and less manoeuvrable than the Carthaginian ships but they contained one significant improvement, a wooden gangway which could be hauled up like the jib of a crane and then dropped on to an enemy ship so that soldiers could cross over into it. (Its shape earned it the nickname *corvus*, 'crow'.)

The war could now be fought by Rome at sea and possibly even taken into the heart of the Carthaginian empire. The first encounter of the two fleets at Mylae off the coast of Sicily in 260 was a Roman victory. It was followed by an even more crushing success off Cape Ecnomus (on the southern coast of Sicily) in 256 when eighty Carthaginian ships were sunk or captured. In each case the *corvus* gave the Romans the advantage. So long as the Romans avoided being rammed as the ships closed they could get troops on to an enemy deck and capture it. The way was now open for an invasion of Africa. Troops were landed there in 256 and at first moved successfully towards Carthage. However, the Carthaginians imported a Spartan mercenary to train their army and, using their cavalry to surround the Roman infantry, crushed the Roman invaders in 255. Further disasters struck Rome when a fleet sent to rescue the survivors was destroyed in a storm and many thousands of trained oarsmen drowned. The year 249 was again disastrous for Rome with a major defeat at the Battle of Drepana off the west coast of Sicily and the loss of almost all the remaining fleet in a storm later in the year.

The war now became one of attrition, symbolized by a nine-year siege by the Romans of the Carthaginian fortress of Lilybaeum on the west coast of Sicily. The attacking forces were harassed by the only outstanding commander of the war, the Carthaginian Hamilcar, who successfully tied them to their bases. By 242 Rome seemed exhausted but a final effort was made to raise a new fleet. At a battle off the Aegates Islands in the following year it met what was also the last of the Carthaginian forces, a fleet heavily laden with supplies for Sicily. A great Roman victory in which most of the Carthaginian ships were sunk or captured finally decided the outcome of the war. Carthage could no longer protect Sicily and in the peace that followed Carthage ceded Sicily to Rome. Syracuse survived as an independent ally of Rome.

The Beginnings of Provincial Administration

The victory confirmed Rome as an extraordinarily resilient and determined power, now with a foothold outside Italy and a fast maturing naval tradition. Within three years Rome had taken advantage of a mutiny among Carthaginian mercenaries to seize Sardinia and Corsica from the Carthaginians. The possession of overseas territories presented her with a new challenge. Her first concern may have been to protect them against a Carthaginian counter-attack, and troops were probably left on each island for this purpose. At some point Rome must also have become aware that there were local systems of taxation, in Sicily at least, whose fruits could be diverted to Rome. The form of the earliest administration is unknown, but from 227 the number of praetors elected annually in Rome was increased to four and two of these were selected as governors, one in Sicily and the other in Sardinia and Corsica. It was already the custom when magistrates were sent out of Roman territory for the senate to assign them a *provincia*, a defined responsibility (the pacification of a tribe, for instance). A magistrate sent overseas was similarly given a defined *provincia*, perhaps the collection of tribute or the defence of the area. Gradually the word *provincia* came to refer to a specific territory rather than just the task the magistrate was expected to achieve within that territory.

The Second Punic War

In 225 BC central Italy was faced with an invasion of Celtic war-bands. The Romans crushed them at the Battle of Telemon and exploited their advantage by conquering the Po valley and establishing Roman colonies at Cremona and Placentia (218). Roman control of the valley was still precarious, however, as was seen in 218 when Italy was unexpectedly invaded from the north by a Carthaginian army led by Hannibal, the son of Hamilcar.

In the years after their defeat the Carthaginians under Hamilcar had been energetically building a new empire in Spain, whether as a replacement for their lost territories or to gather resources for a new war is not clear. One of Rome's oldest allies, the city of Massilia, had clearly become concerned about the expansion. Rome needed her support against the Celts and it was probably for this reason she made an agreement with the Carthaginians that they would not move north of the River Ebro. During these years, however, Rome also made an alliance with the town of Saguntum, well south of the Ebro, evidence that she was concerned about Carthaginian resurgence. When Hannibal, who had succeeded his father, besieged and took the city in 219, probably in the belief that Rome had given him a free hand as far as the Ebro, Rome quickly protested. Neither side appears to have had any inhibitions about going to war again and the Second Punic War (218–202) was the result.

Rome's first plans were ambitious, to go on the offensive and fight the war in both Spain and Africa. An army and fleet under Publius Cornelius Scipio, the consul for the year, was sent round the coast to the north of Spain with the aim of defeating Hannibal there. Hannibal, however, had also decided that his best strategy was an offensive one, to strike at Italy, in the hope of humiliating Rome and destroying her links with her allies. As his army made its way eastwards towards the Alps it just evaded the Romans crossing in the opposite direction. Scipio, however, made the courageous decision to send the army on to Spain under his brother Gnaeus and to return himself to meet Hannibal in northern Italy.

Hannibal was one of those men who seem groomed for greatness. His father had been a brilliant and energetic commander and also a statesman of vision who had reformed Carthage's institutions and been a patron of Greek culture. Hannibal had a tutor from Sparta and was brought up, as was anyone with military pretensions in the ancient world, to admire the campaigns of Alexander.

However, when he trained his army, like all Carthaginian armies one made up of mercenaries, he dropped the standard Greek phalanx of heavily armed infantry and created an army of smaller more flexible units, each based on an ethnic group. It was this, an energetic cavalry, and Hannibal's tactical genius which were to underlie his success.

It is still not known where Hannibal crossed the Alps. The Col de Clavier is a recent choice of scholars. It was a gruelling ordeal with hostile tribes harassing his men (and the elephants they brought with them) as they passed. Perhaps a third of his army was lost on the way, with some 25,000 men finally descending on the Po plain, where the Celts rallied to Hannibal as their liberator. In the first major encounter with the Romans at Trebia, west of the new Roman colony at Placentia, over half the Roman army was lost and with it the north of Italy. The next year, 217, Hannibal, now in central Italy, lured a large Roman army into the narrow plain between Lake Trasimene and the mountains and then slaughtered it. A consul, Gaius Flaminius, and perhaps 15,000 men died in the disaster. The only consolation for Rome was that her allied cities of central Italy, those of Latium, Umbria, and Etruria, stood firm. Their traditional fears of the Celts and the belief that the fiery mercenaries of Hannibal were little more than barbarians kept them loyal.

In an emergency such as this the constitution allowed a dictator to be appointed for a limited, six-month, term of office. Quintus Fabius Maximus was chosen and he argued that the only policy was to avoid the fixed battles of which Hannibal was clearly the master and instead wear him down gradually (through what became known as Fabian tactics). A policy of avoiding battle was so alien to Roman thinking that at first Fabius had little support and when, in 216, after his term of office was over, two new consuls were appointed to replace him they resumed the traditional policy of direct confrontation. According to one source, the senate raised eight legions each of 5,000 men and, together with allies, 80,000 men marched south to Apulia where Hannibal was ravaging the land. Hannibal drew the Roman armies on to an open plain at Cannae where he knew he could use his cavalry effectively. The Romans hoped that the sheer weight of their numbers would be enough and drew their infantry together in a close formation so that it could overwhelm the Celts and Spaniards who were holding Hannibal's centre. However, although the Carthaginian centre retreated it did not break, and the Romans found themselves enveloped by African infantry stationed on the two wings and the Carthaginian cavalry who had routed their Roman coun-terparts. In a devastating defeat all but 14,500 of the Roman army was wiped out.

His victory at Cannae now allowed Hannibal to consolidate his position in southern Italy. His greatest prize was Capua, the second city of Italy, and a num-ber of other cities of Campania either came over to him or were captured in the aftermath of the battle. Hannibal was now in a position to march on Rome but he never made the move. He must have realized that the subjection of the city would be a very different matter from defeating its forces in the open field and there is no evidence he wished to destroy Rome. He appears to have stuck to his original aim of humiliating her and destroying her allies, probably in the hope that she would be forced to surrender Sicily and Sardinia and be reduced to her original territory in Latium.

In Rome the news of the catastrophe shocked the city. It was hard to escape the feeling that the gods had deserted Rome. Even the oracle at Delphi was consulted as to the correct procedure for regaining their trust, and there was a ritual sacrifice of appeasement in which a pair of Gauls and a pair of Greeks were buried alive. Yet Rome's nerve held. The historian Polybius later picked this moment as the one in Rome's history when her resolution was at its strongest. Hannibal had sent to ransom his prisoners, but the senate refused to make any concessions, to the despair of the prisoners' families. Instead four new legions were raised from the city's youth and 8,000 slaves were freed for service. The policy of Fabius (who was to serve as consul twice in the years immediately following Cannae and again in 209) now became predominant as the Romans counted their advantages. Whatever the losses in the south, the centre of Italy with all its manpower remained loyal and the Roman armies could be rebuilt. Most significantly Hannibal held no major ports. He captured the town of Tarentum in 212 but the Romans managed to hang on to its citadel and with it control over its important harbour until Fabius recaptured and sacked the city in 209. In 212 Capua had also come under siege and the following year Hannibal marched on Rome in the hope of forcing the Roman armies to raise the siege. When he saw how confidently the city was defended he retreated and Capua fell. Hannibal was now on the defensive and it was significant that each winter he was now forced to withdraw to the south of Italy. In a final attempt to break the deadlock Hannibal's brother Hasdrubal marched from Spain to join his brother but he was intercepted in the north of Italy by both consuls and defeated at the battle of the River Metaurus in 207. This was the last major engagement of the war on Italian soil. It left Hannibal unable to break out of southern Italy.

Meanwhile, the most significant fighting of the war was taking place in Spain. It was difficult country for both Romans and Carthaginians not only because of the terrain but because the local tribes were hostile to outsiders (the Carthaginians had treated them particularly badly) and unrest was common. The Romans enjoyed an unbroken run of successes until in 211 three separate Carthaginian armies converged on their forces, which had been split into two under Gnaeus Scipio and his brother Publius (sent by the senate to join Gnaeus in 217). At the ensuing defeat, which saw the deaths of both Scipios, the Romans almost lost their hold on Spain. The situation was saved when Publius Cornelius Scipio, the son of Publius, was appointed to take command. It was a major break with precedent as he had not yet held either a consulship or praetorship.

Scipio was perhaps the most brilliant Roman commander to date, energetic, charismatic, and imaginative. In 209 he achieved the capture of New Carthage, a supply base of immense strategic importance, by launching a surprise attack across a lagoon at low water. (His claim that Neptune, the god of the sea, had promised him success in a dream led to rumours that he was divinely inspired.) A decisive victory at Ilipa in 206 and the surrender of another strategically important port, Gades, saw the end of Carthaginian dominance in Spain and the beginning of centuries of Roman hegemony in the peninsula. Scipio had himself hailed as *imperator*, a title of honour offered by troops immediately after a victory. He had now gained the status with which to return to Rome and be elected consul in 205, despite the fact that he had never been praetor, a normal precondition for election.

Scipio now argued that he should take the war to Africa. There were those who opposed him, worried over the growth of his personal power and concerned that Hannibal, still at large in Italy, should be defeated first. However, Scipio set off for Africa in 204 and it was his first success there which forced the Carthaginians to recall Hannibal (who had not been 'home' since he was a child of 9 in 237). The final showdown between the two commanders came at the Battle of Zama (202). For the first time the Roman cavalry played a major part in a victory. Scipio's horsemen drove the Carthaginian cavalry off the field and the Roman infantry was able to hold the Carthaginian lines until the Roman cavalry returned from the chase to attack them from behind. Hannibal's army was destroyed and the war was effectively at an end. Carthage was reduced to her territory in Africa, from which she was forbidden to expand and she was burdened with an indemnity of 10,000 talents to be paid over fifty years. Rome inherited her empire in Spain. In Sicily, Syracuse, who had joined the Carthaginians, had been taken and sacked by Romans in 212. The most notable casualty was the celebrated scientist Archimedes, whose ingenious war machines had delayed the city's capture. Scipio himself was awarded the name 'Africanus' in recognition of his victory.

The Roman Pacification of Spain and Northern Italy

Italy had been devastated by the sixteen years of Hannibal's occupation, and one of the legacies of the Second Punic War was a lasting fear of invaders from the north. However, victory had been won and much of the credit was due to the senate, whose resolve had proved unshakeable. The next fifty years saw its greatest prestige. Moreover, there had been no concessions made to any of Rome's allies and Rome went on to deal ruthlessly with cities which had defected. Capua was treated with especial fury. The city ceased to be a *municipium* and all its land was declared Roman property. The forcible removal of much of the population of Campania was also ordered, though it is probable that this was never fully carried out. Meanwhile in the north of Italy the Celts were marked out for final subjection. From 201 to 190 the senate assigned one or both consuls to the north, and the two main Celtic tribes, the Boii and Insubres, were dealt with ruthlessly. The Insubres submitted and they survived. The Boii resisted. The richest part of their land was confiscated and their presence so effectively eliminated that there is virtually no archaeological evidence for La Tène culture in north-west Italy after this period. Roman settlers were moved in to take their place. In the north-west, another tribe, the Ligurians, were also conquered so that by 180 BC northern Italy was finally under Roman control.

Control had also to be consolidated over Spain. Two further praetors were appointed each year from 197 and Spain divided into two *provinciae*, Hispania Citerior, Nearer Spain, along the eastern coast, and Hispania Ulterior, Further Spain, stretching inland from the southern coast. At first the situation in Spain seemed so calm that the two legions stationed there were withdrawn to Rome. It was a serious miscalculation. Very soon the tribes had risen in revolt and for the next twenty years there were continual wars of pacification in Spain before Roman control was established well into the interior. The Roman commitment was not enormous. Spain was clearly not seen to be as important as Italy or, later, Greece. In most years four legions were deployed there, about 22,000 men, with an equal number of allies. Alongside the desire to keep order a major incentive for pacification was the plunder of silver and slaves. One commander, Tiberius Sempronius Gracchus, brought back 40,000 pounds of silver with which to celebrate a triumph. The mines themselves were given to the censors to farm out to local contractors and they soon made Spain the richest source of raw materials in the empire. Even Judas Maccabaeus, the defender of Israel against the Seleucids, had heard of 'all the Romans had done in the province of Spain to gain possession of the silver and gold mines there' (1 Maccabees 8: 3).

In the 150s revolt broke out again in Spain, sparked off by an invasion of Roman territory by a still independent people, the Lusitanians. Pacification was renewed, often with great brutality, the Roman commanders taking the opportunity to raid into unconquered territory. Enslavement of whole peoples was normal and in at least one city, Cauca, surrender in 151 was followed by the massacre of the entire male population of 20,000. Yet the fighting was not easy in the mountainous country and reports which reached Italy were disquieting enough to seriously affect recruitment and dampen national morale. The final Spanish stronghold to be conquered, Numantia, only fell when the most gifted of the Roman commanders, Scipio Aemilianus, subdued it in 133 with an army expanded to 60,000 men. He spared fifty of its inhabitants for his triumph, sold off the rest, and razed the city to the ground.

Rome Becomes Involved in Greece

While these testing campaigns were continuing Rome had also become involved in the east. In 215 Hannibal had made an alliance with Philip V of Macedon. Rome had sent a small fleet to Greece but primarily used the Aetolian League (see p. 337), traditionally hostile to Macedonia, to contain him. Peace had been made in 205, but many senators felt that Philip had not been sufficiently punished and so they responded when in 201 the king of Pergamum, Attalus, supported by Rhodes, came to Rome to appeal for help against the intrusions of Philip. There may also have been some who saw an attack on Macedonia as a chance for plunder to refill Rome's treasury, and the senate persuaded the assemblies that despite the exhaustion of the state war was justified. The official pretext for war was that Rome was protecting the liberty of the Greeks against Macedonian expansionism. Rome was aware that the Greek city states were much more sophisticated than the tribal peoples she was subduing elsewhere and seems to have had no interest in the annexation of Greek territory.

The war was entrusted to Titus Quinctius Flamininus, a commander who had proved so effective against Hannibal that he had won a consulship for 198 when still only 30. He managed to get his command in Greece renewed for a further three years (the consuls who succeeded him were both needed in Italy) and while he was there he was in a strong position to define Roman policy on his own initiative. After destroying Philip's army at Cynoscephalae in Thessaly in 197, he used the Isthmian Games of 196 (over which he was asked to preside) to proclaim that Rome intended to leave Greece, including the coastal cities of Asia Minor, free and independent. The Greeks greeted the news with joy. It was, in fact, a shrewd move. Each city was now dependent on Rome for its protection and from this time onwards the inter-city embassies which were so much part of the Hellenistic world were directed at Rome. Flamininus himself was loaded with honours from grateful cities.

Rome now had direct links with the Greek world and regarded Greece as a sphere in which her interest, even though informal, was exclusive. It was the Aetolian League which found this out to its cost. The League had hoped to resume control over a number of cities surrendered by Philip. In this they sought the support of the Seleucid king Antiochus III. Antiochus had set himself the task of reviving the Seleucid kingdom and in 196 had crossed into Thrace, an area once held by the Seleucids. Roman suspicions had already been aroused and they had warned him not to come further. When, in 192, Antiochus agreed to support the Aetolian League and crossed with a small army to the Greek mainland, the Romans reacted vigorously. In 191 at Thermopylae he was easily defeated by a Roman army twice his size. The following year he was defeated again, in Asia at Magnesia, near the old Lydian capital at Sardis.

Roman troops had now reached Asia, but while some opportunities were taken for plunder (a campaign was launched against the Galatians who had given help to Antiochus), Rome still showed no interest in annexing territory. Again her main aim was to perpetuate her control by building up dependent allies, though her sphere of influence was now the whole Aegean area. Antiochus was excluded from the Aegean by depriving him of all his possessions along the Aegean coastline and restricting him to the east of the Taurus River. His navy was also disbanded. The cities of the coast were given their independence while the remaining territory was shared between Rhodes and the kingdom of Pergamum, which now became the largest state in Asia Minor.

So matters rested in comparative peace for twenty years, until a son of Philip of Macedon, Perseus, came to power on his father's death in 179. Perseus made tentative moves to rebuild a Macedonian relationship with Greece. While Rome was happy to leave the small Greek cities to their own devices, she could not afford to allow a rival focus of power to emerge in Greece. In 172 the Romans shipped over an army and forced Perseus into a war he had never desired. He held out successfully for some time but once again Roman manpower and resilience triumphed. In 168 Perseus' army was destroyed at the battle of Pydna on the Macedonian coast.

It was in the settlement after Pydna that Roman power was first imposed effectively in Greece, and in that sense 168 marks a turning point. Macedonia was split up into four republics, each ruling itself through elected representatives and allowed only limited contact with the others. At least this was some kind of survival, with the Romans stopping short of creating directly administered provinces. Others were treated more harshly. The Molossians of Epirus who had aided Perseus found their cities plundered and, according to one source, 150,000 of their inhabitants sold into slavery. Rhodes, which had done nothing to support the Romans in the war, was undermined by the creation by the Romans of a free port of Delos which took much of its trade (and developed into one of the major slave-trading markets of the ancient world, capable of handling 10,000 transactions a day). The Seleucid king Antiochus IV, who had invaded Egypt in 168 without Roman approval, suddenly found himself confronted on the spot by a Roman envoy, Gaius Popillius Laenas, who drew a circle around the astonished monarch and forbade him to leave it until he had agreed to make peace and withdraw. He acquiesced. Other kings allowed even greater humiliation to take place. Polybius talks of Prusias II of Bithynia, who visited Rome in 166 and threw himself before the senators addressing them as ' "Saviour Gods!"'; thus making it impossible', Polybius goes on, 'for anyone after him to surpass him in unmanliness, effeminacy and servility,' while Eumenes, king of Pergamum, who had been a staunch ally of Rome until 168, was humiliated in his own country by a Roman commissioner who encouraged his subjects to publicly vilify him.

The final subjection of Greece was not far off. In 150 a revolt in Macedonia was met with the reduction of the kingdom of Philip II and Alexander into a Roman province (148). The Achaean League had also aroused increasing irritation in Rome. The League had been involved in a dispute with Sparta, whose independence had been upheld by Rome. Rome also insisted that other cities, including Corinth and Argos, be allowed to leave the League. The League realized its survival was at stake and it must make its final stand. Its hopes were quickly dashed by Lucius Mummius, consul for 146, who defeated the League's forces. The senate singled out one of its cities, Corinth, for such complete destruction that the site remained deserted for a hundred years.

The same fate had already overtaken Carthage. The loss of the city's territorial empire in 202 had not meant the end of its prosperity and its trade routes still stretched as far as the Red and the Black Sea. Evidence from excavations shows that the city may even have grown during the second century, and a population of 200,000–300,000 has been guessed at. Militarily, however, the city was weak, its men totally inexperienced in war after the peace enforced on the city by Rome fifty years before. When a Carthaginian army was mustered against the neighbouring king Massinissa of Numidia in 150 it was annihilated. The very fact that Carthage had raised an army was now to be used by Rome as an excuse for declaring war, even though Rome's consistent support of Massinissa against Carthage had contributed to the Carthaginian attack. There was no strategic need for such a war and it may simply have been that Roman hard-liners in the senate refused to countenance the continued existence of an old and still prosperous rival. After three years of siege, Carthage was finally stormed, appropriately by Scipio Aemilianus, the grandson by adoption of Scipio Africanus. The city was razed to the ground, at least 50,000 of its inhabitants sold into slavery, and its land ritually cursed against any rebirth. For many Romans, however, this was a less than honourable war, and even Scipio was said to have had a premonition that the terrible fate of Carthage would one day be followed by a similar one for Rome. Carthage's territory became the new province of Africa.

Within a few years, therefore, the balance of power in the Mediterranean had been transformed with both the Carthaginian empire and the Hellenistic monarchs humbled. The Romans held *provinciae* in Spain, Africa, and Greece. In 133 the last king of Pergamum bequeathed his kingdom to Rome and it became the province of Asia.

Polybius and *The Universal History*

One contemporary of the events, the Greek historian Polybius (*c.*200–after 118 BC), was so impressed by the triumph of Rome that he set out in his *Universal History*, the only example of Hellenistic history to survive, to explain how it had happened. Polybius was a talented young aristocrat from Megalopolis, one of the members of the Achaean League. He had become a leader of the League's cavalry by 170, but after Pydna he was one of a thousand nobles from the League taken as hostages to Italy. Rather than brood in exile, as many of his fellow hostages did in remote cities of Etruria, Polybius managed to get to Rome and become friendly with Scipio Aemilianus (later the victor over Carthage and Numantia). He soon had access to the leading families of the city while also managing to keep his contacts with Greece.

Polybius was also a man of action. During his exile he travelled widely, through Italy, Africa, Spain, Gaul, and through the Straits of Gibraltar. He was with Scipio at the destruction of Carthage. He had been allowed to return to Greece in 150, and after the humiliation of the Achaean League by Rome in 146 he was appointed to mastermind the settlement of their affairs which followed. He did this so successfully that he was honoured in many of the League's cities and an inscription in Megalopolis pays tribute to the way he quenched the anger of the Romans. He was extraordinarily well placed to write the history of the conquest of Greece, though he extended his history to take in the two Punic Wars as well.

It was the seriousness with which Polybius took his task which marks him out as one of the greater Greek historians. He had no doubt that the Romans deserved to defeat the Greeks. Their highly disciplined army, their resolute spirit, and, above all, their balanced constitution gave them an overwhelming superiority. In that sense, the Roman victories were comprehensible. However, at the same time, Polybius recognized that chance, Tyche, always played a role in the unfolding of the events, and he sought to establish through a careful analysis of events, how far chance had contributed to the Roman victory. Polybius was scrupulous in his search for the truth and appears to have been an avid interviewer of those who had witnessed the events of the past.

Motives for War and Imperialism

Polybius had attempted to explain why Rome had been so successful in war. It is perhaps more difficult to explain what her motives were for engaging in so many wars in the first place. A traditional view has seen Rome primarily as a defensive power, reacting to events rather than creating them. According to this view the Carthaginians, Philip of Macedon, the invading Celts, were all threatening forces to which Rome had to respond as she had had to respond early in her history to those who had threatened her on the exposed plain of Latium. In 1979 this view was challenged by William Harris in his book *War and Imperialism in Republican Rome* (Oxford, 1979), in which Harris argued that Roman society was naturally attuned to aggression. For the aristocratic elite war provided the main avenue to political success, the only way an individual could achieve glory and status, while the fruits of victory, in plunder and slaves, made war attractive for the luxurious lifestyle and status it brought. In Italy the confiscation of land allowed the surplus population of Rome to be settled away from the city so that social tensions could be contained. Insofar as the only obligation that Rome expected from her allies was the provision of men for war, her continuing supremacy over them also depended on frequent campaigns. A number of forces, economic, social, and political, thus combined to create an active will for war and this explains why Rome was seldom at peace.

Rome was certainly a militaristic state, a touchy power, confident of her military prowess and quick to seek revenge for insults. She had access to large forces, showed no inhibitions about using them, and once she was engaged in a war fought it through to a conclusion, normally in her favour. It does not follow, however, that because Rome had an unrivalled mechanism for winning wars and a range of incentives for doing so that every war she engaged in was of her seeking. The events described above show a rather more complex pattern. Once Rome had stumbled into war with Carthage she was tied to winning the war or risking humiliation. After the First Punic War she knew that Carthaginian revenge was possible and she took active steps against it. Her consolidation of control in the western Mediterranean can be seen, in this sense, as defensive. It is also true, however, that Rome showed an abnormal sensitivity to any slight or any perceived threat to an area she had defined as a sphere of interest and was quick to use war in retaliation. This is how she became embroiled in Greece. How much the desire for individual glory and plunder was an element in her reaction is difficult to gauge. Victory was certainly enjoyed to the full by those who had achieved it, but there is little evidence that Rome set out to acquire permanent control of territory overseas. The empire appears to have grown piecemeal, with marked reluctance in Greece at least to annex territory until there was no alternative way of maintaining Rome's supremacy in the area. Insofar as there was a turning point from piecemeal expansions, the unpremeditated acquisition of an overseas empire, to a more deliberate policy of humiliation of enemies and determined annexation of further territory, it can placed in the period between 148 and 133 when Macedonia and Greece were absorbed, Carthage sacked, and the wealthy kingdom of Pergamum inherited. By now Rome had a Mediterranean-wide empire which she had to defend and administer and an ideology which appeared to set no limits to its size.

The Impact of the East

The impact of Rome's victories was profound. Not only did vast amounts of plunder, including some hundreds of thousands of slaves, pour into Italy but the city was open now to the rich cultures of the east. Rome had always been part of a cultural matrix which included access to Greek culture either through the mediation of the Etruscans or directly via the Greek cities of southern Italy which had now been absorbed. While most of the Roman gods had been introduced by the Etruscans, Apollo had been adopted directly from Greece in 433 when his help was needed to avert a plague. In 291, Apollo's 'son' Asclepius, the god of healing, was imported and a temple to him erected on the Tiber island. The first history of Rome was written at the end of the third century by the Roman Fabius Pictor, but in Greek, as if it were the older culture which needed to be impressed. Fabius actually claimed that a Roman festival, the *Ludi Romani*, was based on a Greek model.

It was the fall of Syracuse that saw the first major influx of Greek art to Rome. The historian Plutarch exaggerated when he writes, 'Prior to this, Rome neither had nor even knew of these exquisite and refined things . . . rather it was full of barbaric weapons and bloody spoils', but the great triumphant process of booty must have made their mark and seemed to many to mark a new phase in contact with Greece. The eastern wars brought the first plunder from mainland Greece, engraved plate and inlaid furniture, music girls, and the conception that cooking was an art. The victor of Pydna, Aemilius Paullus, carried off the royal library of Macedonia as a gift for his sons. He brought back so many statues and paintings that they took three days to pass in his triumphal procession. Greek art was exhibited to the public for the first time in a portico set up by Quintus Metellus, the destroyer of Macedonia, in 148. Soon Greek artists were copying Hellenistic statues for Roman patrons. The sack of Corinth resulted in a flood of bronze decorative objects into Rome which became favourite collectors' pieces. The earliest Roman temple in marble was put up in 148 BC and although the Etruscan model of a high podium and decorated façade was retained the decoration was now in Greek and the Greek architectural orders became common. Rome itself was transformed in the second century with three new aqueducts, a mass of new temples, and for the first time grand houses for the nobility. One vast warehouse, the Porticus Aemilia, on the left bank of the Tiber, south of the Aventine, was 487 metres long and 60 metres wide with 294 pillars. (It could only have been constructed with the help of a Roman invention, *opus caementicium*, a mortar of lime and sand strengthened by stones which appears for the first time about 200 BC.)

Greek culture infiltrated Roman at many levels. Athletic games following a Greek model were staged for the first time in Rome in 186 by Scipio Africanus' brother, the victor over Antiochus. Greek drama was introduced by Livius Andronicus at the end of the third century (Livius was born Greek and had probably been brought to Rome as a boy after the sack of Tarentum in 272), but the most lively adaptations were those of Plautus (*c.*250–184 BC), who translated a mass of Greek plays into a series of fast-moving musical comedies, full of stock characters, thwarted lovers, swaggering soldiers, and slaves with more wits than their masters.

The greatest poet of the period, Quintus Ennius (239–169 BC), who was trilingual in Oscan, Greek, and Latin, introduced the Greek epic into Roman literature in his celebrated *Annales*, a verse history of Rome. Its sombre tone caught the mood of the educated classes and it became a standard text from which Roman schoolboys learnt of the exploits of their ancestors. Later Terence (193?–159 BC) followed Plautus in adapting Greek comedies for the Roman stage, although he kept more closely to the originals and was altogether more highbrow than Plautus.

By the middle of the second century BC, therefore, the average upper-class Roman knew a great deal about the Greek way of life and would have met Greeks in a variety of contexts. Individual Romans adopted Greek ways with varying degrees of enthusiasm. Many, however, were very conscious of a traditional system of values which was under threat. These values were rooted in a dimly remembered past where the typical citizen lived a life of austerity on a small-holding. (The archetypal and probably mythical hero was Cincinnatus, who became dictator for sixteen days during the fifth-century wars with the Aequi, returning to his plot of land as soon as the state had been saved.) In war he would show *virtus*, unflinching courage, at home he would be marked out by his *pietas*, correct observance of the religious rituals by which the protection of his home and the state would be assured. To his clients he would be known for his *fides*, good faith, and he would never be corrupted by bribes. These virtues would combine to make up his *dignitas*, his status, and they would achieve their greatest value in public service. 'He achieved the ten greatest and best things which wise men spend their whole lives seeking,' proclaimed Quintus Caecilius of his father Lucius, the *pontifex maximus*, on his death in 221 BC:

He wished to be the first of warriors, the best of orators, and the most valiant of commanders; to be in charge of the greatest affairs and held in the highest honour; to possess supreme wisdom and to be regarded as supreme within the senate; to come to great wealth by honourable means; to leave many children; and to be the most distinguished person in the state. (Translation: T. P. Wiseman)

Many feared that these values were threatened by the influx of Greek culture. Plutarch blamed Marcellus, the victor of Syracuse, for 'filling the Roman people, who had hitherto been accustomed to fighting or farming . . . with a life of soft-ness and ease . . . with a taste for leisure and idle talk, affecting urbane opinions about the arts and about artists, even to wasting the better part of a day on such things'. A famous passage from Polybius chronicles the supposed decay:

Some young men squandered their energies on love affairs with boys, others with courte-sans, and others again with musical entertainments and bequests and the extravagant expenses that go with them, for in the course of the war with Perseus and the Macedonians they had quickly acquired the luxurious habits of the Greeks in this direction. So far had the taste for dissipation and debauchery spread among young men that many of them were ready to pay a talent for a male prostitute and 300 drachmae for a jar of Pontic pickled fish. (Translation: Ian Scott-Kilvert)

There were fears that physical hardiness would be undermined by these activities, that a weakness for wealth would lead to corruption, and that family fortunes would be wastefully squandered. In retaliation a number of laws curbed spending at banquets, while in a famous case in the 150s the seats of a theatre were destroyed on the insistence of a conservative senator who believed standing was more manly. (Rome was not to have a stone theatre until Pompey constructed one a hundred years later.) A group of philosophers from Athens who arrived in 155 were ridiculed when it appeared that philosophical arguments could be applied to destroy the justification for the Roman empire. Earlier, in 186, there had been a witch-hunt against the participants in Bacchanalian orgies, the Roman equivalents of the riotous celebrations in honour of Dionysus.

The Older Cato

The opposition to the trends was spearheaded by one of the most interesting and complex figures of the period, Marcus Porcius Cato (234–149 BC). Cato was a native of Tusculum, a small town near Rome, who through the help of a noble patron and his own considerable ability was able to win a consulship in 195 BC. His command for the year was in Spain and here he excelled himself, returning to Rome to celebrate a triumph. He was later sent to Greece with the Roman army which defeated Antiochus at Thermopylae. In 184 as a respected former consul he was elected to the prestigious post of censor and he revived the traditional role of the office as a guardian of public morals. For the next thirty-five years he stood out as the figurehead of resistance to the influx of ideas from Greece and to luxurious living and corruption. In his last years he became increasingly obsessed with the continuing survival of Carthage and it was his often-repeated pronouncement 'Carthage must be destroyed' which helped create the atmosphere that led to the city's final destruction. Cato wrote the first history of Rome in Latin and the earliest surviving treatise on agriculture, *De Agricultura*, which despite its idealization of the rural past of Rome was very much concerned with the new commercial farming of the present. His narrowness and vindictiveness on public occasions was offset to some extent by a real affection for his son, for whom he composed a history of Rome written out in large letters for easy reading and whose bath-time he never missed.

Yet Cato was not simply a narrow-minded Roman traditionalist. He had at least been to Greece even if only as a soldier. Although he showed no deep understanding of Greek culture there are hints in his writings that he had read Homer, Demosthenes, and Xenophon. When he contributed to the building of Rome it was with a basilica, the all-purpose assembly hall used for law cases, commercial dealings, and markets which was derived from the Greek stoas. Probably it was not so much Greece itself that he feared as the loss of self-control by those who took on Greek ways.

In his *Culture and National Identity in Republican Rome* (Ithaca, 1992), Eric Gruen provides a balanced assessment of the relationship between Greek and Roman in which he stresses how often the Romans used Greek culture to sustain their own cultural identity. Greek statues were often rededicated in Roman temples, for instance. It was the maintenance of the dignity of the Roman elite and of good public order which seems to have been behind the rejection of specific Greek customs, such as exercising naked. The same could be said of the suppression of the Bacchanalian cults in 186 BC. It was not so much that they were Greek in origin as they broke down conventional notions of authority and threatened state control of religious affairs.

The Great Period of Senatorial Government

The stability of the state over which Cato remained so concerned was, however, little threatened during his lifetime. In the fifty years after the Second Punic War the senate proved remarkably successful in maintaining collective oligarchical rule. The careers of Scipio Africanus and Flamininus had shown that an individual commander away from Rome could achieve a position of immense influence. Both had come close to being treated as kings in Spain and Greece. After the Second Punic War, the lure of plunder and glory led to increasing competition for the magistracies which could provide them. However, the senate successfully contained these ambitions. A law in 180 prescribed minimum ages for the praetors and consuls and there had to be an interval of at least two years between holding these posts. In the 150s second consulships were forbidden. Commanders might celebrate their triumphs and flaunt their plunder, they could not, however, translate them into long-term political power.

Although the senate retained enormous prestige in these years there is also evidence that the popular assemblies were vigorously involved in politics. There may have been 250,000 citizens by now and only a tiny proportion could have attended meetings, but the assemblies took their powers of election and legislation seriously. They also sat in judgement in the private prosecutions which became increasingly prevalent in this period. Accusations that a commander had taken plunder which was not his due, or extorted excessive tribute, were an accepted part of the political infighting which took place among rival candidates for power.

Intimations of Popular Unrest

After 150, however, there is evidence that the prestige of the senate was being undermined. Some individuals appear to have been defying its power. When the war against Carthage became stalemated in 148 Scipio Aemilianus, whose early career in Spain and Africa had been brilliant, won a consulship and the command on the behest of a tribune, who threatened to use a veto to block the consular elections if Scipio did not get the command. Scipio was under age and had never been praetor but the senate was unable to block the appointment. In 134 he gained a second consulship, again through popular support, in order to finish off the Spanish war at a time when second consulships were forbidden by law. In 143 Appius Claudius Pulcher celebrated a triumph even though the senate had refused him one.

These developments probably reflected growing popular unrest. The long wars in Spain, where soldiers served for an average of six years, were increasingly unpopular (hence the desire to appoint commanders to finish the job even when they were technically not qualified to take command). Recruitment was faltering and there was growing tension between the consuls, whose interest was in raising large armies, and the tribunes who, in their role of representatives of the people, resisted new levies of citizens.

These tensions were intensified by changing patterns in agriculture. The most stable and prestigious investment for those with wealth to spare was in land, and the conquest of Italy and the widespread confiscations after the Second Punic War had made large areas of public land available for purchase. The new farms which emerged were geared to commercial production. In the south they were *latifundia*, ranches on which sheep and cattle were grazed. Their wool and leather found a good market with the armies. In central Italy, especially Latium and Campania, the farms tended to be smaller and concentrated on cash crops, olives, and vines. In both cases they were now worked by slaves, who had been imported into Italy into such numbers that one estimate is that there were between two and three million by the end of the first century, over a third of the population. Slave labour was all the more attractive to landowners as slaves could not be called up for military service.

It was the peasant producers, whose plots had always been small, who most suffered. Some returned from service overseas to find their land swallowed up in larger estates, others were simply squeezed off the land. Opportunities as free labourers probably also declined as slaves swelled the labour force. Many areas of Italy were comparatively unaffected by these changes but there was an increasing pool of disaffected citizens, some of whom must have made their way in desperation to Rome, where they would have put extra stress on the city's resources. There is evidence of hurried attempts to improve the water supply in 144 and a crisis in the corn supply in 138. Evidence for actual unrest is limited but it was in these years that the tribunes appear to have become more active on behalf of the citizenry, as has already been seen in relation to military recruitment. In 139 a tribune managed to get a law passed introducing a secret ballot for the annual election of magistrates, the first of several ballot laws. In 133 this revival of tribunate power was to drive the Republic into political crisis.

Note: The introduction of Roman coinage. The earliest unit of coinage was the as, issued as a pound (324 grams) of bronze in the early third century BC. Not long afterwards the first silver coins appeared and about 214 the two metals were given an equivalent by setting a silver denarius as equal to ten asses. The as was gradually reduced in weight until it was the equivalent of 54 grams in bronze. The denarius was also revalued (in 141 BC) so as to be equal to sixteen asses. As the as became less valuable a new coin, the sestertius, 2.5 asses, was minted and this in its turn was later revalued to four asses. The sestertius was used freely as a measure of wealth or an annual payment, such as a soldier's salary. With the Romans absorbing so much silver from booty and mines in Macedonia, production of the denarius soared. By the middle of the second century BC Rome was minting as many denarii in a year as some Greek cities would in a century and the silver denarius became the standard coin of the Mediterranean world until the third century AD. (See the entry 'Roman coinage' in *The Oxford Classical Dictionary* (revised third edition, Oxford, 2003) for further details.)

FURTHER READING

On the Phoenicians/Carthaginians, S. Moscati, *The World of the Phoenicians* (London, 1999), and as editor, *Phoenicians* (London, 2001). See also Maria Aubet, *The Phoenicians and the West* (Cambridge, 1994), and G. Markoe (ed.), *Phoenicians* (London, 2002). The *Cambridge Ancient History* covers the Punic Wars. The first is covered by H. Scullard in vol. vii, Part 2, and the second by J. Briscoe in vol. viii (Cambridge, 1989). For a good overview of the period see Michael Crawford, *The Roman Republic* (2nd edition, London, 1992). Andrew Lintott, *Imperium Romanum: Politics and Administration* (London, 1993) provides a solid introduction to Roman provincial administration from the republican period onwards. For Polybius see F. Walbank, *Polybius* (Berkeley, Calif., 1972).

On politics in Rome after the Punic Wars, the chapter by A. Astin in the *Cambridge Ancient History*, vol. viii: *Rome and the Mediterranean to 133 BC* (Cambridge, 1989), provides a fine overview. Crawford, *The Roman Republic*, is good on the Roman aristocracy. See also A. Astin, *Cato the Censor* (Oxford, 1978). On Roman attitudes to the Greeks see E. Gruen, *Culture and National Identity in Republic Rome* (London, 1993). For the artistic transformation of Rome see the chapter by J. Pollitt in the *Oxford History of Classical Art*. For changing land use see K. Hopkins, *Conquerors and Slaves* (Cambridge, 1978), which looks at the economic changes brought by the transformation into empire, and Tim Potter, *Roman Italy* (London, 1987). E. Salmon, *The Making of Roman Italy* (Ithaca, NY, 1982) takes the story from 350 BC through to the Social War. P. Brunt, *Italian Manpower 225 BC–AD 14* (revised edition, Oxford, 1987), provides important background material.

The Gracchi and the Challenge to Senatorial Government

Social reformers were rare in Roman politics and this makes the attempts by two brothers, Tiberius and Gaius Sempronius Gracchus, to tackle the social and economic problems of land hunger in Italy in the late second century BC all the more remarkable. The Gracchi were a noble family, with five consulships to their credit, and Tiberius and Gaius' mother, Cornelia, was none other than the daughter of Scipio Africanus. She was a formidable woman, mother of twelve children, of whom only three survived. When widowed, she transferred her ambitions on to her sons and the result was two men, nine years apart in age, who were the nearest republican Rome ever produced to Greek reformers such as Solon and Cleisthenes.

Tiberius Gracchus was elected a tribune in December 134. The traditional powers of his post allowed him not only to pass laws ('plebescites') through the *concilium plebis* but to veto, on behalf of the people, any acts of the magistrates and any decree of the senate. It was thus, in contrast to the *comitia centuriata*, a genuinely popular assembly—in 188 it was recorded as having 258,318 eligible voters—and while the *comitia centuriata* met out on the Campus Martius, the *concilium* assembled on or alongside the Capitoline Hill, right in the centre of the city. Used with determination the tribunate could thus prove a lever for creating or resisting political change. Tiberius was set on using his powers to achieve land reform. What his motives were is hard to say. His critics saw him as one who was exploiting popular unrest for his own advantage. Tiberius claimed purer motives, no less than the restoration and consolidation of the small landowner whose position was being undermined by the growth of large estates and who was, therefore, being lost for military service (for which landownership was a precondition).

Tiberius' plan for land reform centred on the *ager publicus*, land owned by the state (much of it originally the territory of defeated Italian cities) which was available for distribution to citizens. Theoretically there was a maximum allocation of 500 *iugera* (120 hectares) for any individual but many citizens and some members of allied communities had acquired much more. Tiberius proposed that they should surrender the extra in return for a formal confirmation of their right to the rest. The surrendered land would then be distributed among the poor in small plots (of 30 *iugera*, 7 hectares) to which they would be given an inalienable right. They would thus be protected from being bought out by their richer neighbours as well as being retained for military service. The whole procedure would be overseen by a commission of three men.

Politically the cleverness of the proposal was that it did not threaten the concept of private property. Those who would lose out would be those who had been caught out. However, any vigorous use of the *concilium plebis* was bound to be unsettling, particularly when it affected richer landowners. Tiberius showed little regard for the sensitivities of the senate. He broke convention by not consulting with them over his proposals and then by deposing one of the tribunes who opposed him. When news came that the kingdom of Pergamum had been bequeathed to Rome by its last ruler, Tiberius suggested that its treasure could be used to provide money grants for those receiving allotments and that the *concilium plebis* not the senate should discuss the future of its income. This was intruding on the traditional role of the senate as the body responsible for foreign affairs. Most provocatively of all, Tiberius then announced he would stand for a second tribunate, another clear breach of convention which he may have tried to hide under further promises of popular reform.

Tiberius maintained his influence in the *concilium plebis*, whose meetings were swollen by a mass of poor citizens crowding into the city to vote, but he had isolated himself from the ruling classes. The Roman state valued precedent above all things. More astute reformers in Rome, as in Greece, always claimed that they were simply restoring things as they once had been, but Tiberius was too impetuous for such ploys and when, on one day in the summer of 133, discussion began on his eligibility for a second term, tensions were already high. The *concilium plebis* met on the Capitoline Hill, the senate was meeting at the same time in the nearby Temple of Fides. As confused stories of developments in the *concilium* were relayed to the senate, the *pontifex maximus* (the head of the priesthood), Scipio Nasica, urged the presiding consul in the senate to have Tiberius killed for attempting to set up a tyranny. The consul refused to use force but Scipio Nasica, convinced of the justice of his case, gathered a crowd of supporters who surged towards the Capitoline Hill, where Tiberius was still holding sway. The result was a pitched battle fought with cudgels and sticks. Perhaps 300 died in the crush, including Tiberius, struck on the head, it was said, by a stool wielded by a hostile fellow tribune. The first popular reform movement in Roman history had been crushed but with methods which could only discredit its opponents.

Despite this debacle, the land commission survived, with Tiberius' brother Gaius as one of its members. There is evidence that in some areas of Italy it succeeded in setting up considerable numbers of small farms. However, there was, inevitably, some opposition from the larger landowners, particularly those from allied cities who did not see why they should surrender their land to the Roman poor. The opponents of the bill exploited this discontent and in 125 a consul, Fulvius Flaccus, proposed that citizenship should be offered to allied cities. The proposal came to nothing but the aspirations of these cities were raised and their frustrated hopes were later to develop into a major threat to Rome.

In 124 Tiberius' brother Gaius was elected a tribune for 123. Gaius was altogether a more formidable man than his brother. He was endowed with enormous energy, personal charisma, and impressive skills as an orator. Descriptions survive in Plutarch's *Life* of Gaius striding backwards and forwards across the speaker's platform, ripping his toga at the height of his emotion, and at work surrounded by a crowd of enthused professionals. (A comparison might be made with the twentieth-century Welsh politician David Lloyd George.) Gaius was also more astute as a politician, and when elected tribune his early reforms were aimed at strengthening his power base. For the poorer citizen access to cheap grain was essential and Gaius stabilized corn prices by instituting a system of bulk buying and storage for sale at a fixed price (thus protecting the poor from variations in the weather and the exploitation of speculators). He attempted to alleviate land hunger by setting up new citizen colonies within Italy and he pushed on with his brother's land reforms.

Gaius' legislation suggests he wished to move power away from the senate towards the popular assemblies. To isolate the senate he courted the *equites*, the equestrians, a class originally composed of those able to provide a horse for the cavalry but now defined by a wealth qualification. It was this class which monopolized state contracts (senators being forbidden to take them). Gaius ensured that the right to raise the revenues of the new province of Asia, which had now been created around the wealthy kingdom of Pergamum, should be auctioned in Rome among the equestrians. In Italy itself he initiated road-building projects which were also highly attractive to equestrian contractors. More daringly Gaius allowed equestrians to participate in the courts, first set up in 149, which judged cases brought by provincials against the rapacity of governors. Since many of the complaints came from equestrians in any case, the equestrians had become judges in their own cause, in effect a boosting of their political position within the state. In other laws passed in the *concilium* Gaius confirmed and extended certain popular rights. The scale of his success could be seen when he was elected to a second tribunate without any of the opposition his brother had run into.

Gaius' success was not to last. The problem was once again the opposition of allied communities to the work of the land commission. Gaius hoped to buy them off with the promise of Roman citizenship for Latin communities around Rome and the grant of Latin rights, including citizenship for those who migrated to Roman territory, for other allied communities. The proposal was statesmanlike and if implemented might have warded off the damaging Social War which was to break out between Rome and her allies in 91. However, there was no real constituency in support of Gaius' reforms. No citizen, rich or poor, had any interest in sharing citizenship and the senate knew that an influx of new citizens would make their own control of elections harder to maintain. While Gaius was abroad planning another of his schemes, the foundation of a large overseas colony, to be known as Junonia, near the site of Carthage, the senate backed a rival plan to create more citizen colonies within Italy. This was of much greater interest to citizens and Gaius' power base crumbled. His franchise bill was lost and he failed in an attempt to secure a third tribunate.

Without office, any Roman, even one of Gaius' stature, was vulnerable. When an attempt was made in the following year to repeal the law setting up Junonia, Gaius appeared with a crowd of supporters to oppose the repeal. In a scuffle which broke out the servant of one of the consuls, Opimius, was killed and the senate seized on the incident to support Opimius in seeking revenge for what was magnified into an attack on the state. For the first time in Rome's history a decree, the *senatus consultum ultimum*, was passed urging the consuls to see that the state came to no harm. Gaius withdrew his followers to the Aventine Hill, a traditional gathering place of the people, but it offered no protection. Opimius attacked ruthlessly and some 3,000 citizens died. Opimius offered a reward for Gaius' head of its weight in gold. When it was finally produced, the story goes that its brains had been scooped out and the cavity filled with lead.

Only a few years before, Polybius had written in praise of the Roman constitution and the balance it maintained between aristocratic (the senate), monarchical (the consuls), and popular (the assemblies) elements. Now the image of harmony had been shattered. The senate's authority had been shown to be hollow, defensible in the last resort only through force. The *concilium plebis* had emerged as an alternative centre of power which could be manipulated by ambitious tribunes. The equestrians had also gained a new sense of identity, one they could exercise in the courts and, in the upper orders of the *comitia centuriata*, at the elections of consuls and praetors. Outside Rome the allies, offered but then denied the possibility of citizenship, simmered with new discontent. The failure of the Gracchi marked a watershed in the political history of the Republic.

Marius and the Defence of the Empire

Any chance of restoring some harmony to the state and respect for the senate was hindered by the continued expansion of the empire. In 133 alone there had been the capture in Spain of Numantia and the bequest of a whole kingdom, Pergamum, now the province of Asia. In the north Roman businessmen were expanding across the Alps into Gaul. Roman administration had to follow to protect them and by 120 a network of roads and towns, many of them colonies, stretched along the coast towards Spain and inland up rivers such as the Rhône, making up the new province of Transalpine Gaul. In the south, across the Mediterranean, the province of Africa was being settled by Italians for the first time. Aerial surveys show a vast area, 160 kilometres broad, which appears to have been set aside for land division in these years.

It was unlikely that Roman rule over these vast territories would remain without some challenge. In 111 one came. The throne of Numidia, a client state of Rome, which neighboured the province of Africa, had been seized by a usurper, Jugurtha. In the struggle some Italian businessmen had been massacred and their supporters in the equestrian class demanded action from the senate. The senate's response was hesitant, largely, said the historian Sallust (whose *History of the Jugurthine War* adopts a high moral tone on the matter), because of massive bribes distributed by Jugurtha among Roman senators. However, it is also likely that the senate was reluctant to initiate a war in a distant and unknown territory. It was only when it was clear that Jugurtha had little respect for Roman authority that war was joined in earnest (110).

However, the war went slowly and frustration with the senate's control of it grew both among the equestrian class and the people as a whole. In 107 the assembly presented their own candidate for the consular elections, Gaius Marius, an equestrian, now nearly 50 years old, with a solid record of military and public service. Marius not only won but, following the precedent established by Scipio Aemilianus in 147, he secured the command in Africa, where he had already served, through a law passed by the *concilium*. This was a direct challenge to the senate which normally allocated provincial commands. Then, instead of going through the normal procedures of conscription, he called for volunteers for his army and, in a break with the tradition of centuries, was prepared to take men without property. Marius had defeated Jugurtha by 105, and returned to lead him through the streets of Rome in chains in his triumph.

Africa was not the only part of the empire under threat. In 113 news came of two Germanic tribes, the Cimbri and Teutones, who had embarked on a long and seemingly undirected migration from central Europe to France which intruded from time to time into Roman territory. Each time they met a Roman army they defeated it. After the final catastrophe, at Arausio in 105, Italy lay completely open to invasion and was only saved by the failure of the Germans to follow up their advantage. Marius seemed the only hope. In 104 he secured a second consulship and then, in defiance of all precedent, another four successive consulships. In two great battles, Aquae Sextia in Provence (102) and Vercelles in northern Italy (101), he defeated the Germans. Even the senate now accepted him as the saviour of the nation.

Marius' problem was the settlement of his troops. Those without land to return to could not simply be disbanded, and he gained the help of one of the tribunes for 103, Lucius Appuleius Saturninus, in securing land for them in Africa. Saturninus had his own plans for using the issue to gain public support and, with Marius' veterans called into Rome to overawe his opponents, forced laws through the *concilium* which would have given Marius' men, including those from the allied communities, access to land in Italy as well. The laws were bitterly opposed by the senate. Disorder increased and Saturninus was killed by a lynch mob. Marius' men never got their land in Italy and Marius himself went into exile, now a somewhat discredited figure. Once again violence had infiltrated the political system.

Marius' career had shown that the rules allowing a man only one consulship could be subverted by a determined *concilium* at a time of crisis and the senate could do little to prevent it. Marius' new-style army also marked an important development. If soldiers were without land they were totally dependent on their commanders to look after them after their campaigns had ended. The commander might be encouraged to use them to force land from the state, as Saturninus had attempted to do on Marius' behalf. The failure of the senate to recognize this problem and deal with it was a serious one. It was to leave itself vulnerable to determined commanders.

The Revolt of the Allies

The very success of Marius had intensified another problem. He had relied heavily on allied support to win the war in the north and the allies were deeply conscious of their indispensability. Certainly their alliances with Rome had not been without their advantages. Allied cities had shared in the general prosperity of the new empire. Campania, for instance, was more advanced than Rome. Theatres, baths, basilicas, and amphitheatres were being built here long before they were known in the capital. At Pietrabbondante in Samnite territory and at Praeneste near Rome imposing shrines had been built. Some of the wealth came from the allied cities' own activities overseas where their businessmen appear to have mixed with Romans on equal terms. Yet in Italy allies were still treated as second-class citizens. Cities had to provide troops at Rome's behest, and while most were happy to join in resisting an attack on Italy itself, service in distant territories such as Spain was increasingly resented. Within Italy they experienced a steady extension of Roman power. Land confiscated by Rome was settled by Roman citizens, Roman roads spread through the peninsula, Roman colonies intruded on allied land. Often individuals treated the locals with contempt—one consul, for instance, ordered a local magistrate to be flogged when the local baths were not cleared and cleaned out fast enough to satisfy his wife.

The hopes of the upper classes of the allied cities now rested on Roman citizenship. Citizenship would give them a chance to participate, through the *concilium plebis*, in the government of the empire and also the rights enjoyed by any citizen against the power of the magistrates. Their hopes were soon dashed by the intransigence of the Roman ruling classes. In 95 a law was passed which allowed the censors to seek out and expel any inhabitant who had falsely claimed citizenship. It was bitterly resented. In 91 one of the tribunes for the year, Livius Drusus, proposed in the *concilium* that citizenship should be extended to the

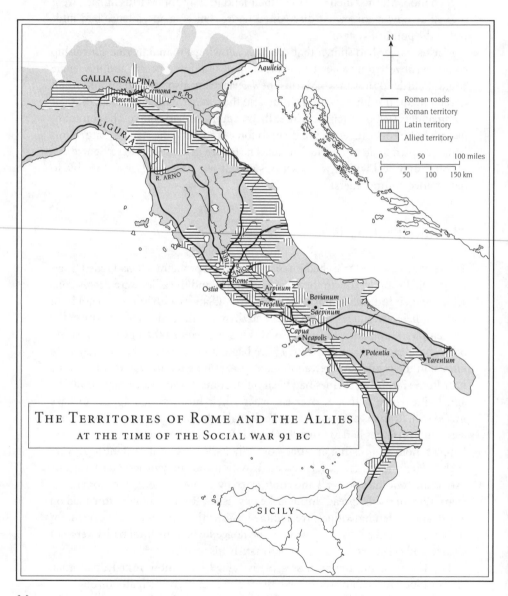

THE TERRITORIES OF ROME AND THE ALLIES
AT THE TIME OF THE SOCIAL WAR 91 BC

MAP 10

upper classes of the allied cities. This move had more support as it would help create a larger body of rich citizens to balance the multitudes of poor, but many felt Drusus was only interested in building up his own power base. In October 91 he was assassinated.

This new dashing of allied hopes was a catalyst for revolt. The grievances of the allies were so deep-rooted that over the winter of 91–90 twelve major peoples, prominent among them Rome's old enemies the Samnites, joined to form the state of Italia, with its capital at Corfinium, a city to the east of Rome well protected by mountains. (The word Italia originally applied only to Calabria, home of a people called *Itali* by the Greeks, but was now extended to the new state.) As an interesting sign of how deeply Roman culture had penetrated, the separatists chose to be governed by two consuls, twelve praetors, and a senate, and their hastily struck coins were clearly imitations of those of Rome. An army of 100,000 men, many of them soldiers well hardened by service in Rome's wars, gathered to defend the new state.

Rome managed to raise 150,000 troops but for the first year of the war was put on the defensive by the determined and well-organized rebels. The pressure was such that in 90, in a major political concession, Rome granted citizenship to all those allies who had stayed loyal and probably as well to those who agreed to lay down their arms. With the opposition split she then crushed the remaining insurgents, whose unity disintegrated with time. As in earlier times the Samnites proved the hardest to defeat but throughout Italy the economy was disrupted, land ravaged, and thousands killed as the war was brought to a close. Eventually when peace came citizenship had been extended to all communities south of the Po. Italian unification had been achieved but the price, in terms of disruption and lingering bitterness, was high.

Sulla

The Social War ('social' from *socii*, allies) lasted longest in the south. The rebels had looked for help from outside and had made contact with a new enemy of Rome, Mithridates, king of Pontus, a mountainous yet fertile kingdom on the edge of the Black Sea. Mithridates was shrewd and manipulative with the aspirations, though not the military talents, of an Alexander. Over a long reign (it had begun in 120) he had noted the growing arrogance of the Roman equestrians and their unashamed plundering of Asia and he sensed the overconfidence of rulers who had not been seriously challenged in battle in the east for eighty years.

Mithridates may have been pushed into action when the Romans unwisely instigated an invasion of his territory by his neighbour, Nicomedes of Bithynia, but his timing was probably conditioned by the knowledge that Rome was tied up with the Social War. In 89 he invaded Bithynia and by 88 he had reached the province of Asia where he called on the Greeks to slaughter Italian citizens and their families. It was said that some 80,000 were killed in a night, so deep-rooted was the hatred of Roman exploitation. The Asian Greeks rallied to Mithridates as a saviour, and further afield, in Athens, there was a democratic coup in his support.

A consul was needed to restore control and one of those elected for 88, Lucius Cornelius Sulla, was granted the command. Sulla was of an old but not particularly distinguished patrician family and his main claim to fame was his success as a commander in the south of Italy during the Social War. As he was about to leave for the east he found his position challenged by a tribune, Publius Sulpicius. Sulpicius had developed a plan to distribute the newly enfranchised allied citizens among the existing tribal groups into which Roman citizens were divided in the *concilium*, doubtless in the hope of calling on their support when he needed it. (The alternative was to marginalize them by placing them in new tribal groups which would vote after the original groups when most issues had already been decided. This was the option preferred by conservatives.) In order to gain Marius' support for his plans he promised Marius, now aged 70, that he would secure him the eastern command in place of Sulla.

Sulpicius' plan was clearly unconstitutional as Marius was not even one of the consuls for the year. Sulla would have been completely humiliated if it had succeeded and was left with little option but to defend his dignity. He persuaded his legions to follow him to Rome. It was a momentous decision, understandable in terms of Sulla's frustration, but outrageous otherwise. For the first time a Roman army was being led into Rome, across the sacred *pomerium*, to be used against other Romans. There was no effective force to resist it though citizens pelted the troops from the rooftops. Sulla was triumphant. He pushed through a decree in the senate outlawing Sulpicius, Marius, and their supporters. Marius fled to Africa where he knew his veterans would welcome him. Sulpicius was betrayed by a slave and killed. Sulla dealt ruthlessly with the remaining opposition before departing at last for Asia.

However, once Sulla had left Italy fresh unrest broke out, again over the distribution of citizens. A consul for 87, Lucius Cornelius Cinna, tried to revive Sulpicius' proposals but was obstructed by the other consul, a nominee of Sulla's. Cinna was forced to flee the city but now sought out Marius and the two returned to besiege Rome. They captured the city and in 86 Cinna and Marius held the consulships, Marius' seventh. Marius died shortly afterwards but Cinna managed to hold four successive consulships and, although the details are obscure, appears to have maintained stability. Sulla was declared an outlaw.

In Asia Sulla, despite having been 'officially' deprived of his command, was rebuilding his position with the harshness that was his hallmark. Athens was retaken and the supporters of Mithridates slaughtered. The Piraeus was burnt down and treasures, including one of the great libraries and columns from the temple of Olympian Zeus, carried off from the city. In Asia the reconquered cities were crushed with enormous indemnities. Mithridates, whose popularity among the Greeks collapsed as soon as the scale of the Roman retribution became clear, surrendered all his conquests and retreated to his kingdom. This was enough for Sulla. He now had the glory of victory to back his return to Rome for revenge. As soon as he landed in Italy in 83 he initiated a civil war in which communities and peoples who had supported Marius, which included the Samnites, were crushed. Then Sulla set out on the systematic elimination of his remaining opponents. Cinna had already died in an army mutiny in 84. A list of between 2,000 and 9,000 equestrians and senators was drawn up, any of whom could be freely killed for reward. Their land was confiscated and distributed among Sulla's veterans, a process which caused renewed disruption in Italy on an immense scale. In 82 Sulla entered Rome yet again with an army and declared himself dictator, a post normally held only for six months but held by Sulla with no declared limit.

Sulla, however, was more than a revengeful tyrant. He had a plan for constitutional reform based on the restoration of the power and prestige of the senate. It was to be enlarged to 600 members (from the traditional 300). The extra 300 members had to come from the equestrian class and their appointment gave Sulla the chance to pack the senate with those loyal to himself. Meanwhile the equestrian class lost their right to sit on juries, which were from now on to be reserved for senators. To hinder the rise of popular leaders Sulla insisted that the traditional rules about magistracies be restored. No one could be praetor before the age of 39 or consul before 42, an age when ambition might be already on the wane. No one could hold the same magistracies twice within ten years. Finally Sulla decreed that anyone who had held the position of tribune could hold no other magistracy, neutralizing the post as a stepping-stone to the more senior magistracies. Tribunes could no longer introduce legislation in the *concilium* without the prior approval of the senate. His new system complete, Sulla then, to the surprise of many, retired from office. He died in 78.

It was during these years that violence had entered the political system and begun to corrode it. Armies had fought within Rome, the constitution had been subverted by force, Italy had been unsettled by massive confiscations of land. Sulla's restoration of the senate was, in the circumstances, an artificial one and almost immediately it came under pressure. The tribunes started agitating for the restoration of their powers and clashed on several occasions with the consuls. Among their most popular campaigns was one against the corruption of Sulla's senatorial courts after it became clear that massive bribery was being used to secure verdicts. Popular unrest was fuelled by several years of high corn prices. There were also direct challenges to the state. One of the consuls for 78, Lepidus, having quarrelled with his fellow consul, put himself at the head of a mass of dispossessed landowners in Etruria, while a former supporter of Marius, Quintus

Sertorius, returned to Spain (where he had originally been governor) and built up such effective support among the native peasantry that senatorial control of the province was lost.

The Rise of Pompey

It was clearly a desperate time, and Sulla's senators failed to match up to the role the dictator had created for them. In fact, in a fatal abdication of responsibility, they undermined the whole purpose of Sulla's reforms by turning to a young commander who was not even a member of the senate to save them. This was Gnaeus Pompeius Magnus, Pompey the Great. Pompey, the son of a former consul, had made his entry into public life by raising three legions in support of Sulla in 83 and using them so effectively that he earned himself the nickname *adulescentulus carnifex*, the teenage butcher. After campaigns on behalf of Sulla in Sicily and Africa Pompey persuaded the dictator to allow him a triumph and the cognomen Magnus, 'the Great'. (An attempt to hold the triumph in appropriate style failed when the elephants he had secured to pull his chariot failed to fit through the city gate.) He was still only 25 and like Mithridates, later to be his adversary, he had aspirations to be an Alexander. (A celebrated marble head of Pompey dating from an original of about 55 BC portrays him, in fact, with a hairstyle similar to that given by Hellenistic sculptors to Alexander.) Now the senate granted him a special command to deal with Lepidus. What pressures Pompey put on the senate to secure his command are unknown, but it was a rash decision to entrust troops to a man whose personal ambitions seemed without limit.

Pompey's career had already shown that he would not be easy to control, but it was equally clear that he was one of the most able men in the state, energetic, ruthless when he needed to be, and with fine administrative skills. He cleaned up Lepidus' revolt quickly and then departed for Spain. Sertorius was a much tougher adversary and victory only came in 72 when, worn down by the strain of continual fighting he was assassinated by a rival commander, whom Pompey soon defeated. As soon as Pompey returned to Rome the senate asked him to mop up another revolt, the massive uprising of slaves led by the Thracian gladiator Spartacus. This had been an extraordinary success. In 72 both consuls had been defeated by the 70,000-strong force of slaves (mostly drawn from the countryside) which Spartacus had forged into a fighting force. If he had managed to discipline them more effectively he might have achieved even more, but in 71 no less than six legions were sent against him, his forces were split, and the revolt ended with a grisly row of 6,000 crucified slaves lining the road from Rome to Capua where the uprising had begun.

Pompey arrived back just as order was being restored but typically he claimed the glory for the suppression of the revolt. In fact the final assault on Spartacus had been led by an older man of more noble background than Pompey, Marcus Licinius Crassus, who was furious at being upstaged by this young adventurer. Crassus could not be ignored by Pompey. He was a man of immense wealth, much of it gained through unscrupulous profiteering during the reign of Sulla. He had built a network of clients among the senate and equestrian businessmen. Pompey realized that Crassus had his uses and the two men agreed to stand for the consulships of the year 70. Both retained their armies to make sure the senate acquiesced.

This was yet another example of Pompey's ambition and arrogance. He had not even held a quaestorship, let alone a seat in the senate, yet such was the influence he held over an overawed and grateful senate that the senate decreed he could be excused from these requirements. When he arrived to take his seat as presiding officer he had to follow the instructions from a book specifically composed for him by a scholarly friend, the writer Varro. He and Crassus then proceeded to undo Sulla's reforms by restoring their original powers to the tribunes and opening the juries once again to equestrians, giving non-senators a majority on each jury. These reforms were widely welcomed and enhanced Pompey's popularity among the people, though they did nothing to gain him the trust of the senate.

After his consulship Pompey retired into private life. His motives can only be guessed at. Even those who were close to him always found them difficult to fathom. He must have known that he had little popularity in the senate and he was not one to bother with the constant nurturing of political relationships which were essential if he was to create a following there. He saw himself above such trivialities and he probably sensed that simply by waiting on events new crises would arise which he would be the only one able to solve. He was soon proved right. In the east Mithridates was on the move again. In 74 king Nicomedes of Bithynia, the kingdom neighbouring Pontus, had bequeathed it to Rome. Mithridates, angry at this extension of the Roman empire, invaded Bithynia and a force was sent under the consul for 74, Lucius Licinius Lucullus, to oppose him. Lucullus was remarkably successful. He forced Mithridates out of Bithynia, invaded Pontus and captured two of its major cities, then led his troops on a gruelling campaign through Armenia, whose king Tigranes was the son-in-law and ally of Mithridates. Finally, Lucullus, conscious of the need for long-term stability in Asia, curbed the excesses of the equestrians, reducing the heavy burdens imposed on the Asian cities by Sulla. This was to be his undoing. In Rome a campaign against him was instituted by those furious at this intervention in their concerns and much was made of the exhaustion of Lucullus' troops and his failure to destroy Mithridates. (Lucullus had wisely decided not to pursue him into the mountains of Anatolia.) There is little doubt that Pompey had his contacts among the campaigners.

A problem which was more immediately pressing was that of pirates who were causing havoc in the eastern Mediterranean. Even the corn supplies to Rome were being disrupted. The confidence of the pirates was such that they even dared penetrate inland, sacking shrines in Greece, burning part of the harbour at Ostia and, on one of their raids into Italy, successfully capturing two praetors. Someone was needed to take the problem in hand. The senate was bitterly opposed to giving Pompey yet another command and it was left to one of the tribunes, Gabinius, who proposed to the *concilium* in 67 that someone chosen from among the former consuls should be appointed. Everyone knew that Pompey was the man intended and there was fierce opposition from both senators and other tribunes before the law was passed. Once it was through, however, it was followed by another which specifically appointed Pompey, with the enormous force of 500 ships, 120,000 infantry, and 5,000 cavalry to support him. His command was to cover the sea and all islands, and to run 80 kilometres inland.

Pompey had broken free of senatorial control but more than repaid the trust the people placed in him. The Mediterranean was divided into thirteen areas, each under a legate, a deputy, and the pirates were driven eastwards, releasing the important corn-supplying provinces of Sardinia, Sicily, and Africa from their grip. Within three months (rather than the three years which had been expected) the pirates had been chased to their strongholds in Cilicia and the problem was under control. Even Pompey's enemies were impressed, and when the command against Mithridates finally came his way in 66 its award aroused much less opposition. (Like the previous command, it was actually granted through the *concilium*.) Once again Pompey was given wide-ranging powers, the absolute right while he was in Asia to make peace and war and any necessary political settlements on condition that these were ratified by the senate on his return home.

Commands were there to be used not just to save the empire but to boost personal prestige and wealth and Pompey was determined to use his powers to maximum effect. Once he had relieved Lucullus of his command (Lucullus angrily told Pompey that he was like a vulture feasting on the carrion other beasts had killed), Pompey scotched an attempt by Mithridates to come to terms by asking for impossible conditions in return. It would do no good to bring the war to an end too soon and deprive himself of glory and plunder. Mithridates was driven northwards to the Bosporus and then Pompey dealt with Armenia, reducing it to the status of a client kingdom of Rome. Further campaigns in 64 and 63 saw the annexation of Syria, the last remnant of the Seleucid state which had already been occupied by king Tigranes of Armenia. Further south, in Judaea, Pompey captured Jerusalem after a siege of three months. Although he left the treasures of the city intact he insisted on entering the Holy of Holies in the Temple, a blatant act of desecration. Judaea became a client kingdom of Rome and the process by which Judaism was to come under Roman control had begun. News then came through that Mithridates had committed suicide.

Pompey could now organize the east as he wished. Three new provinces were created. Cilicia, hitherto held by the Romans along the coast, was extended inland so that its western border ran alongside the province of Asia. Cyprus was added to the province in 58 after the Romans had extracted it from Egyptian control. The province of Syria included the former Seleucid capital of Antioch and extended southwards along the coastline to take in the ancient Phoenician cities of Tyre and Sidon and inland to the Euphrates. Beyond lay Parthia, and it was one of the few weaknesses of the settlement that Syria remained vulnerable to attack from the Parthians, attacks made more likely by the contemptuous way Pompey and others had treated the Parthian kings. Along the southern shores of the Black Sea ran the province of Bithynia and Pontus carved from the former kingdoms of Nicomedes and Mithridates. Pompey divided the province into eleven communities, each with an urban centre for easier administration. Flanking these provinces to the east was a series of client kingdoms, Colchis, Commagene, Judaea, and Armenia among them. All were required to pay tribute to Rome.

It was an extraordinary achievement. Pompey had created a stable eastern empire which now provided a vast income from taxes and tribute for Rome. For himself he had gained wealth (military victory was always a provider of riches as there were few legal restrictions on what the commander took for himself), political glory, and a host of men and territories which now counted themselves as his clients. There is little wonder that back in Rome the senators and many others were apprehensive about his return. If he kept his armies intact he was unchallengeable. This was how vulnerable the republic had become.

Cicero and the Catiline Conspiracy

In fact while Pompey was away there had been another political crisis in Rome. Among the contenders for the consulship of 63 had been one Lucius Sergius Catilina, usually known as Catiline. Catiline was of an obscure patrician family but his fortunes had benefited, like many others, from the proscriptions of Sulla. In the early 60s he had been accused of extortion and it was not until 64 that he was free to stand for the consulship. Having failed then he tried again in 63 (for the year 62), campaigning on a programme which included the abolition of all debts. The hope was that Pompey's settlement in the east would finance the purchase of land on which the landless poor could be settled. A variety of discontents, including spendthrift nobles and unsuccessful farmers, were attracted to Catiline and when he was once again unsuccessful in the elections there was talk of an armed uprising among his frustrated followers in Etruria.

One of the successful consuls for 63 was Marcus Tullius Cicero, perhaps the most gifted and versatile orator and man of letters Rome was ever to produce. Cicero had been born outside Rome, at Marius' birthplace, Arpinum, in 106 and had come to Rome as a boy, to study law. He spent only a short time in the army and was soon back in Rome making his way as an advocate in the courts. There was no shortage of opportunities for those with talent. The confiscations of Sulla had left a host of embittered landowners while continued Roman expansion overseas had allowed all manner of corruption and extortion to flourish. Within Rome bribery at elections had become frequent. Prosecutions for these excesses could be brought both by the state and private individuals but usually became entangled in the personal rivalries of aristocratic families. As cases were decided by juries, much depended on swaying their members with impassioned oratory. Cicero excelled at the forensic speech where facts were combined with emotion to destroy an opponent. After some initial success in Rome he developed his talents through two years' intensive study of rhetoric in Greece. Back in Rome his fame grew and in 75 he became the first man to be elected as quaestor without the normal ten years of military service. He spent his term in office in Sicily and it was as a result of contacts there that he was asked, in 70, to take on the prosecution of a notorious governor, Gaius Verres, who had ruthlessly plundered the island in the late 70s. Cicero's opening speech was so devastating that not only was Verres forced into exile but his own defending counsel, Hortensius, hitherto the most respected in Rome, never recovered his reputation. Cicero was now seen as the leading orator in the city. He was elected praetor in 66 and then a consul for 63.

It was Cicero's duty as consul to defend the state and he took on the job with relish. His experience of exploiting the emotional volatility of the juries had taught him how to project himself to crowds and he appeared in the senate, dramatically arrayed with armour under his toga, to denounce Catiline to his face. Catiline fled to Etruria where an uprising had already begun, whereupon Cicero unmasked five fellow conspirators in Rome itself and with the support of the senate had them executed. Catiline assumed leadership of the Etrurian rebels but they were no match for the legions sent against them. Catiline and his followers were wiped out.

For Cicero it was his finest hour and many among the senators agreed, heaping him with titles, 'father of his country', 'the new founder of Rome'. Cicero himself never tired of retelling the story (he wrote a long letter to Pompey on the subject, which was received with some coolness by a man who was understandably sensitive to any threat of being upstaged), and from now on saw himself as some kind of senior statesman with a particular responsibility for guiding the state through the turbulent times that confronted it. But the adulation did not last. For many senators Cicero remained a social parvenu, moreover one who had never held military command. His support was destined to remain limited. More ominously, as the emotions of the moment faded, there were those who questioned whether it was correct to put to death Roman citizens, in this case those conspirators rounded up in Rome, without trial. It was a question which was to return to haunt Cicero.

The year 62 was overshadowed by the return of Pompey. No one knew what he would demand when he reached Italy. His feelings had always been well concealed and his contempt for normal constitutional practice well known. In the event as soon as he landed at Brundisium in December he disbanded his army, to the genuine amazement of all. His reasons remain unclear. He may have simply decided that from now on he was going to act as a senior figure within the constitution and must be seen therefore to be acting correctly. More likely he felt that his prestige was so high that he did not need to bother with armed force. He set out, virtually alone, for Rome to seek the official confirmation by the senate of his settlement in the east and a law to allow him to settle his veterans.

Here he was in for a shock. His first speech to the senate fell completely flat. In effect, the senate, led by such figures as Lucullus, whose command Pompey had relieved in Asia, and Marcus Porcius Cato, great-grandson of the censor and as petulant in his conservatism, would have nothing to do with a man they still considered an upstart who had broken all the sacred conventions of the constitution. (This Cato is normally referred to as Cato of Utica, a north African port where he served as governor.) When Pompey tried to win over Cato by proposing himself as a husband to one of Cato's unmarried relations he was coldly rejected. Despite several attempts to pass it through the senate Pompey's settlement remained unratified and his troops, though disbanded, without land. Even an attempt in 60 by a tribune to push through a land bill failed when a consul, Metellus, rallied the senate in opposition to it. Only a magnificent triumph held in 61 briefly revived the glory Pompey had once known.

The Political System in the 60s: An Overview

Recent archaeological excavations in the area between the Roman Forum and the Arch of Titus have revealed the foundations of a series of grand aristocratic houses dating from the middle of the first century BC. There is some continuing dispute about the ownership of each, but one study identifies those of Cicero, his brother Quintus, and his arch rival Clodius (see below). The lavish decoration of the homes and the large slave quarters found in one have suggested not only the opulence of the elite in the later republic but the ways in which their homes were used as a form of propaganda in support of their political ambitions.

The finds support the view that the 60s and 50s were years of increased aristocratic competition for election to the magistracies. The consulships and praetorships (elected by the conservative *comitia centuriata*) remained the goal of every ambitious man but they had to be reached through the lower magistracies (elected by the *concilium*). At each step of a political career further advancement became more difficult. Under half of those who became quaestors could become praetors and only two of each set of six or eight praetors a consul. Men standing for the lower magistracies had also to sell themselves to an electorate which after the Social War was much larger and more volatile. The disruptions of the Social War and the civil wars of Sulla had led to Rome being packed with refugees from the upheavals. The contenders for the magistracies could, as they had always done, play on the antiquity and achievements of their family and their own military record. However, effective oratory now had a greater impact, one reason why a 'new man' such as Cicero had been able to gain a consulship. The crowds also responded to those who would spend on their behalf. This is why the post of aedile, whose responsibilities included the administration of games, became so sought after. Spectacular public entertainment was always popular. Behind the scenes the direct bribery of voters seems to have been on the increase and was a common subject of private prosecutions between rivals.

There were no political parties or platforms as such in Rome but there were certain policies which were bound to appeal to the mass of citizens. They warmed to military victory and expected wars to be fought competently. (It had been popular initiatives which had led to the appointment of Marius to his commands in the military crisis at the end of the second century.) They valued their own rights and the defence of these by the tribunes and were correspondingly suspicious of the powers of the senate. They were always ready to respond to those who would offer land or, in the city, a more effective and cheaper supply of corn. As competition for the magistracies increased there was every temptation for candidates to appeal to these popular concerns. Those who did so were dubbed by their opponents *populares*, 'those pandering to the people'. Those, on the other hand, who wished to uphold traditional senatorial authority against the demands of the assemblies, called themselves optimates.

Traditionally a consulship had been followed by little more than a respected position in the senate for life but from the time of Sulla it had become more common for the consuls to stay at home and be sent overseas *after* their term of office. Such overseas commands could be granted by either the senate or the assemblies and, most significant of all, they could be prolonged. In the 70s Metellus Pius had spent nine consecutive years in Spain and Lucius Lucullus eight in the east. These special commands presented an extended opportunity to achieve military glory and wealth as well as allowing the commander concerned to build up a dependent and therefore loyal army. They thus offered a potential threat to the republic. As Pompey had shown in Asia, once abroad a commander operated largely beyond the control of the senate. It was only when he returned that the senate could refuse to ratify any decisions he had made overseas or hinder the settlement of his troops. Such obstruction resolved nothing. It was true that Pompey, faced with opposition from the senate on his return, had not overthrown the state, but somehow his business had to be settled and this is why he now turned to a newly elected consul, Julius Caesar, for help.

The Young Caesar

Julius Caesar is perhaps the best known of all the Romans, his name transmitted into later European history as Kaiser and Tsar and incorporated into the western calendar (July), with his assassination remaining one of the most vivid folk memories of European culture. He had been born in 100 BC to a family which was patrician in origin (and actually claimed a divine founder, Venus) but at the time of his birth not a distinguished nor a rich one. He had had to make his own way and showed no hesitation in doing so. He was talented, ambitious, and a particularly fine speaker ('the most eloquent of the Romans', as Cicero generously described him). One of his finest qualities was a magnanimity towards those he had defeated, a rare trait among commanders of the time. However, what now marked him out from his many rival candidates for office was his consistent use of the cause of the *populares* in support of his ambitions. In 69 he made a public declaration of his commitment to the cause of the people by making the funeral oration at the death of his aunt, the widow of their hero Marius, and when he was elected aedile in 65 he replaced the trophies of Marius which Sulla had removed from the Capitoline Hill. His popularity was consolidated by massive spending, and it paid off in 63 when he was elected *pontifex maximus*, a post of great dignity held for life and traditionally reserved for former consuls. It was an extraordinary achievement for such a comparatively young man. It was followed in 62 by his election as a praetor.

Caesar's electioneering had left him heavily in debt. His best hope now was a command overseas, and one as governor of Further Spain was assigned to him in the ballot through which provinces were allocated. In order to escape his creditors Caesar had to have his debts underwritten by Crassus, who had become a specialist in the business of buying political support through loans, before he could leave Rome. Once in Spain Caesar had few difficulties in engineering a campaign which took him beyond the western border of his province as far as the Atlantic coast. It was his first taste of successful generalship and as a victorious commander he was entitled to most of the plunder. He returned home with enough wealth to finance his next ambition. This was to become one of the consuls for 59. By now the optimates were becoming wary of his ambitions and the elections were bitterly contested. However, there was no stopping Caesar now that he was backed by money and fame, and the most the optimates could do was to have their own candidate, Bibulus, elected as Caesar's fellow consul.

Consulship and Command: Caesar Consolidates his Position

By 59, therefore, Caesar had marked himself out as a remarkable man, a supporter of the cause of the *populares* who was both consul and *pontifex maximus*.

He saw the advantage of an agreement with Pompey which could harness the latter's popular appeal to his own cause. Crassus had also to be brought in although he was bound to be an uneasy bedfellow. The agreement the three made was little more than an offer of mutual support in achieving their immediate aims. For Pompey this was, naturally, ratification of his settlement and land for his veterans, for Crassus favourable treatment for a group of his supporters who found they had bid too high for the privilege of collecting taxes in Asia. In return for using his consular power to achieve these ends Caesar expected support for a further overseas command at the end of his consulship.

Caesar was not to disappoint his allies. He introduced in the senate a land law to allow for the settlement of Pompey's veterans. It was a moderate one. Some of the wealth Pompey had brought home from his conquests was to be used to purchase land from willing sellers. The senate, however, would do nothing to support Caesar and he was forced to turn to the people. With Pompey's veterans crowding the Forum he pushed the land law through the *concilium*. Caesar then secured a law revising the terms for Crassus' tax collectors and another ratifying Pompey's settlement in the east. All the while Bibulus attempted to obstruct Caesar through what was in fact the perfectly legal device of scanning the skies and declaring the omens were unfavourable for business. Even the *pontifex maximus* could not counter such tactics and many of Caesar's laws were technically invalid. He was open to prosecution by the optimates if at any time he lost the protective power of *imperium* which he enjoyed as consul or would enjoy as holder of a subsequent command.

Caesar, however, was in no mood to change course. In April 59 he embarked on a much more provocative land law, one which would distribute public land in Campania to some 20,000 citizens, mostly veterans and urban poor. In effect Pompey was having his own supporters settled not far from Rome. Fears of what Pompey and Caesar were up to were intensified when Pompey married Caesar's only daughter Julia (a political alliance which, in the event, proved a genuine love match). Many now believed that Pompey and Caesar were after some form of dictatorship. Pompey, who was acutely sensitive to disapproval, found to his horror that his name was hissed in the theatre and his speeches in the senate greeted with silence. Caesar meanwhile had rewarded himself with a special five-year command in Gaul and Illyricum, one which would give him every opportunity to enhance his glory. (It was pushed through the *concilium* by a friendly tribune.) Governorship of the province of Transalpine Gaul was later added by the senate at the behest of Pompey.

Among those who were apprehensive about the growing power of Pompey and Caesar was Cicero. In a speech in the courts as early as March 59 he dared to complain about the political situation. In the hopes of containing Cicero, Caesar and Pompey engineered the election as tribune of an enemy of Cicero's, a raffish aristocrat, Publius Clodius. Cicero had testified against Clodius when the latter had been on trial for sacrilege. It was now clear that Clodius could use his new position to attack Cicero over the execution of the Catilinian conspirators. Caesar offered Cicero protection (he had, in fact, some personal admiration for him) but Cicero was having none of it. However, he turned out to be particularly vulnerable. He was reluctant to support Pompey and Caesar, yet it soon became clear that, as a *novus homo*, he had no real standing among the optimates. Having used him as their figurehead during Catiline's conspiracy, they now had few inhibitions about discarding him.

Once a tribune (for the year 58), Clodius quickly showed he was no mere creature of his patrons Caesar and Pompey. He had a clearly worked out programme specifically designed to win the support of the urban *plebs*. The two most popular measures were a law which allowed free corn handouts for the poor and another allowing the trade associations, the *collegia*, which had been banned in 64 after they had become centres for electoral bribery and intimidation, to operate freely once more. Exploiting his popularity, Clodius was also able to pass in the *concilium* a law exiling anyone who had condemned a citizen to death without trial. He could hold this over Cicero, who now found that neither Pompey nor Caesar felt obliged to support him. Without waiting for the prosecution which was now inevitable he left Rome for exile in Macedonia. Once he had left, Clodius allowed his personal gang of roughs to ransack Cicero's magnificent house near the Palatine.

In 58 Caesar left Rome to take up his commands. The potential for the glory of victory was immense. There had been continuing unrest among the tribes in Gaul and reports of a migration by one of them, the Helvetii, towards Roman territory. Memories of Hannibal and the Cimbri and Teutones had made Romans exceptionally sensitive to any threat of attack from the north and Caesar was able to exploit these sensitivities to the full. It was to be another nine years before he returned to Rome. The Helvetii were defeated in 58 and the remnants of the tribe forced back into what is now Switzerland. Caesar, with general support from the Gaulish tribes, now went north to take on a German tribe, the Suebi, who had spread across the Rhine into Gaul. By the end of 58 they had been pushed back across the Rhine. Caesar was now established in Gaul itself and made no pretence of staying within the provinces allotted him. The lure of further conquest was too strong. Some tribes, the Belgae in the north-west of Gaul, for instance, were provoked by the Roman intrusion and eager to resist. Others were embroiled in rivalries with neighbouring tribes which could be exploited. In his next year of campaigning, 57, Caesar brought virtually the whole of Gaul under Roman control. Back in Rome the news of his victories aroused such enthusiasm that even the senate recognized them, by the granting of fifteen days of public thanksgiving. (It had never given Pompey more than ten.)

In the senate the vote of thanks to Caesar was proposed by none other than Cicero. Cicero had returned from exile in September 57 thanks to the unremitting hard work of Pompey. As Clodius' confidence had grown he had set upon humiliating Pompey and the restoration of Cicero was one way Pompey could reassert his authority. The senate naturally supported the return and so, it turned out, did the mass of citizens outside Rome who had no particular reason to support Clodius and who favoured the recall of a man who stood for order. By summoning these citizens to Rome and using the *comitia centuriata*, with its bias towards the wealthy, to pass a decree allowing Cicero to return, Pompey eventually succeeded. Cicero was greeted with some popular enthusiasm although it was clear that he was now in Pompey's debt.

Clodius had been outmanoeuvred and he resorted to using gangs of his supporters, many of them runaway slaves, to intimidate his enemies. The atmosphere in Rome was vividly described by Cicero in a letter to his friend Atticus in November 57. Cicero was in the process of rebuilding his house, a move naturally opposed by Clodius.

On 3rd November an armed gang drove the workmen from my site . . . smashed up my brother's house by throwing stones from my site, and then set it on fire. This was by Clodius's orders . . . Clodius was running riot even before, but after this frenzy he thinks of nothing but massacring his enemies, and goes from street to street openly offering slaves their freedom. (Translation: D. R. Shackleton Bailey)

A rival gang organized by one of the tribunes for 57, Milo, offered some resistance but the effect was simply to escalate the use of violence in a city where the senate had no effective means of keeping order. Unrest was fuelled by shortages of corn, the inevitable result of Clodius' policy of handing it out free. The only man seen as able to resolve the situation was Pompey, and Cicero, in one of his first public appearances since returning from exile, steered the proposal that Pompey be granted the task of restoring corn supplies through the senate, despite widespread opposition from the optimates. However, attempts to give Pompey his own troops for his task failed, and his hopes that he would also be given a command to restore the exiled ruler of Egypt, Ptolemy Auletes, to his kingdom came to nothing. When Pompey failed to reduce the price of corn quickly he also began losing his support among the people.

This was all to Caesar's advantage as it meant that Pompey would remain dependent on his support. It was probably for this reason that in April 56 Pompey agreed to go north to Luca, just inside Caesar's province of Cisalpine Gaul, to meet with Caesar and Crassus to renew their understanding. The agreement made at Luca was that Crassus and Pompey would become the consuls for 55. This would enable them to secure commands to follow their year of office. In return they agreed to use their influence to secure a further command in Gaul for Caesar once his allotted five years were completed in 54. The Luca agreement shows how far the senate had lost the initiative and was at the mercy of those with the commands. Caesar even sent some of his men 'on leave' to Rome to allow Crassus and Pompey to bully their way into the agreed consulships. There was no pretence of holding an open election. In the other elections for the magistracies feelings ran so high that on one occasion Pompey returned home spattered with blood. Moderates such as Cicero were now completely impotent, simply there to be used by Pompey and Caesar as their mouthpieces. 'What could be more degrading than our present life, especially mine,' Cicero wrote in 55. 'I am regarded as a madman if I say what I ought on public affairs, as a slave if I say what I have to, as a prisoner of war if I say nothing . . . I am as miserable as you'd expect.' (Translation: David Lacey.) With the senate and the moderates reduced to impotence the stage was set for the last act of republican history.

FURTHER READING

Further reading for this chapter and the following interlude and Chapter 23. Vol. ix of the *Cambridge Ancient History* (Cambridge, 1994) provides an authoritative overview. M. Crawford, *The Roman Republic*, is excellent on many areas but peters out at the end of the period. The story is taken up by Colin Wells, *The Roman Empire* (2nd edition, London, 1992). David Stockton's *The Gracchi* (Oxford, 1979) gives a thorough account of the reforming brothers. Marius' army reforms are dealt with in L. Keppie, *The Making of the Roman Army* (London, 1984). On the Social War see A. Keaveney, *Rome and the Unification of Italy* (Oxford, 1988) and the essay on the war by P. A. Brunt in his *The Fall of the Roman Republic* (Oxford, 1988). On Sulla, E. Badian, *Lucius Sulla: The Deadly Reformer* (Sydney, 1970), and A. Keaveney, *Sulla: The Last Republican* (London, 1982). On Pompey there is Robin Seager, *Pompey: A Political Biography* (Oxford, 1979), which may have too much political detail for the general reader and Pat Southern, *Pompey the Great* (London, 2002).

On Cicero, Elizabeth Rawson, *Cicero: A Portrait* (London, 1995) is a fine treatment of every aspect of Cicero's life. See also D. Stockton, *Cicero: A Political Biography* (Oxford, 1971) for Cicero as a politician. Anthony Everitt, *Cicero: The Life and Times of Rome's Greatest Politician* (London, 2002), is a recent popular biography. An attractive selection of Cicero's letters to various recipients is provided by L. Wilkinson (London, 1949). On Cicero's philosophy see J. G. F. Powell (ed.), *Cicero the Philosopher* (Oxford, 1995). T. Wiseman's *The World of Catullus* (Cambridge, 1985) is particularly useful for showing the seamier side of life in Rome. For intellectual life in general see E. Rawson, *Intellectual Life in the Late Republic* (Baltimore, 1985). On Lucretius and Catullus see the chapter 'The Poets of the Late Republic' by R. Nisbet in the *Oxford History*; D. N. Sedley, *Lucretius and the Transformation of Greek Wisdom* (Cambridge, 1998).

Caesar is the subject of a short study by J. Balsdon, *Julius Caesar and Rome* (London, 1967) while there is a longer, much respected, study by Matthias Gelzer, *Caesar: Politician and Statesman* (Oxford, 1968). A recent biography is C. Meier, *Caesar* (London, 1995). The transition to Augustus' principiate is covered by Colin Wells (see above) and there is Ronald Syme's classic *The Roman Revolution* (Oxford, 1939). I have also drawn on the first two chapters of Paul Zanker's *The Power of Images in the Age of Augustus* (Ann Arbor, 1988).

For analysis of the republic's collapse see the title essay in P. Brunt's *The Fall of the Roman Republic* (Oxford, 1988); David Shotter, *The Fall of the Roman Republic* (London, 1994), short but helpful; E. Gruen, *The Last Generation of the Roman Republic* (Berkeley, 1974); and M. Beard and M. Crawford, *Rome in the Late Republic: Problems and Interpretations*

(London, 2000). See also D. Braund's essay 'The Legacy of the Republic' in vol. i of John Wacher (ed.), *The Roman World* (London, 1987) and Fergus Millar, *The Crowd in Rome in the Late Republic* (Ann Arbor, 1998).

INTERLUDE FIVE

Voices from the Republic

Cicero has already been introduced as an orator and as the consul who defeated the conspiracy of Catiline. He was also a man of learning and culture who thought deeply about the political system of Rome. In 55 BC he produced his first literary work, on oratory, and then in 54 began one of his most celebrated works, *De Republica*, a study of the republican state, which now survives only in fragments. It was written as a dialogue set in the 120s and is an exercise in nostalgia, a lament for an idealized past when the various components of the Roman political system, the democratic, aristocratic, and monarchical, existed in harmony.

By the time he was writing Cicero's ideal world was no more. The republic was disintegrating around him and he was acutely sensitive not only to its destruction but to his own deteriorating political position. Much is known of his feelings as some 800 of his letters have survived. They provide an incomparable insight into the period. Cicero's own personality, with its mixture of vanity and self-doubt, a love of peace and books (April 59 BC: 'I have so fallen in love with leisure that I can't be torn away from it. So either I enjoy myself with my books . . . or I sit counting the waves . . .'), set against a yearning for the approval of a public audience, captivates the reader.

The main recipient of Cicero's letters was an old schoolfriend, Atticus, though many letters also survive to Cicero's brother, Quintus, and to Brutus, later to be one of the murderers of Caesar. Atticus (the name comes from Atticus' long residence as a young man in Athens) was a wealthy and cultured man who avoided politics and concentrated on his academic interests and his friendships. When he later came to live in Rome he published Cicero's works. Cicero could write to him without reserve, yearning for his company and his advice when the two were separated. In the tense months when civil war broke out in 49 BC (see below, p. 433) Cicero's dependency on his friend becomes all the more acute. He writes in March 49:

I have nothing to write about, having had no news and having replied to all your letters yesterday. But since my distress of mind is such that it is not only impossible to sleep but torment to be awake, I have just started this scrawl without any subject in view, just in order as it were to talk to you, which is my only relief.   (Translation: D. Shackleton Bailey)

Cicero was as much concerned with his own position as with that of the state. He was a republican by temperament, a believer in the ancient liberties of Rome, but had to admit, even in *De Republica*, that the breakdown of order required a strong man to take control. (Cicero had Pompey in mind.) Yet strong men often act in a tyrannical way, and in another of his letters to Atticus Cicero agonizes over what is the proper course to take in these situations. Is it right to risk the future of the state by opposing a tyrant? Is it legitimate to put the safety of one-self and one's family before one's duty to oppose tyranny? What measures can a ruler use to keep order without becoming a tyrant? As Caesar emerged as dicta-tor in the 40s these questions took on a new urgency (see below, p. 438).

Cicero's letters are also remarkable for their accounts of the everyday life of a cultured and leisured man determined to create harmony and good taste around him. He writes to his brother Quintus in 54 BC about progress on a new villa Quintus was building:

At your Manilian place I found Diphilus [the architect] going slow even for Diphilus. Still he had finished everything except the baths, the cloister and the aviary. I liked the house enormously for the dignity of its paved colonnade, which I only realised when I saw the whole length open and the columns polished. It will all depend on the stucco harmonising and I will see to that. The pavement seemed to be getting well laid. I did not care for some of the ceilings, and ordered them to be changed . . I admired the topiary work: the ivy has so mantled everything, both the foundation wall and the spaces in the colonnade, that now those Greek statues look as if they were the topiary artists pointing it out for our approval. Again the bathing-place is as cool and mossy as can be . . . (Translation: L. P. Wilkinson)

Perhaps inevitably, as political and family affairs took their course, Cicero became burdened with his personal disappointments. He divorced his wife Terentia after many years of marriage when he found her meddling with his money. He saw his beloved daughter Tullia married three times, the first time to a man of integrity who soon died, the third time to a rake. Then, in 45 BC, she died in childbirth. It was a bitter blow. His son, Marcus, also proved a disap-pointment, ending up with the reputation of the hardest drinker in town. Yet it is also clear from the letters that Cicero himself cannot have been easy to live with. He could be fussy, self-pitying, and ambivalent in his loyalties. At the same time he displays an undoubted, if rather lofty, humanity in his distaste for the slaughter of animals in the shows, in his affection for his freedman, Tiro, who takes down his dictated letters and arranges his books in a new home, and his concern over the deaths of those he loves. Cicero emerges as a fully human indi-vidual, one caught in a political turmoil over which he has no control and of which he eventually becomes a victim (see p. 440).

One of the themes of *De Republica* is Cicero's preoccupation with the duty of citizens, in particular those of the richer classes, to uphold high standards of personal morality and to take an active part in government. Others in these troubled times took a different path and were attracted by the philosophy of

Epicurus with its emphasis on withdrawal from private life and a concentration on personal qualities of friendship (see p. 351). They took their inspiration from one of the great poems of the period, *De Rerum Natura*, 'On the Nature of Things', by Titus Lucretius Carus (98–*c*.55 BC).

Virtually nothing is known about Lucretius. He was clearly a passionate admirer of Epicurus and much of *De Rerum Natura* is devoted to praising the man who had freed the human race from superstition and religion and the fear of death. In what Alexander Dalzell has called 'one of the rarest of literary accomplishments, a successful didactic poem on a scientific subject', he also managed to expound the atomic theory of Epicurus. (In fact this is the fullest account of the atomic theory to have survived and Lucretius remains to this day a hero for chemists.) Yet the whole poem is also infused with the richness of the natural world and contains a non-theological explanation for the development of life, with grass and shrubs appearing first and then the first animals from wombs in the earth. Even in the early brutish period of humanity's development there is room for human affection and friendship, one of the cherished beliefs of Epicureanism. Lucretius never allows his rational approach to the physical world to erase an emotional response to its riches. Seldom has a system of beliefs been expressed so powerfully and with such imagination in what is one of the few original works of Roman philosophy.

Lucretius' sensuous approach to life is echoed in the poems of another of the 'voices' of the period, Gaius Valerius Catullus (*c*.84–*c*.54 BC). Catullus came from a wealthy family in Verona but moved south to join in the literary circles of fashionable Rome. Like any 'modern' poet of the day he was steeped in Greek literature and among his surviving works are translations of Sappho and Callimachus. While drawing heavily on the metres and legends of Greece he was versatile enough to develop a voice which is entirely his own. In his own time he was best known for his erudite and finely crafted poems, such as the short epic 'The Wedding of Peleus and Thetis', which require an understanding of Greek myth to achieve their fullest impact. (The marriage is described in sensuous detail as the height of happiness but the educated reader knows that the child of the marriage, Achilles, is doomed to die young.)

The modern reader has, however, been attracted by Catullus' record of his experiences in the 'bohemian' circles of late republican Rome. His poems detail the characters which surround him with all their eccentricities, pretensions, and betrayals. The most celebrated is Lesbia, the woman he loved and lost. 'Lesbia' is probably Clodia, the sister of the dissolute Publius Clodius. The affair is detailed from its first rapture to the despair of rejection.

You ask Lesbia, how many kissings of you are enough and to spare for me. As great the number of the sands of Libya to be found in silphium-bearing Cyrene between Jove's torrid oracle and the sacred tomb of legendary Battus; or as many the stars which in the silence of the night behold the stealthy loves of mankind: so many kisses to kiss you would be enough and to spare for love-crazed Catullus, too many for the inquisitive to be able to count or bewitch with their evil tongues.

As he is betrayed he bitterly asks his friends to

take back to my sweetheart a brief and not kind message. Let her [Lesbia] live and be happy with her lovers, three hundred of whom at once she holds in her embraces, loving none truly but again and again rupturing the loins of them all; and let her not count on my love as in the past, for through her fault it has fallen like a flower at the meadow's edge, after being lopped by the passing plough.   (Translations: T. P. Wiseman)

This is the world of the sophisticated, the erudite, and the malicious. Catullus is adept at sending off obscenities to those he dislikes. (Even Caesar, who was rumoured to have had a homosexual relationship when young in the east, was the target of a lampoon.) There is also the genuine anguish of an age where personal relationships have become shallow and transient. These are the private voices of an age of uncertainty.

23 | The Fall of the Roman Republic, 55–31 BC

Caesar and Pompey: The Showdown

Withdrawal into a private world of cultivated friendships was the last thing on the minds of Pompey and Crassus. They both wanted to use their consulships of 55 BC as stepping-stones to further commands. Pompey secured one in Spain, for five years. So as not to lose his position in Rome he sent legates to govern Spain on his behalf, something which had never been done before by a governor. He then began raising troops but retained them in Italy on the pretext that they were being trained there for Spain. Meanwhile he kept his name before the public by building a massive theatre, the first stone one to be erected in Rome, in the Campus Martius. Such was the breach in convention involved (no permanent stone theatre had ever been allowed before) that the auditorium had to be built as if it were a glorified annexe to a temple that stood in the centre at the top of the steps.

In 54 Pompey's wife, Julia, died in childbirth. It was a major personal blow to Pompey but the death also symbolized the growing distance between Caesar and himself. They were now actively competing against each other for popular support. Alongside Pompey's new theatre in the Campus Martius Caesar began to build a massive voting enclosure in marble while also planning to make a huge extension of the Forum on the north side. He continued to relay reports of his successes to Rome. The year 56 had been spent campaigning through Brittany and along the Atlantic seaboard and Gaul was now quiet enough for him to take the dramatic step in 55 of crossing to Britain, an exploit he repeated in 54. It was a foolhardy adventure which, in 55 in particular, almost ended in disaster when his fleets were destroyed in storms. These setbacks were glossed over in Caesar's deliberately dramatized accounts of his crossing of a distant ocean. They aroused enormous enthusiasm in Rome.

Crassus, unable to compete with these two showmen, now set out on his own quest for military glory. Although nearly 60 and with little experience of command he determined to lead an army to Parthia. There was no immediate reason for war although relations with Parthia had been strained since Pompey had failed to hand over territory he had promised the Parthian king. Crassus led seven legions into the interior. He had some success in 54 in Mesopotamia but in

53, heading east beyond the Euphrates, he allowed his forces to be surrounded by the expert Parthian archers. Both his cavalry and legionaries were overwhelmed. Plutarch chronicles the horrifying last days of the army as, forced to abandon 4,000 wounded men in the town of Carrhae, it was cut down by the Parthians. Crassus' head was carried off in triumph to be thrown at the feet of the Parthian king. Only a quarter of the original force of 40,000 managed to struggle back to Roman territory.

Carrhae was one of the most humiliating of all Roman defeats and news of the disaster filtered back to Rome at a time of escalating disorder. The political system was in such disarray that in 53 no consuls were elected before July. The elections for 52 were also delayed. In January 52 Clodius and Milo's gangs met on the Appian way. Clodius was wounded, taken to an inn, and there murdered on the orders of Milo. His body was taken to the Forum for the customary speeches and the incensed crowds began raging against Milo. The fire consuming the body got out of hand and the senate house and an adjoining basilica were burnt down.

In the chaos the crowds began calling for Pompey's appointment as dictator. The senate was trapped. If they gave in they would be giving absolute power to one they still feared and distrusted. As a face saver they devised a formula by which Pompey would become sole consul and he remained so from February 52 until a fellow consul was elected in August. This astonishing breach of convention showed once again how dependent the senate had become on Pompey. Pompey immediately set in hand measures to restore order. Corrupt practices were outlawed and violence curbed. Milo, deserted now by Pompey, was put on trial in 52 for his murder of Clodius. The court was so overawed by Pompey's troops and supporters of Clodius that Cicero, who had agreed to defend Milo, lost his nerve for the first time in his life and only spoke briefly. Milo was forced into exile. (He later wrote to thank Cicero for not using his rhetoric effectively on his behalf. If he had been acquitted he would have missed the chance to enjoy the excellent seafood of Massilia.) Many of Clodius' supporters were also convicted. In 51 elections were resumed according to the normal schedule.

It is possible Pompey might have restored control but there was still Caesar to contend with. Caesar, in fact, had been in trouble. After the first shock of defeat the Gauls had regrouped and recovered their confidence. In 54 an entire Roman legion had been lured from their camp by the Eburones, a northern tribe, and massacred. Caesar had had to borrow a legion from Pompey's forces to replace it as well as recruit two more from Cisalpine Gaul. Unrest among tribes in the north of Gaul had continued into 53 and then in 52 there had been a far more formidable revolt which had covered much of central and south-western Gaul. It had been led by Vercingetorix of the Arverni, the first leader able to transcend tribal loyalties and unite the Gauls in defence of their freedom. Even tribes such as the Aedui who had been allies of the Romans had been drawn in as well as others who had not yet faced Roman forces. Vercingetorix had concentrated on depriving the

Romans of food supplies, hoping to isolate them within Gaul so that they could be dealt with more easily. Caesar's leadership skills and the discipline of his legions had been tested to the full before Vercingetorix was brought to bay on a high plateau at Alesia in eastern Gaul. The Romans surrounded the stronghold with several kilometres of ditches dotted with forts and then fought off a large relieving army. Vercingetorix finally surrendered and was carried off as captive to Rome. (He eventually graced a triumph of Caesar's in 46 and was then strangled.) The year 51 was spent successfully mopping up the remnants of opposition. For the first time the Roman empire had moved beyond the Mediterranean. The new border of the empire in the north was the Rhine and here, despite occasional attempts at further expansion, it was to remain for over 400 years.

It was in 51 that Caesar also published his masterly account of his campaigns, his *Commentaries on the Gallic War*. Told in the third person, they give a vivid picture of the Roman legions in operation and the tribes of Gaul in their final moments before defeat. Caesar, as general, is at the forefront and the account highlights his skills, his calmness, determination, and the speed with which he acted at moments of crisis. There is no doubt that the work was focused on a public audience, but at the same time the simple and lucid prose in which the *Commentaries* are written convince that this is a fairly reliable account of what actually happened on the campaign.

Despite popular acclaim, Caesar remained vulnerable to counter-attack by the optimates. It is not clear, and does not seem to have been even to contemporaries, when his command should have come to an end (the law giving him the command may not have specified a date) but when it eventually did so he would be vulnerable to prosecution unless he could secure another *imperium*, either a command overseas or a consulship. In 50 a political struggle broke out with the optimates trying to bring Caesar's command to an end without any renewal and a tribune, Gaius Scribonius Curio, a heavily indebted optimate who seems to have been bribed into the support of Caesar, vetoing any law which threatened him.

Pompey's third consulship had come to an end at the end of 52 although he continued to hold his command in Spain. He seems to have hoped that he could hold the balance between the optimates and Caesar by, in some way, making Caesar dependent on him. However, the time when Caesar would submit to the influence of Pompey was by now long past. After his successes in Gaul it would be below his dignity to accept any relationship with Pompey that was less than one of equality. Pompey seems to have become aware of this during 50 but was confident that in a showdown he would win. In May 50 he had fallen dangerously ill and his recovery was greeted with such apparent enthusiasm that he assumed support from the towns of Italy would not be hard to find. He also received misleading reports that Caesar's armies were on the point of mutiny. His military position was improved when it was decreed that two legions, one from each of Pompey's and Caesar's armies, be sent as a precaution to the Parthian border. Pompey asked Caesar to

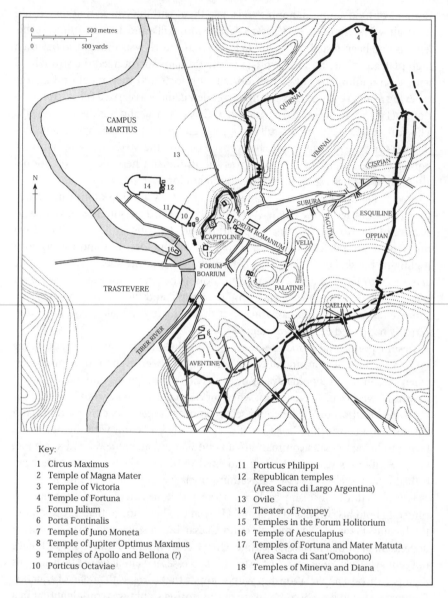

Key:

1   Circus Maximus
2   Temple of Magna Mater
3   Temple of Victoria
4   Temple of Fortuna
5   Forum Julium
6   Porta Fontinalis
7   Temple of Juno Moneta
8   Temple of Jupiter Optimus Maximus
9   Temples of Apollo and Bellona (?)
10 Porticus Octaviae
11 Porticus Philippi
12 Republican temples
    (Area Sacra di Largo Argentina)
13 Ovile
14 Theater of Pompey
15 Temples in the Forum Holitorium
16 Temple of Aesculapius
17 Temples of Fortuna and Mater Matuta
    (Area Sacra di Sant'Omobono)
18 Temples of Minerva and Diana

MAP 11 The City of Rome, 52 BC. The centre of popular politics was in the Forum and on the neighbouring Capitoline Hill. In this relatively small area the senate and the concilium plebis met and major law trials were held. One can understand why politics became so volatile in the late republic and why there was such a premium on effective speaking. The Comitia Centuriata held its meetings and elections on the Campus Martius, outside the walls of the city.

surrender the legion which he had lent to him in 54 in addition to surrendering one of his own. When news came that the Parthian threat had receded both were retained in Italy and Pompey treated them as his own.

All these moves fuelled the increasing sense of crisis. It was clear that a power struggle was under way—'the greatest struggle that history has ever known,' as Cicero put it as he agonized over which side he should take. 'Victory will bring many evils in its train including the certainty of a despot.' Towards the end of the year Curio, fearful of what would happen to him when he stopped being tribune, proposed that both Caesar and Pompey should surrender their commands. The motion was passed by the *concilium* with an overwhelming majority but no date for the surrender was set. By the end of the year rumours were circulating that Caesar was about to march on Rome, and in December 50, the consuls, on their own initiative, approached Pompey to ask whether he would save the city against Caesar. He accepted in what was now an alliance with the optimates in defence of the Republic. On 1 January 49 Caesar suggested in a letter to the senate that both he and Pompey should lay down their commands. The optimates, now in league with Pompey, would not agree and tried, against opposition from tribunes friendly to Caesar, to get his armies (and his alone) disbanded. On the 7th the senate passed a *senatus consultum ultimum*, the emergency decree calling all magistrates to defend the city. If he was to preserve his dignity Caesar was now left with little choice but to take the initiative. On 10 January 49 he crossed a small river, the Rubicon, which marked the boundary of Cisalpine Gaul within which he could exercise *imperium* and the rest of Italy where he could not. He had, in effect, declared war on the republic.

The Civil War

Once Caesar had taken the initiative there was no reason to delay. The defenders of the republic could call on the two legions in Italy and then on a further seven in Spain where Pompey still had a legitimate command. Caesar had to seize Italy before these could be brought home. As he marched south he found little opposition. After all the disruptions of the previous years the mood was one of apathy and Pompey and his supporters were horrified to find that there was no uprising in their favour. In March the consuls, Pompey, and the republican army managed to leave Italy. Strategically, but perhaps not psychologically, it was the right move. Pompey's strengths lay not only in the east (where he had grateful clients from his campaigns of the 60s) but in his command in Spain, and in the provinces of Sicily and Africa which were controlled by optimate supporters. His best hope was to stretch Caesar's resources and communications to breaking point.

In the event Pompey lasted little more than eighteen months. The summer of 49 was spent by Caesar eliminating Pompey's armies in Spain and this important success was followed by the submission of Sicily and Sardinia. A major setback

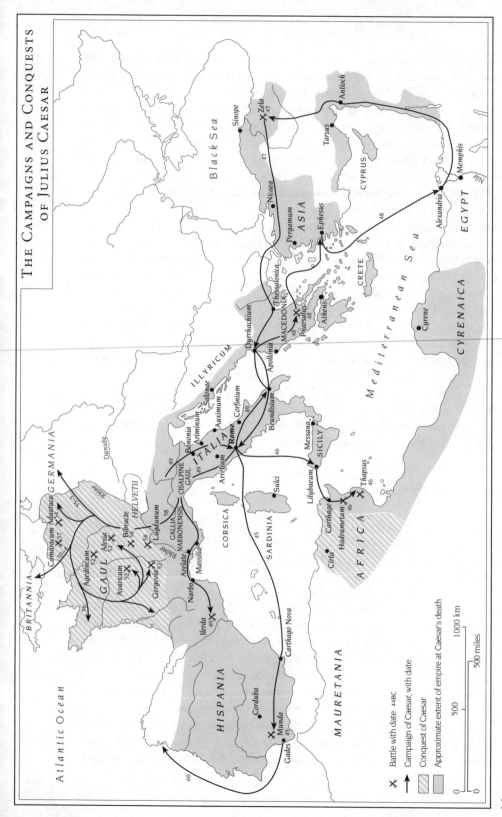

THE CAMPAIGNS AND CONQUESTS
OF JULIUS CAESAR

Atlantic Ocean

BRITANNIA

GERMANIA

Rhine

Danube

GAUL

Camaracum 53
Aduatuca 57 54
Alesia 52
Agedincum 52
Avaricum 52
Bibracte 58
Gergovia 52
Lugdunum 58
GALLIA NARBONENSIS 58
HELVETII
Arelate
Massilia
Narbo

CISALPINE GAUL 49

Rhône

HISPANIA

Corduba
Gades
Carthago Nova
Ilerda 49
Munda 45

CORSICA

SARDINIA
Sulci

MAURETANIA

AFRICA
Cirta
Carthage
Hadrumetum 46
Thapsus 46

ITALIA
Bononia
Ariminum
Auximum
Corfinium
Arretium
Rome
Brundisium
Salonae
ILLYRICUM

Black Sea

Sinope
Nicaea
Pergamum
ASIA
Ephesus
Zela 47

Tarsus
Antioch

CYPRUS

Thessalonica
MACEDONIA
Pharsalus 48
Apollonia
Dyrrhachium 48
Athens 48
CRETE

Messana
SICILY
Lilybaeum

CYRENAICA
Cyrene

Mediterranean Sea

Alexandria 48
Memphis
Nile
EGYPT

Battle with date 44 BC
Campaign of Caesar, with date
Conquest of Caesar
Approximate extent of empire at Caesar's death

0   500   1000 km
0   500 miles

MAP 12

took place, however, in Africa. Here Curio, Caesar's bribed tribune from the year 50, was sent with four legions. He found himself facing not only the local Pompeian commander but King Juba of Numidia. It was the king who lured the inexperienced and impetuous Curio into the desert on the pretence that the Numidian forces were in retreat. Curio was killed in the counter-attack and most of his army destroyed: Africa, for the time being, was lost to Caesar.

It was a direct confrontation with Pompey, now training up his legions and cavalry in Macedonia, which was important. Here Caesar's emphasis on speed and surprise paid off. The Adriatic was well guarded by Pompey's fleet (which was led by Caesar's old adversary, Bibulus) but Caesar shipped 20,000 legionaries and 600 cavalry across to Epirus in the middle of winter and escaped capture. It was a risky operation particularly as there would be little food to feed the troops in Greece and it nearly ended in disaster two months later when Pompey, attempting to break through fortifications which Caesar had erected between him and his naval base, Dyrrachium, inflicted heavy casualties on Caesar's smaller army. It took all Caesar's formidable powers of leadership to regroup his forces and finally bring Pompey to bay at Pharsalus in northern Greece in August. Although he was outnumbered by 47,000 to 24,000, Caesar inflicted a crushing defeat on Pompey. Fifteen thousand of Pompey's men died, another 24,000 were captured. Pompey fled, first to Lesbos, where his wife and younger son Sextus were sheltering, and then with them on to Egypt. The people of Rome had been made guardian of the young Egyptian king Ptolemy XIII by Ptolemy's father, who owed some gratitude to Rome for having restored him to his throne in 55, and Pompey must have hoped for some support. However, as he stepped ashore he was murdered on the orders of the Egyptian authorities, who understood that Caesar was now the man to please. When Caesar arrived a short time afterwards he was presented with Pompey's head, embalmed. He was magnanimous enough to weep at the sight.

For seven months Caesar stayed in Egypt. It was still an independent kingdom ruled, in theory, jointly by a 21-year-old queen, Cleopatra, and her brother, the 15-year-old Ptolemy XII, but the two had fallen out. At the time Ptolemy and his courtiers and generals had the upper hand over Cleopatra, who had been forced to flee to Syria to raise troops against him. She was, however, a formidable rival. The surviving portraits of her do not confirm her as a conventional beauty but she must have had both charisma and intelligence. She was the first Hellenistic ruler of Egypt to have learnt the language (she knew nine altogether) and to have participated in Egyptian religious festivals. She grasped where her chances lay, and when Caesar boldly installed himself in the royal palace in Alexandria, she smuggled herself in wrapped in a rug. She was soon his mistress. Together Caesar and Cleopatra withstood a siege by Ptolemy's supporters (it was then that Caesar, trying to destroy his opponents' ships, succeeded in burning down part of the famous library of Alexandria) and when he was relieved by troops from Syria Caesar managed to defeat Ptolemy and install Cleopatra as sole ruler. There are legends of them cruising the Nile together and she claimed a boy born to her later as Caesar's son. He was named Caesarion.

However, the civil war was not yet over. By April 47 Caesar was on the move again. He returned to Italy via Asia Minor, where in one of the easiest victories of his career at Zela in Pontus he crushed an army led by Pharnaces, a son of Mithridates ('I came, I saw, I conquered,' as he succinctly put it), and Greece. Pompey's Adriatic fleet had also been eliminated. Caesar paused in Rome and then set out in late 47 to Africa, still resolutely held by supporters of Pompey and the old senatorial order. The troops gathered there were commanded by Quintus Metellus Scipio, last survivor of one of the noblest Roman families, and Titus Labienus, an officer of Caesar's who, though trusted throughout the Gallic War, had thrown in his lot with Pompey in 49. With them was Cato of Utica, who personified the old conservative Rome which Caesar was now in the process of destroying. Again it was a brilliant campaign. Caesar faced immense logistical problems in landing a force large enough to take on the fourteen legions awaiting him, but as he gathered strength (he received some support from descendants of the veterans of Marius' armies) he rounded on his enemies and the final battle at Thapsus in April 46 was a massacre. Cato committed suicide, becoming in the process a hallowed martyr of a vanishing world. Plutarch describes the nobility of his death in detail and it haunted later generations (including some of the Founding Fathers of the United States). Scipio also committed suicide when facing capture as he escaped westwards to Spain. Labienus actually reached Spain, where, with one of Pompey's sons, Gnaeus, he mounted a last stand. Caesar arrived in late 46 for a short but savage campaign which ended in the Battle of Munda (March 45), a hard-won victory which led to the deaths of both Labienus and Gnaeus. The old order was dead.

Caesar and the Search for a Political Solution

Caesar's thoughts now had to turn to a political settlement. He had paid brief visits to Rome during the civil wars and as his dominance over the empire grew he had assumed greater political powers. In 49 he had himself established as dictator and used the power of the post to ensure he achieved the consulship of 48, the consulship he had always intended to hold. He also held the dictatorship for short periods in 48 and 47 before it was given to him for a period of ten years in 46 and for life in 44. This was a clear breach of convention—the post was designed only to be held for a short period during an emergency—but now Caesar acquired on a permanent basis all its powers, which included the right to overrule all other magistrates and to be immune from the vetoes of the tribunes. In 46 he was again made consul and never surrendered the post. He remained *pontifex maximus* and strengthened his influence over Roman religious life by becoming an augur (one of those responsible for divination) in 47.

The powers of 46 were granted by an enthusiastic if obsequious senate after the news of the victory at Thapsus had reached Rome. Caesar was awarded no less than four triumphs. The fact that he had won a civil war against fellow citizens was glossed over by allocating each triumph to a victory over foreigners, the Gauls, the Egyptians, Pharnaces, and King Juba of Numidia. They were held with appropriate splendour in September 46. The celebrations ended with gladiatorial games (as gladiators could only fight in honour of the dead the games were dedicated to the memory of Julia) and the opening of the magnificent new basilica and forum which Caesar had been building since 54. Each citizen was granted a cash handout together with a special issue of grain and oil.

Caesar was, in fact, acquiring the aura of a Hellenistic monarch although he was careful to scotch any attempts to make him divine or to allow the charged word *rex*, king, to be used of him. The question remained whether he could sustain this new role, eliminate the old order completely, and stabilize the state. He did set about tackling some of the abuses and tensions of society. A system for the fair settlement of debts had been decreed in 48. Disorder in Rome was curbed by banning the *collegia* and the problem of the poor tackled by reducing the number of families eligible for free corn. At the same time new colonies were set up overseas. Some 80,000 citizens were persuaded to emigrate, forming permanent centres of Roman culture in the provinces. Citizenship was also granted to loyal provincial communities. Taxes in the provinces were to be collected directly, no longer through tax farmers, and measures were taken to eliminate the bribery of juries. The traditional Roman calendar, which was made up of a year of 355 days, with an extra month of 22 or 23 days added every other year, was replaced on the advice of an Alexandrian astronomer, Sosigenes, by one of 365 days with one extra day added every four years. (This calendar lasted until it required further reform in the sixteenth century.)

None of this solved the crucial issue of Caesar's position within the state. It seemed to be becoming increasingly absolutist, and opposition began to grow, particularly among the noble families of the senate who saw the house packed with those Caesar wished to reward, many of them army officers or provincials. The changing mood towards Caesar can be seen through the eyes of Cicero. He had agonized over which side to take in the civil war and had then chosen Pompey's. Once Pompey had been defeated he threw himself on the mercy of Caesar, who treated him with the clemency and consideration which remained one of his most attractive qualities. Cicero had hoped against hope that Caesar's rule might lead at last to the stable and united republic of which he had dreamed. In a speech in the senate in late 46 he praised Caesar for his generosity and ability to bring reconciliation to the state. Yet, although he never lost an admiration for Caesar as a man, he inevitably became disillusioned with the stifling of political life as Caesar's behaviour became more overtly monarchical. After his daughter Tullia died he wrote a moving letter to a friend Servius Sulpicius which set out his despair:

Now I cannot escape from the sorrow of my home into public affairs, and find anything in them to console me, whereas before I always had a place at home to cheer me up when I came home depressed from public life. So I'm not at home, and I'm not in public life; my home cannot console me for the sorrow I feel for the free Republic, nor can public life compensate for the grief I feel at home.   (Translation: Elizabeth Rawson)

Fortunately Cicero's intellectual powers remained intact. In his misery he set himself the task of presenting the fruits of Greek philosophy in Latin for an audience which could not read Greek for itself. There was also a personal motive, seen in one lost work, *Consolatio*, of trying to come to terms with his grief through exploring his emotions through the similar experiences of others. These final works of his life tackled epistemology (*Academica*), the ultimate aim of life (*De Finibus*), the nature of the gods (*De Natura Deorum*), and moral philosophy (*De Officiis*), with shorter works on friendship and old age. Many concepts proved untranslatable into Latin and so Cicero had to coin words to express them. Words such as 'quality', 'essence', and 'moral' (*qualitas*, *essentia*, and *moralis*) all appear for the first time. In these works Cicero's prose achieved a range and precision which made it a model for those who came after him.

In his exposition of philosophy Cicero adopted a tone of intellectual detachment. (It was exactly this which made these final works so influential. In the long centuries when original Greek texts were unknown in Europe they formed the only substantial record of Greek philosophy.) He believed in countering superstition by reason yet at the same time doubted whether there was such a thing as certainty. Insofar as he warmed to any school of philosophy it was to Stoicism with its emphasis on endurance and commitment to public life for the good of all. While he was prepared to believe in some form of divine being, Cicero felt that the traditional gods of Rome and the variety of new gods which were entering Rome from Egypt and the east were no more than human creations, of real use only to the credulous.

For the final months of Caesar's life Cicero was absent from public life. Although there were claims that he was involved in the plot to kill Caesar there is no direct evidence for it. The plot was hatched at a time when Caesar's future ambitions were arousing increasing concern. The senate continued to pile honours on him, the dictatorship for life, the renaming of the month Quinctilis after him (it survives today in English as July), a gilded chair and triumphal robe for his public appearances. At one festivity a crown was placed on Caesar's knees. Caesar's fellow consul for the year, Marcus Antonius (Mark Antony), attempted to place it on his head but Caesar threw it into the crowd. He may simply have started to become irritated by the ceremonies of public life. When a delegation from the senate approached him with the offer of new honours he did not even stand up. By early 44 his energies were being taken up by the more congenial task of planning a major campaign in the east.

It is hard to know how Caesar saw his own position and whether he had any clear concept of himself as ruler. In his last months he seems to have been attracted to the idea of himself as divine (as Alexander was). In the east he was already accepted as a god ('descended from Ares and Aphrodite', as one acclamation from Asia put it). There was nothing unusual in this, but things seem to have been taken further than usual in Rome when Caesar accepted the idea of a temple dedicated to him and the appointment of Mark Antony as his *flamen* or priest. More provocative to the average Roman were the accumulation of honours and trappings which hinted of kingship. Here Caesar's behaviour was deeply ambiguous. Some have argued that more public enthusiasm for the idea would have encouraged him to declare himself as king, others that he never intended to breach the most sacred concept of republicanism, that of freedom from royal tyranny. It may have been that he felt himself trapped between rival expectations and that the planned trip to the east was an attempt to escape the impasse.

For many, however, the notion of *libertas* was one which was sacrosanct. It proved a powerful rallying call even if it did not offer a clear alternative for political stability. A varied group of conspirators were inspired by it. There were committed republicans such as Cassius and Brutus, the leaders, former supporters of Pompey whom Caesar had forgiven, and others with more personal resentments. The secret was well kept. Caesar was due to attend a meeting of the senate in a great hall adjoining Pompey's theatre. One of the conspirators was delegated to throw himself at Caesar's feet with a petition, pulling Caesar's toga downwards so he could not defend himself. The others were then to stab him. On 15 March 44, three days before Caesar was due to leave on campaign, the murder took place as planned. Caesar fell bleeding to death at the foot of a statue of Pompey. (His body was burnt in the Forum and flowers, left by unknown admirers, are still to be found today on the supposed spot of the cremation.)

The Aftermath of Caesar

The conspirators claimed that they had killed Caesar in the cause of republican liberty. It now became clear that what they meant was the liberty of the optimates, a concept which had long since forfeited popular support. The crowds did not rise in support of the conspirators and they were forced to take refuge on the Capitoline Hill and then hammer out a compromise with the surviving consul Mark Antony and supporters of Caesar. The dictatorship was abolished and the murderers given an amnesty but in return all Caesar's acts were confirmed and there would be no prosecutions for activities in the Civil War. Cicero emerged to preside over the reconciliation. However, when it was discovered that Caesar had left his gardens to the city and a sum of money to each of its citizens, popular fury against the murderers grew and Brutus and Cassius were forced to leave Rome.

It was Antony, with the support of Lepidus, Caesar's Master of the Horse, who now held the initiative. To his dismay Antony found that Caesar had adopted his 18-year-old nephew, Octavian, as his son and heir, and Octavian, despite family pressure to keep out of politics, arrived in Rome to claim his inheritance. He soon began appealing for troops to join him, with some success. It was Cicero, once again leaving his writing desk, who now came forward to play his final role in Roman politics. He flattered himself that he could woo Octavian and use him against the growing power of Antony, who had secured a command in Transalpine and Cisalpine Gaul to follow his consulship. In the senate Cicero launched into a series of speeches against Antony which he called his *Philippics* after the great speeches of his hero Demosthenes against Philip of Macedon (see p. 312). His plot was to send the new consuls and Octavian, with a special command, against Antony.

The plan backfired. Antony was indeed defeated in Cisalpine Gaul but both consuls were killed and Octavian found himself commander of an army of eight legions. These he refused to give up and marched to Rome to demand and receive a consulship from the humiliated senate. He was aged 19. He now threw off the patronage of his elders and marched north on his own initiative to meet Antony and Lepidus. Between them they could muster forty-five legions and so there could be no argument when in November 43 they set up a triumvirate, a government of three. The west of the empire was divided between them and they took on the responsibility of making laws and appointing magistrates. This liquidation of the republic was ratified by a meeting of the *concilium* held in a Forum ringed by troops. The senate, by allowing Octavian to raise his own troops and then recognizing him as a consul, had once again helped bring about its own demise.

There was a nasty aftermath. All three of the new rulers owed their position to Caesar and they now took the opportunity to rid themselves of Caesar's and their own enemies. It was as important to them to seize land in Italy to settle their large armies. A death list of 300 senators and 2,000 equestrians was drawn up. There was only one name of consular rank, Cicero. He hesitated over his escape and was caught in his litter and beheaded. The final scene is recorded by Plutarch in one of the most evocative passages of his *Lives*. (The approaching end is signalled by a flock of crows cawing around Cicero.) In a grisly aftermath Antony ordered the hands which had written the *Philippics* to be hacked off and nailed alongside Cicero's head on the speaker's rostrum in the Forum. It was a grotesque end to Rome's greatest orator and one of the founding figures of European liberal humanism.

Lepidus was now left to keep order in Italy while Octavian and Antony headed east. Their quarry was Brutus and Cassius to whom the senate had given commands in Macedonia and Syria in 43. They had acquired a total of nineteen legions between them but these proved no match for the larger forces of the triumvirate. At successive battles at Philippi in Greece in the autumn of 42 they were defeated by Antony and both committed suicide. (Octavian played very little part in the battle and was haunted for years to come by taunts of cowardice.) The only focus of opposition to the triumvirs was now Pompey's son, Sextus Pompeius, who was based with a fleet on Sicily where he styled himself 'the son of Neptune'.

He was not the only one to claim divine inheritance. In January 42 the senate had recognized Caesar as a god. After his death a cult had sprung up focused on the spot where his body was burned and the appearance of a comet confirmed to those who wished to believe that a new god had arrived in the heavens. Octavian eagerly appropriated his father's status and from now on called himself *divi filius*, the son of a god.

There was no love lost between the triumvirs. Lepidus was soon pushed aside. Antony tried to outmanoeuvre Octavian by allocating him the west of the empire where he would have the unpopular task of settling veterans in Italy and dealing with Sextus. When Octavian simply confiscated the land he needed and wiped out his opponents Antony reacted and attempted to land in Italy. The two would have fought each other in 40 if their armies had not been so sick of war. At Brundisium in September 40 they agreed on a new division of the empire. Octavian was to take the west of the empire, from Illyricum westwards, while from Macedonia to the east was to stay with Antony. Lepidus was to remain in the triumvirate with a command in Africa. The agreement brought universal relief. In his fourth *Eclogue* the poet Virgil talked of a new era of peace which would be consolidated by the birth of a young child. Later Christian writers argued that this was Christ but Virgil probably meant the expected child of Mark Antony and his wife Octavia, the sister of Octavian.

The third member of the triumvirate, Lepidus, did not last long. In 36 he was involved in the final defeat of Sextus Pompeius in Sicily but unwisely then made an attempt to challenge Octavian, whose own part in the fighting had been less successful. His troops simply melted away at Octavian's approach and he was forced to capitulate. Octavian, in merciful mood, confirmed him in his post of *pontifex maximus* which he had been given on Caesar's death and Lepidus lived out the remaining twenty-four years of his life quietly in Africa.

Antony versus Octavian: The Final Struggle of the Republic

In the early 30s both Antony and Octavian were preoccupied with the consolidation of their rule. Although Octavian had been as guilty as anyone of bringing disruption to Italy he now sought to portray himself as a man of peace wedded to the restoration of traditional Roman values. His background as the son of a wealthy landowner from the town of Velitrae in the Alban Hills equipped him to understand the needs of provincial Italy and the deep longing there was for stability but he also showed himself an adept propagandist. He associated himself with the god Apollo, the god of reason and order. One of the symbols of Apollo was a snake and rumours spread as to how Octavian's mother (like Olympias, the mother of Alexander) had been impregnated by one. Octavian's comparatively modest house on the Palatine was attached to an imposing temple to the god.

By fostering traditional Roman values Octavian was implicitly condemning the influence over Rome of the east. Here Antony played into his hands. When Antony had assumed command in the east after Philippi he had worked hard to restore order among the client states of the empire. One of these was Egypt, and so Cleopatra, who had strengthened her position by murdering her younger brother and placing the 4-year-old Caesarion as co-ruler in his place, was summoned to Antony in 41. She upstaged him by appearing in a magnificent barge, weighted with gold and suffused with the perfumes of the Orient. (The vivid description of her arrival in Plutarch's life of Antony proved a direct inspiration for Shakespeare in his *Antony and Cleopatra*.) Antony, who, in contrast to the austere Caesar, had a weakness for opulence, succumbed. He spent the winter of 41 to 40 with Cleopatra in Alexandria and she bore him twins. It is impossible to disentangle the components of their relationship. Undoubtedly it depended partly on the exotic setting of their romance and sexual attraction, but Antony certainly had his eye on the wealth of Egypt as well. For Cleopatra Roman support was essential if her kingdom was to survive and she was prepared to grant her favours to the strong man of the day. (Whatever the bond between the two, it was not indissoluble. The couple spent four years apart between 40 and 36, a period when Antony was married to Octavian's sister, Octavia.)

The major threat to the stability of the eastern empire now came from Parthia, the only well-organized state on its borders. In 39 Parthian forces invaded Syria and even entered Jerusalem. They were repulsed. Antony, who had sent Octavia home when she had become pregnant and renewed his relationship with Cleopatra, now planned a major invasion of Parthia. It was launched in 36 and ended in disaster. Antony was forced to withdraw his forces with the loss of 22,000 legionaries, a third of his men.

Little help could be expected from Octavian and from now on Antony was increasingly dependent on Cleopatra. In 34 he and Cleopatra staged a great ceremony in Alexandria. They sat together on a pair of golden thrones with Cleopatra robed as the goddess Isis. Caesarion was declared the true heir of Caesar (an obvious affront to Octavian) and, with his mother, joint ruler of Egypt and Cyprus. Antony had already granted Cleopatra the rich timber-bearing coastline of Cilicia. (Egypt was as short of timber as it had been 2,000 years before.) Their three children, the twins and a son now 2 years old, were each proclaimed rulers of eastern provinces. Antony claimed no royal powers for himself, but when the news of the ceremony reached Rome in 33 it was easy for Octavian to damn him as the plaything of a powerful woman who was corrupting Roman virtues with the decadence of the east. Although Antony retained some support in Rome, Octavian was winning the propaganda battle. Antony too had associated himself with a god, Dionysus. Dionysus was acceptable as a role model for a ruler in the east but in Rome he was seen only as a god of indiscipline and decadence and Octavian played on the connotations. The campaign paid off. A swell of support for Octavian in provincial Italy gave him the *auctoritas*, the status, to cancel the consulship promised to Antony for 31. When Cleopatra crossed with Antony to Greece in 31, the move could be sold as an invasion of the empire to which Octavian as consul himself for the year must respond.

The final act was in many ways an anticlimax. Both Antony and Octavian mustered vast forces. Antony had thirty legions and 500 ships, Octavian a fleet of 400. They met at Actium, a cape on the western coast of northern Greece. Octavian's forces managed to cut Antony off from the Peloponnese and Antony was reduced to trying to break out with his fleet. When the breakout failed he and Cleopatra abandoned their forces and fled to Egypt. Octavian was able to take the surrender of both army and navy. A year later Octavian arrived in Egypt, and seized Alexandria and the treasures of the Ptolemies. In one of the more memorable death scenes of history (Plutarch once again excels himself) Antony stabbed himself, while Cleopatra had herself bitten by an asp. Caesarion was later murdered. Egypt, the last of the great Hellenistic kingdoms, was now in the hands of Rome. At last, wrote the poet Horace in one of his *Odes*, the time for drinking and dancing had come.

Why did the Republic Collapse?

Politically the most successful years of the Republic had been those when the senate's authority had been respected and deferred to by the other participants in the Roman political system. In the third and early second centuries it had maintained an aura of competence and stability and although its legal powers were limited it had dominated the decision-making process. Unfortunately the senate's aura was easily dissipated through its own incompetence and political clumsiness. The growth of the empire with its demands for good administration and effective defence and rising social tensions at home, between rich and poor, Romans and allies, offered a variety of challenges which the body had proved unable to meet. The Gracchi, for instance, had been met with nothing more visionary than violence. At the same time, and crucially, the senate did not have a monopoly of coercive power and was thus vulnerable to those who did, the consuls and praetors during their term of office and afterwards if their commands were prolonged. When outsiders, such as Pompey, also acquired commands, the senate was rendered impotent. It survived because the conventions of the constitution remained astonishingly powerful. When the crunch came Pompey did not overthrow senatorial government even though he undoubtedly had the power to do so.

In the 50s, however, the constitutional conventions came under renewed strains. The people had never been totally quiescent in the state (the *concilium plebis* was influential even in the heyday of the senate in the second century) but now with an enlarged and volatile urban population there were opportunities for unscrupulous manipulators such as Clodius to engineer popular unrest. The senate, now increasingly marginal to events, had to rely on its former enemy Pompey to defend it not only against street disorder but also against the ambitions of Caesar.

Ultimately he who dared won. Caesar could argue that he was only defending his threatened dignity as a Roman when he crossed the Rubicon. However, he had used his magistracies and commands to achieve a political supremacy whose logical end, if he triumphed over his enemies, was dictatorship. What kind of dictatorship perhaps even Caesar did not know, so powerfully did the heritage of republican liberty limit the possibilities of one-man rule. In the event Caesar failed to replace the republic with an alternative while his acclaimed quality of clemency left his enemies, and those who still cared for 'liberty', at large. His assassination was the result and it was followed, inevitably, by a new power struggle. The old republican concept of *libertas* died finally on the battlefields of Philippi and from then on there was only a struggle between competing dynasts. The winner of this, Octavian, now promised that he had no other interest than the restoration of the republic. It was a promise which a shattered senate and a weary people were ready to accept.

FURTHER READING

In addition to the reading listed at the end of Chapter 21, see Susan Walker and Peter Higgs (eds.), *Cleopatra of Egypt* (London, 2001), and on the impact of Cleopatra through history Lucy Hughes-Hallett, *Cleopatra, History, Dreams and Distortions* (London, 1990).

Women in the Roman Republic

The Romans of the late republic preserved an idealistic picture of early Rome with life centred on steady toil in the fields, piety to the gods, and loyalty to the state in peace and war. There was also an ideal of womanhood. Women, in their role as the wives of farmers and soldiers, were expected to be tough and frugal home-keepers, the mothers of future citizens. Most valued was the virtue of *pudicitia*, a word which had connotations both of fidelity and fertility. The *univira*, the woman who had slept only with her husband and never remarried after his death, was the sexual ideal, encapsulated perhaps in Lucretia, who, raped by the son of the last of the Roman kings, killed herself rather than live with the dishonour of providing an unchaste example to others. Absolute loyalty to their menfolk was also expected. The women of the neighbouring Sabine tribe served as the ideal here. They had been forcibly carried off as wives by Romans but when, in the next campaigning season, their kinsfolk tried to rescue them, they appeared, now with their 'Roman' babies, to reconcile the invaders.

By the second century BC Rome was being overwhelmed by the riches of conquest and the cultural impact of the east. Already the Romans had a much more relaxed attitude towards the appearance of women in public than the Greeks did. Women could eat with their husbands and even preside over meals at which both sexes were present. Now there were other role models available for women of the richer classes and many were able to indulge in extravagances which deeply offended the more traditional Roman. It was, not unsurprisingly, the elder Cato who emerged to defend traditional Roman womanhood against the pernicious influences of the east which, he argued, would undermine men's control of their wives. Others, however, argued that it was fitting that the heroes of Rome's wars should set their wives up in state, as a glittering appendage to their own status. Polybius has left an account of the lifestyle of Aemilia, the widow of the great Scipio Africanus:

When Aemilia had left her house to take part in women's processions, it had been her habit to appear in great state, as befitted a woman who had shared in the life of the great Africanus when he was at the height of his success. Apart from the magnificence of her personal attire and the decoration of her carriage, all the baskets, cups, and sacrificial vessels or utensils were made of gold or silver, and were carried in her train on such ceremonial occasions, while the retinue of maids and men—servants who accompanied her—was proportionately large. (Translation: I. Scott-Kilvert)

In a parallel development the wars had led to more and more women being widowed, and so emerges the strong independent woman, of whom Cornelia, the daughter of Scipio Africanus and Aemilia, and mother of the Gracchi, is a prime example. (She was even wooed in her widowhood by the king of Egypt.) By the first century a few aristocratic women were also well educated. Of Cornelia, the wife of Pompey, it was said (by Plutarch):

The young woman had many charming qualities, apart from her youth and beauty. She had a good knowledge of literature, of playing the lyre, and of geometry, and she was a regular and intelligent listener to lectures on philosophy. (Translation: R. Warner)

The shift in attitude was mirrored by changes in marriage customs. There was never any pretence that romance played much part in the making of a marriage which, in aristocratic circles, normally saw an older man, perhaps in his twenties, being joined to a girl who had just reached puberty. Political considerations were important, with families using their marriage links to sustain alliances. The marriage of Pompey with Caesar's daughter, Julia, is an obvious example and it is good to report that it developed into a genuine love match—one ending tragically, however, when Julia died in childbirth in 54 BC. A major purpose of marriage was to produce male heirs who could extend the family line and, according to Lucretius, the committed wife was expected to lie still during sexual intercourse as this was the best way to ensure conception. The achievement of a pregnancy came before sexual pleasure. Prostitutes, who did not want to conceive in any case, could be more forward in their love-making, says Lucretius, and they and their partners were assumed to enjoy it more.

In Rome's early history the most common form of marriage was *in manus*. Here the father of the bride transferred her, with her dowry, into the hands of her husband's family and abdicated all responsibility for her. It is probable that in early times the dowry was in land which would be added to the husband's plot which the family would then work together. If the husband died his widow and any children would inherit the plot intact and their livelihood was preserved. An alternative way of marriage, *sine manu*, allowed the wife to retain membership of her own family, and thus the right to any inheritance due to her from it, even though married into another. Her husband no longer had formal control over her. By the first century BC, for reasons which are not wholly clear, this had become the most popular form of marriage. Although the woman retained a *tutor*, a member of her family who was responsible for her affairs, she had some independence in the management of her business. She could carry out cash transactions, own property, and accept inheritances.

Women also retained some control over their dowries. A husband was supposed to keep it intact and could even be sued by his wife if she suspected it was being put at risk by his financial misdealings. At his death it was returned to her, even if it meant the estate had to be broken up to extract it. On her death it was the convention that the dowry would pass down to the children. The dowry would even be repaid in cases of divorce and Cicero, divorcing his wife Terentia, found himself financially embarrassed at having to do so. He promptly married a very young and rich girl, Publilia, but this marriage also ended in divorce. By the first century AD divorce had become common and had lost much of its stigma (from the days when it was largely the result of a wife's adultery). Mere incompatibility seems to have been enough.

There is some evidence, therefore, that even within a male-dominated world women were given some margins within which they could maintain an independent life. It is clear that women did participate in decision-making in the family. A mother expected to be consulted over arrangements for her daughter's marriage and, in one of his letters, Cicero reports a family conference held by his friend Brutus after the assassination of Caesar. (Such a family meeting was known as a *consilium*, literally 'consultation'.) Brutus' mother, Servilia, seems to have actually presided. There is also evidence that Romans did see marriage as having a companionate quality, as acting as a satisfier of emotional needs. Much of the evidence comes from tombstones. Their conventional phrasing often makes them hard to interpret but there is enough personal feeling surviving to suggest marriages were often very happy. ('You who read this,' one epitaph to a wife concludes, 'go bathe in the baths of Apollo, as I used to do with my wife. I wish I still could.') There is also the long inscription, dating from the late republic and conventionally known as the *Laudatio Turiae* ('funeral speech to Turia'), in which a husband recaptures the virtues of his dead wife and the care and loyalty she showed to him during the turmoil of the civil wars. Unable to produce children she had even offered him a divorce, but he had rejected the offer, preferring, he said, to live with her than with another who could bear him children. A century later Pliny the Younger writes with real tenderness to his young wife, Calpurnia.

It is incredible how much I miss you, because I love you and then because we are not used to being separated. And so I lie awake most of the night haunted by your image; and during the day, during the hours I used to spend with you, my feet lead me, they really do, to your room; and then I turn and leave, sick at heart and sad, like a lover locked out on a deserted doorstep . . . (Translation: Jo-Ann Shelton)

Women had their own festivals and cults. In the festival in honour of Fortuna Virilis (the Fortune of Men), for instance, women offered incense and a drink of honeyed milk and poppyseed and then bathed together in the men's bath. Ovid claimed the ritual blinded men to the bodily defects of their womenfolk. At the time of the wars with Hannibal there are several accounts of women collectively sacrificing for the good of the state. Marriage had its own rituals. Unlike men,

women had no rite of passage at puberty and their wedding seems to have fulfilled this role. The bride sacrificed her childhood toys before being taken off in
procession from her own home to that of her groom who was awaiting her.
There were ceremonies of welcome and the couple sat together hand in hand on
a couch as these were completed before retiring to the bridal chamber. A small
group of women never experienced these ceremonies. These were the Vestal
Virgins chosen before the onset of puberty to live for thirty years in celibacy
tending the flame of the temple to the goddess Vesta in the Forum. They were
given a public status, with special seats reserved for them at public banquets and
games, and were allowed to handle their financial affairs without the intrusion
of a *tutor*. On the other hand, if they broke their vow of virginity, the punishment
was death. An offender was walled up alive in an underground chamber.

The late republic was an unsettled time and this had its impact on sexual relationships. Many women had lost their husbands through wars or the proscriptions which followed them, others were left alone while their men were on
campaign. (There must have been hundreds of thousands of women and
children whose sufferings in these disturbed times have passed unrecorded.)
Some took to a life of promiscuity, freely using their sexuality to enjoy a succession of lovers. Catullus and his 'love' for the dissolute Clodia have already been
recorded. The Umbrian poet Propertius (*c*.50 BC–after 16 BC) vividly records his
tortuous love affair with Cynthia, the sex snatched at odd moments. ('We used
to make love then on street corners, twining our bodies together, while our
cloaks took the chill off the side walk.') These women have their sexual power
and well they know it. They are all too ready to deride their hapless lovers.
Cynthia says to Propertius:

> So you've come at last, and only because that other woman
> has thrown you out and closed the doors against you.
> Where have you spent the night? That night that belonged to me?
> Look at you creeping back with the dawn, a wreck.
> It'd do you good to have to spend the sort of night
> you make me spend! You'd learn what cruelty is.
> I sat up over my loom, trying to stave off sleep
> then tired of that and played the lyre a little.

(Translations: J. Warden)

Cynthia's adept, and somewhat manipulative, presentation of herself as
weaver and musician reminds the reader that the loom and the sober lyre was the
symbol of the virtuous wife. When Augustus, as part of his campaign to restore
social order, instituted a return to the traditional decorum of marriage he
insisted that his wife Livia should be seen to be making the family's clothes. So,
despite the dislocations of the late Republic, the old traditions persisted. As
Gillian Clark points out in her *Women in Late Antiquity* (Oxford, 1993) they are
found surviving even in the late empire.

FURTHER READING

Sarah Pomeroy's *Goddesses, Whores, Wives and Slaves* (New York, 1975) remains the classic introduction. Now see E. Fantham and others, *Women in the Classical World* (New York, 1994). There is a wealth of new research on Roman women and family life in general. For good overviews see Suzanne Dixon's *The Roman Family* (London, 1992) and her *The Roman Mother* (London, 1988). Also J. Gardner, *Women in Roman Law and Society* (London, 1986). On Roman marriage now see S. Treggiari, *Roman Marriage* (Oxford, 1991). Two important conferences are reported in B. Rawson (ed.), *The Family in Ancient Rome: New Perspectives* (Ithaca, NY, 1986), and B. Rawson (ed.), *Marriage, Divorce and Children* (Oxford, 1991). See also J. Evans, *War, Women and Children in Ancient Rome* (New York, 1991) and K. Bradley, *Discovering the Roman Family* (Oxford, 1991). On upper-class Roman women see E. Hemelrijk, *Matrona Docta* (London, 1999).

24 | Augustus and the Founding of Empire

In the first of his *Georgics* the poet Virgil, whose homeland around Mantua had been laid waste in the conflicts of the late republic, pleaded with the ancient gods of Rome to allow Octavian, 'this youthful prince', to save a world which was in ruins. There had now been periods of disruption in Italy since the Social War of 90 BC with the years 49 to 31 being ones of almost continuous civil war. Octavian appeared to be in a position to offer peace. He had a monopoly of armed force, with some sixty legions under his command and the means to maintain them from the wealth of Egypt and taxation from the empire. Yet this did not assure stability. The loyalties of so many troops could not be guaranteed for ever, particularly if there were no further enemies for them to confront, and their commanders were to conceive other ambitions. It was essential to have most of them disbanded and settled as soon as possible.

Octavian's position with the senators was also uncertain. Even though many had died at Pharsalus and in the proscriptions of 43 BC the survivors still retained a belief in their role as the defenders of *libertas* against anyone who threatened to become a dictator or monarch. There was much the senators could do to make Octavian's position untenable. Even his aura as military commander was not unblemished. Accusations of cowardice at the Battle of Philippi lingered, while Actium had been a scrappy victory. Octavian had to enhance his image by emphasizing the acclamation he had received as *imperator* (the accolade given to a victorious commander by his troops) during campaigns in the Balkans in the late 30s. He adopted the title, from which the word emperor is derived, as a *praenomen*. In 29 BC, in an attempt to further dignify his image as a commander, he celebrated three glorious days of triumph: one for victory in the Balkans, one for Actium, and one for Egypt.

Whatever his failings as a commander (and his next campaign, in Spain in 26 BC, was no more than a temporary success), Octavian now proved a consummate political operator. In the years that followed he was to forge a permanent settlement with the senators which transformed the collapsed republic into an empire while still maintaining the pretence that republican ideals and institutions persisted. While never using a title grander than *princeps*, first citizen, one which had honourable precedents in the republic, Octavian was to emerge with senatorial approval as 'Augustus', with a package of powers which gave him, and, as it turned out, his successors, the status of an emperor.

Octavian's Character

Octavian's ambition and self-confidence had been obvious from his very first entrance into the troubled world of Roman politics at the age of 18, but unlike Alexander the Great, whose megalomania and frenetic lifestyle had destroyed him by his early thirties, he had kept himself tightly disciplined. He was conservative by instinct, a reflection of both his temperament and his upbringing in a small provincial town outside Rome. The historian Suetonius tells that he lived frugally on cheese and olives and that his house, on the Palatine Hill, was simply furnished. (Recent excavations have shown that the house, though modest in size, was in fact part of a much larger complex directly linked to a major temple in honour of Octavian's 'favourite' god, Apollo.) He appeared distant, even touchy, except when in the company of close friends or advisers. According to Suetonius, his adulteries were always for reasons of state (he used his intimacy with men's wives to find out what their husbands were thinking), although in his later years he did develop a liking for young girls. There is no evidence of a man of strong sexual passions and his relationships with his wives appear to have been reserved, although he does seem to have developed genuine affection for the second, Livia, whom he had married for political reasons when she was already pregnant by her first husband.

In short, there was something calculating, even cold, about Octavian. Suetonius quotes the words he is supposed to have said to his family on his deathbed, the traditional words of a departing actor, 'If I acted well, applaud me and send me off with unanimous praise.' It seems clear that most of his public actions were carefully calculated for effect. Only on a few occasions, such as when three Roman legions were massacred in the German forests in AD 9, or when he became aware of his daughter Julia's adulteries, do his emotions seem to have broken through in some kind of nervous breakdown. He could also be superstitious.

The 'Restoration' of the Republic

Octavian's immediate aim in 29 BC, when he arrived back in Rome, was to play down any fears among senators that he might be a military dictator. He had soon disbanded over 100,000 men and discharged them with land bought out of his own wealth, notably from the treasury of Egypt which he had appropriated for himself. It was a shrewd move as it bound the veterans directly to him and at the same time avoided the need for new taxes or confiscations of land. It was not until AD 6 that Octavian transferred responsibility for paying for the discharge of soldiers to the state. A more manageable peacetime army of twenty-eight legions, probably 150,000 men, remained and with some fluctuations this was to remain the standard size of the army for most of the next century. Then, in 28 BC, as if closing the door on the many brutal events which had brought him to power, Octavian issued an edict declaring an amnesty and an annulment of any unjust orders he had given during the wars. The ambitious upstart, still only 34 years old, was now free to create a new role for himself as senior statesman.

Octavian's opening move in January 27 was a surprising one, made with the support of his close advisers. He proclaimed that it was now safe to restore the republic and that he would surrender all the powers he held back to the senate. He was, in effect, asking the body to resume its traditional role. It was an astute move. The senators knew, as did Octavian, that they could not keep order without him and that they would have to offer him something back. An elaborate game followed in which both sides pretended to be acting according to republican precedents while at the same time powers were transferred, temporarily it seemed at first but, as it turned out, permanently, into Octavian's hands. Following the precedent by which Pompey had been given a command in Spain without actually having to go there, Octavian was offered the administration of the provinces of Syria, Cilicia, Cyprus, Gaul, and Spain for ten years. It was in these provinces that the bulk of the remaining legions were now stationed. Octavian was thus being tacitly confirmed as the supreme military commander. The remaining provinces were to be administered, as they had been under the republic, by senators selected by lot. A few days later came the grant of a new name, Augustus, the name by which Octavian became known through history. It was a highly emotive word evoking both dignity and piety and its adoption by Octavian added powerfully to his aura. More significantly, however, Octavian remained consul, his position renewed from year to year until 23 BC. In this case he was certainly breaking with republican tradition and risking alienating those senators who would normally have sought the post for themselves.

Now confident of his position, Augustus spent the next three years away from Rome, campaigning in Spain and Gaul, but by 23 he was back in Rome where at the beginning of the year he fell seriously ill. One result was that in July he surrendered the post of consul. This proved a wise move. It released Augustus from a heavy administrative burden and opened the post again to ambitious senators. (It became the custom after this to elect several consuls a year, thus allowing the honour of the post to be shared more widely.) In return Augustus was given *imperium maius*, 'greater proconsular power', which gave him greater authority than other proconsuls. Unlike traditional proconsular power it did not lapse when he entered the city of Rome.

As important was the grant of the powers of a tribune. Augustus may have been given individual tribunician powers earlier (there is some scholarly dispute on what specific powers and when) but now all these were consolidated. Like any tribune he could summon the senate and the *concilium*, propose measures to them, and veto any business he disapproved of. He could be appealed to by any citizen and like any magistrate had the right to insist on his orders being obeyed. The grant of full tribunician powers proclaimed Augustus as guardian of the people's rights. The years that followed showed that he retained enormous popularity with the people of Rome. When he gave up the consulship, the crowds mistook the move as an abdication of power to the senate and rioted. Between 22 and 18 BC Augustus had to take on a variety of roles, including some of the powers of censor, to placate them. The most useful was that of supervising grain supplies, a position held by Pompey in the 50s. Public order in Rome, and thus the survival of the emperor, was so dependent on efficient distribution of food that this became a responsibility taken on by all subsequent emperors.

By 17 BC there was a feeling that stability had returned and the *Ludi Saeculares*, games traditionally held in the republic every hundred years to commemorate relief from national danger, were held with great ceremony in Rome. They were followed by more honours for Augustus. He had shown immense respect for the traditional religious life of Rome, commissioning images of himself at prayer or veiled for sacrifice, and in 12 BC he became *pontifex maximus*, the official head of the priesthood. (It was characteristic of Augustus' continuing sensitivity that he allowed the former *pontifex*, Lepidus, to die before taking the post.) His new status was celebrated by one of the most fascinating complexes of Augustan Rome, a giant sundial which has only recently been rediscovered.

The whole complex was designed so that on the date of Augustus' birth the tip of the shadow from its needle (an obelisk brought from Egypt which still survives in Rome) pointed towards another celebrated building of Augustan Rome, the Ara Pacis, the Altar of Peace. This great altar, itself only rediscovered in the last century, had been commissioned earlier by the senate (in 13 BC) to welcome Augustus back from campaigns in Gaul and Spain. The imperial family, including Augustus and his grandchildren, are seen in procession on their way to sacrifice. The altar is important in showing how the senate was by now prepared to accept Augustus and his family as a 'first family' which had been fully integrated into the religious and political life of Rome. As with all the finest Roman sculpture, it was the work of imported Greek craftsmen and echoes the serenity of Classical art, which Augustus preferred to the more ornate Hellenistic styles.

The responsibility of providing a model of family life was one which Augustus took seriously (although the means by which he had acquired Livia were scarcely praiseworthy). He seems to have been reacting against the breakdown of family life among the elite in the late republic. Adultery was made a criminal offence in 18 BC, though in effect only for women. A husband was supposed to reveal his wife's infidelities and then prosecute her. If he failed to do so he could himself be prosecuted for living off immoral earnings. Any outsider could also report adulteries and the law thus gave informers a field day. Augustus also encouraged marriage, rewarding those who had children and restricting the rights of inheritance of those who had not. His motive here must have been to restore the breeding-stock of upper-class families which had been so depleted by the civil wars.

The final honour given to Augustus was the one which he himself said meant most to him, the title *Pater Patriae*, 'Father of the Fatherland'. It came on the initiative of the crowds who forced the request on the senate in 2 BC. It was said that the normally restrained Augustus was in tears as he received the title.

Augustus' formal powers were rooted in republican precedent and there was the knowledge that they had been granted freely to him by the senate and the people of Rome. In combination and duration they extended beyond anything known in the republic. Added to them was his own *auctoritas*, that indefinable charisma and authority which enabled Augustus to achieve so much without having to rely on his formal powers. In effect he controlled the business of government. He could influence elections to the magistracies and supervise the governors of even the senate's provinces. He was commander of all the empire's armies. There was no longer any independent centre of decision-making and, almost without realizing it, the senators had surrendered their traditional role as the dominant force in Roman political life. Henceforth, the *princeps*, first citizen, the title Augustus preferred for himself, was the focus for all political activity. (*Princeps* was a form of honorary title without specific powers, a forerunner of the later *Duce* or *Führer*.)

Whatever the realities of his power, Augustus remained scrupulous in his dealings with senators. He knew the importance they attached to being addressed correctly and how much they appreciated his attending their family celebrations. He boosted the dignity of the body by expelling its more dissolute members and insisting on good birth, respectable wealth (a minimum sum of a million sestertii, a purely nominal amount for many grandees), and integrity. Numbers were reduced to 600 but, in accordance with republican traditions, senators continued to fill almost all the senior posts in the empire, including the governorships of the provinces and the commands of the legions. An exception was Egypt. The province was treated as the personal conquest of Augustus, the source in fact of much of his wealth, and it was governed on his behalf by an equestrian. No senator was allowed to visit the province without the express permission of the emperor.

Augustus was also sensitive in the use of his formal powers and he used them sparingly. One decree sent to Cyrene in 7 BC is typical. It gave orders which were effective only 'until the senate deliberates about this or I myself find a better solution'. It gradually became common practice, however, for Augustus to write directly to governors, and soon the cities and provinces themselves began by passing the senate and appealing directly to him. This was quite natural for petitioners in the eastern provinces who had become used over centuries to appealing to monarchs when things needed to be done. Augustus was also integrated into local ruler cults and became the focus of their prayers. In Egypt his statues were placed in the temples as those of the pharaohs and Ptolemies had been in the centuries before. In the west of the empire, where there was no tradition of monarchical rule, the imperial cult was a more artificial creation, often established through an imposing temple. A temple to Rome and Augustus was consecrated in Lugdunum (Lyons), the administrative capital of Gaul in 12 BC for instance, and others were to be found elsewhere.

As has been seen earlier (Chapter 19), the Hellenistic monarchs had traditionally made their capitals, Alexandria and Pergamum, for instance, showpieces of their rule. In Rome Augustus followed their example. During the years of political breakdown in the first century BC the city had fallen into decay. (The poet Horace claimed that the gods had unleashed the civil wars on Rome as revenge for the neglect of their temples.) Caesar had attempted to build a new forum for the capital and characteristically it was this that Augustus finished first when he returned to Rome. (Augustus never forgot that it was his divine heritage that had given him entry into Roman politics.) Next, according to his boast in the *Res Gestae*, the record of his achievements which he had inscribed on the great Mausoleum he had built for himself and his family, he set to work to restore eighty-two temples. It was only then that he began on his own work, the Forum Augustum, dominated by the great temple of Mars Ultor, the god of war portrayed as the avenger of his adopted father's death. It was dedicated in 2 BC. Augustus was supported by his lifelong friend Marcus Vipsanius Agrippa, who carried out the first building of the Pantheon (see below, p. 521) and the construction of the first great city baths. By Augustus' death much of central Rome had been filled with new building and what was a city of brick had become, in another of his boasts, 'a city of marble'. The buildings, statues, and decorations of the city were carefully designed to project the image of a new revived Rome, proud of its past and its reputation as a world conqueror. In the Forum Augustum the history of Rome was proclaimed in the form of statues of its great commanders leading up to Augustus himself whose victories were inscribed under a great *quadriga*, a triumphal four-horse chariot erected in the Forum's centre. In the famous Prima Porta statue, Augustus presented himself in a military cuirass as supreme commander.

The title *Pater Patriae* reflected Augustus' supremacy not only in Rome but in Italy. Control of the peninsula from Rome still remained comparatively weak in a country where local loyalties had always been strong. Cisalpine Gaul had been formally integrated into Italy only in 42 BC and in the south the Greek cities still retained their own cultures. Italy had suffered heavily in the first century, in the civil wars and endless confiscations of land as rival commanders attempted to settle their veterans. In the latest civil wars no less than sixteen major towns had been razed to the ground. A period of stability and a policy of integration was desperately needed to unify the peninsula. In his great building programme Augustus looked beyond Rome to the rest of Italy. He repaired roads and bridges, improved the security of travel by setting up guard posts along the main routes, and encouraged the building or reconstruction of towns. Many of the new towns, among them Aosta and Turin, were built to consolidate Roman control over the rich plain of the Po and they retained the atmosphere of frontier towns in an area still perceived to be vulnerable to attack from the north.

Augustus himself never forgot his own provincial roots and he was determined to integrate the wealthier Italian families into the government of Rome, not only to use talent more effectively but also to dilute the power of the Roman aristocracy. Italians were now welcome in the capital either as aspiring senators or as equestrians who could be given administrative jobs. Meanwhile in the countryside the end of conflict brought new prosperity. Probably no part of the empire benefited from Augustus' reign as much as Italy. One of the most common themes in the works of Horace and Virgil is the peace and fruitfulness of the land now order had been restored. Stability also allowed the continued spread of Latin, which acted as a *lingua franca* among the many local languages of the peninsula and gradually displaced many of them.

The army proved another unifying force in the peninsula. The legions could only recruit from among citizens and in this period this meant mostly from Italy and overseas citizen colonies. The Celtic tribes of the north proved one of the best recruiting grounds and army service was an excellent way of integrating them into the Roman way of life. Augustus realized the importance of establishing a professional army loyal to the state with formal conditions of service and arrangements for discharge. In 13 BC the normal period of legionary service was set at sixteen years, with annual pay of 900 sestertii. In AD 5 it was raised to twenty years with a discharge payment of some 12,000 sestertii. Increasingly it was a sum such as this rather than land which became the standard payout. From AD 6 the cost of this was borne by a military treasury. Augustus paid in 170 million sestertii of his own money to get it established but it was maintained by a 5 per cent inheritance tax on all citizens and a 1 per cent sales tax. As support to the legions Augustus formalized the setting up of auxiliary units raised in the provinces from non-citizens. In most cases they drew on local military traditions and skills such as archery or horsemanship. To provide an incentive to serve, citizenship was granted to auxiliaries and their families when they retired.

An elite group among the legionaries was the Praetorian Guard. Under the republic, generals such as Marius, Caesar, and Antony had raised their own bodyguards but Augustus established a more formal and permanent unit of nine cohorts each of six centuries, about 5,400 men in all. Three of the cohorts were stationed in Rome, the other six in surrounding towns. They were commanded by equestrian Praetorian Prefects. The Guard had higher wages than legionaries, 3,000 sestertii a year, and had only to serve sixteen years. As the only first-class fighting force in the vicinity of Rome their role was to become crucial at times of instability, such as when an emperor died and there was no obvious successor. Their normal duties included accompanying the emperor both in Rome and when he was on campaign and on occasions keeping order in the city itself.

Augustus and the Empire

Beyond Rome and Italy stretched the empire. In the east it was still bounded by client kingdoms. In the civil wars they had been loyal to Antony, and one of Augustus' first tasks had been to tour the east gaining their allegiance for himself (22–19 BC). They were gradually to be absorbed into the empire itself. Further east, beyond direct Roman control, was Parthia, the only state which could meet Rome as an equal. The disastrous invasions of Crassus and Antony had shown how formidable an enemy the Parthians could be. It was one of Augustus' major achievements that he came to terms with Parthia, in 20 BC bullying her into returning the captured Roman standards, and then setting up Armenia as an independent buffer state between the two empires. The event was trumpeted throughout the empire. A large issue of denarii bore the image of a kneeling Parthian offering up the coveted standards. On the cuirass of the Prima Porta statue the Parthian king himself is shown offering back the standard to a figure in military dress and the surrounding motifs suggest a world united in peace thanks to the dominance of Rome.

In the west Roman control was still limited. Some areas such as Spain were still unpacified, even though the Romans had nominally controlled the peninsula for 200 years. Others such as Gaul still had not been consolidated for tax purposes. All this was put in hand. Spain was pacified with great brutality while Caesar's Gallic conquests were consolidated into three provinces. The southern borders of the province of Africa were also stabilized, an important achievement in an area which, along with Italy, Sicily, and Egypt, supplied most of the grain of Rome.

In the north the borders of the empire, from the Balkans to Germany, had never been properly defined. It was here the empire was most vulnerable. The tribes, some of whom were Celtic, some German, and one, the Sarmatians, Asiatic in origin, were fiercely independent and able to offer determined resistance to the Romans. The dilemma, one which was to haunt Roman policy-making for four centuries, was whether to try and subdue them or whether to exclude them from the empire by a defended frontier. In 17 or 16 BC German tribes spilled over the Rhine, which had marked the limit of Caesar's conquests.

Augustus himself went north to rally the defence and so began years of fighting along the borders. In 16 and 15 the Alps were subdued to secure Roman control along the Danube and allow better communication between the Rhine and the east of the empire. An initial pacification of the Balkan tribes took place between 12 and 9, with the eventual formation of the provinces of Dalmatia and Pannonia. Meanwhile Roman armies were advancing across the Rhine towards the Elbe, which was reached about 9 BC.

However, Roman control was not as complete as it seemed. A great revolt broke out in Pannonia in AD 6 which took four years of hard fighting to subdue. (The historian Suetonius believed it was the toughest war Rome had to fight since the great struggle with Carthage.) Just as the fighting ended (AD 9) a Roman commander, Varus, who was organizing tax collection in what is now north-western Germany with three legions to support him, was ambushed and massacred with all his men. It was an appalling humiliation and the news shook Augustus more than any other of his reign. The legions were never replaced, their numbers left unused. (One of Tacitus' most graphic descriptions is of Roman armies raiding in the area seven years later coming across the whitened bones of the dead soldiers still lying in the forest. The site of the disaster, in the Teutoberger Wald, is now marked by a monument.) Retreat had to be made to the Rhine, where no less than eight legions were left stationed to guard what now had to be accepted as a permanent border. In a message left at his death Augustus warned his successors not to try to expand further. With the exceptions of the conquest of Britain (from AD 43) and Dacia (finally in 105–6), and the absorption of client states, no further permanent additions were to be made to the empire.

The Poets of the Augustan Age

The opportunity to act as patron of the arts was too good to miss for a politician as astute as Augustus. He was especially lucky with his writers. Two of the greatest poets of the age, in fact of any age, Horace and Virgil, were already well established in Rome before Actium. By then they were also members of the cultivated circle enjoying the patronage of Maecenas, an Etruscan aristocrat, who was in his turn an intimate of Octavian. After Actium a complex relationship developed between these two independent and sensitive poets, their patron, and their ruler, who must have hoped they could be persuaded by his achievements to enhance his personal glory.

Quintus Horatius Flaccus, Horace, was born in 65 BC. His father had been a slave, freed before Horace's birth, who had made enough money to give his talented son the best education possible, first in Rome and later in Greece. Horace's debut in public life, however, was inauspicious. He had sided with Brutus against

Mark Antony and Octavian at Philippi and he was lucky to be able to return to Rome and find a post as secretary to the quaestors. It was from this that Maecenas, recognizing his genius, plucked him and gave him the support needed to become a full-time poet. The support included a farm in the Sabine Hills which Horace was to immortalize as a retreat of rural bliss.

Like all Roman poets Horace was immersed in Greek poetry. Its influences run through his verse at such deep and complex levels that they are often impossible to disentangle. He is a poet's poet, fascinated by the actual art of making poems and this becomes more obvious as he matures. Among his earliest work, the *Satires*, written in the 30s, are conversation pieces. Already the central themes of his later poems are there, above all the joys and agonies of friendship and sexual relationships, and the problem of finding balance, between peace in the countryside and stimulation in the town, between independence as an individual and support by a patron. In the *Epodes*, published in 29 BC, many of the same themes are developed, but in a denser and more complex way. They lead on to Horace's supreme achievement, the *Odes* (published together probably in 23 BC), short lyrical poems, using Greek metres, in which each word is placed to provide alliteration or to play off against another. The composition is often so sophisticated and polished that many have continued to resist satisfying translation.

The translator's greatest challenge has often been seen as the fifth ode in Book I. Horace describes his 'shipwreck' at the hands of an unscrupulous lover, Pyrrha, and wonders now who struggles to enjoy her favours. This is the translation of the English poet John Milton.

> What slender youth bedewed with liquid odours
> Courts thee on roses in some pleasant cave,
> Pyrrha; for whom bind'st thou
> In wreaths thy golden hair,
> Plain in thy neatness; O how oft shall he
> On faith and changed gods complain: and seas
> Rough with black winds and storms
> Unwonted shall admire:
> Who now enjoys thee credulous, all gold,
> Who, always vacant, always amiable,
> Hopes thee; of flattering gales
> Unmindful? Hapless they
> To whom thou untried seem'st fair. Me in my vowed
> Picture the sacred wall declares t'have hung
> My dank and dripping weeds
> To the stern god of sea.

The *Odes* cover many subjects, from the very personal, the fear of death, the satisfaction, even glory, of being a poet, the intricacies of relationships, to grand public themes such as the celebration of Augustus' achievements. At one level Horace's life as expressed in his poetry seems calm and unhurried. He loves the contrast between the peace of the countryside, with its simple rustic virtues, and the sophisticated bustle of town life, but within a very limited range of venues he explores every nuance of personal feeling. He comes across as a sensuous man, enjoying sex, good wine, the warmth of the sun, and the fertility of the land, but underlying his work is an anxiety about being accepted socially, about his relationship with his patrons, the perennial dilemma of a man of intellectual brilliance who is dependent on support from men more wealthy than himself. He never married.

Horace's relationship with Augustus was particularly complex. Augustus, who had few intimate friends, warmed to him and even asked him to become his secretary. (The relationship provides a good example of how Augustus, despite his new grandeur, continued to be approachable.) Horace refused. He was acutely aware of the need to preserve his integrity as a poet although at the same time he knew that his way of life depended on the stability that Augustus had brought. It is only in Book III of the *Odes* that he allows himself to give unashamed support to the regime, but even here he still hints at the precariousness of power, a theme which is never far from his thoughts. Finally, in 17 BC, Horace agreed to compose the Centennial Hymn for the *Ludi Saeculares* and appeared in public to conduct it. When he died, in 8 BC, he left everything he had to Augustus.

While the poems of Horace present an absorbing picture of the sensitivities of a gregarious and highly talented man living off his wits, his contemporary, Virgil, comes across as shy and less socially adept. He was born in 70 BC to what appears a well-off family near Mantua, an area which was to suffer badly in the civil wars. (His family estates appear to have been confiscated to provide land for veterans after the battle of Philippi.) The experience of disruption helps explain the intensity which Virgil brings to his poetry, the conviction with which he writes of the importance of stability and the sacrifices which are needed to bring order.

Like many talented provincials, Virgil was attracted by the cultural beacon of Rome and finished his education there. With his first poems, the *Eclogues*, published about 38 BC, he followed most Roman poets in taking a Greek model, in this case the Hellenistic poet Theocritus, the father of pastoral poetry (see p. 346). The *Eclogues* are pastoral poems in which peace on the land is contrasted with the threat of the disruption of war. It is this theme which is developed in Virgil's first great work, the *Georgics*, written after he had become a member of Maecenas' circle.

In contrast to the fashion of the time, the *Georgics* form a long poem, in four books, with a total of over 2,000 lines. They masquerade as a practical handbook in verse for farmers but their main purpose is very different. Virgil was writing just as the civil wars were coming to an end (the *Georgics* were completed in 29 BC). He was preoccupied, like so many Italians, with the need for peace and the work is suffused with the hopes raised by the emergence of Octavian. ('Surely a time will come when . . . the farmer heaving the soil with his curved plough will come on spears all eaten up with rust or strike with his heavy hoe on hollow helmets, and gape at the huge bones in the upturned graves.' Translation: L. P. Wilkinson.) In the *Georgics*, the measured toil of farming life, its steady cultivation of crops, its frugality in the midst of fertility, which peace makes possible, echo back to the mythical past of Rome when the state was made up largely of farmers. Farming, suggests Virgil, creates morally good men, those who form the backbone of a stable society. To argue his point Virgil has to romanticize. The farmer as Virgil sees him is not worn down by back-breaking toil, as must have been the case of the typical peasant farmer: he seems to be perpetually active, sensitive to the fruitfulness of the earth and even invigorated by the routine of labour in the fields.

The *Georgics* broke new ground by their length and the intensity with which their theme is presented but Virgil's masterpiece was still to come. The *Aeneid*, written between 29 and 19 BC, comes at a culmination of his life, a rare instance when an artist happens to end on the highest note possible, without a decline into old age. (In fact the work was unfinished and only saved on the direct orders of Augustus.)

Virgil had the same problem as Horace. He was deeply grateful for the order that Augustus had brought (and fearful that it would end) but unwilling to surrender his independence as an artist simply to glorify the new regime. After the *Georgics* his ambition was to write an epic. An obvious theme was the rise and triumph of Octavian but Virgil knew that in doing so he would have to gloss over the brutal realities involved in the struggle for power. It was much better to look further back into Roman history and eventually Virgil chose the legend of the Trojan Aeneas. The legend, as Virgil adapted it for his purposes, told how Aeneas, fleeing from the capture of Troy, voyaged across the Mediterranean and eventually arrived in Italy after a celebrated love affair with Dido, queen of Carthage. After bloody struggles for supremacy, he founded the family which was itself to found Rome. The attraction of the story was that Augustus' adoptive family, the Julians, claimed their own descent from Aeneas and so indirectly Virgil was glorifying his emperor.

The *Aeneid* is consciously modelled on Homer. The wanderings of Aeneas in the first part echo the *Odyssey* and the battles of the second the *Iliad*. It was an audacious undertaking, particularly from a man who, in famous lines from Book VI of the *Aeneid* (see below, p. 497), acknowledged the supremacy of the Greeks in all the arts, but it was a subject which allowed Virgil to use his powers to the full. The greatness of the *Aeneid* lies not just in the majesty and beauty of its language but in its courage in tackling the agonies involved in power and destiny. Rome has been given its tasks by the gods and must not flinch from achieving its empire. Virgil captures the emotional force of Aeneas' separation from his homeland, his loneliness, and what seems to be a refuge in the arms of Dido, before duty and the will of the gods drive him on to the hostile shores of Italy. Here the battles he wages to establish himself are ruthless and destructive. Virgil is free, as he would never have been if he had written directly about Augustus, to dwell on the pity and waste of war and to write sympathetically of the victor's opponents. Yet there is an end, order established and the rise of Rome foretold. Taken into the underworld, Aeneas sees the future Octavian: 'This is the man, this one, of whom so often you have heard the promise, Caesar Augustus, son of the deified, who shall bring once again the Age of Gold to Latium. . . .' A past prophecy has been fulfilled in the present. Virgil's respects have been paid and his hopes for the future expressed without any compromise to his independence.

There were other important poets of this generation, Propertius and Tibullus, for instance, but the third major star of the reign was a much younger man, Publius Ovidius Naso. Ovid came from a peaceful and fruitful part of central Italy which had been left relatively untouched by the civil wars. He was still only a boy of 12 when the wars ended and, as a member of a well-off provincial family, he was free to make his way in a society much more settled than that known by Horace and Virgil. When he came to Rome to study rhetoric, he seemed set on a conventional career. His father's hopes were that he would progress to the senate.

However, Ovid's greatest love was the use of language and he engineered his life so that it became one of full-time writing. He never committed himself to the imperial establishment to the same degree as Horace and Virgil and he emerges as a freer and less inhibited poet as a result. His first published work, the *Amores* (around 20 BC), explores the life of young lovers let loose in a large metropolitan city. Trips are made to the races and theatre against a background of all the frustrations, delights, joys, and sufferings of young love. The *Amores* are elegies (elegies took their name from the metre in which they were written and were used, in classical times, to express a wide range of subjects, not only the 'songs of lamentation' with which the word is now associated), and they set a standard of the genre for later generations.

In *The Art of Love* (possibly around 1 BC), a much more cynical and world-weary poet writes of the stratagems to be used by both men and women to seduce those they desire. 'The first thing to get in your head', writes Ovid, 'is that every single girl can be caught and that you'll catch her if you set your toils right. Birds will sooner fall dumb in springtime, cicadas in summer, or a hunting dog turn his back on a hare, than a lover's bland inducements can fail with a woman.' (Translation: Peter Green.) This is the world later portrayed for the eighteenth century by Laclos's *Les Liaisons Dangereuses*, where love is treated as conquest by men and women who are otherwise bored with life. As it follows its decadent theme, the *Art of Love* is filled with the detail of everyday life in Roman society, the devices with which women make themselves look beautiful, the skills of hair-dressing, and the appropriate lover's gift.

PLATE 44

The triumph was the climax of a Roman general's career and here Julius Caesar is shown enjoying his victory over the Gauls, acclaimed as one of the greatest military achievements of the Republic. Beyond his chariot an arch stands as a symbol of triumph while a slave holds a laurel wreath over his head. The wreath will later be placed on the statue of Jupiter on the Capitoline Hill. This portrayal is by Andrea Mantegna (1431–1506), one of nine canvases detailing the procession. Mantegna lived at Padua, a centre for the new humanism spreading through Europe, and was one of the first painters of the Renaissance to become obsessed by the correct portrayal of antiquity, the ruins of which still littered the Italian landscape. Mantegna was haunted above all by the clash between Christianity and the pagan antique culture he revered.

PLATE 45

PLATE 46

The opulent Roman home-owner of the first century BC delighted in portraying the natural world on his walls. This example (Plate 45 above) comes from the so-called Villa of Livia, the wife of Augustus, on the Palatine Hill and shows a profusion of fruits, shrubs, and bird life.

The hippodromes, the scene of the great chariot races, formed a focus for social life (as in the poems of Ovid) but were also arenas which allowed political energies to be diverted into the support of rival teams (the Blues and Greens of Constantinople, for instance). The example shown is a nineteenth century painting of a third century AD mosaic from Gaul. Note the starting gates on the left and the "eggs" in centre of the *spina* (barrier), one of which was removed after each lap.

The theme of the Parthenon frieze, one of the great masterpieces of classical sculpture, is a grand procession. A group of elders (*right*) pause on their way to the Acropolis (440s BC). In the Ara Pacis, the Altar of Peace (*below*), commissioned by the Roman senate in 13 BC, Augustus is honoured as the upholder of the religious traditions of his fore-fathers. This section shows members of the imperial family including Livia. (The child may be the young Claudius.)

PLATE 47

PLATE 48

PLATE 49

PLATE 50

'Aphrodite's sphere of activity is the joyous consummation of sexuality' (Walter Burkert). Aphrodite, known as Venus to the Romanas, originates with the Semitic goddess of love, Astarte. Legend suggested that she rose from the sea out of the castrated genitals of Uranus. Nothing of this origin is suggested by the relief on the lovely 'Ludovisi' throne (*above left*), of Greek workmanship but possibly made in Italy, *c.*460 BC.

This statue of Venus (*left*), now in the Capitoline Museum in Rome, appears to be a second century AD copy of a Hellenistic copy of the famous statue of Aphrodite of Cnidus. (See the interlude on the Classical Age in Art.) The original set a model for the inviolable female nude which lasted for centuries. The 'Capitoline Venus' was rediscovered in Rome in the seventeenth century and gained new importance when Napoleon took it to Paris as part of the plunder he exacted from Rome in 1797.

The nude Venus was easily accepted by the Romans and the Esquiline Treasure of *c.* AD 380 (above right), part of a wedding gift to a Christian couple, shows that pagan and Christian motifs could still co-exist in late antiquity. Later a nude Venus was seen only as a manifestation of sin.

PLATE 51

PLATE 52 ⇨

⇩ PLATE 53

The goddess of hunting, Artemis (Diana to the Romans), was surprised when bathing by the hunter Actaeon. Outraged by the intrusion, she set his own dogs on him and completed his punishment with her arrows. In a version of 460 BC (top) by the so-called Pan Painter the iconography is established. In the 1550s the painter Titian follows in the tradition although he draws on a story from Ovid's Metamorphoses that Actaeon was transformed into a stag before his dogs set on him. This is an illustration of the enduring influence of Greek and Roman mythology in later European art.

PLATE 54

Timgad in north
Africa (*right*) was built
for legionary veterans
in the second century
AD. The Forum is in
the centre of a typical
grid plan with the
theatre to the left.
A triumphal arch
crosses the road at the
top. The Colosseum
in Rome (*below*),
designed to hold
50,000 spectators, was
built on marshy land
in just ten years
(70–80 AD).

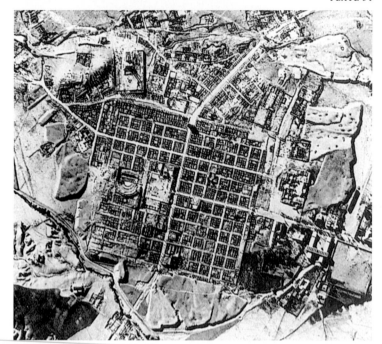

⇩ PLATE 55

PLATE 56

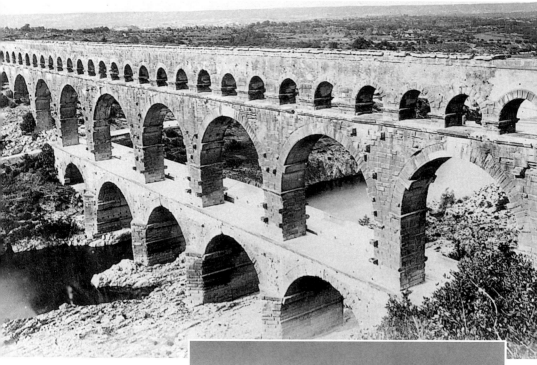

The aqueduct with its simple stone arches is one of the most effective and enduring symbols of Roman rule. The Pont du Gard at Nimes (*above*), was built by Marcus Agrippa in 20–16 BC. The skill of the engineers lay in keeping the gradient constant, often over long distances. Typically, however, an aqueduct ran underground to better protect the water. The surviving surface of a Roman road (*right*): well-founded and drained Roman roads allowed swift communications by land. Speeds of up to 200 kilometres a day are recorded, though any heavy goods were better transported by sea.

PLATE 57 ⇨

PLATE 58

PLATE 59

PLATE 60

The Pantheon (120s AD) is one of the great architectural achievements of antiquity, impossible without concrete. This eighteenth century portrait of its interior (*facing*) shows how the inside of the dome was carved out so as to lighten the building as it rose. Through the door the great columned entrance can be glimpsed. The basilica was another type of Roman building especially popular for early churches. The fifth-century Santa Sabina in Rome (*above*) is a superb example. (*Below*) citizens of fifth-century Constantinople, the emperor Theodosius II and his pious sister Pulcheria among them, receive the bones of the martyred St Stephen.

PLATE 61

PLATE 63

PLATE 62

⇦ PLATE 64   ⇧ PLATE 65

Part of the success of early Christianity lay in the way it incorporated Christ into traditional iconographies. Christ as the Good Shepherd (*facing main picture*) echoes similar representations in eastern art and that of Archaic Greece (*facing inset*). Christ could also be shown as a Roman military hero trampling animals (*above right*, a mosaic from Ravenna). (The allusion is to Psalm 91 in which God will protect by treading on a lion and an adder.) On a mid-fourth century sarcophagus (*above, top* Plate 63), Jesus' passion becomes a Roman triumph with a laurel wreath being offered to him instead of a crown of thorns.

This apse mosaic from the Church of Santa Pudenziana in Rome (*c.*AD 390) (Plate 65, *above right*) is the first to show Christ in Majesty. It draws heavily on pagan mythology and conventions of authority and shows how fully Christ had been integrated into a Roman context by this date, even being described as a leader of the Roman legions. To the left of Christ sits Paul, an indication of the rising importance of the apostle in the fourth century. See further Chapter 30 for these developments.

PLATE 66

Raphael's celebrated portrayal of Greek philosophers, the School of Athens (AD 1510–11), shows Plato (*centre left*) pointing his hand towards heaven while Aristotle, always the empiricist, points down towards the earth. On Plato's right, Socrates disputes with the young of Athens and, below him, Pythagoras demonstrates 'his' theory from a slate.

PLATE 67

The relationship between Christian and pagan art was a complex one as can be seen by this representation above (from a mosaic from Nea Paphos, Cyprus, dated to the first half of the fourth century AD) of the baby Dionysus being offered for adoration by his protector, the god Hermes (e.g. Hermes was not his father; Zeus, the 'father of the gods', was). Attending Hermes on the far right is a woman named as Theogonia, 'divine birth'.

Once Paul had brought the denunciation of idols into Christianity, it became a mark of Christian commitment to destroy them. Here (Plate 68, left) the third century saint Apollonia of Alexandria assaults a statue of Dionysus. The story is recounted in the fourth century Ecclesiastical History by Eusebius, hence the inscription on the balcony. Painting attributed to Antonio Vivarini, c.1450.

PLATE 68

PLATE 69

In this superb relief, dating from the late 170s AD, and one of a set of eleven, the emperor Marcus Aurelius is shown in triumph in a four-horse chariot. A flautist is about to lead the procession through an arch. The original relief depicted an actual triumph of Marcus Aurelius and his son Commodus (as portrayed in the film Gladiator!) which took place in Rome in 176. After Commodus' assassination in 192, his figure was removed from the chariot and the steps of the temple extended to fill the space. Three of the eleven reliefs are at present in the Capitoline Museums in Rome, the remaining eight were reused on the Arch of Constantine.

⇧ PLATE 70

PLATE 71 ⇨

One of the finest bronze statues from the ancient world is that of the emperor Marcus Aurelius (*above left*). It survived being destroyed by Christians as it was originally believed to be of Constantine and as such stood for many centuries before his Church of St John Lateran. It was transferred to the Capitoline Hill by Michelangelo in 1538. It acted as a model for statues such as that of Bartolomeo Colleoni by Verrocchio set up in Venice in 1496. (*above right*)

The four horses of St Mark's, Venice, are the only surviving set of four horses from the classical period. The method used to apply the gilding dates them to the second or third century AD, but their style, notably their cropped manes, is Greek, an illustration of how traditional styles were used and reused. Their casting suggests they were placed on a triumphal arch, possibly one erected by the emperor Septimius Severus to mark his conquest of Byzantium in 195 AD. Byzantium becomes Constantinople in 324 and this is where they were first recorded before being taken by the Venetians to Venice in 1204. They are now under cover in St Mark's.

PLATE 72

PLATE 73

PLATE 74

PLATE 75

The triumphal arch provides a powerful symbol of Roman military success. (*Facing above*) the arch built by the senate to commemorate the victory of Constantine at the Milvian Bridge (AD 312). Napoleon, characteristically, exploited the arch for his own ends; included here (*facing below*) is one he erected for a festival in Venice (1807). The British architect Lutyens borrowed the model for his First World War memorial to the missing of the Somme at Thiepval, France (*above*). Here, perhaps, Pericles' famous Funeral Speech (431 BC) in which the loss of Athens' young men is compared to the taking of spring from the year provides a more appropriate allusion.

PLATE 76

PLATE 77

The appropriation of original material for the museums of Europe was a major feature of nineteenth-century collecting. The Englishman Austen Henry Layard began excavating at the Assyrian palace of Nineveh in 1846 and (above) he is shown supervising the removal of sculptures for the British Museum. Below, King Ludwig of Bavaria (1825–48) stands before the galleries he created in Munich for his collection of Greek art. The art historian Johann Winckelmann is shown resurrected (he had died in 1768), extolling the virtues of Greek antiquities to him.

PLATE 78

PLATE 79

The emperor Justinian in a sixth-century mosaic from San Vitale in Ravenna. The emperor never visited Ravenna and the model may be an imperial procession from Santa Sophia in Constantinople. The Christian emperor is shown with a paten, the dish on which the eucharistic bread is laid. To his left are a bishop (Maximianus) and a deacon carrying a jewelled gospel cover. Note the chi-rho sign on the soldier's shield, another indication of the absorption of Christianity into Roman militarism.

'St. Agnes hovers silently and alone, set against a bottomless sea of gold, above an apse made as exquisite and translucent as a honeycomb by marble columns' (Peter Brown). The fourth-century Christian writer Prudentius remarked that through Agnes's martyrdom, following her refusal to submit to the sexual demands of a Roman official, she trampled on all the vanities of the world, pomp, gold, and silver. In this seventh-century mosaic where Agnes is arrayed as a Byzantine princess and flanked by two popes who built her church, she receives in heaven what she has scorned on earth. From the church of St. Agnes in Rome.

PLATE 80

Giovanni Pannini (1691–1765) provided travellers on the Grand Tour with carefully composed momentos of their visit to Rome. In his *Roman Capriccio*, the Colosseum and Trajan's Column are seen through the ruined halls of one of the great city baths.

Ovid's hunger for new forms of expression was also to find a rich source in Greek mythology. In his *Metamorphoses* (about AD 2) he constructs a rich tapestry of stories from the time of creation to his own day. The common theme is the transformation of the characters into new shapes, from human to animal or plant. It is a highly inventive work which remained Ovid's most popular throughout the Middle Ages (and provided the inspiration for Roberto Calasso's modern reinterpretation of classical myth, *The Marriage of Cadmus and Harmony*).

Ovid was sensitive and cynical by turns, but always brilliant and ready to break new ground. Finally he fell foul of Augustus' regime. His 'crime' is not known. Augustus certainly disliked Ovid's celebration of sexual freedom for women at a time when he was trying to uphold more austere moral codes, but there was some other more serious offence, possibly association with political opposition. Augustus summoned him personally in AD 8 and sent him into remote exile to the Black Sea. He was separated from everything he loved, the bustling *demimonde* of Rome, even his third wife. He was never allowed to return, and died about AD 17, after composing a final set of poems bemoaning his exile.

The Problem of the Succession

Augustus' powers had been granted personally to him by the senate for life. There was no imperial constitution and theoretically the Republic could have been revived on his death. However, by the time that moment came in AD 14, forty-five years after Actium, the principate had become too firmly entrenched for the republic to be restored. In fact long before his death Augustus had been trying, in true monarchical fashion, to designate an heir. His hopes rested on his only daughter Julia, whom he exploited shamelessly in the hope of producing male grandchildren. In 23 BC she was forced into a second marriage to Augustus' closest colleague Agrippa, who was old enough to be her father. In the short term the aim of the marriage seemed to have been met. Three sons were born. For years the hopes of the succession rested on the two eldest, Gaius and Lucius Caesar. However, by AD 4 both were dead. Another son, known as Agrippa Postumus (because he was born, in 12 BC, after Agrippa's death) was passed over by Augustus as not being suitable for the throne and subsequently, it appears, murdered.

In 11 BC Julia was bullied into a third marriage to Tiberius, the son of Augustus' wife, Livia, by her first husband. It was not a success, there were no surviving children, and Julia took refuge in a string of adulteries which caused so much scandal she was eventually exiled by her father from Rome. On the death of his second grandson, Augustus was forced to adopt his stepson Tiberius as his own son and designate him as heir. As a mark of his special status Tiberius was granted the tribunician power (this became a normal way in which an emperor designated his successor). By the time of Augustus' death in AD 14 his position as successor was undisputed. Tiberius, however, conscious that he was not Augustus' first choice and now in his fifties, accepted only out of his sense of duty.

Augustus had been ailing for several years before his death. (His last years, with defeat on the northern borders of his empire and the deaths of so many of his family, are uncannily like those of another great monarch in history, Louis XIV of France.) When the moment finally came, everything was in hand for the succession. Augustus died at Nola in August (the month named in his honour, as July had been named in honour of Caesar). After cremation his ashes were buried in his Mausoleum with great ceremony, and when a senator reported having seen his spirit ascending through the flames of the funeral pyre to heaven it was decreed by the senate that the Divine Augustus should be ranked among the gods of the state. His divinity, the decree ran, rested on 'the magnitude of his benefactions to the whole world'.

FURTHER READING

A sourcebook on this period is K. Chisholm, and J. Ferguson, *Rome in the Augustan Age* (Oxford, 1981). R. Syme, *The Roman Revolution* (Oxford, 1960), is the classic study. Martin Goodman, *The Roman World, 44 BC–AD 180* (London, 1997) is a reliable introduction. On Augustus himself see A. H. M. Jones, *Augustus* (London, 1970), and D. Shotter, *Augustus Caesar* (London, 1991). See also K. Raaflaub and M. Toher (eds.), *Between Republic and Empire: Interpretations of Augustus and his Principate* (Berkeley, 1990), and F. Millar and E. Segal (eds.), *Caesar Augustus: Seven Aspects* (Oxford, 1984). F. Millar, *The Emperor in the Roman World, 31 BC–AD 337* (London, 1977) is fundamental. Paul Zanker's *The Power of Images in the Age of Augustus* (Ann Arbor, 1988), is penetrating and original. On Rome, see Diane Favro, *The Urban Image of Augustan Rome* (Cambridge, 2003). On the development of the imperial cult see S. Price, *Rituals and Power: The Roman Imperial Cult in Asia Minor* (Cambridge, 1984).

On the background to the cultural life in Augustus' 'reign' see Karl Galinsky, *Augustan Culture* (Princeton, 1996). A readable introduction is G. Highet, *Poets in a Landscape* (London, 1957). There is also J. Griffin, *Latin Poetry and Roman Life* (London, 1985), and T. Woodman and D. West, *Poetry and Politics in the Age of Augustus* (Cambridge, 1984). On Virgil, Charles Martindale (ed.), *The Cambridge Companion to Virgil* (Cambridge, 1997), and the magisterial study by Richard Jenkyns, *Virgil's Experience* (Oxford, 1998). On the *Aeneid* there is the translation by Robert Fitzgerald (London, 1974). On Horace, try D. Armstrong, *Horace* (New Haven, 1989) for a lively overview and J. D. McClatchy (ed.), *Horace, The Odes: New Translations by Contemporary Poets* (Princeton, 2002). For Ovid, S. Mack, *Ovid* (New Haven, 1988), and P. Hardie (ed.), *The Cambridge Companion to Ovid* (Cambridge, 2002). Ovid's poems from exile, often overlooked by those who go for the earlier erotic poems, have recently been translated by Peter Green in a Penguin edition and Ted Hughes, *Tales from Ovid, Twenty-Four Passages from the 'Metamorphoses'* (London, 1997), is an acclaimed verse translation.

25 | Consolidating the Empire, AD 14–138

Augustus had created a new political system which had brought peace and stability to the empire. This stability was achieved at the expense of the old republican liberties, the traditional powers of the senate and the assemblies, and the direction by noble families of government through the magistracies. The risk was that the new system would degenerate into tyranny and in several reigns that followed it did. Yet no alternative form of government ever emerged in the Roman empire and emperors stretched in an almost unbroken line to the final overthrow of Constantinople in 1453. This is the measure of Augustus' achievement.

Suetonius and Tacitus

There are two major sources for the political developments of the early empire, the equestrian Gaius Suetonius Tranquillus (born *c.* AD 70), and the senator Publius Cornelius Tacitus (AD 56 to after 117). Both worked in the early second century AD when the more tolerant rule of Trajan allowed them to write more freely than had been possible under the 'tyranny' of Domitian (see below). Suetonius' most celebrated surviving work is his set of biographies of the emperors, *On the Lives of the Caesars* (from Julius Caesar to Domitian). In each biography he follows a similar pattern: the early life of his subject, his public career, physical appearance, and private life. For the early lives Suetonius had access to the imperial archives (he was an imperial secretary until dismissed by Hadrian) and he also drew on gossip and reminiscences though often without much discrimination. The result is a highly readable collection of vignettes whose accuracy is open to question.

A far greater historian is Tacitus. Tacitus' career, as a senator, began under Vespasian but it was his experience of the tyrannical reign of Domitian which defined his attitudes to the past. Tacitus wrote his accounts of the first century AD from the perspective of one who was nostalgic for the ancient liberties of the republic and who saw many of the emperors as destroyers of these liberties. Yet he is also aware of the underlying problems in writing any kind of history at all. 'Some', he writes in the Annals 'hold as true whatever they hear, others twist truth into fiction, and both types of perversion become more extreme with the passing of time.' It may be that one of the points that Tacitus is making is that the 'perversions' are the direct result of a government which has lost its contact with the masses and become secretive. 'Truth' becomes lost within the machinations of those in power.

Tacitus' earliest work is a panegyrical life of his father-in-law, Agricola, governor in Britain, whom he felt Domitian had betrayed. This was followed by the *Germania*, a study of the German tribes. Many of the details of their daily life compiled by Tacitus have been confirmed by archaeological research although the whole is set within an ideological framework in which the 'virtuous' German is set against the 'decadent' Roman. In his *Histories* of the period AD 69–96, of which only the first part survives, and his *Annals*, which cover AD 14–68 (though here again much is missing), Tacitus shows the same ability to distance himself from the Romans and to understand that not all their subjects had cause to welcome Roman rule.

There is a strong moral undertone to Tacitus' writings and he is fascinated by the problems caused by tyrannical rule, in particular for those 'good' men who manage to survive under it. Thucydides is the nearest equivalent among the Greek historians. This makes for an absorbing and penetrating narrative shaped by Tacitus' determination to expose his villains and glorify his heroes. As Ronald Mellor puts it in his study of Tacitus, 'If other ancient writers examined the human psyche as affected by war (Homer), by love (Ovid), by suffering (Sophocles), and by religion (Euripides' *Bacchae*), Tacitus above all others probes the individual personality transformed by political absolutism. . . .' Even Augustus failed to escape his acute analysis:

He seduced the army with bonuses and his cheap food policy was successful bait for civilians. Indeed, he attracted everybody's good will by the enjoyable gift of peace. Then he gradually pushed ahead and absorbed the functions of the senate, the officials, and even the law. Opposition did not exist. War or judicial murder had disposed of all men of spirit. Upper-class survivors found that slavish obedience was the way to succeed, both politically and financially . . . (Translation: Michael Grant)

Tiberius

By concentrating on the personalities of the emperors and their relationships with those around them in Rome neither Suetonius nor Tacitus does full justice to his subjects as rulers of a Mediterranean empire (although, of course, Tacitus shows in his earlier works that he is fully aware of politics at and beyond the limits of Roman imperial power). This particularly affects Tacitus' portrayal of Tiberius, whom the historian treated as cynically as he had done Augustus. In fact Tiberius was one of the most gifted men of his age and certainly the most experienced of the possible successors to Augustus. He had borne the brunt of the fighting along the northern borders and had been entrusted with regaining the standards lost by Crassus at Carrhae, one of the greatest diplomatic coups of Augustus' reign. He was a fine administrator and a good judge of men. He knew that the empire needed peace and stability and that the prosaic tasks of keeping expenditure low, appointing sound generals and administrators, and punishing those who overstepped the mark were essential if the achievements of Augustus were to be sustained. Even Tacitus had to accept that Tiberius' appointments and supervision of the empire were sound. The twenty-three years of Tiberius' reign were crucial ones for consolidating the foundations laid by Augustus.

The death of Augustus provoked a mutiny among the troops on the Rhine, apparently in the hope of better conditions, but this was soon quelled. Otherwise the succession took place peacefully. Tiberius already had the tribunician power and could summon the senate on his own authority. What was surprising was how easily the senators, used to working the republican system in which all magistracies were elected, accepted the principle that the son, real or adopted, of an emperor would be his successor. The recognition of a ruling dynasty, the 'Julio-Claudian', shows just how fundamental the shift in power within the Roman state had become. (Tiberius came from the Claudii, one of the most ancient families of Rome. His adoption into the Julians, Augustus' adopted family, gives the dynasty its name.) When the people of Cyprus swore an oath of loyalty to Tiberius in 14 it was to the emperor 'and all his house'.

However, Tiberius was now 54. His life had been an active one, largely based in the army camps, and he had never been at ease with the senatorial aristocracy who had enjoyed more leisured lives in Rome. It appears that he was reluctant at his age to take on the range of powers held by Augustus. He would have much preferred to have shared responsibility with the senate. When, at the meeting held to confer imperial authority on him, he hesitated in accepting it, the senate felt rebuffed. Without Augustus' personal touch and authority the ambiguities of the imperial role were exposed and Tiberius never found a formula which satisfied the senators. The relationship remained uneasy, or worse, for the whole of his reign.

The people of Rome, hungry as ever for 'bread and circuses', were no better impressed. Squandering resources on shows was not Tiberius' way and the crowds focused instead on Germanicus, Tiberius' nephew, designated by Augustus as Tiberius' heir. Germanicus was campaigning along the German borders in the hope of avenging the defeat of Varus. It was a fruitless task with little in the way of long-term gains. Tiberius felt that the frontiers should be stabilized rather than extended and recalled Germanicus in AD 16. The extravagant triumph Germanicus held in Rome consolidated his reputation as the darling of the masses. Tiberius then sent him east to bring order to the client kingdoms there, but when he died in Antioch in AD 19 there were many who believed

Tiberius had connived with the local governor in poisoning him. When Tiberius, in an effort to calm the hysteria with which Germanicus' ashes were received in Rome, refused to attend their interment, his guilt seemed confirmed.

The new heir was Drusus, Tiberius' own son and his preferred successor. Tragically he died in 23. Tiberius' distress, and perhaps an increasing reluctance to appear in public when he developed a disfiguring skin disease, made him all the more isolated and in 26 he withdrew to an imperial palace on the island of Capri. Suetonius revels in the details of the supposed sex life of the elderly Tiberius, but the companions he chose to accompany him to Capri seem to have been eminently respectable. In Rome, with the senate now apparently unable to take any form of initiative, there was a power vacuum. It was filled by Sejanus, the Prefect of the Praetorian Guard. Although Sejanus was only an equestrian he was not a mere upstart. His father had been the prefect of Egypt and he had links to noble families. He was ambitious and, if Tacitus is to be believed, coldly single-minded in his pursuit of power. He grouped the Guard, the only effective military force in Italy, into one barracks on the edge of Rome, pushed aside rivals, and gained the appointment of supporters to provincial governorships. Tiberius trusted him ('my partner in toil', he described him on one occasion) and had made him fellow consul for part of the year 31. When he discovered later in that year how Sejanus was plotting to succeed him his reaction was immediate. A letter was sent to the senate denouncing Sejanus. The same senators who had fawned to him when he was the emperor's favourite now had no compunction in deserting him. He was executed the same day and his family was included so that his line would be destroyed for ever. To meet the legal requirement that a virgin could not be executed the executioner raped his young daughter before strangling her.

Tiberius was now in his seventies. Old age, isolation, and suspicion of those jockeying for power now that the succession was open made his last years ones of deepening gloom and even terror. Supporters of Sejanus were still being executed two years later. Within the imperial family two of Germanicus' sons and his widow Agrippina were executed or committed suicide. Tiberius eventually designated as joint heirs his great-nephew Gaius, the last surviving son of Germanicus, and his grandson by Drusus, Tiberius Gemellus. (It was now certain that the succession should run on dynastic lines.) He died in 37, at the age of 77. The news was greeted with rejoicing. Certainly the last years of Tiberius had been dispiriting ones overshadowing the real achievements of the reign.

The Prosperity of Italy

It was in Italy that the fruits of good administration were most enjoyed. The field survey of southern Etruria carried out by the British School at Rome shows that

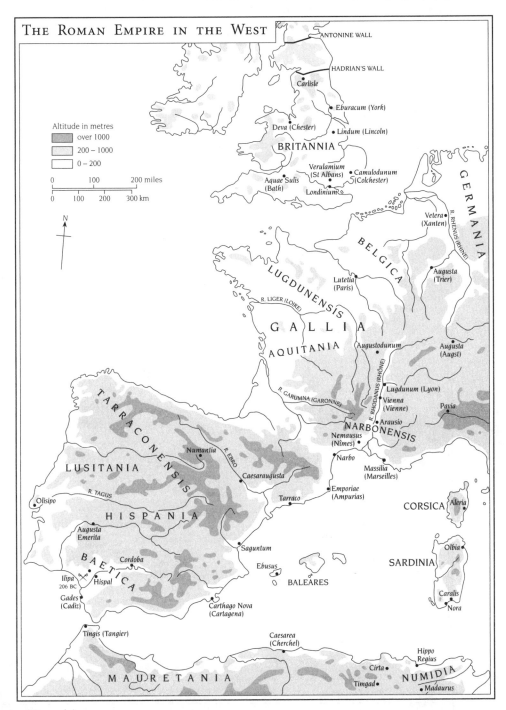

THE ROMAN EMPIRE IN THE WEST

ANTONINE WALL

HADRIAN'S WALL

Carlisle

Eburacum (York)

Deva (Chester)
Lindum (Lincoln)

BRITANNIA

Altitude in metres
- over 1000
- 200 – 1000
- 0 – 200

0   100   200 miles
0   100   200   300 km

N

Verulamium
(St Albans)
Camulodunum
(Colchester)
Aquae Sulis
(Bath)
Londinium

GERMANIA

Vetera
(Xanten)
R. RHENUS (RHINE)

BELGICA

Augusta
(Trier)

LUGDUNENSIS

Lutetia
(Paris)

R. LIGER (LOIRE)

GALLIA

AQUITANIA

Augustodunum
Augusta
(Augst)

R. GARUMNA (GARONNE)

R. RHODANUS (RHÔNE)

Lugdunum (Lyon)
Vienna
(Vienne)
Pavia

Arausio
NARBONENSIS

Nemausus
(Nîmes)
Narbo
Massilia
(Marseilles)

CORSICA
Aleria

TARRACONENSIS

Numantia
R. EBRO

Caesaraugusta

Tarraco

Emporiae
(Ampurias)

LUSITANIA

HISPANIA

R. TAGUS

Olisipo

Augusta
Emerita

BAETICA

Cordoba

Ilipa
206 BC
Hispal

Gades
(Cadiz)

Saguntum

Ebusus

BALEARES

SARDINIA

Olbia

Caralis
Nora

Carthago Nova
(Cartagena)

Tingis (Tangier)

Caesarea
(Cherchel)

Cirta

Timgad

Hippo
Regius

NUMIDIA

Madaurus

MAURETANIA

MAP 13(a)

THE ROMAN EMPIRE IN THE EAST

Augusta
(Augsberg)
Carnuntum
RAETIA
NORICUM
Aquincum
(Budapest)
DACIA
Milan
Drobeta
Pavia
Aquileia
Sirmium
Adamklissi
PANNONIA
Arretium
Ancona
ILLYRICUM
MOESIA
Salonae
(Split)
Perusia
DALMATIA
Adrianople
378 AD
Rome
Philippi THRACIA
42 BC
Capua
MACEDONIA
Doriscus
Brundisium
Thessalonica
Tarentum
Pergamu
EPIRUS
LESBOS
Actium
Thebes
CHIOS
31BC
SAMOS
Messana
Corinth
SICILIA
Athens
ACHAEA
Catana
Sparta
Agrigentum
Carthage
Syracuse
Zama
Hadrumetum
MELITA (MALTA)
202 BC
Thapsus
CRETE
BYZACENA

N

Sabratha
Oea
Leptis Magna
Ptolemais
Apollonia
Berenice
AFRICA
(Benghazi) Barca Cyrene

TRIPOLITANIA
CYRENAICA

Altitude in metres
over 1000
LIBYA
200 – 1000
0 – 200

0   100   200   300 miles
0   100   200   300   400   500 km

Map 13(b)

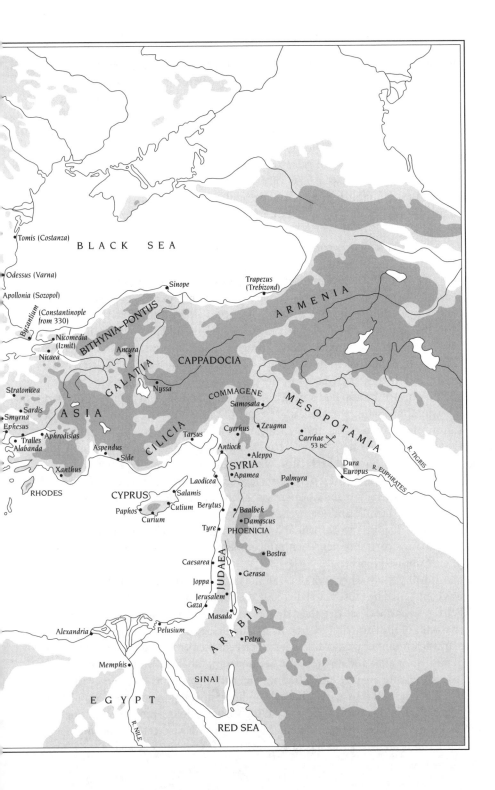

BLACK SEA

Tomis (Costanza)

Odessus (Varna)

Apollonia (Sozopol)

Byzantium (Constantinople from 330)

Nicomedia (Izmit)

Nicaea

BITHYNIA–PONTUS

Sinope

Trapezus (Trebizond)

A R M E N I A

Ancyra

GALATIA

CAPPADOCIA

Nyssa

COMMAGENE

M E S O P O T A M I A

Stratonicea

Sardis

Smyrna

Ephesus

A S I A

Aphrodisias

Tralles

Alabanda

Xanthus

CILICIA

Tarsus

Samosata

Cyrrhus

Zeugma

Carrhae
53 BC

R. TIGRIS

Aspendus

Side

Antioch

Aleppo

SYRIA

Apamea

Palmyra

Dura
Europus

R. EUPHRATES

RHODES

CYPRUS

Laodicea

Salamis

Cutium

Paphos

Curium

Berytus

Baalbek

Damascus

Tyre

PHOENICIA

Caesarea

Bostra

Joppa

Gerasa

JUDAEA

Jerusalem

Gaza

Masada

A R A B I A

Alexandria

Pelusium

Petra

Memphis

SINAI

E G Y P T

R. NILE

RED SEA

the first century saw the countryside dotted with comfortable farmhouses and the villas of a richer class. Campania, always one of the most fertile areas of Italy, thanks to its benign climate and volcanic soil, was particularly favoured. A farmhouse such as San Rocco, near Capua, meticulously excavated by the British archaeologist Molly Cotton in the 1960s, became transformed into an opulent villa during the reign of Augustus and in the first century acquired a grand new bathhouse. Its economic base was also transformed, as commercial opportunities increased. There were new olive presses and tile-making facilities. This seemed typical of much of Italy, with agriculture further boosted by the opportunities to export oil, wine, and pottery, for example, to newly pacified parts of the empire.

As richer landowners consolidated their advantages in an expanding market the distribution of wealth in Italy may, however, have become even more unequal. Not the least of the beneficiaries of imperial rule was the traditional senatorial aristocracy—one reason, perhaps, why they were so politically quiescent. A fine example, if from a slightly later period, is provided in the letters of Pliny the Younger (AD 61?–113). His estates were large and prosperous (in a good year his property in Umbria alone brought in 400,000 sestertii). Although he was busy in public life, in the law courts, as an official in the state treasury, as an augur, and, finally, as governor of the province of Bithynia-Pontus in the early second century, he also had ample time to visit his estates and enjoy a cultivated lifestyle, appreciating the peace and beauty of the countryside, reading books in sunny corners of his villas, and writing letters to friends. He was particularly sentimental about his estates around Lake Como, which had been in his family for generations. Although, like Tacitus, with whom he was friendly, Pliny was overawed by Domitian, he presents a more favourable picture of political life among the elite. His letters make no mention of the grotesque cruelties of the court detailed by Tacitus and he writes with real tenderness of his third wife, Calpurnia. This is a world where leisure brings the time to cultivate relationships. Pliny's correspondence with the emperor Trajan (see below) maintains a tone of mutual respect.

As in all periods when wealth is rapidly increasing, the traditional ruling class was confronted by those who had made their money more recently. One senator, Petronius, chose to satirize the new rich in his novel *The Satyricon*. The central character of the surviving fragments is Trimalchio. Born a slave, he boasts at an extravagant dinner party of how he was freed after satisfying the sexual desires of both his master and mistress and became joint inheritor, with the emperor, of his master's fortune. A lucky trading enterprise gave him the wherewithal to invest in land and thus ape the lifestyle of the aristocracy. In fact, he is completely out of place in their world. He is appallingly ostentatious, enjoys humiliating his slaves, and brags of the monumental tomb he will have erected to his memory, but he indicates, in an exaggerated way, the rich pickings available for a tiny minority. (There is no evidence to suggest that the life of the majority—the tenant farmer or the small peasant producer, for instance—was anything other than hard, even in this time of relative prosperity.)

Caligula

Tiberius' successor, Gaius, often known by the nickname Caligula, 'little boot', given him when he was a small boy with his father in the army camps, proved to be in character closer to Trimalchio than to Pliny. He succeeded to the imperial throne as sole ruler and was granted full imperial powers by the senate within a day, a sign of how readily the senators were prepared to acquiesce in a transfer of power, once it was clear there was no alternative successor. (Tiberius Gemellus was awarded an honorary title and then pushed aside and murdered within a year.)

The senators were soon to regret their enthusiasm. Gaius was only 24 and untried. He had never had the sobering experience of commanding an army, for instance. Now he suddenly had the enormous but still loosely defined powers of an emperor together with a vast fortune (2,300 million sestertii, it was said). He clearly felt he had to make some kind of impact as emperor and so began such a vast spending spree that most of his inheritance was exhausted within a year. In one extraordinary instance he had a bridge of boats three Roman miles long built across the Bay of Baiae, seemingly to disprove a taunt that it was impossible. Favourites—a charioteer, for example—could suddenly find themselves 2 million sestertii richer.

There was more to Gaius' behaviour than mere immaturity. He was certainly unstable with a particularly perverse sense of humour. The accounts suggest that he enjoyed dominating others, humiliating them or inflicting cruelty. He would order men to be killed 'so that they could feel they were dying' or, in one case, a famous actor to be flogged slowly so that he could hear his fine voice shrieking for longer. His power was so unlimited that he believed himself to have transcended mortal life. While Tiberius had turned down an offer from Spain to have a temple dedicated to him ('I am a mere mortal, fulfilling the duties of a man . . . men will give my memory enough,' Tacitus reports him saying), Gaius appeared dressed as a variety of gods. He ordered his head to be placed on a statue of Zeus at Olympia and outraged the Jews by ordering a similar statue for the Temple at Jerusalem.

Extravagant antics were at first popular with the Roman crowds. It was good entertainment and inevitably some of the big spending trickled down to the poor, but as the money ran out and Gaius dreamed up new taxes which fell on the urban poor his popularity quickly slumped. Among the senators disillusion had set in more quickly. Gaius treated the senate with contempt. Senators were arbitrarily accused of treason and forced to commit suicide. It soon became obvious that it was impossible to allow this perverse man in his twenties with possibly fifty years of life ahead to continue in power. With no constitutional means of removing an emperor, the only way was assassination. A conspiracy was organized by members of the Praetorian Guard with support from within the senate and in January 41 Gaius was set upon in one of the galleries of his palace and stabbed to death.

In the constitutional hiatus that followed the old republican cry of the aristocracy, *libertas*, was briefly heard in the senate house. However, the republic was by now past restoration. Once again the senate simply acquiesced in events when the Praetorian Guard proposed as the new emperor Claudius, a brother of Germanicus, whom, it was said, they had found cowering behind a curtain in the imperial palace. Whether this was true or not, Claudius recovered his composure quickly enough to reward the Guard with money, a precedent they were not to forget. That and the magic of his family name was enough to secure his succession.

The Emperor Claudius

Claudius has been immortalized in the novels *I, Claudius* and *Claudius the God*, by Robert Graves (novels brought to life in a masterful television portrayal of Claudius by Derek Jacobi). He may have been born with cerebral palsy. He was unable to control his limbs properly and faltered when he had to speak in public, though his mind was unaffected by these physical problems. In an age where public appearance was so important he had been kept by his family in the shadows and in compensation had developed a range of scholarly interests. He knew better than any emperor before him how the Roman state had evolved and seems to have acquired the conviction that he could do better than his immediate predecessors.

Claudius' weakness was that he had no centre of support, either in the senate, which felt that he had been foisted on it, or in the army, which had never seen him in command. He was to do his best to repair the position with the senators, speaking to them on frequent occasions, but he mistrusted their competence and the more traditional senators resented it when he proposed, as one of his more far-seeing policies, that leading provincials from Gaul should be admitted to the house. The uneasy relationship sometimes broke down into hostility and there were several conspiracies against him. Altogether thirty-five senators are known to have been executed during his reign.

The army offered a more satisfying opportunity. It could be used for a conquest for which Claudius, as emperor, could then take credit. An invasion of Britain had been talked of for decades. Caesar's experience had shown that undertaking the empire's first conquest across the ocean attracted all the prestige later given to launching into space. There were also more practical reasons for an invasion. Continuing power struggles between British tribes threatened the trade routes along which grain, hides, and iron were conveyed across the Channel to the armies of the Rhine and there was always the fear that one chieftain might unite Britain and confront the empire from the west. A Roman conquest would secure southern Britain, stabilize it, and provide plunder to refill the imperial treasury depleted by the extravagances of Gaius. Everything, not least Claudius' political needs, combined to make the invasion attractive.

The conquest of southern Britain was efficiently done. Forty thousand troops were ferried over the Channel in AD 43 and soon the southern part of the country was under Roman control. (Despite his own military inexperience Claudius had an aptitude for appointing sound commanders.) The emperor came from Rome, his presence made more impressive by a troop of elephants he took with him, and was in time to lead his men into the capital of the Catuvellaunian tribe at Colchester. He accepted the homage of eleven defeated chieftains. This was enough to allow him to return to Rome to throw an extravagant triumph. Claudius' small son, born in 41, was renamed Britannicus in the exultation of a victory which was proclaimed on coins throughout the empire. Claudius, like Tiberius, had no particular enthusiasm for being portrayed as a god but he did allow a temple in his honour to be built at Colchester to provide a focus for the emotions and loyalties of a people shattered by their defeat. As Claudius returned to Rome the process of pacification went on. A famous excavation by the British archaeologist Sir Mortimer Wheeler at Maiden Castle in Dorset in the 1930s was able to trace the progress of the final battle for a Celtic stronghold from the hastily dug graves of those killed in the Roman assault.

Claudius was in power for thirteen years. The business of the empire was gradually becoming more complex. In addition to Britain two more provinces in Mauretania, as well as Thrace and Lycia, were added to the empire in his reign. The emperors themselves were becoming men of vast wealth. It had become the custom for those without heirs to leave their possessions to the emperor, particularly if they had been given any patronage. Maecenas and Horace both left property to Augustus, who claimed in his will that his inheritances had totalled 1,400 million sestertii. Claudius was not greedy for more wealth and he forbade those with surviving relatives to make him their heir, but he continued nevertheless to accumulate property.

These developments, added to the failure of the senate to participate in public business, led Claudius to develop his own imperial bureaucracy. Although there is some dispute as to how exactly this worked, it seems that there were four departments, each under a freedman (whose loyalty to Claudius as their emancipator would be guaranteed). One dealt with the emperor's correspondence, one with his personal finances, and another with petitions and legal matters. The fourth was an archivist. From AD 53 imperial procurators, appointed independently of the governors and subject only to the emperor, oversaw the imperial estates. 'Good' emperors increasingly saw their wealth as there to be used for the benefit of the state as a whole. Gradually, through a process which remains obscure, the funds of the republican treasury, the *aerarium*, became merged with the private wealth of the emperor, the *fiscus*.

The consolidation of an imperial bureaucracy further diminished the role of the senate. Senators found it humiliating to have to do their business with the emperor through freedmen, especially when it became clear that these were making fortunes in the process. Narcissus, the chief secretary, reputedly ended up 400 million sestertii richer, the largest fortune recorded for any single Roman. As a further blow to senatorial prestige Claudius transferred other responsibilities, such as the regulation of the grain supply and the care of roads in Rome, to himself, continuing a trend of imperial involvement set by Augustus, but relying on equestrians rather than senators to oversee the work.

One of Claudius' concerns was the more efficient administration of Rome. By the first century Rome was a crowded, bustling, and often dangerous city with a population of perhaps a million. A city of this size was unable to support itself from a pre-industrial economy and the empire's economy and state administration was distorted to keep Rome alive and politically quiescent. It is estimated that 200,000 tonnes of grain had to be imported a year, with much of it distributed free to the poorer citizens of the city. Some of it came from the wealthier parts of Italy such as Campania but the main sources were Sicily, Sardinia, the province of Africa, and, after 30 BC, Egypt. Increasingly the emperors provided some of the grain from their own estates. The emperors took responsibility for the provision of corn through an official, the *praefectus annonae* (*annona*, the corn supply). Transport to Rome was provided by private merchants and, to induce them to provide for the city, Claudius offered privileges, including that of citizenship, to those with large ships who would sign a contract to deliver grain to Rome over six years.

These achievements have been overshadowed by the popular image of Claudius, drawn from the pages of Suetonius. This is of a man at the mercy of his unscrupulous and scheming wives. Intrigue was probably inevitable in the imperial household. Claudius was 50 when he became emperor so that succession was bound to be a live issue. His own son, Britannicus, had been born only in 41, leaving the throne open to many older cousins. His mother, Messalina, the emperor's third wife, knew that if Britannicus was pushed aside she would be as well. She freely used her sexuality to maintain her influence. (There were few alternatives for ambitious women in the male-dominated world of Roman politics.) However, in 48 she went too far and entered into some form of marriage ceremony with a young senator, Gaius Silius. This could only be seen as a blatant attempt to depose Claudius and it failed utterly. She was exposed and executed.

Claudius' next wife was Agrippina, his own niece and the daughter of his popular brother Germanicus. In political terms the marriage was a shrewd move as it consolidated the unity of the family against rivals for power. On the other hand, Agrippina had her own son who was three years older than Britannicus and thus an obvious rival for the succession. He took the all-encompassing name Nero Claudius Drusus Germanicus Caesar. Agrippina seems to have consolidated her position quickly, perhaps because Claudius' powers were failing. She had herself proclaimed Augusta, appeared as an important figure on public occasions, was represented on coins, and gave her name to at least one new Roman colony. Her main aim was to install Nero as successor. In 52 he was awarded the *toga virilis*, the mark of mature adulthood, at 13, a year early. Theoretically he could now become emperor. Britannicus would not achieve the same status until the year 55 and so it was important for Agrippina to act fast. In October 54 Claudius died, the victim, it was said, of a dish of poisonous mushrooms fed to him by Agrippina. Nero, still aged only 16, was proclaimed emperor. Britannicus, four months under age, could not succeed with him but the day before he reached the required age of 14 he died at a banquet. Nero passed off the cause of death as an epileptic fit.

Nero

Nero lives on in legend as a capricious tyrant, but he does seem to have had some kind of coherent view of himself as emperor though his model was Hellenistic rather than Roman. He probably envisaged himself living in immense splendour, enjoying a role as cultural patron. He certainly had some modest talent as a poet and musician and a genuine interest in Greek art, and he inspired what has been seen as a minor renaissance of poetry and prose writing. However, there was still prejudice against the customs of the east. When Nero founded Greek games, the Neronia, in 60, he shocked the more traditional Romans by competing in them himself and then compounded the embarrassment by expecting senators to join in as well. More seriously in Roman eyes, Nero had no military experience and showed no interest in acquiring any. The maintenance of good order in the army was left to the initiative of local commanders.

For the first years of his reign this did not matter so much. Claudius had left a stable and well-governed empire. In his leading adviser, Seneca, and the Praetorian Prefect, Burrus, Nero was well served. Between them they forced Agrippina out of the imperial palace and Seneca made conciliatory speeches to the senate which helped to smooth relationships there. In contrast to what followed these were looked on later as golden years.

Seneca is remembered as the most articulate proponent of Roman Stoicism. As has been seen (p. 351), the Stoics saw the world as one community, a single brotherhood, evolving under the benevolent care of a presiding force. The individual was both part of this force and yet also subject to it. Within a framework which he could not control he nevertheless had a role in helping to bring the whole to fruition. Unlike the Epicureans, for instance, the Stoic had a duty to take part in public life, to uphold the moral order when he could, and to endure the unfolding of events when he could not. This philosophy fitted well with traditional Roman ideals: service to the state, whatever the cost, frugality, and respect for the divine order. Virgil's Aeneas is a model of the Stoic virtues of courage, loyalty, resolution, and piety.

Stoicism was essentially a conservative and paternalistic philosophy. Stoics were expected to treat their slaves well but there was never any suggestion that slavery itself should be abolished in the name of the brotherhood of man. Yet Stoicism could also inspire resistance. The model in the republic was Cato of Utica (95–46 BC), who was unflinching in his defence of senate and republican ideals, committing suicide when he heard of Caesar's triumph over the old order. Later Stoics offered resistance to those emperors who seemed determined to upset the natural evolution of the world by their tyrannical behaviour. Both Nero and Domitian were to face the opposition of Stoics (though it has long been debated as to whether Stoics resisted because they were Stoics or became Stoics to steel their resistance).

The Stoic could appear stern and unbending. The importance of Seneca is that he humanized Stoicism. (Some, looking at his great wealth and his enjoyment of power under Nero, argue that he was all too human.) He wrote voluminously and not only on philosophy. His works include poetry and tragedies as well as scientific treatises (his main work on science, *Naturales Questiones*, was an undisputed authority until the works of Aristotle were rediscovered), and even a satire on the reign of Claudius. His philosophical works deal with such topics as anger, clemency, and what is meant by happiness. It is in his letters to his friend Lucilius, 124 of which survive, that he is most approachable. They present the ideals of Stoicism in an easy conversational style and relate them to actual events, the destruction of the city of Lugdunum (Lyons) in a fire, the everyday treatment of slaves, and how to deal with the unsettling effects of large crowds.

The hopes that Seneca would ensure stability of government proved an illusion. Nero was still very young, inexperienced, and with a childhood which had been poisoned by the morbid tensions and rivalries of the imperial family. Some of his behaviour, escapades through the streets of Rome at night, for instance, was probably no more than adolescent high spirits, and it is hardly surprising that he became impatient with his sober advisers. (Seneca was attacked publicly in 58 with the pointed challenge of explaining how his philosophical beliefs had allowed him to accumulate so much wealth.) Gradually, however, Nero's activities became more sinister. In 59, egged on by his mistress Poppaea, he decided to murder his mother. After the first attempt to drown her in a collapsible boat ended in farce she was beaten to death. In a sense this was Nero's coming of age, but the murder of a woman who was so dominant in his life must have left him with an immense psychological burden. Soon a reign of terror began. Nero's wife Octavia and, probably, Burrus were among the victims. Seneca was dismissed and later forced to commit suicide. (Whatever can be said of Seneca's lifestyle, his death as recounted by Tacitus is an exemplar for all Stoics.) When a fire destroyed much of Rome in 64 it was soon rumoured that Nero had started it. He almost certainly did not but he used as a scapegoat the small Greek-speaking Christian community of the city and persecuted them so brutally that he simply did his own image further damage. His main response to the devastated centre of Rome was the building of a vast imperial palace, the Domus Aurea, the 'Golden House', which covered the centre of Rome and was fronted by an immense statue of the emperor. (Some of the central rooms have survived.) The coinage was debased to help pay for the cost. (Archaeologists working across the German border have found that coin hoarders preferred to accumulate pre-Neronian coins.)

By now lax control at the centre of the empire was having its impact in the provinces. In Britain the callous insensitivity of a procurator had led to a massive uprising by the Iceni tribe under their chieftain, Boudicca, probably in 60. (Recent scholarship has preferred this date to Tacitus' 61.) Control was only regained at the cost of terrible retribution. In 62 a Roman army was once again humiliated by the Parthians and it took a major show of force to achieve a compromise through which Armenia was stabilized as a buffer state between Rome and the Parthian empire with the Romans forced to recognize a Parthian prince, Tiridates, as its ruler. Most formidable of all was a Jewish revolt, set off in 66 by the clumsy behaviour of a Greek governor, appointed under the influence of Poppaea. A million died in the following years as it was suppressed. This provincial unrest was masked by an extravagant display of feasting and games in 66 when Tiridates was received in Rome and formally accepted as a client king. Nero presented what was in effect a setback for Roman power in the east as a triumph for himself. In the east he was to be known as 'Lord and Saviour of the World'.

Within Rome pressure on Nero was increasing. Several plots were hatched against him, many involving respectable senators, but Nero managed to foil them all, eliminating many of his finest administrators in the process. The most effective commander of the age, and a hero to Tacitus, was Domitius Corbulo, who had not only kept order on the German frontier but then had managed a brilliant campaign in Armenia which restored Roman prestige there. Nero grew increasingly jealous of his success and ordered him to commit suicide in 67. Three other provincial governors were killed. Nero must have sensed how vulnerable his lack of military experience left him. Among the motives was his desire to increase his wealth. It was said that he had the six richest men in Africa killed so that he could gain their land, allegedly half the province, for himself.

It may have been to escape the atmosphere of hatred that the emperor decided to head east in the hope of finding an audience which would genuinely respond to his need for applause. Throughout 67 Nero toured Greece, attending the ancient games which he had rescheduled to fit in with his itinerary. Whether performing as charioteer, orator, or lyre player, he inevitably had to be awarded first prize by the overawed judges. Much of this tour was farcical but it was also the first time an emperor had taken a personal interest in Greek culture and perhaps marks the moment when the Greeks began to feel part of the empire. When he returned to Rome, laden with the crowns of his victories, Nero, significantly, celebrated with a show staged as a military triumph. Any residual loyalty in the army must have been undermined by this desecration of the most prestigious ceremony in Roman political life.

There was increasing revulsion among provincial aristocrats at Nero's unworthiness, fuelled by discontent over high taxes imposed to finance his rebuilding of Rome. In 68 a revolt broke out in Gaul. It was led by Gaius Julius Vindex, a Romanized Celtic aristocrat who had established links with the governor of one of the Spanish provinces, the 71-year-old Servius Sulpicius Galba. Galba was acclaimed as *imperator* by his troops. According to Suetonius, Nero heard of the revolt on the anniversary of his mother's death. Firm action might have saved him: the troops of Vindex were attacked by the Rhine legions and easily scattered and Galba had only one legion (although he soon raised another). However, with the fantasy world he had built around himself now crumbling, Nero panicked and set off towards the east, perhaps in a last hope that he would be welcomed there. The senate and the Praetorian Guard (once again rewarded handsomely for their pains) rallied to Galba and proclaimed him the new emperor. Nero, waiting in a suburban villa for a boat to take him from Italy, killed himself.

AD 69: A Long Year of Revolt

With Nero died the last of the Julio-Claudians. He had no obvious successor within the family and the imperial throne was there to be fought over. Autocratic rule was now the established order, no one proposed any alternative system of government, and the senate did little more than react to events. Galba threw away his advantage. He was slow to reach Rome, refused to spend money to consolidate his position, and offended almost every potential supporter. By early 69 the legions along the Rhine had revolted and declared their own candidate for the throne, the governor of the province of Lower Germany, Aulus Vitellius. In Rome, however, one of Galba's leading supporters, Marcus Salvius Otho, the governor of Lusitania and, incidentally, former husband of Nero's Poppaea, was so frustrated by events, especially when a younger senator was proposed as

Galba's heir, that he won over the Praetorian Guard, who proclaimed him emperor, and then used them to assassinate Galba in the Forum.

It now looked as if the bad days of the Republic were back with two rival army commanders fighting over the spoils of the empire. With the Julio-Claudian dynasty extinguished there was no other way of determining the succession. The conflict between Vitellius and Otho appeared to be shaping up as one between east and west. Vitellius had the support of Spain, Gaul, and Britain, Otho of Italy, Africa, and the east. In the event the war ended quickly. Vitellius' troops invaded Italy and defeated Otho at Cremona in April. Otho committed suicide. The senate dutifully proclaimed Vitellius emperor.

In his turn, however, Vitellius threw away his victory. He never built up any support beyond the legions of the Rhine and yet another contender was allowed to come forward. This was Titus Flavius Vespasianus. Vespasian had had a dazzlingly successful career, first as a commander in the invasion of Britain, then as consul, and subsequently as governor of Africa. The background of his family was modest. His Italian grandfather had been a centurion, his father a tax collector in Asia. Nero had appointed Vespasian commander to suppress the revolt in Judaea precisely because his provincial origins made him an unlikely rival. He was first proclaimed emperor by the prefect of Egypt but he found the border legions of the Danube and Syria and his own legions in Judaea and Egypt rallying to him. He made his way to Egypt knowing that he could exert pressure on Rome through threatening its grain supply. Meanwhile the legions of the Danube had taken the initiative. They marched down into Italy, defeating Vitellius' army almost at the same spot where Vitellius had defeated Otho. In a passage worthy of Thucydides, Tacitus details the appalling slaughter the victorious troops unleashed on the town of Cremona. They continued on to Rome, where civil war had broken out between the supporters of Vitellius and those of Vespasian. The Praetorian Guard, whose fickle allegiance was now to Vitellius, was wiped out and peace was finally restored by one of Vespasian's supporters, the governor of Syria, Mucianus, who had arrived in Italy with his legions. Vespasian was in his turn recognized by the senate, but showed what little respect he had for their role by dating his reign from his proclamation by the troops in Egypt. In a decree the senate meekly accepted that everything that had already been enacted by Vespasian should be legally binding.

What perhaps was most remarkable about the political struggles of the year 69 was how little they shook the institutions of the empire. Vespasian was a usurper, 'an emperor', in Tacitus' celebrated phrase, 'made elsewhere than at Rome', but he fitted without difficulty into the imperial framework. There is no evidence of any hesitation in the way the senate granted him the rights of the earlier emperors to convene and make proposals to the senators and to put forward the magistrates for formal acceptance by the increasingly impotent popular assemblies.

The Flavian Emperors

There were three Flavian emperors, Vespasian (69–79) and his sons, Titus (79–81) and Domitian (81–96). They personified a new phase in the development of the empire, one when the emperor could come from outside the traditional noble families of Rome and make his way to power through sheer merit. Vespasian was not to disappoint. He was the first emperor since Augustus to maintain good relationships with those varied constituencies, the senate, the army, and the people of Rome. Although severe in tone and cautious with his spending, he also had a sound awareness of what the empire needed—the defin-ition of boundaries, stable provincial government, and a widening of citizenship so that its subjects could be progressively drawn into loyalty.

Nero's reign and the disruption of the year 69 had left the empire unsettled. In Judaea Vespasian's son, Titus, brought the revolt to a bloody end with the capture of Jerusalem in 70. Elsewhere the most restless provinces were in the north-west, in Britain and along the Rhine, where the shattering of Vitellius' legions had left the Roman presence weaker and encouraged revolt. On the Rhine border the auxiliary troops, raised from local peoples, defected *en masse* and rallied to one Julius Civilis, a native of Germany. Julius incited local nobles to proclaim a local 'Gallic' empire. It is unclear what his motives were. In the event the empire proved to be a fantasy and soon collapsed. Nevertheless it took eight legions to restore order. These legions were then transferred to Britain, where they moved to the north, to subdue the powerful tribe of the Brigantes, and westwards into the Welsh mountains. In the early seventies the modern cities of York, Chester, and Carlisle were founded.

It was in the reigns of Vespasian and Domitian that the German borders were defined by permanent barriers. (The provinces of Upper and Lower Germany were formally constituted in the 80s.) Archaeologists have been able to plot the stages by which Roman control was pushed northwards and eastwards from the Rhine so as to forge better communications in the difficult territory between the Rhine and the Danube. A *limes*, a road, was cut through the forest with observation towers every 500 or 600 metres and small forts between them. By the 90s, if not earlier, it was complete. It was manned by auxiliary forces who, after the revolts of the early 70s, had been reconstituted under Roman officers.

As the borders were stabilized there was a gradual shift of troops from Britain and the Rhine frontier towards the Danube. There was a threat here from the Dacians. The Dacians were well established as agriculturalists in the plain of Transylvania, north of the Danube, and also exploited the iron, gold, and silver of the Carpathian mountains north of the plain. A self-confident chieftain, Decabalus, had united the local tribes under his control and shown that he had no fear of Roman power. The threat he offered meant that attempts by the governor of Britain, Agricola, to conquer Scotland had to be curtailed. A temporary fortress built in wood on the banks of the River Tay at Inchtuthil was abandoned (and, archaeological evidence suggests, dismantled about 88) and one of the four legions in Britain was transferred to the Danube some time between 85 and 92. Tacitus' biography of Agricola portrays the retreat as a betrayal typical of Domitian's high-handedness, but the conquest of the Scottish Highlands was hardly feasible at a time of danger elsewhere and Domitian's decision seems wise. Domitian was able to conduct a war against Decabalus in 88 and reduce him to the status of client king.

Vespasian was known for his distaste of extravagance but his political instincts told him when it was justified. It was during his reign that one of the great surviving monuments of ancient Rome, the Colosseum, was begun. Amphitheatres were the largest constructions undertaken by the Romans. Most were built to house 20,000–25,000 spectators though some, such as the well-preserved examples at Thysdrus (modern El Djem) in Africa and Verona, could take 30,000. The Colosseum with a capacity of 50,000 dwarfed them all. Its building was remarkable in many ways. It was built over the site of an artificial lake constructed by Nero for his Golden House, yet the foundations were laid so successfully that there is still, 2,000 years later, no trace of settlement. (By restoring land taken by Nero from the city of Rome Vespasian was in effect returning to the people what they considered theirs, and when he created a Temple to Peace to commemorate his victories in Judaea, he transferred works of art from the Golden House to it.) The building could take in and disperse its thousands of spectators efficiently while also containing the victims, both animal and human, of the slaughter they had come to see. The construction work was so effectively organized that the Colosseum was ready for service just ten years after its inception. The emperor Titus was able to throw a hundred days of inaugural games, one of which involved the sacrifice of 5,000 animals. (It was a display of munificence which proved typical of Titus' short reign. Faced with a disastrous fire in Rome, the destruction of Pompeii and Herculaneum by the eruption of Vesuvius, and plague in Italy, he proved particularly generous in his relief of suffering.)

By the first century AD, gladiator fights predominated at the games. These combats had originated in republican times, at funerals. There appears to have been a belief that the souls of the dead needed to be propitiated by human blood. A staged armed contest provided the blood. Gradually the combats became more ostentatious and figured among the public entertainments offered by aspiring politicians. Under Augustus the shows, even those held outside Rome, became associated with the largesse of the emperor and an essential part of his patronage (partly no doubt to prevent ambitious nobles upstaging him). At the dedication of the Colosseum Titus had 3,000 gladiators on hand and Trajan celebrated his victory over the Dacians with 123 days of games with a total of 10,000 men involved. Alongside men came a constant need for animals—tiger, crocodile, giraffe, lynx, rhinoceros—the more exotic the better so that ever more bizarre battles between men and beasts (these animal shows were known as *venationes*) could be staged.

The world of the gladiator was a strange one. Many gladiators were condemned criminals and their deaths in the arena simply a form of execution, others were prisoners of war or former slaves. They were carefully trained by a *lanista*, who might be a retired gladiator himself and in the arena could be presented in various ways. The *murmillo* was heavily armed with a long shield, visored helmet, and a short sword, the *retiarius* wore hardly any armour but had a net and trident while the Thracian had a round shield and a carved scimitar. Successful gladiators would become celebrities and their skills might earn them pardons, even when they had been technically defeated in a battle, so that they went on to have distinguished careers from one games to the next. The courage involved and the aura of physical strength and sexual potency was so powerful that many ordinary Romans were attracted by the profession. Senators and equestrians had to be forbidden by law from debasing themselves in this way.

Alongside the southern side of the Palatine Hill where the emperors had their palaces was the Circus Maximus, founded in Rome by the Etruscans as a circuit for chariot racing. It is now a deserted and rather desolate site and it is hard to imagine that in its final form, in about AD 105, it was over 600 metres long and 140 wide with a capacity of 150,000 spectators, three times the number who could fit into the nearby Colosseum. 'It amazes me', wrote Pliny the Younger, a senator and provincial governor, 'that thousands and thousands of grown men should be like children, wanting to look at horses running and men standing on chariots again and again', but they did. In a typical day's racing there would be twenty-four races and, with four horses to a chariot, each race would need forty-eight horses, over 1,150 in total. The demand for horses was so heavy, in fact, that whole herds of wild horses were set aside to help the emperors to meet it. The tight circuit and the use of four horses to a chariot ensured that this was a risky sport but it must have been thrilling to watch. As with most aspects of Roman life the proceedings were highly ritualized, with processions of the gods before the contests began and ceremonies to mark the victories of the drivers who, like successful gladiators, became major celebrities.

The gladiatorial contests and other games were not just shows for the public's amusement. They were also political events, ones in which the emperor confronted his people in a way which was no longer possible elsewhere now that the popular assemblies had lost their powers. (There is no record of the *concilium plebis* meeting after the end of the century.) The emperor was expected to attend (at the Circus Maximus he had a box on the edge of the Palatine Hill), be attentive to the proceedings, and listen to any complaints expressed by the crowd. In his decision as to whether to allow wounded gladiators to live or die he exercised an absolute power. 'It was', as Keith Hopkins remarks, 'a dramatic enactment of imperial power repeated several times a day before a mass audience of citizens, conquerors of the world.'

The emperors fulfilled their role with varying degrees of enthusiasm. Augustus was always correct and punctilious in his attendance, aware that Caesar had attracted a bad reputation by conducting his official correspondence while in his box. He actually enjoyed the games. Tiberius was less enthusiastic and attended only out of duty, while Gaius, typically, lost his temper when he felt the crowd was supporting the gladiators rather than himself. Claudius, on the other hand, was so enthusiastic about the games that his behaviour was considered to lack the decorum required of an emperor.

Like Claudius before him, Vespasian involved equestrians more fully in the administration of the empire but he appears to have done this without offending the sensitivities of senators. The equestrian class was large and drawn from the same wealthy and educated landowning groups as the senators. It thus represented no threat to the established order. Equestrians were much more socially acceptable as administrators to the provincial notables than freedmen and it made good sense to draw on their skills, a process which was to continue over the next centuries. While Vespasian did this without losing his good relationship with the senate, Domitian, who was altogether less sensitive than his father, flaunted his use of equestrians, even allowing them to sit in judgement over senators. It was only one of many ways in which he earned the hatred of the senators. He was arrogant and autocratic by nature, preferring to be addressed as 'Lord God'. He took the old republican office of censor, with its right to control the membership of the senate, permanently, and he used it to rid himself of those he disliked or feared. He was particularly suspicious of foreign cults such as Judaism and Christianity but his increasing absolutism also aroused opposition from conventional senators inspired by Stoicism. Such a man was better appreciated by the army, and outside Rome the empire was well administered and maintained. However, the antagonism to him in Rome itself became so acute that a conspiracy to kill him was hatched by disaffected senators, the Praetorian Prefects, and Domitian's own household. He was stabbed to death within his palace in September 96. In its exultation the senate ordered that every reference to him on public monuments should be erased.

Trajan: The Model Emperor

The conspirators had been shrewd enough to designate a successor, Marcus Cocceius Nerva, an elderly senator of impeccable lineage whose career had been one of modest achievement but whose geniality and mildness had offended no one. It was felt he could be trusted to deal well with the senate and provide a period of calm after the terror of Domitian's last years. He succeeded. He was conciliatory and unobtrusive, attempting in his short reign to stabilize the empire's finances and restore good working relations between the emperor, senate, and people of Italy (whose tax burden he seems to have lightened). Whether he would have survived in the long term is more questionable and his wisest move was to have a strong successor already installed as joint emperor at the time of his death in January 98.

The new emperor was Marcus Ulpius Traianus, known to history as Trajan. Trajan's family was not unknown among the ruling families of Rome, as his father had been a consul and governor of Syria, but its origins were long-established settler stock in Spain. His accession marked a further widening of the circle from which emperors could be drawn and once again the choice proved more than justified. Trajan was to be extolled down the ages as the ideal emperor, the monarch that medieval rulers took as their example. He adopted Hercules, with his image of perpetual labour for the good of the community, as his model but also allowed himself to be portrayed on his coins with Jupiter. He intertwined respect for the emperor with that for the traditional gods of Rome, and temples to Jupiter built in his reign typically also display a dedication to the emperor.

When he was appointed emperor Trajan was governor of Upper Germany and it is interesting that he lingered there for over a year before returning to Rome. Ostensibly he was securing the borders but he was probably boosting his reputation as a military commander, now that that seemed an essential attribute of a successful emperor. (It would give him prestige with the senators and the support of troops who could effectively prevent a challenge to him.) It was a sign, too, that the business of an emperor was no longer necessarily centred on Rome. Trajan marks the shift towards the emperor as one who is expected to confront Rome's enemies in person. He was back again in the north for the winter of 98–9 and then again in 101 to launch an invasion of Dacia.

The senator Pliny, who had shared the common hatred of his class for Domitian, rejoiced at this new emperor and eulogized him for the efficient way he dealt with his business:

We see how he meets the desires of the provinces and even the requests of individual cities. He makes no difficulty about giving them a hearing or delaying in replying. They come into his presence promptly and are dismissed promptly, and at last the emperor's doors are no longer besieged by a mob of embassies who have been shut out.   (Translation: Betty Radice)

A famous correspondence between Trajan and Pliny, when the latter was governor of Bithynia and Pontus, illustrates Trajan's attention to the smallest detail. He shows no irritation in dealing with a range of queries. He was assiduous in intervening in the affairs of cities, settling disputes and telling them how to

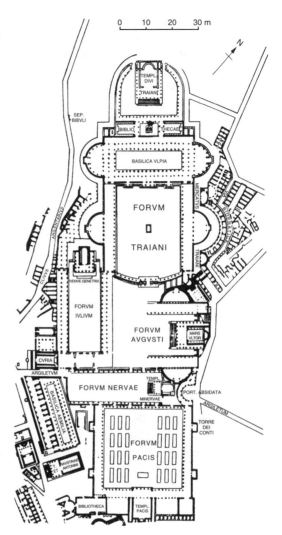

FIG. 6 The Imperial Fora. Trajan used the plunder of his Dacian campaign to construct an enormous new Forum, complete with basilica and library, to the north of those fora already constructed in memory of Caesar (Forum Iulium) and by Augustus to commemorate his victories. It was this massive array of public buildings which was to so overwhelm the emperor Constantius when he visited Rome for the first time in AD 357.

arrange their affairs. He was in fact a paternalist and the most famous example of his concern is the system of *alimenta* instituted by him in Italy. Farmers could apply for loans from the imperial treasury at 5 per cent interest (instead of the usual 12 per cent). The interest was then placed in a special account and used to pay for grain rations for the children of the poor.

Trajan also proved to be the last great conqueror of the Roman empire. His reasons for extending Roman rule over Dacia, the kingdom north of the Danube, and into Parthia, where he added two new provinces to the empire, may be linked to his desire to enhance his military reputation. However, the campaigns were also justifiable on the grounds that both kingdoms offered a threat to Rome. Decabalus was still set on revenge of his defeat by Domitian and probably no emperor could have left him unchallenged. Trajan fought two wars in Dacia, in 101–2 and 105–6. The first war ended in an armed truce, the second in the complete defeat of the Dacians. Decabalus' royal palace was sacked, he himself was killed, and his head sent back in triumph to Rome. Following it was plunder in silver and gold on a scale reminiscent of the great republican conquests. Scenes from the campaign—the bridging of the Danube, the assault on the Dacian capital, the setting up of camps—are portrayed on Trajan's column, which still stands in Rome. It provides the most vivid picture to survive of the Roman army in action. Dacia was incorporated as a province in 106 and the Transylvanian plain soon attracted settlers.

In the east Trajan had strengthened the frontier by incorporating Nabataea into the empire as the new province of Arabia. When a new dispute with Parthia over Armenia arose in 110 this made an invasion of Parthia all the easier. Whether the emperor, now buoyed up by his success in Dacia, was simply after glory (as the original sources suggest) or whether he was prudently aiming at the cowing of another enemy of Rome remains disputed. In its early days the campaign was a success. Armenia was overrun and made into a province and then Trajan extended Roman control over Mesopotamia, established as another province, and further south towards the Persian Gulf. As with other Roman commanders Trajan's model was Alexander, and when at the end of his Parthian campaign (116) he reached the mouth of the Euphrates he is said to have wept that he could go no further and equal the exploits of his hero. It was simply not feasible to do so. The newly incorporated territories were restless and there was also trouble elsewhere in the empire, tribal uprisings in Britain, a Jewish rebellion, and unrest on the lower Danube. In any case Trajan was ailing. He died in 117.

Hadrian

The succession of the next emperor, Hadrian (ruled 117–38), proved controversial. Hadrian was a cousin of Trajan's (and also his great-nephew by marriage). He was certainly the most favoured of Trajan's associates and had the advantage of being in command of the eastern armies. He also claimed that he had been officially designated his successor by Trajan on his deathbed. While he was still in the east four senators appeared to challenge his succession in Rome and they were executed. It is not known whether Hadrian was involved in their deaths but it proved an episode which permanently damaged his relationship with the senate.

It may never have been a stable one in any case. Hadrian was a versatile but restless man. His character has proved impossible to fathom. 'Changeable, manifold, fickle, born as if to be a judge of vice and virtues, controlling his passionate spirit by some kind of artifice, he expertly concealed his envious, unhappy and wanton character, immoderate in his urge for display; feigning self-restraint, affability and mildness and disguising his desire for glory' was the account of one who was clearly exasperated by him. He was certainly much happier away from Rome. No less than twelve of his twenty-one years of rule were spent in the provinces. After two or three years in Rome he embarked on a tour which lasted five years. It took in Gaul, the German border, Britain, Spain, Mauretania, and finally two years in Greece, the emperor's favourite part of the empire. (The god to whom he felt closest was the Olympian Zeus and several hundred statues or altars are known to have been dedicated to him in this role.) He returned to Italy in 126 but between 128 and 134 he was away again. This time his travels included Greece but also Egypt and Palestine, where he refounded Jerusalem, a deserted site since 70, as a Roman colony. (The intrusion on to this sacred site led to yet another Jewish uprising, suppressed in the usual ruthless way.)

Hadrian is remembered above all as a builder. In Rome there is the Pantheon, and his mausoleum (now the Castel San Angelo). Outside Rome is his villa at Tivoli where his eastern tastes were allowed full sway. (See further Interlude Seven.) However, he was a benefactor throughout the empire. Many cities, particularly those in the east, enjoyed his patronage (200 benefactions in no less than 150 cities have been recorded) and Athens gained a whole new suburb through his generosity. In short, his patronage was critical in fostering the integration of the Greek provinces more fully into the empire. When his beloved favourite Antinous was drowned in the Nile, Hadrian decreed that he should be worshipped as a god and throughout the empire thousands of statues of Antinous were produced, as permanent reminders of the emperor's loss.

However, Hadrian was more than just a builder and cultural inspiration. He recognized that the empire was becoming overstretched and it was vital that it should be settled within defensible frontiers. He quickly surrendered Trajan's conquests in the east (it may have been this that affronted the senators who conspired against him) and established the first unbroken border fortifications. A wooden palisade was constructed between the Rhine and the Danube and this was followed by one of his most famous creations, Hadrian's Wall, crossing northern Britain from sea to sea. One of the implications of the settled borders was that the army's role became more limited and thus there was a risk of declining morale. Hadrian understood this and there are surviving accounts of him inspecting troops and insisting on regular manoeuvres to maintain discipline.

One consequence of Hadrian's continuous travels was that imperial decision-making was consolidated independently of the senate in Rome. When they were in Rome the more sensitive emperors worked with the senate. The normal practice was for the emperor to outline a desired policy and for the senate then to accede to it. The fiction was maintained that the senate was involved in the making of policy (and it continued to make decisions on its own account when the emperor was not present). However, by Hadrian's reign it is clear that the emperor's decisions on matters brought to him directly were now also considered to have the force of law. Such decisions were known as rescripts and some of Hadrian's are quoted in Justinian's great Digest of Roman law (see p. 637). The range of matters an emperor dealt with were wide and there was certainly no area of public life to which the senate could any longer claim exclusivity. A possibly ironical comment attributed to Tacitus sums it up well. 'What need is there for long speeches in the senate when the top people come swiftly to agreement? What need for endless harangues at public meetings, now that policy is settled not by the inexperienced masses but by a supremely wise man and one alone?' Increasingly the magistracies became ceremonial posts whose main function was the demanding one of distributing largesse and games. The philosopher Epictetus wrote:

If you want to be consul you must give up your sleep, run around, kiss men's hands . . . send gifts to many and daily tokens to some. And what is the result? Twelve bundles of rods [the fasces carried by the twelve lictors, the consul's attendants] sitting three or four times in the tribunal, giving games in the circus and distributing meals in little baskets.   (Translation: Fergus Millar)

These posts were, however, important as stepping-stones to governorships and military commands.

The 'Good' Emperor

An adviser to the Roman emperor Marcus Aurelius, Marcus Aurelius Fronto, listed the duties of a Roman emperor as follows: 'to correct the injustices of the law; to send letters to all parts of the globe; to bring compulsion to bear on kings of foreign nations; to repress by edicts the faults of the provincials, give praise to good actions, quell the seditious and terrify the fierce ones'.

There was by this time a paradigm of a good emperor. He should work tirelessly in the service of the state and be resolute in the maintenance of public order and in the defence of the empire. He should be sensitive to those with ancient privileges, such as senators, and munificent in the giving of games and benefactions to cities. In the old traditions of the republican magistracies he was expected to be approachable. There is a good story of Hadrian who was petitioned by a woman as he was passing by on a journey. He said he had no time to hear her. 'Then, stop being emperor,' she retorted. To his credit Hadrian turned to listen to her. He and his successor, Antoninus Pius, made some modest attempts to bring humanity into the law. Hadrian is supposed to have forbidden the castration of slaves and the practice of shackling agricultural slaves in 'prisons'. Antoninus tightened the conditions under which torture might be used. One of the finest reliefs of this period (now in the Palazzo dei Conservatori in Rome), shows the emperor Marcus Aurelius extending clemency to defeated enemies.

The very quality of the Marcus Aurelius relief, which is one of a set, shows the importance of imperial propaganda. It was not only that the emperor had to be capable in practice, he had to continually remind his subjects of the fact. So in eastern cities such as Ephesus and Aphrodisias there are major cultural projects honouring particular emperors. In Aphrodisias, which benefited greatly from imperial patronage in the first century AD, the Julio-Claudian family is honoured in the Sebasteion (the name derived from *sebastos*, the Greek equivalent of the Latin Augustus), a complex which unites cult worship of Aphrodite (the Roman Venus from whom the Julio-Claudians claimed inheritance) with the imperial family itself. On one relief Claudius is shown personally vanquishing a personified Britannia, a good example of how the conquest of this distant province was presented to the people of the eastern empire. In Ephesus an altar to Lucius Verus (who ruled as emperor AD 161–9 alongside Marcus Aurelius) presents three generations of the Roman imperial family in their roles as protectors of the eastern empire, the stress being as much on the continuity of the family as on their role as defenders. (The fragments of the altar are now in the Kunsthistorische Museum in Vienna.) Often these commissions were paid for by local notables and underline how the generosity of the emperors was proclaimed as much by subjects of the empire as by the emperors themselves. It was this common interest of emperors and the provincial elites in sustaining imperial power which underpinned the survival of the empire. (See the following chapter for a fuller treatment of this theme.)

While legitimacy as emperor could be earned through success in war, the acclamation of troops and the acquiescence of the senate, an emperor would normally seek to install his own heirs as his successors. As will be seen this remained as important in the fourth and fifth centuries AD as in the first and second. The emperor also needed to assert his legitimacy as the one favoured by the gods. This was stressed through the development of the imperial cult through which the emperor was seen as a divine figure largely because of his seemingly boundless power. The emperor's name was normally linked to the traditional gods of Rome. In the province of Africa it was common for a temple to the three gods of the Capitol, Jupiter, Juno, and Minerva, to be inscribed with the name of the emperor as well, and joint dedications to the Divine Augustus (or another emperor) and Rome were common. Gradually the emperor's name became integrated in all major religious rituals, appropriated as it were as a talisman for the security of the state. By the third century a calendar of festivals celebrated by the garrison at Dura-Europus on the Euphrates, in the far east of the empire, was made up largely of anniversaries of the accessions, deifications, or victories of emperors. By the end of this century emperors such as Diocletian are stressing their relationship with a favoured god, in Diocletian's case Jupiter, although as the emperor drew closer to the chosen god, whether pagan, or in the later empire, Christian, so he became more removed from his subjects, no longer a Hadrian, accessible personally to his subjects, but a personification, 'Your Majesty', 'Your Serenity' or even 'Your Severity', and approaches to him in his audience halls were ritualized so as to preserve his remoteness. (See further p. 560.)

Underlying all this was the emperor as successful warlord. Tradition and the practical politics of governing a far-flung empire made this the central role, the one on which ultimately success depended and Hadrian's successors were to be sorely tested by events to come.

FURTHER READING

Reading on Chapters 25–8. Colin Wells, *The Roman Empire* (2nd edition, London, 1992), comprehensive and with a fine bibliography. Martin Goodman, *The Roman World 44 BC–AD 180* (London, 1997). John Wacher (ed.), *The Roman World* (London, 1987), is a two-volume survey of most aspects of the empire (cited from now on as Wacher). F. Millar, *The Roman Empire and its Neighbours* (London, 1967) and P. Garnsey and R. Saller, *The Roman Empire: Economy, Society and Culture* (London, 1987), also provide excellent overviews.

For Tacitus see R. Mellor, *Tacitus* (London, 1993). The older classical study not just of Tacitus but on the age in which he lived is R. Syme, *Tacitus* (Oxford, 1958). See also T. Wiedemann, *The Julio-Claudian Emperors* (London, 1989). F. Millar, *The Emperor in the Roman World, 31 BC–AD 337* (London, 1977), is essential. On ruler worship, in addition to Price (Further reading, p. 464), an overview is provided by J. Ferguson in chapter 31 (vol. ii) of Wacher. On individual emperors see B. Levick, *Tiberius the Politician* (London, 1976); A. Barrett, *Caligula: The Corruption of Power* (London, 1989); B. Levick, *Claudius* (London, 1990). On the conquest of Britain see P. Salway, *The Oxford Illustrated History of Roman Britain* (Oxford, 1993). On Nero, a fine study is Miriam Griffin, *Nero, the End of a Dynasty* (London, 1984); see also Miriam Griffin on Seneca, *Seneca: A Philosopher in Politics* (Oxford, 1976). K. Wellesley deals with the events of AD 69 in *The Long Year, AD 69* (London, 1975). For the later emperors see B. W. Jones, *The Emperor Titus* and *The Emperor Domitian* (London, 1984 and 1992), and B. Levick, *Vespasian* (London, 1999). On Trajan see J. Bennett, *Trajan, Optimus Princeps* (2nd edition, London, 2001) and on Hadrian Anthony Birley, *Hadrian, the Restless Emperor* (London, 1997) is excellent.

On the empire itself Janet Huskinson (ed.), *Experiencing Rome: Culture, Identity and Power in the Roman Empire* (London, 2000), is the best starting point. Andrew Lintott, *Imperium Romanum: Politics and Administration* (London, 1993), is a scholarly analysis of the empire's administration. See also Susan Mattern, *Rome and the Enemy: Imperial Strategy in the Principiate* (Berkeley, 1999), for a rethinking of the aims of Roman foreign policy. See also the relevant chapters in Wacher. Greg Woolf, *Becoming Roman* (Cambridge, 1998), is important. See also Mary Boatwright, *Hadrian and the Cities of the Roman Empire* (Princeton, 2000). An introduction to Roman law is provided by J. Crook, *The Law and Life of Rome* (London, 1967). On roads see R. Chevallier, *Roman Roads* (London, 1976). The Iceni revolt is covered in Salway's *Roman Britain*, cited above. Garnsey and Saller, cited above, deal with the question of status in the empire (in chapter 6). On citizenship, in addition to the standard work, A. N. Sherwin-White, *Roman Citizenship* (2nd edition, Oxford, 1973), see the essay by M. Hassall, 'Romans and Non-Romans', in Wacher (vol. ii). There is an essay on the Romanization of elites in P. Brunt, *Imperial Themes* (Oxford, 1990).

The standard introduction to the army is G. Webster, *The Roman Imperial Army of the First and Second Centuries AD* (3rd edition, London, 1985). See also J. Campbell, *The Emperor and the Roman Army* (Oxford, 1984) and the chapters in Part 3 (vol. i) of Wacher. See also Anthony Birley, *Garrison Life at Vindolanda* (Stroud, 2002). Detailed descriptions of the empire's frontiers are also provided in Wacher (vol. i) but for the east see B. Isaac, *The Limits of Empire: The Roman Empire in the East* (Oxford, 1990). For Hadrian's Wall see S. Johnson, *Hadrian's Wall* (London, 1989). On the Romans and Celts see Barry Cunliffe, 'The Impact of Rome on Barbarian Society, 140 BC to AD 300', in Cunliffe (ed.), *The Oxford Illustrated Prehistory of Europe* (Oxford, 1994). For a fuller account see Cunliffe's *Greeks, Romans, and Barbarians: Spheres of Interaction* (London, 1988), and see also M. Todd, *The Northern Barbarians, 100 BC–AD 300* (revised edition, Oxford, 1987). For the strategy of the empire see the stimulating but controversial E. Luttwak, *The Grand Strategy of the Roman Empire* (London, 1983). On the particular problems of language J. N. Adams, *Bilingualism and the Latin Language* (Cambridge, 2003).

On particular provinces. Italy: T. Potter, *Roman Italy* (London, 1987). On changing land use in Italy see T. Potter, *The Changing Landscape of South Etruria* (London, 1979), and, for the villa at San Rocco, M. Cotton and G. Metraux, *The San Rocco Villa at Francolise* (Rome, 1985). Pompeii and Herculaneum are covered in M. Grant, *Cities of Vesuvius: Pompeii and Herculaneum* (London, 1971). See also the catalogue of an exhibition of the latest finds, *Rediscovering Pompeii* (Rome, 1990), and Paul Zanker, *Pompeii, Public and Private Life* (Cambridge, Mass., 1998). On Africa: Susan Raven, *Rome in Africa* (London, 1969), and D. J. Mattingly, *Tripolitania* (London, 1995); on Britain, Peter Salway, already cited above. On Gaul see J. Drinkwater, *Roman Gaul: The Three Provinces 58 BC–AD 260* (London, 1983). E. Wightman, *Gallia Belgica* (London, 1985), is regarded as a classic study and there is also A. King, *Roman Gaul and Germany* (London, 1990). On Spain there is S. Keay, *Roman Spain* (London, 1988), and on Greece S. Alcock, *Graecia Capta: The Landscapes of Roman Greece* (Cambridge, 1993). On the east F. Millar, *The Roman Near East, 31 BC–AD 337* (Cambridge, Mass., 1993). For Egypt see A. Bowman, *Egypt after the Pharaohs, 322 BC–AD 642* (London, 1986) and N. Lewis, *Life in Egypt under Roman Rule* (Oxford, 1983).

On gladiators T. Wiedemann, *Emperors and Gladiators* (London, 1992) but see also the chapter in Keith Hopkins, *Death and Renewal* (Cambridge, 1983). J. Carcopino, *Daily Life in Ancient Rome* (originally New Haven, 1940, also Harmondsworth, 1956), and J. Balsdon, *Life and Leisure in Ancient Rome* (London, 1969) have lasted well. Andrea Giardina has edited a series of essays on different types of Romans in *The Romans* (Chicago, 1993). On slavery Keith Bradley, *Slavery and Society at Rome* (Cambridge, 1994) provides an excellent overview. For patronage see A. Wallace-Hadrill (ed.), *Patronage in Ancient Society* (London, 1990).

On cities see articles in Wacher, Part 5 (vol. i) but for a general overview see E. Owens, *The City in the Greek and Roman World* (London, 1991). A well-received popular introduction is J. Stambaugh, *The Ancient Roman City* (Baltimore, 1988).

The empire's economy. M. Finley, *The Ancient Economy* (Berkeley, 1973), set off a major debate. Keith Hopkins's views on the debate are usefully summarized in his introduction to P. Garnsey, K. Hopkins, and C. Whittaker, *Trade in the Ancient Economy* (Berkeley, Calif., 1983). See now David Mattingly and John Salmon (eds.), *Economies beyond Agriculture in the Classical World* (London, 2001). R. Duncan-Jones has attempted to provide accurate statistical background for the Roman economy. His calculations are to be found in *The Economy of the Roman Empire: Quantitative Studies* (2nd edition, Cambridge, 1982) and more recently in *Structure and Scale in the Roman Economy* (Cambridge, 1990). A longer overview is now provided by K. Randsborg, *The First Millennium* AD *in Europe and the Mediterranean: An Archaeological Essay* (Cambridge, 1991). On farming the chapter 'Agriculture and Horticulture' by S. Rees in Wacher (vol. ii) is a good introduction but K. White, *Roman Farming* (London, 1970) is the older standard work. The grain supply to Rome is dealt with by Peter Garnsey in *Trade in the Ancient Economy*, cited above. For an analysis of one port see G. Milne, *The Port of Roman London* (London, 1985). The shipwreck evidence is dealt with by A. Parker, *Shipwrecks of the Mediterranean and Roman Provinces* (Oxford, 1992). The standard work on the villa is J. Percival, *The Roman Villa* (London, 1976) and he has written the chapter in Wacher (vol. ii). There is a good essay on 'Townships and Villages' by Andrew Poulter in vol. i of Wacher.

On the sophists, G. Bowerstock, *Greek Sophists in the Roman Empire* (Oxford, 1969), is the standard introduction. Now Simon Swain, *Hellenism and Empire, Language, Classicism and Power in the Greek World, AD 50–250* (Oxford, 1996) is important and new thinking is to be found in Simon Goldhill (ed.), *Being Greek under Rome* (Cambridge, 2001). On Plutarch see C. Jones, *Plutarch and Rome* (Oxford, 1971). For the Second Sophistic in art see J. Elsner, *Imperial Rome and Christian Triumph* (Oxford, 1998).

26 | Administering and Defending the Empire

In his *Agricola*, Tacitus imagined the speech of a British chieftain to his men:

Plunderers of the world, they [the Romans] are, and now, that there is no more territory left to occupy their hands which have already laid the world waste, they are scouring the seas. If the enemy is rich, he is termed greedy; if the enemy is poor, he is dubbed as power hungry. Neither east nor west has been able to sate them. Alone of all men they covet rich nations and poor nations with equal passion. They rob, they slaughter, they plunder—and they call it 'empire'. Where they make a wasteland they call it 'peace'. (Translation: Jo-Ann Shelton)

Maintaining Control

As Tacitus acknowledged, the Roman empire had been won and, in the last resort, was held by force. Control was not imposed easily. Spain suffered nearly 200 years of campaigning before it was finally subdued and even provinces which appeared peaceful might still rise in revolt. An example was the great rebellion in Judaea in AD 66 which began with the massacre of a Roman garrison in Caesarea and then spread to the whole of Palestine. It was fuelled by the strong sense of national identity preserved by the Jews and by tensions between rich and poor. By the time Jerusalem was stormed by Titus in 70 the Romans may have inflicted a million casualties. Those insurgents who were captured alive were distributed as victims to the amphitheatres of the east (600 of the fittest were reserved for Rome) and the treasures of the Temple carried off as booty. (Some of them, including the great candelabrum, can still be seen portrayed on the triumphal arch of Titus in Rome.) Lingering resistance in the mountain fortress of Masada continued until 74 when, according to the historian Josephus, its last defenders committed mass suicide. (In their honour Israeli tank crews were for many years sworn in on the site.) Around the fortress the remains of a carefully built ramp and a ring of army camps still show the methodical and determined approach of the Romans to warfare and suppression of revolt. A second Jewish revolt in 132–5 was crushed with equal brutality.

The suppression of the Jewish revolts showed that the earlier traditions of ruthlessness were not dead. Officially the day-to-day administration of the empire was less brutal. The process of punishment was regulated and restrained by law. In the provinces the governor alone had the right to pass a capital sentence, while citizens maintained the right to appeal to the emperor, in his role as tribune, in Rome. However, all the evidence suggests that violence was routine in the conduct of the administration. Suetonius' and Tacitus' histories preserve the memory of the megalomanic behaviour of Caligula and Nero against their subjects and the lives of Tiberius and Domitian also ended in reigns of terror. Non-citizens had no protection against the arbitrary decisions of magistrates and there is evidence that governors would order executions to appease local pressure groups (the trial and crucifixion of Jesus on the authority of Pontius Pilate can be viewed in this context) or simply to clear overcrowded gaols.

Capital punishment was used not only to eliminate undesirables but to act as an example to others. Crucifixions provided a slow death in public. The execution of criminals was institutionalized as public display on a far greater scale in the arena. Seneca visited the amphitheatre one day just as the latest crop of criminals was being dealt with:

All niceties were put aside, and it was pure and simple murder. The combatants have absolutely no protection. Their whole bodies are exposed to one another's blows and thus each never fails to injure his opponent. Most people in the audience prefer this type of match to the regular gladiators. The spectators demand that combatants who have killed their opponents be thrown to combatants who will in turn kill them, and they make a victor stay for another slaughter. For every combatant, therefore, the outcome is certain death. (Translation: Jo-Ann Shelton)

The use of terror as example was deeply embedded in the Roman mind. Like most societies of the ancient world Rome was very brutal, but the brutality was carried out with more efficiency than in most. In the original conquests of the empire one defiant city was often singled out for particularly harsh treatment in an attempt to cow the rest into quick submission. The same procedure was used to keep order at home. When a slave murdered his master, for instance, it was the custom to execute all the other slaves in the household. In AD 61 the wealthy City Prefect Lucius Pedanius Secundus was murdered by one of his slaves. He had 400 altogether and once news spread that all of them, including women and children, were to be put to death crowds gathered to protest. The matter was debated in the senate. The depth and rigidity of Roman conservatism can be seen in the speech of Gaius Cassius Longinus, quoted by Tacitus:

When wiser men have in past times considered and settled the whole matter, will you dare refute them? . . . The only way to keep down this scum is by intimidation. Innocent people will die, you say. Yes, and when in a defeated army every tenth man is flogged to death, the brave have to draw lots with the others. Exemplary punishment always contains an element of injustice. But individual wrongs are outweighed by the advantage to the community. (Translation: Michael Grant)

His views prevailed. The unlucky 400 were led off to execution with the Praetorian Guard called out to line the route and hold off the protesting crowd.

Records of the persecutions of Christians (covered in Chapter 29) suggest that torture and ill-treatment of suspects was routine. When Lucius, the hero of Apuleius' novel *The Golden Ass* (second century AD), is suspected of murder, instruments of torture, including hot coals and a rack, are produced in order to force him to reveal the names of his accomplices.

The Administration of the Provinces

The Romans had never shown any hesitation in declaring that their wars of conquest were justified and they showed a similar confidence in their right to rule others. In his *Res Gestae* Augustus boasted of 'the achievements by which he subjected the whole world to the *imperium* of the Roman people'. His confidence in Rome's destiny found justification in the famous words of Virgil in Book VI of the *Aeneid*.

> Others will cast more tenderly in bronze
> Their breathing figures, I can well believe,
> And bring more lifelike portraits out of marble;
> Argue more eloquently, use the pointer
> To trace the paths of heaven accurately
> And accurately foretell the rising stars.
> Roman, remember by your strength to rule
> Earth's people—for your arts are to be these:
> To pacify, to impose the rule of law,
> To spare the conquered, battle down the proud.
>
> (Translation: Robert Fitzgerald)

The beginnings of provincial rule have been covered earlier (Chapters 20–3). In the early years there were few restraints on plunder. The election system made it inevitable that governorships would be used to recoup election expenses and individual governors went well beyond fulfilling this need. The misdeeds of Gaius Verres, the corrupt governor of Sicily between 73 and 70 BC, stand out because of the remorseless way they were catalogued by Cicero in his celebrated speeches of prosecution. Cicero details the exactions which were possible:

I affirm [said Cicero] that in the whole of Sicily, in a province which is so wealthy and old, which has so many towns and so many rich family estates, there is no silver vase, neither Corinthian nor Delian, no gem or pearl, no object of gold or of ivory, no bronze, marble or ivory statue, no picture either painted on a tablet or woven on a tapestry, which he has not sought out, inspected, and, if it pleased him, stolen. (Translation: John Boardman)

It was common for governors to collaborate with the equestrian *publicani* who collected the taxes, if only to acquire valuable allies to support them if prosecuted. The depth of resentment which resulted can be seen in the alacrity with

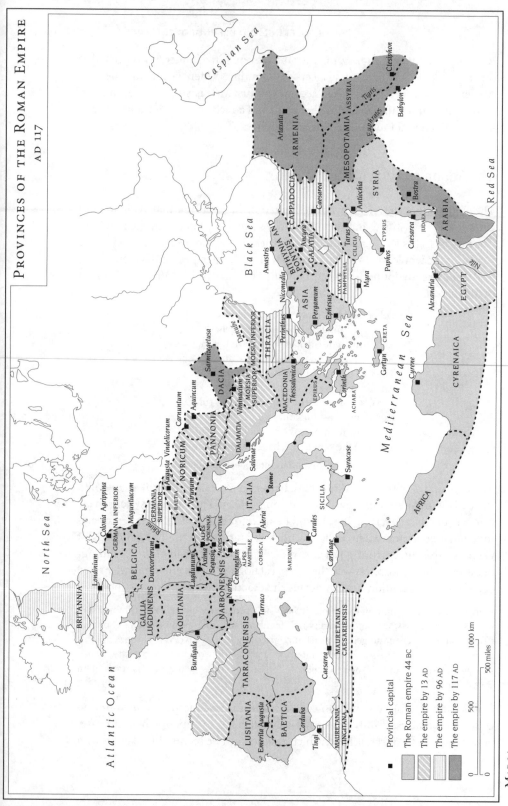

PROVINCES OF THE ROMAN EMPIRE
AD 117

North Sea

Atlantic Ocean

Caspian Sea

Black Sea

Mediterranean Sea

Red Sea

BRITANNIA
Londinium

GERMANIA INFERIOR
Colonia Agrippina
Moguntiacum
GERMANIA SUPERIOR
Rhine
BELGICA
Durocortorum
GALLIA LUGDUNENSIS
Lugdunum
AQUITANIA
Burdigala
NARBONENSIS
Narbo
Tarraco
TARRACONENSIS
LUSITANIA
Emerita Augusta
BAETICA
Corduba
MAURETANIA TINGITANA
Tingi
MAURETANIA CAESARIENSIS
Caesarea

RAETIA
Augusta Vindelicorum
NORICUM
Virunum
ALPES POENINAE
ALPES COTTIAE
Axima
Segusio
ALPES MARITIMAE
Cemenelum
CORSICA
Aleria
SARDINIA
Carales
ITALIA
Rome
Salonae
DALMATIA
Carnuntum
Aquincum
PANNONIA
Viminacium
MOESIA SUPERIOR
Sarmizegetusa
DACIA
Danube
MOESIA INFERIOR
THRACIA
Perinthus
MACEDONIA
Thessalonica
EPIRUS
ACHAEA
Corinth
CRETA
Gortyn
SICILIA
Syracuse
Carthage
AFRICA
CYRENAICA
Cyrene

Nicomedia
Amastris
BITHYNIA AND PONTUS
Ancyra
GALATIA
CAPPADOCIA
Caesarea
ARMENIA
Artaxata
ASIA
Pergamum
Ephesus
LYCIA & PAMPHYLIA
Myra
CILICIA
Tarsus
CYPRUS
Paphos
SYRIA
Antiochia
MESOPOTAMIA
ASSYRIA
Ctesiphon
Babylon
Tigris
Euphrates
ARABIA
Bostra
JUDAEA
Caesarea
EGYPT
Alexandria
Nile

Legend:
- ■ Provincial capital
- The Roman empire 44 BC
- The empire by 13 AD
- The empire by 96 AD
- The empire by 117 AD

0 — 500 — 1000 km
0 — 500 miles

MAP 14

which Greeks massacred Roman businessmen in Asia when called on by Mithridates to do so (p. 410).

The republic was not, however, totally corrupt. Verres' misdeeds are recorded because he was successfully brought before a Roman court after an appeal by the Sicilians for justice. The evidence was so overwhelming that Verres, despite having influential supporters, went into exile after Cicero's opening speech. There was in fact a tension between those who indulged in or condoned exploitation of the empire and those who had the vision or prudence to see that unrestrained plundering was immoral and self-defeating. Lucullus, who commanded the Roman armies in the east against Mithridates between 73 and 70 BC, the same years that Verres was governor in Sicily, worked hard to stem the abuses of the equestrians of Asia. (It did him little good as the embittered equestrians simply stirred up opposition to him in Rome.) In 59 BC, as part of his legislation in his first year as consul, Caesar passed a law (the *lex Iulia de repetundis*) which brought together and enhanced existing legislation on how a governor should behave. Its many clauses dealt with such varied topics as bribery, the unfair requisition of grain, abuse of local privileges, and unjustified demands for 'hospitality'. At the end of his term of office a governor had to deposit copies of his accounts both in his province and at Rome. Pompey attempted to break the link between election expenses and the subsequent governorship to recoup them by introducing a five-year break between a magistracy and a governorship (the *lex Pompeia de provinciis*, 52 BC).

The five-year gap meant that there was a temporary shortage of qualified magistrates to act as governors, and it was in the following year, 51 BC, that Cicero was persuaded to become governor of Cilicia. He was reluctant to leave Rome ('All service in the provinces, as I realized long ago when I was young,' he later wrote in his urbane manner, 'is dull and sordid for one who is able to shine in the city') but once arrived in Cilicia he set about becoming a model governor. He took on the two main tasks of any governor, maintaining good order, through the courts if possible, but by armed force if necessary, and ensuring the raising of taxes. He arrived in his province in July and decided to use the remaining summer months for what fighting needed to be done and the winter for court work. He was accompanied, as every governor was, by legates (the term refers to one who holds delegated authority), in his case all experienced soldiers, to whom he entrusted the pacification of the borders between Cilicia and Syria. (He hoped, in vain as it proved, that their success might enable him to be given a triumph.) Much of his work lay in resolving disagreements between tax collectors and provincials. The previous governor had been, in Cicero's words, 'a beast' and much needed to be done to soothe discontent. He tried to encourage cities to solve their own disputes when these did not involve Roman citizens (these cases the governor normally judged himself) and to sort out their financial muddles. (He was also asked to provide panthers for shows in Rome but reported back that he was unable to trap any.) Just how much of a gold mine provincial government had become for most of its administrators could be seen at the end of his term of office when he proposed paying back his unused expenses to the treasury in Rome. His quaestor, the deputy responsible for financial affairs, and legates were furious at being deprived of what they had come to see as their legitimate dues.

On the whole the emperors brought a more stable pattern of provincial administration. As Tacitus wrote in the *Annals*:

The new order [of Augustus] was popular in the provinces. There government by Senate and People [had been] looked upon sceptically as a matter of sparring dignitaries and extortionate officials. The legal system had provided no remedy against these, since it was wholly incapacitated by violence, favouritism, and, most of all, bribery.   (Translation: Michael Grant)

The more conscientious emperors, such as Augustus, Tiberius, Claudius, and Vespasian in the first century, took special care that administration was fair and oppressive governors punished. Intrinsic to stable imperial government was the development of the emperors' legal powers. These had been inherited from the magistrates of republican Rome. So, for instance, the emperor had the right to issue edicts proclaiming laws of a general character such as the granting of citizenship to the whole Roman world by Caracalla in 212. Decrees (*decreta*) were rulings by the emperors on specific legal issues and although not binding on all cases came to have the force of law. Later in the empire edicts and rulings were synthesized in law codes e.g. those of Theodosius II (438) and Justinian (534).

The Structure of Administration

Since the reign of Augustus a distinction had been made between those more vulnerable border provinces (twenty-two of them in 138) where the governor, usually a senator, was appointed directly by the emperor as his legate, typically for a period of three years, and the remaining 'senatorial' provinces (ten of them in 138) where appointment was by lot from among senators of sufficient seniority. (They were granted proconsular powers.) Equestrians could serve as imperial legates, and in Egypt an equestrian (referred to as a prefect, a term officially used for one granted a military command) was always appointed, a reminder that this had been a personal conquest of Augustus. The term procurator refers to one who had been given legal authority to act in civil (rather than military) matters by the emperor. It was used as a title by equestrian governors of minor provinces such as Judaea and of those who collected the taxes in the 'imperial' provinces (often referred to as 'fiscal procurators') or oversaw the emperor's estates.

A governor was provided with a remarkably small staff. The proconsul of Asia, for instance, had no more than two or three junior senators to help with day-to-day administration of justice and a quaestor to oversee financial matters. There would also be attendants, messengers, scribes, and a bodyguard who could also be used to track down offenders. In addition a governor would also select a group of friends, chosen perhaps as much to provide company as for any administrative skills they might have. This would be his entire retinue. The total number of senior officials was no more than 150 for the whole empire, perhaps one for every 600,000 of its subjects. (Estimates for the population of the empire at its height reach 100 million.)

The official business of the empire travelled along its roads and across its seas. The original purpose of the roads was military, to provide a fast means for the legions to reach areas where trouble brewed, but once established they provided a means of uniting the peoples of the empire. They were built in a standard method by which a paved surface rested on three layers of foundation, which included broken stone and rammed chalk. Good drainage was essential if a surface and foundation was not to break up and was provided through a cambered surface and good ditching. (The roads really did last. I was once on an archaeological survey in my native Suffolk where the line of a Roman road was plotted across a hillside. A trial dig at the top of the hill revealed the road was still there, surface and all, nearly 2,000 years after it was built.) Travel could be fast. A special messenger sent from Mainz, on the German border, to Rome in AD 69 made the 1,500-kilometre journey in about nine days. The emperor Claudius averaged nearly 90 kilometres a day as he crossed Gaul on his way to his 'conquest' of Britain in AD 43. As seen in Chapter 7 sea travel was not so predictable for those wanting to move fast as winds and weather fluctuated so widely.

There was always a critical time in a new province when order was imposed. Any combination of mismanagement and greed at this moment could be disastrous. The revolt of the Iceni in Britain in AD 60 is a good example. Their home, the east of England, was nominally under Roman control and their king, Prasutagus, had left his estates in his will to the Roman emperor (Nero), probably so that on his death his subjects and heirs would be treated fairly. Local Roman officials took a different view and interpreted the bequest as if it was the surrender of a defeated enemy. Plundering began and Prasutagus' widow, Boudicca, was flogged and his daughters raped. This was the signal for revolt. Other tribes which 'had not yet been broken by servitude' (Tacitus) joined in. The fury of the insurgents was directed first at Colchester, centre of the imperial cult, and then at London, now probably the main administrative centre of the province, and Verulamium (the modern St Albans). Tacitus gives a total of 70,000 Romans and loyalists killed. 'The Britons took no prisoners, sold no captives as slaves, and went in for none of the usual trading of war. They wasted no time in getting down to the bloody business of hanging, burning and crucifying.' It was some time before the Roman governor, Suetonius Paulinus, could bring up his legions and use their discipline to crush the disorderly mass of British warriors. He then set about laying waste to their lands. On some sites, such as

Colchester and South Cadbury in Somerset, archaeologists have been able to identify the layer of destruction. The 'desolation' the Romans made did in fact lead to peace. Archaeological evidence shows that when construction resumed on these sites, it was more likely to be of civilian than military buildings.

Once order had been secured in a province a census was put in hand. The purpose of the census was to provide the basis on which two taxes, a poll tax and a tax on property, could be assessed. When Judaea became a Roman province in AD 6, for instance, the governor of the neighbouring province of Syria, Quirinius, moved in to make the assessment. (It must have been this census that Luke mistakenly links in his gospel to the birth of Jesus. Galilee was not a province of the empire at the time of Jesus' birth, it was subject to the taxation of Herod and later his son Herod Antipas not the Roman authorities. Even if it had been Mary and Joseph would have been taxed where they lived.) It would have been impossible to take the census without local help and so the local ruling classes were given much of the responsibility for compiling the details. In the third century the jurist Ulpian recorded the procedure. Each farm had to be named and described in relation to its neighbours and local town or village. The use of the land had to be entered, the amount of plough land, the number of vines and olive trees, and the extent of meadow and pasture. Houses and slaves were included. The amount of tax due was then computed and increasingly it was the city officials who were then responsible for its collection. The *publicani*, the notorious tax farmers of the republic, disappear from the historical record, though their successors cannot have been much more welcome. Italy and Italian colonies remained exempt from these two taxes, a legacy of the days when republican plunder had balanced public expenditure. The exemption was finally ended by the emperor Diocletian.

There were other taxes. Augustus had instituted an inheritance tax, payable only by citizens, specifically to fund discharge settlements for the army. There were indirect taxes on goods in transit, charged at a rate which was usually between 2 and 2.5 per cent and often collected by teams of imperial slaves, and a 1.5 per cent sales tax. They were very unpopular and Nero was tempted in a fit of generosity to abolish them altogether until he was persuaded that the state could not have borne the loss of revenue.

Provinces remained liable to other impositions, the requisitioning of supplies by those on official business, the use of local labour and money for local building projects such as roads, and the provision of free hospitality to governors or soldiers. The benefits to the local population of Roman rule may not have been immediately obvious. A conversation of Jewish rabbis survives. 'How fine', says one, 'are the works of these people! They have made streets, they have made bridges, they have erected baths.' Another rabbi replies, 'All that they have made they have made for themselves; they have built market places to put harlots in, baths to rejuvenate themselves, bridges to levy tolls for them.'

The taxation system had the advantage of being easy to administer and cheap to run. The revenue, normally in denarii, but also in kind, was transferred upwards to the imperial treasury and could then be distributed according to the needs of the empire. This enabled resources to be allocated from the richer provinces such as Asia and Africa to the poorer such as Britain, which required a permanent and expensive garrison. The overall burden was probably not oppressive. In the east the amount of grain raised seems to have been similar to that raised by the Seleucids. The weakness of the system was its inflexibility and perhaps the relatively low level at which taxation was set. If there was a sudden crisis, an attack on the borders, for instance, the system had few spare resources and could not raise new ones quickly. There was naturally resentment if any extra exactions were suddenly imposed. (Increased provincial taxation had been behind the revolt against Nero.) Until Diocletian reorganized the financial system in the early fourth century and instituted a more efficient system of taxing the empire's wealth emperors in difficulties were tempted to debase the coinage or encourage the legions to collect their food and supplies directly from the local population.

The scope of the governor's powers and any specific responsibilities attached to his post were normally set out before he left Rome although he could make his own statement of his priorities. Central was his responsibility for maintaining order. Ulpian sums it up well:

It is the duty of a good and conscientious governor to see that the province he rules is peaceful and tranquil, and this result he will achieve without difficulty if he takes careful measures to ensure that the province is free from criminals and searches them out. He should search out persons guilty of sacrilege, brigands, kidnappers and thieves and punish them according to their offences; he should also repress those who harbour them, without whom a brigand cannot long be concealed. (Translation: Graham Burton)

In some cases the maintenance of order necessitated military campaigns but by the second century small-scale criminal cases predominated. Certain towns were designated as assize towns. (The status was eagerly sought after as the influx of claimants, petitioners, and other hangers-on would be substantial and bring in a great deal of business.) The governor normally depended on cases being brought before him and local magistrates were relied on to search out brigands and wrongdoers. Justice was clearly rough. Although a governor could order a full investigation if he had doubts about any case, he often bowed to popular pressures and many criminals seem to have been condemned without much of a hearing. (Again the case of Jesus comes to mind. He seems to have been flogged almost as a matter of course, and Pontius Pilate, the governor, put up little opposition to his crucifixion.)

Private citizens could also bring their civil cases, petitioning the governor to have them heard according to Roman law when there seemed an advantage for them in doing so. There is an Egyptian record of one prefect receiving no fewer than 1,804 petitions in three days. Gradually the use of Roman law became more popular, particularly when individuals from different cities or opposing legal systems were involved. It had well-set-out procedures and the use of precedent gave it some stability. Citizens could appeal from local decisions direct to the emperor. (A recently discovered inscription details the responses of the emperor Marcus Aurelius to a batch of appeals from Athens.) In addition to using Roman law as established by statute in Rome or by precedent the governor could create local laws himself. This was inevitable when he might be faced with unique circumstances in an outlying province two months' travel from Rome. Communication did go on, however. In the famous correspondence between Pliny, governor of Bithynia, and the emperor Trajan, Pliny asks advice on a wide variety of issues: how to deal with Christians, how to punish slaves who tried to enlist in the army, whether he should put in hand the building of a canal between a lake and the sea, and at what age the emperor recommended entry to a local senate. Trajan's courteous replies insist that the administration should be in the interests of the people and that local tradition should be respected. (There has been some argument over whether the replies are genuinely those of Trajan or those of his officials.) Altogether there were forty issues on which Pliny wrote for advice in two years. Many of them seem trivial but it can be assumed that on many more everyday matters he made up his mind himself. More formal edicts of the emperor or records of decisions made by the senate could be recorded in inscriptions. These acted not only as a permanent reminder of Rome's power but as propaganda for the emperor concerned. So the *Res Gestae*, the record of Augustus' achievements, which is in fact a proclamation of the legitimacy of his rule, is found inscribed on the temple to Rome and Augustus in Ancyra, the capital of the province of Galatia and copies were probably distributed throughout the provinces.

The Frontiers

In his speech of praise to Rome (quoted below, p. 509) Aelius Aristides portrayed the inhabitants of the Roman empire as safe inside well-guarded and impenetrable frontiers. This was misleading. The concept of frontier took some time to mature. During the republic the vision of world conquest persisted and the idea that the empire should set limits to its expansion was never articulated. It was during the reign of Augustus that the concept first took root in face of the difficulties and disasters experienced in conquering the German tribes. Tiberius consolidated the policy and from then on the frontiers of the empire began to stabilize. Britain and Dacia were the only new areas conquered and held for any length of time after the reign of Augustus. Trajan may have dreamed of emulating Alexander in achieving new conquests to the east but his successor Hadrian recognized the impossibility of maintaining control of so vast an empire if its armies were also set on further conquests. So he called a halt and began to consolidate the frontiers, most famously in the wall he built across northern Britain.

By the time the empire had reached its fullest extent, in the second century AD, there were in fact thousands of kilometres of boundaries to defend. From the mouth of the Rhine to that of the Danube is 2,000 kilometres. The borders of the north African provinces ran for a total of twice that. The eastern frontier still had a number of client kingdoms and no fortified frontier was necessary until these had been absorbed, as Cappadocia, Nabataea, Commagene were in the first century AD and Palmyra and Osrhoene in the second. (Armenia remained as a buffer state between Rome and Parthia.) The shortest marching route between the Black Sea and the Red Sea was then 3,000 kilometres by road. Sometimes the frontiers were natural boundaries, such as rivers or mountains. Others ran over open desert or through woodland. It was obvious that these could not all be protected by military force, nor was there any particular wish to close the empire off from the world beyond. Rome needed its luxuries, amber and fur from the Baltic, silks from China, and spices from elsewhere in the east and gold from deep within Africa. Barry Cunliffe argues that Rome's greatest need was for slaves—an estimated 140,000 were required annually to maintain the supply of the empire, and so contacts had to be sustained outside the empire. In effect, except in a few defined trouble spots, the frontiers of the empire were permeable. Even Hadrian's Wall, the most sophisticated and complete barrier between the empire and the outside world, was designed to be crossed by traders entering or leaving under Roman supervision and its main purpose may have been to control this communication more effectively.

This does not mean there were not fortifications along the borders of the empire. Hadrian's Wall in Britain is, as just noted, the best-known example, but in Germany there was the *limes*, originally a military road overseen by watchtowers. Under Hadrian continuous palisades were constructed to strengthen it. In Africa ditches and watchtowers were built to protect the prosperous grain- and olive-growing areas from raids by nomadic tribes. (These tribes were never a serious security threat and no more than 45,000 troops (legionaries and auxiliaries) were allocated for the entire 4,000-kilometre frontier.) In the east there were no formal lines of defence but roads were built running back from the frontier with Parthia so that troops could be hurried to the front if needed.

In reality the defence of the empire depended not on walls but on a mixture of diplomacy and the ultimate threat of armed force. The native tribes could be bought off by gifts of money or luxury goods, or offered special protection. The sons of leaders could be brought into the empire, 'civilized' in the emperor's household and then returned home, hopefully as lifelong friends of the Roman people. Disputes between tribes could be fostered so that they did not unite against the empire. Tacitus, as usual, put it shrewdly: 'May the tribes ever retain, if not love for us, at least hatred for each other.' There were always dangers along the northern border simply due to the shifting allegiances and relationships of the various tribes and when pressures built up among them from the end of the second century diplomacy was not to be enough. It was easier, in theory, to deal with Parthia, a centralized state with only one ruler with whom to negotiate.

The Army

As the frontiers of the empire stabilized the role of the army changed. Gone were the days of continuous conquest and now the army could expect to be largely immobile for years at a time. Augustus had settled the number of legionaries at about 150,000, and a total of twenty-eight to thirty legions was maintained in the first two centuries AD. They were stationed along the more vulnerable frontiers of the empire. The Rhine had been allocated eight legions in 23 BC but as things became calmer four were seen to be enough. Further east along the Danube was the most vulnerable area, and in AD 150 ten legions, a third of the entire army, were stationed there. Eight legions were allocated to the eastern border, three to Britain, and two to the whole of north Africa. Thus over half of the legions were strung along the Danube–Euphrates axis. This was why Rome became increasingly marginalized as a command centre and why, in the fourth century, Constantine was to choose what had hitherto been the Greek city of Byzantium, at the fulcrum of this axis, as his new capital, Constantinople.

Figures from the end of Augustus' reign suggest that the army absorbed some 70 per cent of the state's resources and it was the focus of an enormous official bureaucracy which kept records of every detail of its day-to-day life, its effective strength and its operations. It offered a well-defined career for those who joined it, and as citizenship, the main criterion for entry to the army, spread, it drew on a larger and larger pool of the subject peoples of the empire. Legions could now raise men locally instead of having to wait for recruits from Italy. There was adequate pay and a set period of service, though there were complaints on occasions that soldiers were not released when their period of service was over. Emperors would supplement the pay with bonuses on special occasions. The main drawback to army life was that a legionary could not contract a legal marriage, though, in practice, stable relationships appear to have been common and the male children of these accepted as recruitable citizens. In the reign of Septimius Severus (193–211) marriages were finally allowed.

Each legion had a nominal strength of some 5,000 infantrymen and 120 cavalry. (The evidence from the Vindolanda tables (see below) suggests that the fighting strength of a unit was significantly lower as a result of secondment, illness, desertion, or leave.) The infantrymen were well protected and heavily armed. Their helmets were made of bronze with an iron skull-plate inside and the upper parts of their bodies were covered in a cuirass. They carried two javelins with which to make first contact with an enemy and a sword for hand-to-hand fighting. Discipline was rigid and training, in theory, constant. A hand-book on military training by Flavius Vegetius Renatus, written in the fourth and fifth centuries AD but referring back to earlier times, sums up the legions' strengths.

The Roman people owed the conquest of the world to no other cause than military train-ing, discipline in their camps, and practice in warfare. What chance would the small number of Romans have had against the multitude of Gauls? How could they have ven-tured, with their small stature, against the tall Germans? It is clear that the Spaniards excelled our men not only in numbers but in physical strength . . . and no one doubts that we were surpassed by the Greeks in skills and intelligence. But against all these we prevailed by skilful selection of recruits, by teaching, as I have said, the principles of war, by harden-ing them in daily exercise, by acquainting them beforehand through field manoeuvres with everything that can happen in the line of march and in battles, and by severe punishment for indolence. For knowledge of military science nourishes boldness in combat. No one fears to do what he is confident he has done well . . . (Translation: N. Lewis and M. Reinhold)

The legions were normally stationed at or close to the frontier, in those provinces allocated to the emperor in Augustus' settlement of 27 BC. The emperor was thus, in effect, their supreme commander and at times of crisis was expected to lead them in battle. In some cases, such as Claudius' conquest of Britain, this leader-ship was token. In others—the Flavian emperors, for instance—the emperors were military men and probably more at home in the army than elsewhere. Marcus Aurelius is the classic example of an emperor with no military experi-ence or pretensions taking his duties as supreme commander with great serious-ness. The legions always showed special respect for an emperor who shared their life with them while on campaign and throughout the empire military success was fundamental to the emperor's status.

Each legion was commanded by a senator who had reached the status of a praetor. Like the emperor he might have had little military experience, but by the third century, as pressures built up on the empire, command was increasingly given to those, many of them equestrians, who had such experience. Under the commander were six tribunes, younger men, most of them equestrians, some of whom would be seeking a senatorial career. The career officers were the centuri-ons who had made their way up from the ranks. These were graded by seniority and the most senior, the *primus pilus*, was a man of great authority and experi-ence who was paid a substantial salary and enough on discharge to make him eligible for equestrian status. In a society where inherited status remained important, the army was a major instrument of social mobility, a means by which a man could achieve respected status purely through merit. A fine example is Quintus Lollius Urbicus, the son of a Berber landowner from the small town of Tiddis in the province of Africa. His career as an army officer took him to the ends of the empire. He served first in Asia, then in Judaea, where he was involved in the suppression of the Jewish revolt of 132–5. He then served along the Rhine and Danube borders before being made governor in Britain, from where he campaigned into Scotland. Finally he was made prefect of the city of Rome, an extraordinary career for one whose origins were so modest.

With the changed conditions of the first and second centuries the legions became settled in bases, normally stone fortresses laid out on a standardized pattern. Civilian settlements often grew up around them. The trappings of Roman culture, baths and amphitheatres, would appear and the whole complex would have a major impact on the local economy. With time the legion would become integrated with the local community, even recruiting its men locally. It is a myth to suggest that the Roman army was made up of monoglot Romans—despite the ability of most soldiers to speak some Latin in everyday life local languages appear to have continued. The local administration could call on their skills as engineers, surveyors, and builders.

The danger was lax discipline. Hadrian recognized that if a halt was called to expansion there was danger of demoralization and stagnation among the troops and he was assiduous in preventing this breakdown of order. He is recorded travelling through one province after another inspecting all the garrisons and forts. According to the historian Dio Cassius:

He personally viewed and investigated absolutely everything, not merely the usual installations of the camps, such as weapons, engines, trenches, ramparts and palisades, but also the private affairs of everyone, both of the men serving in the ranks and of the officers themselves—their lives, their quarters and their habits—and he reformed and corrected in many cases practices and arrangements for living that had become too luxurious. (Translation: N. Lewis and M. Reinhold)

Such continual supervision was essential for keeping the empire's defences in good order.

From Augustus' reign there was also increasing reliance on auxiliary troops. The auxiliaries were recruited from non-citizens and grouped in units of 500 or 1,000 men. The emphasis was on skills, in archery or horsemanship, for instance, which were lacking in the heavy infantry of the legions. Gaul, Spain, and Thrace were important recruiting grounds. At first auxiliary units would serve under their own native commanders but gradually they were integrated into the structure of the Roman army, with equestrian commanders, fixed rates of pay, and the promise of citizenship at the end of service. They served in a variety of roles. On the march they protected the cumbersome legions from attack by probing the countryside ahead of their line of march and guarding their flanks. On the other hand, they were quite capable of fighting battles on their own. The Battle of

Mons Graupius, the greatest victory of Agricola's incursions into Scotland, was entirely an auxiliary affair. In peacetime auxiliary units were normally given guard duties along the frontiers. Hadrian's Wall was manned by auxiliary units, for instance.

The Integration of Local Elites

During these centuries of relative stability, a process normally referred to as 'Romanization' took place. The word, in its loosest sense, describes the interaction of Roman and local cultures with the implication that a 'Roman' culture came to predominate. Insofar as the Roman city (this chapter) and in the countryside, the Roman villa (see below p. 532) became the focus of life for local elites in many parts of the empire this is certainly true but it would be wrong to assume that local cultures provided nothing of their own. In cases such as Greece and Egypt, there were civilizations much older than that of Rome and these retained a sense of cultural superiority. In the east, in the so-called Second Sophistic, Greek culture was revived in the second century, primarily, it seems, as a *response* to Romanization. One must also avoid the assumption that what was 'Roman' was unchanging. After all Roman culture was already deeply imbued with Greek elements and the interaction between the two cultures continued to be important throughout the history of the empire. So the interplay between Rome and other cultures was bound to be fluid and to have varied from one part of the empire to another. Archaeology is also showing how Romanization spread outside the empire's boundaries, making the later relationship between Roman and barbarian far less confrontational culturally than they might have been. This chapter will look at the cultural and religious aspects of Romanization, the next at the economic underpinnings of the process.

As a generalization it could be said that the Roman empire survived because it gained the allegiance of the provincial elites who came to understand that their own status not only depended on the security provided by the Romans but could be enhanced by it. As part of this process 'Romanization' was an important development. The shock of recognition that a local elite had much to gain from Roman rule was expressed at its most eloquent in Greece in the second and third centuries AD. A panegyrical speech to Rome by the Greek orator Aelius Aristides survives from about AD 150 in which he dwells on the advantages to the Greek cities of their subject status:

Your subjects relax in utmost delight, content to be released from troubles and miseries, and aware that they were formerly engaged in aimless shadow boxing. Others do not know or remember what territory they once ruled . . . Now under you all the Greek cities emerge . . . all other competition between them has ceased, but a single rivalry obsesses every one, to appear as beautiful and attractive as possible.   (Translation: N. Lewis and M. Reinhold)

Underlying this famous piece of rhetoric (Aelius Aristides was one of the leaders of a revival in Greek oratory, described below) is an emphasis on status within the empire. 'You have divided all the people of the empire in two classes,' he goes on; 'the more cultured, better born and more influential everywhere you have declared Roman citizens: the rest vassals and subjects.' This was the crucial point. Rome had allied herself so successfully with provincial ruling classes that they collaborated in keeping order and maintaining a common front against threats from below. Even in the revolt of 66 the more conservative of the Jewish authorities sided with the Romans. In one of his letters Pliny congratulated a fellow senator on the way he had shown 'consideration for the best men', and went on, 'nothing could be more unequal than that equality which results when these distinctions are confused or broken down.' One of the developments of the second century was a more formal distinction, enshrined in law, between those citizens who were *honestiores*, of higher status, and the *humiliores*, the rest. The *honestiores*, who included senators, equestrians, and local magistrates as well as army veterans, were likely to have their cases heard first and avoid imprisonment while awaiting trial while witnesses of poorer status were routinely tortured. A convicted *honestior* was usually exiled, his poorer fellow subjects executed by crucifixion or murdered in the arena. (For the distinction between slave and free, which provided the most rigid and important mark of status for the mass of the population, see below, p. 527.)

If one is looking for the focus for the sense of shared values, it must be, as Aelius Aristides stressed, the city. The Romans did not, of course, create the idea in the Mediterranean and in their conquest of Carthage, Greece, Egypt, and the Near East they brought under their control a vast array of cities, many of them with impressive histories of their own. However, there were Roman cities which were deliberately planted as part of the system of imperial control. First there were the *coloniae*, garrison towns of legionaries or veterans, established primarily for strategic reasons. So Aquileia, eventually one of the great cities of the empire, was founded in 181 BC as a military settlement on the coast of the northern Adriatic where migratory Celtic peoples could cause havoc. *Coloniae* could be founded on existing urban sites. *Colonia Augusta Nemausus*, the modern Nîmes in southern France was founded on the urban centre, *oppidum*, of the Arecomici tribe. In imperial times, the emperor could bestow the status of a *colonia* on a city as a mark of honour. Vespasian, for instance, granted this status to the city of Caesarea, the administrative capital of Palestine, originally built by Herod. In addition to the *coloniae*, were the *municipia*. The term was originally used of a self-governing community which had become an ally of Rome but again developed into a mark of status which could be conferred by the emperor. The term *civitas*, community, was used to designate a free-standing community, of non-citizen status, often based on a local ethnic group but not necessarily on a town, although it was rare in the middle or later empire to find a *civitas* without its urban centre. There were also the *vici*, often translated as 'villages' though the larger were the size of towns and the term could be used to denote a district of a particular city—Rome had its *vici*. The *vici* had no formal status within the empire and remained subordinate to the local administrative centre. They could, however, be raised to the status of *municipia* with a constitution provided by Rome, often at the request of local aristocrats who wanted their loyalty to be formally recognized. An example of such a promotion, of the late first century AD, survives from the town of Irni in Spain. The town is made a *municipium* with Latin rights (see p. 377) and a Roman style constitution in which detailed regulations are laid down for the election of magistrates, the conduct of a senate, and the procedures for raising taxation, using local labour, and administering justice. On the completion of their term of office magistrates would become Roman citizens, and with time a *municipium*, whatever its native origins, would become an integrated part of the empire.

Tacitus mocked the process of urbanization as he saw it happening in Britain during the time his father-in-law, Agricola, was governor:

Agricola had to deal with people living in isolation and ignorance, and therefore prone to fight: and his object was to accustom them to a life of peace and quiet by the provision of amenities. He therefore gave private encouragement and official assistance to the building of temples, public squares and good houses, he praised the energetic and scolded the slack; and competition for honour proved as effective as compulsion. Furthermore he educated the sons of the chiefs in the liberal arts . . . . The result was that instead of loathing the Latin language they became eager to speak it effectively. In the same way, our national dress came into favour and the toga was everywhere to be seen. And so the population was led into the demoralising temptations of arcades, baths and sumptuous banquets. The unsuspecting Britons talked of such novelties as 'civilization', when in fact they were only a feature of their enslavement.   (From *Agricola*, translation S. A. Handford)

Such may have been the view of a sophisticated and cynical Roman but the process succeeded in building loyal provincial elites. The steps by which a particular family could become integrated into the administration of the empire can be seen through the descendants of a Gallic aristocrat, Epotsorovidius. After the conquest of Gaul by Caesar, Epotsorovidius' son emerges as a Roman citizen and combines Caesar's name (an indication that citizenship was a result of Caesar's patronage) with a Gallic one to become Caius Julius Agedomopas. Two generations later the family has become completely Romanized, suggesting the Latin may have become their preferred language. Gaius Julius Rufus, of the fourth generation, was a priest of the cult of Rome and Augustus at Lugdunum (Lyons) and a *praefectus fabrorum*, an army official concerned with building works. His wealth was such that he was able to donate two quintessential Roman buildings, an amphitheatre to Lyons and a triumphal arch to his native town Mediolanum Santonum (modern Saintes).

Alongside the integration of the local elite into city government went the spread of Roman citizenship. Citizens acquired status and privileges including the right to take part in the administration of many cities, join the legions, or enjoy the benefits of Roman law. The physical mark of citizen status was the right to wear a toga. Until 212, when Caracalla declared that all subjects of the empire (except slaves and some categories of freedmen) were citizens, the process developed naturally as an individual, by virtue of a magistracy in a city or service in an auxiliary army unit, for instance, acquired citizenship and then passed it on to his descendants. A freed slave would also eventually acquire citizen rights if his master was a citizen himself. Whole communities could also be granted citizen rights. More common was the grant of Latin rights to a community which allowed it rights of trade and intermarriage with similar communities. Vespasian gave Latin rights to some 400 urban communities in Spain. The spread of citizenship did lead, in the eyes of the emperors at least, to a requirement of shared obligation in return. This was particularly important when the empire came under stress and one can see the insistence by emperors such as Decius in demanding sacrifice by all (which placed communities such as the Christians who refused to sacrifice to pagan gods under immense pressure) as an attempt to reinforce a common loyalty to the empire through respect for its traditional gods.

The Survival of Greek Culture

While citizens enjoyed a common legal status, Roman citizenship did not transcend cultural or ethnic background and older citizen families would tend to look down on 'provincials'. Among the 'provincials' the Greeks occupied a special place. The Romans could show contempt to the Greeks for their lack of fighting spirit but had to respect their intellectual achievements. After the shock of defeat by the Romans Greek culture remained intact even if, at first, the Greeks were hesitant about becoming involved in the empire's politics. Greek senators are not recorded until the end of the first century AD and none appears to have achieved consular rank until the second century. However, some Roman emperors, Nero, and, notably, Hadrian showed their own enthusiasms for Greek culture, and it seems to have been the gradual realization that the empire offered the best protection for their own status which led to a drawing together of Greek and Roman upper classes. By the second century one can find members of both the Greek and Roman elites being aware of a common *paideia*, the Greek term for the educated man's way of being in terms of a shared education, attitudes, and mannered relationships with others. The fourth century orator Libanius talked of the young man with *paideia* as one 'who has installed Demosthenes in his soul [in other words, mastered rhetoric] . . . He will think it is his duty to make the cities happy; he will rejoice when the executioner's sword lies idle; he will make the citadels beautiful with buildings; and he will remain throughout as servant of the Muses.' An educated Roman such as Marcus Aurelius Fronto, tutor to the emperor Marcus Aurelius, would have concurred in these values.

An early example of a Greek who led the life both of a public servant and a cultured intellectual in 'Roman' Greece is Plutarch (AD 46–120). Plutarch was a wealthy native of the city of Chaeronaea in Boeotia and he spent most of his life there and at Delphi where he was a priest. However, he studied in Athens and also lectured in Rome. He appears to have been completely at ease with the new balance of power, accepting Rome as the ruler of Greece, while insisting that Greece remained the more sophisticated of the two cultures. In his *Political Precepts* he advises his fellow members of the elite to acquiesce in the dominance of Rome (and deliberately cultivate patrons in the capital itself) while never abasing themselves before their rulers. He knew the Roman mentality well enough to know that self-abasement would only encourage contempt.

In his *Lives*, which have been drawn on earlier in this book, Plutarch compares celebrated Romans with selected Greek equivalents (the orator Demosthenes is compared to Cicero, for instance, and Nicias, who led the ill-fated Sicilian expedition, with Crassus, who suffered a similar disaster in Persia). His eye for detail is exact and he is adept at creating the drama of a death scene, the murder of Cicero or the suicide of Cato of Utica or Antony and Cleopatra. His real interest is in the characters of individuals and the moral attributes of each of his subjects matter more to him than whether they were Greek or Roman. In short his sympathies range beyond the confines of his native Greek culture.

Plutarch was the forerunner of a cultural movement which its adherents termed the Second Sophistic. The sophists of the second century AD were not philosophers as such but rather rhetoricians specializing in formal declamations modelled on earlier Athenian examples. In this sense they were conservatives rather than innovators. They were without exception wealthy men and from some of the most prosperous and sophisticated cities of the Greek world, Athens, Ephesus, Pergamum, and Smyrna. They were Greek and proud of it but, like Plutarch, realized the contribution of Rome to allowing their class and their cities to survive. The speech of praise of Aelius Aristides emphasizes that it is *Greek* culture which flourishes as a result of Roman rule. One important role of these men was to represent their city to the imperial government and gain respect and honour from doing so. When an earthquake devastated Smyrna, Aristides took some pride in appealing to the emperors Marcus Aurelius and Commodus for help which was then granted. There are many other examples of status being acquired or maintained in this way.

One of Plutarch's surviving works, *Of the Face of the Orb of the Moon*, describes a dinner party in Rome where the participants discuss the somewhat recondite problem of whether there is a face on the moon. In fact their discussion is erudite; they know their earlier Greek philosophers well, can formulate difficult questions and attempt answers to them, and they lace their conversations with references to

Homer and the great tragedians. It is a reminder that the Greek intellectual adventure was still alive. Among the most significant figures of the period are Ptolemy, an astronomer and geographer, who worked in Alexandria between AD 127 and 141, and the physician and logician Galen (AD 129–*c*.200 or later).

Ptolemy's astronomical work is contained in his *Syntaxis*, later known by the Arabs as the *Almagest*. The *Syntaxis* begins by rehearsing the arguments for the earth being the centre of the universe and then goes on to develop the earlier explanations of the movements of the planets. Although, like his predecessors (see above, p. 348), Ptolemy worked with a geocentric model of the universe, he went beyond them in positing another point, the equant, around which the circles which each planet followed revolved, and through this he was able to account for even more observed phenomena. His work was, in the words of Geoffrey Lloyd, 'extraordinary for the rigour of its mathematical arguments, for the range of ideas encompassed and the comprehensiveness of the results proposed' and, absorbed into the Christian tradition, was to dominate astronomy for another 1,500 years. Even Copernicus, who supplanted it with his heliocentric system in the sixteenth century, relied heavily on Ptolemy's own observations. Ptolemy's contributions to science extended beyond astronomy to mathematics (he devised new geometrical theorems), optics (he was the author of the first treatise on refraction), music, mechanics, and geography. A recent review of his work *Geography* reminds one that he introduced minutes and seconds into degrees, insisted on the continual rechecking of observations, and tackled the perennial problem of how to represent the globe on a flat surface.

Galen was born in Pergamum where among his earliest experiences as a doctor was the patching up of wounded gladiators. After study in a number of Greek cities, including Alexandria, he sought his fortune in Rome, and spent most of the rest of his life there until his death. The range of his work is staggering: something like 20,000 pages of it survive, covering every aspect of human health. There are extensive commentaries on his predecessors, and the main reason why Hippocrates was so highly regarded by later generations is that Galen showed immense respect for the works attributed to him. Galen was the supreme exponent of dissection, even though, unlike his Alexandrian predecessors (see p. 349 above), he was forced to rely on animals for his experiments. He refuted the traditional view that the arteries hold air, even if he did not grasp the principle of circulation. (He had the blood passing through invisible pores.) Nevertheless, he was able to distinguish some of the functions of the liver, heart, and brain and to observe contractions of the stomach in digestion and the peristalsis of the alimentary canal. He carried out experiments on spinal cords to try and pinpoint the relationship between parts of the cord and specific motor functions of an animal. He certainly deserves the title of founding father of experimental physiology. Recent work is also emphasizing his importance as a logician. 'Galen', to quote Geoffrey Lloyd again, 'is probably unique among practising physicians in any age or culture for his professionalism as a logician . . . conversely he is also remarkable among practising logicians for his ability in, and experience of, medical practice.' Like Ptolemy his work became incorporated into the Christian tradition (from a text of his collected works compiled about AD 500).

The interaction of Greece and Rome took place at many different levels including art and literature. Just as Greeks were able to revive ancient skills such as rhetoric, and continue to make progress in scientific thought, so the Romans were able to use Greek styles to advertise their good taste. In the words of the art historian Jas Elsner we see in the second century the emergence of 'a sophisti-cated antiquarian classicism drawing on eclectic sources to demonstrate its scholarship, taste and expertise'. Often the style is so eclectic that dating of a work of art from this period becomes difficult. The fine set of four horses, a *quadriga*, which stand inside (formerly, before the advent of industrial pollution, outside) St Mark's in Venice were dated until recently to as early as the fourth century BC by some scholars on the grounds that they were so characteristically Greek. An understanding of the method of their gilding shows that they are probably from the second or third century AD. Hadrian's idealizations of his beloved Antinous, in statues found throughout the eastern empire, show the same use of earlier forms.

By the time of Ovid Roman and Greek mythology were inextricably mixed. This openness to other gods did not mean that traditional Roman cults and rit-uals were undermined—they were too closely tied to the ethos of the state—and they travelled with Roman rule as part of the process of Romanization. The con-stitution of the *colonia* of Urso in Spain shows that gods, rituals, and priesthoods were modelled on those from Rome, and, as has been seen the imperial cult was also ubiquitous. What was important for the survival of the empire was the readiness of the Romans to tolerate local gods alongside their own. 'Each province and city has its own god: Astarte in Syria, Dusares in Arabia, Belenus in Noricum, Caelestis in Africa', noted the Christian church father, Tertullian. The standing of these local gods depended on their prestige and the culture within which they were set. Even the most elite Romans were attracted by ancient Greek cults, and at Eleusis one finds emperors and senators applying for admission to the mysteries. In the west, local gods seldom had the prestige or cultural resilience to stand up to those of Rome and a common practice was for a Roman god to absorb a local deity. In Gaul dozens of Mars with a suffix of a local god are to be found and the attributes of this Mars might actually expand with the absorbed powers of the local gods. The Platonist Celsus wrote in the second cen-tury that 'it makes no difference whether we call Zeus the Most High or Zeus or Adonis or Saboath or Amun like the Egyptians, or Papaeus like the Scythians.' One temple to Zeus in Libya honoured him in the unexpected role of protector of caravan routes across the desert. The point to be made is that Roman toler-ance to local cults and even the readiness to join them was one important way in which the empire was cemented. (See further on Roman religion especially as it related to Christianity in Chapter 29 below.)

'Instead of loathing the Latin language they became eager to speak it effectively.' As Tacitus noted, Romanization involved, for many, some mastery of Latin. As mentioned earlier, one of the most unexpected finds in recent British archaeology has been the series of documents written in ink on thin wooden tablets preserved in waterlogged deposits at Vindolanda, a fort manned by auxiliaries of the late first century AD, near to the future site of Hadrian's Wall. The letters contain official requests for more money to buy supplies, reports of military strength, personal correspondence between soldiers and their relations, and even women writing to each other to arrange a birthday party. The auxiliaries were not British but mainly from northern Gaul and the number of individual hands suggests that literacy was quite widespread. What is particularly interesting is that these native Gauls wrote in colloquial Latin, with much use of army slang. While some of their language remains untranslatable there are marked similarities with the colloquial Latin of graffiti from Pompeii from just a few years earlier and a similarity in the use of Latin (which is written in the 'Old Roman' cursive script of Vindolanda) has also been seen in texts on third-century AD papyri from Egypt. Here were subjects of the same empire, but of very different backgrounds, using their second language, Latin, in a recognizably uniform way.

In the modern town of South Shields in northern England, a 'Roman' tombstone has been found. It commemorates one Regina, the British wife of a trader by the name of Barates from Palmyra at the furthest eastern extreme of the empire. The inscription is both in Latin and in the dialect of Aramaic spoken in Palmyra. The Latin, however, is unorthodox in that some of the words are given Greek endings. The stone cutting suggests that while the sculptor is happy to cut Aramaic inscriptions he has some difficulty with Latin script. (Just as an English-speaking stone cutter might have difficulty getting an Arabic inscription right.) It has been suggested that Barates' first language was Aramaic but that he knew Greek well and when he learnt Latin he transferred Greek grammatical forms to the language. It is a reminder of just how complex the process of Romanization was.

FURTHER READING

See the suggestions at the end of Chapter 25, but I would also strongly recommend 'Becoming Greek with Lucian', chapter two of Simon Goldhill, *Who Needs Greek?: Contests in the Cultural History of Hellenism* (Cambridge, 2002). It provides excellent insight into the relationship between outsiders and Greek culture in this period.

The Romans as Builders

If there was a birthplace of Roman architecture it was not Rome, nor even Greece, but the cities of coastal Campania, wealthy settlements along the Bay of Naples to the south of Rome. The sheltered coastline had been open to eastern influences for centuries and the cultural development of the area was in many ways more advanced than that of Latium. It is to this area that the emergence of the typical Roman stone building types, the amphitheatre, the theatre (in its Roman form), and almost certainly the Roman bath, the market building, and the basilica can be traced. Here too the typical Roman house with its *atrium* (central court) and enclosed colonnaded garden was born.

Of these the most obviously Greek in conception was the basilica, a long hall framed on each side by a colonnaded aisle. Its origins were probably in the Greek-speaking cities of southern Italy but a very early example (early second century BC) has been found beside the Forum at Pompeii. The preservation of Pompeii as a result of the great volcanic eruption of Vesuvius in AD 79 has allowed the architectural development of a Campanian city to be studied in detail. In the second and early first centuries BC Pompeii, whose heritage was Greek but which had been overrun by the Samnites in the fifth century, had already acquired a full complement of urban buildings, including theatres, an amphitheatre, bathhouses, and market buildings. Two of the bathhouses predate any in Rome by a century, while Rome had no stone theatre before Pompey's in 55 BC (and even that had to be disguised as a temple) and no stone amphitheatre before the Colosseum (dedicated in AD 80). Even a small Campanian town such as Pompeii had achieved a sophisticated lifestyle long before the same was available in Rome.

By the first century BC Rome did, of course, have its great public buildings around the Forum, its temples, senate house, halls for the public assemblies, and state offices. There were market halls and great warehouses. However, it was not until the reign of Augustus that the city was transformed 'from brick to marble'. From this time on imperial patronage was to be an essential component in architectural development. Only the emperors had the resources and political need to make a major impact on architecture while the stability of imperial rule stimulated

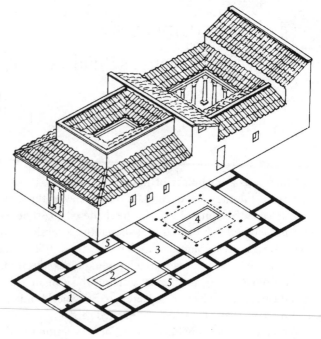

Fig. 7 A typical house from Pompeii. An entrance (1) leads to an inner hall or atrium (2) and a reception room (3) beyond. At the back is an enclosed colonnaded garden (4). Family portraits would have been placed in recesses (5).

the spread of building throughout the empire. Earlier traditions of town planning from the Greek world combined with this stimulus and the renewed prosperity of a settled empire to create the typical Roman town, with its grid plan, central forum, and surrounding public buildings.

One of the inspirers of this urban renewal was an engineer, Vitruvius, responsible for a great basilica in the town of Fano on the Adriatic coast. He left a famous treatise, *De Architectura*, in which he set out a shopping list of buildings and urban accessories which any self-respecting Roman town ought to have. (It was much admired by Renaissance architects and an inspiration to Palladio.) Among the essentials were paved streets and drains, an aqueduct to bring in fresh water (not least to supply the public and private baths), an amphitheatre and a theatre, a forum, temples, and basilicas for public business. City walls were to be built, in some cases for defence, but more often as a mark of civic pride, and the centre of the town might be graced with commemorative arches and statues of its prominent citizens and benefactors. Many Italian towns achieved all these buildings quite rapidly.

Large cities depended on efficient water supplies. The earliest Romans drank from the Tiber but by the late fourth century BC alternative sources were needed. While the aqueduct was not a Roman invention (earlier examples have been found in Persia and seventh-century Assyria) it was a building form Roman engineers made their own. The first aqueduct of Rome, the Aqua Appia, had been constructed as early as 312 BC. It was 17 kilometres long. As the city grew engineers began probing ever further into the Campagna, the countryside round Rome, for water. The Aqua Marcia of 144 BC, for instance, ran for 92 kilometres from the east of the city and is estimated to have brought in a million litres of water an hour. The problem facing the engineers was how to secure a regular flow from higher to lower ground. The Aqua Marcia had a fall of 260 metres, one metre for every 354 metres in length, and the route had to be planned to keep this fall constant. (Roman architects were also able to use a siphon system to take water from lower to higher ground.) Aqueducts seldom ran in a straight line as they had to negotiate the changing levels of countryside. The visible remains of the great aqueducts, the thousand arches which led Claudius' aqueduct into Rome, the imposing Pont du Gard near Nîmes, the two-tiered structure at Segovia (which still carries part of the city's water supply), give the impression that aqueducts ran largely above ground. In fact whenever possible they were run underground to protect the purity of the water and its possible contamination by enemies. The Aqua Marcia only ran above ground for 11 of its 92 kilometres and the water which crossed the Pont du Gard then ran underground for the next 50 kilometres. Aqueducts needed constant supervision if water was not to leak out, and in imperial times a task force of slaves was kept by the emperors specifically to keep them in repair. The building of aqueducts was another area in which emperors took a leading role. Augustus built a major aqueduct on the Campania to supply Naples and the cities of its Bay.

The typical aqueduct ran along an arched foundation. The arch was not a Roman invention. It is used in the mudbrick buildings of the east. The Greeks preferred rectilinear designs and so shunned the arch but, by the fourth century, even they were prepared to use it for city gates. These gates are found in central Italy from the early third century BC onwards and the arch then becomes part of the Roman builders' repertoire. One particularly powerful manifestation of it is the triumphal arch, erected by emperors to commemorate their victories. The first of these arches dates from the reign of Augustus (with the earliest example actually to survive at Rimini in Italy (27 BC)). Tiberius erected a particularly elaborate arch with three openings and a mass of decoration, at Orange in southern France in AD 26 after he had suppressed a Gallic rebellion. In Rome the emperor Titus erected an arch (in concrete, faced with Pentelic marble) to celebrate his conquest of Jerusalem. Another elaborate example in Rome is the arch of the emperor Septimius Severus (built in AD 203). The form of the triumphal arch became a symbol of Roman imperialism which spread throughout the empire but which was adopted with particular enthusiasm in the eastern and north African provinces.

The transformation of cities such as Rome was helped by the development of a strengthened form of concrete, which used local volcanic ash (known now as *pozzolana*) mixed with lime as mortar. The combination was first used in the late republic but it took two generations of trial and error before the best kind of lime was isolated and the right mix was perfected. One of the qualities of volcanic ash, as compared to the sands used in earlier Etruscan and Roman concretes, for instance, was that it produced a mortar which would set under water and so could be used as the base for bridges and harbour works. To create a standing wall the mortar was mixed with stone. A typical method was to lay a course of stones boxed in with planks. The mortar would then be poured in and when it was dry a new layer of stones added and so on. The finished rough wall was then faced with patterned stone. In the larger buildings the content of stone fill would be lightened as the building rose.

The new concrete provided the possibility of a totally different approach to architecture, one in which the encapsulation of space, rather than just the construction of a structural mass, became possible. It was the emperors who alone had the resources to develop this possibility to the full in a succession of great public buildings that now began to fill Rome.

The first developments can be seen in the Domus Aurea, the 'Golden House', built by Nero as a palace for himself after the burning of Rome. The style was that of an opulent seaside villa of the type well known along the coast of Campania but here transported into the centre of the city. What was revolutionary about its design was one room, the central chamber of the east wing, where a dome was raised from an octagonal base. (The concept of a dome may have been inspired by the tent canopies of Achaemenid Persia.) Radiating out from the central chamber were a series of vaulted rooms. The whole was lit by a circular opening in the dome and by windows placed high in the walls of the surrounding rooms. This was a truly revolutionary way of using space and light.

This initiative was developed in the palace the emperor Domitian built for himself at the end of the first century AD, the ruins of which still stand on the Palatine Hill in Rome. Like Nero, Domitian was seeking a setting in which to display his autocracy. The Domus Augustana was a grand building with two majestic façades, one overlooking the Circus Maximus, the race track, the other the Forum. The site was an awkward one and vast foundations had to be laid before the building could rise on two different levels. Its grand public rooms, in particular the Aula Regia where the emperor displayed himself on ceremonial occasions, could not have been constructed without concrete. This vast room (possibly 30 metres across) was roofed in timber but the adjoining basilica had a concrete vault which spanned over 14 metres. The whole was an elaborate interplay of vaults, domes, and half-domes, still set, however, within a traditional rectangular exterior.

In Trajan's reign the plunder of Dacia provided the opportunity for another massive building programme in Rome. Trajan decided to benefit the city directly with a huge complex including a Forum and library as well as a market hall and shopping precinct. In the Forum and library, Trajan stuck to traditional forms and they were built on levelled ground at the foot of the Esquiline and Capitoline Hills. Trajan's column, faced with its great unravelled scroll of the events of his Dacian campaigns, was built to a height of 40 metres to show how much the ground had been lowered. The market area had to be built behind, within the cuttings of the hills, and this required considerable imagination and expertise. Trajan's architect, an easterner, Apollodorus of Damascus, created a masterpiece of design which exploited the difficult site to create a complex which still exists on three different levels each with its terrace and entrance from the surrounding slopes. Again this would have been impossible without concrete, but here it is used in the service of the community in a set of buildings which are elegant but which, unlike the Forum and its accompanying buildings below, have no pretensions to grandeur.

With Hadrian comes the culmination of these developments. Like Trajan, Hadrian was sensitive to the Roman past and when he built a temple to Trajan he followed traditional models. Likewise the Mausoleum he built for himself by the Tiber (now the Castel San Angelo) was modelled on that built by Augustus. With the Pantheon, the temple to all the gods, however, he exploited to the full the confidence with which Roman builders now used concrete. It was erected on the site of an earlier temple built by Augustus' colleague, Agrippa, and Hadrian modestly preserved Agrippa's name at the top of the columned façade. The Pantheon appears simple in design, no more than a drum roofed with a huge dome, the world's largest until modern times, over 43 metres in diameter. (The largest dome built in *stone* in antiquity, the sixth-century Mausoleum of Theodoric at Ravenna, is only 9 metres across.) The problem was how to support the vast weight of this dome. It was done by lightening the type of stone used as the structure went higher and narrowing the masonry skin so that while 6 metres thick at the foundation it is only 150 centimetres thick around the opening at the top of the dome. Recesses carved inside the completed dome lightened the load still further. The whole building (mercifully saved by transformation into a Christian church in the seventh century) stands today as the supreme achievement of Roman architecture.

Hadrian is also remembered for the complex of buildings which make up his villa at Tivoli (built between AD 118 and 134). It is the largest villa known from the Roman world and, like the English country house of the eighteenth century, set in landscaped surroundings. The whole is an extravaganza of the new tastes in architecture and the skills needed to realize them. Domes, vaults, and almost every form of curved surface are used in the succession of buildings, which are set alongside pools, fountains, or cascades of water. Some echo buildings Hadrian had seen in the east, a stoa from Athens, the temple to Aphrodite (the Roman Venus) at Cnidus, for instance, while along the galleries and colonnades were set copies of antique statues. The villa is a public display of the emperor as connoisseur.

Among Trajan's many benefactions to Rome was a vast bath complex. There had been earlier baths in Rome (both Nero and Titus had built some for the city) but Trajan's set a pattern which was to become copied through the empire. The centre of the baths was the *frigidarium*, a cold room, which now, through the use of concrete, could become vaulted and vast. From the *frigidarium* the bather would proceed to smaller rooms where the water was warm or hot (the *tepidarium* and the *caldarium*). There was much more to bathing than this. The Romans incorporated the concept of the Greek gymnasium into the bath complex so that, typically, there were *palaestrae*, exercise areas, on either side of the *frigidarium* and libraries, galleries, and even shops. The Roman could satisfy not only his or her physical requirements, but also his social, intellectual, and sexual needs (from the many prostitutes who frequented the baths). In the first century AD there was no prohibition on women bathing at the same time as men, although those women who particularly valued their reputation normally

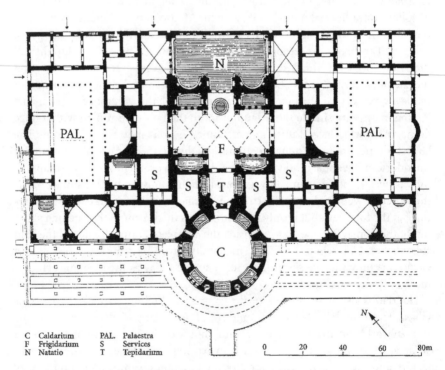

C	Caldarium	PAL.	Palaestra
F	Frigidarium	S	Services
N	Natatio	T	Tepidarium

FIG. 8 The baths of Caracalla show how a typical bath complex had evolved by the early third century. In the central rooms bathers had a choice of hot or warm baths (*caldarium* and *tepidarium*) or a cold plunge (*frigidarium*). There was also a larger pool for swimming (*natatio*). On either side of the complex were exercise yards (*palaestra*). The whole complex provided a massive display of grandeur which inevitably became associated with its donor whether he was an emperor or wealthy provincial.

patronized separate establishments. There were, inevitably, scandals, and Hadrian eventually had to decree the segregation of the sexes. In the large city baths it now became the custom to institute separate bathing times for men and women.

The imperial baths built in Rome in the later empire are the most monumental of all. The baths of Caracalla (built AD 212–16) covered 2 hectares and were set in an enclosure of 20 hectares. They could accommodate 1,600 bathers. Those of Diocletian (built AD 298–306; the short time-span an indication of the efficiency of the whole building operation) were even larger. Their great central hall was later converted by Michelangelo into the church of Santa Maria degli Angeli and survives today, its eight vast supporting pillars still faced in the original Egyptian marble. The central hall baths of Maxentius, begun in AD 307 and completed by Constantine, rose to a height of 35 metres above ground level. There was no better way to make the ordinary citizen of Rome feel he was part of a proud empire, and baths became part of Romanization throughout the provinces. In the west, where they were an innovation, great baths are found at Timgad and Leptis Magna in north Africa, at Trier, near the Rhine border, and at Aquae Sulis, the modern Bath, in Britain where the local hot springs fed the bathing pools.

The Romans may not be remembered for the beauty of their architecture—the impulse to create effect was probably too strong—but they impress with the confidence with which they handled their materials and the sheer monumentality of their creations. When the empire became Christian the basilica became the most popular of the designs for churches, while Justinian's great church St Sophia in Constantinople has been seen by some as inspired by the Pantheon and the Baths of Maxentius. When the Venetian architect, Piranesi, created his prints of real or imagined Roman buildings in the late eighteenth century, he scandalized some by his insistence that Roman architecture was more inventive than Greek, but inspired others so that one finds the dome and the arch reappearing in early nineteenth century architecture as far afield as Washington. Even into the twentieth century the Roman architectural legacy has persisted, in creations such as the war memorial at Thiepval, France, and the great booking hall of Pennsylvania Station, New York, which drew on the triumphal arch and the bathhouse respectively.

FURTHER READING

See the general studies on Roman architecture cited after Chapter 20. Rabun Taylor, *Roman Builders: A Study in Architectural Process* (Cambridge, 2003) is now the best starting point for building techniques. See also J.-P. Adam, *Roman Building: Methods and Techniques* (London, 1999). Aqueducts are dealt with by A. Trevor Hodge, *Roman Aqueducts and Water Supply* (London, 2002). On Hadrian's Villa, William MacDonald and John Pinto, *Hadrian's Villa and its Legacy* (New Haven, 1995) is excellent.

27 | Social and Economic Life in the Empire

Wealth and Identity

The Roman world was one in which traditional status remained important. The most important distinction remained between slave and free, but there was, as mentioned in the last chapter, among free men the further distinction between the *honestiores* and *humiliores*. Senators and the equestrian class were *honestiores* by virtue of their status and so was the growing class of *decuriones*. Originally this was a status awarded to the councillors of *coloniae* and *municipia*, nominally a hundred of them in a typical city. As with the senators and equestrians there was a wealth requirement and a man needed to be of high local reputation. With time the *decuriones* became a hereditary class but the demands associated with the status also became a burden as the weight of taxation (which the *decuriones* played an important part in collecting) and the maintenance of their cities became more onerous.

Even if there was a wealth requirement for all these classes, that wealth had to be displayed within conventional ways. High living could be openly despised, as it was by the immensely rich Stoic philosopher Seneca, and vulgar display of wealth would be ridiculed. The classic example in literature is the ostentatious and boorish Trimalchio in Petronius' *Satyricon* (see above, p. 472). An acceptable approach to lavish spending lay in patronage of one's local city. The opulent library given to the city of Ephesus by the family of one Celsus who became consul in AD 120 is a fine example. Its façade still stands even if its 12,000 volumes or rolls have long since gone. An alternative was to stage games for the the city. On a day-to-day level a great man would have an open house in the sense of making his wealth available for others to enjoy rather than shutting it away behind closed doors. The size of a man's entourage bound to him as patron was an important mark of his public status. Status was reinforced in the public arena by customs such as reserving sections of the theatre for each class.

The patron–client relationship was central to Roman society. It reflected a harsh world in which advancement was difficult without the help of a man of higher status. In the verses of Martial and Juvenal (see below) the client is presented as in a permanent state of humiliation. He abases himself before his patron in order to get fed. However, some accounts give a more sympathetic view of the personal element involved. So the senator Pliny the Younger reports of one client Julius Naso whom he was supporting for office:

He has made friends and cultivated friendship, and in my own case, he singled me out for his friend and model, as soon as he could trust his own judgment. He is at my side full of concern when I plead in court or give a reading; he is there to take an interest the moment my trifling works see the light. (Translation: Betty Radice)

A patron would gain added status from his ability to place his clients and Pliny the Younger goes on to describe his own feeling as he waits for the vote of the senate on a post for Julius. 'I hang in suspense: I am worried by hope and excited by fear; I do not feel like an ex-consul. For I once more seem to be a candidate myself for all the offices for which I ran. In short, if Naso wins the position he seeks, the honour is his; if he is denied, the rejection is mine.' The relationship was found throughout Roman society, the emperor had his clients as did rich senators and provincial grandees. It was so deeply engrained that with the coming of Christianity bishops become patrons (petitioning the emperor for exemptions from tax for their clergy) and even clients in the sense of adopting 'patron saints' to represent them at the 'court' of the Last Judgement.

However much the patron–client relationship may have helped make everyday life more bearable for some, for the mass of population of the empire this remained a cruel and unforgiving world. For Rome itself the reality of daily life in a city where the gap between rich and poor was immense is vividly documented in the work of two poets of the late first century, Martial, a native of Spain who arrived in the city about AD 64, and Juvenal, from Latium itself. (Martial is best remembered for his numerous surviving *Epigrams*, Juvenal for his *Satires*.) Both describe the streets blocked with people, the decaying tenements, with the roof tiles falling from them on to passers-by, the appalling noise of the city. Before dawn it is the bakers who disturb you, says Martial, then the schoolteachers, while all day there is the hammering of coppersmiths, the clinking of the coins of the money changers, the chanting of priests, and the patter of beggars. The rich can move around freely, says Juvenal. They have tall litter-bearers who lift them above the crowds. The poor have to struggle through the mud, being jostled, stepped upon, and subjected to violence. Their homes are no more than flimsy boards, vulnerable to fire and collapse. It is only the rich who can buy peace, the space of a garden, and the security and status provided by a mass of attendants.

Literary sources also provide some details of everyday life in the eastern half of the empire. The gospels, for instance, provide a vivid picture of life in first-century Palestine (see Chapter 29). For the mid-second century there is Apuleius' *The Golden Ass*, the only full-length novel in Latin to have survived. Not much is known of Apuleius. He was a native of the city of Madaura in Africa and appears to have travelled widely in the African provinces lecturing in philosophy. *The Golden Ass* draws on earlier Greek tales of one Lucius who, while travelling in Thessaly, becomes transformed into an ass. He can only be restored to human form by chewing roses and much of the tale describes his adventures in search of them. He is eventually drawn into a festival to the goddess Isis where he finds the roses he needs. Human again, he becomes an initiate into the mysteries of the goddess (see p. 571).

Both the gospels and *The Golden Ass* record the life of the small dusty towns of the east and the countryside surrounding them. It is not a wealthy world and there is little in the way of luxury. Some comfort is provided for the more prosperous inhabitants by the local baths and by the ministrations of servants and slaves. There are social gatherings, weddings, evening dinner parties, and festivals. In the small town of Hypata, the setting for the first part of *The Golden Ass*, the inhabitants join in the local Festival of Laughter with enthusiasm, crowding into the theatre for a mock trial of Lucius (still at this point in human form). Alongside such diversions, however, there are continual reminders of the insecurities of life, the prevalence of poverty and disease. As the extraordinary range of medical concoctions outlined in, for example, the *Natural History* of the Elder Pliny (AD 23–79) shows ('For fractures of the ribs, goat's dung applied in old wine is especially extolled . . . recurrent fevers are cured by wearing the right eye of a wolf, salted and attached'), there was no understanding of disease and most afflictions must have remained without effective treatment. This explains why there was such heavy reliance on magic makers and miracle workers. The everyday use of magic pervades *The Golden Ass* (its setting, Thessaly, was seen as the home of magic and enchantment), and the gospel accounts show how quickly stories of successful healing spread through the local community. There is a persistence of everyday violence. In *The Golden Ass* adolescents from the local 'first families' are apt to rampage through Hypata in the early hours, picking out foreigners to terrorize. Those with luxury goods keep them secure in a strong room at the centre of their houses with the outside doors barred and guarded by porters. Outside the towns bandits haunt the roads. The authorities bring out the instruments of torture as soon as they have a suspect to question.

Despite the insecurities of everyday life there remains, however, some sense of an overriding order. There are magistrates and local Roman garrisons. There is some attempt to provide justice, even though little sympathy is given to supposed troublemakers and punishments are cruel. It is possible to travel from one part of Galilee or Thessaly to another. There are inns to welcome the traveller or the possibility of an introduction to a local notable who will provide hospitality. There is the sense of a shared cultural background. In short, society in the empire did have some form of cohesion, even if only of a limited kind.

The mass of the population of the empire remained poor. There was simply no way in which sufficient surplus wealth could be generated to benefit more than a lucky few. Very little is known about the way of life of the free poor or the margins on which they survived. Most lived on the land, as landless labourers, tenants, or peasant owners and were subject to all the fluctuations of the seasons and climate. Famine must have been common, and was probably accentuated by the power of the cities to draw in what surpluses of crops remained. For those who were labourers four sestertii seems to have been the maximum possible wage, three or even two sestertii more likely. A miner from Dacia is recorded in an inscription as earning one and a half sestertii a day plus keep. Some prices recorded in Pompeii suggest that a sestertius might buy 2 kilograms of wheat, while one as, a quarter of a sestertius, would buy a plate, a lamp, or a measure of wine. In one Spanish example an as would buy admission to the baths. This suggests a modest but sufficient way of life for a labourer in full-time employment, but much of the work must have been seasonal and unpredictable, the labourers waiting in the market place, as in the gospel parables, in the hope of finding a master to employ them. It is also clear that the prices of necessities fluctuated wildly and, at times of shortage, wheat could soar to six or seven times its normal price.

Slavery in the Roman World

> The principal distinction in the law of persons is this, that all men are either free or slaves, next free men are either freeborn or freedmen, free born as those born free, freedmen those manumitted from lawful slavery.
>
> Gaius, *Institutes*

The labourers just described were free men but it is difficult to gauge what the concept of freedom meant in a world which was poor and, despite some overall improvement in order, insecure. Slavery was an integral part of this world. It had existed in the east for centuries. In Italy slaves had been accumulated as the plunder of war. In his *Slavery and Society at Rome* Keith Bradley points out that in the early days of Rome slaves were defeated enemies whom the victor had the right to kill but chose to preserve, under a suspended death sentence as it were. The defeated were also, in Roman ideology, seen as abject in themselves. From there it was possible to argue that slaves were slaves because they were, or had become through misfortune, servile in nature. (It needs to be remembered that, in reality, slaves, particularly those from the Greek world, must often have been more culturally sophisticated than their Roman masters.) For historical reasons slavery remained most prevalent in Italy. An estimate is that there were 2–3 million slaves there, up to 40 per cent of the population, at the end of the first century BC. In much of the west slavery remained less common. There are relatively few references to slaves in Britain, for instance, and in Gaul slaves are to be found only in cities.

There is virtually no evidence of any challenge to the institution of slavery in the Greek or Roman world during this period. Some Stoics did advocate that the slave be recognized as a human being. 'Remember, if you please, that the man you call slave springs from the same seed, enjoys the same daylight, breathes like you, lives like you, dies like you ... You can as easily conceive him a free man as he can conceive you a slave,' writes Seneca in one of his letters. This was, however, no more than prudent and paternalistic humanitarianism and shows no concern with the institution itself. Christianity made little difference. The author of Ephesians (probably composed about AD 90) simply transfers the institution into a new context. 'Slaves, be obedient to the men who are called your masters in this world, with deep respect and sincere loyalty, as you are obedient to Christ, not only when you are under their eye, as if you only had to please men, but because you are slaves of Christ and wholeheartedly do the will of God.' Freedom comes for the Christian in the next world, not this one.

There was little economic rationale for slavery. In a society where the mass of the population was very poor, it was probably as cheap to employ casual labour when needed as to buy a slave and maintain his or her fitness throughout the year. Rome was not a slave society in the sense that the economy was dependent on slavery for its survival. The mines in Spain may have been worked largely by slaves but those in Gaul were probably not. No section of the economy would have collapsed if there had been no slaves. Rather, as Keith Bradley puts it: 'The social and economic benefits that accrued to owners derived from their almost limitless abilities to control and coerce human property.' Such control not only made life easier, with every comfort catered for, but reinforced the owner as a free and hence socially respected individual. Throughout his banquet Trimalchio enjoys playing with his slaves' feelings, sometimes threatening force, sometimes promising a grant of freedom, conscious that by doing so he is displaying his new-found power.

Attitudes to slaves must have been conditioned by their large numbers and memories of the great slave revolts of the republic, those in Sicily in the 130s BC and the uprising of Spartacus in 73 BC, both of which attracted more than 70,000 slaves. The custom of executing all the slaves in a household when the master had been murdered by one (see p. 496) again shows the depth of fear and how, characteristically, the use of terror was the means of dealing with it. There was nothing (until a few humanitarian measures introduced by the emperors in the mid-second century AD) to restrain the brutality of owners who were that way inclined. An example of how horrifying things could be is found in one of Cicero's cases where he describes how a mistress, Sassia, tried to force a slave to incriminate her son on a charge of murdering her stepfather. The slave, as was customary, was tortured in front of witnesses to tell the 'truth'. When the required 'confession' was not forthcoming Sassia urged the torturers on so sadistically that in the end the witnesses could not stomach the ordeal any longer and had to force her to desist.

In the writings of the agriculturalist Columella (mid-first century AD) slaves are treated as if they are naturally deceitful and need constant supervision. He mentions in passing the practice of keeping slaves chained together while they work and secured in prisons (*ergastula*) at night. It must have been in those situations where slaves were employed in the mass, whether on the farms or in the mines, that everyday treatment would have been at its most harsh. In the domestic setting the position of individual slaves was more ambiguous. A large household might have several hundred and their jobs would range from those requiring specific skills, such as doctors, teachers, and secretaries, those concerned with administration, such as the steward or household chamberlain, down to the most menial sweepers and cleaners. Many of these jobs offered the opportunity of direct human contact on a one-to-one basis with the master or mistress and slaves may have taken pride in belonging to one of the grander families of Rome. A secure and well-managed household might actually offer a better life for the slave than the streets and farms outside. While slaves could not be legally married, liaisons, with children born to them, were common, and many owners condoned these 'family' arrangements, preferring slaves who had been born into slavery to those bought in from the outside world. (Columella also refers to the civilizing influence of women in the otherwise all-male world of the agricultural slave.) However, there was never a guaranteed protection from violence, ill-treatment, and sexual harassment. The children of slaves could be sold separately from their parents and the plucky slave-girl, Fotis, who initiates and enjoys sex with the 'hero' Lucius in Apuleius' *The Golden Ass*, cannot be assumed to be typical. Every form of sexual abuse must have been common. Trimalchio boasts that his freedom was granted after he had satisfied the desires of both his master and mistress.

Manumission and Freedmen

Where Rome differed from Greece was that slaves could be freed and their descendants become full citizens. Manumission was an ancient concept found as far back as the Twelve Tables of the fifth century BC. An owner could set a slave free by means of a declaration in front of the magistrate or through the terms of his will. Alternatively a slave could buy his freedom, if the owner agreed, by offering the owner compensation from whatever he might have saved. The number of slaves an owner could free through a will was, however, limited by a law of Augustus. An owner of between thirty and a hundred slaves could free no more than a quarter of them, one with over a hundred slaves only a fifth. Manumission brought freedom for only a minority of slaves and inevitably those who were freed during an owner's lifetime tended to be those who had earned his respect. Cicero's freedman, Tiro, enjoyed the genuine affection of his former master. The freedman was subject to some continuing restrictions, in his choice of marriage partners (marriages between freedmen and freedwomen were common) and in the way he could leave his wealth, but his children enjoyed the full rights of any citizen and within a generation or so their ancestry would be of little consequence.

Most freedmen remained close to their previous owners and were supported by them in their new lives, often as tradesmen and craftsmen in the cities, and even buried in their family tombs. In return their former owners could expect complete loyalty. This explains why emperors such as Claudius used freedmen so extensively. Traditional Romans, however, viewed the rise of the freedman to a position of wealth with horror. Again, the depiction of Trimalchio in Petronius' *Satyricon* is the classic example from literature. The old arguments enunciated by Theognis 700 years earlier (see p. 215), that no amount of wealth could create nobility, reappear in this context. 'He had the wealth and spirit of a freedman,' comments Seneca of one Calvisius Sabinus. 'I never saw a man whose good fortune was a greater offence against propriety.' However, the Romans were a pragmatic people. The emperor Diocletian may have himself been a freed slave or at least the son of one.

It remained one of the paradoxes of Roman society, that for a tiny minority slavery might provide a mechanism for social advancement. Horace's father was a freedman, his son ended up as an intimate of Augustus. The philosopher Epictetus was born a slave in Asia (in the middle of the first century AD), suffering the extra handicap of being lame. Yet after being freed he spent much time in Rome mingling with the elite and later in his life he may even have been introduced to Hadrian.

Land and Survival in the Roman Empire.

> We note with certainty that the world grows better cultivated and better supplied with everything than it used to be. Everything is accessible, everything is known, everything is used; delightful rural domains have forced famous deserts to retreat, furrows have tamed the forests, herds have put wild animals to flight; stretches of sand have been sown with seed, roads are opened through the rocks, marshlands are drained, there are as many towns as there once were houses, . . . Everywhere there are dwellings, peoples, cities, life.
>
> (Tertullian, *c*.210)

The economy of the Roman empire depended overwhelmingly on agriculture. Throughout the Roman period the staples of the Mediterranean 'dry farming' economy remained, as they had been in earlier times, olives and grapes, supplemented by cereal crops, and cattle, sheep, and goats for meat, milk, wool, and leather. In the north of Europe, where the sun is limited and the soils are heavier, olives would not grow at all and vines only on specially favoured sites. Here cereal and vegetable production was predominant. In many areas little happened to change the traditional mix of crops. In Egypt, for instance, the centuries-old methods of production of grain continued and it appears that the emperors (whose 'personal' province this was) actively discouraged any economic development which might threaten the grain surplus with which they maintained the political stability of Rome and other parts of the empire. The cities of the east had long-established relationships with their hinterlands and there was no incentive to disturb these. In Britain the native field systems were largely preserved intact (with some lengthening of the fields as ploughing became more efficient) and the concentration on cereals, which had produced a surplus for export to the Continent even before the Roman conquest, continued.

The long centuries of settled Roman rule did, however, have their impact, perhaps in some areas as marked as that noted by Tertullian. Its extent is not easy to determine, however, as the evidence is fragmentary. For agriculture in Italy there are some literary sources—Cato's *De Agricultura* in the second century BC and Columella's *De Re Rustica* in the first century AD. Both are instruction manuals specifically aimed at the larger landowner hoping to exploit local markets (there is much on the processing of goods for market and the management of slaves) and the information they give is of only limited relevance, even for Italy. The *Natural History* of the elder Pliny, the uncle of Pliny the Younger, does range beyond Italy but not in any systematic way. Increasingly it is the archaeologist, working through field surveys and the analysis of villa sites, who has provided the significant evidence for agricultural change.

The evidence suggests that farmers as a whole benefited from the *pax romana*, the centuries of stable Roman rule. In normal times they could get on with their work without interruption. Keith Hopkins suggests, from analyses of pollen and settlement patterns, that the amount of land cultivated increased and that population grew to be higher in the first centuries AD than 1,000 years earlier or 500 years later. Hopkins also argues that there is evidence for some increase in productivity, that is the yield of crops per unit of land. He cites a variety of improved methods including the diffusion of iron tools and screw presses (for oil production) along an axis from the south-east to the north-west of the empire.

A surplus may have been stimulated by the emergence of urban centres (see below). The main incentive for increased production at local level was, however, provided by the state itself, through its demands for tax or rent in money or in kind. Further afield large cities, such as Rome and, later, Constantinople, could not support themselves and the emperors took on the task of diverting supplies to them either from their own estates or from the richer areas of the empire. Rome drew on grain from Sicily, Egypt, and the African provinces. In Africa, in particular, vast new areas of olive groves were planted once the land was properly irrigated. Recent research, covered in D. J. Mattingly's *Tripolitana*, shows that it was not a Roman but a native Phoenician and Libyan elite which was responsible for promoting the expansion of agriculture into the desert. Syria was another area of the empire where the imposition of Roman rule coincided with the introduction of olive cultivation. (The appearance of the olive is particularly significant as it takes ten to twelve years before the tree bears fruit so cultivation would attract only those with capital and confidence in the long-term stability of an area and its markets.) The legionary bases drew on these sources but also invariably had a direct impact on the land around them. A careful study of the settlements around Hadrian's Wall in Britain, for instance, suggests that a third of them expanded in the second century AD, with an increase in production of, on average, about 37 per cent.

The Villa

Although it is impossible to generalize across the empire as a whole over several hundred years, it appears that there was a growth in the number of medium-sized or large estates farmed by tenants, slaves, or free labour at the expense of smaller peasant farms although these never disappeared. It was these estates which supported the most pervasive symbol of Roman influence in the provinces, the villa. The term 'villa' is a broad one covering both the palatial establishments of the Roman rich on the Bay of Naples and the comfortable farmhouses found throughout the provinces. (The finest literary description of a grand country villa comes in the letters of Pliny the Younger (Book II, Letter 17).)

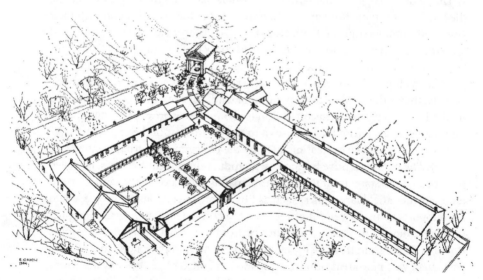

FIG. 9 The villa at Chedworth in Britain, c.AD 300. This is a good example of a comfortable domestic home with its own secluded courtyard alongside an open courtyard where the business of the estate would be carried on.

Field surveys are showing just how widespread the villa became in the more fertile areas of the empire, particularly in the west. One recent survey of the Somme valley, for instance, found over a thousand examples. For a farmhouse in the provinces to qualify as a villa, there has to be some evidence of Romanization, either in the design of the building or in its furnishings. This process of Romanization was often cumulative, and can sometimes be traced by excavation. A native farmhouse might originally consist of a single large room shared by animals and people. The first sign of progress would be the segregation of the owner from his animals. Then rooms for living and sleeping would be built to separate him from his workers. If prosperity continued luxuries could follow—baths and heating systems, corridors, mosaics, and painted wall-plaster. Finally the façade of a grand villa might be turned away from the farmyard and graced by a portico. A larger villa would extend its rooms so as to enclose a court-yard or garden where the the family could enjoy the open air in some seclusion. These were all improvements which spread in the first instance from Italy. The process often began in the west a generation or two after conquest—in Gaul, for instance, at the end of the first century BC, in Britain not until the end of the sec-ond century. (British villas enjoyed their finest period of prosperity only in the fourth century.) It was not uniform. In many cases a villa was built from scratch, perhaps by a resident official, while other villas remained modest working farms.

Villas required craftsmen, builders, plasterers, tilers, and mosaic layers. Typically the owners would also buy in all the trappings of civilized Roman liv-ing, including glass and silverware, and the fine Samian pottery (*terra sigillata*) with its red gloss and raised designs. (The presence of the last on a site is partic-ularly important for the archaeologist because the styles can be dated.) This sug-gests links with local market centres and provides further evidence for Hopkins's thesis that there was a surplus of agricultural produce which could be sold to buy these skills and goods. There is no doubt that there was an economic symbiosis between villa and urban centre. It has been shown that in Britain, for instance, almost all villas are within half a day's ride of an urban centre. The French archaeologist Michel Ponsich has traced the varied links between villas in the valley of the Guadalquivir in Spain and local townships. The produce brought into the towns might then be taken downriver to the sea (near the Straits of Gibraltar) and shipped north to Britain and Gaul or eastwards into the Mediterranean. (Ponsich's work is cited by Kevin Greene in his *The Archaeology of the Roman Economy* (London, 1986).)

Cities and the Economy

The vast majority of the cities of the empire supported themselves through the fruits of local agriculture, either brought in directly for sale or transferred from the landed estates of the elite into building programmes. A few benefited directly as sea or river ports from the increase in trade which the *pax romana* brought to the empire (see further below). The commercial city able to maintain itself from trade or industry was unknown although some cities such as Aquileia in the northern Adriatic gained substantial wealth as an entrepôt for trade (in this case from northern Europe) and from local metal resources such as gold and the manufacturing of gems and amber goods. Those cities which had aspirations for grandeur were acutely dependent on outside patronage, which is why their loyalty could be bought so easily by a generous emperor. The system worked well until the third century when stresses on the empire undermined the surplus of resources and the willingness of the provincial elites to shoulder the burden of continual repair. The relative lack of economic resources within each city suggested another weakness. The second-century physician Galen, writing on how disease spread among the poor, mentions in passing that at times of famine the city dwellers would strip the local countryside of its food, bringing starvation to its inhabitants. There is not the evidence to support or reject this view but some exploitation of the countryside may perhaps have been the price the Romans paid for maintaining the local provincial elites intact. The extent to which the empire was undermined by the alienation of the mass of its population living in rural areas through the depredations of the wealthy and the demands of taxation is still debated but it certainly seems to have been a factor in later decline.

No city had a more artificial economic status than Rome, with its population of over a million by the time of Augustus. Rome fulfilled many roles beyond that of the purely administrative which had to be maintained for the psychological well-being of the empire. It was the showcase of the empire, its monumental buildings deeply embedded in ancient rituals and enduring reminders of its great emperors and many victories. It had to be kept stable through outside support and this required the importing of an estimated 190,000 tonnes of grain a year. Wheat was preferred to the less nutritious barley but this limited the areas of the Mediterranean to be exploited (wheat requires more rainfall than barley does). Although the city was supplied through private enterprise, at first from grain surpluses in Italy and Sicily, the emperors came to exercise substantial control over the process of supply, even providing the surplus of their own estates. The grain of Egypt, the emperor's personal province, was increasingly drawn on with the grain being collected from peasant farmers directly as tax. (Alexandria became the most important exporting centre of the empire.)

A major problem was finding carriers and Claudius showed his pragmatic approach to such matters by offering citizenship or exemption from tax to those who signed six-year contracts to bring ship loads of at least 70 tonnes of wheat each year. In Hadrian's day the corn traders could gain exemption from other public duties. In Rome itself a *praefectus annonae* had overall supervision of supplies but the emperors also played a major role in developing the port of

Ostia. Originally Ostia had been a river port but its frontage was too small to take the number and size of ships now required to supply Rome so under Claudius and then Trajan a seaport was constructed and this eventually became the focus of commercial activities. By the middle of the second century Ostia had a population of some 50,000 and its mass of merchants, shipowners, trade associations, and supporting clerical staff made it one of the few 'middle-class' cities of the empire. Its Square of the Guilds has mosaics illustrating its main trades, rope makers, tanners, timber merchants, shipowners among them. There is even a record of an elephant importer!

The relationship between cities, such as Rome, and local economies elsewhere can be plotted from another part of the empire which helped sustain Rome through its grain and other produce, north Africa. The hungry population of Rome was a short voyage away across the Mediterranean with Carthage acting as the connecting port with Ostia. (Shipowners from Carthage are notable in inscriptions in Ostia itself.) Like elsewhere, the basis of Africa's wealth was agricultural, predominantly olives and grain, but it was also an important source of marble. (Particularly favoured was the veined yellow and red marble from Smitthu in Numidia, used, for instance, in the Pantheon.) From the second century AD African pottery was also sold throughout the empire. The overall effect was to stimulate and sustain a large number of towns. In origin these were a mix of ancient Phoenician cities, Roman garrison towns, citizen colonies, and local market towns (many of whom were to be given the status of a *municipium*). What is remarkable is their number. In what is now northern Tunisia there were some 200 towns at an average distance from each other of only 10 kilometres. A typical population of one of the north African cities might be between 5,000 and 15,000. About a dozen had a population of over 20,000 (the rebuilt Carthage may have had 100,000, Leptis Magna 80,000). The remains of these cities, with their theatres, temples (often dedicated to the Roman pantheon, Juno, Jupiter, and Minerva), triumphal arches, and gateways still scattering the landscape, attest to the success of the Romans in creating a common imperial culture but all this prosperity rested ultimately on exploiting the artificial 'pull' of Rome.

A good example of a small port growing prosperous on the fruits of agriculture and associated products is Pompeii on the Bay of Naples. The city was destroyed in August AD 79 by a colossal eruption of the volcano Vesuvius. Much was preserved under the ash and it has been possible to piece together the details of almost every aspect of social and economic life in the city.

The wealth of Pompeii originated in the surrounding countryside of Campania and came predominantly from wine and olive oil. In the mid-first century AD wool-processing also seems to have been an expanding industry with raw wool being brought down from the Samnite highlands for treatment in the city. As the main port of its stretch of the coastline Pompeii was ideally placed to export these goods throughout the Mediterranean and wine amphorae from the town have been found in France. Business must also have benefited from the local villas of the rich with all their needs for building materials and other supplies. What industry there was in Pompeii was related to the marketing of agricultural goods. Pottery production, for instance, centred on the amphorae in which wine, oil, and other local produce could be exported. At the time the city was destroyed, however, there are some indications that its traditional export markets were declining as provincials began developing their own vineyards and making their own pottery. The reversal in trading relationships has been demonstrated in Pompeii by a crate of imported red-gloss pottery newly arrived from southern Gaul. (Some scholars are now challenging the thesis that Italy underwent an agricultural crisis in the first century as a result of provincial competition and argue instead that the prosperity of the peninsula remained intact.)

If north Africa showed a whole region could benefit from access to Rome and the wider Mediterranean economy, the army also had its own economic impact. Soldiers were comparatively well paid and there could be several thousand men in a single garrison, such as Vetera (modern Xanten) on the Rhine. So there were rich pickings to be had, and evidence from the sprawling townships which emerged near the camps suggests that traders were attracted from far afield. Most of the early occupants of the township around the fortress at Noviomagus (modern Nijmegen) were immigrants and on military sites along the Rhine and Danube the remains of luxury goods, fine tableware from Italy and Gaul, spices from the east and exotic glassware from Egypt, have been found. Legionaries often kept their families in the townships and in some cases went to live in them when they retired. Although some of the townships appear to have developed their own form of government (complete with magistrates) they normally remained subject to the camp. On occasions a township might be fortified by the legion but there were instances (at Vetera, during the revolt of Julius Civilis, for instance) when a township was razed by the legions to prevent it being used by insurgents.

Trade Routes

An analysis by R. Duncan-Jones of transport costs in the empire concludes that carriage costs by sea were a fifth of those by river and one-twenty-eighth of those overland. Overland transport was slow and expensive. Thus those goods which could not be produced locally travelled by water, and any analysis of trade routes of the empire has to disregard roads and concentrate on routes across the sea and along rivers. It used to be believed, for instance, that trade with the German tribes went eastwards overland from the Rhine. In fact it made better economic sense to take goods around Denmark and into the Baltic and this helps explain why the Baltic area is so unexpectedly rich in Roman finds. Knowledge of sea and river transport is being revolutionized by developments in the excavations of waterlogged sites and in underwater archaeology. Evidence of shipwrecks is being used to piece together routes and the types of goods carried, while the recent discoveries of the great wharves of cities such as London and Xanten (on the Rhine) show the importance of riverside ports. Ships were also becoming larger. Although shipwreck analysis suggests that the average Roman merchant ship had a capacity of about 100 to 150 tonnes, those in the grain fleet may have been in the range of 300 to 500 tonnes, while one exceptional vessel, the *Isis*, described by the second-century AD writer Lucian, has been calculated at 1,200 tonnes, a size not equalled until the sixteenth and seventeenth centuries.

Most trade was in the everyday commodities of life: grain, of course, preserved fish, wine, and oil, supplemented by smaller decorative items such as glass, pottery, and metalware. The stamped amphorae in which wine and oil were transported suggest a discriminating market for the better-quality goods, claret-type wine from southern Italy (marked with the name of the estate and the vintage), Spanish fish sauce, and oil from Baetica (in the province of Further Spain). The important cloth industry had its own specialist centres, Sicily and Malta for the most luxurious cloths, for instance. In the first century AD many commodities could command an empire-wide market but the trend was for local production to rival these foreign imports. The origin of Samian ware was Arezzo in central Italy where the clay was especially fine. By the first century AD, however, new centres of production appeared in Gaul, first at Lugdunum (the modern Lyons) and later southern Gaul. An analysis of amphorae found in shipwrecks show that Spanish and Gallic Samian ware became more important during the first century. From this period on it is now only occasionally that a local industry achieves an empire-wide market, perhaps as a result of a change in taste. One example is the astonishing success of African pottery after the second century AD. It is found penetrating the eastern Mediterranean and even the Black Sea. Gallic cloth and clothing became the fashion in Italy in the third century.

In addition to the agricultural products which remained the staples of small towns such as Pompeii, the empire also provided a market for luxury goods. As only a tiny section of the population had the spare capital to buy such items, it was, inevitably, small as a proportion of the whole, though some items such as silverware were popular among a wider clientele. Spain was an El Dorado for precious metals, including gold, silver, copper, tin, and lead. They were transported to be worked up at specialist centres. The area around Capua in Campania was particularly known for its work in copper and silver, for instance. Many luxury goods came from beyond the empire's borders: ivory from eastern Africa (via Nubia), incense and myrrh from Arabia, amber from the Baltic coast, pepper from southern India, and silk from China. Much was accumulated in Rome itself, in the case of pepper in vast warehouses. In AD 408 when the Goth leader Alaric forced a ransom from the city he was able to demand 3,000 pounds of pepper and 4,000 silk garments.

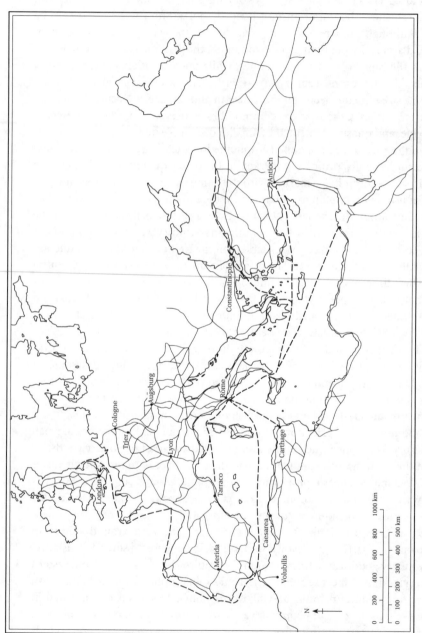

MAP 15 The Principal Land and Sea Routes of the Roman Empire. The sea routes were crucial for the transport of heavy goods and most of the major ports gave river access to the interior. Note how Rome, with its enormous demand for grain, was the centre of a network of both road and sea routes.

The Social and Economic Impact of Trade

There has been intense controversy in recent years over the social and economic impact of trade on the empire as a whole. In *The Ancient Economy* (Berkeley, 1973) Moses Finley suggested that trade had a very limited role to play in the social and economic development of the empire. The staples of the agricultural economy were uniform throughout the Mediterranean basin, he argued, so there was little incentive for one area to trade with another. The cost of transport was another factor inhibiting exchange as it would price traded goods well above the same goods produced locally. (This would explain why the development of oil, wine, and pottery production in the provinces in the settled years of the empire might threaten the traditional centres of production such as Italy.) Finley also pointed out that the status of traders remained low and that as soon as they had made profits they tended to invest them in land. It was not the lure of money as such which stimulated economic activity but the search for status, achieved through landownership, public office, and displays of largesse in the city centres. Finley concluded that the forces which dictated the movements of goods were not those of the market but those imposed by the state in its determination to keep the imperial structure, the prestigious cities such as Rome, and the legions, intact through the provision of grain and other basic necessities.

Finley's thesis has been challenged by Keith Hopkins. Hopkins's views on the growth of agricultural production have already been cited. He goes on to argue that much of the surplus which he believes was extracted from agriculture was actually traded. He draws on the archaeological evidence described above and also stresses how widespread was the use of coins with evidence also for commercial loans and shared risk investment. Coins would not have been found in so many contexts if small-scale trading had not been significant. In short, in contrast to Finley, Hopkins argues that there are clear signs of a market economy with its own dynamism. He is supported by recent work, surveyed, for instance, in David Mattingly and John Salmon (eds.), *Economies beyond Agriculture in the Classical World* (London, 2001), which shows how archaeology provides evidence for the intensification of every aspect of the traditional Mediterranean economy, including trade, during the first centuries AD.

The term 'intensification' rather than transformation needs to be stressed. The Roman economy provides only a few instances of technological innovation in any area. The invention of glass-blowing in Syria revolutionized the industry and made glassware widely available at a reasonable cost for the first time. There is some evidence for water mills, although they do not seem to have been widely used and donkeys remained the main motive power for milling. In Spain, Portugal, and Gaul the Archimedes screw (a revolving cylinder up which water can be drawn) appears to have been adopted for the drainage of mines. In Gaul a remarkable harvesting machine was developed. It was pushed by a donkey and its iron teeth cut the corn at mid-stalk. It would have been wasteful to operate and must have been developed as a response to the short harvesting season when speed mattered more than thoroughness. These are exceptions. More important in bringing about any rise in productivity was probably the growing availability of better tools and the knowledge—accumulated over many years of stability—of how to maximize the potential of any given piece of land. In short the economy of the empire had many areas of modest growth and commercial success. What seems to have been lacking was any empire-wide political and administrative structure able to transform it into anything more substantial. The Roman economy remained overwhelmingly dependent on the land and as such was severely limited by the natural forces which conditioned Mediterranean agriculture.

It is within this context that the achievements of the empire must be assessed. They amounted to some greater security for the farmers, some increase in demand for goods, and so employment, some opportunities for those with talents to find service in the army or the bureaucracy of the empire. For a tiny few there was the chance of real opulence and significant social status. All must have shared, however remotely, the awareness that they were part of an enormous empire whose aegis stretched across much of the known world. This was all possible because the Romans had the vision and skill to integrate the leaders of those they had conquered into an interlocking society which not only provided stability over time but acted as a recruiting ground for new leaders when the empire was under threat. This explains the resilience of the empire in the crises which were now to follow.

FURTHER READING

See the suggestions given at the end of Chapter 25 above. Specifically on the city of Rome, see now Catherine Edwards and Greg Woolf (eds.), *Rome, the Cosmopolis* (Cambridge, 2003).

28 | Transformations: The Roman Empire 138–313

The contrast between Hadrian and his successor Antoninus Pius (emperor 138–61) could not have been greater. Antoninus, whose family originated in Gaul but whose father and grandfather had been consuls in Rome, was already in his fifties when he succeeded. He had been a proconsul in Asia and an adviser of Hadrian (who designated him as successor shortly before he died). His reign was a peaceful one. The only recorded campaign was an unsuccessful attempt to conquer Scotland (the so-called Antonine Wall was built to the north of Hadrian's but abandoned twenty years later). Antoninus remained in Rome, 'like a spider in the centre of a web' as one observer put it, and ruled autocratically but benevolently. For Edward Gibbon this represented the moment when the human race was more prosperous and contented than at any other time in history, and it was in Antoninus' reign that Aelius Aristides delivered his famous panegyric of Roman rule.

Yet the equilibrium between Rome and the provinces, between the emperor and the senate and the provincial elites, was very delicate. Above all, it depended on peace. The empire was, in fact, exceptionally vulnerable to war and invasion. The defences along its extended borders were not designed to withstand major attacks, while roads ran from them towards cities whose riches lay unprotected by walls. Its armies were by now accustomed to fixed bases and would take some time to deploy, especially if they had to be moved large distances. The subjects of the empire had enjoyed relatively low levels of taxation for decades and the resources needed to meet a challenge could not be easily raised at short notice.

Threats to the Empire

Trouble was now building up from two sources. First there were the tribes of northern Europe. The Romans gave the name German to the wide variety of peoples who occupied the area from the Rhine and Danube valleys to the North Sea and the Baltic and as far east as the river Vistula. The Romans had long accepted that the Germans could not be incorporated into the empire.

Experience had shown that their heavily wooded lands were impossible to conquer. Instead a variety of relationships had been built up. Many of them were peaceful, trading and diplomatic relationships underwritten with Roman subsidies. On occasions there was conflict but shrewd emperors realized the importance of playing the tribes off against each other rather than risking direct confrontation. As a result many Germans had adopted aspects of Roman culture and in some activities, metalworking, for instance, were as adept as the Romans. The Germans lacked an efficient centralized system of administration, but in certain respects their standard of living may not have been far below that of many parts of the empire. Romanization was not confined to the empire.

However, during the second and third centuries there were important changes taking place in the societies of northern and eastern Europe, although these are still impossible to define clearly. The difficulty lies in relating Roman sources which talk of large, relatively well-organized tribes assaulting the empire and the archaeological evidence which, insofar as it can give a stable interpretation, suggests a much wider range of interactions on both sides of the border, many of which may not have involved any destruction. There seems to have been steady population growth together with the emergence of new, often expansionist, tribal groups. In the Black Sea area the Goths appear in the early third century. Traditionally they have been seen as a single people with origins in Scandinavia but more recent research suggests that they were an amalgam of various migratory peoples, eastern German tribes and the original settlers of the Black Sea region. The term probably never fairly described an ethnic grouping but rather those whom Gothic leaders managed to forge into a fighting force. (This should be borne in mind when the term is used later in this book: the tribal groups which gave their allegiance to Gothic leaders probably shifted with time.) They gathered their resources around the Black Sea and eventually were strong enough to threaten Asia Minor and the Balkans. In south-east Europe they came into conflict with the Sarmatians, nomadic peoples of Asian origin, who had established themselves on the Hungarian plain. The Sarmatians in their turn were pushed towards the Roman frontier.

This period also sees the emergence of new Germanic cultures further north. One of them, the so-called Przeworsk culture which appeared in the late second century between the Vistula and Oder rivers, stands out because of its rich warrior burials. Another is the so-called Oksywie culture on the lower Vistula. These cultures were more highly militarized than was usual with the German tribes (for whom warfare was typically low level and seasonal) and it has been suggested that they were organized around the capture and trading of slaves. Although the evidence is still controversial there is some that indicates these cultures were expansionist. Archaeological evidence suggests that a new tribe, the Burgundians, emerged on the Elbe to the west of the Vistula about the same time as the home of the Oksywie culture became deserted. Similarly another German tribe, the Vandals, may have been the successors of the people of the Przeworsk culture. All these attempts to link peoples to defined cultures need to be taken with great caution, allegiances to tribal chiefs shifted easily, and groups of warriors broke up and reformed often without leaving archaeological traces.

The emergence and expansion of these peoples put the German tribes along the Roman frontier under increasing pressure. One result was to force the smaller scattered peoples into larger tribal units. The process probably began in the early third century. The central German tribes were drawn together as a confederation known as the Alamanni ('all men'), first attested in 213. The Franks emerged slightly later along the lower Rhine while the Saxons appear along the coast of the North Sea. The Germans also seem to have become more sophisticated fighters, probably as a result of service in the Roman armies. They had originally used short slashing swords which would not have been effective against Roman infantry. Now they were using long two-edged swords or rapiers which could penetrate armour more easily. There is also evidence of skilled bowmen armed with weighted arrows, again an effective weapon against armoured troops. For the first time the Germans could face the Romans with some confidence, and as pressures built up on them from the north the riches and lands of the empire became more alluring. By the middle of the third century the Romans were vulnerable along the whole northern border from Saxons, Franks, Alamanni, Sarmatians, Goths, and other smaller tribes. Their raids were often small scale with the limited objective of obtaining plunder but they were bound to be frightening (which is why the Roman sources may have exaggerated them) and if left unchecked might lead to the gradual dislocation of the empire.

The strategic problems involved in meeting the threat were considerable. The border was so extended it could not be effectively guarded along its whole length. So long as the pressures from the north and north-east and the endless regrouping of peoples beyond the borders continued, even a major victory over the German tribes could not bring a lasting peace. The Romans were to try a variety of policies from straightforward military confrontation to making treaties with individual tribes or buying them off with payments of cash. Garrisons were sometimes stationed over the border in German territory so that trouble could be snuffed out before it reached the empire, while on other occasions invaders were allowed to settle within the empire in the hope that they would defend their land against any future incomers (as well as providing troops for the Roman armies). None of these policies provided a permanent solution.

It was unlucky that the empire also faced a fresh threat from the east. Campaigns by the Romans against the Parthians in the 160s and 190s were relatively successful but this was partly because the Parthian empire was in decay. It was under threat from the Kushan empire in the east and it also faced internal disintegration because of its policy of relying on independent local leaders who were allowed their own armies and control of their own finances. In the early third

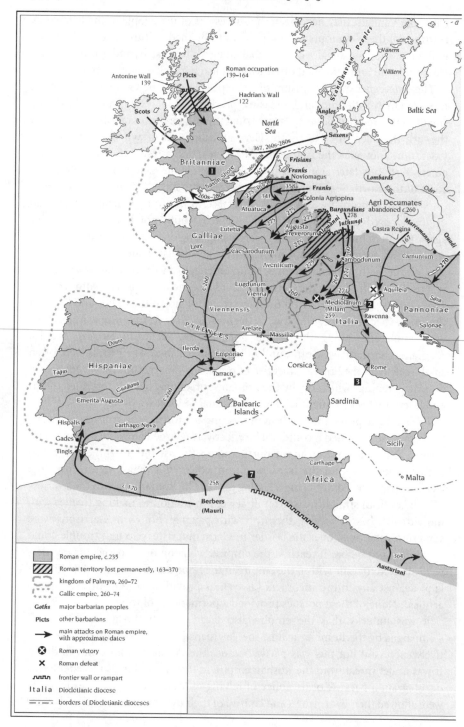

MAP 16 Invaders of the Roman Empire, AD 117–376

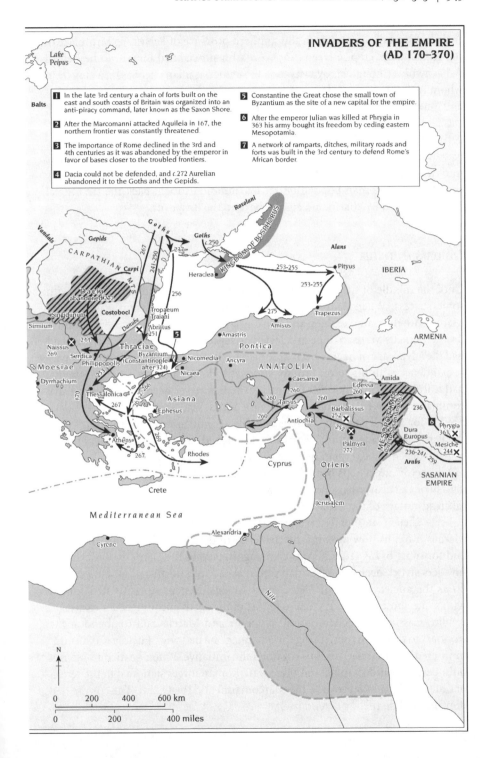

INVADERS OF THE EMPIRE
(AD 170–370)

1 In the late 3rd century a chain of forts built on the east and south coasts of Britain was organized into an anti-piracy command, later known as the Saxon Shore.

2 After the Marcomanni attacked Aquileia in 167, the northern frontier was constantly threatened.

3 The importance of Rome declined in the 3rd and 4th centuries as it was abandoned by the emperor in favor of bases closer to the troubled frontiers.

4 Dacia could not be defended, and c.272 Aurelian abandoned it to the Goths and the Gepids.

5 Constantine the Great chose the small town of Byzantium as the site of a new capital for the empire.

6 After the emperor Julian was killed at Phrygia in 363 his army bought its freedom by ceding eastern Mesopotamia.

7 A network of ramparts, ditches, military roads and forts was built in the 3rd century to defend Rome's African border.

century the last of the Parthian kings, Artabanus V, was overthrown by one Ardashir, king of a tiny state in the southern province of Persis, the birthplace of the Achaemenid empire (see p. 105). Ardashir proclaimed himself to be heir of Achaemenids (though his dynasty took the name Sasanian after Sasan, a king from whom Ardashir claimed descent) and he was crowned in the tradition of Darius and Xerxes as King of Kings at Ctesiphon, on the Tigris, in 226. The Sasanian state was fervently nationalist, purged Persia of foreign influences, including those lingering from the Greeks, and revived the traditional religion of Zoroaster. Ardashir was succeeded by Shapur I (AD 239–70), a forceful ruler who extended the state into Armenia and Georgia and there was some talk, perhaps again exaggerated by the threatened Roman population, of his ambition to win back the traditional boundaries of the Achaemenid empire beyond the Bosporus.

Marcus Aurelius

Until the middle of the third century the empire managed to defend itself with some success. When Antoninus Pius died in 161 the succession was smooth. Marcus Aurelius, the nephew and son-in-law of the emperor, and his adoptive brother, Lucius Verus, had been selected as successors by Hadrian and they had had the advantage of having been groomed for their roles. (Marcus Aurelius' correspondence with his tutor, Fronto, survives.) However, while Marcus Aurelius had learned the conventions of court life, he had never been given any military command and at first he relied heavily on Verus, who seemed to have the dash needed for military action. Marcus Aurelius' confidence was misplaced. When the Parthians invaded in 161, Verus was dispatched east to deal with them but he only managed to beat them off with difficulty. When the war was finally over in 166 the returning troops brought plague back into the empire and meanwhile a variety of German tribes, the Chatti, Marcomanni, and Quadi among them, had taken advantage of the weakened northern frontier to raid into the empire.

Verus died in 169 while on the northern frontier. Despite his inexperience Marcus Aurelius now took on the challenge of defending the empire in person and for most of his reign he was campaigning along the Danube borders. The invaders struck deep. One German raid reached into northern Italy, another as far as the ancient shrine of Eleusis near Athens. Marcus Aurelius struck back with some success but in 175 a false report of his death encouraged an easterner, Avidius Cassius, to declare himself emperor and Marcus had to abandon the frontiers to deal with him, losing the advantage he had won. Luckily Cassius was murdered and Marcus Aurelius regained the initiative. When he died in 180 not only were the borders intact but there were Roman forces stationed in the territory of two of the major tribes, the Marcomanni and the Quadi. The empire had done more than merely defend itself.

Something of Marcus Aurelius' personality survives in his *Meditations*, random jottings put down in Greek, and never intended for publication, which he made while on campaign. They are grouped in twelve books compiled between 172 and 180 and show a man preoccupied with his own thoughts, seemingly hardly affected by external events. The *Meditations* have evoked a mixed response from later generations. Many readers find them cloying and sentimental and are depressed by the pervading sense of melancholy and preoccupation with death. Others are attracted by the genuine concern Marcus Aurelius shows for the unity of life around him ('For all things are in a way woven together and all are because of this dear to one another') and by his attempts to live as a good man in a bad world, taking the initiative in acting with kindliness and dignity whatever the response of others. To the senatorial class he was the perfect emperor, and it is particularly appropriate that one of the few great bronze statues of the Roman world which survives is that of him on horseback. (It was saved because later generations thought it was of the Christian emperor Constantine. Pollution has now taken its toll and the restored original is now permanently under cover, with a copy having taken its traditional place in Michelangelo's Piazza del Campidoglio on the Capitoline Hill.)

Marcus Aurelius had made his son Commodus co-emperor three years before he died. In this he was reasserting the traditional desire of emperors to set in place a dynasty. However, the appointment was, said Marcus Aurelius' admirers, the only failure of his life. Commodus was, according to the historian Dio Cassius, 'a greater curse to the Romans than any pestilence or crime'. He abandoned the idea of extending Roman rule over the frontier, made peace, and returned to Rome. He was much condemned for this although in fact the peace held (thanks to resolute local governors and a policy of settling Germans on land in return for military service). Handsome and athletic, he then devoted himself to pleasure. Favourites took over power and an atmosphere of intrigue pervaded the court. The carefully cultivated image of family piety encouraged by Antoninus was shattered. In its place Commodus attempted to create an image of himself as a divine emperor. He portrayed himself as Hercules, not in the guise adopted by Trajan, as a hero labouring on earth for humanity, but as a god who had already completed his labours and who stood alongside Jupiter. It aroused little support, and without allies in the army, the senate or even within his family, he was acutely vulnerable. He was assassinated in 192.

Septimius Severus

The assassination had taken place within Rome and was followed by a provincial *coup d'état*. While various senators fought over the imperial purple in the capital, the governor of Pannonia Superior on the Danube, Septimius Severus, an

African from Leptis Magna, exploited the loyalty of the legions. His own always provided the centre of his support but he soon had those of the Rhine and his native Africa behind him. A possible rival, the governor of Britain, Albinus, was temporarily bought off by offering him the title of Caesar with the implication that he would be Septimius' successor. Septimius now marched on Rome and the senate, in a manner reminiscent of the year 69, jettisoned their own candidate. Severus was greeted in magnificent style, flattered the senate, tricked the Praetorian Guard into surrendering its arms, and replaced it with one drawn from his own legions. From now on the Praetorian Guard was to be hand-picked by the emperor.

Severus had already shown that his political and military skills were considerable and he combined energy with astute opportunism. However, what he had done could be done by any resolute commander and the governor of Syria, Pescennius Niger, also chanced his luck and declared himself emperor. Severus set off to the east, defeated and killed Pescennius in 194, and then, amalgamating Pescennius' legions with his own, led them into Parthia (possibly to consolidate their loyalty through victory). The campaign was only interrupted when Albinus, who had discovered that he had been duped when Septimius designated his own son as successor, proclaimed himself emperor and crossed to Gaul. He was defeated and killed outside Lugdunum (Lyons) and Severus then strengthened his position in the west through the sacking of cities and mass confiscations of land.

Severus knew the importance of mixing ruthlessness with lavish generosity. The people of Rome were won over by donations and games and a great triumphal arch dedicated in 203 is one of only three in Rome to remain largely intact. Coins show that he was placed in a triumphal chariot drawn by no less than six horses, with, as a sign of his dynastic ambitions, his sons beside them. His patronage included a massive rebuilding of his native city Leptis Magna. In a relief of a triumphal procession at Leptis there is what can be interpreted as an innovation in imperial art. The emperor faces away from the crowds and stares forward at the onlooker. He is carved slightly larger than those around him. Here was the elevation of the emperor as superhuman. Like Commodus, but much more successfully, Severus portrayed himself as a companion of the gods. Severus was determined to set in place a dynasty and his son Antoninus (better known as Caracalla, from the Celtic hooded cloak he wore) was made co-emperor in 198 when only 9.

Severus was an expansionist emperor, a sign that when the empire was led with determination it had not lost its vigour. In 197 he was back campaigning against Parthia and plundered some of the great cities of the empire, Seleucia, Babylon, and the Parthian capital Ctesiphon. Although the campaign then faltered, Severus added two more provinces to the empire in northern Mesopotamia and Roman rule now stretched as far as the Tigris. In 207 news arrived of another revolt, this time in the far west of the empire, among the northern tribes of Britain. Severus was ailing but he travelled north with his sons Caracalla and Geta and they shared in the suppression of the revolt. Archaeologists have found the remains of the camps which supplied the Roman armies as they penetrated north of Hadrian's Wall.

Severus died in York in 211. He had shown what ruthlessness and incisive leadership could achieve in defending the empire. His reign marked important shifts in the balance of power. Severus' wife, Julia Domna, was from Syria (she identified herself with Cybele, the great mother goddess) and most of his advisers were easterners. Provincials were preferred to Italians and soldiers to civilians. The army was given a pay rise and soldiers allowed to make legitimate marriages. Promotion from the ranks became easier. Severus' alleged last words to his sons, 'Stick together, pay the soldiers, and despise the rest', have something of the ring of truth about them. This was certainly a more militarized empire and possibly even a fairer one, although it could be argued that by his defeat of the Parthians Septimius unwittingly added to the long-term problems of the empire. The weakened Parthians were replaced by the far more powerful Sasanians.

Caracalla and the Later Severan Emperors

In his last years Severus had been increasingly concerned with the instability of Caracalla. According to one source he had even considered killing him. However, while in Britain he had appointed his younger and more popular son Geta as co-emperor and the two sons succeeded together. They loathed each other, even setting up separate households in the same palace in Rome. In 212 Geta was murdered by Caracalla and, it was said, some 20,000 of his supporters were massacred. (A fascinating reminder of the murder can still be seen on Septimius' arch in Rome where Geta's name has been chiselled out.) Caracalla himself survived until 217 when he was murdered by a Praetorian Prefect. Although he was not a great commander he had earned some popularity among the soldiers for his readiness to share their hardships while on campaign along the northern borders. The ruins of the vast baths he built in Rome remain and his reign is also remembered for the extension of citizenship to all subjects of the empire (except slaves and certain freedmen) through the *constitutio Antoniniana*. The historian Cassius Dio reports that his motive may have been no more than to make all liable to the taxes, such as inheritance tax, paid only by citizens, but the edict is also a reflection of the more egalitarian mood of the empire under the Severans.

Severus' dynasty lasted until 235. A Praetorian Prefect, Macrinus, reigned briefly after Caracalla's death before the family regained control in the shape of a nephew who shrewdly took the name Marcus Aurelius Antoninus. The power behind the throne was Julia Domna's sister, the new emperor's grandmother, who claimed the new Marcus Aurelius was Caracalla's illegitimate son. He proved to be a devotee of an eastern sun god and is normally known by the title of this god, Elagabalus. His adherence to oriental practices and public exhibitionism were found deeply offensive. His grandmother had him murdered in 222 and provided another grandson, Severus Alexander, then only 13, to take his place. That there was still some residual loyalty to the family of Severus is suggested by Alexander's survival for another thirteen years, but he in his turn was murdered by his troops when he decided to negotiate rather than fight with the German tribes.

The Crisis of the Mid-Third Century

With the death of Alexander the empire enters one of its most complex periods. The literary sources are inadequate and offer little detail of a period of major instability with a pattern of attacks from both the German tribes and the Sasanian Persians over fifty years (234–84). Something can be learned from the study of coin hoards (the assumption being that they were hidden at times of trouble and can be roughly dated by the year of the latest coin), destruction levels, and the building of fortifications or the walls of cities, but the sequence of events is still unclear.

There were at least eighteen emperors in these years who could lay some claim to legitimacy. Their average reign was only two and a half years. It is not difficult to find the reasons for this high turnover. The geographical extent of the attacks on the empire ensured there were several armies campaigning at any one time. Their commanders might chance their luck at seizing power or even proclaim themselves emperor to make themselves more effective as leaders. The armies themselves had every incentive to declare their commanders emperor in the hope that this would give them access to greater plunder. There were also power struggles within the armies between rival commanders and several emperors died at the hands of their own men. Others died fighting invaders. The crisis of the third century was as much an internal as an external one. It showed up the inherent vulnerability of the emperors at a time of military stress. As many resources were used fighting rivals as in confronting invading enemies. The toughness and resolution needed to survive are vividly portrayed in the portrait busts of these emperors. They are among the more impressive achievements of Roman sculpture. (As examples one might pinpoint the bust of Philip the Arab (emperor 244–9) in the Vatican Museums or the head of Trajan Decius (emperor 249–51) in the Capitoline Museums in Rome.)

Attacks by German tribes were renewed in the 230s but they were relatively small scale and tackled with some ease by the new emperor Maximinus, a rough outsider from Thrace. The real threat to Maximinus came from Rome where there were still

Severan supporters in the senate. They exploited a revolt in Africa against taxation led by a local governor, Gordian, and eventually proclaimed his grandson, later Gordian III, as Caesar. Maximinus rushed south to deal with the situation but drove his men so harshly that they mutinied and killed him in 238. Gordian III, though still only a boy, emerged as sole emperor in the same year. He relied heavily on strong military men of whom the most prominent was an Anatolian, Timesitheus. While raids on the empire continued along the Danube border, the most troublesome was a series of attacks by the Sasanians on Roman border towns which provoked a major Roman counter-attack by Gordian in 243. It ended in his death and the withdrawal of the Roman army, after it had paid a huge ransom, under the Praetorian Prefect, Philip the Arab, who had been hastily declared the new emperor. It was Philip who faced the large-scale attacks on the Danube borders, including the first launched by the Goths. One of his commanders, Decius, was, however, so successful that his men elevated him to emperor and Philip died confronting him (249). Decius died, in his turn, in 251 fighting the Goths.

From 253 there was comparative stability in leadership as power was shared by Valerian, an Italian emperor of great aristocratic distinction, and his son Gallienus. Valerian's main concern was to stem the advances of the Sasanians, who in 253 (or possibly 254) had sacked Antioch, one of the great cities of the eastern empire. His own reign ended, however, in disaster in 260 when he was seized by the Sasanian monarch, Shapur I, during negotiations. Shapur humbled the proud Valerian by using him as a footstool from which to mount his horse and he eventually died in captivity. The Sasanian triumph was trumpeted by Shapur in a magnificent series of rock reliefs. The king is shown humiliating his Roman enemies. Gordian is shown being trampled underfoot by Shapur's horse. Philip pleads before the king for his release. Valerian, on foot, is held by his wrist by his conqueror.

The 250s and 260s were a time of almost continual unrest as invasions struck ever deeper within the empire. In 253 Goths reached as far south as Ephesus while in 260 the Alamanni reached Milan (the Roman Mediolanum) where they were defeated by Gallienus, emperor between 253 and 268. (It was probably now that the importance of Milan and the inadequacy of Rome as a base for the defence of Italy first became apparent.) In 259–60 other German tribes devastated eastern Gaul and made their way down to the Mediterranean. Some bands even penetrated Spain and Mauretania. In 267 the Heruli, a people not recorded on any other occasion—a reminder, in fact, of how transient many of these raiding groups were—took an invasion fleet of 500 ships into Greece and sacked Athens. The great Odeion of Agrippa and the Hellenistic stoas were destroyed and the survivors had to hurriedly construct a new wall for the city from the debris. Athens never fully recovered from the attack.

Gallienus was a man of enormous energy. Despite the range of attacks he managed to maintain peace in the central part of the empire for some six or seven years in the 260s. One of his innovations was a specialized cavalry force. He was also prompted into realizing that the empire might be better defended by dividing the imperial command. The prompt came from one of his commanders on the Rhine frontier, Postumus, who was declared emperor by his troops in 260. He soon found himself in control along the northern frontier, with a 'capital' at Trier, and with influence as far south as the Alpine passes. The next step, and that taken traditionally by usurpers, would have been to march towards Italy to challenge Gallienus but Postumus hesitated. He may have been wanting to consolidate his position in the west before he moved and he did win over the legions of Britain and Spain. However, even then he did not move and he seems to have been happy with a 'Gallic empire', which he ran as if it was a Roman state. It is probable that his rule depended not just on the legions but on the support of the local aristocracy, whose main concern would have been the defence of their lands. They may have offered him the taxation he needed to survive on condition he remained there to defend them. In fact Postumus campaigned so successfully against the Germans that between 263 and 271 they gave no more trouble. Although Postumus' 'empire' was an affront to the centralized traditions of the empire, it did provide a model to follow. Gallienus, in fact, realized the advantages of the arrangement and left Postumus alone until 265 when he tried unsuccessfully to defeat him. When Gallienus was murdered his successor Claudius II (268–70) also tolerated Postumus and his successors. The 'Gallic empire' survived until 274 when it was reconquered by the emperor Aurelian.

Another area of the empire to achieve independence during this period was Palmyra. This great trading city on the eastern border of the empire had been incorporated into the province of Syria in AD 18 but its ruling families, who depended on trade with the east, had always preserved its separate identity. Its king, Odaenath, successfully harried the Sasanians as they retreated from the campaign of 260 and Gallienus was prepared to allow him to coordinate the defence of the east. Odaenath then declared himself 'King of Kings' and held sway over much of Syria, Palestine, and Mesopotamia. Under his redoubtable widow, Zenobia, who probably murdered him in 267, the 'empire' annexed Egypt and much of Asia Minor. It was when Zenobia declared her son Augustus in 271 that the Romans moved to crush her. Palmyra was regained for the empire in 273.

The Effects of the Crisis

The effects of this continuous unrest are difficult to quantify. It has proved particularly difficult to assess the economic impact of the crisis. One response to the increasing costs of war had been the debasement of coinage. Marcus Aurelius had cut the silver content of coins by a quarter and Septimius Severus and

Caracalla had reduced it even further. By the reign of Gallienus a typical 'silver' coin only contained 2 per cent silver. This led to the hoarding of old coins, the fact of hoarding itself reflecting insecurity and breakdown, and the rejection of the new with a resulting breakdown of the currency and soaring inflation. With vast masses of new coins of increasingly poor quality being issued, forgeries became common as there was no standard by which to judge official coins. Increasingly the army had to be supplied in kind rather than in coin. It was those who relied on state 'salaries' who probably suffered most while those who had access to their own food supplies may have been less affected—in other words many may have survived by reverting to barter—but the evidence is so limited and its interpretation so difficult that even this is hard to prove.

It is certainly clear that communities living along the northern borders were disrupted and many of their inhabitants may have sought refuge in the cities. The insecurity of the times can be seen in the building of defensive walls, across the Isthmus at Corinth, in Athens, and in Rome (by the emperor Aurelian, ruled 270–5), though many smaller cities did not complete theirs until later in the century or beyond. In general, other building in cities is now rare and few dedicatory inscriptions survive. There is not a single one at Olympia after 265. Large cities, filled with imposing buildings, had already become increasingly difficult for their councillors to maintain and the invasions may only have hastened developments which were taking place in any case. On the other hand, some cities, Trier, Milan, and Sirmium (in the Balkans), gained new importance as centres of defence and administration. In general the cities of the east appear to have been more resilient than those of the west: Antioch was able to survive and flourish despite being plundered twice by the Sasanians.

The decline in city life and the general unrest may also have encouraged a move of the richer classes to the countryside although the evidence varies from one part of the empire to another. Generally in Europe the small and medium size villa appears to have been in decline and the larger villa on the increase. In the more ravaged areas of the empire there may have been the opportunity for speculators to buy up land and it appears that some of the great fortunes of landowners who appear in the fourth century were built up this way. Agriculture as a whole was not significantly threatened by the upheavals of the century. Pannonia on the upper Danube seems, despite its exposed position, to have benefited from new economic contact with the east. The construction of country villas there continued throughout the century. In less vulnerable areas of the empire prosperity continued. Syria and Asia were hardly affected by the unrest and olive production in north Africa increased. Spain also prospered. Overall, despite the instability at the centre, the empire proved astonishingly resilient, which is why scholars are reluctant to exaggerate the scale of the crisis.

One sign of this resilience is the appearance of revived or new local cultures. With the establishment of Roman rule local cultures had often been undermined, first by conquest and then through an influx of goods from Italy. As the shock effect of Roman victory wore off, local cultures regained their confidence. In the Celtic parts of the empire divinities such as the equestrian goddess Epona reappear and Roman towns are renamed with Celtic names. In other parts of the empire there are the first literary works in local languages, in Egypt in Coptic (popular Egyptian speech but written in Greek letters) and Syriac. There are economic revivals. Roman artefacts—pottery, for instance—became produced locally and trade links with Italy declined. In the third century many routes must have been disrupted, further encouraging the growth of regional trade. This new vitality, which reflected a shifting but enduring balance between imperial and local cultures, was, without doubt, a factor strengthening the empire.

The Romans Regain the Initiative

Gallienus was killed by his officers in 268. They probably resented his acquiescence in the independence of the Gallic empire and Palmyra. His successor, a cavalry-general, Claudius II (268–70), won a great victory over 'the Goths' which was to keep peace for decades, but died in the following year at his Balkan headquarters, Sirmium, of the plague. After his death a series of emperors continued the struggle to resume control of the empire. They were of Balkan stock (the Balkans had become a major source of recruits) and their loyalty to the empire showed how successful it had been in integrating its subject peoples in a common cause. The first of these emperors was Aurelian. Aurelian defeated an invasion by the Alamanni and finally brought to an end the two independent parts of the empire, the Gallic empire and Palmyra. He also rationalized the boundaries of the empire by withdrawing from Dacia and so re-establishing a frontier along the line of the Danube. To restore the confidence of the people of Rome, who had become increasingly aware of the vulnerability of their city, he built a massive wall round it, much of which still stands today. Once the empire was restored he brought back riches plundered from Palmyra to display in a great triumph in Rome with Zenobia and the last of the Gallic emperors, Tetricus, among the prisoners.

A successor of Aurelian, Probus (276–82), achieved further success against the Germans through a mixture of victories and concessions and the inclusion of Germans in his armies. In the hope of recultivating the devastated borderlands of the empire defeated barbarians were settled there. Both Aurelian and Probus were killed by their own soldiers and Probus' successor, Carus (282–3), who had continued the fight back by launching a successful invasion of Persia, died on campaign. Much had been done in these short reigns but there needed to be a period of consolidation if the empire was to regroup its resources for long-term survival.

Carus was the first emperor not to seek formal recognition by the senate (and his successors followed suit). This was a significant moment as the emperors were now freed from any need to leave the frontiers for Rome. Carus had also attempted to strengthen his position by appointing his sons as Caesars, his deputies and successors. The elder, Carinus, was given charge of Italy and the western provinces. The younger, Numerian, accompanied his father on campaign against the Sarmatians and then on the invasion of Persia. When his father died he was declared emperor but while the army was returning home he was found dead in his litter. The chief suspect was the Praetorian Prefect Lucius Aper and he was soon challenged by the commander of the household cavalry, one Diocles.

Diocletian

Diocles' background remains obscure but he may have been born about 243 in the Dalmatian town of Solona near Split. Some stories suggest he was a freed slave or at least the son of one. Whatever his origins his character, like that of the earlier Balkan emperors, was reminiscent of that of the traditional Roman of the republic, self-disciplined, frugal, with a complete, somewhat arrogant, confidence in his abilities. Aper was summoned before the assembled armies at Nicomedia in November 284 and Diocles, after obtaining the support of the troops, stabbed him to death himself. Acclaimed as Augustus, Diocles defeated Carinus six months later and found himself sole emperor. He took the name Diocletian.

The third-century 'crisis' had been tackled with some success, but it was still unresolved when Diocletian came to power and there was no reason to expect he would last any longer than his predecessors. However, he had the good fortune to stay in power for twenty years and he was to establish the empire in a form which was to survive in the west for almost 200 years and in the east for very much longer. Many of his reforms depended on creating a coherent system out of what had been a series of improvisations by earlier emperors but he did this with immense determination and great organizational flair. His first concern was the succession. Here he may have been influenced by memories of the joint emperorship of Valerian and Gallienus and the example of the Gallic empire and Palmyra. Imperial responsibilities, he realized, were better shared. A fellow Balkan commander, Maximian, was appointed as a joint, but clearly junior, Augustus in 286. Seven years later two more younger commanders, Constantius and Galerius, were added as Caesars and they were designated as successors to the Augusti. The Tetrarchy, or 'rule of four', was consolidated through marriage alliances between the four families. (There is a moving statue of the four, each with one hand on another's shoulder, the other on the hilt of his sword, embedded in the wall of St Mark's, Venice, after it had been looted from Constantinople in the Fourth Crusade of 1204.) Although the empire remained a single political entity each was given a sphere of operation. Diocletian took the east, Maximian, Italy and Africa, and the two Caesars, Galerius and Constantius, the Danubian provinces and Britain and Gaul respectively. Four new imperial capitals appeared, Trier near the Rhine, Milan in northern Italy, Sirmium on the Danube border, and Nicomedia in Asia Minor. Rome was now a backwater so far as the practical needs of the empire were concerned although Diocletian built a vast bath complex there (see p. 523) and provided a senate house in red brick (which still stands) on his only visit to the city. It was little more than a sop to the senators, who had done nothing to sustain him in power.

In the 290s the Tetrarchs achieved between them a succession of victories which quelled the Germans, dealt with a wide range of local insurgents who were taking advantage of the breakdown of order, and ended in 297 with a massive defeat of the Persians by Galerius. There was to be peace on the eastern frontier for decades to come. These victories and the absence of civil war meant that resources could be used more effectively in the defence of the empire. The archaeological evidence suggests that a massive programme of building took place along the frontiers involving the construction of much more sophisticated forts and barriers. Walls now had projecting towers and fewer, narrower gateways, with extra forts being used to thicken the line of defence. The well-preserved walls of the 'castle' at Portchester on the southern coast of Britain provide a good example. They were probably built by Carausius, a local commander, who was entrusted by Diocletian with the defence of the Channel. (A similar fort was built at Boulogne.) The walls are over 3 metres thick and 6 metres high with twenty bastions. They were originally surrounded by a double ditch. These were much more substantial fortifications than anything known earlier in the empire.

A recent view is that these fortifications may not have been aimed at the Saxons but intended instead to protect goods in kind which had been collected for the armies. Indeed, if the empire was to survive in a strengthened form it was essential that it exploited its tax base more efficiently. When there was a sudden demand for resources it had been met by the requisitioning of local produce in what could only have been a haphazard and deeply resented way. Diocletian developed a system under which each individual was assessed on the production potential of his land rather than its extent. Each piece of land was given a value in units known as *iuga* from which the tax required could be computed, and this would remain the same over five years after which time another census would take place. For the first time a budget could be planned. From the little evidence that survives, most of it from Syria and Egypt, it does not appear that the weight of taxation increased. Rather it was more efficiently collected. The burden continued to fall on the poor with the rich able to claim a variety of exemptions.

Traditionally the governor of a Roman province had also been its military commander. Diocletian developed a policy, probably initiated earlier in the century, of splitting the civilian and military commands. The number of provinces was doubled and each now had a civil governor and a military leader (*dux*). The aim was probably to allow the civil administration to concentrate on efficient tax collection without the distractions of defence. The system was consolidated at the top under Constantine when military commands to the *duces* were transmitted via *magistri militum* (Masters of the Soldiers) and civil instructions via the Praetorian Prefects who now lost their traditional military role. In between the central administration and the provinces was another tier, the dioceses, of which there were twelve, each headed by a vicar. While the new system took some time to settle as governors and local officials learnt their new roles, it was to stay in place until the collapse of the western empire in the fifth century.

While many of the armies' needs were met by supplies in kind, some had to be bought in and the soldiers also received cash payments. So it was essential to stabilize the money supply. In 293 Diocletian did this in characteristic fashion by sweeping away all vestiges of local currencies and replacing the devalued coins by a currency based on pure gold coins of 5.20 grams in weight with pure silver coins for lower denominations. Constantine followed him by introducing a gold coin lower in weight (4.45 grams), the solidus, which was still being used in the Byzantine empire as late as the eleventh century. However, the mass minting of bronze coins continued (largely, it seems to provide the soldiers with spending money) and this meant that inflation remained rampant. Again it was typical of Diocletian that he should launch an empire-wide campaign to bring it under control.

The Edict of Prices of 301 is a fascinating document. In it are listed the proposed maximum prices for a vast range of goods and the highest wages each type of craftsman and labourer should receive. For a sewer-cleaner this was 25 denarii a day, for a top-quality scribe the same amount for every hundred lines of script. A teacher of rhetoric was entitled to charge 250 denarii a pupil, an elementary teacher 50 denarii a boy. Different grades of wheat, fish, wine, and olive oil all had their prices. A 600-pound camel-load could not cost more than 8 denarii a mile to transport, an ass-load 4 denarii. Shoes fit for a senator would cost 100 denarii a pair, for a patrician 150 denarii, while for an equestrian only 70 (so far did traditional marks of status survive). However, such an attempt to control the minutiae of every transaction, especially when there was not true money economy in any case, was bound to fail. A hostile witness, the Christian writer Lactantius, records that goods were simply hoarded and prices soared even higher. Even the threat of death or exile for offenders did not deter the speculators and the Edict soon became a dead letter.

There has been much controversy over how Diocletian organized his army. It had certainly swollen since the second century and may have numbered between 350,000 and 400,000 men. There are records of new legions but some of these may

BRITANNIA II

BRITANNIA
INFERIOR

FLAVIA CAESARIENSIS

BRITANNIAE

BRITANNIA SUPERIOR

BRITANNIA I

Londinium

MAXIMA
CAESARIENSIS

Atlantic Ocean

GERMANIA
INFERIOR

BELGICA II

GERMANIA II

Trier

BELGICA

BELGICA I

GERMANIA

Rhenus

AGRI DECUMATES

Danuvius

LUGDUNENSIS II

Sequana

RAETIA II

NORICUM
RIPENSE

PANNON

G A L L I A E

Liger

LUGDUNENSIS I

GERMANIA
SUPERIOR

RAETIA

NORICUM
MEDITERRANEUM

NORICUM

PANNON
SUPERIC

AQUITANICA II

SEQUANIA

ALPES
GRAIAE

RAETIA I

AQUITANICA I

AQUITANIA

NOVEM POPULI

VIENNENSIS

Lugdunum

VIENNENSIS

Rhodanus

ALPES
COTTIAE

AEMILIA

VENETIA AND
HISTRIA

Mediolanum

Ticinum

Padus

Aquileia

Ravenna

SAVIA

PANNO

GALLAECIA

NARBONENSIS I

Arelate

NARBONENSIS

NARBONENSIS II

ALPES
MARITIME

LIGURIA

FLAMINA

HISPANIA

Durius

Iberus

TARRACONENSIS

TUSCIA
AND
UMBRIA

Tiberis

PICENUM

DALM.

LUSITANIA

Tagus

CARTHAGINIENSIS

Anas

CORSICA

SARDINIA

** I T A L I A**

Roma

SAMNIUM

CAMPANIA

APULIA AN
CALABRI

H I S P A N I A

BAETICA

LUCANIA AND
BRUTTII

MAURETANIA
TINGITANA

MAURETANIA
CAESARIENSIS

MAURETANIA
TABIA

NUMIDIA
CIRTENSIS

Carthago

PROCONSULARIS

SICILIA

Catania

MAURETANIA CAESARIENIS

NUMIDIA

NUMIDIA
MILITIANA

BYZACENA

Mediterranean S

A

F

R

I

C

A

AFRICA

TRIPOLITANIA

ASIA

‑ ‑ ‑ ‑ ‑   Severan province boundary

CARIO

....   Diocletianic province boundary

•   Principal Roman mint in the time of Diocletian

AFRICA   Diocletian's dioceses are shown in bold capitals

0   1000 km

0   500 miles

Map 17

DIOCLETIAN'S DIOCESES AND PROVINCES
IN THE EARLY FOURTH CENTURY AD

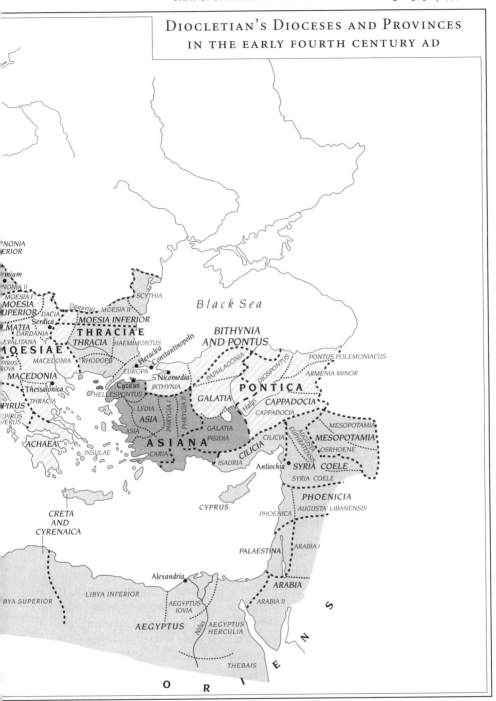

PNONIA
ERIOR

rmium

NONIA II

MOESIA I
MOESIA
UPERIOR DACIA

Danuvius MOESIA II

SCYTHIA

Black Sea

MOESIA INFERIOR

LMATIA
DARDANIA

Serdica

THRACIAE

EVALITANA THRACIA HAEMIMONTUS

BITHYNIA
AND PONTUS

OESIAE

IRUS
IOVA MACEDONIA RHODOPE

Heraclea EUROPA Constantinopolis PAPHLAGONIA

PONTUS POLEMONIACUS

MACEDONIA Nicomedia DIOSPONTUS ARMENIA MINOR

Thessalonica Cyzicus BITHYNIA

PIRUS
EPIRUS
VERUS THRACIA HELLESPONTUS

PONTICA

PONTICA

LYDIA GALATIA CAPPADOCIA

ACHAEA ASIA PHRYGIA I PHRYGIA II Halys CAPPADOCIA

MESOPOTAMIA

INSULAE GALATIA

ASIANA PISIDIA CILICIA MESOPOTAMIA

CARIA AUGUSTA EUPHRATENSIS OSRHOENE

ISAURIA CILICIA

Antiochia SYRIA COELE

SYRIA COELE

PHOENICA

PHOENICIA

CYPRUS PHOENICA AUGUSTA LIBANENSIS

CRETA
AND
CYRENAICA

PALAESTINA ARABIA I

Alexandria

BYA SUPERIOR LIBYA INFERIOR AEGYPTUS
IOVIA

ARABIA II

ARABIA

AEGYPTUS AEGYPTUS
HERCULIA

Nilus

THEBAIS

O R I E N S

have appeared only because the size of each original legion was reduced. (The legionary forts of the period seem to have held only some 1,000 men as against the traditional 5,000 of a full-strength legion.) This would have allowed the men to have been used more flexibly (and also made it easier to supply them from local resources) but how they were actually deployed is still a mystery. An argument that small forces on the frontier acted as delayers while more mobile forces were rushed up from behind has not been backed by archaeological evidence.

Diocletian sensed that the power of the emperor needed to rest on something more than military might. Earlier emperors had associated themselves with the gods (Commodus with Hercules, Aurelian with the sun god, for instance). The problem for someone of obscure birth was how to establish the link. As Sabine MacCormack has pointed out in her *Art and Ceremony in Late Antiquity*, surviving panegyrics to the emperors suggest that it was their very success that could be used to show that they were the favoured of the gods. (There is an echo here of Pindar and his hymns of praise to successful athletes.) The choice of god was also important, as the fiasco of Elagabalus had shown, and here Diocletian chose shrewdly. He proclaimed himself as none other than the son of Jupiter, while Hercules, whose successful labours had made him the symbol of those who claimed to be labouring to free humanity of its terrors, was associated with Maximian. On Maximian's coins Hercules was often portrayed slaying the many-headed hydra, an appropriate symbol for Rome's many enemies. (The hydra was a flexible symbol—Christians were later to talk of a hydra of heresies confronting orthodoxy.)

The emperor had now become something different. The pretence that he was no more than an elevated magistrate was exploded as ceremonial became more important. Accessibility was renounced in favour of inaccessibility. Diocletian did not invent the new ceremonial. A famous description of Aurelian meeting a delegation from a German tribe has the emperor dressed in purple sitting on a tribunal surrounded by a crescent of troops, his commanders on horseback and the imperial standards arrayed before him. The scene was carefully set before the Germans were allowed into the emperor's presence. Diocletian also dressed himself in purple and suppliants had to grasp the robe and kiss it before they could be heard. The emperor was treated as if he was the personification of virtues such as majesty or serenity (and thus would be addressed as Your Majesty or Serenity). Audience chambers were designed to show off the emperor while court officials made access to him an obstacle course of elaborate ritual. His replies were fed back by officials. As the identification between emperor and the traditional gods of Rome was consolidated there was increasing suspicion of those who refused to respect traditional rituals, and the last years of Diocletian's reign were marked by persecution of Christians, a persecution carried out with special fervour by Galerius in the east.

In 305 Diocletian abdicated, persuading a reluctant Maximian to do likewise. He retired to a palace at Split, parts of which still stand. Although his achievements were remarkable, they depended on his eventual successor Constantine to bring them to fruition. The fourth and fifth centuries were, as a result, not, as they might have been, solely a period of decline but one in which imperial government was reinvigorated and set in new directions. As Peter Brown has written, 'Far from being a melancholy epilogue to the classical Roman empire, a fleeting and crudely conceived attempt to shore up a doomed society, the first half of the fourth century witnessed the long-prepared climax of the Roman state.' For this Diocletian must take much of the credit.

The Emergence of Constantine

When Diocletian and Maximian abdicated Diocletian's carefully structured system of succession was put into operation with Constantius and Galerius being appointed Augusti and they in their turn naming two new Caesars. However, the system fell apart almost immediately. Constantius died in 306, but, instead of one of the Caesars succeeding him, the troops of Britain and Gaul acclaimed his son, Constantine, as Augustus. Meanwhile in Rome the son of Maximian, Maxentius, also had himself proclaimed emperor. By 308 there were no less than seven rival emperors contending for power.

The winner was to be Constantine, an intensely ambitious and determined man with little time for power sharing. By 312 he was in Italy and advancing towards Rome, which was defended by Maxentius. The rival contenders for the western empire met at the Milvian Bridge, which ran across the Tiber just north of the city. It was a decisive battle. Maxentius and his men were trapped against the Tiber and forced into headlong retreat across the river where many, Maxentius among them, were crushed or drowned.

Constantine now entered Rome as victor and the senators soon voted him a triumphal arch which still stands near the Colosseum. Its decoration is a mixture of styles with much of the material reused from earlier imperial monuments. The reused material seems to have been picked specifically from monuments to 'good' emperors such as Trajan, Hadrian, and Marcus Aurelius, presumably so as to associate Constantine with them. What is perhaps most interesting is the contrast between these older reliefs and those created specifically for the arch. A panel from an arch of Marcus Aurelius shows this emperor in his role as dispenser of justice and largesse, sitting informally surrounded by petitioners. A newly carved panel shows Constantine in the same role but now represented sitting formally and staring to the front with the gathered petitioners carved at only half his size and gazing up at him. It is the pose of Septimius Severus at Leptis taken a stage further. The arch marks the appearance in art of the new imperial ethos, the emperor as demigod, removed from his people.

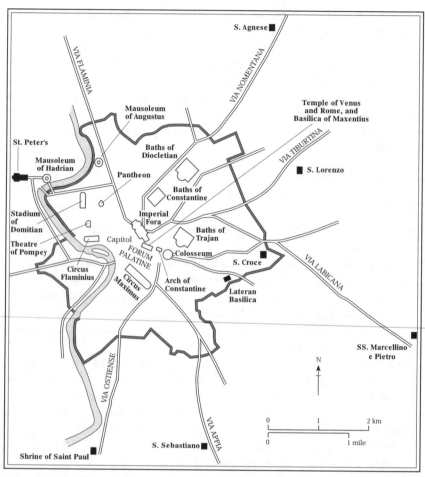

MAP 18 Rome at the death of Constantine, AD 337. Note how Constantine had added traditional buildings such as a complex of baths, his triumphal arch, the basilica of Maxentius, which he completed, in the historic centre while his churches such as the Lateran Basilica (later St John Lateran) and Santa Croce were placed on the edges of Rome on sites already owned by the imperial family. This suggests Constantine's determination to exercise his Christian patronage without offending pagan tradition-alists. Other early churches (St Peter's, San Lorenzo) were built on the burial places of martyrs.

The inscription on Constantine's arch attributes his victory to 'the inspiration of the divinity and the nobility of his own mind'. It appears that the emperor is being associated with a single god as his third-century predecessors, Elagabalus, Aurelian, Diocletian (Jupiter), had been. The senate did not specify which divin-ity. On the arch Constantine is shown making a sacrifice to the goddess Diana but there is also a representation of the sun god shown alongside his head. In fact, from about 310, the sun god seems to have been Constantine's favoured divinity, perhaps partly because the god was especially popular among the Balkan troops and their officers. Constantine was to issue coins with *Sol Invictus*, the unconquered sun, portrayed on them, as late as 321.

The most remarkable feature of the victory at the Milvian Bridge was that Constantine later claimed he had had a vision, or dream—the accounts are confused—that the God of the Christians had effected his victory. There followed an extraordinary reversal of policy towards Christians. In the so-called 'Edict of Milan' of 313, Licinius, Augustus in the east since 308, joined Constantine in proclaiming 'that no one whatsoever should be denied freedom to devote himself either to the cult of the Christians or to such religion as he deems best suited to himself, so that the highest divinity, to whose worship we pay allegiance with free minds, may grant us in all things his wonted favour and benevolence'. It was a remarkable proclamation and can be interpreted as the culmination of the traditional Roman tolerance of religious cults, now extended even to Christianity. Yet Constantine's own commitment to Christianity and the effective way in which the Christians themselves exploited their new status led, ironically, to the elimination of all pagan cults over the next 200 years. In this sense the Edict of Milan marks a significant turning point in western history. To understand its significance, Christianity itself needs to be explored.

FURTHER READING

On Marcus Aurelius see the fine biography by A. Birley (London, 1987). The same author has provided the equally good *The African Emperor: Septimius Severus* (London, 1988). On the emergence of the Germans see M. Todd, *The Northern Barbarians*, already cited, and B. Cunliffe, 'The Impact of Rome on Barbarian Society, 140 BC–AD 300', in Cunliffe (ed.), *The Oxford Illustrated Prehistory of Europe* (Oxford, 1994). See Peter Wells, *The Barbarians Speak: How the Conquered Peoples Shaped Roman Europe* (Princeton, 1999) on the archaeological evidence for the absorption of Roman culture. On the third-century crisis there are short overviews in Millar, *The Roman Empire and its Neighbours* and Averil Cameron, *The Later Roman Empire* (London, 1993) but I am grateful to John Drinkwater for sharing the draft of his chapter for the relevant *Cambridge Ancient History* volume. It will provide an excellent overview of this exceptionally difficult period when the volume finally appears. See A. King and M. Henig (eds.), *The Roman West in the Third Century: Contributions from Archaeology and History* (Oxford, 1981). John Drinkwater's *The Gallic Empire: Separatism and Continuity in the North-Western Provinces of the Roman Empire* (Stuttgart, 1987) provides a thorough analysis of Postumus while Palmyra is now dealt with by R. Stoneman, *Palmyra and its Empire: Zenobia's Revolt against Rome* (Ann Arbor, 1992). Diocletian is dealt with by S. Williams, *Diocletian and the Roman Recovery* (London, 1985), though the trend is now more towards stressing how much Diocletian relied on earlier precedents. See chapter 3 of Averil Cameron's *The Later Roman Empire*. On the elevation of the emperor see S. MacCormack, *Art and Ceremony in Late Antiquity* (Berkeley, 1981). For Constantine see the suggested reading for Chapter 30.

29 | The Foundations of Christianity

Bâ€‰y the time of the Edict of Milan (313) Christianity had survived in an empire which had been at best indifferent to it and at worst actively hostile for nearly 300 years. Its origins, like so many of the religious beliefs that spread into the Graeco-Roman empire after the first century, lay in the east. It was inspired by Jesus, a Jew who lived and preached in Galilee, part of Palestine, before being crucified in Jerusalem in the reign of Tiberius. (Jesus was his given name— Christ, from the Greek *Christos*, the messiah or anointed one, came to be used when his movement spread into the Greek world.)

The Gospel Evidence

The sources for Jesus' life are, like those for most aspects of the ancient world, inadequate. References to Christianity in contemporary non-Christian sources are very few, just enough to give confirmation that Jesus existed. Of the twenty 'gospels' believed to have been written (the word derives in English from the Anglo-Saxon 'godspell', the Greek original means 'good news'), only four, those of Matthew, Mark, Luke, and John, have survived in full since antiquity while another, later, collection of sayings of Jesus (the so-called 'gnostic' gospel of Thomas) was rediscovered only in 1945, among the documents of the Nag Hammadi library, so called from the Egyptian town near where they were found. Parts of the later part of a gospel of Peter also survive and offer a fuller picture of the events immediately after Jesus' death. (Most of these other gospels were composed in the second century and were rejected as the 'canon' of accepted New Testament writings was consolidated in later centuries.)

As historical (rather than theological) sources the gospels have serious drawbacks. They were first written down two generations after Jesus' death (most scholars date the gospels to between 65 and 100 with John's account traditionally placed much later than the other three) and for local Christian communities distant from Jerusalem and Galilee where the events they describe took place. (Tradition relates that Mark's gospel was written in Rome and Matthew's in Antioch.) They appear to be based on collections of sayings, some of them in the form of parables. With the exception of a few surviving phrases in Aramaic, the language Jesus spoke, they are written in Greek. Inevitably much of the original meaning of what Jesus said and the context in which he said it must have been lost in the transfer from one culture and language to another.

In any case the gospels were not written primarily as biographies. Their aim was to emphasize the special importance of Jesus so as to distinguish him from the other holy men and cults which pervaded the ancient world. An important preoccupation, therefore, was to establish Jesus' status. This was done through highlighting stories of a virgin birth, of a 'Transfiguration' (the moment when God himself appears to have recognized Jesus' status), and of his powers as a miracle worker. Jesus' death and his resurrection are also given special prominence, with a focus on his mission as an innocent man, put to death but come to life again to proclaim God's message of salvation. There was also a concern with establishing Jesus as the longed-for messiah (see below). To do this, stories from his life were probably shaped to correspond with prophecies from the Hebrew scriptures. The first chapters of Matthew, for instance, outline the events of Jesus' birth and early life with constant reference back to earlier prophecies. Matthew may, in fact, have seen Jesus as a leader who aimed to bring redemption to Jews alone but who like earlier 'prophets' was rejected by them.

The degree to which such needs and pressures shaped the 'facts' presented in the gospels is the subject of immense scholarly dispute. The trend of recent scholarship pioneered by such scholars as Emil Schürer and, more recently, Geza Vermes, has been to seek to accept the historical reality of Jesus but to place him more securely within his Jewish background. This background has been put into sharper focus by the growth of understanding of the Jewish world of the first century, particularly as a result of the discovery of the Dead Sea Scrolls (see below).

The Life of Jesus

Jesus emerges about AD 27 after a 'baptism' by an itinerant preacher, John the Baptist. He had been brought up in Galilee, a northern region of Palestine, in the village of Nazareth, a peasant community with a population estimated to have been between 200 and 400. Galilee was governed not by the Romans but by a series of client kings, first, at the time of Jesus' birth around 4 BC, Herod, and then his son Herod Antipas. So, contrary to popular belief it was never one of the provinces of the empire during Jesus' lifetime. Herod Antipas raised his own taxes and kept order himself and archaeological evidence of any Roman influence is very limited. (There is rather more evidence of Greek and Phoenician settlement.) Even though Galilee was a reasonably fertile area and not cut off entirely from the outside world, the Galileans had the reputation of being a tough and rather unsophisticated people, looked down upon by the more highly educated Jews of Jerusalem to the south. They had their own pride, and several of Jesus' recorded sayings stress his own distrust of outsiders. Straightforward and direct, he had little in common with the devout Jewish sectarians such as the Pharisees who laid immense emphasis on rigid adherence to Jewish law, the Torah. He was more in the tradition of the *Hasid*, the holy man, an individual who has the power to cure illnesses, exorcize devils, and heal the sins which Jewish teaching believed was their root cause. He had no inclination to distance himself from ordinary people and moved freely among the local outcasts. In Mark's gospel especially his miracles are rooted in his compassion for others. His success was dependent on his preaching in terms his fellow Jews could identify with but his God was more immediate than the traditional one of the Jewish world. His coming was promised soon, his kingdom might even be already on the way, and he would have special care for the poor and rejected. The news of Jesus' healing powers and his message spread quickly and crowds gathered to listen to him. They may have been drawn in particular by his promise of the restoration of traditional values at a time when Galilean peasant society was under acute pressure from population growth, Herodian rule, and the influx of Greek settlers.

Certainly the world in which Jesus moved was a tense one. Judaea to the south had been a province of the Roman empire since AD 6. Although Roman rule had been comparatively light, and the province administered not from Jerusalem but from the coastal city of Caesarea, the Roman governor (technically he was a prefect) appointed in AD 26, Pontius Pilate, had outraged Jews by his insensitivity. In Jerusalem itself the chief priest, Caiaphas, was in charge (a good example of how provincial government was left to the local elite) but there was always the fear of Roman retaliation if he mishandled any local unrest. The trickiest time of year was when thousands of Jews attended the Passover in Jerusalem. Then the governor himself moved up from the coast to supervise good order. So when Jesus moved his ministry out of Galilee to Jerusalem for the Passover he was entering a volatile situation. Any apparent threat to good order, as when Jesus entered into the temple, was likely to lead to a reaction by the conservative priesthood, who relied on Roman acquiescence for its survival. It may have been to save themselves that the priests handed Jesus over to Pilate. Pilate, never a sensitive or merciful man, had little hesitation in ordering the crucifixion.

Jesus' followers were shattered by his death, in particular by its humiliating form. (It was to be 300 years before Christians could bring themselves to represent Christ hanging on the cross, although there may have been other cultural reasons for this inhibition.) However, early on stories circulated that, though taken down dead from his cross and buried, he had come to life again and had been seen by a favoured few before ascending into heaven. The belief in this 'resurrection' persisted to become a central doctrine of Christian belief. Meanwhile Jesus' closest disciples remained in Jerusalem and struggled to keep their community intact. An early leader was the former fisherman Peter, who, according to Matthew's account, had been picked out by Jesus as the first leader of his movement. By AD 40, however, the dominant figure in the community appears to have been Jesus' brother, James. The preoccupation of the small community at this time was to wait together until the coming of God, predicted by Jesus, took place.

Another role for Jesus emerged in these early years, that of messiah. The coming of a messiah, 'the anointed one' who would deliver the Jews from bondage, had long been part of Jewish belief but the Jewish messiah had always been seen as a powerful king coming in triumph. Jesus' life and death could hardly give him this status but he could be seen in a different sense, as a messiah who redeemed (freed humans from the consequences of their own sins) through his own suffering. (Several of the Psalms of David provide precedents for a suffering messiah.) In this sense Jesus marked a fresh beginning in God's plan for mankind. Christians now talked of a 'new' covenant between God and his people to replace the traditional one of the Hebrew scriptures (see p. 101). (These different conceptions of messiah were to be one of the issues which helped maintain a division between Christians and Jews.)

The impulses which led to the acceptance of Jesus as the messiah were not unique to Christianity. On the north-western shore of the Dead Sea to the east of Jerusalem in 1947 some shepherd boys stumbled upon a cache of leather and papyrus manuscripts hidden in caves around Qumran, the first of the celebrated Dead Sea Scrolls. More manuscripts were discovered and gradually the life of a Jewish community, members of the Essene sect, was revealed. The Essenes rejected worship in Jerusalem and lived as small communities in monastic seclusion in the wilderness, rigidly observing Jewish law. They shared their property, may have practised celibacy, and identified themselves strongly with the poor. They saw themselves as a privileged group, God's elect, who were also waiting for a messiah who would usher in the kingdom of God. Meanwhile they studied the scriptures assiduously for prophecies of his coming (a vast amount has been learned about the formation of the Hebrew scriptures, the Christian Old Testament, from the surviving Scrolls). No direct links have been traced between the Qumran community and Christianity but the parallels are many and show that the Christian community was not alone in its sense of being a privileged people waiting for the coming of their god.

The Early Christian Community and the Missions of Paul

The small Christian community of Jerusalem must have felt isolated. It was viewed with suspicion by many traditional Jews, particularly when early Christians such as Stephen argued that the new covenant brought by Christ was needed because Jews had failed to adhere to the old. (Stephen was stoned to death by the Jews and thus became Christianity's first martyr.) Its converts were mainly among Greek-speaking Jews, and soon small congregations appeared outside Jerusalem in the Jewish communities of large cities such as Damascus and Antioch, the capital of Syria and third city of the empire. (The term Christian appears to have been first used in Antioch.) The synagogues in these large cosmopolitan cities traditionally attracted gentiles (non-Jews) to their services and it must have been in this way that the story of Jesus first leaked out into the gentile world.

At first it had little impact. The Jerusalem leaders, Peter and James, wedded to their Jewish background, insisted that Jesus was only for those who were circumcised and who obeyed Jewish dietary laws. Uncircumcised gentiles could not be admitted to the sect. It took one of the most remarkable figures of early Christianity to break this taboo. This was Paul, a Greek-speaking Jew from Tarsus in Cilicia and a citizen of the empire. Paul was a Pharisee who had come to Jerusalem to train as a rabbi. At first he had shared the Pharisees' distrust of Jesus and joined in persecution of Christians but then, on the road north from Jerusalem to Damascus, he had a vision of Jesus and became a believer.

Interestingly it was some time, at least three years, before Paul made contact with the Christian community in Jerusalem. He was probably much younger than its leaders (he may have been born as late as AD 10) and, unlike them, had never known Jesus. In his letters to the early Christian communities, the earliest surviving documents of Christianity, he makes almost no reference to Jesus as a historical person. However, Paul had few doubts as to who Jesus was and what his message meant. He was the Christ who had come to redeem those, Jew and Greek, slave and free, male and female alike, who showed faith in him. Those who put their trust in Jesus would be saved. Paul's emphasis is thus on faith rather than rigid adherence to Jewish law. Many of Paul's letters (those to the Corinthians in particular) are concerned with the problems which arise when believers are freed from the rigid constraints of a moral code and have to define a new code of behaviour which is compatible with their faith in Jesus.

Paul insisted that uncircumcised gentiles could become Christians and he argued his case against the restrictive attitudes of the Jerusalem community with vigour. He only got his way when he agreed that his gentile churches would collect money for the church in Jerusalem. There followed broad agreement that the Jerusalem leaders would continue to preach to Jews while Paul would be leader of the mission to the gentiles. Nevertheless, the relationship between the two missions was a tense one. Paul later told the Galatian Christians of a public row he had had with Peter in Antioch. Peter had been prepared at first to eat with gentiles but when joined by fellow Jewish Christians from Jerusalem withdrew from doing so. His behaviour infuriated Paul, who felt in the circumstances that Peter had no right to make gentiles follow Jewish ways.

The doings of Paul and the early Christian community are described in the Acts of the Apostles, composed, probably in the 60s AD, as sequel to his gospel, by Luke. An educated Greek, he was writing within the historical traditions established by Thucydides and he may have been present at some of the events he records. He probably had no written sources and it is believed that the speeches he places in the mouths of his main characters are, like those of Thucydides, shaped to the personality of the speaker and the occasion on which he was speaking with the result that scholars view the historical accuracy of Acts with some caution ('vivid but unreliable' in the words of the scholar Philip Rousseau). Luke has a wider message. He attempts to place the Christian story within the context of world history and, more than any other gospel writer, he shows a detailed knowledge of the Roman world. His account of Paul's ship-wreck on the way to Rome, for instance, is a valuable piece of historical evidence in its own right (see earlier p. 115). It was to be 250 years before another such detailed work of church history (that by Eusebius) was to be composed.

Paul is the central character in Acts and it was his energy and beliefs which transformed the young Christian communities. He moved on his missionary journeys through Galatia, Asia, Macedonia, Greece, and even as far west as Rome, inspiring the first Christians and struggling tirelessly to achieve some coherence and unity in their beliefs. He was so successful that the Jerusalem Christian community was soon eclipsed. It had no real future within the Jewish world and in the revolt against Rome of AD 66 it was accused by traditional Jews of being unpatriotic. The break between church and synagogue was complete by about AD 85 although scattered and isolated communities of Christian Jews con-tinued to exist in Syria and elsewhere for some time.

Paul's impact on the shape Christianity took was profound. He laid a new emphasis on the importance of 'faith', specifically condemning the pagan philosophers for their 'empty logic' and thus arguably setting in place a conflict between Christianity and the Greek tradition of rational thinking. His abhor-rence of sexuality (especially homosexuality) was much more pronounced than that of Jesus (who laid a greater emphasis on the sanctity of the marriage bond rather than any distaste for sexuality as such). While Jesus appears to have been relaxed about his exercise of authority, Paul was much less secure, partly because often he has no direct contact with the scattered recipients of his letters and con-stantly feared that in his absence they were losing their way. His stress on the importance of Christian authority was to become influential in the fourth cen-tury when the church needed to consolidate its own position. Equally influential for the Christian tradition was Paul's depiction of the human personality as at war with itself. 'I have been sold as a slave to sin. I fail to carry out the things I want to do, and find myself doing the very things I hate . . . I know of nothing good living in me,' as he told the Romans. As seen earlier (p. 284) this sense of internal struggle was also intrinsic to Plato's concept of the soul and by the fourth century Plato and Paul's conceptions of inner conflict had coalesced to provide a specifically Christian psychology of sin.

By the second century the gentile communities represented mainstream Christianity. Their separation from Judaism was a tortuous process, with Christians claiming that God had forsaken the Jews, but Judaism nevertheless provided an enduring influence. Christians believed, like Jews, that there was only one god, who deserved exclusive worship, and that those who believed were a people set apart. It is hard to imagine the later success of Christianity without this cohesion and sense of exclusiveness. The elders of a Jewish synagogue may have provided a model for the priesthood and the Jewish condemnation of idols was transferred into the Christian tradition, again by Paul. It left ambiguities in the way Christians approached art as they increasingly used decoration in catacombs, meeting places, and, later, churches. Could, for instance, a line be drawn between a work of art which helped viewers understand the divine and a work which was venerated for its own sake, as icons tended to be? As Christianity gained official status in the later empire pagan art became vulnerable to outright destruction by extremists (and the tensions over art erupted within the Christian world in the iconoclasm controversy in eighth-century Byzantium and at the Reformation).

There was also a shared ethical tradition. Jews valued chastity and the stability of family life. They visited the sick, and supported the poor. Sometimes, as with the Qumran community, they held property in common. This was echoed by early Christian behaviour. 'We Christians hold everything in common except our wives,' said the second-century Tertullian. Christians retained the Hebrew scriptures, valuing them for what were seen as references—in Isaiah, for instance—to the coming of Jesus. It was important for a religion derided by many as having no roots to secure itself a past. The Old Testament remained an integral part of the body of Christian scripture, even if the God of the Old Testament, with his exclusive relationship with one people and a heavy emphasis on the destruction of his enemies, sits ill at ease with the more gentle and approachable god preached by Jesus. (In the 140s one Marcion, the son of a bishop from Pontus, did in fact argue that the Gods of the Old and New Testament were distinct, with the God of the New Testament altogether a superior entity to that of the Old. Marcion, who had come to live in Rome, was excommunicated from the Christian community there in 144, but his ideas continued to be highly influential. They were eventually declared heretical.)

Christianity within the Spiritual Life of the Empire

The spiritual life of the empire at this time was one of extraordinary variety. Traditional Roman religion remained highly ritualistic with the emphasis on the propitiation of the gods through ceremonies which had to be carried out with absolute precision. This approach was reinforced through the rise of the imperial cult, which took different forms in different reigns according to the demands of the ruling emperor and the degree to which he was prepared to foster the worship of his predecessors. In Africa, dedications to emperors were inscribed on temples alongside those to Jupiter, Juno, and Minerva. As Augustine was to point out in his critical assessment of paganism in *The City of God*, these traditional religious activities were primarily concerned with the maintenance of the glory of the state. They did not, in themselves, have an ethical content although this continued to be supplied by philosophical movements such as Stoicism.

A mass of temples, oracles, centres of healing, and remote shrines also survived alongside the official religion of the state. In Egypt animal worship persisted. At Didyma on the coast of Asia a great temple to Apollo remained crowded with worshippers seeking the advice of the oracle there. (The continuing popularity of oracles sustained the belief that the will of a god could be known and that there were gifted individuals who might be able to proclaim it, an approach which was to have its own influence on Christians.) Judaism remained strong, despite the impact of diaspora and Hellenization. In Syria people honoured a Holy and Just Divinity, who was portrayed with attendant angels. In the Celtic world water and river gods remained popular. As seen earlier (p. 515) Roman cults either coexisted with or were superimposed on these beliefs and a variety of cults could be followed by an individual without any sense of impropriety.

Then there were the mystery cults appealing to those who sought a more personal salvation. These cults shared common features which may be traced back in the Greek world, for instance, to the ceremonies involved in the worship of Demeter at Eleusis (see above, p. 238). Typically, initiates had to go through ritual purification. There was the promise of some form of personal communion with the god or goddess on earth and of a reward after death. In Apuleius' *Golden Ass* (see above, p. 525) the rites of initiation to the cult of Isis are described in detail. The initiation itself included a ritual bath, the transmission of secrets, and ten days of fasting before the ceremony. The climax for Apuleius (it is assumed his account is autobiographical) was one of intense mystical experience. 'I approached the borders of death, I was borne along through all the elements and then I returned. At midnight I saw the sun blazing with bright light, I came into the presence of the gods who dwell above the earth and those who dwell below.'

The gods and goddesses who were worshipped in these mystery cults tended to come from outside the Greek world. The cult of Isis spread from Egypt and vied with the long-established cult of Cybele (whose origins were in Anatolia) for those, not necessarily women, who wanted the protection of a mother goddess. Mithraism, a popular cult among soldiers and men of business, had its origins with a Persian god, Mithras. Evidence of Mithraism is found in army camps throughout the Roman world and some 400 Mithraic 'temples' are known. The intensely personal nature of the relationship between worshipper and god acted to elevate the favoured deity above the other gods. Isis tells Apuleius: 'I am Nature, the universal mother, mistress of all the elements, sovereign of all things spiritual, queen of the dead, queen also of the immortals, the single manifestation of all gods and goddesses that are.' (Translation: Robert Graves.) By the second and third centuries AD this elevation of one god or goddess above all others was a common feature of religious belief and many pagans were quite happy to deal with the concept of a 'Supreme deity'.

The early Christians were both in this world and outside it. Much of the imagery of the New Testament—light and darkness, faith compared to flourishing crops—is similar to that found in mystery religions. The 'facts' of Jesus' life were presented in a format which was not unique to him. With the gospel of John (written c.100) he is presented as divine but he was not alone in this. Humans had been conceived by gods in both the Egyptian and Greek world. It was said that Mithras had been incarnated and been visited by shepherds after his birth in a cave. Stories of miraculous healings, shared meals of believers, and even resurrections (in the legends surrounding Cybele, her beloved Attis, a shepherd, is mutilated, dies, but is reborn to be reunited with the goddess) and the promise of an afterlife for the initiated would have been commonplace to anyone who had contact with mystery religions. The development of the cult of Mary, the mother of Jesus, acquires a new richness when placed in parallel with the worship of other mother figures in these religions (although the most influential development was to be the cult of Mary's perpetual virginity). Many of the attributes of Isis, as a protectress of sailors, for instance, reappear in worship of Mary, 'the star of the sea'.

Yet there were major differences. While belief in one mystery religion did not preclude involvement in another, Christianity did require rejection of other gods and an exclusive relationship with Christ and his God. Another problem, and one which lasted until Constantine's acceptance of Christianity, lay in the relationship between Christianity and the state. The Romans were traditionally suspicious of religious activities which took place in private. It is interesting that in Apuleius' description of the worship of Isis the ceremonies begin with public prayers to the emperor and senate. This was doubtless a precautionary measure to ward off suspicion. The Christians made no such compromises and their worship of a man who had claimed to be a king aroused instant distrust. 'These men all act against the edicts of Caesar, saying there is another king, Jesus,' shout hostile crowds in Thessalonica in the first century AD (Acts of the Apostles 17: 7). The isolation of the Christian communities and garbled accounts of their activities (including free love and cannibalism) led to a consensus by authorities that this new sect (its newness arousing suspicion in itself) needed to be kept tightly under control. The letters of the emperor Trajan to Pliny (see above, p. 504) show that the punishment of Christians who came to the notice of the authorities and who refused to repent was already the norm in the early second century.

The Early Christian Communities

The distinct identity of the early Christian communities and their insistence on welcoming and offering support to all must have been attractive to many who needed protection in a harsh world. Women seem to have made up a large part of the membership of the early communities, as they probably did in the mystery religions. An ascetic streak in early Christianity appears to have attracted virgins and widows in particular. It was precisely women of this status who were most marginal in traditional Graeco-Roman society with its focus on marriage and childbearing and so the church offered them a home denied elsewhere. The poor were also welcome. In Rome 1,500 poor were being fed by the church by the middle of the third century while fifty years later the community at Antioch was providing food for 3,000 destitute people.

Later Christian writers argued that God had put the Roman empire, with its wide-flung trading routes, in position specifically so that Christianity might spread more easily. The openness of the empire certainly helps explain the geographical range of the early communities. The first Christian communities were spread mainly over the eastern part of the empire, especially in the cosmopolitan cities of the coasts, though there was a Greek-speaking Christian church in Rome by the middle of the first century. These communities were exclusively urban (among the meanings of the word 'pagan', eventually used in a derogatory sense by Christians of non-Christians, is country dweller, though the word also means civilian as against a soldier) and most kept a low profile so as not to invite persecution. An opponent, Celsus, whose attack on Christianity, written about 180, was influenced as much by his sense of social superiority as distrust of Christianity *per se*, recorded woolworkers, cobblers, and laundry-workers among the congregations, going on to argue that Christianity was only suitable for the most ignorant, slaves, women, and little children. Recent scholarship suggests that individuals of wealthier backgrounds were, in fact, members of the church from its earliest days, some providing their houses as meeting places. With time there is more evidence of converts of higher social status, and Robin Lane Fox has pointed out how the background of Mary, the mother of Jesus, was 'upgraded' in the third century so as to make her appear of high status. (A fictional account of her life gave her rich and well-born parents. Political and cultural factors combined to elevate her even higher. By the fifth century Mary is being presented, in the mosaics of Santa Maria Maggiore in Rome, for instance, in the robes of an empress.) It is important, however, not to overestimate the success of early Christianity. Perhaps 2 per cent of the empire were

Christians by AD 250 (though there are some estimates as high as 10 per cent), with virtually no Christian presence in the west of the empire or along its northern frontiers. The boundaries between what was Christian and what was pagan were not clearly drawn nor was conversion necessarily permanent. There was considerable diversity of belief, understandably so in an empire where there were so many local communities remote from each other and with their own traditions. Inevitably many Christian communities failed and their members lapsed. A major issue in the third and early fourth centuries was how to deal with those who left the churches when persecution threatened.

The Christian communities required meeting places where worship could be carried on and baptisms take place. The need for discretion meant that these early 'churches' were converted from homes. An early example has been found at Dura-Europus on the Euphrates, right on the eastern edge of the empire. Here a 'middle-class' home was transformed into a simple Christian meeting place in about 230. In the decorated baptistery the earliest known representation of Christ survives. He is portrayed as a beardless young man extending his hand over the man 'sick of the palsy'. In the western empire there are examples of the next development, the enlargement of the meeting hall so that it becomes the dominant part of the building. At the villa at Lullingstone in Britain, domestic rooms on one side of the villa were sealed off and reconstructed as a Christian meeting place in the fourth century. Perhaps the most atmospheric example of a very early church is the first phase of San Clemente in Rome, reached by descending below the eleventh-century church. There was a large hall for Christian worship here by the early third century which was transformed into something grander a hundred years later by the addition of an apse at one end and a porch at the other. However, in contrast to, say, Judaism, Christianity was remarkable for its lack of 'holy places', and even prided itself on the fact. While the Jews were confined to one 'promised land', argued the church historian Eusebius in the fourth century, Christians had a 'much greater land, truly holy and beloved of God, not located in Judaea'. There was some lingering distaste for Jerusalem as the place of the humiliation of the crucifixion and it was not until 451 that it was given its own patriarch.

Christians took care over their burials, favouring the Jewish custom of preserving the body rather than burning it. Around Rome the soft tufa rock allowed galleries to be cut into it with recesses for bodies carved out of their walls. One early Christian burial site by the Appian Way bore the name 'by the hollow' and the Greek for this gives the word 'catacomb'. The word was used to describe the hundreds of galleries constructed around Rome as the Christian community in the city grew in the second and third centuries. The catacombs are moving places to visit and they are also treasuries of very early Christian art. There are scenes from both the Old and New Testament. Jonah being saved from the whale and Daniel from the lions' den are common Old Testament themes emphasizing the

THE FOUNDATIONS OF CHRISTIANITY | 575

power of God to save those in peril. Particularly interesting are the representations of Jesus. Here pagan art provides the models for Jesus as Good Shepherd or the Sun of Righteousness, in one instance being carried up to heaven in the chariot of the sun. In some cases he is portrayed as if he were the pagan hero Orpheus who had the ability to calm beasts through the playing of a lyre. The suggestion is that Jesus will also bring peace to those around him.

The scattered Christian communities needed leadership. As suggested above Christians inherited from Judaism the concept of elders, known as presbyters, from the Greek *presbuteros*, 'old man'. This confirmed the early church as male dominated. (The evidence suggests that women did have some place in the very early church but that as Christianity spread into Greek and Roman communities traditional attitudes to women reasserted themselves.) By the early second century it appears that many communities had appointed one of the presbyters to the role of president with responsibility for the affairs of the community, overseeing baptisms, managing the offerings, and corresponding with local churches, for instance. The Greek term used for this was *episkopos*, an overseer, which had hitherto been used only of secular office. This was the origin of the bishop and by the middle of the second century it was accepted that there should be a single bishop at the head of each community. There was no supreme bishop, although those of the larger cities, Jerusalem (in very early days), Antioch, Ephesus, and Alexandria, claimed some form of pre-eminence in their region. Particularly important in this respect was the concept of apostolic succession through which a bishop received his status as a result of unbroken descent from an apostle's foundation of that bishopric. If, drawing on Matthew's account of Jesus proclaiming Peter as the rock on which he would build his church, Peter could be seen as the leader of the apostles, then Rome, where by tradition Peter ended his days in martyrdom, could claim primacy over the other bishoprics. The difficulty lay in asserting this primacy. In the late second century other bishops were affronted when Victor, bishop of Rome, tried unsuccessfully to impose the date of Easter adopted in Rome on the rest of the church.

Ironically it was just as Christianity entered a period of vigorous growth in the third century that Rome was losing its strategic importance within the empire. Even within the city the bishops were marginal figures so long as the pagan senatorial aristocracy remained powerful as it did until the end of the fourth century. Moreover the Christian communities in Rome, which at first were Greek speaking, gradually attracted native Latin speakers so that eventually, in the 380s, Bishop Damasus changed the liturgy from Greek to Latin. It may have been a pragmatic move but as Greek died out in the western empire, it left Rome increasingly unable to assert its authority over the east. A papacy able to sustain its authority over a defined area, in effect western Europe after the Islamic invasions had swept through north Africa, was a medieval development. (See in particular the section on Gregory the Great, p. 625 below.)

Christianity and the Greek Philosophical Tradition

In the diatribe he launched against Christianity, Celsus had complained of the ignorance and credulity of Christians, and by the late second century it was a charge that educated Christians began to take seriously. Already Christians had had to defend themselves against Gnosticism, a movement which reached its height in the second century. The Gnostics taught that the souls of human beings were imprisoned in their earthly bodies but could be liberated through the acquisition of 'knowledge' (*gnosis*). Christ, whom the Gnostics believed had had no earthly existence, was one of the mediators between man and the divine. Another second-century movement, Montanism, which arose in Anatolia, relied on charismatic prophecy, with its main adherents, Montanus and two women, Prisca and Maximilla, claiming their utterances were the words of the Holy Spirit. This too was rejected by the mainstream church, which now sought a more rational basis for belief. This was partly because Christianity was attracting more highly educated converts but also because of the need to find a secure basis for doctrine. So, in the Greek world, in particular, Christians began adapting Greek philosophy for their needs.

The first century AD had seen a revival of Platonism. (Platonic philosophy of the first to third centuries AD is normally known as Middle Platonism to distinguish it from the later Neoplatonism of Plotinus (205–70) and his followers (see p. 596).) Plato's 'the good' (see p. 283) was for these later followers a supreme reality, whose existence transcended human thought. It was possible to grasp the nature of 'the good' but only through a rigorous intellectual quest, an intense and penetrating meditation on what 'the good' might be. An appreciation of 'the good' helped, however, give the physical world meaning and value. Middle Platonism gave the name *theos* to 'the good' and this can be translated as 'God'. In this sense Platonism was echoing the elevation of deities seen in the mystery religions. Plato's Forms were seen by these philosophers as 'the thoughts of God'. (From now on 'the Good' will be given a capital, to suggest its elevation to a supreme spiritual force.)

Middle Platonism began to permeate the writings of Christians. Clement of Alexandria, writing around 190–200, was determined to show would-be converts that Christians were well able to hold their own intellectually with pagans and had no fear of Greek philosophy. Plato and the Platonists, argued Clement, had grasped the nature of God (possibly, he said, through reading the Hebrew scriptures) and had shown that his existence could be defended through the use of reason. This was a magnificent answer to the likes of Celsus who argued that Christianity was based on no more than woolly emotion and credulity.

The Platonists did not, however, mention Christ. The idea that 'the Good/God' could influence human history through the activity of a human being, whether divine or not, born in one specific place and at one point of time, was, in fact, alien to Platonism. Christians had therefore to find their own method of integrating Christ into the Platonist principles they had absorbed. One view first articulated in John's gospel, but later taken up by the church in Alexandria, was that Jesus represented the *logos*. *Logos* was a concept developed by Greek philosophers (Stoics as well as Platonists) to describe the force of reason which, they argued, had come into being as part of creation. *Logos* is a complex term, used in many different contexts and it was precisely the range of these which provided flexibility for the theologians. (The conventional English translation as 'the Word' conceals the wealth of its original meanings in Greek.) *Logos*, for instance, was described as the intellectual power with which human beings were able to understand the divine world so, in this sense, *logos* overlapped both the physical world and the divine. Christ could be portrayed as *logos* created by God in human form and sent by him into the world to act as an intermediary between God and man. This still left aspects of Christ's relationship with God unclear. Those who followed John in accepting Christ as *logos* had then to determine whether he was an indivisible part of God, of the same substance with the father, or a separate entity distinct from the father as in an earthly father–son relationship. Justin Martyr (*c.*100–165) argued for the second option. Jesus may have been God from the beginning of time but separate from the father in the same way that one torch lit from another is separate. Tertullian (*c.*160–*c.*240) from Carthage followed him in arguing Jesus as *logos* was only part of God and subordinate to him.

The most intellectually brilliant of these early theologians was probably Origen (184–254). Origen was an austere figure, deeply affected, it was said, by the martyrdom of his Christian father. His life's work lay in biblical scholarship, bringing together and commenting on different versions of the Old Testament, but he also made important contributions to the concept of Christ as *logos*. For Origen God had originally created all souls as equal parts of his goodness but gradually all failed to worship him and they fell from union with him into the material world. From here they had to be redeemed and restored to union with God in the original state of goodness. How was this to be done? Luckily, argued Origen, there was one soul which had never fallen away from God and which remained bound to him in adoration. It was this soul united to the *logos* which became incarnated in the body of the Virgin Mary and was born as Jesus. He was the instrument of redemption. Those souls who had fallen into human bodies could use him as inspiration for the long climb back to God. Origen was also important for following Plato in distinguishing the few (those whom Plato had called Guardians) who could grasp the reality of 'the Good' and the masses who were diverted by their sensual natures and lack of commitment from being able to do so. For them it was vital to stress the importance of faith. As Origen, in a passage deeply influenced by Plato, put it, 'As this matter of faith is so much talked of, I have to reply that we accept it as useful for the multitude, and that we admittedly teach those who cannot abandon everything and pursue a study of rational argument to believe without thinking out their reasons.'

Origen's views that Christ as *logos* was distinct from God the Father were among those which led to his being condemned as a heretic by the late fourth century (see the Arian controversy, p. 584 below). Origen had also argued that no one, even Satan, was beyond the redeeming power of God's love. There was, therefore, no need for a hell to contain the irredeemably evil. By the late fourth century, when scholars such as Jerome and Augustine were arguing for the reality of hell as a place of everlasting torment for those who have rejected God, the less forbidding views of Origen and his followers had been superseded.

The adoption of Platonism by Christian theologians was of immense importance. Plato had always argued that a minority could, through reason, grasp the eternal truths, which were ultimately more 'real' than any truth in this transient world, and impose them on the rest of society. This provided a rationale for church authority if the Platonic minority could be equated with the church hierarchy or the bishops meeting in council. Moreover Plato's denigration of those who let their souls be ruled by sensual pleasure also fitted well with the ascetic impulses of many Christians. Later his view that things of beauty or grandeur on this earth could provide an imitation of heaven was used to justify opulent church buildings.

The Persecutions

These speculations may have helped gain Christianity intellectual credibility but they did little to help the security of individual communities at times of tension. As early as 64 Christians were used as scapegoats by the emperor Nero when seeking to allocate blame for the fire at Rome. Nero could exploit the distrust of Christians as easterners and the seclusion in which their activities took place. There was seldom, however, any concerted activity against the early Christians and no empire-wide decree against them. Those who were considered troublesome were prosecuted under the traditional powers given to governors to maintain good order but, as Trajan had told Pliny, Christians should not be sought out specifically and those who had lapsed were of no concern at all.

The real problem was the renunciation by Christians of all other cults, including those involving worship of the emperor. Accounts of trials show that it was not so much what Christians believed that worried local governors as their refusal to honour traditional gods. The more flexible judges tried to find compromises, some gesture which could be passed off as recognition of these gods, but many Christians would refuse. In 177 the governor of Lugdunum (Lyons) asked the emperor Marcus Aurelius' advice on how to deal with the Christian community. Marcus Aurelius, who was highly conventional in his religious beliefs, believed Christianity offered a threat to the state and he was prepared to condone local persecutions. He replied that those who recanted could be set free but those who did not could be condemned to the arena or, if they were citizens, beheaded. Among the forty-eight put to death a slave girl, Blandina, stood out for her courage. It was said that her death aroused enthusiasm among other Christians, for whom a painful but sudden death seemed little price to pay for the guarantee of eternal bliss in heaven.

One of the most moving of early Christian documents is the prison diary kept by Perpetua, an early martyr who died with her slave girl, Felicity, in the arena at Carthage in 203. Perpetua's father desperately tried to persuade her to renounce her faith, especially as she was still nursing her infant daughter, but Perpetua stood firm and in prison appears to have exercised a leadership role over other Christian prisoners. She met her death with dignity, even, it was said, guiding the gladiator's sword to her throat. It could be argued the very specific context of martyrdom shaped a role for women as leaders which was denied to them in the everyday activities of the churches. There were clearly complex psychological elements of martyrdom. In north Africa in particular, there are signs of a collective willingness among communities to face death for their beliefs, with others attracted to Christianity as a result of their example. Tertullian put it succinctly, 'The blood of the martyrs is the seed of the church.'

The persecution of Christians reached its fullest extent in the third and early fourth centuries. The intensity of these persecutions reflected the tensions of the age. It was inevitable that those who refused to sacrifice to the gods would be confronted when the continuing defeats of the empire suggested that those gods were deserting Rome. The refusal of converted soldiers to honour the cult of the emperor was particularly intolerable. There was a major persecution under the emperor Decius in 250–1, with bishops as the prime targets, and another under Diocletian and his successor Galerius between 303 and 312. Persecution was not applied consistently. Many Christian communities escaped it completely. However, the random nature of the attacks, in which official backing was often given to the activities of lynch mobs, was frightening. Christians really were thrown to the lions in front of howling crowds. (The Christian Lactantius, writing in the early fourth century, told of the terrible punishments God would exact in retaliation for these enormities.)

Persecution can also be seen as a response to the success of Christianity in infiltrating official institutions such as the civil service and the army. Origen had argued that the spread of Christianity was a natural development willed by God and by the end of the third century he was apparently being proved right. In many large cities there were now so many Christians that they overflowed into public life, acting as councillors and imperial officials. Christianity was winning converts higher in the social scale so that even Diocletian's wife was rumoured to have Christian sympathies. Bishops were becoming well-known local figures, running large and well-organized communities and distributing alms among their members, while Christian communities may also have been filling gaps left by the decay of traditional institutions.

Cohesion was also being established between the Christian communities although it was a slow and often painful development. There was general agreement by 200 on a basic creed affirmed by all seeking baptism which included acceptance of God as the father, Jesus Christ as the son, the Holy Spirit, and the resurrection. (The Holy Spirit refers to the activity of God shown in the world, typically as the power of healing, casting out devils, or prophesying through the medium of ordinary human beings, but also as the instrument through which Mary conceived Jesus.) Gradually the sacred writings of the church were gathered into a Bible of selected books of the Old and New Testament (the Greek word *biblia* means 'the books'), although the disputes over which early Christian writings should or should not be included took some time to resolve. Those not accepted were gradually discarded or in some cases declared heretical. Most have now disappeared.

There was still, however, no supreme human leader of the church. The bishops of Rome, Antioch, and Alexandria had gained some prominence in their local areas with the right to consecrate the bishops of smaller cities, although they still vigorously refused any submission to each other. This was recognized by Cyprian, bishop of Carthage, who argued in his treatise on the unity of the Catholic church (251) that all bishops should act in consensus with no one bishop supreme over others. For Cyprian the church was the only body capable of authoritative Christian teaching and no true Christian could exist outside it. 'He no longer has God for his father, who does not have the church for his mother.' This definition of a church claiming exclusive authority over all Christians had immense implications for the future of Christianity. One indication of how deeply Christianity was becoming integrated in Roman society can be seen in Cyprian's definition of his authority as if he was a Roman provincial governor with heretics portrayed as rebels against that authority.

So when Constantine and Licinius offered toleration for all sects including Christianity in 313 the church, even though it still contained only a minority of the population, was in a strong position to take advantage of it. With the added support given by Constantine, Christianity came into its own and enjoyed a political and social respectability it had always lacked. Over the next century it was to become the only officially tolerated religion of the empire.

FURTHER READING

A good general introduction to early Christianity, which provides a full analysis of the written sources, is John and Kathleen Court, *The New Testament World* (Cambridge, 1990). *The*

Cambridge History of Judaism, especially vol. iii edited by W. Horbury, W. D. Davies, and John Sturdy (Cambridge, 1999), is essential for more advanced work. A scholarly overview of the Jewish world is G. Vermes and F. Millar's revised edition of E. Schurer, *The History of the Jewish People in the Age of Jesus Christ* (Edinburgh, 1973–87). A thorough and balanced assessment of the historical evidence for Jesus' life is to be found in E. P. Sanders, *The Historical Figure of Jesus* (London, 1993). See also, from a mass of recent work, G. Vermes, *The Changing Faces of Jesus* (London, 2000); J. R. Porter, *Jesus Christ: The Jesus of History, the Christ of Faith* (London, 1999); Paula Fredriksen, *Jesus of Nazareth, King of the Jews* (London, 2000); and Markus Bockmuehl (ed.), *The Cambridge Companion to Jesus* (Cambridge, 2001). For a clear account of how early concepts of Jesus as 'the Christ' developed see the excellent (as much for the quality of writing as anything else) John Macquarrie, *Jesus Christ in Modern Thought* (London, 1990). John McManners (ed.), *The Oxford Illustrated History of Christianity* (Oxford, 1990), has fine introductory surveys but does not include any discussion of the early historical sources. Peter Brown's *The Rise of Western Christendom* (2nd edition, Oxford, 2003) is outstanding (but starts in AD 200). B. Metzer and M. Coogan (eds.), *The Oxford Companion to the Bible* (Oxford, 1993), is essential as a record of up-to-date research. For the Dead Sea Scrolls, see Philip R. Davies and others (eds.), *The Complete World of the Dead Sea Scrolls* (London, 2002). For Paul, see E. P. Sanders, *Paul* (Oxford, 1991), as an introduction. Jerome Murphy-O'Connor, *Paul, A Critical Life* (Oxford, 1996), is a more detailed scholarly overview. For an overview of other religions see J. Ferguson, *The Religions of the Roman Empire* (London, 1970), and, essential for further study, Mary Beard, John North, and Simon Price, *Religions of Rome* (Cambridge, 1998). See also P. Athanassiadi and M. Frede (eds.), *Pagan Monotheism in Late Antiquity* (Oxford, 1999), for the rise of the idea of the 'supreme deity', and J. W. Liebeschuetz, *Change and Continuity in Roman Religion* (Oxford, 1979). Henry Chadwick, *The Early Church* (Harmondsworth, 1967), is a standard introduction and see now his magisterial *The Church in Ancient Society: From Galilee to Gregory the Great* (Oxford, 2001). P. Esler (ed.), *The Early Christian World*, 2 vols. (New York, 2002), has reliable articles on the main figures. E. Ferguson (ed.), *An Encyclopaedia of Early Christianity* (Chicago, 1990), provides background information. For the emergence of Christian doctrine Jaroslav Pelikan, *The Christian Tradition*, vol. i: *The Emergence of the Catholic Tradition (100–600)* (Chicago, 1971), is outstanding. For the relationship between Greek philosophy and Christianity see Christopher Stead, *Philosophy in Christian Antiquity* (Cambridge, 1994). Robin Lane Fox's *Pagans and Christians* (London, 1986) is essential for placing Christianity in a wider context. See also J. Rives, *Religion and Authority in Roman Carthage* (Oxford, 1995), which includes a study of Cyprian. Marina Warner has written on the cult of the Virgin Mary in *Alone of all her Sex* (London, 1976). Also useful for this chapter is R. MacMullen, *Christianizing the Roman Empire (AD 100–400)* (New Haven, 1984), and the classic E. R. Dodds, *Pagan and Christian in an Age of Anxiety* (Cambridge, 1965).

30 | The Empire in the Fourth Century

Constantine and Christianity

In histories of the Roman empire it has been traditional to make a chapter break between Diocletian and Constantine so that the latter could be welcomed as the first Christian emperor. It is certain that without imperial support Christianity would never have been more than the religion of a minority and to this extent the toleration and active support of Christians by Constantine does mark an important turning point in the history of the western world. However, making a break here tends to underestimate the continuity between Constantine and Diocletian and his predecessors. Constantine was preoccupied, as Diocletian was, with defending and financing the empire and securing a stable succession and many of Diocletian's reforms were sustained and consolidated by Constantine, in particular in the years 324 to 337 when he was sole emperor.

It may also be misleading to talk of Constantine as a converted Christian in the conventional sense of the word, even though this is the picture painted in the main source for his life, the biography by the church historian Eusebius (died 338/9). Constantine was not baptized until shortly before he died (although this was a common practice, with baptism delayed in the hope that the purified soul would be untouched by sin before death) and most of his advisers were not Christians. There is remarkably little mention of Christ in his recorded speeches or decrees or awareness of Christian doctrine. One could see Constantine's attitude to Christianity as a pragmatic one, the deliberate use of his victory at the Milvian Bridge as a platform from which to dismantle the structure of persecution and integrate the cohesive Christian communities in the service of the state. This is not to deny that Constantine showed a genuine commitment to Christianity but he was certainly unwilling to follow Christians in rejecting paganism. No committed Christian could have supported the degree of toleration given to such cults by the Edict of Milan and Constantine himself did not even abandon traditional worship. Towards the end of his reign he sanctioned the building of a large temple to his family on the Flaminian Way and it was to be endowed with theatrical shows and gladiatorial fights. Most remarkable of all, Constantine continued to portray himself on coins and in the statues of himself used at the dedication of Constantinople as a sun god. Many of his decrees were 'written in terms of a neutral monotheism which would be acceptable to Christians and pagans alike' (J. W. Liebeschuetz). Tellingly Constantine once informed a group of bishops: 'You are bishops of those within the church, but I am perhaps a bishop appointed by God over those outside.' Constantine was never to allow the church to interfere in the way he exercised his rule.

Whatever his motives Constantine's support for Christianity was crucial in establishing the religion's respectability and ensuring its continued spread. Not only could Christians now operate freely but in numerous ways Constantine gave them effective help. The clergy were relieved of any obligation to serve on city councils (a move which led to a mass of ordinations so onerous had these posts now become) and taxation. There was financial help for the building of churches and as bishops were now able to receive bequests some congregations became extremely wealthy. In Rome and Palestine the emperor and his family funded the first great Christian buildings. Constantine donated land from the old imperial palace of the Lateran to provide a cathedral for Rome, now St John Lateran, while on the Vatican hill a basilica (the traditional all-purpose hall of Roman public life now adapted to hold Christian congregations) was built over the supposed resting place of the apostle Peter. The martyrs were now given great prominence, their feastdays dominated the church calendar, and their shrines became centres of pilgrimage. The first St Peter's, like St John Lateran, no longer survives but Rome still has two fine fifth-century examples of basilicas, those of Santa Maria Maggiore and Santa Sabina. The former is adorned by magnificent mosaics while the latter boasts a finely carved set of cypress-wood doors with scenes showing the links between the Old and the New Testament, and one of the earliest known scenes of the crucifixion. Meanwhile the mother of the emperor, Helena, visited Palestine in 326 and set in hand the building of appropriate memorials to the life of Jesus at Bethlehem and on the Mount of Olives. Constantine himself was responsible for the great Church of the Holy Sepulchre at Jerusalem over the supposed burial place of Jesus. As early as 333 pilgrims were visiting these sacred sites. Parts of the diary of one of these, a well-born Spanish nun, Egeria, survive from her visit of 384 and show that, with official help, even remote sites in Judaea, Egypt, and Galilee could be visited by those determined enough to do so.

In her diary Egeria left a description of the Church of the Holy Sepulchre. 'The decorations really are too marvellous for words. All you can see is gold and jewels and silk . . . You simply cannot imagine the number and sheer weight of the candles, tapers, lamps and everything they use for services . . . They are beyond description, and so is the magnificent building itself. . . .' There is 'gold, mosaic and precious marble, as much as his [Constantine's] empire can provide.' These great new buildings, with their fantastic decoration and aura of sanctity around the shrines of the martyrs, brought 'a Christianization of space' (in the words of Robert Markus). In theory God might be everywhere. In practice he now seemed especially close once a worshipper entered a church. Yet the diversion of so many resources into religious building, although the norm in the pagan world, was an aberration for Christianity which had never proclaimed the need to display opulence. Until recently few books on church architecture have noted the radical reappraisal required to justify the glittering mosaics, the gold lamps and the extravagant domes by a community which in earlier times had been described as 'a crowd lurking in corners shunning the light'. In his fine study *God and Gold in Late Antiquity* (Cambridge, 1998), Dominic Janes has explored how the adaptation was made. Relevant texts were dug out from the Old Testament and if further theological justification was needed, churches could be seen as imitations of what might be expected in heaven. (Here again the influence of Platonism was strong.) Most (but not all) bishops acquiesced in the wealth which came their way and some, like Ambrose of Milan, revelled in the opportunity to create their own vast buildings. The abrupt shift to opulence, however, left its tensions. Well might the ascetic scholar Jerome complain of how 'parchments are dyed purple, gold is melted into lettering, manuscripts are dressed up as jewels, while Christ lies at the door naked and dying'. These tensions were to erupt in the iconoclasm of the eighth-century Byzantine empire and at the Reformation, which saw a widespread destruction of Christian art and imagery.

Few churches, of course, enjoyed the magnificence of the basilicas of the capitals of the empire. The three rooms found at the villa at Livingstone in Britain must have been more typical. Christians were still in a minority in every part of the empire even though the support of the emperor had led, in the words of Eusebius, 'to the hypocrisy of people who crept into the church' to win his favour. Moreover individual churches still enjoyed a large degree of independence and there was no effective way of settling doctrinal and other disputes between them. To this extent Christianity was still not a coherent force in Roman society. This was to change as successive emperors took the lead in consolidating a unified church.

The Arian Controversy

The nature of the Roman empire with its mass of local cultures made it impossible to impose uniformity and it is increasingly clear that Christianity had taken different forms in the different cultural niches in which it settled. By granting tax exemptions and other privileges to 'Christian' clergy, Constantine and his successors laid themselves open to petitions for exemption from a mass of different communities all claiming to be Christian. This meant that the state, anxious to control its tax base, was impelled to take the leading role in defining what was Christian orthodoxy. As early as 313 Constantine had to decide which of two rival Christian churches in north Africa to privilege. One, the Donatists, so called from one of their bishops, Donatus, claimed to be the 'true' church as they had stood firm against all persecution. Their rivals were made up of Christian communities which had buckled under persecution but had then asked for readmittance to the church. Constantine consulted bishops on the matter and eventually ruled against the Donatists, depriving them, in effect, of state patronage. It is arguable that Constantine preferred to work through the more flexible communities which had compromised themselves with the state rather than with the rigid and anti-imperialist Donatists. Even without patronage, however, the Donatists survived as a vigorous church in north Africa until destroyed by persecution by their fellow Christians in the early fifth century.

The Donatist controversy had not been a doctrinal dispute but in the 320s, as Constantine became ruler over the eastern empire with its much higher proportion of Christians, another major issue arose among the churches which certainly was. It concerned the relationship of Christ to God the Father. The question hinged on whether Christ had been part of God from the beginning of time or whether he had been created by him at a later date and with a distinct substance. The latter view, which had substantial support from earlier Christian tradition (Origen, for example), was argued by one Arius, a priest in Alexandria. The slogan of the Arians was 'There was [a time] when he [the *Logos*] was not'. Christ, in this tradition, occupied an indeterminate position somewhere between the creator and what had been created, neither fully god nor fully man. The issue was brought to the front when Arius was attacked by his bishop, Alexander, who argued an alternative view that the son had existed eternally and that there was no separate act of creation. (The rival slogan was 'Always the God, always the Son'.) The dispute was complex and the church provided no satisfactory way of resolving it. Constantine was concerned that such issues threatened his dreams of the church as a stable support for his rule and, having failed to cow the factions into silence, he took the initiative in convening a council of bishops in order to reconcile the opposing groups. It was eventually to meet at Nicaea, near to Constantine's eastern base at Nicomedia (Constantinople was still under construction) so that the emperor could attend in person.

The council of Nicaea, 325, was the first great ecumenical council of the church with 220 bishops in attendance, most of them from the east where the dispute was most intense. (The bishop of Rome, still on the margins of the largely Greek-speaking Christian world, did not appear.) The details of the council are obscure but it seems that it was Constantine himself who urged the declaration that Christ was 'consubstantial, of one substance, with the father', in effect a refutation of Arius' view. Constantine's aim was clearly to achieve consensus—he showed no interest himself in the minutiae of doctrinal disputes—and, in the short term he was successful. Only Arius and two bishops opposed the resolution. There was, however, an unhappy sequel to their opposition. Constantine used his imperial powers to exile the two bishops, the first indication that an emperor, with all the influence at his disposal, had assumed responsibility for upholding Christian doctrine. In fact the issue was unresolved. Arianism remained strong in the eastern empire and Constantine himself, in what seems to have been his overriding concern, to maintain the unity of Christianity, made no further move to condemn it. He even showed personal sympathy towards Arians and in fact his own baptism was carried out by an Arian bishop.

The Founding of Constantinople

After his victory at the Milvian Bridge, Constantine was prepared to recognize Licinius as Augustus in the east. The joint meeting at Milan which saw the issue of the Edict of Toleration was followed by a marriage alliance. Licinius married Constantine's sister and later they were jointly to declare their sons as Caesars. By this time, however, they had begun to quarrel over the borders between them, Licinius had renewed persecution of the Christians, and the relationship broke down completely. In 324 Constantine, as single-minded as ever in his pursuit of power, moved east to defeat Licinius and so became sole emperor.

Ostensibly the city of Constantinople, capital of the Byzantine empire for over a thousand years, was founded to commemorate Constantine's victory but a powerful motive must have been the need to create a base from which the defence of the empire in the east could be directed. The centuries-old Greek town of Byzantium was an ideal site. It was relatively close to both the Danube and Euphrates borders. There were excellent road communications both to east and west (though those in the west were vulnerable to disruption by invasion) and the city could also be supplied by sea. The Tetrarchic capitals with their palaces and adjoining hippodromes provided one model for the city, but a mass of statuary was looted from the Greek world (as it had been for Rome by earlier conquerors) and Constantine's creation of a second senate and the provision of a free grain supply for its inhabitants (much of which came from Egypt) also suggested that this was more than just a subsidiary capital. The city's hippodrome was directly modelled on the Circus Maximus in Rome and it was in its imperial box that Constantine, weighted with precious stones, displayed himself at the city's inauguration in 330. One can hardly avoid the impression that the self-glorification of Constantine ranked high among the motives for the city's foundation—a great statue of the emperor, with the rays of the sun emanating from his head, stood on a column in the Forum. Constantine spent much of his time in his new capital until his death in 337 although the city was still small at the time of his death.

Interestingly Constantine gave low priority to the building of churches in Constantinople and some, Vasiliki Limberis, for example (in *Divine Heiress: The Virgin Mary and the Creation of Christian Constantinople* (London, 1994)), have argued that one motive for building the city was to retain its founder's independence from the ancient Christian bishoprics. The only church completed by Constantine's death, that of the Holy Apostles, was his own mausoleum where he had himself buried as no less than 'the thirteenth apostle'. This somewhat provocative nomination provides further evidence of an emperor determined to maintain his own interpretation of his favoured religion. Even late in life Constantine kept his links with paganism. Coins issued on his death show him being welcomed into heaven with the same imagery as his pagan predecessors while the first 'Christian' churches in the city were dedicated to 'Wisdom' (the great Santa Sophia, still surviving today in its sixth-century form) and 'Peace', terminology acceptable to both Christians and pagans.

Constantine's Successors and the Problems of Defence

When Constantine died in 337 he left three sons to succeed him. All three were Christians. Constantine II took the west of the empire, Constantius the east, and the central provinces of Africa, Illyricum, and Italy went to the youngest, Constans. To secure their position they eliminated many of their close relatives but when, in 340, Constantine invaded Italy in the hope of adding it to his share he too was killed. Constans died in his turn in 350 when fighting a usurper, Magnentius. The following year Constantius and Magnentius met in the great battle of Mursa where Magnentius was defeated but both armies suffered enormous losses. 'Thus perished', wrote the historian Eutropius, 'large forces that could have conquered any enemy and assured the security of the empire.' After the battle the Alamanni who had been recruited by Constantius to help him went on the rampage in Gaul.

The truth was that the fundamental problems of the empire, the threats from outsiders from north and east and the instability of leadership, remained. Constantius ruled as sole emperor until his death in 361 and proved a conscientious ruler and commander but did not have the flair and charisma to galvanize the empire's defence. For much of his reign he was preoccupied in the east where the Sasanian king Shapur II was energetically raiding into Mesopotamia. This meant that the northern borders of the empire were neglected and Gaul, in particular, was frequently ravaged. For the first time the Germans were able to take cities. The Gauls only enjoyed some respite when a young cousin of Constantius, Julian, nominated by him as Caesar and given the charge of Gaul in 355, surprised everyone by proving a highly effective commander. Both the Franks and the Alamanni suffered major defeats at his hands. By 360 order had been restored to the borders and Roman forces were stationed along them.

Constantius, still hard pressed in the east, now tried to remove some of Julian's troops. They revolted and declared Julian an Augustus (360). Despite a half-hearted plea of loyalty to Constantius, Julian was ambitious enough to seize his chance and he was soon heading east. It was by chance that Constantius died before they could meet in battle and Julian found himself sole emperor by default. Julian was the last of the pagan emperors and he attempted to re-establish the traditional cults of the empire (see below). However, he was only to survive eighteen months before dying at the hands of an unknown assailant in 363 while on campaign against the Sasanians.

Julian's successor was a Christian army officer, Jovian, who, caught in enemy territory, was forced into a humiliating surrender of border territory to the Sasanians. He died on the way back to Constantinople. The army now chose Valentinian, a native of Pannonia, as the new emperor. Valentinian (emperor 364–75) was perhaps the last of the 'great' emperors. He was a tough man, often brutal, and completely intolerant of any challenges to his authority. However, he was a fine soldier and fought with success along the northern borders while at the same time quelling revolts in Britain and Africa. Archaeological evidence shows that he undertook a systematic programme of fort construction along the Rhine and Danube and on the main roads leading inland from the borders. For perhaps the last time the borders of the empire were effectively defended. Valentinian shared power with his inexperienced and much weaker brother Valens, whom he installed in the east of the empire.

Ammianus Marcellinus

The details of the period 354 to 378 are so well known because they are covered by one of the finest of the Roman historians, Ammianus Marcellinus (330–c.395). Ammianus was Greek by birth, a native of Antioch, but he provides a good example of how the empire had imbued Greeks with loyalty to a Roman ideal. Having served with the Roman army he spent the last years of his life in Rome and wrote in Latin. He has a nostalgia for the earlier days of Rome, contrasting the frugal habits of the early republic with the decadence of the grandees he observed around him in the city. His descriptions of their wealth and alleged corruption and their passage through the streets surrounded by a mass of slaves are among the most evocative portraits in his work.

Ammianus' history began in AD 96, the date at which Tacitus' history had ended. However, all the early books are lost. Those which survive (from 354) are based on personal experience and contemporary evidence and provide by far the best non-Christian perspective on an empire which was overwhelmingly concerned with political survival. Ammianus' work is remarkable at many levels, quite beyond the wealth of detail it provides. He can create, as Tacitus could, the atmosphere of terror emanating from a man who had absolute power, and in the closing chapters of his work he explains the feelings of impotence engendered by the hordes of 'barbarians' who swept into the empire before the cataclysmic defeat of the Roman armies at Adrianople in 378 (see below).

Ammianus' world, therefore, is one where pressures crowd in on those in power and their reactions are often brutal in return. For instance, he details the cruelty which spread from the top down during the reign of Constantius, for whom he had a particular aversion. In Pannonia one of the prefects, Probus, attempted to ingratiate himself with the emperor by gathering taxes with such force that the poor were sometimes reduced to suicide while the rich moved to escape his depredations. This is the picture which has survived of the fourth century in general, one in which Roman rule became increasingly brutalized. Whether it is the full truth is difficult to say. As has been suggested in earlier chapters, Roman rule had always been weighted towards the elites at the expense of the poor with little mercy shown for those who offended the state.

The Imperial Administration

In the second century the administration of the empire had been carried out by the provincial governors and their staff, a few hundred in all. By the fourth century government had become something very different. A mass of office holders had been created around the emperor himself, who now enjoyed being centre of a court. There were masses more at a subordinate level. (One estimate is that there were 30,000–35,000 officials by the late fourth century.) Now that urban life was in atrophy and the *decuriones* ever less willing to give patronage to their cities, government office became the most certain way of achieving status. As in any such system there was an obsession with rank, each level of the imperial service being minutely graded. The competition for these posts encouraged the buying and selling of offices and the emergence of new patterns of patronage as those with power and influence exercised them on behalf of dependants. As the administration became more complex corruption also appears to have spread.

The proliferation of official posts at the centre of the administration placed an even greater focus on the emperor. There was a paradox here. Just as the emperor had become in theory a semi-divine figure with almost absolute power, the post itself increasingly became the plaything of the soldiers. Julian, Jovian, and Valentinian all owed their elevation to the army. Emperors tried to secure their sons as their successors, appointing them as Caesars or even Augusti when they were still small, but it was hard to sustain a dynasty against pretenders or strong men who ruled from behind the throne. Insofar as the survival of the empire rested with energetic and talented emperors who were capable of mobilizing resources and men in its defence, it depended to a large degree on chance.

These weaknesses have traditionally been seen as among the causes of the fall of the empire in the century to come. However, it can hardly be said that the government of the fourth century lacked vigour. A mass of legislation survives, much of which tries to freeze the subjects of the empire into their role as tax-payers. Entry to those positions which carried tax exemption—the clergy, civil service, and even the army—was restricted and in many occupations sons were required to follow their fathers rather than escape elsewhere. Tenant farmers (*coloni*) were increasingly tied to the land and if they did move to other estates the landowner became liable for their poll tax. In extreme cases the *coloni* may have been little different from the slaves who still existed in large numbers.

If there was an area where the state was losing control it was over the traditional elites. These city elites were already under strain, a strain intensified by the growth of the court as an alternative focus for able men. The state tried desperately to keep them in place. As the empire became Christian the morale of those cities which remained pagan was undermined, especially as power centred increasingly on the bishops. As one pagan notable lamented, 'All the temples that are in the city will fall, the religion of the town will cease, our enemies will rise against us, our town will perish and all this great honour which you see will pass away.' Other potential centres of resistance were among the large landowners whose position in the west strengthened in the fourth century. The old senatorial class living around Rome was especially powerful now that the western emperors tended to be based in Milan. They preserved a mannered way of living, maintaining their relationships with each other through gifts and other courtesies and sustaining the traditional pagan cults of the city. How far their estates were cultivated efficiently and what proportion of any surplus ended up in the state's hands is uncertain but small-scale peasant production would probably have been easier for the state to exploit, as it certainly seems to have been in the east.

The evidence for the overall prosperity of the empire is ambiguous. The church (helped by tax exemptions and the renunciation of wealth in its favour by aristocrats who espoused asceticism) and many landowners in the west certainly became richer. The cities of north Africa were flourishing while the villa estates of Britain enjoyed their greatest period of opulence. (Most of the surviving mosaics from Roman Britain date from this century.) Yet there is also a mass of evidence complaining of the weight of taxation and traditionally a picture has been painted of an empire groaning under the oppressive demands of tax collectors and soldiers. This may be the result of better sources and voices not heard before at last having their say. It is also clear that conditions varied widely between different parts of the empire and that while some must hardly have been aware of the depredations of invaders, others knew the horror of the sudden raid all too well. Only patient detective work on the archaeological and epigraphic sources is likely to develop a fuller picture of what life really was like in the fourth century.

Pressures on the Borders

The problem, in fact, was probably not so much lack of the will to survive on the part of the government as the continued pressures of these invaders. The ongoing wars with the Sasanians were manageable in the sense that Sasanian Persia was a centralized state which could be negotiated with, although there were other factors involved, including the ambitions of leaders on both sides, which prevented peace. However, there was no easy way to control the northern borders of the empire. Valentinian had managed to preserve the frontiers but had died suddenly in 375, from an apoplectic fit brought on when negotiating with some intransigent Germans. His successor, his son Gratian whom he had made an Augustus when only 8, was now 16. (The troops also declared Valentinian's 4-year-old son, another Valentinian, as Augustus. There was a clear clash here between the needs of the empire for strong rulers and the determination of those emperors in power to start a dynasty.) Gratian and his co-emperor, his uncle Valens, now faced a massive incursion of Goths, as a hitherto unknown people, the Huns, appeared from the east. The Huns were nomadic peoples who, for some reason, possibly major economic changes in the steppes of central Asia, had been forced into migration. Ammianus is at his best as he describes this 'wild race moving without encumbrances and consumed by a savage passion to pillage the property of others'. The Goths were pushed helplessly towards the boundaries of the empire and soon a mass of refugees was struggling to cross the Danube.

Faced with this incursion Valens in fact saw it as an opportunity to recruit men for the overstretched Roman armies. However, far from organizing the recruitment in an orderly way, local soldiers treated the new arrivals with contempt. There were reports of Roman officers offering the Goths' leaders dogs for food in return for the surrender of their men as slaves. The Goths were outraged, broke free from Roman control, and were soon rampaging through Thrace. Valens had to march from Constantinople to subdue them, but at the Battle of Adrianople, 9 August 378, the Romans were caught by an overpowering mass of armed Goths and defeated. Two-thirds of the Roman army, possibly 10,000 of its best troops, died in the humiliating defeat. Valens fell among them.

This humiliation is often seen as a turning point in the history of the empire, the moment when the Romans finally lost the initiative against the invaders. This may be an exaggeration. The armies had been under pressure for decades and the defeat at Adrianople may have been no more than one further step in a continuous process of the weakening of the empire. However, a significant development in the relationships between Romans and barbarians now took place. Gratian appointed an efficient general, Theodosius, to succeed Valens and in 382 Theodosius signed a treaty with the Goths under which they were allowed to settle in the empire, in

Thrace, in return for providing troops for the Roman armies. Their position was to be one of privilege. They were to be exempt from taxation and able to serve under their own leaders. There were precedents for such compromises but this was the first time that an area within the borders of the empire had been passed out of effective Roman control. Within a few years the Goths were to be once again on the move, causing havoc as they searched for new land (see below, p. 609).

Gratian was killed in 383 when fighting a western usurper, Maximus. Theodosius tolerated Maximus until the latter invaded Italy, when Theodosius rushed westwards and defeated and killed him at Aquileia in 388. He was now sole emperor until his death in 395.

The Christian Emperor

Despite the support of Constantine the church was still relatively weak. After the pressures of the Nicene Council, there was increasing recognition that the formula of consubstantiality (expressed by the Greek word *homoousios*) had no backing from the scriptures and went against earlier teaching. Constantine's sons, though Christian, had continued to tolerate paganism. (Historians still use the word 'paganism' as a general term for non-Christian beliefs but they do so with increasing uneasiness. The connotations attached to the word unfairly degrade a range of beliefs, many of which were highly sophisticated.) They continued to hold the traditional title of *pontifex maximus* and subsidized pagan temples. A law of 342 prohibited the destruction of temples so as to protect the traditional entertainments associated with them. It was only in the 350s that Constantius launched a determined attack on paganism, in particular the practice of divination. (Emperors were always wary of those able to predict their successors.) However, even this campaign had its limits. When Constantius visited Rome in 357 (in one of his most famous passages Ammianus describes how the emperor struggled to maintain his self-control when faced for the first time with the magnificence of the city), he realized the enormous strength of paganism there and refrained from upsetting the privileges of the senators and the revenues of their temples. Archaeological evidence shows that temples in Rome were being restored as late as the 380s.

Like his father, Constantius was determined to achieve an agreed creed around which he could group the Christian communities and in 360, at a council of bishops he called to Constantinople, he did secure a somewhat unstable consensus for a compromise creed in which Jesus was declared to be *homoios*, 'like', the Father with the Nicene term *homoousios* specifically condemned on the grounds that 'it was not familiar to the masses, caused disturbance and because the Scriptures do not contain it'. Constantius' achievement was short-lived in that his successor Julian was determined to reintroduce paganism. Julian had been brought up a Christian but the elimination of most of his immediate relations by Christian emperors had shaken him. He was further disillusioned by the Christian infighting over doctrine. 'Experience', wrote Ammianus Marcellinus, 'had taught him that no wild beasts are so dangerous to man as Christians are to one another.' So he 'converted' back to paganism. As the orator Libanius put it in a panegyric to the emperor: 'You quickly threw aside your error [Christianity], released yourself from darkness and grasped truth instead of ignorance, reality in place of falsehood, our old gods in place of that wicked one and his rites.' From now on, Julian proclaimed, Christians were to confine their teachings to their churches. Julian was an intellectual, a philosopher emperor whose opposition to Christianity rested as much on a rejection of its teachings as on his personal experience of it as a faith torn by dissension. He mounted a powerful critique of Christian belief in his *Contra Galilaeos* (362–3) which analysed the scriptures for contradictions. He argued instead that a diverse empire needed a diverse set of gods to represent its many different cultures and traditions. (He followed this through by encouraging the rebuilding of the Temple in Jerusalem although, to the joy of the Christians, the building was halted by a great fire.) However, it was one thing for Julian to dissect the scriptures, it was another to find a stable alternative around which to rally the empire. His own religious ideas were complex and incoherent, a mixture of sophisticated philosophy with a personal enthusiasm for pagan sacrifices, at a time when many pagans had rejected them. Fascinating though he remains, Julian was not able to reverse the growth of Christianity.

With Jovian came a restoration of Christian privilege and there were to be no more pagan emperors. The church was able to resume its progress. Increasingly its influence was based on the emergence of strong bishoprics headed by men of character and power. The church had acquired great wealth, mostly in land donated by the faithful, while the bishops had been given rights of jurisdiction (they could order the release of slaves, for instance) and often had an important role in the distribution of alms. Administrative expertise was essential. For this reason bishops were normally chosen from the traditional ruling classes and in some cases were appointed even before they were baptized. One such was Ambrose, bishop of Milan from 374 to 397, and perhaps the most influential bishop and preacher of his age. He had been an effective governor of north Italy and when there was some dispute over the succession to the bishopric of Milan, he was asked to be bishop. Once baptized, he quickly mastered his new role, adopted the Nicene creed, and showed he was much more than an administrator. In the twenty-four tempestuous years of his rule he waged a formidable campaign against moral laxity, heresy (especially Arianism), and paganism. The council he held in the basilica at Aquileia in 381 was a superbly stage-managed condemnation of the Arian bishops summoned to attend apparently as equals but then browbeaten into submission. Ambrose insisted that it was the church which should define orthodoxy and set the standards of morality and the duty of the state to act in support. He first worked on the young Gratian, inducing him to surrender the post of *pontifex maximus*. His *cause célèbre* was his battle with the Roman senate over the statue of Victory which adorned the senate house in Rome. Gratian was persuaded to order its removal despite the most impassioned opposition from the pagan senators. Ambrose was also important in encouraging the cult of relics. Having found the supposed bodies of two martyrs, Protasius and Gervasius, in 386 he buried them in his own cathedral but also distributed parts of them to others he wished to impress. By 393 Ambrose had sent 'blood and earth' from the two as a gift to his fellow bishop, Victricius, at Rouen while 'dust' soaked in the martyrs' blood had been dispatched to Bishop Gaudentius of Brescia. This was the old practice of gift relationships extended to the Christian world.

After Julian's death the debate over the relationship between Jesus the Son and God the Father had revived. It was embittered by the lack of any secure foundation on which it could rest. Scripture, tradition, the teachings of rival schools of theology, and Greek philosophy were all used by the contenders. In the western empire there was general sympathy for a united Godhead on the Nicene model. In the east debate was more vigorous and varied but in the 370s the Nicene position received impressive intellectual backing from the works of the three theologians from Cappadocia, Basil of Caesarea, Gregory of Nazianzus, and Gregory of Nyssa, who developed a formula through which the Holy Spirit was integrated in a Trinity in which three distinct persons, God, Jesus, the Holy Spirit, shared a common substance. However no solution could have been imposed on the warring factions without the support of the emperor. It was Theodosius I who decided to back a revised Nicene creed. Although the Council he called to meet in 381 in Constantinople was relatively small (some 150 bishops, all from the east as Theodosius had no jurisdiction over the western empire) and its proceedings tempestuous, it was here that Nicene orthodoxy was passed and then imposed by imperial decree. The Arians were ordered out of their churches. Among the losers were the 'barbarian' peoples who had been converted to Christianity at a time when Arianism was dominant and who now found themselves classed as heretics (although most were to use their rejection to strengthen their own sense of identity). It is possible, in fact, that Theodosius' support for the creed was part of a deliberate policy of consolidating an 'orthodox' empire against 'heretical' 'barbarians'.

After Gratian's death Theodosius I became sole emperor and thus for the first time subject to Ambrose's influence. He first encountered Ambrose in Milan in 388 where he found himself forced to defend a Christian community at Callinicum on the Euphrates who had sacked a Jewish synagogue. The emperor had ordered restitution but Ambrose insisted that he should not restore a building where Christ was denied. Ambrose's influence increased. When the emperor ordered a massacre of some rioters in Thessalonica, Ambrose threatened to excommunicate him and took the credit for forcing him to repent. (Although Theodosius' acquiescence may well have been a calculated public relations exercise, the incident was later used by popes in their struggles with European monarchs as a precedent for the primacy of the church over the state.) Theodosius became a Christian emperor of the type desired by Ambrose. It was in his reign that a wide variety of heresies were first defined and a vigorous onslaught launched against pagan cults. In Egypt bands of fanatical monks wrecked the ancient temples. The Serapeum, near Alexandria, one of the great temple complexes of the ancient world, was dismantled in 392. In north Africa Christian vigilantes raided pagan centres and ridiculed traditional beliefs. Another element of the growing intolerance was the opposition to the Jews, given some official backing by the Callinicum episode and further inflamed by Christian preachers such as John Chrysostom. By the beginning of the fifth century Jews were banned from the civil service. In a masterly funeral oration for Theodosius in 395 Ambrose told his listeners that there was no doubt that such a committed Christian emperor 'enjoys everlasting light and eternal tranquillity' with God.

So new relationships between the churches and the imperial state were being forged. When Hilary, bishop of Poitiers and one of the more formidable supporters of the Nicene cause, was asked his views on the emperors, he replied that 'he [the emperor] does not bring you liberty by casting you in prison, but [now] treats you with respect within his palace and makes you his slave'. Despite Ambrose's apparent triumph over Theodosius, the church had now become the servant of the state in a way that many Christians, such as Hilary, deplored. Bishops were increasingly used by the state to keep order and the benefits offered for acquiescence in this role were many. It was Ammianus Marcellinus who talked of the bishops of Rome as 'enriched by the gifts of matrons, they ride in carriages, dress splendidly and outdo kings in the lavishness of their table'. This is much too simplistic a picture as it was precisely this opulence which drove many bishops to reassert their moral authority through charitable building programmes (as with Basil of Caesarea's leper colonies) or personal austerity (Martin, bishop of Tours, is a good example). However, the church did take on attitudes which were supportive of traditional values and customs. Constantine's victory at the Milvian Bridge had raised the possibility that the Christian God sanctioned success in war. (The church historian Eusebius called Constantine 'God's Commander-in-Chief'.) By the late 370s, Ambrose was able to declare that 'the army is led not by military eagles or the flight of birds but by your name, Lord Jesus and Your Worship'. Remarkably, Jesus who, of course, had in reality been crucified by Roman soldiers, is portrayed as one in the Archiepiscopal chapel in Ravenna (c.500)! Depictions of Christ in Majesty—the earliest is in the late fourth-century church of Santa Pudenziana in Rome—show him displayed as an emperor or even the God Jupiter might be. The result was a tension in the

Christian tradition, between those who saw Christianity essentially as part of the natural conservative order of things (slavery, remarked Augustine, was no less than God's punishment for sin) and those who were inspired by the gospels to reject worldly status and power.

The Survival of Pagan Culture

The triumphalist nature of much Christian writing of the period tends to over-shadow the continuing vitality of pagan thought. The variety of pagan belief meant that there had never been any exclusivity. Membership of one cult did not preclude membership of another and the spiritual heritage of paganism remained rich and capable of fertile development. As the senator Quintus Aurelius Symmachus, a leading protester against the removal of the statue of Victory from the senate house, put it, 'What does it matter by which wisdom each of us arrives at the truth? It is not possible that only one road leads to so sublime a mystery.' His fellow senator, Praetextatus (died 384), is described on his tombstone not only as an initiate of the Eleusinian mysteries but as a priest of the cults of Hecate at Aegina (in the Aegean), the Egyptian god Serapis, as well as Mithras, Cybele, and Sol. When he addressed an audience on the nature of the gods, 'he alone, they declared, knew the secrets of the nature of the godhead, he alone had the intelligence to apprehend the divine and the ability to expound it'.

The most popular belief of intellectual pagans remained Platonism, as developed by the greatest of the Greek religious philosophers, Plotinus (AD 205–70). Plotinus may have been Egyptian by birth (his early studies took place at Alexandria), but his later years were spent in Rome, where he attracted a circle of devoted admirers. Plotinus developed the idea of 'the Good' beyond the meaning given it by the earlier Platonists. For Plotinus 'the Good' was an entity which had existed since before the creation of the physical world. Within 'the Good' was the power of love, which reached out to those who searched for it. (The searcher could only find 'the Good' through this emanating love.) Once the mind of the human believer met with 'the Good', a transformation, a profound mystical experience, could take place. As Plotinus put it, 'when in this state the soul would exchange its present state for nothing in the world, though it were offered the kingdom of all the heavens: for this is "the Good" and there is nothing better.'

It was clear, therefore, that orthodox Christianity did not have a monopoly of spiritual experience, or even of the person of Christ who could be found in cults such as Manichaeism. It is worth asking exactly what separated the ordinary Christian from his pagan counterpart. There was a vast shared territory. Christians, sometimes to the despair of their bishops, continued to take part in pagan celebrations, attend the games, and indulge in traditional superstitions.

(Pope Leo I is found in the 440s denouncing a group of 'Christians' whom he found worshipping the sun from the steps of St Peter's!) There is no evidence that Christian marriage customs were any different from pagan ones. The text on Praetextatus' tomb describes his wife Paulina as 'partner of my heart, nurse of modesty, bond of chastity, pure love and loyalty produced in heaven . . . united by the pact of consecration, by the yoke of the marriage vow and perfect harmony', a description of a happy marriage as much Christian as pagan. Christians continued to own slaves (a slave collar found in Sardinia, and dated to about 400, is stamped Felix the Archdeacon) and as late as 580 the emperor Tiberius, launching a persecution of pagans, used the traditional Roman punishment of crucifixion (in the case of one pagan governor, Anatolius, after he had first been thrown to wild beasts).

The art of the period also shows the extent of shared territory. The basilica was one traditional Roman building adapted to Christian use, another was the circular mausoleum, traditionally used as the resting place of emperors. Constantine created one for himself in Constantinople while in Rome the mausoleums of his mother Helena and his daughter Constantina (Santa Constanza) survive. The mosaic decoration of Santa Constanza (354) shows no Christian influence whatsoever. There are cupids, cherubs picking grapes, and vine leaves (in fact, archaeologists once believed the mausoleum to be a temple to Bacchus). The first public Christian art (as distinct from that concealed in the catacombs) shows Christian themes mingled with pagan symbolism and motifs. In one sarcophagus of the mid-fourth century from Rome, the twins Castor and Pollux, traditionally seen in Roman mythology as guardians of the dead and symbols of immortality, are placed alongside reliefs of the feeding of the 5,000 and an incident in the life of St Peter. In the marriage casket from the Esquiline treasure (of *c*.380) a Christian inscription surrounds artwork which is still rooted in classical mythology with a nude Venus occupying a prominent position. Other sarcophagi show Christ receiving such traditional classical emblems as a laurel crown or depicted as a pagan god, Apollo, while images of the Virgin and Child appear to be derived from those of the Egyptian goddess Isis and her son Horus. In this sense Christianity was drawing on the cultural background it shared with paganism. It was a gradual process by which Christian art was to develop its own distinct systems of iconography and ritual. (If one walks across from Santa Constanza to the neighbouring church of St Agnes, the magnificent early seventh-century mosaic of St Agnes shows the difference. In the evocative words of Peter Brown: 'St. Agnes hovers silently and alone, set against a bottomless sea of gold, above an apse made as exquisite and translucent as a honeycomb by marble columns.') Even if pagan themes were eventually eclipsed or subsumed, they survived much longer than traditional accounts have suggested.

The Growth of Asceticism

While many Christians enjoyed being in and of the world, exercising their power as bishops or as advisers to the emperor, a minority saw the world as a haven of wickedness. This was perhaps reinforced by the new-found wealth of the church which appeared to many to be a betrayal of its ideals. Their response was to leave the world. The Egyptian Antony, so-called 'father of the monks', lived seventy of his purported 105 years in the desert, remote from any human contact. (A life of Antony, ascribed to Athanasius, bishop of Alexandria, was the first in a long line of hagiographical accounts of holy men and women which provided exemplars for those who wished to renounce the world.) In Syria some holy men climbed pillars and lived on top of them for years with thousands of curious or devout visitors coming to stare. Not all could bear the lack of immediate human contact. In Egypt the withdrawal from the world took place in communities. Thousands of ordinary men, most of them villagers by birth, crowded into settlements where they lived according to a routine of prayer and manual labour. These were the first monasteries.

However successful an individual might be in escaping from other human beings he or she still had a physical body to contend with. It was a problem well known to the Greek philosophers, who had long asserted that the desires of the flesh hampered them in their search for the spiritual world. So asceticism was not a Christian invention although Christians were more preoccupied with sexual desire than the Greek philosophers were. Peter Brown in his *Body and Society* traces this preoccupation back to Paul and it seems that celibacy was also practised by some Jewish communities such as that at Qumran. By the fourth century the preoccupation had become an obsession, part of the more widespread movement of renunciation of physical pleasures followed by the first hermits and monks. The act of sex in itself was now viewed by many with intense distaste. Some extremists, such as the Egyptian Hierakas, even doubted that married couples who had enjoyed the sexual act would be admitted to heaven. The more conventional view adopted by the church was that sex between married couples was acceptable but only as a means of creating children (or as Jerome put it more humans who could consecrate themselves to virginity!). The fulfilment of sexual desire as an end in itself was morally wrong.

This left women in an ambiguous position. On the one hand they could be cast, in the tradition of Eve, as temptresses to be avoided. The works of the church fathers are filled with dire warnings of the perils offered by glimpses of female flesh. On the other, those who made a commitment to virginity could achieve a certain status denied to their more carnal sisters. Even Jerome, who was more troubled by sexuality than most, could accept the company of virgins who were prepared to devote themselves to pious study. A minority of women, usually from upper-class backgrounds, discarded their wealth and founded hospitals or monasteries. Melania the Younger is the best-known example. She and her husband surrendered vast estates and Melania later founded a religious community on the Mount of Olives.

The Christian Intellectuals

The late fourth and early fifth centuries produced a number of profound thinkers who had been brought up in the traditional world of classical learning, converted to Christianity, and then deployed their penetrating intellects in the service of the church. The hero of many of these men was the apostle Paul who enjoyed an important revival in the late fourth century. In Constantine's day he had been honoured in Rome by no more than a shrine over the supposed place of his martyrdom. In the 380s this was transformed into a great basilica, San Paolo fuori le mure. Paul's attraction lay in his stress on authority at a time of apparent social and political breakdown and he was used as an intellectual battering ram against the pagan elites who remained strong in Rome until early in the fifth century. His distaste of sexuality also appealed to the more ascetic Christians.

Perhaps the most fervent supporter of Paul was John Chrysostom, 'the golden-mouthed' (c.347–407). John was born into the Greek-speaking elite of Antioch in Syria. From an early age he was such a gifted speaker that it was assumed that he would become a lawyer or civil servant like his father. However, he was baptized when 21 and then took to a life of solitude in the caves around Antioch. He emerged, his health permanently damaged, with a loathing for finery and self-indulgence. Any hint of greed or arrogance aroused his anger and it was said that he would sternly fix his eye on the women in his congregation who appeared overdressed. His harshness was modified, however, by his concern for the poor of his congregations, many of whom welcomed his denunciations of the rich. His sermons were full of powerful imagery. 'Do you pay such honour to your excrements as to receive them in a silver chamber pot when another man made in the image of God is perishing of cold?' On Paul he told his congregations, 'If I am regarded as a learned man, it's not because I'm brainy. It's simply because I have such a love for Paul that I have never left off reading him. He has taught me all that I need to know. And I want you to listen to what he has to teach you. You don't need to do anything else [sic].'

Until he was 50 John served in Antioch, earning an empire-wide reputation as a preacher. However, Paul was not his only concern. It was during these years that he preached his eight sermons warning Christians against Judaism. The context appears to have been the continuing vigour of Judaism in Antioch and the readiness of Christians to attend synagogues. John's invective bordered on the deranged and his sermons, translated into Latin and transferred to the west, later fuelled anti-Jewish hysteria in medieval Europe. In 398 John was forced to accept the bishopric of Constantinople. It was an unhappy move. He was never at ease in the shadow of an opulent court, offended many by his habit of eating alone, and aroused the anger of many clergy for his insinuations about their sex lives. A determined attempt to unseat him by Theophilus, bishop of Alexandria (who remained incensed by the elevation of Constantinople above his ancient see), proved successful when John forfeited any remaining support in the court by what appeared to be attacks on the worldliness of the empress Eudoxia. Only the poor remained loyal but their rioting in his favour was never likely to secure his survival. Finally he was exiled to a remote village on the coast of the Black Sea where he died in 407.

John Chrysostom operated in a Christian world which was gradually being divided into Greek-speaking east and Latin-speaking west. An important symbolic moment came in the 380s when Bishop Damasus of Rome ordered the use of Latin rather than Greek for the liturgy in the western empire. As Greek became less widely spoken in the west, many of the works of the eastern church fathers never reached Rome. A letter survives from Augustine, whose Greek was minimal, pleading for more translations. This linguistic isolation was reinforced by the distance of Rome from the Greek-speaking Christian communities and the decline of the city as an administrative centre of the empire. The bishops of Rome were outraged when the Council of 381 affirmed that 'the bishop of Constantinople has the privileges of honour after the bishop of Rome because it is the new Rome'. Things were not helped by the administrative division between the eastern and western empires which became permanent in 395 (see p. 608 below). Even if neither side was as yet prepared to recognize the fact, two distinct churches (later, of course, the Roman Catholic and Orthodox churches) were in the process of emerging.

Jerome and Augustine

One of the last of the major Christian thinkers to be at home in both east and west was Jerome. He had been born in the Balkans about 347 of Christian parents but by the age of 12 he was studying philosophy and rhetoric in Rome. He developed a profound love of classical authors and one of the most shattering events of his life was a dream in which God accused him of preferring Cicero to the Bible, for which failing he was flogged. He resolved never to read a pagan author again (though his letters remain full of classical allusions).

Jerome's life was restless and tormented. He travelled incessantly and underwent periods of severe asceticism. In Peter Brown's words, 'The human body remained for Jerome a darkened forest, filled with the roaring of wild beasts, that could be controlled only by rigid codes of diet and by the strict avoidance of occasions for sexual attraction.' His letters to adversaries are deeply vindictive. At the same time, however, he studied assiduously and mastered both Greek and Hebrew in addition to his native Latin. It was this breadth of knowledge which recommended him to Bishop Damasus of Rome, who employed him first as his secretary (382–4) and then as the translator of the Greek and Hebrew texts of the Old and New Testaments into Latin.

A unified and authoritative translation had long been needed. There were all too many Latin translations of varying quality circulating in the western empire. Jerome faced formidable problems in achieving his task. In Rome his censorious personality and suspicion over a new translation made him so unpopular that after the death of Damasus he was forced to leave the city. The last thirty-four years of his life were spent in Bethlehem in a monastery and it was here that his translation was finally brought to a conclusion. At first it received little recognition but by the eighth century it was accepted by the church as the authoritative Latin version of the original texts. As the Vulgate (the 'common version') it lasted unchallenged in the Catholic church for centuries and remains one of the great achievements of early Christian scholarship.

It was to Jerome that Augustine sent his letter asking for more translations of the Greek Christian texts. Augustine can be seen as the founding father of a distinctive western tradition of theology. (His influence in the west remains immense, in the east it is negligible.) His experiences are detailed in the *Confessions*, a brilliant account of a tortured mind searching for absolute peace. The central chapters of the *Confessions* are concerned with his spiritual experiences in Milan and his eventual conversion to Christianity. They were written in the late 390s after he had returned to his native Africa. Augustine presents himself as a deeply unworthy man, tormented by his sexuality and harried, although he took some time to recognize the fact, by the looming power of God.

I broke your lawful bounds and did not escape your lash. For what man can escape it? You were always present, angry and merciful at once, strewing the pangs of bitterness over all my lawless pleasures to lead me on to look for others unallied with pain. You meant me to find them nowhere but in yourself, O Lord, for you teach us by inflicting pain, you smite so you may heal and you kill us so that we may not die away from you. (Translation: R. Pine-Coffin)

Augustine came to accept that God's love becomes available to sinners only when they make complete submission to him. The moment of conversion came after many struggles when he heard the voice of a child asking him to take up the New Testament. He opened it at the words of Paul, 'put on the Lord Jesus Christ and make no provision for the flesh to gratify its desires'. Suddenly he had found his true haven, in the church. Once he had renounced the satisfaction of his sexual desires for ever, he was able to be baptized. (For Augustine too Paul was a dominant influence, to the extent that the scholar Paula Fredriksen has claimed that 'much of western thought can be seen as one long response to Augustine's Paul'.)

After his conversion and baptism, Augustine returned to his native Africa and became bishop of Hippo, where he remained until his death thirty years later. While he preferred the life of the monk, he cared deeply about the needs of the ordinary Christians who thronged his churches and was more sensitive than most church leaders to their earthly desires. (He was prepared, for instance, to accept sexuality as an intrinsic part of marriage.) In the remaining years of his life, he applied the brilliance and clarity of his mind to some of the major theological issues of the day. Perhaps the most famous was the dispute with Pelagius, an ascetic who may have been of British birth, over the nature of free will.

Pelagius had argued that each individual had the freedom to follow God's will or not. The hope, of course, was that he or she would choose to aim for a life of perfection, with Christ as the model. In such a case, argued Pelagius, God would support these efforts. Augustine, on the other hand developed a different approach, one that had only been dimly formulated before his time. This was the view that as a result of Adam and Eve's transgressions in the Garden of Eden God had burdened all human beings with an 'original sin' which was passed on from generation to generation. The concept of original sin had never been mentioned by Jesus and Augustine relied on one verse from St Paul (Romans 5: 12) for support. The consequences of the sin were, however, profound. Even the power of human reason, suggested Augustine, had been reduced to a spark and as a result (as Plato would have agreed) human beings were drawn to the earthly pleasures of the world. Only the grace of God could liberate them from the burden of these pleasures. This grace could be passed on through the sacraments, especially those of baptism and the Eucharist, but it was always a gift from God, not the right of any individual, however good his or her life.

Augustine's God was, therefore, selective. Only a few would be saved. This left uncomfortable questions to be resolved. Was it possible to live a good life and still be deprived of the grace of God? What would happen to those who did not receive this grace or who were never baptized? When challenged by his opponents over what would happen to the souls of babies who had died before they were baptized Augustine was forced to accept that their original sin left them unprotected and they could never be admitted to heaven. Independently Augustine also came to reject Origen's view that eternal punishment was incompatible with the goodness of God and became one of the foremost defenders of a hell where punishment would be harsh and eternal. There would be no mercy for those to whom the grace of God was not extended. (Augustine's thoughts on these issues can be found most easily in the closing chapters of his *The City of God*.)

Augustine's concept of original sin was, in the early fifth century, a minority view held only by some of his fellow bishops in north Africa. As another opponent commented, the whole idea was improbable, making it seem as if the devil, not a loving God, had created man. What was remarkable, however, was that through sheer persistence and intellectual energy Augustine managed to get his view accepted as the official doctrine of the western church after the emperor Honorius insisted the Italian bishops adopt it. The concept of original sin received no support elsewhere. It never travelled to the east (Augustine wrote only in Latin), nor was it adopted by any other monotheistic religion.

Augustine attempted to define what was meant by the 'church'. Joining the church and receiving its sacraments presumably increased the chance of receiving the gift of God's grace but the logic of Augustine's views suggested that membership of the church did not guarantee salvation and that those who did not join the church were not necessarily deprived of it. The church, however, had a duty to ensure that all who wished to join and receive the benefits of its sacraments could do so. Augustine's main opponents here were the Donatists (a majority of the Christians in Hippo and north Africa as a whole), who continued to insist that the orthodox church had been fatally damaged during the persecutions and that they were right to keep Christians from joining it. To counter this attack Augustine argued that the validity of the orthodox church did not depend on the worthiness of its members. The sacrament of baptism given by an unworthy priest was still valid in the eyes of God. It followed that the Donatists, through their intransigence, were depriving those who might be eligible for God's grace from receiving it through the sacraments. Therefore it was legitimate to destroy the sect and release its followers to their proper home in the church. This approach reinforced the view taken by Theodosius and Ambrose, that the church, backed by the state, had the right to deal with heresy. Although Augustine cautioned restraint in the methods employed against heretics, his words were used in later centuries to justify the persecutions of medieval and Reformation Europe.

Augustine's last great work, *The City of God*, was prompted by the sack of Rome by the Visigoths in 410 (see next chapter). Although the physical damage was not immense (and the Christian Visigoths left the city's churches untouched), the psychological shock certainly was. It seemed as if the world as all had known it was at an end. Much of the book is concerned with pointing out the failure of traditional Roman religion to save the city or provide anything more than a self-glorification of the state. Augustine argued that the true 'city' was, instead, that inhabited by the believers loved by God, a community which extended from earth into heaven. An earthly city, even one so great as Rome, was only a pale reflection of the heavenly one and it was to the heavenly city that the aspirations of men and women must be directed. The fall of Rome was thus of little significance in the eyes of God. In *The City of God*, Augustine makes a dramatic break with the Graeco-Roman conception of the city as the context in which human beings achieve their highest state of being. Now the city is no more than a backdrop to their lives although the church can hope that it will be given tolerance. In his description of society Augustine comes across as a social conservative, supporting traditional hierarchies and slavery and cynical about the possibilities of social progress.

Augustine's influence on the church was profound. His writing and sermons had a clarity and majesty which was unrivalled. His mind penetrated every nook and cranny of Christian thought. Much of his writing, in Book IX of *The Confessions*, for instance, where his last conversations with his mother are recorded, is deeply moving. He was not a cold intellectual but a human being acutely aware of the power of his emotional feelings. It is hard not to feel some sympathy for him in his agonizing searches for his God. Ultimately, however, his message was a chilling one. There was no salvation without divine grace and this could not necessarily be gained through living a 'good' life. The church had the right to prosecute heretics and call on the state to support it. Only those who are convinced that divine grace is theirs and who through it have liberated themselves from their body's desires can read his works with total ease.

Conclusion: A Transformed Society

In 394 the emperor Theodosius had been challenged by a usurper in Gaul, Eugenius. Eugenius was a pagan and attracted the support of many leading Roman senators. Theodosius met their forces at the River Frigidus in the Alps and crushed them. The battle was seen by contemporary Christians as the confirmation of the triumph of their faith. (The arrival of the bora which scattered Eugenius' forces was interpreted as a miraculous intervention.) Certainly a different world now existed, with new concepts of spiritual authority and different visions of God and morality. The church was by now largely integrated into Roman society. It had been associated by Constantine and his successors with success in war. Its bishops were powerful figures and expected to uphold the authority of the state. A vast building programme of churches contrasted with the decay of other public buildings. A growing preoccupation with the elimination of paganism and heresy meant, inevitably, that the rich diversity of Graeco-Roman spiritual experience was stifled, with the result that eventually spiritual aspirations could no longer be expressed outside a specifically Christian context. Jews were increasingly isolated, and the fourth century marks for them, in the words of Nicholas de Lange, 'the beginning of a long period of desolation'. In his *The Decline and Fall of the Roman Empire* Edward Gibbon blamed this narrowing of perspective on Christianity but this is too simplistic. The Christianity of the fourth century was far removed from that of the gospels and it reflects the degree to which it had become the servant of the state, with the bishops, as the perceptive Hilary of Poitiers had put it, the 'slaves' of the emperors.

FURTHER READING

Reading for chapters 30–2. This has been one of the more exciting areas of study in recent years with renewed emphasis on the continuity of 'Roman' ways in the west and the survival of the empire in the east. Research has moved on from A. Jones's pioneering *The Later Roman Empire 284–620: A Social, Economic and Administrative Survey* (Oxford, 1964), which was the standard overview for many years. Now as wide-ranging introductions see G. W. Bowersock, Peter Brown, and Oleg Grabar (eds.), *Late Antiquity: A Guide to the Postclassical World* (Cambridge, Mass., 1999), and Peter Garnsey and Caroline Humfress, *The Evolution of the Late Antique World* (Cambridge, 2000). See also Averil Cameron's *The Later Roman Empire* (London, 1993), which takes the story from 284 to 430, and her *The Classical World in Late Antiquity, AD 395–600* (London, 1993). A clear and up-to-date account is also given by Roger Collins, *Early Medieval Europe 300–1000* (2nd edition, London, 1999). As a sourcebook, see Michael Maas, *Readings in Late Antiquity* (London, 2000). Many readers will have been drawn to this period by Peter Brown, whose *The World of Late Antiquity* (London, 1971) and *The Making of Late Antiquity* (Cambridge, Mass., 1978) are superb evocations. The power of his writing is such that, as Averil Cameron memorably puts it, the period is 'in danger of having become an exotic territory, populated by wild monks and excitable virgins and dominated by the clash of religions, mentalities and lifestyles', but his work is constantly entertaining and full of insight. On Constantine, see H. Pohlsander, Constantine *the Emperor* (London, 1997); T. Barnes, *Constantine and Eusebius* (Cambridge, Mass., 1981); and D. Bowder, *The Age of Constantine and Julian* (London, 1978). On Constantine and the church H. A. Drake, *Constantine and the Bishops: The Politics of Intolerance* (Baltimore, 2000), is important. Fergus Millar makes the point about Constantine continuing the traditional role of the emperor as solver of disputes in his *The Emperor in the Roman World* (London, 1977). Sabine MacCormack, *Art and Ceremony in Late Antiquity* (Berkeley, 1981) is important. An introduction to Constantinople can be found in R. Krautheimer, *Three Christian Capitals* (Berkeley, 1983).

Robert Markus's chapter in the *Oxford Illustrated History of Christianity* takes the story from 330 to 700 and usefully concentrates on the process of 'Christianization'. See also his *Christianity in the Roman World* (London, 1974) and *The End of Ancient Christianity* (Cambridge, 1991). Averil Cameron's *Christianity and the Rhetoric of Empire* (Berkeley, 1991) explores the way rhetoric was used to Christianize late Roman society. Peter Brown's *Power and Persuasion in Late Antiquity* (Madison, Wis., 1992) shows how the bishops, in particular, absorbed the role of the old city elites and see also his *Poverty and Leadership in the later Roman Empire* (Hanover, NH, 2002). On Ambrose, N. McLynn, *Ambrose of Milan; Church and Court in a Christian Capital* (Berkeley, 1994) is excellent. On early Christian art I have found R. Milburn, *Early Christian Art and Architecture* (Berkeley, 1991) very useful. There is now J. Elsner, *Imperial Rome and Christian Triumph* in the Oxford History of Art series (Oxford, 1998) and his *Art and the Roman Viewer: The Transformation of Art from the Pagan World to Christianity* (Cambridge, 1995). See also Robin Margaret Jensen, *Understanding Early Christian Art* (London, 2000).

On the religious controversies see the works by Brown, Stead, and Pelikan cited in the last chapter as well as F. Young, *From Nicaea to Chalcedon* (London, 1983) There is much good material in J. Herrin's excellent *The Formation of Christendom* (Oxford, 1987). On the important subject of the continuation of paganism see P. Chuvin, *A Chronicle of the Last Pagans* (Cambridge, Mass., 1990); G. W. Bowersock, *Hellenism in Late Antiquity* (Ann

Arbor, 1990); and Ramsay MacMullen, *Christianity and Paganism in the Fourth to Eighth Centuries* (New Haven, 1997). Stephen Mitchell's *Anatolia: Land, Men and Gods in Asia Minor*, 2 vols. (Oxford, 1993) is a superb study of the spread of Christianity at local level. On the end of public debate Richard Lim, *Public Disputation and Social Order in Late Antiquity* (Berkeley, 1995), and Charles Freeman, *The Closing of the Western Mind: The Rise of Faith and the Fall of Reason* (London, 2002, New York, 2003).

On asceticism, Peter Brown, *The Body and Society: Men, Women and Sexual Renunciation in Early Christianity* (New York, 1988; London, 1989), is essential reading. See also Philip Rousseau, *Ascetics, Authority and the Church in the Age of Jerome and Cassian* (Oxford, 1978); V. Wimbush and R. Valantasis (eds.), *Asceticism* (Oxford, 1995) and S. Elm, *Virgins of God* (Oxford, 1994). For emotional changes Richard Sorabji, *Emotion and Peace of Mind: From Stoic Agitation to Christian Temptation* (Oxford, 2000) is masterly. Gillian Clark deals with women, both Christian and pagan, in her *Women in Late Antiquity* (Oxford, 1993).

For John Chrysostom, J. Kelly, *Golden Mouth: The Story of John Chrysostom* (London, 1995). On Jerome J. Kelly, *Jerome* (London, 1975). Augustine is again the subject of Peter Brown's insights in his *Augustine of Hippo* (2nd edition, London, 2000). An introduction is also provided by Henry Chadwick, *Augustine* (Oxford, 1986), reissued as part of *Founders of Thought* (Oxford, 1991). A. D. Fitzgerald (ed.), *Augustine through the Ages* (Michigan, 1999) is an encyclopaedia, essential for further study. Also recommended are C. Harrison, *Augustine: Christian Truth and Fractured Humanity* (Oxford, 2000), and J. Rist, *Augustine: Ancient Thought Baptised* (Cambridge, 1994). A fine biography which covers many of the themes here is Dennis Trout, *Paulinus of Nola: Life, Letters and Poems* (Berkeley, 1999).

Looking at the nature of administrative harshness from a gloomy perspective is R. MacMullen, *Corruption and the Decline of Rome* (New Haven, 1988). Ammianus Marcellinus is dealt with in R. Blockley, *Ammianus Marcellinus: A Study of his Historiography and Political Thought* (Brussels, 1975), and J. W. Drijvers and D. Hunt, *The Late Roman World and its Historian: Interpreting Ammianus Marcellinus* (London, 1999). On the Goths, P. Heather, *Goths and Romans* (Oxford, 1991) is important not only for its reinterpretation of the written sources but for its stress on the difficulties facing the Goths once they had entered the empire. Patrick Geary, *The Myth of Nations* (Princeton, 2002) is essential. See the chapter by M. Todd, 'Barbarian Europe AD 300–700', in B. Cunliffe (ed.), *The Oxford Illustrated Prehistory of Europe* (Oxford, 1994). On Julian there is the biography by R. Browning, *The Emperor Julian* (Berkeley, 1976) and R. Smith, *Julian's Gods: Religion and Philosophy in the Thought and Action of Julian the Apostate* (London, 1995). On the accommodations between Roman and invaders see W. Goffart, *Barbarians and Romans, AD 418–584* (Princeton, 1980). On the successor kingdoms see Roger Collins, cited above. Also Marcia Colish, *Medieval Foundations of the Western Intellectual Tradition, 400–1400* (New Haven, 1997). A thorough study of Theodoric is offered by J. Moorhead, *Theodoric in Italy* (Oxford, 1992). On Ravenna, R. Milburn, *Early Christian Art and Architecture* (Berkeley, 1991) offers a sound introduction. John Moorhead, *The Roman Empire Divided, 400 to 700* (Harlow, 2001), and L. Webster and M. Brown (eds.), *The Transformation of the Roman World AD 400–900* (London, 1997). On Gregory Robert Markus, *Gregory the Great and his World* (Cambridge, 1997), is an excellent starting point. The transition from Latin to Romance is covered in the essay by R. Posner in R. Jenkyns (ed.), *The Legacy of Rome* (Oxford, 1992).

On the changes in the economy the standard for the debate has now been set by Michael McCormick, *Origins of the European Economy AD 300–900* (Cambridge, 2002). It uses new methods to try and understand the movements of men and ships which led eventually to a Mediterranean economy by the end of the millennium. K. Randsborg, *The First Millennium AD in Europe and the Mediterranean: An Archaeological Essay* (Cambridge, 1991). Averil Cameron outlines the problems of assessing urban life in chapter 7 of *The Mediterranean in Late Antiquity*, and there is also J. Rich (ed.), *The City in Late Antiquity* (London, 1992) and the important survey by J. W. Liebeschuetz, *Decline and Fall of the Roman City* (Oxford, 2001).

31 | The Creation of a New Europe, 395–600

On the death of Theodosius in 395 his two sons were declared joint emperors and the empire was split into two administrative areas with one son nominally responsible for each. Both were still young: Arcadius, emperor in the east, was only 18, Honorius even younger. In the north the division was made along the boundary of Illyricum, roughly where Greek replaced Latin as the predominant administrative language, a reminder that despite centuries of apparent unity the empire was still made up of two distinct linguistic cultures (as well as, of course, of a mass of minor ones). The split became consolidated by other forces: a more buoyant economy in the east, based on peasant production rather than large estates, more defensible frontiers and less intractable enemies, perhaps the preservation of civilian rather than military rule for everyday administration, even an element of luck in that the emperors in the east lived longer and were more resolute characters than those in the west. The two halves of the empire were never to be reunited.

The 'Fall' of the Western Empire

The western empire was to 'fall' eighty years later in 476. The 'fall' when it came was hardly a major or unexpected event in itself. By the 470s the western emperors had lost control of virtually all their territories outside Italy and relied on German soldiers to lead their own depleted troops. A boy emperor, Romulus Augustulus, was deposed by a Germanic soldier, Odoacer, who then got in touch with the emperor in the east, Zeno, asking for a position as *patricius*, in effect a high-ranking subordinate with the status of consul. Zeno had hopes that his own nominee for emperor, one Julius Nepos, who had been expelled from Italy shortly before, might yet be restored so he hesitated. By the time Julius died, unrestored, in 480 Odoacer was firmly in place as ruler of Italy and effective control over the last remnants of the western empire had been lost. (It is good to report that Romulus' life was spared and there is some evidence that he was still living on a private estate in Italy thirty-five years after his deposition.)

The fall of the western part of the empire has gripped the imagination of later generations. Edward Gibbon's magnificent *Decline and Fall of the Roman Empire* must bear some of the responsibility, within the English-speaking world at least, for creating an image of a cataclysmic event in human history which requires some kind of special explanation (although Gibbon was not only concerned with the west and continued the story up to the fall of Constantinople in 1453). Gibbon himself laid the blame on Christianity, which he claimed had undermined the ancient warrior traditions of the Romans and, through the influence of monasticism and asceticism, turned them away from earthly things. This thesis does not explain why the east, more fully Christianized than the west, survived. There have been innumerable other theories—one book lists 500 of them—but behind many of them lurks the assumption that the Roman empire had some magic element, a moral superiority, for instance, which should have protected it for ever against the processes of historical change. (The idea was not new. Theodosius I was once told by one local Gallic magnate, 'We know that no revolution will ever overthrow the state because the Roman empire is foreordained to remain with you and your descendants'.)

Every explanation, however, must include the fact that the empire in the west faced continuous pressures along its extended borders on the Rhine and Danube. By 395 these pressures had lasted over 200 years, ever since the first wars against the Marcomanni in the 160s. What was remarkable was that the Roman armies had managed to hold the borders intact (with the surrender only of Dacia in the third century). The empire had continually found the resources to build forts and raise new armies while in the late third and early fourth century it had undergone a major restructuring under Diocletian and Constantine. Modern scholars have now re-established this period of 'late antiquity' as one of vitality and achievement. The old convention by which histories of the Roman empire were allowed to peter out after Diocletian can no longer be sustained.

The 'Goths' in the Western Empire

It was the appearance of the Huns in the 370s which placed new and overwhelming pressures on the empire as groups referred to in Roman sources as Goths were forced across its borders. By 382 these had been given some degree of independent status (see p. 591 above). As suggested earlier (p. 542) there is increasing reluctance among scholars to see the Goths as in any way an ethnic people. The term is perhaps most accurately used of those peoples who were bound into allegiance to a particular Gothic leader. In the 380s one of these leaders, Alaric, emerged as a highly effective commander who secured widespread support among the peoples who had migrated south of the Danube. His Goths are conventionally termed the Visigoths (in contrast to the Ostrogoths, those Goths who remained north of the Danube and outside the empire) but if they were to survive as a distinct group it was essential that they forged their own identity. After the declaration of Nicene orthodoxy by Theodosius in 381, this was through their adherence to Arianism, but they also had their own language (into which the Bible was translated). To further preserve their identity they were forbidden to intermarry with Romans. Alaric's aim was to achieve, through diplomacy or force, a permanent settlement for his followers within the empire. When diplomacy failed he used the only weapon he had, the plundering of neighbouring land. By 395 he was moving his men into the Balkans through Thrace and Greece, using them as pressure points on the east. In 397 he seems to have been recognized by the eastern empire as a military commander in Illyricum but this recognition was not sustained and by 402 he was on the move again. This time he went west towards Italy.

Here his adversary was Stilicho, Theodosius' former *magister militum*, Master of Soldiers. Stilicho was half German but had himself married Theodosius' niece and later married his daughter to Honorius, an indication of how complex the relationship between Roman and German had now become. Stilicho claimed that, on his deathbed, Theodosius had asked him to act as guardian of both his sons, in other words become the regent of the empire. His attempts to intrigue to this end in the east and, in particular, to secure Illyricum, a rich recruiting ground, in his half of the empire, were unsuccessful and simply consolidated the split between the two halves of the empire.

The extent of Stilicho's power in the west was shown in 402 when Honorius moved his court from Milan to Ravenna, a city surrounded by marshes and so almost impregnable. Honorius was in effect abdicating the traditional role of emperor as commander of his troops and from now on the western empire was normally fronted by a strong military figure, often German in origin, while the emperors lived isolated lives in pampered seclusion. No wonder soldiers were said to yearn for the days of Valentinian when the emperor fought alongside his own men and shared their discomforts.

When confronted by Alaric Stilicho repulsed him but the Visigoth forces remained intact and probably settled back in Illyricum. By 405, however, Stilicho appears to have realized that the Visigoths could be sensibly used as soldiers within his own armies, possibly even as a means of entering the east. Before an agreement could be made Alaric was threatening Italy once more, and in 407 Stilicho persuaded the senate to pay him over 4,000 pounds of gold and recognize him as an allied force. This agreement infuriated both the east, who recognized the threat Stilicho now posed, especially after the eastern throne became vacant on the death of Arcadius in 408, and Honorius, who had no wish to compromise with the 'barbarian' Goths. In 408 Stilicho's enemies persuaded the emperor to assassinate him and the agreement with Alaric was disowned. A wave of anti-barbarian hysteria led to a massacre of many of the Germans who now made up a large part of the Roman armies.

Alaric's bluff had now been called. He desperately needed a settlement if he was to retain credibility with his people. While Honorius refused to bargain Alaric was forced to negotiate with the senate in Rome in the hope that the senators would put pressure on Honorius. It was when all the negotiations proved fruitless that, in 410, Alaric led his men into Rome and carried out the sack of the city, the first for 800 years. It was a move which had a devastating shock effect on the Roman world, far beyond its importance as an act of destruction. Rome was no longer an eternal and inviolable city. Yet the sack achieved nothing for Alaric and he now appears to have considered moving his men to Africa. On the way south he died and his brother-in-law Athaulf, who succeeded him, decided to move the Visigoths northwards to Gaul.

A Disintegrating Empire

The preoccupation with the Goths had left the western government paralysed while far more serious incursions were taking place to the north. At the end of 406 there had been a major invasion of northern Gaul, over the frozen Rhine, by Vandals, Sueves, and Alamanni. This time they were largely unopposed (although the Franks, now settled along the border, did honour early promises and offer some resistance) and spread quickly southwards. The Romans were forced to replace their command centre at Trier with Arles in the far south of Gaul. The collapse of the Roman defences was viewed with dismay in Britain, which was itself suffering raids from Saxons and others. The British legions took matters into their own hands. An abandoned Gaul meant an isolated and indefensible Britain. They elevated one of their number, Constantine, as emperor and it was Constantine who crossed into Gaul to lead a counter-attack. In the short term he was astonishingly successful. He gained some kind of control over both Gaul and Spain and in 409 Honorius was temporarily forced to accept him as a fellow Augustus. His 'empire', which he ruled from Arles, was, however, short-lived. His Spanish commanders proclaimed their own emperor and Britain was simply too far from Arles to be controlled. The Roman administration there seems simply to have fallen apart and was never revived. (By 430 coinage had ceased and urban life was already, with some exceptions, in decay. Rival invaders, Scots, Saxons, Angles, and Jutes, took over the country and no central rule was to be reimposed for centuries.) In Gaul itself another German people, the Burgundians, appear now to have crossed into the empire and established themselves south of Trier. Constantine was reduced to holding out in Arles, where he was eventually captured by Honorius' new *magister militum*, Constantius, in 411 and put to death.

It appears that from now on the western empire was unable to launch any major military initiatives with its own troops. Quite what had happened to the

Roman armies is difficult to discover. The *Notitia Dignitatum*, the Register of Civil and Military Dignitaries, compiled some time after 395 and surviving in a western copy, lists military units with a nominal total of 250,000 men in the west but in reality there seem to have been only about 65,000 troops, perhaps 30,000 each in Gaul and Italy. Most of these were probably Germans, on whom the armies were now dependent. Germans had served as mercenaries for centuries, making their fortunes in Roman service and then returning to their homes. More recently prisoners of war, Sueves, Sarmatians, and Burgundians among them, had been settled and bound to military service but now there were also whole contingents of Franks and Goths serving under their own officers. (The cemeteries of Roman forts of the late fourth and early fifth centuries in Belgium show a proportion of German troops ranging from 20 to 70 per cent.) The Germans had usually proved to be loyal and hardy fighters but by the early fifth century the armies do not seem to have operated as effective and controlled units. Increasingly the administration had to rely on the unsatisfactory alternative of using one tribe directly against another. The Visigoths, for instance, were used against the Burgundians in the north and then sent into Spain against the Vandals. They were then settled in 418 in Aquitaine between Toulouse and the Atlantic as a 'federate' kingdom.

The details of this new arrangement, in effect the recognition of a German kingdom within the empire, remain obscure. One view put forward by Walter Goffart in his *Barbarians and Romans* is that a proportion of the tax revenue from the area they settled in was diverted directly to Germans, in effect depriving the Roman state of it. In this sense the Visigoths had secured some independence. The trouble was that the Visigoths had no incentive to remain within the boundaries allocated them and they were soon set on further expansion. The same was true of the Sueves who had settled in Galicia (north-western Spain). They too were given federate status but by the 430s were expanding further into Spain.

The Vandals, who had crossed into Spain with the Sueves in 409, had come to rest in the south of the country. In 429 they moved on. Their leader Gaiseric, perhaps the most successful of all the German leaders, led them across the straits into Africa. Twenty thousand men and their families, 80,000 in all, made the crossing. It was a shrewd move. Not only was the land fertile but Italy still drew on its surplus of corn. Gaiseric knew that by holding Africa he could put direct pressure on the centre of the empire. Once ashore the Vandals moved quickly along the coast taking the main ports. (The elderly Augustine died in Hippo in 430 while the city was under siege.) In 435 the Romans were forced to give the Vandal kingdom federate status but this did not stop further expansion. Carthage was sacked in 439 and Gaiseric then seized the islands of the western Mediterranean. These were the greatest loss the empire had yet suffered.

Aetius, 'The Last of the Romans'

Honorius had died in 423. The western army elevated one John to succeed him but the eastern emperor, Theodosius II, disapproved and installed a 6-year-old, Valentinian III, as his choice. In effect power was in the hands of Valentinian's mother, Galla Placidia, the granddaughter of Valentinian I. Galla Placidia had had a most unsettled life. Taken off by the Visigoths as a hostage after the sack of Rome, she had married the Visigothic leader, Athaulf. Returned to the Romans after his death she then married Constantius, Honorius' new strong man. The young Valentinian was the result. His father had died in 421 and Galla Placidia had taken refuge in Constantinople. It was from there that she was restored to Italy. She was a strong woman and for ten years she held her own against her army officers. In 433, however, she was outmanoeuvred by her *magister militum*, Aetius, who now became the dominant figure in the western empire and remained so for the next twenty years.

Aetius had spent some years of his youth as a hostage with the Huns but he had managed to build such good relationships with his captors that he was able to raise his own armies from them. It was these forces he used in his attempts to defend the empire. Aetius' focus remained a narrow one. He made no attempt to defend or regain Africa, Spain, or Britain and in 442 he acquiesced in a treaty between the emperor and Gaiseric in which Valentinian's daughter, Eudocia, was to marry Gaiseric's son, Huneric. His main concern was to hold some imperial control over Gaul. By this time both the Visigoths and the Burgundians were well established there and Aetius felt it crucial to exercise more effective control over them. He had some success in containing the Visigoths and in 443 he also crushed the Burgundians and set them up as a third federate kingdom around Lake Geneva (doubtless hoping that they would be more controllable there than in the north).

Aetius' success depended on a constant supply of Hunnic mercenaries drawn from a society which had remained small-scale and decentralized. However, in the 430s the Huns seem to have undergone the same sort of transformation as the Goths had in the 380s with consolidation under a central leader. By 445 this was one Attila. Under his leadership the Huns took a more aggressive attitude towards the empire. For instance, they now started raiding the Balkans and the eastern emperor Theodosius had to pay them subsidies to desist. When Theodosius died in 450, however, the new emperor in the east, Marcian, refused to continue the subsidies and the Huns turned their attentions to Gaul. The attacks meant the total collapse of Aetius' strategy. The main source of his troops was being turned against him and concentrated on the area he was most determined to preserve within the empire. He had no option but to call on his former enemies the Visigoths and Burgundians to join with other German tribes in repulsing the Huns. This they did successfully at the Battle of Catalaunian Plains (west of Troyes in Champagne) in 451 after which Attila retreated. In the following year, however, he was back raiding Italy. Significantly there was little resistance: Aquileia was one of the provincial capitals sacked, and only a resolute stand by the bishop of Rome, Leo I, appears to have dissuaded Attila from attacking Rome. The empire seemed at his mercy when, fortuitously, he died in 453 and his empire collapsed. (Leo's intervention marks, perhaps, the moment when Rome can truly be said to be under Christian rather than pagan authority—by now most of the senatorial aristocracy had converted.)

The strategy of Aetius was now thoroughly discredited. He had not even been able to defend Italy. His enemies now saw their opportunity. Aetius was summoned to the emperor's presence in Ravenna and executed, possibly by Valentinian himself. Six months later some officers loyal to Aetius had their revenge and struck down Valentinian. His death brought to an end the dynasty founded by Valentinian I ninety years before.

The Final Years of the Western Empire, 455–476

Aetius has been called the last of the Romans. It is perhaps an appropriate description as during the twenty years of his dominance the empire had disintegrated still further. Its survival was now dependent on a variety of volatile peoples none of whom had any interest in remaining a loyal ally, especially when they had the chance to extend their own lands. Italy had become especially vulnerable to attack from the sea. The new emperor Petronius Maximus tried to consolidate his position by marrying his son to Valentinian's daughter Eudocia. Gaiseric had been promised Eudocia for his own son back in 442 and so now had a fine excuse to send a fleet to Rome in 455 and sack it once again. In 458 he took Sicily, held as a Roman province for nearly 700 years.

The effectiveness of their seapower had established the Vandals as the main threat to the empire. The new *magister militum*, a Gallic aristocrat, Avitus, determined to use the Visigoths to invade Africa. In the event the Visigoths exploited their indispensability to move into Spain, where the structure of Roman administration had by now collapsed. Britain, Spain, Africa, and much of Gaul had now fallen out of Roman control.

After the death of Petronius Maximus in 455 Avitus declared himself emperor but his continuing failure to tackle the Vandals and his Gallic origin meant he had little support among the senators of Rome, to whom the Vandal threat was the main concern. When a German commander of half Visigothic and half Suevic origin, one Ricimer, defeated the Vandals in a sea battle, the senators were impressed enough to choose him as the empire's new strong man. An emperor, Marjorian, a former army officer, was also provided and the two combined to depose Avitus.

Between 456 and 472 it was Ricimer who managed what remained of the western empire. Emperors survived only with his support and were deposed or murdered when they lost it. Marjorian was executed in 461, probably as a result of attempts to make peace with the Vandals. His replacement, Severus, died, possibly poisoned by Ricimer, in 465. In 467 Ricimer saw the advantage of making an alliance with the east, accepting an eastern nominee, Anthemius, as emperor in the west in return for effective help against the Vandals. However, an expedition launched by the east against the Vandals in 468 proved a disastrous failure and relationships between Ricimer and Anthemius broke down so completely that Anthemius ended up as another of Ricimer's victims, dragged from a church in Rome where he had sought sanctuary, and executed. When Ricimer himself died in 472 the empire outside Italy was effectively lost for good.

The eastern emperor, Zeno, now tried to impose his own nominee as emperor, one Julius Nepos, but he was expelled to Dalmatia where he had been previously the *magister militum*. His successor, his own *magister militum*, Orestes appointed his son, Romulus Augustulus, as emperor and it was he who was deposed by Odoacer in 476.

The story of the last years of the empire of the west is one in which Roman administration gradually disintegrated. In many areas, as has been seen, the administration was simply delegated to German tribes, in others it atrophied. In the life of Severinus by Eugippius there is an atmospheric account of the last days of imperial rule in the province of Noricum. As late as the 470s there were still army units stationed in the main cities of the province. At one point their pay failed to arrived. One unit sent off a delegation to Italy to collect the money but no more was heard of it and the unit disbanded itself. Others followed and the defence of the frontier was, in effect, abandoned. Germans soon moved over the frontier to take control.

Coming to Terms with a New World: The Survival of Roman Culture in the Late Fifth Century

With the collapse of the old administration local populations were now coming to terms with their new Germanic rulers. The degree of change involved may not have been enormous especially as in many areas accommodation had been taking place over decades and without major disruption. Economic evidence is notoriously difficult to judge. There might be vastly reduced trade but still made up of a wide diversity of goods. There is some archaeological evidence that long-range trading routes remained intact, certainly between cities, until the early sixth century. At the Schola Praeconum in Rome a refuse dump dating from about 430–40 contained amphorae with oil from Tunisia, wine from the eastern Mediterranean, and lamps and red-slip table ware from north Africa. The trade does not appear to have been disrupted by the Vandal invasion of Africa. Naples was also importing olive oil from north Africa as well as perfumes from Asia Minor, though trade with north Africa appears to have declined after 500. However, overall the picture in Italy is of serious economic decline. The port of Ostia was already in decay by 350—when cracks appeared in the walls of the theatre they were patched up by using the inscribed plinths of statues of former notables, a certain sign of a city which had lost its pride. The villa economy around Monte Cassino in Italy seems to have collapsed as early as AD 400. By the sixth century there was no longer any navigation up the Tiber and the Via Ostiense, the main road into Rome from Ostia, was described as totally overgrown. Rome's population shrank dramatically in the sixth century, from perhaps 100,000 at the beginning of the century to 30,000–40,000 by the end. (Part one of Michael McCormick's *Origins of the European Economy* (Cambridge, 2002) now provides a full review of the archaeological evidence for the decline in trade.)

The collapse of the administrative structure did not mean that Roman culture vanished. In most areas 'Romans' continued to form the vast majority of the population and many of the incoming German peoples were already Romanized through service in the Roman army or through trading contacts. If Walter Goffart's understanding of the arrangements between the federate Germans and local populations is correct, Germans were thrown into close contact with those local taxpayers whose tax was assigned to them. It was in their interest to maintain the systems of landownership which provided the tax. Throughout the former empire there are, in fact, very few cases of barbarians actually dispossessing 'Roman' landowners. (The confiscation of estates by the Vandals around Carthage is an exception.) In short, accommodation between Romans and newcomers rather than confrontation seems to have been the norm.

The letters of the Gallic aristocrat Sidonius Apollinaris provide a fine picture of how a sophisticated man, schooled in classical traditions, could survive. Sidonius, the son-in-law of Avitus, had inherited a beautiful if remote estate in the Auvergne. Here he cultivated the life of a landowner and, like many of his class, became a bishop, of Clermont in 470. In 475 when his city was besieged by Visigoths he directed its defence, but after its defeat he worked hard to cultivate relationships with his new overlords. He recognized that the Visigoths offered the best hope of defence against other attacks and to sustain the relationship he was even prepared to visit the Visigothic king Theodoric to play backgammon with him. The appearance and manners of those Germans billeted on his estate he found less palatable.

Sidonius' experiences provide a reminder that the church survived with its administrative structure intact. Its estates were large and could support its clergy. As the clergy were exempt from taxation and military service there was no shortage of recruits. As Childeric, king of the Franks, put it, 'Our treasury is bankrupt and all our wealth has been transferred to the church. Only bishops have any power.' In fact the church took an important role as protector of the poor. In Gaul and Italy a quarter of the church's revenue was earmarked for widows and the poor. The fifth and sixth centuries saw the emergence of a range of charitable institutions, hospitals, hospices for reception of pilgrims, and orphanages, and this role of the church was to be sustained in the centuries that followed.

While the church survived as a force for cohesion, so then did Roman law. The church used it (as the law code of the Franks put it, *ecclesia vivat iure Romano*, 'the Church lives according to Roman law'). One of the last joint achievements of the eastern and western empires had been, in fact, the Law Code issued by Theodosius II (emperor in the east 408–50). It was a definitive collection of imperial laws issued from the time of Constantine onwards, proclaimed throughout the empire in 438. Many German rulers now adopted it for their 'Roman' subjects. King Alaric II made an abridgement of the Code for his Aquitanian subjects in 506 while the Ostrogoth king Theodoric promulgated it in Italy about 500. The use of Roman law perpetuated the concept that the state should take responsibility for justice on behalf of an individual and that there were personal rights which should be protected. However, it also meant that other features of Roman society such as slavery persisted with legal support. (The trade in slaves in England was forbidden for the first time only in 1102.)

The administrative functions of the church may have helped to sustain urban life but most towns in the west were mere shells of what they had been. In the north-west of the empire towns had virtually ceased to exist after AD 400. One finds cities such as Aquileia which simply fade away, in Aquileia's case its magnificent fourth-century mosaics preserved under the silt with which they were slowly covered. Others were reduced to little more than markets for peasant exchanges, temporary barracks for soldiers on campaign, and fortified refuges to be used in times of trouble. Lugdunum (Lyons) had covered 160 hectares in its heyday—by the sixth century it was down to 20. Cathedrals might still be built in cities but in Gaul the Franks tended to build their churches on the sites of Roman estates with villages growing up later around them. Communities now centred on the courts of the Germanic kings or monasteries. This was now a rural world and its horizons were inevitably narrower than they had been.

Theodoric and the Ostrogoths in Italy

The best-documented example of how Roman and German lived alongside each other is the kingdom of the Ostrogoth Theodoric in Italy (493–526). 'The Ostrogoths' is the term conventionally used of those Goths who had remained north of the borders of the empire under the domination of the Huns, in contrast to the forerunners of the Visigoths who had fled over the border in the 370s.

Again it is not clear how much the Ostrogoths were a clearly defined group but certainly peoples from north of the Danube migrated into the Roman empire after the collapse of Attila's empire in the 450s, and by 484 had been united under a new leader, Theodoric. As with the Visigoths their adherence to Arianism and their own language helped maintain their sense of a separate identity from the Romans. Theodoric had spent ten years of his early life as a hostage in Constantinople (461–71) and so had absorbed some elements of classical culture. However, when back in Italy, he showed no inhibitions in attacking the eastern empire. It seems that the eastern emperor Zeno decided, in 488, to divert him by sending him to Italy to overthrow Odoacer. After enduring a long siege in Ravenna Odoacer surrendered but was murdered by Theodoric. Theodoric was now the most powerful man in Italy.

It has been estimated that Theodoric may have had a following of some 100,000 men. Archaeological and literary evidence combine to suggest they were settled mostly in the north-east of Italy, probably to protect Theodoric's new kingdom against invasion from the north by other German tribes. Theodoric consolidated his position steadily. He guarded against counter-attack from the east by assuming control over Pannonia in 505. When the Visigothic kingdom collapsed in Provence in 508 Theodoric annexed the province and also annexed Visigothic Spain in 511. Marriage links were made with the Burgundians and Vandals.

Theodoric's 'Roman' subjects numbered some 4 million so accommodation with them was essential. In fact, Theodoric showed much sympathy for classical civilization. After he took over Provence he wrote to its 'Roman' inhabitants, 'Having been recalled to your old freedom by the gift of God, clothe yourselves with manners befitting the toga, eschew barbarism and put aside the cruelty of your minds, because it is not fitting for you to live according to strange customs in the time of our just rule' (translation from Cassiodorus: John Moorhead). The Romans were encouraged to use their own laws for disputes among themselves. It helped that Theodoric took a personal interest in Rome, even restoring some of the buildings there and allowing the senators to retain their status and prestige. Although Rome, like other cities in the west, was in decline there was a revival of the city's ancient pride. The corn handouts were resumed and games were held when Theodoric visited the city in 500. Images of the emperor were replaced by pictures of Romulus and Remus suckled by the wolf and the motto *Roma invicta*.

In short, Theodoric quickly gained the respect of Romans (even being compared by some to the emperors Trajan and Valentinian). A number, including the scholar Cassiodorus (whose letters provide one of the best sources of the reign), the senator Symmachus (descendant of the pagan Symmachus of the fourth century), and Symmachus' son-in-law, the senator and philosopher Boethius, served the regime as senior civil servants. Although the Ostrogoths were Arians and proud of it, Theodoric tolerated orthodox Christianity, and in Ravenna, which Theodoric made his capital, orthodox and Arian churches co-existed, though their very splendour suggests some rivalry between the two churches. (There was no lack of sophistication in Arian Christianity. An exquisite gospel book, the *Codex Argenteus*, survives as well as the fine mosaics from the Arian church of San Apollinare Nuovo in Ravenna.) With time the distinction between Ostrogoth and Roman began to break down. Many Ostrogoths moved from being warriors in one generation to landowners in the next. Some took Roman names, converted to orthodox Christianity, and intermarried with the Roman nobility. Cassiodorus was able to write to some of his Gothic correspondents in Latin. By the sixth century the Ostrogoths as a group disappear, apparently absorbed into the Roman majority.

Boethius and Cassiodorus

In such an atmosphere classical culture could survive and even be transmitted to future generations. The major intellectual figure of Theodoric's Italy was Anicus Manlius Severinus Boethius. Boethius was from an aristocratic family which had links to at least two emperors and one bishop of Rome. He showed great intellectual promise from an early age and his life was divided between service of Theodoric and philosophical study. Among his achievements was a translation into Latin of all Aristotle's works on logic which kept Aristotle's name alive in the medieval west when all knowledge of Greek had disappeared. Boethius had hoped to go on to translating the *Dialogues* of Plato and then show how the works of the two philosophers could be reconciled, but in 524 he was arrested on a charge of treason and bludgeoned to death after Theodoric confirmed the death sentence passed by a court in Rome. The affair is normally regarded as a black stain on Theodoric's otherwise tolerant treatment of Roman aristocrats although it is difficult to sort out who actually made the accusations against Boethius and exactly what they consisted of.

It was while awaiting his death in prison that Boethius composed the work for which he is most famous, *The Consolation of Philosophy*. It is a purely classical work which, despite being religious in tone, has not a single mention of Christ or Christianity. (In fact, in one of the poems which break up the prose text Boethius praises the achievements of Agamemnon, Odysseus, and Hercules.) Boethius as he lies in prison is visited by a shadowy woman, old in years but still vigorous in spirit, who engages with him in a dialogue reminiscent of those of Plato. The background of the *Consolation* is Platonic too. Boethius is led towards an appreciation that there is a higher 'Good' which transcends his present suffering. One of the major themes explored in the *Consolation* is the apparent contradiction between the existence of an ultimate 'Good' and the everyday vagaries

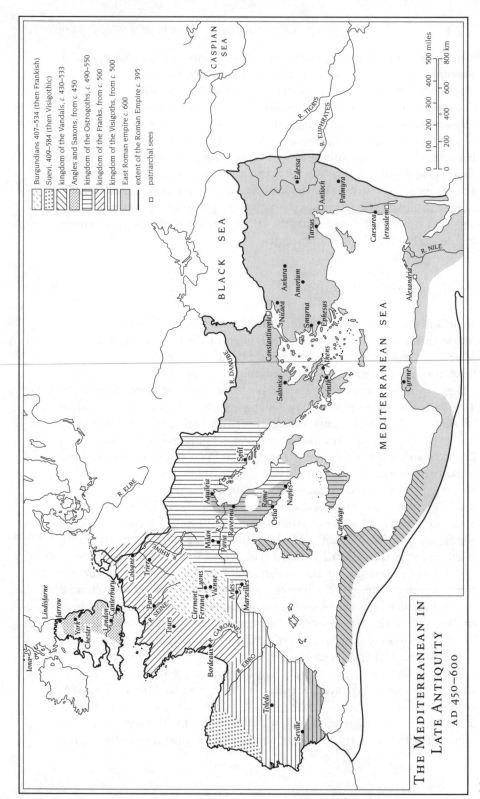

THE MEDITERRANEAN IN
LATE ANTIQUITY
AD 450–600

Burgundians 407–534 (then Frankish)

Suevi, 409–584 (then Visigothic)

kingdom of the Vandals, c. 430–533

Angles and Saxons, from c. 450

kingdom of the Ostrogoths, c. 490–550

kingdom of the Franks, from c. 500

kingdom of the Visigoths, from c. 500

East Roman empire c. 600

extent of the Roman Empire c. 395

patriarchal sees

MAP 19

of fate. The individual has to lift himself above the injustices of everyday life so that he can be united with the stability of 'the Good'. (There are shades of Plotinus here.) *The Consolation of Philosophy* became one of the most read books of medieval Europe, its comparative simplicity providing an attractive contrast to the intricate quarrels of the medieval schools of philosophy. Dante claimed that it provided him with consolation after the death of his beloved Beatrice.

A century before, Augustine had argued that a training in the classics, particularly in grammar and rhetoric, was essential for any Christian. The most distinguished of Theodoric's 'Roman' civil servants, Cassiodorus, agreed. Cassiodorus (490–c.585) drew on Greek models for his argument that the best training for higher studies in Christian theology was provided by the seven liberal arts, grammar, logic, rhetoric, music, geometry, arithmetic, and astronomy. When in retirement in his fifties, he founded his own monastery at Vivarium on his family estates in southern Italy. Here he collected manuscripts both Christian and pagan and encouraged the monks to copy them, even providing a manual, *De Orthographia*, to help them resolve textual difficulties. A large number of Latin authors were preserved in this way and even some Greek texts such as Eusebius' *History of the Church* and the medical works of Galen and Hippocrates. It was partly thanks to Cassiodorus that an education in pagan classical texts was enshrined as part of the church's own education system at a time when secular schooling was in decline. After Cassiodorus horizons narrowed so that eventually only the works of the Latin church fathers were collected. The library of the venerable Bede (672–735) in Northumbria, for instance, one which was considered important for its age, had virtually no classical authors, perhaps not even a copy of Virgil's Aeneid. Although, in western Europe, monks played an important role in copying texts, by the twelfth century no more than one text by Plato, the *Timaeus*, was available while Aristotle was only known through one or two of his works of logic. The works of Galen and Ptolemy became frozen into a Christian perspective of the world and their achievement as the fruit of individual empirical observation and reason was forgotten until the sixteenth century. This move away from rational thought reflected a shift in consciousness. As the fourth-century Christian writer Lactantius had put it: 'What purpose does knowledge serve—for as to knowledge of natural causes, what blessing is there for me if I should know where the Nile rises, or whatever else under the heavens the "scientists" rave about?' The old spirit of curiosity so much part of the Greek world was by now dead.

The Frankish Kingdom

While Theodoric was holding court in Italy other Germanic peoples were successfully setting up kingdoms. As early as the fourth century the Franks had been used by the Romans to keep order on the Rhine frontier, and in the disastrous years 406–7 they played some part in resisting the influx of other German invaders. Between 430 and 440 Franks are found settled between Tournai and Cambrai and it was in Tournai in 1653 that the tomb of the early Frankish 'king', Childeric, was found intact. The king was surrounded by a treasury of gold and silver, two great swords with scabbards inlaid with garnets, and a rich cloak, in short all the paraphernalia of royalty. It was Childeric's son Clovis who was to expand the kingdom. He threw back the Alamanni towards the Upper Rhine and energetically disposed of rival kings. His shrewdest move was to become converted to orthodox Christianity, possibly in 498 or 499. This immediately gave him a link with the 'Roman' populations under Burgundian and Visigoth rule (the Burgundians and Visigoths remained Arians) and the support of their bishops. He now marched triumphantly into Aquitaine and, at the battle of Vouillé in 507, defeated and killed the Visigothic king, Alaric II. By the time of his death, probably in 511, Clovis had laid the foundations of a large Frankish kingdom underpinned by orthodox Christianity.

The events of the next two centuries are confused. In his important book *The Myth of Nations*, Patrick Geary explains how nineteenth-century nationalist historians revived legends of the Franks, Germans, and other European peoples as having a coherent ethnic identity by the fifth century. Geary shows how simplistic this view is (and how easily it was used by racists in the nineteenth and twentieth centuries to talk of an ancient 'pure' France or Germany). Most 'kings' may have been little more than warriors enjoying the temporary allegiances of a mass of different peoples. So Frankish history should be written in terms of leaders controlling specific territories rather than of a Frankish nation forging its identity. After Clovis' death his kingdom was split between four of his sons although these seem to have worked together in comparative harmony. Between 533 and 548 there was once again strong centralized rule under Clovis' grandson, Theudebert I. Theudebert eliminated the Burgundian kingdom in 534 and gained Provence from the Ostrogoths in 536. He also expanded north of the Rhine and even across the Alps into Italy. For the first time in European history the peoples of western Europe lived together in some form of political unity without the Rhine as a barrier between 'Germans' and others. Theudebert deliberately cultivated an imperial presence in the old Roman style. He presided over games in the hippodrome at Arles and for his coinage adopted the eastern solidus (first minted by Constantine) with his name and title substituted for that of the eastern emperor. The kingdom disintegrated after Theudebert's death but was reunited again by a great-grandson of Clovis, Chlothar I, in 558. Under Chlothar II (584–629) and Dagobert (629–38) the Frankish kingdom was to survive as the most effective kingdom of the west.

The Visigoths in Spain and Vandals in Africa

The Visigothic kingdom in Spain had to endure annexation by the Ostrogoths and invasion by the Byzantines (see below), before it re-emerged as a strong and centralized kingdom at the end of the sixth century. Leovigild (569–86) achieved the reunification of most of the peninsula through military means, finally defeating the Suevic kingdom in 585. The problem that remained was the division between the Arian Visigoths and the orthodox Christians who made up the majority of the population. Leovigild may have been edging towards conversion to orthodoxy before his death but it was his son Reccared (586–601) who took the plunge. Summoning the bishops to Toledo in 589, Reccared not only proclaimed his conversion but formed an alliance with the church through which church and state worked together to consolidate the political unity of the state. As in Italy the distinction between Visigoth and Roman appears to have faded with time although it is interesting that the names of the rulers remain Gothic ones well into the seventh century. This perhaps reflects that fact that Gothic had become synonymous with elite status.

As a result of this integration, the Visigothic kingdom was to compete with the Frankish as the most stable and intellectually fertile in Europe. The most influential of its scholars was Isidore, bishop of Seville from about 600 to 636. Isidore's main contribution to political life was the development of a theory of Christian kingship in which the ruler must shine through the exercise of his faith. However, his contribution to scholarship was as great. In his twenty-volume *Etymologies*, Isidore collected a vast range of earlier material to serve as a foundation for the understanding of the meanings of Latin words. He was a determined advocate of a traditional classical education for the clergy, insisting that it was better for Christians that they read the pagan authors than remain ignorant of them. Like Cassiodorus in Italy, he set in hand the copying of manuscripts, and classical learning was preserved as a feature of education more successfully in Spain than in any other western state. Yet there is already a sense of the classics of the past vanishing. The authors stood, Isidore said, like blue hills on the far distant horizons and he found it hard to place them even chronologically.

In contrast to these two European kingdoms, Vandal rule in Africa was less stable. The Vandals ruled as overlords, for the most part isolating themselves as garrison forces in the coastal cities. Landowners had their estates confiscated and orthodox Christians were vigorously persecuted (the Vandals, like the other German tribes, were Arians). As a result there was little hope of accommodation between Germans and Romans. It was the fate of the local Christians, written up in lurid detail by one of their bishops, Victor of Vita, which aroused the interest of the east, in particular the emperor Justinian (527–65). It seems to have been his initiative, based on a desire to help the oppressed Christians as well as to make a final, if anachronistic, attempt to revive the western empire, that lay behind the decision made in 533 to invade Africa, an invasion which was astonishingly successful (see below, p. 639). It was followed by an invasion of Italy in 535.

Italy in the Late Sixth Century

The attempt to reconquer Italy was not a success (its events are described in the next chapter). Justinian had hoped to restore some form of classical, albeit Christian, civilization to the west but wars often achieve the opposite of their hopes. One result of the eastern intervention in Italy was the disappearance of the senatorial aristocracy. Many were simply eliminated by the Goths as suspected traitors. In 547 the Gothic king, Totila, had taken Rome, now reduced to a population of some 30,000, and seized the treasures of the senatorial palaces. Many senators had simply fled with all they could carry. The last of the Gothic leaders, Teias, massacred some 300 children of senatorial families whom he was holding as hostages. The villa economy, on which the senators' wealth depended, also seems to have disappeared at the same time, doubtless dislocated by the protracted wars. The senate ceased to meet in the 580s and it is in these years that the image of Rome as an abandoned city, its great monuments falling into ruin, first emerges.

There is, however, one magnificent set of survivals from these troubled years, the churches of Ravenna. The city had been the emperor's capital from 402 but achieved its full glory under Theodoric, one which was sustained when Ravenna came under eastern control after 540. The splendour of these churches lies in their mosaics. Mosaics had originally been used only on floors, but from the fifth century they were increasingly used for walls and vaults with the tesserae set at an angle to each other to produce a shimmering effect. The earliest mosaics at Ravenna are to be found in the mausoleum built for herself by Galla Placidia (425). They are Hellenistic in style, Christ as the Good Shepherd being shown relaxing among a group of sheep. When Theodoric came to build his palace church, San Apollinare Nuovo, in 490, he used mosaics to cover the whole length of the walls and with a much more formal composition of rows of saints facing the altar. There is also, above the saints, the earliest known extant cycle of gospel scenes. The whole is lit for effect by large windows in the clerestory. San Apollinare Nuovo retains the traditional basilica shape as does a slightly later Ostrogothic church, San Apollinare in Classe (in Ravenna's port) begun in the 530s. Here again there are fine mosaics (in particular of St Apollinaris, the first bishop of Ravenna, in a wooded and green landscape surrounded by sheep) in what remains one of the most harmonious of early Christian interiors.

A different and individual approach was taken in San Vitalis, begun under the Ostrogoths in the 520s. The church is essentially an octagon surmounted by a cupola but there are the additions of a chancel and entrance porch. The interior is broken up by a series of columns and arches superimposed on each other. The whole is beautifully integrated and given even greater magnificence by its mosaics, which were added after Justinian's reconquest of Italy. Here are the celebrated portrayals of Justinian and his consort Theodora bringing gifts to Christ, but they are only a few of the host of images and symbols which blend in with the architecture of the church.

When Justinian had finally achieved some sort of victory in Italy in 554 he attempted to reimpose an imperial system of administration, staffed by eastern officials. It was bitterly resented by the demoralized population. In any case, there was little in the way of an administrative structure left outside that provided by the church. Yet here there were also difficulties after the rejection by most Italian clergy of Justinian's condemnation of the so-called Three Chapters, texts which supported the Nestorian view that Christ had a distinct human nature. (See next chapter.)

Up to the fifth century the bishops of Rome, though maintaining some authority in the church as a whole as the proclaimed successors of Peter, had played little part in formulating Christian doctrine. The Christian world was predominantly Greek, the great councils of the church at which doctrine had been decided took place either at Constantinople (381, 553) or even further east (Nicaea (325), Ephesus (431), Chalcedon (451)). The dominant figures in these councils had been the emperors, who had called them and proclaimed their findings through imperial decrees, rather than the bishops. With Christianity now the official religion of the state, it mattered as much to the emperors as to the bishops that there was doctrinal unity and it was hard, in any case, to see how this could have been achieved without imperial backing.

Rome's attempts to exert influence were not helped by the comparative isolation of the city from the east and the persistence in Rome of a strong pagan elite. There were individual Italian bishops, Ambrose in Milan, for instance, who found themselves closer to the western emperors and thus in a position to exercise greater power than a bishop based in Rome. It was not until the Council of Chalcedon in 451, when the so-called *tome* (letter) of Leo was read (in his absence), that 'for the first time Rome took a determining role in the definition of Christian dogma' (Judith Herrin) and even here there was a challenge to Rome's claims to primacy when, to Leo's fury, Constantinople's status was confirmed as second only to that of Rome (a move designed as much to raise its authority above the older Christian bishoprics of Antioch and Alexandria as to challenge Rome). The council held in Constantinople under Justinian's auspices in 553 conducted its business totally independently of Rome.

When in 590 a new bishop of Rome, Gregory (540–604), was consecrated, it seemed that the supremacy of the Greek east in defining Christianity would continue. Gregory had spent several years in Constantinople and had expressed some sympathy for the eastern position on doctrine. The emperors must have hoped that he could be controlled. These hopes were soon dashed. Gregory was a Roman aristocrat (in fact a former City Prefect) and his affection and concern for the city remained strong. He fed its often starving population from his own estates. Despite his stay in Constantinople he was not learned in Greek and represented the new clerical culture of the west, in which learning in the Latin classics was combined with a devout and somewhat austere Christianity, but remained always subservient to it. His happiest days, he recalled, were those when he was living as a monk in a community he had founded in Rome.

Gregory is undoubtedly one of the greatest spiritual leaders the west has ever produced. He restored to Christianity a moral integrity which had risked being lost in the vindictive debates of the fourth century and he knew the value of moderation in pastoral care. It was he who endorsed the rule of Benedict, which in contrast to the extreme asceticism of the fourth century, accepted that measured discipline was the way forward if monasteries were to remain settled and humane communities. His ideal pastor must, he wrote in his *Condescensio*, learn 'to be intimately close to each person through compassion, and yet to hover above all through contemplation'. It was a nice mix. Yet there was no compromise on papal authority. Gregory exploited his freedom from imperial control and doggedly set out on a new path which was to define the nature of western Christendom. The bishop of Rome was to be the presiding force in Christian Europe with his fellow but subordinate bishops strengthened as leaders of the Christian communities. The authority of the church rested jointly on the four gospels and the four ecumenical councils (Nicaea, Constantinople (381), Ephesus, and Chalcedon) but 'without the authority and consent of the apostolic see [Rome]', insisted Gregory 'none of the matters transacted [by a council] has any binding force'. It was a sophisticated rationale for papal power which owed much to the theology of Augustine but rested ultimately on the direct succession Gregory claimed from the apostle Peter. The foundations had been laid of the medieval papacy. They were reinforced by the widening doctrinal split with the east, and a growing isolation from the traditional Greek-speaking centres of Christianity as the leading members of the western church (Augustine, as has been seen, is one example) were unable any longer to understand Greek. Later, in the seventh century, Rome's position was further strengthened by the eclipse of two traditional rivals, the bishoprics of Alexandria and Antioch, by the Arab invasions so that one can justly talk of 'the Roman see as the single isolated, religious centre of the barbarian west' (Robert Markus).

Yet few in the late sixth century could have predicted the later supremacy over Europe of the popes. Rome as a city was by now isolated, little more than a few churches encircling the ruined centre. The Lombards had overrun many of the larger Italian cities and Gregory had only the most fragile of contacts with the rest of Europe. The mission he sent to England which successfully converted the Anglo-Saxons was in the circumstances a magnificent achievement. The acceptance of papal authority was slow (the Irish St Columban was still arguing in the seventh century that if any one bishop had the right to exert supreme authority in the church that was surely the bishop of Jerusalem), but there is no doubt that Gregory's reign marks a turning point in the history of Christianity and it is a fitting point with which to end this chapter.

Not least of the achievements of Gregory and his fellow bishops was to ensure the survival of classical Latin as the language of church law and administration in the Middle Ages and beyond. There was also a more colloquial Latin, the language of ordinary people of the empire. (In 813 a council of bishops at Tours ruled that sermons had to be in *rustica romana lingua*, colloquial Latin while, presumably, the rest of the service continued in classical Latin.) It was from these local dialects that the Romance languages appear to have emerged in those areas where the Roman population was a majority, the Iberian peninsula, Italy, France, and Romania. A barrier between these areas and those further north where German became the majority language has lasted from the sixth century to the present day and is a fine reminder that despite the collapse of the empire its legacy in Europe persisted.

Historians should always be sensitive to continuity. Yet the mentality of life in the early medieval centuries was dramatically different from that of the classical world. While secular rulers struggled to keep their authority, the church consolidated hers in the west through the well-established network of bishops. There was an increasing preoccupation with preparation for the afterlife and the rise of the patron saint as a mediator at the court of the Last Judgement. Relics become important symbols of prestige offering protection to cities as they struggled to keep their identity in a precarious world. In place of the vibrant pagan mythologies, a new set of mythologies based on the holy deeds of saints or the miracles of relics take their place. This was indeed a new world, no less fascinating than the old but markedly different from it.

FURTHER READING

See the suggestions at the end of Chapter 30.

32 | The Emergence of the Byzantine Empire

The Eastern Empire: Cultural Complexity in the Late Empire

The half of the empire which was placed under the rule of the young emperor Arcadius in 395 was one of some geographical and cultural complexity. It included not only the Danube provinces, as far west as Illyricum, the Balkans, and Greece but also Asia Minor, Syria, Palestine, and Egypt. Latin remained as a language of the army and law. Some emperors, such as Justin I and Justinian, came from a predominantly Latin cultural background and the language was kept up by the courtiers and lawyers of the imperial palace in Constantinople. However, the main spoken language of administration was Greek, which had spread widely in the east after Alexander's conquests. Antioch, the second city of the empire, and Alexandria were both Greek speaking and, as former capitals of the Seleucid and Ptolemaic monarchies, prided themselves on a Greek heritage which was much older and richer than that of Constantinople.

Although Greek had spread outside the cities (and is found as the normal language of inscriptions even in rural areas) local cultures had become more prominent since the third century. Christianity was a religion where the written text was important and local languages developed their own Christian literature. Syriac was used for a wide variety of Christian writings, including lives of the saints, sermons, and church histories. Greek texts were translated into Syriac and vice versa while Syriac texts were in their turn translated into Armenian, Georgian, and even in later times into Arabic. In Palestine the Jewish teachers understood Greek but debated in Hebrew and conversed in Aramaic. In Egypt Coptic, which is essentially Egyptian written in a Greek script, had appeared in the late third century as the medium used by the Christian church to communicate with the Egyptian-speaking masses. Many Egyptians were bilingual in Greek and Coptic and Coptic became more widespread century by century until the Arab invasions of the seventh century.

Yet despite its cultural complexity the eastern part of the empire saw itself as the proud heir of Rome. Its inhabitants called themselves *Romaioi*, or Romans, right up to the fall of Constantinople to the Turks in AD 1453. The court at Constantinople also served as a haven of Greek classical culture. A scholarly elite survived in Constantinople for centuries. It is through their careful copying of

Greek texts, for instance, that so much of the work of Plato, Euclid, Sophocles, and Thucydides has been saved. The fact that an empire with its own distinct ethos emerged in this area and sustained itself as a multicultural entity for over a thousand years was a remarkable achievement and the comments of the Irish historian William Lecky writing in 1869 that 'Of the Byzantine empire, the universal verdict of history is that it constitutes, with scarcely an exception, the most thoroughly based and despicable form that civilization has yet assumed' has long been superseded.

Constantinople and the Christian Emperors

So long as imperial rule survived in Italy Constantinople could not be the true capital of the empire, but by endowing it with a senate, one of the empire's two consuls, and its own grain supply (the *annona*) on the Roman model, Constantine had ensured that it was the natural successor to Rome as government in the west collapsed. At first Constantinople had few Christian buildings but the announcement after the Council of Constantinople (381) that its bishop was second only to the bishop of Rome, a decision which offended Rome and Alexandria in particular, gave it the status of a Christian capital. This was enhanced by the steady accumulation of relics. Those of the first Christian martyr, Stephen, were welcomed into the city with great ceremony in 417. Under the long reign of Theodosius II (408–50) in particular, Constantinople was consolidated as the centre of administration for the east. The population grew steadily and Theodosius built a massive line of walls, much of which still stands, to defend the larger city. For the first time the emperors come to reside permanently in the Great Palace and court ceremonies become part of the life of the city. The most lively of these ceremonies were the settings for the meetings of the emperor with his people in the vast hippodrome which had been built by Constantine alongside the Palace. Gladiator fights had by now died out and the races were of chariots, but the games had a serious political aspect. The emperor was on display and could be acclaimed or derided by the city's population. The integration of the crowds into political life, particularly in the charged atmosphere of the races, where two factions, the Blues and the Greens, championed opposing teams of charioteers, brought an explosive element to city life and several emperors found themselves the focus of massive unrest when they misjudged the popular mood.

In the fourth century Eusebius, the historian of the reign of Constantine, had developed a model of Christian kingship which was adopted by Constantine's fifth-century successors. The emperor was God's representative on earth. God regulates the cosmic order, the emperor the social order, bringing his subjects together in a harmony which mirrors that which God has designed for all creation. In Theodosius' reign the image of imperial sanctity was reinforced by the emperor's pious elder sister, Pulcheria, who, while her brother (aged 7 at the time of his accession) was a minor, took the traditional Roman title of Augusta and maintained her position on Theodosius' death by marrying his successor, Marcian (450–7). (Her austere lifestyle brought her into conflict with Theodosius' wife, Eudocia, an intellectual beauty from Athens and reputedly a pagan by birth, who was more extravagant by nature.) The continuing importance in the eastern Orthodox churches (a capital 'O' denotes the distinct eastern churches, e.g. Greek or later Russian Orthodox churches which were now emerging) of a single ruler as one chosen by God contrasted strongly with the situation in the west where bishops of Rome such as Gregory were free to consolidate their authority independently of state control.

Marcian had no heir and it was the *magister militum*, a German, Aspar, who determined his successor, Leo I (457–74). There was still, after all these centuries of imperial rule, no agreed way of arranging the succession. The emperor could be the nominee of the armies or German strong men. Leo was the first of the emperors to be crowned by the Patriarch of Constantinople, a ceremony which took place before 'the people' in the hippodrome. Although chariot races continued as the city's most popular form of entertainment, the hippodrome gradually developed its role as the centre of imperial display. Leo also tried to reduce the dependency of the empire on 'barbarian' troops by recruiting a native mountain people, the Isaurians, instead. It was a choice fraught with its own difficulties. The Isaurians had been long known for their lawlessness and had been highly disruptive during the troubles of the third century. (The 'sophisticated' citizens of Constantinople had the habit of assailing visiting Isaurians with stones.) Even so Leo married his daughter Ariadne to one of their military leaders, Zeno, who then succeeded Leo as emperor in 474. Zeno's was a particularly unstable reign. He faced major challenges from rival factions of his native Isaurians as well as renewed pressures in Thrace from the Goths.

When Zeno died in 491 his widow made the choice of emperor. It was of a courtier, Anastasius, who was already 61 years old. Anastasius came from Epirus, on the fringes of the Latin-speaking world. He was a fine administrator whose career had included a period in Egypt. He married Ariadne and then consolidated his position by crushing the Isaurians. Anastasius was a devout man described in one source as 'the good emperor, the lover of monks and the protector of the poor and afflicted', in short a truly Christian emperor. He was drawn to Monophysitism (for which see below) but reluctant to impose his beliefs on others. The people of Constantinople, however, who always expected the emperor to be their own, were offended by his lack of religious orthodoxy and the clear preference he showed for the eastern provinces, in particular Syria.

Anastasius' most impressive achievement was the steady accumulation of capital. When he died there were 32,000 pounds of gold in the imperial treasury.

(Gold was the favoured metal of the empire drawn from sources in the Balkans, Armenia, and apparently, in the sixth century, from the Sudan. One pound of gold was made up of 72 solidi, the coins first minted by Constantine which were to survive as a stable unit of currency for several hundred years.) It was the result of an effective and steady administration of an empire which remained relatively prosperous. Although the evidence for this prosperity remains fragmentary, archaeological research has uncovered a flourishing area of olive oil cultivation along the Syrian limestone massif, for instance, while in the Hauran and Negev areas in Syria and Palestine there are signs of new areas being taken into cultivation as population increased. Trade continued along an axis from Egypt and north Africa to Constantinople even after the collapse of the west. Solidi have been found on sites from Sweden to the Ukraine and in Ceylon they were said to be favoured above Persian silver.

This prosperity was tapped through an effective consolidation of the administration, with a shift of power towards provincial governors at the expense of the town councils, which were by now in decay. The classical city entered a period of decline and disintegration, similar to that seen in the west. There is a sense in the sources of life being sucked out of it. 'Now we have no more meetings, no more debates, no more gatherings of wise men in the agora, nothing more of all that made our city famous', lamented Basil of Caesarea in the late fourth century. A city such as Aphrodisias, always vulnerable to earthquakes, was able to repair the damage caused by them in the fourth and fifth centuries. In the seventh the resources and will to build have evaporated and the buildings are left to lie in ruins. By the eleventh century Venetian captains are being encouraged to pick up discarded columns from among the detritus of dead classical cities—many of them still embellish the portals of St Mark's, the city's opulent basilica.

The taxation system remained unbalanced and harsh. Senators were exempt from some taxes while the heaviest burden seems to have fallen on the peasantry. There are accounts of recalcitrant taxpayers being flogged or imprisoned and their children sold into slavery. Through sheer ruthlessness the system worked well enough to transform surplus produce (payments of which could be commuted into gold) into the means by which the army and administration could be financed. A supply of free corn to Constantinople was also maintained, much of it coming from Egypt.

The Defence of the Empire

The heaviest financial burden on the state was that of defence. The empire remained under continuous military threat. While Constantinople itself was virtually impregnable the Danube provinces to the west were not and were ravaged by a succession of Goths, Huns, and, later, Bulgars, Avars, and Slavs. Yet the defence policy of the eastern empire, unlike that of the west, never became dictated by outsiders. The people of Constantinople made the point in 400 when they launched a successful uprising against the city garrison, which was under the command of a Goth, Gainas, who appears to have had the ambition to become an eastern Stilicho. Gainas was killed. The lesson was learnt and no emperor allowed a military strong man to take his place. The court of the eastern empire remained civilian rather than military in temper and mixed diplomacy with military confrontation. Perhaps as a result the strategy of dealing with the barbarians was often muddled and inconsistent. An agreement was made with the Visigoth Alaric (397) but it was then repudiated. Similarly Attila's Huns were bought off by Theodosius II (to the tune of 6,000 pounds of gold in 443) but on Theodosius' death Marcian refused to continue paying. The eastern empire was fortunate in that in both cases the barbarians then headed to the west, adding to the overwhelming pressures on that part of the empire. There was little the east was able to offer the west in support. The one major attempt at intervention, the invasion of Africa in 468, was a disastrous failure. When Odoacer deposed the last of the western emperors he was allowed to survive through default. His overthrow at the hands of Theodoric the Ostrogoth was not as a result of the eastern empire's strength but, instead, its weakness in not being able to remove Theodoric from its own territory in any other way.

The empire also faced a continuing threat from the east. The Persian Sasanian empire remained powerful and prided itself on its cultural superiority over the Romans. (It saw the Roman empire as the moon in comparison to itself as the sun.) Neither side was now set on the conquest of the other but low level conflict persisted. There was continuous dispute over the definition of the borders between the empires in Mesopotamia. Further north, Armenia, traditionally a buffer state, also proved a source of tension. Armenia had been Christian since the early fourth century and was increasingly oriented towards the west. The Persians, resentful that Armenia's autonomy was being compromised, tried to impose their own cultural and religious values in return. The Persians were also, like the Romans, under intense pressure from the north from nomadic peoples. This made Lazica, on the eastern edge of the Black Sea, another area of conflict. The Persians feared that if they did not control the area nomads would use its passes to attack the fertile lands along the Caspian Sea. The Romans, in their turn, feared the Persians would use the passes to penetrate into the Black Sea, giving them the opportunity of threatening Constantinople.

Christianity in the Eastern Empire

Theodosius I had launched a determined attack on paganism but many areas of the eastern empire still remained pagan and only gradually succumbed to

Christianity. Even orthodox Christianity was difficult to impose. Arianism remained strong and there were many Christian communities (especially, inscriptions show, in Anatolia) where local traditions of worship were resistant to decrees from far-off emperors. In fifth-century Athens it was still possible for a Platonist such as Proclus to have his own school and conduct his own pagan rituals, including prayer to Asclepius, the Greek god of medicine, whose temple remained in use. The Athenian school of philosophy survived in fact into the sixth century when it was finally closed down by Justinian. However, classical Greek culture was on the defensive. By the late fourth century the gymnasia of the Greek world had disappeared. There was a marked decline in the use of books and church leaders freely abused 'philosophers' and the Greek tradition of empirical thought. In this Christianity linked itself back to older traditions of pre-scientific thinking which had, of course, always predominated in everyday life. The Asclepium in Athens eventually becomes a Christian church in which the healing rituals were little different from those of Asclepius. Local temples continued to be closed down by determined bishops or sacked by vigilante groups made up of monks. The centuries-old culture of Egypt was also finally stifled. The temple of Isis at Philae was closed in AD 536 and at Karnak wall paintings and reliefs were covered with rough plaster and the temple buildings adapted to the use of convents and monasteries. 'See what blessings God's Christ came to bestow on us, since through His teachings in the gospels he has redeemed even the souls of the Egyptians from such a disease of lasting and continued blindness so that most of the people of Egypt have been freed from this insanity,' exulted the church historian Eusebius.

The spread of Christianity was reflected in many important social changes. In the cities it was the bishops who assumed the responsibilities of the old classical elites. As in the west bishops tended to come from the traditional ruling classes and preserved the *paideia*, the civilized ways of behaviour of a leisured elite for whom personal relationships were an art form in themselves. Through launching energetic building programmes the bishops were also assuming a traditional role of the elite, although there was a tension between their role of builder of churches (which were now opulently adorned with fine marbles and mosaics) and the explicitly Christian role of providing for the poor. (One bishop, Theophilius of Alexandria, was accused of diverting money given to buy shirts for the poor to his building programme.) The demise of the old city governments also left the bishops responsible for the maintenance of order. The bishop of Antioch excused his late arrival at the Council of Ephesus in 431 on the grounds that he had been busy suppressing riots and another bishop of Antioch wrote to a colleague, 'It is the duty of bishops like you to cut short and to restrain any unregulated movements of the mob.' On occasion bishops even had to defend their cities against marauding bands of monks.

A glimpse of the relationship between church and state can be seen in surviving records from southern Egypt. When raids into the empire from Nubia caused a mass of refugees to flee northwards up the Nile the well-known abbot Shenoute took responsibility for feeding them for three months from the bakehouses of his monastery. His gesture was recognized by the imperial authorities, who granted him a tax exemption on the lands of his monastery. Again, further south, on the exposed frontier itself, Bishop Apion of Syene is found petitioning the emperor for more troops with which to protect his churches and people. The petition went all the way to Theodosius II, was endorsed by him in his own hand, and then sent to the military commander of southern Egypt for action. In both cases church initiatives receive state responses.

While the bishops may have been appropriating the traditional roles of the elite, others were turning their backs on society, by withdrawing and adopting an ascetic lifestyle. Some, the monks of the Syrian desert, for instance, lived alone, courting death through the acute deprivations they imposed upon themselves. Their conquest of their bodies gave them immense spiritual charisma. Symeon Stylites, perched on the top of a sixty-foot pillar on a mountain ridge at Telnesin, drew vast crowds. Even the bishops became disturbed by the unsettling energies released by these holy men who seemed to be beyond any form of social control. The social impact of asceticism is difficult to gauge. For some it offered a form of freedom. Women who took a vow of virginity could escape from the traditional confinement at home and gained a status not seen in the east since the days of Homer. There was no longer the fear that they would dishonour their family by sexual misbehaviour abroad, perhaps the main reason for seclusion in the first place. There is no corresponding improvement for women who chose the married state, at least not until the reign of Justinian when divorce laws were equalized for the sexes and women given greater rights over their own children.

Most ascetics chose to live in communities. The word 'monastery' perhaps fails to convey the diversity of living arrangements which could be found. Some 'monasteries' were little more than private homes, often in a city, where the owner and a few adherents lived a life of asceticism. At the other extreme were substantial buildings set in the desert and surrounded by defensive walls. In Egypt many thousands, both men and women, are said to have lived in this way. Some cultivated contact with the outside world, some did not. St Basil of Caesarea (333–79), the most influential of the early monastic leaders in the east outside Egypt, believed hospitality was an essential element of monastic life. Monastic communities should work and live in poverty passing on all surplus produce to the poor. Basil himself founded a whole complex of buildings outside Caesarea including a hospital and a leper colony. Some monks took more overtly political roles, in the destruction of pagan temples, for instance; others followed more withdrawn lives of prayer.

The Christian world remained divided by doctrinal disputes. The most divisive dispute of the fourth century, the Arian controversy (see p. 584), had theoretically been settled with the condemnation of Arius but many, including those Germans and Goths who had been baptized before the condemnation, tended to be Arian and remained so. Now a new dispute arose within the orthodox church ('orthodox', small 'o' is used here to describe correct doctrine). It was over the nature of Christ. His divinity had been emphasized by the Nicene creed, now established as orthodoxy, but while the Nicene creed had settled one problem it highlighted another, the extent to which Jesus could be human as well. Nestorius, installed as patriarch of Constantinople in 428, argued that Christ was one person but had two distinct natures, one human and one divine, both coexisting in the same body. Nestorius himself tended to emphasize the human nature of Christ, stressing, for instance, that when Christ suffered on the cross he did so as a human being. Nestorius was bitterly opposed by the Patriarch Cyril of Alexandria, whose own interpretation was that Christ, while appearing in human form, was predominantly divine. (The bitterness of Alexandria over the elevated status of Constantinople lurked behind this conflict.) Those who emphasized the divinity of Christ were later to be known as Monophysites. Intertwined with this dispute was the complementary one over the correct title for Mary. Cyril and Monophysites wished to proclaim Mary as *Theotokos*, bearer of God, Nestorius preferred *Anthropotokos*, man-bearer, but was prepared to compromise with Christ-bearer.

These debates were intensified by the granting of tax exemptions and patronage to those who accepted what was defined by the emperor of the time as orthodoxy. Disputes over doctrine could easily degenerate into struggles over the control of resources. As Gregory of Nazianzus observed of a conflict between two rival bishops. 'The pretext was souls, but in fact it was desire for control . . . of taxes and contributions which have the whole world in miserable confusion.' These disputes risked upsetting the good order of the empire, one reason why the emperors played such a large role in enforcing an agreed orthodoxy and were so eager to use councils as a means of settling them. A council held in Ephesus (where by tradition Mary had spent her later life) in 431 accepted the concept of Mary as *Theotokos* thus by implication condemning Nestorius. Nestorius, who had not attended the Council, was forced into exile for the rest of his life and Theodosius ordering the burning of his writings in 435. The issue was still not settled, however. A second Council of Ephesus, held in 449, took the Monophysite position but was then condemned by the bishop of Rome, Leo I, as 'a robber council'. These two councils had, in fact, operated largely free of imperial control, but now the emperor, Marcian, was taking no chances and another council was held, this time at Chalcedon, in 451. It was rigidly controlled by imperial officials and Marcian himself put in an appearance. Here the pendulum swung back and Christ was proclaimed to have the two natures, human and divine, within the same undivided person. This was, in fact, close to what Nestorius had argued in the first place. As a concession to the supporters of Cyril of Alexandria Mary's title as mother of God was confirmed.

The Chalcedonian formula was welcomed by the west but Leo, who did not attend the Council himself, took offence at another decision, that the patriarch of Constantinople should be second in authority only to the bishop of Rome. There were other lasting divisions. Doctrinal disputes had by this time aroused such bitterness and involved so many personality clashes that no solution would ever have satisfied everyone. By taking a compromise position the Council of Chalcedon had isolated extremists of each side. One group, taking its inspiration from theologians of the east Syrian city of Edessa, continued to emphasize the distinct human nature of Christ. (They are sometimes called the Nestorians, but their emphasis on Christ's humanity was more pronounced than anything put forward by Nestorius.) They eventually formed the separate 'Church of the East', most of whose adherents were in Persia. The church survived successfully for many centuries, even managing to send missionaries as far east as China in the thirteenth century. Meanwhile the Monophysite position claimed the adherence of many in Syria and Egypt and separate churches, the Coptic and Syrian Orthodox churches, eventually emerged.

The Council of Chalcedon had therefore succeeded in creating a religious division which made a mockery of the emperor as ruler of a people united in a single church. The whole debate had been marked by high levels of violence and intimidation and any further compromise was to prove impossible. The Monophysites, in particular, were intransigent and any move to accommodate them within the church now risked offending the church in the west, which remained (and still remains to this day) resolutely Chalcedonian.

Justinian

On the death of Anastasius in 518 a 70-year-old Latin-speaking soldier from the Balkans, Justin, the commander of the palace guards, became emperor. Virtually illiterate himself, he groomed his sophisticated nephew, Justinian, as his successor and Justinian duly succeeded in 527. So began one of the most memorable reigns (527–65) of late antiquity. Justinian inherited a stable and prosperous state. He had a vision of how it could be raised to new heights of glory through the revival of a Roman empire incorporating its old capital and whatever else could be regained of the west. It would be united under a single orthodox Christianity with the Arianism of the barbarian successor kingdoms destroyed. This was history-making on a grand scale, but despite the underlying stability and prosperity of the state it was carried out against a backdrop of continued pressures from both the east and north and, less predictably, natural disasters of earthquakes and plague. The final effect of Justinian's awesome ambitions may well have been to weaken the empire and the question remains as to how much Justinian himself has to shoulder the blame for this. Responsibility was not his alone. The influence over him of his beautiful, worldly-wise, and supremely self-confident wife Theodora, whom he raised from mistress to empress, must have been strong.

Justinian's Law Codes

The first 'great' achievement of Justinian was his codification of Roman law. Over the preceding 500 years Roman law had become an unwieldy accumulation of imperial decrees interspersed with the opinions of jurists. The result was a mass of contradictions and uncertainties. For Justinian a unified system of law, based on Roman tradition, was essential to the security of the state and in 528 he set codification in hand. It was masterminded by a senior administrator, Tribunician, a man of great erudition and intellectual energy. The work was completed in three parts. The *Code* brought together all imperial decrees in a single volume. Henceforth, only those cited in the *Code* could be used in the courts. A first version of the *Code* was ready as early as 529 but what now survives is a second version promulgated in 534. The *Digest* is a compilation and rationalization of the opinions of jurists. Three million words of opinion were reduced and consolidated into a million. (The wording of earlier opinions was often retained, so that the *Digest* is not as coherent as it might be.) In order that there should be no further confusion Justinian forbade any further commentaries on these opinions. They had to be used as they were without further interpretation (though translations into Greek were allowed). In order that lawyers would be able to use the *Code* and *Digest*, a separate volume, the *Institutes*, was drawn up to serve as a textbook for students. The *Digest* and *Institutes* were promulgated in 533.

It was this codification (together with a fourth volume of the laws which Justinian enacted after 534) which was to pass through the medieval Italian schools of law (the *Digest* survived in one single sixth-century copy which passed around several Italian cities before coming to rest, permanently, in the Biblioteca Laurenziana in Florence) and become part of the legal tradition of countries as varied as South Africa, France, and Germany. More immediately it was a symbol of Justinian's determination to bring an administrative unity to his empire based on Roman, not Greek, principles.

The Nika Riots

To centralize and simplify his administration Justinian chose ruthless ministers. The most prominent was John of Cappadocia, a poorly educated but determined man who had no respect for the privileged. John set to work to destroy the tax exemptions enjoyed by the elites and the cosy relationship many of them had established with the civil service. Those who continued to defy him could even be subjected to the humiliating ordeal of being flogged. Meanwhile the civil service was slimmed down and, in breach of the traditions established by Constantine, some civil and military posts were combined. Not surprisingly John's rigour aroused discontent among the professional classes. In 532 they found growing support among the population of Constantinople, who were unsettled by food shortages. An outburst of anger (voiced by the Greens) could probably have been contained by encouraging each faction to focus their traditional hostility towards each other, but a bungled attempt by the authorities at hanging one Green and one Blue supporter led to the factions combining against the government (with cries of 'Nika', victory). There was widespread rioting and the crowds, whose political perspectives remained highly conventional, attempted to install a rival emperor. Justinian wavered. He dismissed John of Cappadocia and Tribunician and appeared in the imperial box to take the blame, all without avail. He would have fled the city if the empress Theodora had not stiffened his resolve with her famous statement that a winding sheet of imperial purple was as good as any. It was the generals, Belisarius and Narses among them, who now came to the fore. The hippodrome was stormed and an appalling massacre, of perhaps some 30,000 of the city population, was carried out only a few yards from the imperial palace. Justinian was saved.

No emperor of imperial Rome had ever treated the people of his capital in such a ruthless way and the experience must have been a sobering one. How it related to Justinian's decision to launch his expedition to Africa in 533 is not clear. Justinian was no stranger to war. The first years of his reign had been marked by a series of campaigns along the Persian frontiers from Lazica in the north to Arabia in the south. At the same time he had conducted a defence of the Danube borders and engaged in conflicts with the Huns along the Black Sea coast. The empire had been able to sustain the cost and now the ambition of regaining the west and 'rescuing' orthodox Christians from the persecutions of Arians became more prominent. Already in 532–3 an 'Endless Peace', underwritten by a large payment of tribute, had been made with the new Persian leader, Khrusro, leaving Justinian free to move westwards. The Nika riots may have strengthened his determination, either by giving him a sense of omnipotence or by providing him with a reason for rebuilding his popularity with the masses. Whatever the motives, campaigns to Africa and Italy were now set in hand.

The Campaigns in Africa and Italy

As the emperor's advisers, aware of the debacle in 468 (see above, p. 615), warned him, an expedition to Vandal Africa was a risky enterprise but in the event their fears proved unjustified. Justinian's general Belisarius landed in the bay of Tunis with 10,000 infantry and 5,000 cavalry. A revolt had been provoked beforehand in Sardinia which diverted many of the Vandal troops there. As a result the Vandals' control of Africa collapsed after two battles and all traces of their presence soon disappeared, another indication of how shallow were the roots of their occupation. (It is assumed that the defeated Vandals were gradually absorbed into their conquerors' armies.) The Vandal king, Gelimer, was taken back to Constantinople where he was paraded in a triumph reminiscent of those of republican Rome. The local population rejoiced at their liberation but now found themselves, somewhat incongruously, under a Greek-speaking administration. Heavy taxation and the raids of nomadic tribes hindered the return of the province's natural prosperity, which does not seem to have been assured until the seventh century. Eastern control survived until the Arab conquest of north Africa in the late seventh century.

In 535 Justinian, buoyed up by his success in Africa, a success he celebrated in Constantinople with a triumph held in the hippodrome, attempted an invasion of Italy. His motives, the elimination of Arianism and the restoration of the western empire, remained the same, but everything was different in Italy. The country was difficult to fight in, the Ostrogoths were resilient, while the local population was ambivalent about being rescued by Greek-speaking easterners. Furthermore the invading force, once again under Belisarius, was only half the size of that sent to Africa. In all the war was to drag on for almost twenty years. Belisarius found himself besieged in Rome (the cutting of the aqueducts by the Goths finally closed the city's great baths) and was only relieved when a second force, still only 5,000-strong, managed to reach the Ostrogoth capital, Ravenna. Complex negotiations eventually resulted in the surrender of the city in 540 but no permanent settlement was made and the Ostrogoths still retained the cities of northern Italy. War soon broke out again just at a time when Justinian faced pressures on his own eastern borders from the Persians. Victory for the east came only in 554, but soon afterwards northern Italy was invaded by the Lombards, who drove out the eastern armies and established their own kingdom in the Po valley, which was to last until 774 (and which still sends echoes to northern separatists today). The empire retained control only of Rome, Ravenna, a fragile corridor between them and a scatter of cities and fortresses. Apart from an intervention in a Visigothic civil war in Spain, Justinian's attempt to revive a western empire had come to a halt.

Procopius of Caesarea

The fullest source for the early part of Justinian's reign (up to the early 550s) is that provided by the historian Procopius of Caesarea, a cosmopolitan city, with Jewish and Christian communities, celebrated as a centre of education. Procopius was born into the Christian upper classes but nothing is known of his life until he surfaces in 527 on the staff of Justinian's most gifted general, Belisarius. It was the career of Belisarius which gave him his opportunity to see, at first hand, fighting in the east, the great expedition to Africa and the longer campaign in Italy (536–40). By 542, at the latest, Procopius was in Constantinople and spent much of the rest of his life there. He may have returned to Italy in 546–7 but he had fallen out of the emperor's favour and does not seem to have held any other official post. There is no work of his which can be proved to be written after 554.

Procopius left three main works. The most substantial is his account of Justinian's wars in the east, Africa, and Italy. *The Wars* is primarily a narrative with a mass of detail on the armies, battles, and personalities involved, much of it gathered at first hand. Procopius' model is Thucydides. He even provides a detailed account of the plague in Constantinople which is reminiscent of that described by Thucydides in Athens. As with Thucydides, Procopius' great strength is the vivid depiction of great events and at first his story has all the excitement it needs, as Procopius' hero, Belisarius, destroys the Vandals and returns home to Constantinople to celebrate his victory. In the later volumes, however, with the sack of Antioch, the outbreak of plague (see below), and stalemate in Italy, Procopius' optimism fades and his disillusionment with imperial policy grows stronger. He, like so many of his class, was naturally suspicious of the ambitions and autocracy of an emperor (at one point he compares Justinian to Domitian) and his resentments were piled up to be eventually vented in his *Secret History*, composed perhaps around 550 (before he had finished *The Wars*). This, the best known of Procopius' works, is a vitriolic tirade against Justinian (and to some extent Belisarius) though it is most often read for its descriptions of the alleged sexual cavortings of the empress Theodora in her early life as a circus artiste. The *Secret History* was intended to be kept unpublished during Justinian's lifetime and contrasts with the third of Procopius' surviving works on Justinian's building programme (*Buildings*). This is a straightforward panegyric, probably also written in the early 550s, in which the great achievements of the emperor as patron of such majestic buildings as St Sophia and other churches (but also of a vast range of fortifications) are praised.

Procopius was writing consciously within classical Greek literary traditions. Both the invective and the panegyric were recognized forms to which a writer could turn when it suited his purpose. Averil Cameron has deconstructed

Procopius' works to show that they have an underlying unity within this tradition. Procopius was writing for an elitist minority who understood the conventions and who would not have been as disturbed by the disparity between the three surviving works as later generations have been. The tradition was a constraining one, however. It focused on secular history in a period when religious debate was endemic and spiritual power a major element of Justinian's hold over his people. Procopius makes only marginal references to religion.

It is, in short, the narrowness of Procopius' perspective which is the main drawback of his writings. In his description of the Nika riots he cannot see the rioters as anything more than a rabble—the expected response of his class, perhaps, but not an adequate analysis of an event which incorporated some form of coherent political programme. Procopius' suspicions of Justinian were understandable but became so exaggerated that it is impossible to understand the motives of the emperor for putting in hand his great campaigns. This is part of a more general weakness, Procopius' failure to deal with causation in history. Years of triumph could be presented as part of God's divine favour for the empire or as the result of the qualities of the empire's leaders; years of catastrophe, such as 540, left the historian overwhelmed and reduced to making banal statements about Fate. Nevertheless Procopius remains a major historian. It can even be said that he is too successful a source, providing a picture of the reign which has been too easily absorbed by those who have read him.

The Church of St Sophia

The Nika riots had done extensive damage in Constantinople with many of the public buildings along the Mese, the ceremonial concourse of the city, destroyed. Among the ruins was the great church of St Sophia, the Holy Wisdom, traditionally one of Constantine's foundations and the church in which emperor and patriarch met on the great feast days of the church. Justinian was inspired to rebuild it in a form which would make it the most awe-inspiring church in Christendom. The rebuilt St Sophia still stands today, without doubt one of the great surviving buildings of antiquity (rivalled perhaps only by the Parthenon and Pantheon). Its centrepiece is a great dome rising from four massive piers joined by arches. In its final form the dome rises 55 metres above the ground. (The first dome collapsed and a new one was dedicated in 563.) The space over each pier between the arches is filled with spherical triangles on which the dome is supported. This left the space under the arches free on the east and west sides and two huge semi-domes were added to fill them. The eastern semi-dome was, in its turn, extended by semicircular apses while the western one led to the vast entrance beyond which lay an open cloister. The north and south arches incorporated columned arcades at two levels. In antiquity the whole was covered with

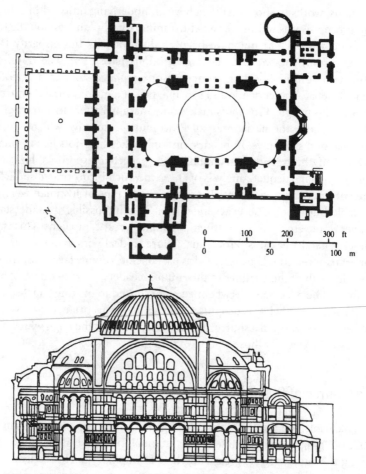

FIG. 10 Santa Sophia, Constantinople, built AD 532–7. The majesty and complexity of its design can be seen in this plan and section. Procopius described the great dome as giving the impression that it was suspended from heaven.

marble and mosaic. It was the sense of space and mystery, as well as overwhelming opulence, which gripped contemporaries such as Procopius, who described the dome as if suspended from heaven. Even now that much of the decoration is lost the building retains its capacity to amaze, its imaginative use of space presenting a real challenge to the eye.

There was no exact precedent for St Sophia. Some have seen Roman influences, the dome of the Pantheon combined with the hall of the great Basilica of Maxentius near the Forum (early fourth century), for instance. Others see precedents in Persia. The architects, Anthemius of Tralles and Isidore of Miletus, a physicist who had made a special study of domes and vaults, were clearly expected to provide something original and Justinian himself took the closest interest in their design. Their method of basing the dome was new and became the most significant contribution of the Byzantines to structural engineering.

St Sophia was only one of a mass of churches built across the empire by Justinian. It may not have been the most influential. The now destroyed Church of the Apostles in Constantinople, built as a cross with one dome in the centre and others on each arm of the cross, influenced the design of St Mark's in Venice, the Church of the Hundred Gates on the island of Paros, and a great church built by Theodora in Ephesus. Justinian's other buildings varied between the use of the squared dome and the traditional basilica plan. The great monastery church, later known as St Catherine's, set behind defensive walls at the foot of Mount Sinai was a traditional basilica for instance, as were many smaller churches on the Syrian border. Not least of Justinian's achievements was the completion of the church of San Vitalis in Ravenna, where the famous mosaic portraits of himself and Theodora surrounded by their retinues are not the least of the church's glories.

The Last Years of Justinian

In his *Buildings*, Procopius devotes more attention to Justinian's fortifications than to his churches. It is a reminder of an empire under continuous military pressure. After 540 the successes in Africa and Italy were overshadowed by a devastating attack by the Persians on Antioch (from which the second city of the empire never fully recovered), the ravaging of Thrace by Huns, Bulgars, and Slavs, and the mounting problems in the campaigns in Italy. Added to this was the first of recurring outbreaks of bubonic plague. It spread from Egypt through Syria and Asia Minor, reaching Constantinople in 542. One theory is that an enormous volcanic eruption at Krakatoa led to a deterioration in climate—tree-ring growth was exceptionally low in many parts of the world between 530 and 550—and famine led to a population especially vulnerable to infection. Although it is difficult to spot the impact of the disease in the archaeological record it is estimated that between a third and a half of the population died in the worst-affected cities. The effect on the morale of the empire and the manpower it could provide must have been profound. It is all the more remarkable that in the 550s the empire took the initiative once more and with some success. A fifty-year peace with Persia, which confirmed Lazica under Byzantine control, was signed in 561 and fighting was finally concluded in the empire's favour in Italy in the 550s.

The most intractable border was the northern. A whole range of peoples, Bulgars, Avars, Slavs, pressed on the empire. Raids reached well into Greece and, on occasions, to the walls of Constantinople itself. This was the period when the cities of Greece went into permanent decline. Athens was raided by Slavs and Avars in 582 and the sites of ancient Sparta, Argos, and Corinth were abandoned with the inhabitants of Corinth seeking refuge on Acrocorinth. The only effective way of dealing with such a range of peoples was to play one off against another, and from the 550s Byzantine diplomacy was employed to foster enmities between them. An Avar delegation was received in Constantinople in 557, for instance, and allied by treaty to the empire. The Avars then subdued a mass of people north of the Danube borders, although they later returned to exact further subsidies from the empire.

In 548 Theodora had died. Justinian was aged 66. Traditionally, the years that followed have been seen as ones in which he withdrew from public affairs and became preoccupied with religion. (The comparison has been made with Philip II of Spain toiling night after night in his office in the Escorial.) This cannot be wholly true. The diplomatic manoeuvres in the north of the 550s suggest a man still in control of policy-making and foreign affairs. Nor did a preoccupation with spiritual matters necessarily imply withdrawal from public affairs. The maintenance of religious unity was fundamental to Justinian's rule and he had, therefore, powerful reasons for being preoccupied with achieving it.

The main barrier to unity within the empire was Monophysitism, still strong in the eastern provinces of the empire. As early as the 530s Justinian had been trying to find a way of bringing back the moderate Monophysites into the orthodox church. His best hope seemed to be to launch a new condemnation of 'Nestorianism' (of the variety preached by the Church of the East), behind which he could rally the Monophysites. His target was the so-called Three Chapters, texts written by three fifth-century bishops in which sympathy for Nestorianism might be detected. The bishops had, however, been specifically cleared of any heresy at the Council of Chalcedon and so any attempt to condemn them now would undermine the authority of that council. This did not prevent Justinian from calling a new council to meet in Constantinople in 553 to revive the issue. The emperor browbeat the attending bishops into accepting his interpretations of the texts. The result of what Judith Herrin has called 'a hollow triumph of political intrigue and imperial intervention' was to deeply offend the western church, whose bishops believed that the decisions of the Council of Chalcedon should not be discarded at the whim of an emperor. The split between the western (Catholic) and eastern (Orthodox) churches, while only finally confirmed in the eleventh and twelfth centuries, was one step nearer. The Monophysites failed to be reconciled and in fact proceeded with the development of their own hierarchy.

The Emergence of the Byzantine Empire

The late sixth century can be seen to mark the transition from the classical to the Byzantine world, one in which a predominantly Christian, Greek culture was precariously maintained by an autocratic state beset by enemies. (The word Byzantine derives from Byzantium, the name of the Greek city on which Constantinople was built.) Classical culture was by now largely dead and a more intensely Christian atmosphere pervaded the empire. In the 530s Justinian had insisted that all should be baptized on the pain of the loss of all their properties although paganism is known to have still flourished in rural areas. In the cities resources now seem to be targeted almost exclusively at Christian buildings. At Aphrodisias, in what is now south-west Turkey, the theatre is finally abandoned in the late sixth century and by the early seventh is being used as a church. Christian liturgies and the music that accompanied them become an important part of general culture and it is clear that they are used by whole congregations not just an educated elite. The icon, a picture of Christ, the Virgin Mary, or a saint, normally painted on wood, becomes increasingly popular at all levels of society. The most venerated were believed to be 'not made by human hands' and had the ability to effect miracles. When Constantinople was besieged in 626, the city's icons were paraded before the enemy and portraits of the Virgin Mary were carried round the walls. The city survived. In the sixth and seventh centuries miracle stories become associated with particular shrines (as at Lourdes today). There is an increased emphasis on the unknowability of God, especially in the works of the mystic known as pseudo-Dionysus.

The horizons of the state also appear to have become narrower. After Justinian's death Latin gradually becomes forgotten. An important moment comes in 629 when the emperor Heraclius officially titled himself *basileus* rather than the traditional *imperator*. Court titles become Greek. The leading military official is a *strategos*, the leading civilian a *krites*. When the defenders of Constantinople had finally triumphed in 626 they sang the great Greek hymn *Akathistos*, which still survives to be used in services in Lent.

This was a time of increasing isolation. The attacks, from both north and east, were unrelenting. The early seventh century saw the crumbling of the Danube borders and the most successful Persian attack ever on the empire with both Jerusalem and Alexandria lost. Asia Minor was ravaged and even Constantinople was nearly captured. Under the emperor Heraclius (610–41) a miraculous recovery took place which brought the Sasanian empire close to collapse. It was celebrated not by the traditional triumph on the Roman model that Belisarius had enjoyed a century earlier but by the return of a fragment of the True Cross to the recovered Jerusalem. So much had priorities changed.

Hardly had Heraclius' success been celebrated, however, than an onslaught of a totally unexpected nature came from the south. The deserts of Arabia had long been home to wandering nomadic tribes, who shared a rich language spread among them by poets and storytellers, but who had never had the resources to create a settled state. It was their very statelessness that brought the possibility that they could unite if given a common purpose. This was provided by Muhammad, of the Arab tribe of Quraysh, who began preaching in his native town of Mecca on the coast of the Red Sea, 1,600 kilometres south of the Byzantine frontiers, about 610. Muhammad delivered to the Arab people the summation of God's message to mankind, in the Koran, that they must surrender to the will of God (this 'surrender' provides the word Islam) and maintain the message through *jihad*. *Jihad* is often translated as 'holy war' but its connotations are as much of fighting to maintain one's identity or message. In 622 Muhammad moved northwards with his supporters to the oasis of Medina in a *hijra*, an emigration of a people in search of new land to settle. The *hijra* marked the starting year of a Muslim calendar and transformed Muhammad and his followers into a nation in arms. They created their own history (in much the same way Christians had by appropriating the Hebrew scriptures) by presenting themselves as the true children of Abraham. To Christians and Jews, both of whom had their own profound reverence for Abraham, they were difficult to place. Heraclius, faced with an Arab delegation, is reported to have remarked that 'This people is like an evening, between daylight and nightfall, neither sunlit nor dark . . . so this people is neither illumined by the light of Christ nor is it plunged into the darkness of idolatry.'

After the death of Muhammad in 632 Islam exploded northwards in a series of lightning military campaigns under his successors Abu Bakr (632–4) and 'Umar (634–44). Nomadic peoples are used to warfare and moving fast but often fall back when challenged. Islam was different in giving the Arab peoples a cohesive sense of community (*umma*) which they were able to maintain after their conquests. Nevertheless the collapse of vast tracts of the Byzantine empire was startling. The Byzantine rulers had had no time to successfully restore order to their southern provinces after the Persian invasions and their largely Monophysite population remained resentful over the imposition of religious orthodoxy. The Jews, increasingly persecuted by the Christian state, had no reason for loyalty and may even have welcomed the invaders. The overrunning of the southern provinces was swift. The defeat of the Byzantine army at the Yarmuk River in 636 left Syria and Palestine open to Islamic conquest. The Sasanians were crushed shortly afterwards. In 642 Alexandria capitulated to Islam and over the next century the Arabs spread inexorably along the coast of north Africa (eliminating Byzantine rule there) and then across the Straits of Gibraltar. Only the victory of Charles Martel at Poitiers in 733 finally halted an advance which had also destroyed Visigothic Spain.

A major theme of this book has been continuity, so often downplayed by historians who have a natural interest in change. At first the Arabs ruled as an elite

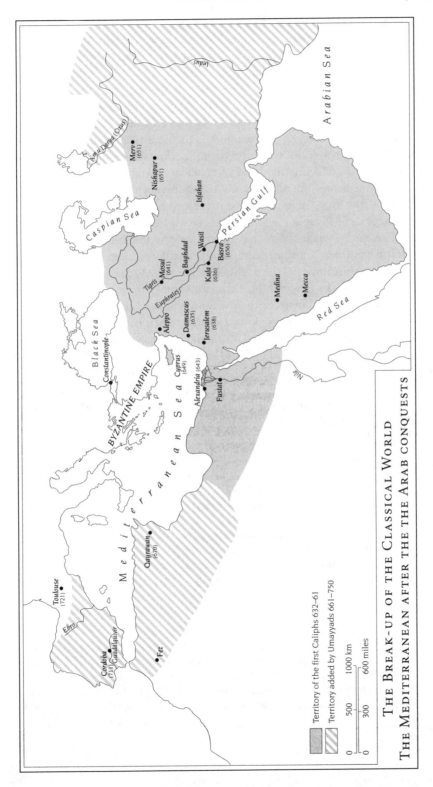

Territory of the first Caliphs 632–61

Territory added by Umayyads 661–750

THE BREAK-UP OF THE CLASSICAL WORLD
THE MEDITERRANEAN AFTER THE ARAB CONQUESTS

MAP 20

for whom conversion was not an immediate priority. They used Greek administrators, and Greek inscriptions, sometimes alongside texts in Arabic, survive
long after the conquest. The Arab tribute to the Greeks was unequivocal. In the
words of the ninth-century scholar Abu al-Hasan Tabith the heathens (i.e. the
Greeks) had contributed much. 'Who made the world to be inhabited and
flooded it with cities except the good men and kings of heathenism? Who has
constructed harbours and conserved the rivers? Who has made manifest the
hidden sciences . . . and it is they who have also made to arise the medicine for
bodies. And they have filled the world with the correctness of modes of life and
with the wisdom which is the head of excellence.' Arab philosophy included
science and medicine built on Greek texts in a way which was not possible in the
Christian world. The Pirenne thesis, which argued from literary sources that the
Arab conquests finally split the Mediterranean world, is not sustained by archaeological research, which shows that the underlying rhythms of life along the
Mediterranean coasts continued although at a vastly reduced level. (Any statement of this nature must now be qualified by reference to the detailed analysis in
Michael McCormick's *Origins of the European Economy AD 300–900* (Cambridge,
2002).) Any moment chosen for the conclusion of this book must therefore be
arbitrary and unsatisfactory. However, culturally a new world was in the making
and it is one which still survives today. Islamic culture remains predominant in
north Africa and the Middle East. There are Orthodox churches whose roots lie
in the events described in this chapter and who remain split from the Christian
churches of the west. Yet underneath the cultural changes an older world had not
been completely eradicated and enough remains of its buildings, art, and literature to ensure that this will always be the case.

The poet Pindar sums it up well in his Fourth Pythian Ode:

> If someone with a sharp axe
> hacks off the boughs of a great oak tree,
> and spoils its handsome shape;
> although its fruit has failed, yet it can give an account of itself
> if it comes later to a winter fire
> or if it rests on the pillars of some palace
> and does a sad task among foreign walls
> when there is nothing left in the place it comes from.

(Translation: Bernard Williams)

FURTHER READING

Many of the works cited after Chapter 30 will be relevant. In addition Cyril Mango (ed.),
The Oxford History of Byzantium (Oxford, 2002) is now the starting point. A. P. Kazhdan
(ed.), *The Oxford Dictionary of Byzantium*, 3 vols. (New York, 1991) for reference. The
atmosphere of the east is provided by Peter Brown in *The World of Late Antiquity*. Justinian
is dealt with by R. Browning, *Justinian and Theodora* (London, 1971) but there is now the

biography by J. Moorhead, *Justinian* (London, 1995). See also J. A. S. Evans, *The Age of Justinian: The Circumstances of Imperial Power* (London, 1996). On Procopius there is Averil Cameron, *Procopius and the Sixth Century* (Berkeley, 1985). On Heraclius, see Walter Kaegi, *Heraclius, Emperor of Byzantium* (Cambridge, 2003). On the Arab conquests, F. M. Donner, *The Early Islamic Conquests* (Princeton, 1981). On popular involvement in the politics of Constantinople, see A. Cameron, *Circus Factions: Blues and Greens at Rome and Byzantium* (Oxford, 1976). As an introduction to Byzantine art, Robin Cormack, *Byzantine Art* (Oxford, 2000). Specifically on icons Averil Cameron, 'The Language of Images: The Rise of Icons and Christian Representation', in D. Wood (ed.), *The Church and the Arts* (Oxford, 1992).

DATE CHART

The Ancient Civilizations of the Mediterranean

BC 5000　4000　3000　2000　1000　0 AD　1000

EGYPTIANS

SUMERIANS

HITTITES

ASSYRIANS

ANCIENT NEAR EAST

ISRAELITES

ACHAEMENIDS

MINOANS

MYCENAEANS

GREEKS

ETRUSCANS

ROMANS

EASTERN EMPIRE

WESTERN EMPIRE

LIST OF EVENTS

Events unspecific to those cultures under discussion are set in italics

BC

EGYPT FROM 4000 BC TO THE ACCESSION OF PTOLEMY I, 305 BC

The chronology of ancient Egypt is subject to constant revision as new evidence
emerges and these dates must be regarded as approximate!

4000	By this date the cultivation of the Egyptian staples, emmer wheat, barley, flax is under way in the Nile valley.
3600	The walled town of Naqada suggests well-established Egyptian trading routes.
3200	Hieroglyphic writing established in Egypt.
3000	First recorded unification of Egypt by King Narmer. Unification initiates Early Dynastic period (3000–2613 BC). Egyptian capital at Memphis.
2650	The tomb of King Djoser at Saqqar, built in the shape of a stepped pyramid, the first large stone monument known.
2613–2130	The Old Kingdom. The Age of the Pyramids.
*c.*2586–2256	Building of the Great Pyramid (for King Khufu) at Giza.
2160–2055	First Intermediate Period. Breakdown of central authority.
2055–1650	The Middle Kingdom. A restoration of stability.
1650–1550	Second Intermediate Period. The rule of the Hyksos.
*c.*1550–1070	The New Kingdom. Egypt as an imperial power. Major exploitation of Nubia and hegemony over the cities of south-west Asia.
1504–1492	Reign of Thutmose I. Thutmose reaches the Euphrates and is the first king to be buried in the Valley of the Kings, near Thebes. The foundation of the workmen's village at Deir el-Medina.
1473–1458	Reign of Queen Hatshepsut.
1390–1352	Reign of Amenhotep III, the zenith of the New Kingdom. Major programme of temple building at Thebes.
1352–1336	Reign of Akhenaten sees an attempt to found a new religion based on the worship of Aten, the sun. Foundation of the new capital at Tell el-Amarna. The new religion fails to take root.
*c.*1327	Death and burial of King Tutankhamun in the Valley of the Kings.
1279–1213	Reign of King Rameses II, the last of the great Egyptian kings.
1275	Battle of Qadesh between Egypt and the Hittites leads to the drawing of a boundary between the two states in Syria.
*c.*1260	Building of the Temple of Abu Simbel. First signs of the weakening of the New Kingdom.
1200	Egypt is among the states of the eastern Mediterranean attacked by the Sea Peoples.
1060	The breakdown of internal administration leads to the world's first recorded strike in the village of Deir el-Medina. The exhaustion of

gold reserves in Nubia and the loss of the Asian empire leave Egypt reduced to its original valley boundaries.

1060–664	The Third Intermediate period. The fragmentation of Egypt.
727	The Kushite king Piankhi achieves a temporary reunification of Egypt.
671	Sacking of Memphis by the Assyrians.
664/3	The Assyrians sack Thebes and establish a loose hegemony over Egypt.
664–610	Rule of King Psamtek I (Greek Psammetichus). Psamtek is installed as a puppet by the Assyrians but manages to sustain the independence of Egypt against its nominal overlords and establish the Saite dynasty, so called from its capital Sais on the Delta.
c.620	Greek traders set up a trading post at Naucratis in the Nile Delta.
525	Egypt is conquered by the Persians.
462–454	An Egyptian revolt against Persian rule is supported by Athens but the Persians regain control.
332	Invasion of Egypt by Alexander the Great leads to the collapse of Persian rule. The city of Alexandria is founded in 332. After the death of Alexander (323) Egypt comes under the control of Ptolemy I and from now on is part of the Mediterranean world.
270	*A list of Egyptian dynasties is compiled by a priest, Manetho, and provides a framework which all subsequent historians have followed.*
196	*The Rosetta Stone, with its trilingual inscription, is inscribed. It later provides the key to the decipherment of hieroglyphs.*

Subsequent references to Egypt will be included in the main date list below.

SUMER

4900–3500	The first urban settlements in Mesopotamia, including Eridu and Uruk, mark the beginning of the civilization of Sumer.
3300	The emergence of cuneiform, the earliest form of writing. Logograms (symbols representing a word) are incised on clay tables with a stylus.
3000	Earliest known wheeled cart found in Mesopotamia.
3000	Discovery, again in Mesopotamia, that copper mixed with tin forms the harder metal bronze. (The so-called Bronze Age lasts until the adoption of iron c.1000 BC.)
2500	So-called Royal Graves at Ur.
2350	The earliest surviving law code, of Urukagina, ruler of the Sumerian city of Lagesh.
2330	The Sumerians are overrun by history's first recorded conqueror, Sargon of Akkade.
c.2150–2004	The Sumerians recover their independence in the so-called Third Dynasty of Ur. Compilation of the *Epic of Gilgamesh*.
c.2000	Collapse of Sumerian civilization as rival cities fight with each other and invading tribes for supremacy in southern Mesopotamia.

1760	The plains of southern Mesopotamia are overrun by Hammurapi, king of Babylon. Hammurapi also sacks the trading city of Mari. The archives of the city remain preserved to provide a major source of information for the period. Babylon now becomes the main centre of civilization in Mesopotamia.
1800	*The appearance of the two-wheeled chariot, an invention which is to transform warfare for the next thousand years.*

THE HITTITES

1650	The Hittites establish their capital at Hattusas in north-central Anatolia.
1650–1400	The Old Kingdom.
1380–1345	Reign of the Hittite king Suppiluliuma I. Conquest of the neighbouring state of Mitanni. The New Kingdom.
1275	The battle of Qadesh between the Hittites and the Egyptians. A boundary is consolidated between the two states.
1200	Collapse of the Hittites under the impact of the Sea Peoples.
1500	*The world's first alphabet (a single symbol representing each of the basic twenty consonantal sounds) is developed in Canaan. Several alphabets are developed in the area in the centuries that follow.*
1300–1000	*The Phoenicians develop their own alphabet. It passes to the Greeks in the ninth or eighth centuries.*

THE ASSYRIANS

1900–1400	The first Assyrian empire.
1300	The emergence of the middle Assyrian empire under King Adad-nirari I. The Assyrians inflict defeats on both the Hittites and Mitannians.
1114–1076	The Assyrians under King Tiglath-Pilaser expand beyond the Euphrates and even reach the Mediterranean. Tiglath-Pilaser's successes are followed, however, by the decline of Assyrian power. The Assyrian state, though limited in size, remains intact with an unbroken succession of kings.
900–850	Revival of the empire under a succession of strong Assyrian warrior-kings. The neo-Assyrian empire.
745–600	Under King Tiglath-Pilaser II and his successors Sargon II and Sennacherib the Assyrian empire expands to include Cyprus, southern Anatolia, Palestine, and Syria.
671	The Assyrians sack Memphis, the ancient Egyptian capital.
664/3	The Assyrians reach Thebes and assume hegemony over Egypt.
615–605	Collapse of Assyrian power after defeat by the Babylonians. The battle of Carchemish, 605, marks the final defeat of the Assyrians by King Nebuchadrezzar II of Babylon. The empire vanishes from history.

THE ISRAELITES

1200	First mention of the Israelites (in an Egyptian document). No other reference survives from before the ninth century BC. The Israelites settle in Canaan, possibly after the disruptions caused by the Sea Peoples. Age of the Judges
c.1000	Possible date of King David.
10th cent.	Rebuilding of cities in Canaan may reflect the activities of the Israelite king Solomon, recorded in the Hebrew scriptures as a great builder.
c.924	The Israelites split into two kingdoms, Israel and Judah.
745–722	Israel is crushed by the Assyrians. Judah comes under Assyrian domination but survives as a state.
627–605	Judah becomes subject to Egypt.
605–562	Reign of Nebuchadrezzar II of Babylon sees the sacking of Jerusalem by the Babylonians and the Babylonian exile, the forcible transfer of many of Jerusalem's inhabitants to Babylon. The religious writings of the Israelites, the Hebrew scriptures, later the Old Testament, are first consolidated in this period.
539	Destruction of the Babylonian state by Cyrus I of Persia. The Jews are able to return from exile.
332	Alexander destroys the Achaemenid empire and Palestine eventually becomes part of the Ptolemies' kingdom.
198	Palestine passes from Ptolemaic to Seleucid rule.
167	The start of the Maccabean revolt.
63	Pompey enters Jerusalem and Palestine is now under Roman hegemony.
c.4 BC	Birth of Jesus.
c. 30 AD	Crucifixion of Jesus in Jerusalem.
66–74	Major Jewish revolt against Roman rule.

THE ACHAEMENID EMPIRE IN PERSIA

560–530	Reign of Cyrus I, the founding king of the Achaemenid empire.
546	Conquest of Lydia by Cyrus. Subjugation of the Ionian Greek cities of Asia Minor.
539	The defeat of the Babylonians and the liberation of the Jews, who are allowed to keep their identity within the Achaemenid empire.
525	Cambyses, son of Cyrus, defeats King Psamtek III and captures Memphis. Egypt is henceforth subject to the rule of outsiders.
522	Darius becomes king after mounting a coup against Cambyses.
514	Darius crosses the Hellespont into Thrace where he conducts inconclusive campaigns against the Scythians but maintains a Persian presence in Europe.
499–494	Revolt of Ionian Greeks against the Persians. The revolt is eventually defeated.
490	Expedition of the Persians against Athens and Sparta. The Persians are defeated at the battle of Marathon.

486	Darius dies. He is succeeded by his son, Xerxes.
480–79	Major expedition of Xerxes to Greece ends in the defeat of the Persian forces at Salamis (480) and Plataea (479).
477–467	Greek campaigns under Cimon of Athens lead to further Persian defeats and the elimination of the Persian threat to the Aegean.
454	The Athenians are defeated by the Persians after they have intervened in support of an Egyptian revolt against Persian rule.
450	Persia faces a revolt in Syria.
449	Probable date of a peace treaty between Persia and Athens.
411	The Spartans receive Persian money to help to rebuild their fleet.
401	Lysander, the Spartan commander, backs a coup against Artaxerxes the new king of Persia (ruled 404–359) by his brother Cyrus. It ends in failure.
395–386	Persia instigates the Corinthian War and by the end of the war has regained her rule over the Ionian Greeks as well as a continuing influence in Greek politics through the King's Peace of 386.
366–360	Revolt of the satraps against the Persian throne.
336	Philip of Macedon launches an invasion of Persia.
335	Accession of Darius III, the last of the Achaemenid kings.
334–330	Alexander conquers Persia and with the death of Darius in 330 the Achaemenid empire is at an end.

Subsequent references to Persia are included in the main date list below.

THE MINOANS

2000	Emergence of the 'palace' civilizations of Crete.
2000–1600	The so-called 'Old Palace Period' of Minoan civilization.
1628/7	Volcanic eruption on the island of Thera (modern Santorini) sees the extinction of the Aegean trading town of Acrotiri which is preserved under the ash.
c.1600	Destruction of the Cretan palaces, followed by their rebuilding on a more magnificent scale.
1600–1425	The so-called 'New Palace Period' of Minoan civilization.
1550	Evidence of Minoan traders at Avaris on the Nile Delta.
1425	New wave of destruction of Cretan palaces, possibly as a result of a Mycenaean conquest.

THE MYCENAEANS

2200–2000?	Arrival of Greek speakers in Greece.
1650	The first use of the shaft graves at Mycenae (rediscovered by Heinrich Schliemann in 1876). The graves are used and reused until c.1500.
1600–1400	Consolidation of power by Mycenaean war leaders in Greece. Their power is sustained by raids overseas.
1400	Possible takeover of Crete by the Mycenaeans. A Mycenaean presence is recorded throughout the Mediterranean from Italy to the coast of Asia and Egypt.

1400	The Mycenaeans adopt Linear B as a syllabic script. (The language in which Linear B tablets were written were deciphered as Greek by Michael Ventris in 1952.)
1200–1100	Collapse of Mycenaean civilization. Invasion of Dorians from the north?

THE GREEKS AFTER 1100

1100–800	**The so-called Dark Ages.**
1050–950	Migrations of Greeks to the Aegean and coast of Asia Minor. In Greece iron is used for the first time.
1100–825	The settlement at Lefkandi provides evidence of the continuation of Greek culture in the Dark Ages. (*c.*975: The 'hero's' tomb at Lefkandi.) Trading links established with Cyprus.
1050–900	Athenian pottery frees itself from Mycenaean influences and develops the so-called proto-Geometric style.
1000–750	*The Phoenicians enjoy widespread prosperity as traders throughout the Mediterranean. 814: Traditional date of the foundation of Carthage by the Phoenicians.*
850	Greeks from Euboea are now involved in extensive trade with the Phoenicians and other peoples of the Near East.
825	A Greek presence established at al-Mina at the mouth of the Orontes river.
900–725	The age of Geometric pottery in Athens. (770–725: The years of the Dipylon master.)
776	Traditional date of the founding of the Olympic Games.
*c.*775–750	First settlement of Pithekoussai (on the island of Ischia off the Italian coast) by Euboean Greeks (and others from the Near East).
753	*Traditional date of the founding of Rome.*
750	The Greeks borrow and adapt the Phoenician alphabet for their own use. It spreads throughout the Greek world.
750–700	The *Iliad* and *Odyssey*, traditionally attributed to Homer, reach their final form.
735	Greek colonization of Sicily begins. (733: Foundation of Syracuse by the Corinthians.)
725	Greeks set up a settlement at Cumae on the Italian coast enabling direct trade with the Etruscans.
720	First Greek colonization of southern Italy and the Chalcidice peninsula in the northern Aegean.
730–680	The Lelantine War between Chalcis and Eretria marks the end of the old aristocratic Greece. Corinth emerges as the most powerful of the Greek cities and is the centre of manufacture of Proto-Corinthian pottery (725 onwards).
730–620	**The so-called Orientalizing Period sees a wide range of eastern influences permeating Greek culture.**
730–710	Spartan conquest of Messenia.
*c.*700	Hesiod's *Theogony* and *Works and Days*.

c.700	First penetration of the Black Sea by the Greeks. (Byzantium founded c.660, although permanent Greek settlements probably not established until c.650.)
675–640	Archilochus of Paros, poet.
669	Defeat of Sparta by Argos at the battle of Hysiae. The defeat, and a subsequent rebellion of the helots in Messenia, probably initiates the militarization of Spartan society.
660s onwards	First Greek traders penetrate Egypt. By 600 Egyptian influences on Greek sculpture are apparent (in the marble *kouroi*, for instance).
657	Cypselus becomes tyrant in Corinth, overthrowing the aristocratic clan of the Bacchidae. Tyrannies becomes the most common form of government in the Greek states in the hundred years that follow.
c.640	The poetry of the Spartan Tyrtaeus reflects the new importance given to loyalty to the *polis*.
630	Cyrene (north Africa) settled by Greek colonists from Thera.
621	Draco's 'Draconian' law code in Athens fails to relieve social tensions.
620–480	**The Archaic Age, an age in which greater order and formality is brought to Greek culture.**
600	Foundation of Massilia (modern Marseilles) by the Phocaeans.
600	The world's first coinage emerges in Lydia. It spreads to the trading island of Aegina by 595 and Athens by 575.
594	Solon is appointed archon in Athens with full power to reform the state. Initiates important social and political reforms.
585	The prediction by Thales of Miletus of an eclipse of the sun is traditionally seen as the starting point of Greek philosophy. Thales' fellow Miletians, Anaximander and Anaximenes, develop his ideas in the decades that follow.
582–573	The spread of pan-Hellenic games (the Pythian Games at Delphi, 582, the Isthmian Games, 581, the Nemean Games, 573).
580	Phoenicians and Greeks clash over spheres of control in Sicily.
575–560	The temple to Hera at Samos, one of the first monumental Greek temples, is possibly influenced by similar monumental Egyptian buildings.
c.570	Death of the lyric poet Sappho.
570	The so-called François vase, made in Athens, marks the re-emergence of Athens as a major pottery-making centre.
560	Defeat of the Spartans by the Tegeans at the Battle of Fetters leads to a more conciliatory approach by Sparta to her neighbours.
c.550	The poet Theognis of Megara laments the threat to traditional aristocratic values.
540	The Etruscans and Phoenicians combine to drive out the Phocaeans from their new colony at Alalia (Corsica).
560–546	Peisistratus struggles, with eventual success, to achieve control as tyrant of Athens.

546–510	The Peisistratid tyranny in Athens sees the emergence of Athens as an important cultural force in Greece, with a major building programme on the Acropolis, the stimulation of religious festivals such as the Great Panathenaea, and the patronage of drama. (534: The first recorded tragedy at the city's festival to Dionysus.) The Peisistratid tyranny continues until Peisistratus' son Hippias is overthrown in 510. Sparta has meanwhile emerged as the champion of oligarchy and collaborates in the overthrow of the Peisistratids.
525	Pythagoras active in southern Italy, after being driven into exile from Samos.
525	Red-figure ware replaces black-figure as the main product of the Athenian potters. Earliest surviving bronze sculpture, a *kouros*, found at Athens. Bronze now becomes the preferred medium for free-standing statues.
520–c.490	Reign of King Cleomenes of Sparta. His active overseas policy leads to a leadership crisis at home and his eventual assassination.
509	Foundation of Roman Republic.
508/7	Reforms of Cleisthenes in Athens lay the foundations for Athenian democracy.
501	First election of the ten generals (*strategoi*) who are to become the most prestigious of the officers of the state in Athens in the fifth century.
500	The philosophers Heraclitus of Ephesus and Parmenides of Elea active.
499–494	Revolt of Ionian Greeks against the Persians. Athens and Sparta provide help. The revolt is eventually defeated.
498	First surviving poem of Pindar. First *Olympian Ode*, 476, first *Pythian Ode*, 470. Pindar remains active until at least 446.
493	Themistocles becomes archon at Athens. He initiates the building of the harbour at the Piraeus.
490	Expedition of the Persians against Athens and Sparta. The Persians are defeated at the Battle of Marathon.
c.490	The so-called 'Kritian boy' from Athens traditionally marks the transition from Archaic to Classical art.
487	Comedies are presented for the first time at the Dionysia in Athens.
487	First recorded use of ostracism in Athens.
484	The tragedian Aeschylus achieves his first victory at the Dionysia festival.
482	The discovery of rich new silver deposits at Laurium allows Themistocles to build an Athenian fleet.
480–336	**The Classical Age, traditionally seen as the culminating years of the Greek achievement.**
480–479	Major expedition of the Persian king Xerxes to Greece ends in the defeat of the Persian forces at Salamis (480) and Plataea (479). The Carthaginians (Phoenicians who have settled permanently in the western Mediterranean) attack Sicily and are also defeated.

477	The Delian League is founded and a period of continuing warfare against Persia under the Athenian aristocratic leader Cimon leads to the elimination of the Persian threat. Sparta acquiesces in Athenian expansion.
475–450	The relief sculptures on the temple to Zeus at Olympia, the major surviving example of early Classical art.
472	Aeschylus' *Persians*, a rare example of a tragedy dealing with a contemporary issue.
471	Ostracism of Themistocles by aristocratic factions in Athens.
470	Naxos forced back into the League after it tries to secede.
468	The tragedian Sophocles successfully challenges the supremacy of Aeschylus by winning first prize in the Dionysia festival.
465	The island of Thasos revolts against the League and is subdued by Athenian forces.
464	An earthquake in Sparta is followed by a revolt of the helots. Cimon takes a hoplite army to help suppress the revolt but his offer is rejected.
461	A democratic revolution in Athens leads to the ostracism of Cimon and the breaking off of relations with Sparta.
461–429	Pericles, one of the leaders of the revolution, maintains his personal supremacy in Athens throughout these years.
461–451	The first Peloponnesian War between Athens and Sparta. Athens builds the Long Walls (458). The first battle between Spartan and Athenian troops is at Tanagra, 457, and is followed by an Athenian conquest of Boeotia.
458	The *Oresteia* of Aeschylus. (456: Death of Aeschylus.)
455	Euripides produces his first play.
454	Heavy defeat for Athens by the Persians in Egypt. The Athenians move the treasury of the League from Delos to Athens.
451	Pericles' citizenship law limits citizenship to those both of whose parents are citizens.
450	Zeno of Elea's celebrated paradoxes develop Parmenides' logic to its extremes.
449	Probable date of peace treaty between Athens and Persia.
447–438	Rebuilding of the Parthenon in its present form. The sculptor Pheidias (490–432) seems to have been largely responsible for the design and decoration of the temple.
447	The defeat of the Athenians at the Battle of Coronea sees Athens lose control of Boeotia.
446–445	Thirty Year Peace signed between Sparta and Athens.
c.445	The Athenian Coinage Decree requires members of the League to use only Athenian weights and measures. The League has in effect become an Athenian empire.
443	Athens founds a colony at Thurii in southern Italy, an indication of new interests in the west.
441	The *Antigone* of Sophocles.
440s	Probable date of Herodotus' *History of the Persian Wars*.

440–430	The atomists, Leucippus and Democritus, suggest that all matter is made up of atoms. The sculptor Polycleitus of Argos stresses the ideal, mathematical, proportions of the human body.
440	Samos revolts against the empire but the revolt is suppressed.
437	Athens founds the city of Amphipolis to give her access to the timber and gold of Thrace.
433–431	Sparta and Athens drift towards war as Athens supports a revolt by Corcyra against Sparta's ally Corinth and the Spartans realize that an Athenian preoccupation with a revolt in Potidaea weakens her at home.
431	Outbreak of Second Peloponnesian War. Thucydides begins his history of the war. Euripides' *Medea*. Hippocrates of Cos, Socrates, and Protagoras of Abdera are all active in this period.
431–430	Pericles' *Funeral Oration*.
430	Plague at Athens kills a significant proportion of the population.
430	The statue of Zeus at Olympia is completed by Pheidias.
430 (or shortly afterwards)	The first production of Sophocles' *Oedipus Rex*.
429	Death of Pericles.
428	Birth of Plato. The *Hippolytus* of Euripides is produced for the first time.
427	The visit of the orator Gorgias of Leontini (Sicily) to Athens fosters the birth of rhetoric.
427	The revolt of Mytilene sparks off the debate on its future in the Athenian assembly.
425–388	The comedies of Aristophanes (*Acharnians*, 425, *Clouds*, 423, *Birds*, 414, *Frogs*, 405).
425	The stalemate of the Peloponnesian War is broken by the capture of the Spartans at Sphacteria but Athenian hopes of controlling Boeotia end with her defeat by the Thebans at Delium (424).
424	The Spartan general Brasidas captures Amphipolis and other Athenian cities in the northern Aegean.
421	Peace of Nicias between Sparta and Athens. It is undermined by continued Athenian intrusion in the Peloponnese.
420–400	Temple of Apollo at Bassae built.
418	Battle of Mantineia. Sparta reasserts her control over the Peloponnese by defeating Argos and her ally Athens.
416	The defeat and enslavement of the island of Melos by Athens.
415	Euripides' *Trojan Women* explores the brutality of war.
415	The Athenian expedition leaves for Sicily.
413	The Athenian expedition ends in disaster and the Spartans regain the initiative by setting up a permanent base at Decelea in Attica.
411	The Spartans seek Persian help to rebuild their navy.
411	The Council of Four Hundred takes over in Athens. Democracy is restored in 410. The Athenians score several naval victories over the Spartans.

406	The Athenian naval victory at Arginusae leads to the assembly's debate on the fate of the generals who left sailors to drown.
406	Deaths of Euripides and Sophocles.
405	The *Bacchae* of Euripides is produced for the first time, after his death.
405	Dionysius I becomes dictator in Syracuse. He maintains himself in power until his death in 367, presenting a new model of government for the Greek world.
405	The Battle of Aigospotamae sees the destruction of the Athenian fleet at the hands of the Persian commander, Lysander.
404	Surrender of Athens. The government of 'The Thirty Tyrants' is imposed on the city by Sparta. Democracy is restored in a counter-coup of 404/3.
405–395	Lysander is dominant in the Aegean although he loses much credibility after the defeat of the Persian prince Cyrus whom he has backed as pretender to the Persian throne (402). The historian Xenophon (*c.*428–*c.*354) extricates the Greek troops from Persia and recounts the expedition in his *March of the Ten Thousand.*
399	Death of Socrates after being found guilty of a charge of corrupting the young.
396–347	The philosopher Plato is active throughout these years. He founds the Academy in 387.
396–394	The Spartan king Agesilaus campaigns to free the Ionian Greeks from Persian control. In retaliation the Persians support Thebes, Athens, and Corinth against Sparta in the Corinthian War (395–386). The Athenians use Persian money to rebuild the Long Walls.
395	Thucydides' *History of the Peloponnesian War* is published.
386	In the so-called King's Peace, the Corinthian War is brought to a close. Persia regains control of the Ionian Greeks and maintains her influence in the Greek world.
382	The Spartans seize Thebes.
379	Thebes is liberated and in 378 Athens forms the Second Athenian League to counter Spartan power.
375–370	The rule of Jason in Thessaly confirms that one-man rule is a serious alternative to city democracy or oligarchy.
371	At the battle of Leuctra, Thebes comprehensively defeats Sparta and Sparta never recovers. From 371 to 362 Thebes is the most powerful state in Greece.
367	Aristotle joins the Academy.
362	With the death of the Theban leader Epaminondas, Theben power collapses. No Greek city state is able to take her place.
359	Philip II becomes king of Macedon. He soon consolidates his control of Macedonia and the surrounding area.
358–330	The theatre at Epidaurus at the shrine of Aesclepius, one of the finest surviving Greek theatres, is built. The sculptor Praxiteles of Athens (born *c.*390), known for his celebrated nude statue of Aphrodite, is also active at this time.

348	The sacking of the north Aegean city of Olynthus by Philip. The excavated remains of the city provide a major source of information on Greek houses.
357–355	Collapse of Second Athenian League.
356–352	Philip achieves hegemony in central Greece. His growing power is criticized by the Athenian orator Demosthenes (384–322).
356	Birth of Philip's son, Alexander, 'Alexander the Great'.
347	Death of Plato. Aristotle leaves Athens but returns in 337 to found his own school, the Lyceum.
340	Athens declares war on Philip.
338	At the battle of Chaeronea (in Boeotia) Philip destroys the army of Athens and her allies. The age of the independent city state is over. The triumph of Philip is welcomed by the Greek orator Isocrates (436–338) who has long advocated the unification of the Greek world under a single leader.
336	Philip launches an attack on Persia but dies in the same year. Alexander succeeds and rapidly establishes his own control of Macedonia and the Greek states. Thebes is sacked.
335	The Cynic Diogenes (c.400–324) reputedly meets Alexander in Corinth and impresses on him the importance of renouncing possessions.
336–31	**The Hellenistic Age. A period when the Greek world is divided between several monarchical states and a more unified Greek culture emerges. It is an age of speculation but also of anxiety which ends with the incorporation of the Greek world into the Roman empire.**
335	Accession of Darius III as king of Persia.
334	Alexander launches his invasion of Persia. His victory at Granicus leads to control of Asia Minor.
333	Alexander cuts the knot of Gordium and defeats the forces of Darius at Issus (September).
332–331	Alexander travels through Syria (siege of Tyre, 332) to Egypt where he is acclaimed as Pharaoh in place of Darius. A visit to the oracles of Ammon at Siwah (Libya) confirms Alexander's belief that he has divine ancestry. The city of Alexandria founded in 331.
331	Alexander's victory over Darius at Gaugamela allows him to take Babylon, Susa, and Persepolis. The great royal palace at Persepolis is burnt to the ground in the following year. Darius is murdered by his own people and the Achaemenid empire is at an end.
330–328	Alexander fights guerrilla campaigns in Bactria and Sogdiana.
326	Alexander reaches India and achieves his last great victory at the Battle of Hydaspes.
325	Alexander returns to central Persia via the river Indus and the Makram desert.
324–323	Alexander shows increasing instability as he attempts to bring order to his conquered territories.
323	Death of Alexander in Babylon.
322	Death of Aristotle in Euboea.

323–276	A power struggle breaks out among the descendants and officers of Alexander. Perdiccas, Alexander's senior cavalry officer, and Antigonous the One-Eyed fail to control the empire as a single unit. Antigonous is killed at the Battle of Ipsus (301). Three major states eventually emerge from Alexander's empire: Egypt under the Ptolemies, Macedonia under descendants of Antigonous, and the Seleucid empire in the east.
321–289	Career of Menander (the New Comedy).
320	Pytheas, from Massilia, makes a circumnavigation of Britain.
307	The philosopher Epicurus founds his school in Athens.
300	Zeno founds the Stoic school, so called because of its meeting place in a stoa, in Athens. The mathematician Euclid, author of *The Elements*, the founding text of modern mathematics, is active at this date. The Museum and Library is founded by Ptolemy I at Alexandria. The first world map is produced by Dicaearchus of Messenia.
290	The Aetolian League occupies Delphi and in the next seventy years emerges as the main political entity in central Greece.
c.287	Birth, at Syracuse, of Archimedes, arguably the greatest mathematician of antiquity.
281	Foundation of the Achaean League, a federation of the city states of the Peloponnese.
280	Pyrrhus of Epirus ships an army to Italy in support of the city of Tarentum and provides the Romans with their first direct contact within the Hellenistic world.
279	Sacking of Delphi by the Celts.
c.275	Aristarchos of Samos suggests that the earth goes round the sun.
274–271	War between Ptolemy II of Egypt and Antiochus I over Syria. There are subsequent Syrian wars between the two powers in 260–253, 246–241, and 219–217.
270	The poets Callimachus and Theocritus (founder of 'pastoral poetry') are active in Alexandria.
263–241	The emergence of Pergamum as a separate kingdom under Eumenes.
260s	Herophilus of Chalcedon and Erasistratus of Ceos conduct experiments into the working of the human body.
238	His defeat of the Galatian Celts inspires Attalus I to rebuild Pergamum as one of the great cities of the Hellenistic world.
235–219	Reign of King Cleomenes of Sparta. Cleomenes integrates helots into the Spartan army.
229–219	Roman campaigns against the pirates of the Illyrian coast lead to the first Roman intrusion into the Hellenistic world.
223–187	Reign of the Seleucid king Antiochus III. Seleucid prestige in Asia is partially restored but Antiochus loses his position in the eastern Mediterranean after humiliating defeats by the Romans 192–188.
221	Philip V becomes ruler of Macedonia.
215	Philip allies with Carthage against Rome.
214–205	Rome declares war on Philip. The first Macedonian War (214–205). The Romans make an alliance with the Aetolian League.

212 or 211	Death of Archimedes in Syracuse after the city is sacked by the Romans.
206–185	Upper Egypt breaks free of Ptolemaic rule.
200	The mathematician Apollonius of Perge active.
200–197	The Second Macedonian War between Philip and Rome ends with Philip's defeat at Cynoscephalae.
196	Declaration of the freedom of the Greeks by the Roman commander Flamininus. The Romans leave Greece in 194.
196	The Rosetta Stone, a record of the thanksgiving of the priests of Memphis to Ptolemy V, is inscribed. It later provides the means by which Egyptian hieroglyphs are deciphered.
191	Defeat of Antiochus III by the Romans at Thermopylae.
189	Following the defeat of Antiochus at Magnesia (190) the cities of the Aetolian League are forced to become subject allies of Rome.
179	Perseus becomes king of Macedonia after the death of his father Philip.
171–138	Reign of Mithridates I, the first Parthian ruler to achieve full independence from the Seleucids.
168	Defeat of Perseus by the Romans at Pydna is followed by the break-up of Macedonia into four republics.
168	Humiliation of Antiochus IV by the Romans when he attempts an invasion of Egypt.
167	Guerrilla warfare breaks out in Judaea under the leadership of Judah Maccabee as a response to the intrusions of the Seleucids.
167	The Greek historian Polybius arrives in Rome.
c.160	Building of the Great Altar of Zeus at Pergamum.
148	Macedonia becomes a Roman province after a revolt is suppressed there.
146	Crushing of the Achaean League by the Romans. Corinth is sacked.
141	The Seleucids accept the independence of Judaea under Simon Maccabee.
133	Pergamum is bequeathed to Rome and becomes the Roman province of Asia (129).
92	The first official meeting between the Romans and the Parthians, on the Euphrates.
88–85	Mithridates of Pontus encourages massacre of Roman citizens in Asia and attempts to liberate the Greeks from the Romans.
86	Sulla captures Athens and Mithridates is forced to retreat. Roman rule restored to the east.
74–63	Campaigns of Lucullus and Pompey in the east lead to the final defeat of Mithridates and the end of the Seleucid monarchy (64). Judaea also comes under Roman rule. Pompey reorganizes the provinces of the east.
55–53	Expedition of Crassus to Parthia leads to the humiliating defeat of Rome at Carrhae. Crassus is killed.
48–47	Caesar installs Cleopatra, daughter of Ptolemy XII, on the throne of Egypt.

41	Cleopatra meets Mark Antony and becomes his mistress.
36	Mark Antony's invasion of Parthia ends in disaster.
34	Antony and Cleopatra try to upstage Octavian by a great ceremony in Alexandria.
31	The forces of Antony and Cleopatra are defeated by Octavian at the Battle of Actium.
30	Antony and Cleopatra commit suicide. Egypt is annexed by Rome.

THE ETRUSCANS

1200	First signs of more intensive cultivation of Etruria.
900	Emergence of scattered villages on the tufa plateaux of Etruria. The 'Villanovan' period.
760	Decorative objects and the increased use of iron in Etruscan burials suggest increasing contact with the east. Burial evidence correlates with foundation of Pithekoussai settlement c.775–750.
700	First fortification of Etruscan settlements with tufa walls. Adoption of the Greek alphabet.
700–550	Evidence suggests widespread trading between Greeks, other easterners, and the Etruscans. The great age of Etruscan prosperity.
c.616	The Etruscan Tarquin I becomes king of Rome. Rome remains under Etruscan influence for over a hundred years and absorbs many elements of Etruscan culture.
600	Emergence of the Etruscan temple form, adopted by the Romans.
550	The Etruscans come under threat from Greek expansionism, especially that of the Phocaeans.
540	The Phocaeans are defeated by a joint fleet of Etruscans and Phoenicians.
525	An Etruscan expedition against Cumae fails.
500	Declining trade along the coast forces the Etruscans to develop new cities in the northern Adriatic. New trade routes open up with the Celts of northern Europe, leading to the development of the Celtic La Tène culture.
474	Hiero of Syracuse defeats an Etruscan fleet. The Etruscan presence in Campania is eliminated during the century by Samnite raiders.
396	Capture of the major Etruscan city Veii by the Romans.
295	The defeat of the Etruscans, and others, at the Battle of Sentinum leads to Roman control of Etruria. The Etruscan trading cities of the north are gradually eliminated under pressures from both Romans and Celts.

ROME

The rise of Rome

| 10th cent. | Possible date of first settlements on the hills of Rome. |
| 753 | Traditional date of the founding of Rome. From the mid-eighth century there is evidence of increasing contact between Rome and the outside world. Rome remains one of the community of Latin cities. |

616–579	Traditional dates for the reign of Tarquin I. Rome is under Etruscan influence.
579–534	Reign of Servius Tullius. Servius Tullius, who was probably Latin rather than Etruscan, appears to expand and integrate the citizen body into the government of the city. Foundation of the *comitia centuriata* and a citizen army (the first legion).
534–509	Reign of Tarquin the Proud. First evidence of a major public building programme.
509	The Republic is founded after the expulsion of the kings. The consuls and other magistrates take the place of the kings.
499	Rome defeats the Latin communities at the Battle of Lake Regillus but later forms an alliance with them to face the neighbouring hostile tribes. Rome and her allies are constantly at war with these tribes during the fifth century.
490–440	The age of the patricians. Patrician families monopolize the consulships but come under increasing pressure to open government to plebeians.
471	The patricians recognize the *concilium plebis*, the assembly of the plebeians.
450	The publication of the Twelve Tables allows all to see the traditional laws of the city.
409	For the first time plebeians are admitted as quaestors (magistrates with financial responsibilities).
390	'Sack' of Rome by the Celts.
343	First war with the Samnites.
342	At least one of the consuls is a plebeian from this date (172: The first year in which both consuls were plebeians.)
340	Latin war ends with Rome's defeat of the Latins and the Campanians. The resulting settlement leaves Rome in control of Latium and Campania.
327	A new Roman colony at Fregellae provokes the Samnites to attack.
327–304	Second Samnite War sees Rome expand for the first time into central Italy.
312	The first of the great Roman roads, the Via Appia, built between Rome and Capua. The first aqueduct into Rome, the Aqua Appia, is also constructed.
298–290	Third Samnite War sees the crushing of the Samnites. (Battles of Sentinum, 295, and Aquilonia, 293.)
287	Resolutions of the *concilium plebis* are recognized as having the force of law.
280–275	Pyrrhus of Epirus lands in Italy in support of the Greek city of Tarentum. Despite initial successes he is forced to withdraw and southern Italy now falls under Roman hegemony.
264	The First Punic War (Rome versus the Carthaginians) begins after Rome intervenes in support of the Mamertines in Messana, Sicily. The war is at first confined to Sicily.
260	First naval encounter between Rome and Carthage ends in a

	Roman victory.
255–249	Rome is put on the defensive after defeats in Africa and at sea.
241	A naval battle off the Aegates Islands finally decides the war in favour of Rome. Carthage cedes Sicily to Rome.
237	Rome seizes Sardinia and Corsica from the Carthaginians.
229–219	Rome establishes a protectorate over the Illyrian coast.
227	The number of praetors (magistrates responsible for judicial affairs) is increased to four with two annually taking responsibility for Rome's new overseas possessions.
225	Celtic invasion of Italy is defeated by the Romans at the Battle of Telamon. The invasion is followed by the suppression of the Celts in northern Italy.
221	Hannibal takes command of Carthaginian troops in Spain.
218	Hannibal's capture of Saguntum, an ally of Rome, leads to the outbreak of the Second Punic War.
218	Hannibal invades Italy. First defeat of the Romans at Trebia.
217	Hannibal defeats the Romans at the battle of Lake Trasimene.
217–216	Fabius is appointed dictator in Rome and urges a less confrontationist approach to Hannibal.
216	Fabius' advice is disregarded and the Romans confront Hannibal at Cannae. A disastrous defeat follows. Hannibal controls most of southern Italy.
215	Alliance of Philip of Macedon with Carthage leads to an inconclusive war between Philip and Rome (214–205).
212 or 211	The fall of Syracuse brings the first influx of Greek art into Rome.
211	Hannibal marches on Rome but fails to take the city. He is on the defensive from now on.
211–206	Roman victories in Spain under Scipio Africanus.
209 (or possibly much earlier)	Livius Andronicus introduces Greek drama and epic to Rome.
204	Scipio invades Africa. Hannibal is forced to return home.
204	First performance of a play by Plautus (active 204–184).
202	Battle of Zama, a victory for Rome, brings the war to an end. Carthage is now dependent on Rome. Rome has gained Spain for her empire.
202	First history of Rome (in Greek) by Fabius Pictor.

Rome and the Mediterranean world

202–150	The senate enjoys its greatest prestige as the governing body of Rome.
202–190	The final suppression of the Celtic tribes of northern Italy.
200–197	Second Macedonian War between Philip and Rome. Ends with Philip's defeat at Cynoscephalae.
196	Declaration of the freedom of the Greeks by the Roman commander Flamininus.
193–133	Continuous wars of pacification in Spain.
191	Defeat of Antiochus III by the Romans at Thermopylae.

189	Following the defeat of Antiochus at Magnesia (190) the cities of the Aetolian League are forced to become subject allies of Rome.
186	Greek-style games held in Rome for the first time. Suppression of Bacchanalian festivities by the senate.
184	Cato the Elder (234–149) becomes censor and launches his campaign against the corrupting influences of the east.
c.180	Ennius composes his *Annales*, an epic poem on the history of Rome.
180	Minimum ages specified for praetors and consuls.
179	Perseus becomes king of Macedonia after the death of his father Philip.
168	Defeat of Perseus by the Romans at Pydna is followed by the break-up of Macedonia into four republics.
168	Humiliation of Antiochus IV by the Romans when he attempts an invasion of Egypt.
167	The Greek historian Polybius arrives in Rome. He is to observe the Roman conquest of Greece and record it in his *Universal History*.
167	The scale of plunder from Rome's wars allows direct taxation in Italy to be abolished.
160s	The plays of Terence performed in Rome during these years.
149	Courts set up in which governors can be prosecuted. Cato publishes his history of Rome.
148	Macedonia becomes a Roman province after a revolt is suppressed there. Vast quantities of booty are brought back to Rome.
146	Crushing of the Achaean League by the Romans. Corinth is sacked. Carthage is also razed to the ground.
139	A secret ballot is established through a law passed by a tribune in the *concilium plebis*. A popular challenge to the senate.
136–132	Slave uprising in Sicily.
133	Pergamum is bequeathed to Rome and becomes the Roman province of Asia in 129.
133	Tribunate of Tiberius Gracchus leads to clashes between supporters of the senate and the people. Tiberius is killed but his land commission survives.
125	Proposal by Fulvius Flaccus that members of allied cities be offered citizenship.
124–122	Tribunates of Gaius Gracchus.
121	Gaius Gracchus is killed after the senate passes a *senatus consultum ultimum* to authorize the massacre of his supporters.
121	Gallia Narbonensis (southern Gaul) becomes a Roman province.
111–110	Outbreak of war with Numidia (the Jugurthine War).
107–100	Marius holds the consulship six times, finishes the Jugurthine War, and then defeats the Cimbri and Teutones, German tribes threatening Rome from the north. Marius goes into exile after he fails to obtain land for his veterans in Italy.
92	The first official meeting between the Romans and the Parthians, on the Euphrates.
91–88	The Social War, a major war between Rome and her Italian allies. Rome cedes citizenship to all communities south of the Po river.

88–85	Mithridates of Pontus encourages massacre of Roman citizens in Asia and attempts to liberate the Greeks from the Romans. Sulla marches on Rome after an attempt to deprive him of the eastern command.
87–84	Cinna, an opponent of Sulla, holds the consulship for four successive years, while Sulla is on campaign in the east. He is supported by Marius until the latter's death in 86.
86	Sulla captures Athens and Mithridates is forced to retreat. Roman rule restored to the east.
83–82	Sulla returns to Rome, seizes power, and eliminates his opponents in a civil war. Remains dictator until 79 and restores the power of the senate.
80–72	Sertorius gains control of Spain. Pompey is used by the senate to regain the Spanish provinces for Rome.
74	Renewal of war on Rome by Mithridates. Licinius Lucullus sent to confront him.
73–71	Massive slave uprising under Spartacus. Order restored by Crassus and Pompey.
70	Crassus and Pompey hold the consulships. Cicero's speeches against Verres establish him as Rome's leading orator.
67	Pompey receives the command, through the *concilium*, to deal with piracy.
66–63	After being given command in the east Pompey engineers the final defeat of Mithridates and the end of the Seleucid monarchy (64). Judaea also comes under Roman rule. Pompey reorganizes the east, establishing the new provinces of Bithynia, Cilicia, and Syria.
63	Cicero, consul for the year, initiates the defeat of the Catiline conspiracy. Julius Caesar is elected *pontifex maximus*.
62	Pompey returns to Italy and disbands his army.
60	Pompey, Crassus, and Caesar form the 'first triumvirate'.
59	Caesar consul. His daughter Julia marries Pompey and Caesar initiates legislation in favour of Crassus and Pompey.
59–54	Catullus's poems to Lesbia.
58–49	Caesar's conquest of Gaul. He recounts the campaign in his *Gallic Wars*.
58–57	Cicero is exiled at the instigation of P. Clodius. He returns through the help of Pompey on whom he is now dependent.
56	Caesar meets Crassus and Pompey at Luca and renews the agreement between them.
55	Pompey and Crassus hold the consulships. Pompey secures the command in Spain but delegates the command and remains in Italy.
55	Death of the poet Lucretius. His *De Rerum Natura* is published posthumously. Cicero produces his first literary work, on oratory, and, in 54, starts *De Republica*. Pompey's theatre is the first stone theatre in Rome.
55–54	Caesar's campaigns in Britain.
55–53	Expedition of Crassus to Parthia leads to the humiliating defeat of Rome at Carrhae. Crassus is killed.

54	The death of Julia symbolizes the breakdown of the relationship between Caesar and Pompey. They are both also seeking popularity through massive building programmes in Rome.
52	Clodius is killed in street-fighting. Pompey is appointed sole consul by the senate in an attempt to restore order.
52–49	Intense political infighting as Caesar attempts to maintain his *imperium*. The senate forms an alliance with Pompey.
49	Caesar crosses the Rubicon and Pompey leaves for the east.
48	At the Battle of Pharsalus Caesar defeats Pompey. Pompey is murdered in Egypt. Caesar installs Cleopatra, daughter of Ptolemy XII, on the throne of Egypt.
47–45	Caesar campaigns in Africa, the east, and in Spain.
46	Caesar assumes a ten-year dictatorship and celebrates his victories with four triumphs.
45–44	Cicero's main philosophical works are written in these years.
45–44	Dictatorship of Caesar arouses increasing concern and eventually leads to his assassination, March 44.
44	Mark Antony controls Rome. Attacked by Cicero in his *Philippics*.
43	Octavian, the designated heir of Caesar, seizes the consulship and forms a triumvirate with Antony and Lepidus. Cicero is murdered at their command.
42	Cassius and Brutus, murderers of Caesar, are defeated at Philippi and commit suicide. The senate declares Caesar a god. Antony remains in charge of the east, Octavian in the west.
42	Cisalpine Gaul formally becomes part of Italy.
41	Cleopatra meets Mark Antony and becomes his mistress.
38	Virgil's *Eclogues* are published.
36	Mark Antony's invasion of Parthia ends in disaster.
34	Antony and Cleopatra try to upstage Octavian by a great ceremony in Alexandria.
31	The forces of Antony and Cleopatra are defeated by Octavian at the Battle of Actium.
30	Antony and Cleopatra commit suicide. Egypt is annexed by Rome.
29	Virgil's *Georgics* are completed. Livy begins publication of his history of Rome. Publication of Horace's *Epodes*.
27	The 'restoration' of the Republic by Octavian. He is granted the name Augustus. Gradually (27–22 BC) Augustus accumulates enough power to emerge, unquestionably, as the dominant figure in the constitution.
26–16	The poet Propertius writes his *Elegies*.
25	Ovid begins writing the *Amores*.
24–23	Publication of the first three books of Horace's *Odes*.
23	Augustus surrenders the consulship and consolidates his political position with the grant of new powers. Completion of Vitruvius' *De Architectura*, later to become the most influential work on Roman architecture.
20	Settlement with Parthia allows the return of the standards lost at Carrhae to Rome.

19	Death of Virgil. The *Aeneid* is preserved for publication by Augustus.
17	Horace's *Centennial Hymn* symbolizes his acceptance of the Augustan regime.
12	Augustus becomes *pontifex maximus*.
12–9	The Balkan tribes are pacified for the first time and the provinces of Dalmatia and Pannonia established. Roman forces reach the Elbe.
9	Dedication of the Ara Pacis.
*c.*4	Birth of Jesus in Galilee.
2	Dedication of the Forum of Augustus. Augustus is declared *Pater Patriae*, 'Father of the Fatherland'.
*c.*1	Ovid's *Art of Love*.

AD

2–4	After many abortive attempts at finding an heir, Augustus appoints his son-in-law, Tiberius, as his successor. The *Metamorphoses* of Ovid.
5–6	The position of the army is consolidated with the normal period of service set at twenty years and the state assuming responsibility for discharged soldiers.
6–9	A major uprising in Pannonia is followed by the massacre of three legions in the German forests (near modern Osnabrück). A frontier on the Rhine is increasingly accepted as the limit of the empire.
14	Augustus dies. Tiberius, the first of the house of Julio-Claudians, succeeds peacefully.
19	Death of Germanicus, Tiberius' designated heir.
23	Death of Tiberius' son Drusus.
26	Tiberius withdraws to Capri.
*c.*29–30	Crucifixion of Jesus in Jerusalem. Foundation of early church.
31	Execution of the praetorian prefect Sejanus after Tiberius discovers the extent of his power.
37	Death of Tiberius aged 77. Succession of Gaius (Caligula).
40	Jesus' brother James becomes leader of the 'Jewish church' in Jerusalem but as a result of the missionary work of Paul Christianity spreads more successfully in Gentile communities.
*c.*42–54	The letters of Paul, the earliest surviving Christian writings.
41	Caligula is assassinated after it becomes clear there is no constitutional way of removing an unsatisfactory emperor. Claudius becomes emperor.
43	Invasion of Britain boosts Claudius' position. Britain becomes a permanent part of the empire.
43–54	Claudius develops an imperial bureaucracy at the expense of the powers of the senate.
49	Claudius marries Agrippina, the mother of the future emperor Nero. Agrippina consolidates her position.

54	After the death of Claudius, Agrippina engineers the succession of Nero and the death of Claudius' son Britannicus.
54–59	Years of stability under the influence of the 'Stoic' Seneca.
59	Nero's murder of his mother Agrippina is followed by his growing instability.
60	Revolt of Boudicca in Britain.
62	Humiliation of the Romans by the Parthians. Rome forced to accept a Parthian nominee as ruler of Armenia, the buffer state between the two empires.
64	A major fire in Rome is blamed on the Christian community. Nero builds his Golden House among the ruins.
65	Seneca commits suicide.
65–100	Composition of the gospels and the Acts of the Apostles.
66	The senator Petronius, author of the *Satyricon*, commits suicide.
66–74	Major revolt in Judaea is suppressed with great brutality.
67	Nero tours Greece.
68	Revolt against Nero breaks out in Gaul. Nero commits suicide.
69	The year of the four emperors, Galba, Otho, Vitellius, and Vespasian. Vespasian eventually wins control of the empire and reigns until 79.
70	Titus, the son of Vespasian, sacks the temple of Jerusalem and brings many of its treasures to Rome. Titus' arch in Rome celebrates his victory. Revolt of Julius Civilis and establishment of a short-lived Gallic empire.
78–86	Major campaigns by Agricola in Britain.
79–81	Reign of Titus.
79	Eruption of Vesuvius destroys Pompeii and Herculaneum. The encyclopaedist Pliny the Elder, author of *The Natural History*, dies in the eruption.
80	The Colosseum is inaugurated.
81–96	Reign of Domitian. Domitian builds a major palace for himself on the Palatine Hill.
80s	The consolidation of the Rhine–Danube frontier with the formation of the provinces of Upper and Lower Germany and more effective fortifications. Domitian invades Dacia and reduces the Dacian king Decabalus to the status of client.
85	The 'Jewish' Christian church in Jerusalem is in decline. The future of Christianity lies with the Greek-speaking Gentile communities.
86–98	The *Epigrams* of Martial.
96	Domitian is assassinated in Rome. The senators move their own nominee, Nerva, into his place.
98	Trajan succeeds as emperor on the death of Nerva. The more relaxed atmosphere of his reign allows the historians Tacitus and Suetonius to write their histories of the first century. The letters of Pliny the Younger cover events from 97 to 113. Plutarch's *Lives* also date from these years.

101–106	Trajan conquers Dacia and builds his forum and market in Rome from the plunder. Trajan's column is decorated with relief sculptures of the campaign.
110–117	The *Satires* of Juvenal.
114–117	Trajan invades Parthia. Temporary annexation of Armenia and Mesopotamia.
117	Trajan dies. He is succeeded by Hadrian.
117–138	Reign of Hadrian. Attempts at expansion halted and the empire settles within its frontiers. The emperor travels widely and his love of Greece helps integrate the east further into the empire. Building of the Pantheon, Hadrian's Villa at Tivoli, and Hadrian's Wall in northern Britain (121).
127–148	Ptolemy of Alexandria, perhaps the greatest of the Greek astronomers, active.
132–135	Major Jewish revolt after a Roman colony is founded by Hadrian in Jerusalem.
138	Death of Hadrian. Succession of Antoninus Pius.
138–161	Reign of Antoninus Pius, traditionally seen as the moment when the empire reached its most perfect form.
150	Panagyrical speech of the Greek Aelius Aristides praises the beneficence of Roman rule. Aelius Aristides is one of the leaders of the Second Sophistic, a revival in the art of Greek oratory. The physician Galen, the founding father of physiology and the greatest scientist of his day, is active.
c.155	Apuleius' novel *The Golden Ass*.
161	Succession of Marcus Aurelius and Lucius Verus as joint emperors. Parthian invasion beaten off with difficulty by Verus. Plague spreads from Persia into the empire.
168–175	Wars of Marcus Aurelius on the Danube end with the repulse of the German invaders.
172–180	*Meditations* of Marcus Aurelius.
177	Marcus Aurelius confirms that Christians who refuse to recant can be put to death.
180	Commodus becomes emperor on the death of his father Marcus Aurelius. Although the borders are secure Commodus' behaviour earns universal condemnation and he is assassinated in 192.
190–200	Clement of Alexandria accepts that Greek philosophy may be of value to Christians.
192–193	Septimius Severus achieves power following an empire-wide struggle over the throne. He consolidates the position of the army.
197	Severus campaigns in Parthia and temporarily adds Mesopotamia to the empire. The Parthian empire is steadily weakening due to external and internal pressures.
200 onward	Consolidation of German tribes into large groupings. (The Alamanni, 'all men', first attested in 213.)
200 onward	Tertullian (died c.225), 'the father of Latin theology', and Origen (died 254), perhaps the most brilliant of the early Christian theologians, active.

203	Septimius Severus' triumphal arch in Rome.
203	Perpetua martyred in Carthage, leaving a diary of her experiences as a Christian.
208–211	Severus campaigning in Britain. Dies at York.
211	Severus' sons, Caracalla and Geta, succeed as joint emperors. Caracalla soon eliminates Geta.
212	Caracalla declares all free subjects of the empire to be citizens.
212–216	Caracalla builds his baths in Rome. The jurist Ulpian is active.
218–222	Elagabalus emperor. His adherence to the sun god arouses universal hostility and he is assassinated.
222–237	Reign of Severus Alexander, last of the Severan dynasty.
226	The crowning of the Persian leader Ardeshir at Ctesiphon establishes the Sasanian empire in place of the Parthian.
234–284	The years of crisis as the empire is under continual pressure from German tribes and the Sasanian (Persian) empire. A high turnover of emperors.
244	Plotinus settles in Rome. Uses Plato's ideas as the basis of Neoplatonism.
249–251	The emperor Decius launches a major persecution of Christians.
251	Cyprian, bishop of Carthage, argues that bishops should act in consensus when determining doctrine.
253 or 254	Sacking of Antioch by the Sasanians. The Goths reach Ephesus.
260	Capture and humiliation of the emperor Valerian by the Sasanians.
260–274	The 'Gallic empire' maintains its independence within the empire as does the separatist state of Palmyra.
267	Athens is sacked by the Heruli.
270–275	Reign of the emperor Aurelian sees the beginning of an effective fightback against Rome's enemies. Aurelian restores unity to the empire by eliminating the Gallic empire and the state of Palmyra.
276–282	Reign of Probus sees a further strengthening of the empire.
282	Carus becomes the first emperor not to seek formal recognition by the senate.
284	A Balkan general, Diocletian, becomes emperor.
286–293	Foundation of the Tetrarchy, rule of two Augusti and two Caesars. Emergence of new imperial capitals at Trier, Milan, Sirmium, and Nicomedia. Diocletian sets in hand a major reorganization of the structure of the empire.
293	Diocletian attempts to stabilize the currency by introducing a gold coinage.
297	A major defeat of the Sasanians brings peace to the eastern frontier.
298–306	Building of Diocletian's monumental baths in Rome.
301	Diocletian's Edict of Prices attempts to eliminate inflation. It proves impossible to administer and has little effect.
303–312	Last major persecution of Christians under Diocletian and his successor Galerius.

305	Abdication of Diocletian. A power struggle ensues.
312	The Battle of Milvian Bridge near Rome establishes Constantine as ruler of the western empire.
313	The Edict of Milan, signed by Constantine and Licinius, emperor in the east, introduces empire-wide toleration for Christianity.
c.314–315	Arch of Constantine erected in Rome.
324	Constantine defeats Licinius and becomes sole emperor. He begins the building of Constantinople and provides material support for the first great Christian churches.
325	Constantine presides over the council of Nicaea, the first great ecumenical council. Condemnation of Arius.
330	Dedication of Constantinople.
333–379	Life of Basil of Caesarea. Basil establishes that the ideal of monastic life is service to the poor. His monastery has a hospital and a leper colony.
337	Death of Constantine. He is succeeded by his three sons.
351	Battle of Mursa sees the emergence of the surviving son, Constantius, as sole emperor. His reign is dominated by campaigns on the Persian border.
356–360	Julian, a cousin of Constantius, restores order along the northern borders.
357	Constantius' visit to Rome, memorably described by Ammianus Marcellinus.
361	Julian becomes emperor on the death of Constantius. The last of the non-Christian emperors, Julian attempts, unsuccessfully, to restore pagan beliefs.
363	Death of Julian while campaigning in Persia. The campaign ends in humiliation for the Romans.
364–375	Reign of Valentinian, probably the last effective emperor in the west.
374–397	Ambrose, bishop of Milan, proves a formidable campaigner against paganism and heresy.
376	Crossing of the Danube by Goths fleeing from the Huns.
378	The Battle of Adrianople. The emperor of the east, Valens, and many of the finest Roman troops, killed in a major encounter with the Goths.
378	Ammianus Marcellinus starts his history of the empire. Only the part dealing with the period 354 to 378 now survives.
381	Condemnation of Arianism by the council of Constantinople.
382	Theodosius, emperor in the east, signs a treaty with the Goths allowing them independent status within the empire.
380s	Jerome begins his Latin translation of the Old and New Testaments. It is completed before his death in 420.
385	Augustine appointed professor of rhetoric at Milan. The experiences leading to his conversion here are described in *The Confessions* (written 397–400). He returns to his native Africa in 388 and becomes bishop of Hippo in 395.

388–395	Theodosius sole emperor. The last reign in which the empire is ruled as a single unit. Under the influence of Ambrose, Theodosius uses his power to uphold orthodox Christianity against heresy and paganism.
390s	John Chrysostom preaching in Antioch. Made bishop of Constantinople in 398.
394	Theodosius defeats a pagan usurper Eugenius at the battle of the river Frigidus. Traditionally seen as the moment when Christianity is triumphant.
395	The death of Theodosius. The empire is split between his two sons, Arcadius and Honorius.

THE WESTERN EMPIRE 395–600

395–423	Reign of Honorius. Honorius moves his court to Ravenna (402) and the empire is now fronted by military strong men.
402–408	Stilicho, the 'master of the soldiers', effective ruler of the western empire.
406–407	Major invasion of Vandals, Sueves, and Alamanni into the empire. One result is the collapse of Roman rule in Britain and Spain. The Vandals reach southern Spain.
410	Sack of Rome by Alaric.
413–426	Augustine writes his *The City of God*.
418	The Visigoths are established as a 'federate' kingdom in Aquitaine.
423–433	Galla Placidia, mother of the young emperor Valentinian, the dominant figure in the west.
425	The earliest mosaics in Ravenna in the mausoleum of Galla Placidia.
429	The Vandals, under Gaiseric, move into north Africa.
430	Death of Augustine in Hippo while the city is under siege by the Vandals.
433	Aetius, Galla Placidia's 'master of soldiers', becomes the new strong man of the west. His main aim is to keep Gaul within the empire.
435	The Vandal kingdom in north Africa is given 'federate' status.
438	Proclamation of Theodosius II's law code throughout the empire.
439	Carthage sacked by the Vandals. Gaiseric then takes over the islands of the western Mediterranean.
443	The Burgundians are given 'federate' status after being defeated by Aetius.
445	Attila becomes leader of the Huns and launches attacks on the empire.
451	Battle of Catalaunian Plains. Attila is forced to retreat but invades Italy in 452. Dies in 453 and his empire collapses.
454	Aetius, discredited by his failure to protect the empire against the Huns, is assassinated.
455	Death of Valentinian. Rome is sacked by Gaiseric.
458	Sicily, the earliest Roman province (241 BC), captured by the Vandals.

458–476	Breakdown of the central authority of the western empire as emperors and 'strong men' struggle for power.
476	The deposition of Romulus Augustus marks the end of the western empire.
c.480–547	Life of Benedict whose Rule for monastic living becomes the most influential of those adopted in the west.
493–526	The Ostrogoth Theodoric establishes a state in Italy which expands to include Provence and Visigothic Spain.
490s	Church of San Apollinare Nuovo in Ravenna, the palace church of Theodoric, begun.
498 or 499	Conversion of the Frankish king Clovis to orthodox Christianity. Clovis lays the foundations of a large Frankish kingdom.
520s	Building of San Vitalis in Ravenna begun.
524	Boethius' *The Consolation of Philosophy*. Boethius is the last Latin speaker to have a comprehensive mastery of Greek and leaves a translation of many of Aristotle's works.
530s	Building of San Apollinare in Classe, Ravenna.
533	Justinian's successful invasion of Vandal Africa.
533–548	Under Theudebert the Frankish kingdom extends over both France and Germany.
535	Justinian invades Ostrogothic Italy but his campaign runs into trouble.
540	Cassiodorus organizes the collection and copying of classical and early Christian manuscripts.
554	Justinian finally achieves control of Italy.
569–586	The reign of Leovigild sees the reunification of Spain.
586–601	Reign of Reccared in Spain. Reccared announces his conversion to orthodox Christianity and establishes an alliance between church and state in Spain.
590–604	Pope Gregory develops the concept of papal authority in the west, laying the foundations of the medieval papacy.
600–636	Isodore, bishop of Seville, urges the preservation of classical learning.
640s onwards	Arab conquests of north Africa and Spain.
733	Victory of Charles Martel at Poitiers finally stems Arab expansion.

THE EASTERN EMPIRE 395–600

395–408	Arcadius emperor in the east.
400	Uprising in Constantinople against Gainas, the Goth commander of the city's garrison.
408–450	Reign of Theodosius II. Constantinople consolidated as the capital of the eastern empire. Image of the emperor as God's representative on earth.
431	Council of Ephesus proclaims Mary to be Theotokos, 'the mother of God', and thus plays down the human nature of Jesus.
450–457	Reign of Marcian.

451	Council of Chalcedon proclaims that Christ had two natures, human and divine, within the same undivided person, but the controversy over the nature of Christ continues.
457–474	Reign of Leo I. Leo attempts to lessen the dependency of the empire on foreign troops. Invasion of Vandal Africa in conjunction with the western empire proves a disaster.
474–491	Reign of Zeno, a period of instability with revolts from the Isaurians and invasions by the Goths.
491–518	Reign of Anastasius. A period of prosperity and stable administration.
518–527	Reign of Justin, formerly commander of the palace guard.
527–565	Reign of Justinian, Justin's nephew.
536	Closure of the temple to Isis at Philae in southern Egypt marks the end of traditional Egyptian religion.
527–534	Justinian's Law Code.
532	The Nika riots, which almost overthrow Justinian, are suppressed with ferocity.
532–537	Rebuilding of St Sophia in Constantinople.
533	Successful invasion of Vandal Africa by Justinian's general Belisarius.
535–554	Invasion and eventual conquest of Italy.
540	The Sasanians sack Antioch. Major outbreaks of plague in the empire.
c.547–554	The historian Procopius writes his history of Justinian's wars as well as his *Secret History* and *Buildings*.
548	Death of Justinian's empress, Theodora.
550s	First Slav penetration of the Balkans.
553	Council of Constantinople fails to resolve the controversy over the nature of Christ.
565	Death of Justinian. The authoritarian and profoundly Christian empire he has sustained is now normally referred to as the Byzantine empire.
620s	Muhammad consolidates power in the Arabian peninsula.
610–641	The reign of Heraclius. Fight back against the Sasanian empire brings it close to collapse but the empire is faced almost immediately by the onslaught of the Arabs.
632	Death of Muhammad. His successor Abu Bakr leads the attack on the Sasanian and Byzantine empires.
636	Battle of Yarmuk sees the defeat of the Byzantines. Arab conquest of Syria and Palestine. The Sasanian empire is also overrun by the Arabs.
642	Alexandria lost to the Arabs.
640s onwards	A reduced Byzantine state maintains its independence until the sack of Constantinople by the Ottoman Turks in 1453.

ACKNOWLEDGEMENTS OF SOURCES

The author and publishers are grateful for permission to include the following copyright material:

Carmina Archilochi, *The Fragments of Archilochus* (University of California Press, Berkeley, 1964), fragment 262, ed. and trans. by Guy Davenport. Reprinted by permission of the University of California Press.

Peter Green, *The Shadow of the Parthenon* (Maurice Temple Smith and University of California Press, London, 1972), translation of a poem by Sappho. Reprinted with permission of University of California Press.

Oswyn Murray, *Early Greece* (2nd edn.; Fontana Press, London, 1993), translations of fragments of Tyrtaios and Solon. Reprinted by permission of Harper Collins Publishers Limited.

PLATES
 1 Temple of the goddess Isis on the island of Philae (Bridgeman Art Library).
 2 Egyptian wall-painting from Luxor, 18th dynasty (AKG-images, London).
 3 Etruscan wall-painting: banquet scene from Leopardi tomb, Tarquinia (AKG-images, London).
 4 Saqqara pyramid (Werner Forman Archive, London).
 6 The Narmer palette (Ancient Art and Architecture Collection, Ltd).
 7 Wall engraving of Queen Hatshepsut (Werner Forman Archive).
 8 Wall engraving of Alexander the Great at Luxor (Hirmer Verlag).
 9 Stone sculpture of Menkaure and his queen (Museum of Fine Arts, Boston).
10 Stone sculpture of Akhenaten (Egyptian Museum, Cairo).
11 The shrine of Anubis at the temple of Hatshepsut (Hirmer Verlag).
12 Doric columns at Corinth (Mansell Collection).
13 An avenue of sphinxes at Luxor (AKG-images, London).
14 Stone lions at Delos (Mansell Collection).
15 A typical Egyptian figure (© The British Museum).
16 The lady of Auxerre (Réunion des musées nationaux, Louvre (Girandon)).
17 Nude *kòuros* figure (Metropolitan Museum of Art, New York).
18 The Critian boy (Acropolis Museum, Athens).
19 Inlaid depiction of a Sumerian chariot (© The British Museum).
20 Impression of a cylinder seal from the cemetery at Ur (© The British Museum).
21 Original of the same seal (© The British Museum).
22 Cuneiform tablet from Amarna (© The British Museum).
23 Relief from Ashurbanipal's palace at Nineveh (© The British Museum).
24 The Rosetta stone (© The British Museum).

25 Stylized geometric vase (National Gallery, Athens).

26 Proto-Corinthian vase (© The British Museum).

27 Chigi vase from Corinth (Hirmer Verlag, Munich).

28 Francois vase, Museo Archaeologico, Florence (Mansell Collection).

29 Early fifth century 'red-figure' pot (AKG-images, London).

30 Late fourth century 'red-figure' pot (AKG-images, London).

31 The Great Sphinx at Giza (Getty Images).

32 Greek female sphinx from the island of Naxos (AKG-images, London).

33 Roman brazier featuring sphinxes. Museo Nazionale, Naples (Mansell Collection).

34 Mosaic of the Nile in flood. Palazzo Baronate, Palestrina (Mansell Collection).

35 Egyptian obelisk in front of St Peter's, Rome (AKG-images, London).

36 Sculpture of Harmodius and Aristogeiton. Museo Nazionale, Naples (Mansell Collection).

37 Prima Porta statue of Augustus, Vatican Museum (Mansell Collection).

38 Sculpture of Alexander the Great (AKG-images, London).

39 Sculptured head of Pompey (Ny Carlsberg Glyptothek, Copenhagen).

40 Temple of Poseidon at Paestum (Mansell Collection).

41 The Parthenon, Athens (Mansell Collection).

42 The *Tholos* at Delphi (Charlie Waite/Tony Stone).

43 Sixth century BC Athenian black-figure vase (AKG-images, London).

44 Mantegna's *The Triumphs of Caesar* (The Royal Collection © 2003, Her Majesty, Queen Elizabeth II).

45 Wall painting from the villa of Livia (AKG-images, London).

46 Third century AD mosaic of hippodrome races (AKG-images, London).

47 Detail from the Parthenon frieze (©The British Museum).

49 The 'Ludovisi' throne (Bridgeman Art Library).

50 Detail from the Esquiline Treasure (© The British Museum).

51 The 'Capitoline Venus' (© Araldo de Luca/Corbis).

52 Fifth century BC vase depicting the story of Artemis and Actaeon (Museum of Fine Arts, Boston).

53 Titian's *The Death of Actaeon* (© National Gallery, London).

54 Timgad in North Africa (Compagnie aerienne de photographie).

55 The Colosseum in Rome (Mansell Collection).

56 The Pont du Gard at Nimes (Mansell Collection).

57 Surviving surface of a Roman road (Mick Sharp).

58 Interior of the Pantheon, Rome by Giovanni Pannini (Image © 2003 Board of Trustees, National Gallery of Art, Washington DC).

59 Basilica of Santa Sabina, Rome (Mansell Collection).

60 Theodosius II and the citizens of Constantinople receiving the bones of St Stephen (Ann Münchow, Aachen).

61 Christ as the Good Shepherd. Museo Laterano, Vatican (Mansell Collection).

63 Fourth century sarcophagus (Mansell Collection).

64 Ravenna mosaic of Christ (Mansell Collection).

65 Apse mosaic of Christ, Santa Pudenziana, Rome (© 1990 Foto Scala, Firenze).

66 Raphael's *School of Athens*. Palazzo Vaticano (Mansell Collection).

67 Nea Paphos floor mosaic (Ancient Art and Architecture Collection, Ltd).

68 *Saint Apollonia assualts a statue of Dionysus*, attributed to Antonio Vivarini, c. 1450 (Image © 2003 Board of Trustees, National Gallery of Art, Washington DC).

69 Relief of the emperor Marcus Aurelius (© Archivo Iconografico, S.A. / Corbis).

71 Verocchio's statue of Bartolomeo Colleoni in Venice (Bridgeman Art Library).

72 The four horses of St Mark's, Venice (Corbis).

73 Arch of Constantine (Mansell Collection).

74 Napoleonic festival arch, Venice (AKG-images, London).

75 Somme memorial arch, Thiepval, France (Hulton Getty).

76 Excavations at Nineveh (Mary Evans Picture Library).

77 Ludwig and Winckelmann before the Glyptothek (Kaulbach, Wilhelm von, Freskenzyklus f.d neue Pinakothek (1848) Ludwig I. Neue Pinakothek. Photo supplied by Artothek, Munich).

78 Sixth century mosaic of the emperor Justinian, San Vitale, Ravenna (Justinian's Court, Ravenna, Church of San Vitale © 1990, Photo Scala, Florence).

79 Apse mosaic of St Agnes, church of St Agnes, Rome (© 1990, Photo Scala, Florence).

80 *Roman Capriccio*, by Giovanni Pannini (Ashmolean Museum, Oxford).

FIGURES

Figure 1 The Doric and Ionic orders, after J. J. Coulton, *Greek Architects at Work* (Cornell University Press, 1983).

Figure 2 The town of Olynthos, after U. Hoepfner and E. I. Schwander, *Haus und Stadt* (Broschiert, 1986).

Figure 3 The Athenian Agora, by J. Travlos and B. Dinsmoor Jnr. Reproduced by permission of American School of Classical Studies at Athens: Agora Excavations.

Figure 4 The Parthenon and the Temple of Artemis at Ephesus, after H. Berve and G. Gruben, *Griechische Tempel und Heiligtümer* (Hirmer Verlag, 1961).

Figure 5 The Imperial Fora, Rome, after G. M. A. Hanfmann, *Roman Art* (Norton, 1964).

Figure 6 A typical house from Pompeii, from E. La Rocca and M. and A. de Vos, *Guida archaeologica di Pompei* (1976).

Figure 7 The baths of Caracalla, Rome, after Ward-Perkins, *Roman Imperial Architecture* (1981). Reprinted by permission of Yale University Press Pelican History of Art.

Figure 9   Reconstruction of the villa at Chedworth, from Boëthius and Ward-Perkins, *Etruscan and Roman Architecture*. Reprinted by permission of Yale University Press Pelican History of Art.

Figure 10   Santa Sophia, Constantinople, after Hugh Honour and John Flemming, *A World History of Art*, 3rd edn., 1991. Courtesy of Laurence King Publishing Ltd.

MAPS

Map 3   The Greeks and the Phoenicians in the Mediterranean, 800–600 BC, adapted from J. Boardman, J. Griffin, and O. Murray, *Oxford History of the Classical World* (Oxford, 1986), 16–17.

Map 4   The Greek world from the seventh to the fourth century BC, adapted from Boardman et al., *Classical World*, 24–5.

Map 5   The Athenian empire at its height, 440–430 BC, adapted from Boardman et al., *Classical World*, 134.

Map 6   The campaigns of Alexander the Great, adapted from Boardman et al., *Classical World*, 318–19.

Map 7   Alexandria, from Ian Shaw, *The Oxford History of Ancient Egypt* (Oxford, 2000), 406.

Map 8   The Hellenistic kingdoms, 190 BC, adapted from John Ferguson, *The Heritage of Hellenism* (Thames and Hudson, London, 1973).

Map 9(a)   Rome and her allies in the third century BC, adapted from Boardman et al., *Classical World*, 388.

Map 9(b)   Etruscan and Roman Italy, adapted from Boardman et al., *Classical World*, 388.

Map 10   The territories of Rome and the allies at the time of the Social War, 91 BC, adapted from Boardman et al., *Classical World*, 389.

Map 11   The city of Rome, 52 BC, from Diane Favro, *The Urban Image of Augustan Rome*, (Cambridge, 1996), 26. Reprinted by permission of Cambridge University Press.

Map 12   The campaigns and conquests of Julius Caesar, adapted from *World of the Romans*. Reproduced by permission of Andromeda Oxford Ltd, Abingdon, UK.

Map 13(a)   The Roman empire in the west, adapted from Boardman et al., *Classical World*, 527.

Map 13(b)   The Roman empire in the east, adapted from Boardman et al., *Classical World*, 528–9.

Map 14   The provinces of the empire, AD 117–376, adapted from *World of the Romans*. Reproduced by permission of Andromeda Oxford Ltd, Abingdon, UK.

Map 15   The principal land and sea routes of the Roman empire, from *The Roman World*, John Wacher (ed.), © 1987 Routledge.

Map 17   Diocletian's dioceses and provinces in the early fourth century, adapted from *Atlas of the Roman World*. Reproduced by permission of Andromeda Oxford Ltd, Abingdon, UK.

Map 18   Rome at the death of Constantine. From Richard Krautheimer, *Rome: Profile of a City*. © 1980 by Princeton University Press. Reprinted by permission of Princeton University Press.

Map 19   The Mediterranean in late Antiquity, AD 450–600, from J. McManners, *Oxford Illustrated History of Christianity* (1990), 86–7.

Efforts have been made to trace and contact copyright holders prior to printing. Oxford University Press apologizes for any errors or omissions in this list and, if notified, will be pleased to make corrections at the earliest opportunity.

INDEX